Mimi

S0-AMN-668

Philadelphia, October 1984

# Eugène Scribe and French Opera of the Nineteenth Century

# Studies in Musicology, No. 6

## Other Titles in This Series

| | |
|---|---|
| *No. 1 Jean-Baptiste de Lully and his Tragédies Lyriques* | Joyce Newman |
| *No. 2 The Operas of Johann Adolf Hasse* | Fredrick L. Millner |
| *No. 3 The Life and Works of Francesco Maria Veracini* | John Walter Hill |
| *No. 4 Music in the Restoration Theatre: With a Catalogue of Instrumental Music in the Plays 1665-1713* | Curtis A. Price |
| *No. 5 John Taverner: Tudor Composer* | David S. Josephson |
| *No. 7 The Creative Process in the Autograph Musical Documents of Hector Berlioz, c. 1818-1840* | D. Kern Holoman |
| *No. 8 Music and Text in the Works of Arnold Schoenberg: The Critical Years, 1908-1922* | Alan Philip Lessem |
| *No. 9 The Comic Intermezzo: A Study in the History of Eighteenth-Century Italian Opera* | Charles E. Troy |

# Eugène Scribe and French Opera of the Nineteenth Century

by
Karin Pendle

RESEARCH PRESS

Text first published as a typescript facsimile in 1970

Produced and distributed by
University Microfilms International
Ann Arbor, Michigan 48106

Library of Congress Cataloging in Publication Data

**Pendle, Karin,** 1939-
Eugène Scribe and French opera of the nineteenth century.

(Studies in musicology series ; no. 6)
Bibliography: p.
Includes index.
1. Opera—France. 2. Operas—Librettos—History and criticism. 3. Scribe, Augustin Eugene, 1791-1861. I. Title. II. Series.

ML1727.P37 782.1'092'4 79-20451
ISBN 0-8357-1004-1

CONTENTS

# THE LIFE OF EUGENE SCRIBE

> It is from the theatre of Scribe that all has grown. For, besides [the fact that] Scribe has reigned as master over the authors and the public for a long time, it is as a reaction against his authority that innovations have resulted: thus, accepted or fought against, his influence has made itself felt everywhere up to the present time. Gifted to excess with all the special talents of a man of the theatre and devoid of all others, Scribe succeeded in making of the theatre a special art which dispensed with sentiments, ideas, and characters. He made of it an empty form. After Scribe, progress consisted uniquely in bringing back to the theatre everything that Scribe had excluded from it or that he had not known how to bring into it.[1]

For some time it has been fashionable to deny Eugène Scribe any talent, to dismiss him as a prolific but barely second-rate hack whose position in nineteenth-centry drama is due more to the amount of work he produced than to the work itself.[2] As Doumic has put it, "because Scribe thought little and wrote badly,"[3] people want to discount his contributions to the stage of his time and of subsequent generations. Stanton further remarks:

> Some detractors admire Scribe's structural craftmanship in the more serious plays . . . but deny him any dramatic merit other than that of '*charpentier*.'[4]

In Scribe's own time Blaze de Bury was among those who particularly attacked the author for his want of style and for his abuses of the French language.[5] The constant use of ellipses and the almost complete lack of true poetry in Scribe's verses, the use of a single language and a single manner for all characters in all situations, indeed the presence of actual grammatical errors in his writing, did not sit well with this critic nor with others of the time. Writing particularly of Scribe's libretti, Blaze commented:

> . . . what he has done is a great deal, but what he has caused to be done is immense. All of our modern lyric theatre comes from his initiative. Without him we would have neither *La Muette, Robert le Diable, La Juive, Les Huguenots,* nor this charming repertoire [of opéra comique] for which Europe envies us and which, at least in part, will survive: *Le Mariage de raison* and *La Calomnie* will have long disappeared from the memories of men while *La Muette* and *Fra Diavolo, Le Macon* and *Le Domino noir* remind them of the

> name of that great composer, his inseparable collaborator. . . . The best thing about Scribe is Auber.[6]

Critic Théophile Gautier, in 1840, referred to Scribe as an "antipoetical nature *par excellence*," and observed: "No author has been more rudely chided than M. Scribe by the severity of that morose and whimsical goddess [criticism]."[7] Before the end of the nineteenth century the name of the man who had once been France's most popular dramatist had fallen into such disrepute that Ernest Legouvé, Scribe's collaborator on *Adrienne Lecouvreur*, felt it necessary to "take up the pen to save him from supercilious indifference and oblivion,"[8] and less than a hundred years after Scribe's death a modern writer could ask, "Who today still knows Eugène Scribe . . . ?"[9]

Such critical comments are easily made at Scribe's expense. Yet despite his weaknesses Scribe exercised a tremendous influence on dramatists for nearly a century, an influence which, as Doumic has pointed out, had both its positive and its negative sides. This influence was strong in both the spoken and the musical theatres and extended beyond the borders of France into England and Germany, among other places.[10] In Paris Scribe was the leading writer of dramas for the four major theatres of his day: the Opéra, the Opéra-Comique, the Gymnase, and the Comédie-Française.[11] In all of them he made decided and far-reaching contributions, particularly in areas of form and subject matter. Indeed, his originality lay not in his poetic style, which was sadly lacking, nor in any great contributions to fine writing, but in the ordered disposition of stage activities to carry out a given theme or action, one which nearly always reflected the people and/or taste of his time. As Matthews has pointed out, Scribe's dramatic range was great.

> He began with the vaudeville, which he improved into the comédie-vaudeville; he rose to the five-act comedy of manners; he invented the comedy drama; he failed in Romantic and historical drama, but he succeeded in handling tragic themes in grand opera; he devised the ballet-opera, and he gave great variety to the opéra-comique. He was ever on the lookout for new dramatic forms.[12]

And, one might add, he was supremely successful in every dramatic form, old or new. Never abandoning one form of drama to devote himself to another, he made simultaneous contributions to all genres.

Was the success of Scribe's "fiction factory" due mainly to "luck" or "good fortune," as Matthews would ask one to believe?[13] It is difficult to see how a man whose active career of some forty years includes over 420 dramatic works, in addition to a number of novels and short stories, could have existed for so long in such great public favor on the chance rays of a lucky star. Scribe's output for the stage includes 244 vaudevilles, 95 opéras comiques, 47 comedies, dramas, and melodramas, 28 opéras, and 8 ballets.[14] The majority of these works enjoyed at least moderate success, and many serve as outstanding examples of their genre. For over three decades, from shortly after 1820, Scribe was the major writer of libretti for opéras and opéras comiques, set by the major French composers of the day: Auber, Adam, Halévy, Boieldieu, Meyerbeer, Hérold, and others. Furthermore, this work was influential outside France. The universality of Scribe's characters, situations, and "local color" whatever the specific setting gave his libretti international appeal and resulted in their being adapted and used as models by writers in foreign lands.[15] His works were the sources of many well known non-French operas. For example, *Le Philtre* served as the basis of Donizetti's *L'elisir d'amore*, and *Le Chalet* was the model for the same composer's *Betly*; while Verdi composed *Un ballo in maschera* on a subject from Scribe's *Gustave III.* Scribe also provided material for Bellini's *La Sonnambula* and Esser's *Die zwei Prinzen* (Munich, 1845), and his style influenced Italian librettists Cammarano and Piave and German writers W. Friedrich, Mosenthal, Charlotte Birch-Pfeiffer, and Richard Wagner. Even Hugo von Hofmannsthal admitted studying Scribe's texts, an activity which is well illustrated by his libretto for *Arabella*.[16]

In such matters as these, good fortune alone can be no substitute for talent and hard work. That Scribe's talent lay outside the realms of poetic inspiration and the loftier reaches of dramatic art cannot be questioned, but the fact remains that he did possess a great gift and a certain originality, a strength of craft, and a discipline which account for his success and lasting influence. A highly intelligent man with a flair for the theatre, Scribe made his work his life, just as many qualities of his life invaded his work.

Auguste-Eugène Scribe was born on December 24, 1791, in Paris.[17] His father, a silk merchant, died in 1806. His mother's death soon followed, and the young Scribe was left in the care of a well known lawyer, Louis-Ferdinand Bonnet. Although Scribe studied law, receiving a Bachelor of Law degree from the Imperial University in 1815, he was already drawn to the theatre by that time. While still in school he met the vaudevillist Jean-François Bayard, who was later to become one of his collaborators, and also became a friend of Casimir and Germain Delavigne, both of whom were to be active in drama and opera. It was in collaboration with Germain Delavigne that Scribe made his dramatic debut in 1811 with the one-act vaudeville, *Les Dervis*, which enjoyed a modest success. Shortly thereafter, in May of 1812, Scribe met with his first real success in *L'Auberge, ou les Brigands sans le savoir*, and wrote his first opéra comique libretto, *La Chambre à coucher, ou une Demi-heure de Richelieu* (April 29, 1813), with music by Guénée. Although Scribe wrote several other vaudevilles and melodramas, political conditions near the end of the Napoleonic era turned people's attention away from the theatre and Scribe's pieces enjoyed no particular distinction. By the end of 1814 Scribe, disheartened by his lack of success and in need of money, decided to return to law for a time. Yet even then he was hopeful of a theatrical career and began to think in terms of how the events and social climate of the day could be put to advantage in his writing.

Throughout his life Scribe, the careful and well-organized dramatist, was in the habit of keeping thorough, ordered accounts and of appending to these accounts a summary evaluation of each year's work. At the end of 1814 he wrote:

> A revolution gives to society a completely new face, completely new needs. The vaudeville, the only genre to which I am devoted, can be conceived from another point of view than the one which people have had up to the present. Instead of following in the tracks of my confrères and imitating them as I have done, I want to try to be myself, to have my genre, my style, my own theatre. I know that I can vegetate for one or two more years before succeeding. But I shall succeed, I feel it strongly despite my misfortunes and catastrophes this year. Up till now I only busied myself with the theatre for relaxation and for my own pleasure; from now on I make it my business. I want no other. I have enough to live on and to wait for successes; I shall wait for them. And whether I succeed or not, I shall at least have a great advantage over many others, that of being free and independent and of not begging for position, help, or pensions from a government which I detest and scorn.
>
> I know that in literature one rarely makes a fortune and that many confrères who are worth more than I have found only misery and ill health. That is because they understood matters badly. There is a way to have talent and money at the same time: the one does not exclude the other. All the directors are rich; why not the authors? Because the former do not share with us a portion of the riches that we make for them? That may be, and that will change, at least if it depends on me! . . . If I ever have successes I say that the public will pay a great deal for them, as will the directors.[18]

Scribe's words have been quoted at some length not merely because they contain predictions of his future success, but because they reveal qualities about the man himself. The fact that he did keep careful accounts and was in the habit of spending one day near the end of each year—usually his birthday—reviewing his personal life as well as his finances shows him to be a practical and methodical man, one who never let life run away with him and who was able to feel himself in full control of his own existence, not subject to the whims of fate or fortune. So too are his dramas and the characters who fill them. Scribe's plays and operas are always well controlled and methodically carried out, no event occurring unexpectedly or without purpose. His characters are their own masters, moving in accordance with their own wills or plans, seldom subject to external control whether from human or superhuman sources. In this lies one of the essential differences between Scribe and the Romanticists, and it is this difference which stems from his own character and background.

The first thing Scribe mentions in the quotation above is, if not an entirely new concept, one which is a driving principle in Scribe's own career: namely, the exploitation by a dramatist of the political and social conditions under which he finds himself working. One can hardly deny that dramatic literature before Scribe's time reflected its own society and politics; one thinks immediately of Scribe's literary ancestor Molière, as well as of Beaumarchais, as prime examples of socially aware dramatists. With Scribe this social awareness is a product of deliberate calculation, and this attitude caused him to change with the time and the regime and in turn caused his enemies to accuse him of having no principles at all. Indeed, precisely his principles caused him to change.

The paragraphs quoted above were written soon after the Restoration of King Louis XVIII and before Napoleon's disastrous return from Elba. In the first few lines Scribe seems to be asking himself: "How can I exploit this political situation to best advantage in the theatre? What can the times offer my pen?" Less than a year later he had tried playing on the socio-political climate and found in it the best of material. Of *Une Nuit de la garde national*, written with Delestre-Poirson, Scribe commented that it was:

> . . . the first piece written according to my new ideas, a piece of the moment, a piece representing a corner of present-day society. Also, it is the first big success I have had to date. The public which had deserted the Vaudeville has returned. May heaven grant that I keep them there![19]

Heaven answered this prayer.

Scribe's desire even at this early stage in his career was not merely to use the theatre as a means of personal expression, while earning his living as a lawyer; nor even to make a reasonable living; but to make a great deal of money. As he says, writers ordinarily did not dream of such things and were not accorded their fair share of the theatrical profits for their work. Scribe opposed this traditional relationship by demanding not only a flat fee for his manuscripts, but royalties as well.[20] The anti-Scribe critics were often quick to attack the dramatist later in his life, when his dreamed-of fortune had become reality, implying that no writer of true artistic merit had ever been rich. In 1830, for example, Stendhal wrote critically of Scribe, saying: "He only loves money; he has earned 150,000 francs in the theatre."[21] Yet Scribe, always a generous man, not only earned his own fortune but made it possible for others to do the same. Through his strenuous and consistent efforts in the 1820s dramatic authors were gradually given a larger and larger slice of the box office pie. Arvin remarks:

> When one realizes the extent to which Scribe was influential in ameliorating the financial condition of his fellow dramatists, in obtaining for them that just recognition of their labors which theretofore they had been largely denied, and when one knows the noble use he was later to make of his own fortune, one likes to see him thus dreaming of wealth and glory.[22]

Even before his first truly successful production, then, Scribe had already set out his aims, both dramatic and financial. That he succeeded more than admirably in accomplishing both is demonstration enough that here was a man of intelligence and talent, for no mere hack could have accomplished what Scribe did. The fact that it was intelligence and talent combined with industry, and not great artistry, that accounted for his later success marks the difference between Scribe and many other dramatists more esteemed by critics of his own day and ours.

Between his first success in 1815 and the decisive year of 1820 Scribe's fortunes continued to mount as he produced an average of eight new works per year, mainly vaudevilles. In 1820 Scribe's friend and sometime collaborator Delestre-Poirson took on the management of a new theatre, the Gymnase, and signed Scribe to a contract which prohibited him from writing for "any theatre in direct rivalry with the Gymnase."[23] Scribe's production in vaudevilles—over a hundred plays between 1820 and 1830—was thus confined to this theatre, but he was still free to write for the Opéra, the Opéra-Comique, and the Comédie-Française. A number of years passed, however, before he spread his influence into these theatres. Only in 1823 did he begin a truly successful career as a writer of opéra comique libretti with *Leicester* and *La Neige*, beginning at the same time his long and prosperous collaboration with Daniel-François-Esprit Auber. As Scribe had broadened and transformed the vaudeville into a true comedy of manners, so he now developed the opéra comique by bringing to it subjects and characters closely aligned with the people of his time and their tastes. He also helped to enlarge the musical portions of these productions, developing more and greater possibilities for the use of truly dramatic music than had been the case in most earlier examples of French comic opera. *La Dame blanche* (1825), written for Boieldieu, is often cited as the first high point of this development.

Scribe and Auber together helped initiate another musico-dramatic form when, in 1828, their *La Muette de Portici* was given at the Opéra. Often considered the first French grand opera, this work became the model for many features of the genre in its use of a theme related to contemporary thought and in bringing together in a modern context the arts of musician, librettist, stage designer, and choreographer. Again, Scribe played a leading role in the transformation and expansion of a dramatic form, one which was to develop throughout the succeeding two-and-one-half decades and to include the works of such composers as Meyerbeer and Halévy.

Earlier, in 1822, Scribe had made his debut at the Comédie-Française with a comedy, *Valérie.* However, it was not until 1827 that he wrote his first five-act play, *Le Mariage d'argent*, for this theatre, and not until the 1830s that he began to produce his most famous comedies, such as *Dix ans de la vie d'une femme* (1832), *Bertrand et Raton* (1833), and *Le Verre d'eau* (1840). By the time of the July Revolution in 1830 or shortly thereafter, then, Scribe was an important writer, if not the principal writer, in four of the most important dramatic genres of his day: vaudeville, comedy-drama, opera, and opéra comique. Despite his long-lasting and continued successes, the July Revolution did have some effect, however temporary, on Scribe's fortunes. The bourgeoisie, a growing force during the Restoration, had been the audience toward which Scribe had directed his work. This group was largely responsible for the overthrow of Charles X and the selection of Louis-Philippe as the new French king. Now, in the face of new literary freedom and the rise of romanticism to greater prominence, Scribe found himself attacked from all sides as a classicist and a reactionary. As earlier, Scribe's reaction to political upheaval took the form of a personal application to his own situation. In his year-end accounts for 1830 he commented:

> A great revolution has just broken out. I neither blame nor approve the causes. I have never meddled in politics, but in literature, and it is only from the latter point of view that I shall examine the consequences of a change which should be more detrimental than useful to me.[24]

As in 1814, Scribe's decision was again to ride with and to exploit the conditions under which he lived and worked, a decision which is illustrated by such works as *Dix ans de la vie d'une femme*, a drama of a woman of the world; *Robert le Diable* (1831) and *Les Huguenots* (1835), grand operas with music by Meyerbeer showing, at least on the surface, the colors of romanticism; and *La Prison d'Edimbourg* (1833), a serious opéra comique with music by Carafa, based on a novel by Sir Walter Scott. Nevertheless, for a time Scribe's great popularity declined as the romanticists forged ahead, and he complained in 1832:

> Politics has killed literature. The theatres have been abandoned; several have even been closed. The Opéra-Comique reopened only last October. The events of June, the republican or Carlist disturbances, have driven the public away from (theatrical) spectacles. The journals themselves seem to have taken on the task of ruining dramatic art. Almost all our confrères aid them only too well. Incest, murder, patricide invade everything, even the French stage. I who have always remained faithful to my literary and patriotic principles, I who have not changed a bit for fifteen years and who have remained stationary when everyone else has moved forward, I now find myself behind the times and people call me *out of date, prejudiced old man, rococo*, etc. Liberal and classical in 1815, I am still liberal and classical in 1832. I therefore have against me the republicans, the Carlists, and the romantics, in a word the *ultras* of all types.[25]

Although discouraged, Scribe was so sure of his own aims that he confidently awaited the end of this period of extremes, all the while incorporating into his own work sufficient amounts of the most outstanding qualities of life and literature to be reasonably up-to-date. By the end of 1833 he began to see the decline of those elements against which he had complained a year earlier, and he took advantage of this to renew his efforts and, eventually, to rekindle his success. That he did overcome this relative low point in his career is evidenced not only by his continued financial health but by his reception in 1834 into the Académie-Française.

Throughout the 1830s Scribe's accounts show him to have been a generous man, bestowing dowries and scholarships on nieces and nephews and assisting friends through financial difficulties. Throughout this time he regretted that he had not yet married and had children of his own, but in 1843 he remedied this situation by marrying a widow with two children. Thus settled, Scribe continued to write a number of new works each year, producing comedies, vaudevilles, operas, opéras comiques, and ballets as before. He was also becoming increasingly well known outside France.

> In Germany the leading theatres make every effort to procure his plays for production, and the competition between directors is so great that, when a new play by Scribe appears in Paris, the German translations are immediately announced, often before the play is printed. The director of the Royal Opera of Berlin begs him to write an opera in five acts, the music to be composed by a distinguished young musician who inspires great hopes, Mendelssohn by name.[26]

And Matthews observes: "As fast as [the vaudevilles] appeared in Paris they were adapted to the London market by Planché, Dance, Poole, or Charles Mathews the younger."[27]

Scribe was a man who lived in and for the theatre. Véron, reporting on Scribe's usual work day, wrote that the author was accustomed to rising early and writing from 5:00 a.m. (or 6:00 in the winter) until about 10:00. Having finished his literary work, he then went to the theatre to sit through long hours of rehearsal, observing how his creations played on the stage and taking note of corrections or changes to be made. Even when not actively engaged in writing or observing rehearsals, Scribe still remained a playwright.

> . . . in his recreation or business affairs he looked for new characters and situations for comedy or drama, he took note of the words of characters, of subjects for plays he happened to find. He observed and listened more than he spoke, and in conversation he claimed less place for himself than for the personalities of others.[28]

One telling example of these habits is to be found in Scribe's own journal entries on a trip to Switzerland, where he observed: "The clouds provided a splendid spectacle which machinists at the Opèra could never have offered us. . . ."[29]

Scribe's output became so vast by the 1830s that the author was practically forced to play a game with himself to keep track of it all. After having produced some 350 works he conceived the idea of attempting to use up all the letters of the alphabet in his titles: hence such works as *Le Kiosque*, *Yelva*, and *La Xacarilla*, so named in order to fill in some missing letters.[30] Yet for the vast number of works he wrote and the influence he was to exercise on both the spoken and the musical theatre, Scribe showed his own particular brand of artistic integrity by remaining his own man throughout his life.

> Scribe was the only dramatist of prominence who took no part in the struggle between the Romanticists and the Classicists, who went quietly on his own way, and who held his public as firmly after the success of 'Antony' and 'Hernani' as before the publication of the preface to 'Cromwell.'[31]

Never one to claim any more for himself than he felt was his due as a capable theatrical craftsman, he remained singularly nontemperamental in and about his work. Véron, as director of the Opéra from 1831 to 1835 Scribe's frequent co-worker, has written:

> M. Scribe never wanted to play the role of a man of genius; he never posed as an innovator; he has never shown the ambition to be head of a school; one cannot reproach him for any charlatanism relating to [the pursuit of] glory; he never wrote a preface, something that is rare enough in these times.[32]

In the face of the overblown artistic pretensions of the romantic era, it is not difficult to respect and even to admire a writer who knew precisely his own strengths and weaknesses, his own financial and artistic worth, and acted accordingly.

The Revolution of 1848 affected Scribe as did most other important political events. He lost prestige and earnings because of the disturbed political climate, a loss from which he did not recover as easily as in the revolutionary 1830s. Scribe's star was waning, but by this time it was not such a serious matter. He had made and secured his fortune, he was the settled head of a middle-class household, and his age and declining health made a leveling off in his production desirable and even necessary. Nevertheless, he continued to write throughout the 1850s, ending his career in the musical theatre with Meyerbeer's *L'Africaine*, staged posthumously by Fétis in 1865.

Scribe died in Paris in February 1861, "after having amused, diverted, enchanted us for half a century."[33] Most of his plays died with him or gradually faded from view. His modern, middle-class characters, even in the historical dramas, left the stages of the Gymnase, the Odéon, and the Comédie-Française for good, and Matthews has observed that "no one of Scribe's people lives after him."[34] Yet in a sense this is only partly true. When the proverbial air had cleared, Scribe's spoken dramas were preserved only in the influence they exercised on such later writers as Ibsen and Shaw, but people still listened to and talked about Raoul and Valentine, Georges Brown and the White Lady, Fra Diavolo, Rachel and Eléazar. If Scribe created—or in some cases recreated—these and other characters for the stages of the Opéra and the Opéra-Comique, it was Auber, Meyerbeer, Halévy, Adam, Carafa, and others who preserved their lives, for without music they too would have been buried with their author. This fact alone reveals something of Scribe's strength as a librettist. His dramas for the musical theatre were even less complete than those for the spoken stage. In the latter he depended primarily upon situations and clever ordering of scenes to produce suspense, whereas his characters were mere shells, their personal qualities expressed not in what they did or the way in which they did it, but in purely external remarks on these qualities made by the characters themselves or by others in the cast. As Matthews has written:

> To Scribe the situations were of first importance, and no more strength was imparted to the characters than was needed to get them through the ingenious intrigue. There is a sharp contrast between the innate and carefully cultivated tact with which Scribe handled the succeeding situations of . . . [the vaudevilles] and the careless way he set on their legs the people whom he was to guide through the labyrinth.[35]

Yet as Lang has generalized, "The French theatre is decidedly more interested in action than in sentiment, and one could go farther by saying that it is even more interested in the outcome of the action than in the action itself."[36] Although there are undoubtedly notable exceptions to this judgment, its applicability to Scribe is without question. Moreover, the fact that it could be made at all may well be indirect testimony to Scribe's strong influence on French dramatic style.

Although Scribe's techniques in writing operas and opéras comiques differed somewhat from those in his spoken dramas, the same general observations could have applied to his libretti. His is an ideal scaffolding for music: a strong, clearly organized plot set in motion by characters to whom a certain humanity—"soul," if you will—is lacking. In such a situation the music would be able to expand, expressing qualities of spirit and emotion absent from Scribe's stick-men. For this basic reason Scribe became, almost by destiny, a popular and sought-after librettist for more than thirty years.

## SCRIBE AND HIS COLLABORATORS

One aspect of Scribe's work worthy of comment is his frequent use of collaborators in writing a drama or a libretto. In all he worked with some 130 literary collaborators.[1] In the areas of opera and opéra comique, these included such names as Germain Delavigne, Mélesville, Saint-Georges, Dupin, Mazères, Varner, Planard, Saintine, many of whom were librettists in their own right. Their working with Scribe, however, was apparently never a matter of Scribe's using their ideas in an unscrupulous fashion, out of laziness or because of the pressures of work. Rather, it seems from all reports as if Scribe did most of the work himself in a collaboration. Véron states: "Ordinary collaborators discuss and draw up together the plan of the work; but all the theatrical pieces to which M. Scribe put his name are entirely written by him."[2] The listing of a collaborator's name was sometimes no more than an act of generosity on Scribe's part, for the collaborator's contribution was not always very large nor equal to that of Scribe. As will be demonstrated later, Scribe's method of adapting a novel for operatic use is a process close enough in essence to what seems to have been his concept of collaboration to serve as a substantiation of this statement. Thus Vapereau's description of the process of collaboration with Scribe is at best a mild piece of slander.

> . . . M. Scribe was obliged to establish a veritable atelier, where a host of ordinary and extraordinary collaborators contributed their several items—one, the idea; a second, the plot; a third, the dialogue; a fourth, couplets. . . . M. Scribe, endowed for his task with an incredible aptitude and perseverance, supervised everything; sometimes he would furnish the sketch, or he would revise or polish the work, or remodel it in part; finally he placed on the playbill the name of his chief collaborator beside his own.[3]

In addition, the general process of collaboration as described by Théophile Gautier, who fundamentally opposed the whole concept as being "one of the plagues of art," also seems not to apply to Scribe.

> . . . a play is manufactured just like a suit: one of the collaborators takes the actor's measurements, another cuts the fabric, and the third assembles the pieces; the study of the human heart, style, language, all that is regarded as nothing. . . . With such a method of working, all inspiration is impossible; genius is essentially solitary.[4]

Bonnefon has observed that "to him [Scribe] the theatre was less a matter of original work than the adaptation of an idea to the taste of the moment."[5] Yet nothing like this sort of assembly line process described by Vapereau and Gautier ever seems to have existed in Scribe's work, as can be substantiated in part by Véron's previously quoted statement on Scribe's constant searching for new material, however incidental, in the actions and conversations of everyday life. The collaboration of Scribe with Legouvé on *Adrienne Lecouvreur* may also be somewhat atypical, since Legouvé appears to have done more of the actual work on the drama than was normal for one of Scribe's co-workers. Legouvé having suggested *Adrienne Lecouvreur* as a suitable subject for a drama, Scribe invited him to return the next morning to discuss some ideas.

> At ten o'clock next morning I was with him. He was being operated on by his barber, who held him by the nose. The moment he caught sight of me, he said quickly, in that peculiar tone of voice of a man who is being shaved, 'My dear boy, I have found what we want.' . . . And while the razor was gliding over his face, his fingers were twitching excitedly; he kept looking and smiling at me. No sooner is the [barber's] back turned than there comes an avalanche of ideas, of more or less defined situations, of outlined characters which had sprung up in his mind during the last four-and-twenty hours, and which were being sketched rapidly by him while he was dipping his face into the water, while he was brushing his hair and putting on his shirt, while he was changing his trousers and tying his cravat, while he was getting into his waistcoat and fastening his watch chain, for he liked to sit down to his work dressed and ready to go out at a moment's notice.[6]

This description and others of Legouvé's comments on Scribe's working techniques seem to indicate that, as usual, the latter did most if not all the work once an idea had been presented to him. Nevertheless, Legouvé's general observations on the subject of collaboration leave this open to some question in the particular case of *Adrienne Lecouvreur*, for he says:

> . . . the primary sketch of a piece is drawn by two authors working in conjunction: it is virtually a conversation between these two on a given subject. . . . The shock of two minds produces the fusion of ideas, and from the fusion springs the plan.

> . . . in some instances, one of the authors undertakes to sketch the whole of the work, while the other fills in and finishes. In others the acts are divided between them.[7]

Legouvé's description is the only one extant concerning the nature of the partnership between Scribe and one of his many collaborators. Nevertheless, it would be a mistake to assume as Longyear does that all collaborations followed some pattern similar to that described below.

> The present writer believes that the collaboration of Scribe with his assistants on *opêra-comique* librettos was a 'conversation . . . on a given subject.' The assistant would furnish the idea from which Scribe would plot out the scenes (*numérotage*). Both writers would work out the *coups de théâtre,* although Scribe would place them in their most effective sequence. Scribe wrote the *poesia per musica* himself and was also responsible for the final literary style of the libretto.[8]

It is hardly likely that a person of Scribe's personal and work habits would consistently rely on ideas from others when he had so many of his own given him by his constant observation of human activity, personality, and conversation. However, the fact that Legouvé makes such a point of Scribe's talent in ordering scenes (*numérotage*), commenting that Scribe would even sketch out the sequence of scenes and the characters involved in each before he knew exactly what information or action each scene would contain, seems sufficient evidence that Scribe was indeed responsible for the ordering of the drama, whether spoken or operatic.[9] In some cases a few details of a collaboration on a given libretto are known. These will be mentioned in connection with the opera in question.

As a postscript to the whole matter of collaboration two items are of interest. First, in spoken drama Scribe very often used a collaborator in his vaudevilles, a practice which was the rule rather than the exception.[10] However, when he wrote the more difficult five-act comedies for the Théâtre-Français he had no assistance whatever.[11] This fact would tend to substantiate other evidence that Scribe had no need to rely on the ideas of others, but rather used his collaborators' ideas in much the same way he would use any piece of information he collected in his daily observations. Second, and of similar importance, Longyear has observed:

> Of the twenty-seven librettos which Scribe wrote for Auber, nineteen were written without assistants. The other composers for whom Scribe wrote librettos . . . generally received texts which were the product of collaboration.[12]

Clearly, not only did Scribe have no essential need for other people's ideas, but his best and most difficult pieces were entirely his own work. The facts speak for themselves in opposition to any adverse criticism of Scribe's "fiction-factory,"[13] and one can rightly consider only as a bit of self-satire the passage in the *comédie-vaudeville Le Charlatanisme* which is taken by Longyear and others as the "aesthetic of the *pièce bien fait[e]*."[14]

> I make *opéras comiques* and *vaudevilles.* One ruins himself in lofty literature, one is enriched by the trivial. Take ten years to create a masterpiece? We take three days to create ours. . . . I know that our masterpieces are worth little more than they cost us, but one sees some that last eight days, some have lasted fifteen days, and when one lasts a month, that is immortality!

## THE THEATRES OF SCRIBE'S PARIS

Paul Henry Lang has observed: "Opera does not belong to the domain of music only, its history is closely connected with the destinies of literature and other arts."[1] This being the case, since Scribe wrote for all the major theatres of Paris and since these theatres often influenced operas by Scribe and others, a few words should be included on the state of these institutions and their audiences during Scribe's time.

The majority of the writers for Paris stages during the period 1827-1848—and indeed for at least a decade before that—did not line up as purely classical or purely romantic in their outlook.

> . . . that which preoccupies above all else the large mass of those who wrote for the stage is, in sum, to follow in everything the vogue of the day to the end of insuring [box office] receipts.[2]

This observation is particularly important in the face of ever-present criticism that chides Scribe for catering too much to public taste. Scribe's writing career spanned as many theatres as it did decades. In the spoken theatre his work included rather trivial vaudevilles for the popular theatres as well as full five-act comedies for the more aristocratic Théâtre-Français, and in musical theatre he wrote libretti for everything from one-act curtain raisers set by minor composers for the Opéra-Comique to grand operas on spectacle-filled historical themes set by the most famous and talented musicians of his day. Yet whenever his works were performed Scribe seems to have attracted the same type of audience: the bourgeoisie. This was the audience Gautier described when he wrote of:

> . . . not the public blasé and disdainful of first presentations, these slaves of mode and of literature, people bound to every dramatic solemnity, but rather the upright bourgeois, more or less head of a household, who without being preoccupied with art, style, poetics, goes to leave behind the cares of the day at the theatre and does not dream, in seeing a new comedy, of Aristophanes' *Clouds* or of *Midsummer Night's Dream.*[3]

This view is seconded by John B. Wolf when he describes the French middle class as being made up of persons of restricted outlook who neither read nor traveled to any degree, preferring instead to concentrate on their day-to-day business and to uphold middle-class virtue while cultivating an equally middle-class vice, the love of money.[4] However, the bourgeoisie was not yet in a dominant position in Paris during the Restoration. It was only after 1830 that this class came to the fore as the political, economic, and social force to be reckoned with.[5] Nevertheless, during the 1820s they were beginning to make their power and tastes known, and the theatre became one of their spheres of influence. The older aristocracy in Paris, although politically powerful during Scribe's first rise to fame, generally was not made up of avid theatre-goers.[6] Scribe could not write for them: they would never have heard him, and he in turn would never have been heard by the larger public. However, the people described by Gautier were interested in the theatre, not for aesthetic reasons, but for entertainment. These people made up Scribe's audience. As Wolf remarks, "They set the tone for society—a tone which, after 1830, was copied by the monarch himself."[7]

The tastes of this audience are reflected in such little variation as exists in Scribe's works with respect to themes and plots. In general, Scribe's work for whatever theatre he was making rich thrives on material from contemporary life and attitudes, even in such supposedly historical works as the drama *Bertrand et Raton* or the operas for Meyerbeer. Yet if there is a slightly greater pro-nobility tone in the works of the Restoration than in those of the July Monarchy, this is due not so much to Scribe's basic conservatism as it is a reflection of what the bourgeois audience itself stood for until the later 1820s. In general, the wealthier members of the middle class, although not extreme royalists, tended to align themselves with the nobility in social and artistic matters, and to some extent political matters as well.[8] Since "the mad scramble for money, the vulgar nouveaux-riches, hardly appeared before the July Monarchy," it is no wonder that Scribe's works do not cater to the more extreme bourgeois forces before that time.

> In general, the middle class was liberal, though not yet Republican, in politics, industrious and cautions, and very fearful of both atheism and clericalism. It loved order, security, and authority, provided this authority were not so oppressive as to throw the country into revolution. It was inclined to philanthropy towards the inferior classes so long as they were inclined to remain inferior. . . . Their favorite organization was the National Guard, . . . in which the bourgeoisie saw themselves as defenders of the state and the home.[9]

Scribe of the 1820s, with his noble soldiers, magnanimous aristocrats, and peaceful peasants, embodied the ideals of this class. When they changed, he changed too—but whatever his stance, his feet were planted firmly in the center. He was outstanding simply because, like the members of his audiences, he was not outstanding. He wrote nothing great, nor did he write anything really bad. He entertained the people, yet his themes generally carried a moral as well. He wrote easily, naturally, but not artistically for, as Gautier observed, "Poetry and form, that is what the public of our day cannot suffer. . . ."[10] Impatient with ideas that did not come right to the point, this audience was composed of people for whom Scribe's well-made plays and their companions in the musical theatre, the well-made libretti, were cut to order. These works held few mysteries, few truly unknown quantities, and yet were structured in such a way as to provide the maximum in suspense. If there was ever a "poet of the bourgeoisie,"[11] it was Eugène Scribe.

Censorship was a factor that influenced some aspects of theatrical art, although its strictness and application varied considerably throughout the period during which Scribe was most active, the years from *ca.* 1820 to 1848. Although theatrical censorship does not seem to have been as strict as that of the press, there were nevertheless set procedures through which each proposed stage work had to pass before it was allowed to be performed. Until 1822 it was the custom that the censors present a collective report to the Minister of the Interior on each new play, which the minister either approved or rejected. After the ascendancy of Charles X in 1822, individual reports were required on all new works. A second person, having summarized and evaluated the reports and added his own opinion of the work, would then send the information on to the minister for approval or rejection.[12]

After 1822 censorship became somewhat less strict than it had been earlier. Previously, certain objectionable details could spell doom for the entire work. Now, however, censors were more willing to allow the work to be performed if the objectionable items were changed. At the same time, however, Charles' government passed a law stating that works had to be performed in provincial theatres in the same version that had been approved for Paris. The reason behind this was that some authors had printed their dramas in the original versions and the provincial theatres had been accustomed to use these uncensored scripts for their productions.[13]

Through at least the first decade of the Restoration the principal aim of censorship was to weed out all undesirable political references, particularly "everything that could call up the memory of Napoleon. The Republic, the Consulate, the Empire did not exist."[14] Especially during the early years of the Restoration, audiences were prone to read political allusions into stage presentations even when they did not exist. Transposition of events to different historical periods and of actions to a nonpolitical arena was often practiced to avoid the censor and to eliminate fights in the theatre by champions of various factions.[15]

By about 1827 the climate was such that the presentation of religious personages and persons in ecclesiastical costumes was barred from the stage.[16] Scribe's *Robert le Diable*, begun at this time, gained its dancing nuns and its monastery only after 1830, under a new regime. Nevertheless, censorship in both theatres and newspapers was loosening up, as a whole, and the later years of the Restoration saw the productions of Auber's *La Muette de Portici*, with libretto by Scribe; Carafa's *Masaniello*, an opêra comique on the same subject; and Rossini's *Guillaume Tell*; while among the newspapers the more liberal journals began to appear without the heavy restrictions of former years.[17] However, the representation of anyone resembling Napoleon was still prohibited.

Interesting enough, the romantic movement in drama generally aroused only the distaste of the censors rather than any spate of administrative action.[18] One notable exception was the prohibition of Hugo's *Le Roi s'amuse* after only one performance on the grounds of immorality and the play's seeming justification of regicide.[19] However vivid the tableaux or the language, romantic writers generally did not transgress the particular political code of the government, and censorship was not applied to judge artistic matters. Some of the more melodramatic items, such as scaffolds, suicides, murders and the like, apparently drew warnings nevertheless, and even the graveyard scene in *Hamlet* was executed as simply as possible.

After the July Revolution theatrical censorship was abolished for a time and such previously prohibited subjects as *Le Jesuite* or *Le Te Deum et le tocsin*, as well as operas and dramas on Napoleonic subjects (*Joséphine, ou le Retour de Wagram* at the Opéra-Comique) appeared.[20] A somewhat later example of an opera on a Napoleonic theme is Scribe's own *Régine* (1839, music by Adam), in which the tone is often explicitly anti-Napoleon. For instance, in Act II, iv, the Countess remarks that "this M. Bonaparte, who commands them [the soldiers], has neither consideration nor gallantry . . . such a leader, such soldiers. . . ." The excesses to which this new freedom led included, as before, the presentation of not-so-thinly disguised political allegories which at times involved persons who were still alive. Indeed, Scribe himself was accused of having done this in his drama *Bertrand et Raton* (1833). In this wave of theatrical license *Robert le Diable* was given its sinful nuns in place of a previously peaceful olympian scene, for now all manner of moral and religious material could be freely presented on the stage.

In 1835 preventative censorship was again reestablished, and one of its earliest victims was Scribe's *Les Huguenots*.[21] The opera was authorized for Paris, but in various Protestant towns—Nimes, for example—the non-Catholic contingent demanded and received an order for its prohibition. This sort of preventative censorship continued until the revolution of 1848, and when a conference on censorship was held after that revolution, Scribe was one of the authors who came out in favor of continued vigilance.[22] Yet even this censorship was insufficient for some. Hogarth remarks on the "vitiated taste for the horrible and the revolting" and the "propensity to profane the most sacred things, now so prevalent on the French stage" and illustrated principally by Scribe's *Les Huguenots* and *La Juive*, both of which Hogarth deemed unfit for performance at any English theatre.[23]

Although censorship was practiced throughout most of the period under consideration, and although Scribe, like every other author, had to submit his works to a more or less thorough scanning by the officials before they could be produced, Scribe's pieces were not among those now famous more for the problems they caused than for their literary merit. Hallays-Dabot, in his survey of theatrical censorship in France, rarely mentions a Scribe work. When he does, it is not cited among the more problematical pieces. At first glance this may seem strange, for Scribe was very much a man of his times and one author has noted his works as "still among the best sources for French social history during this long period from 1815 to 1870."[24] Yet Scribe was a mirror of his times, not a leader or a reformer. When the conservative bourgeois, tired of the uncertainties and destructiveness of war, wanted a settled peace in which to lead a stable existence, Scribe spoke to him of shopkeepers, honorable but not inactive soldiers, domestic scenes, and a people living in harmony with one another and with the world around them. Evil was put down quickly and inevitably, and virtue flourished once more as if nothing had ever disturbed it.

In essence, of course, Scribe's lack of problems with censorship was precisely the result of that censorship and the ideals under which it operated. Some even wanted the censors to go so far as to

> . . . examine the works before their presentation, . . . prohibit any subject drawn from the holy books, any drama representing on the stage dethroned kings, deposed princes, rebellious subjects, homicides, seduced maidens, faithless women, pontiffs, priests, and processions. The worker would no longer take lessons on politics and insurrections from the [theatres of the] boulevards; he would find nothing more, by orders from above, than the pleasant scene of the interior of his home, of his shop, or of his store.[25]

Fortunately, actual censorship was never quite this restrictive, but the possibilities outlined in the above quotation undoubtedly influenced Scribe, however indirectly.

Nevertheless, the peace and prosperity themes of the Restoration changed under a multitude of influences and Scribe changed in response to the same influences. In the years surrounding 1830, when romanticism was making its loudest noises and a new government brought with it a new license in the theatre, Scribe spoke of Masaniello, of Bertrand and Raton, of Robert the Devil and the prison of Edinburgh, of religious wars and history. During this time Scribe also began to deal more stringently with the follies of his time in his vaudevilles, so much so that the Duchess of Berry threatened to withdraw her patronage from the Gymnase for their having presented Scribe's *Avant, pendant, et après* (June 28, 1828), a play she believed should have been withdrawn by the censors.[26] Comparatively speaking, however, Scribe's moves in these new directions were never extreme, and the local or historical color in his works was a veneer. Underneath, the solid bourgeois remains as Scribe knew he would when, after the July Revolution, he patiently waited for the air to clear and his fortunes to rise again from the dust. For Scribe, censorship was a guide but never a threat, for he was what he was: a successful playwright.

In 1817 the population of Paris was some 715,000 people, a figure which rose to 800,000 by 1830.[27] Naturally, not all or even a large majority of these people attended the major theatres with any frequency, but even one per cent of 800,000 people is a considerable number. There were theatres in Paris to cater to every taste and station, and in almost all cases the public dictated the type of entertainment it wanted to see. Each Parisian stage cultivated its own particular clientele, which was often different and distinct from that of other theatres. By means of tacit agreements among theatres and the somewhat restrictive licensing practices of the French government, stages cultivated particular dramatic genres which their audiences expected and for which they became known.[28] Thus the theatres of Paris can be classified under five general headings: the musical theatres, theatres for spoken comedy and drama, the secondary theatres featuring vaudevilles and similar light entertainment, theatres for heavy drama and spectacle, and theatres for farce and extravaganza. Although Scribe was not active in all these types, a discussion of them is important to establish the theatrical climate in Paris during the first half of the nineteenth century and to determine the ways in which the various dramatic genres were mutually influential.

Chief among the spoken theatres in Paris was the Comédie-Française, which served not only as a showcase for the highest forms of contemporary dramatic art, but also as a kind of living museum dedicated to the preservation and continuation of classical traditions in both drama and acting.[29] The Théâtre-Français at the time of Scribe was undergoing changes similar to those at the Paris Opéra. By the mid-1820s classical and neoclassical tragedy had reached an impasse, just as had the operas of the older school of French composers from Gluck to Cherubini, and such entertainment failed to appeal to the large mass of people. However, like the Opéra, the Théâtre-Français gradually began producing plays in the later years of the decade which chose themes from recent history and included such features as local color and more realistic dialogue. These had a much broader appeal than the older topics of classicism and the stilted alexandrines of earlier French tragedy. Under the impact of such romantic plays as Alexandre Dumas' prose drama *Henri III et sa cour* (1829), the Théâtre-Français began once more to be relevant to its age even though the romanticists, exposed to adverse criticism and ridicule on this stage, chose the secondary theatres as the scene of many of the major events of their desired dramatic revolution. As Karl Mantzius has observed, "no fortress is more impregnable to assault by a band of rebellious poets than is a reactionary State Theatre."[30] Although true romanticism did not thrive at the Théâtre-Français, the trend toward updating themes and styles on its stage continued. In Scribe's work this trend is illustrated by his first five-act comedy for this theatre, *Le Mariage d'argent* (1827), a play dealing with contemporary life and the solid bourgeois views on the virtues of a good and proper marriage.[31]

The *deuxième Théâtre-Français* was the Odéon. Given a government subsidy during the Restoration, it came under the direction of Jean-Charles Harel in 1829. This man, although inexperienced in things theatrical, was more sympathetic to the romanticists than the management of the Théâtre-Français had been, and helped promote productions of dramas by Hugo, Dumas, and others.[32]

Below this theatre in rank stood the vaudeville theatres. Those included the Gymnase Dramatique, a theatre opened in 1820 by Scribe's friend Delestre-Poirson and sustained for some ten years thereafter by Scribe's plays. This theatre was also called the Théâtre de Madame because of the patronage by the Duchess of Berry after 1824,[33] and was called by one author "the third Comédie-Française and the second Opéra-Comique."[34] One of its functions was indeed to act as a proving ground for talented young performers desirous of playing eventually at the Opéra-Comique.[35] It thus stood in the same relation to the Opéra-

Comique as did the Odéon to the Théâtre-Français, and in addition helped train actors for the latter stage.

Others in this group of secondary theatres were the Gaîté and the Ambigu-Comique, which also included melodrama and spectacle pieces in their repertoires, and the Vaudeville. The last-named house was first opened in 1792 and "was frequently in trouble for the topical and political allusions found in its productions by the vigilance of the censor," which it avoided by masking these allusions under semihistorical themes.[36] The Vaudeville having burned down in 1838, the troupe moved to the Nouveautés where such authors as Dumas *fils* were included with some success on the playbills. One particularly important work premiered by this company was *La Dame aux camélias* (1852).[37]

The position of the vaudeville on the French dramatic scene is not so much the result of artistic merits or defects as it is of the quantity of such works produced. Since there were two or three vaudevilles produced to each serious play, the popular form was by far more important in the day-to-day theatrical life of Paris.[38] The character of the vaudeville has some elements in common with the opéra comique, enough so that Scribe himself could name them in the same breath in his play, *Le Charlatanisme* (see the quotation on page 16).

> . . . [vaudeville] provided light entertainment for the vast new theatre-going public, and at the same time served as an echo and mirror of the times.[39]

Scribe learned his craft of dramatic construction and general style first in the realm of vaudeville, turning that genre into the dramatically more highly developed *comédie-vaudeville.* Lang has gone so far as to suggest that the secret of Scribe's success "was that whatever form of the theatre he cultivated, he invariably took his inspiration from the vaudeville."[40] No wonder, then, that certain structural elements of the well-made play as well as the popular theatre's modernity turn up in his opéra comique libretti. As Arvin has observed, Scribe transformed the opéra comique just as he had the vaudeville, making its subjects more up to date, its dialogue more natural, its action livelier and more varied. "The *opéra comique* thus renewed became a sort of complement to the company which he had inaugurated at the Gymnase."[41] A landmark in this changed aspect of opéra comique is *La Dame blanche,* with music by Boieldieu, first performed in 1825.

One of the strongest influences on romantic drama—hence both a direct and an indirect influence on grand opera and the more serious opéras comiques—was melodrama. Melodrama was a sensation-filled dramatic form that broke through the domination of the versified classical tragedy, with its three unities, and thrived on "swift, violent action, . . . mingling of bloodshed and sentimentality, . . . elaborate settings and stage effects, and . . . expert manipulations of well-worn themes in which, after the pleasurable excitement of villainy, virtue rose triumphant."[42] It flourished during the postrevolutionary decade and on into the nineteenth century. A particular champion and prolific author of the form was Guilbert de Pixérécourt (1773-1844), who was manager of the Théâtre de la Gaîté in the 1820s and '30s.

In addition to the Gaîté two other theatres particularly cultivated melodrama and spectacle: the Porte-Saint-Martin and the Ambigu-Comique. The former, once the home of the Opéra, devoted itself after 1810 to "strong drama and spectacular works," among them plays by Hugo and Delavigne and fairy tale productions involving spectacular stage effects.[43] An important theatre in the battle between classic and romantic drama in the late 1820s, it saw the first performances of Dumas' *Tour de Nesle* and *Antony*, Casimir Delavigne's *Marino Faliero*, and Hugo's *Marie Tudor* and *Lucrèce Borgia*.[44] The Ambigu-Comique, founded as a marionette and children's theatre in 1769, devoted itself primarily to melodrama from 1797 until it was destroyed by fire in 1827.[45] As for the Gaîté, it has the distinction of being the first French theatre that was not subsidized by the state. Founded in the eighteenth century, it was very prosperous in the first half of the nineteenth century, "sharing the vast output of melodrama with the Ambigu-Comique, and putting on elaborate fairy-plays, pantomimes, and vaudevilles."[46] After 1862 its name was given to a new theatre known particularly for its success under the direction of Offenbach.[47]

The influence of melodrama on romantic opera and drama was great, for melodrama was making use of historical and supernatural subjects, thrilling horror plots, and all the attendant stage effects as early as the 1790s. According to J. F. Mason:

> The mind of the populace of Paris was in such an abnormal state [during the 1790s] that the desire for the strange and the peculiar, for stories of devils, ghosts, and imps in the midst of scenes of battle and murder, seemed insatiable.
>
> When political conditions became more normal this exaggerated romanticism began to disappear, and long before Hugo's Spanish bandit came upon the stage of the *Comédie-Française*, the popular theatres had adopted almost exclusively historical and domestic subjects for their plays.[48]

Thus nearly every element of romantic drama, which in turn influenced such romantic operas as *Robert le Diable* and *Les Huguenots*, was present in the popular theatre years earlier. Mason has summarized:

> The success of *Hernani* marks the advent of the melodrama into literature. With this change of theatre the genre itself underwent certain changes, verse was substituted for prose and *drame romantique* used instead of *mélodrame.* The latter was too closely associated with the *boulevard de Crime* to appear on the bills of the Comédie-Française, and the partisans of the new school were only too fearful lest their enemies should draw invidious comparisons between the plays of the Boulevards and romantic drama. In spite of this change of name, the dramas of Hugo and Dumas stand in close relationship to the melodrama, and *Hernani* marks the culmination rather than the beginning of the new genre.[49]

Music was an important part of the melodrama. It was used to heighten certain dramatc situations, to emphasize entrances and exits, and in general to create a more receptive climate for emotional reactions to the sensations of the drama. Ballet was also employed as the occasion demanded.[50] As early as the short melodramatic monologues of the 1760s and '70s thematic unity in the accompanying music had been used to form the scenes into a well-wrought whole.[51] In the nineteenth century, with the role of the orchestra becoming greater in opera, music in and of itself began to take on independent dramatic functions similar to those of the music in melodrama. Perhaps such use of music as is found in the melodramas of Pixérécourt hastened this development even as the scenic effects in melodrama left their mark on the spectacular staging of grand opera and romantic drama. The lavish settings of the operas of Meyerbeer and Halévy provide examples of the former. As for the latter, an example is to be found in Artz's observations on Dumas' *Henri III et sa cour*, the first truly successful romantic drama: "It seems, if read today, hardly a play at all, but only a series of gorgeous tableaus of the days of Catherine de' Medici and the Guises."[52] Further examples exist in the dramatists' insistence on accuracy of local color in scenery, costumes, and stage properties (e.g., Hugo's statements in the Preface to *Cromwell*), ideas which had been advocated and put into practice by Pixérécourt some twenty-five or thirty years earlier.[53]

Scribe himself did not cultivate the genre of melodrama. Yet as an intelligent man of the theatre, one who made his life the stage, he could not help but be aware of the contributions being made by Pixérécourt and others. It is surely no accident that Cicéri, stage designer at the Opéra when Scribe's greatest grand operas were produced, first worked in the field of melodrama.[54]

The leading companies in the musical theatre during the first half of the nineteenth century were those of the Opéra, the Opéra-Comique, and the Italian opera. It should be emphasized that these groups were companies and not theatres, for each changed its base of operation several times in the course of the period under discussion. The Opéra, a convenient designation for an institution that was called more formally the Académie Imperiale (or later, Royale) de Musique, provides a good example of this point. Immediately after the Revolution the company, under the name of Théâtre des Arts après le Dix-Août, settled briefly at the Porte-Saint-Martin Theatre, moving soon to its new house on the Rue de la Loi (now Rue Richelieu) known as the Salle Montansier. This theatre housed the Opéra from August 7, 1794, until the assassination of the Duke of Berry in the theatre on February 13, 1820. Moving for a few months to the Salle Favart and then to the Salle Louvois, the Opéra soon settled in a new theatre on the Rue Le Peletier which was its permanent residence until 1873, when a fire destroyed the building. Thus, during the greater part of the period under consideration the Académie Royale de Musique occupied the Salle Le Peletier, a theatre seating more than 1700 persons, where it was directed first by Habeneck, then successively by Duplantys (1824), Lubbert (1827), Véron (1831), Duponchel (1835), Monnais (1839), Duponchel and Lèon Pillet (1840), Pillet and Roqueplan (1847), and Roqueplan alone (1849).[55]

The residences of the Opéra-Comique were even more varied. In 1801 the companies that formerly performed in the Théâtre-Feydeau and the Salle Favart banded together under the appellation Théâtre de l'Opera-Comique, and gave their performances in the Feydeau Theatre. The year 1804 saw the company making use of several different theatres: the Salle Favart from July to October; the Théâtre-Olympique during October; and the Salle Favart again until the middle of 1805, when the company moved back to the Feydeau. This theatre remained the home of the Opéra-Comique until mid-1829, when it moved to a new house, the Ventadour, where it stayed until moving to the Théâtre des Nouveautés (1832). In 1840 the Opera-Comique left the Nouveautés to the performance of vaudevilles and took up residence in the Second Salle Favart, where it remained until the end of the century.[56]

In 1879 the Salle Ventadour, which had housed the Théâtre des Italiens since 1841 and had earlier (1829-1832) been the home of the Opéra-Comique, was sold and remodeled for use as a bank.[57] Thus ended the activity of the permanent Italian company in Paris, an activity which had declined in popularity some years before. In its prime, however, the Théâtre-Italien had been a serious competition of both the Opéra and the Opéra-Comique and had enjoyed the services of Rossini as director during the 1820s. Like the other major musical companies, the Italian troupe also had several homes during the first half of the nineteenth century. During the Napoleonic era the troupe performed at the Odéon, a theatre which was later dedicated to spoken drama and was second only to the Théâtre-Francais, for which it was a feed-theatre for both plays and players.[58] At various times during the decade from 1815 to 1825 the Italian troupe played at the Salle Favart, making this theatre its permanent home from 1825 until 1838. Housed in various theatres from 1838 to 1841, the Théâtre-Italien took over the Salle Ventadour in 1841 and remained there until the above-mentioned sale.[59]

A fourth, short-lived company devoted to musical theatre was the Opéra-National, founded by Adolphe Adam and Achille Mirecour in 1847. Like the Théâtre-Lyrique which succeeded it in 1851, the Opéra-National was intended to give younger, unknown composers, librettists, and performers a chance to be heard and to produce works that were not light enough for the Opéra-Comique yet not sufficiently serious or elaborate for the Opéra. The story of the eventual success of this venture belongs to the second half of the century.[60]

Another minor musical theatre was, for a time, the Théâtre de la Renaissance, first opened on November 8, 1838, "with a license for plays both with and without music. This aroused the jealousy of both the Comédie-Française and the Opéra, who finally caused it to close, but not before it had done some good work."[61]

It was the mid-1820s before Scribe and his various musical collaborators began the rise to fame and popularity that was to culminate in their virtual domination of the Paris musical stage. For both the Opéra and the Opéra-Comique these years in the middle and late 1820s were ones of change from older, now well-worn styles and ideals to those that would prevail during the last years of the Restoration and throughout the July Monarchy. In these changes Scribe and his libretti played an increasingly important role.

The state of French opera during the first years of the Restoration was rather dismal. The great composers of the Revolutionary and Napoleonic eras—Méhul, Lesueur, Spontini, Cherubini—were dead or aging, and no new names were rising to take their places. This produced a situation about which Grout could state flatly: "During the eight years after Spontini's *Olympie* (1819) no significant new works were produced at the Paris Opéra."[62] Indeed, Edwards dates this decline as beginning in 1813, after Cherubini's *Abencerrages*, and continuing until Rossini's *Siège de Corinthe* of 1826.[63] Sophie Leo, upon her arrival in

Paris in 1817, noted that although Gluck's works were still performed ("more to the convenience of the company than to the pleasure of the public"), the old masters had been put aside and replaced by mediocre imitators.[64] Sacchini's *Oedipe à Colonne* (1786), "though at first received with enthusiasm, had failed to justify the pretensions to Gluck's heroic manner entertained by its composer," and Catel "had proved a disappointment and was subsequently forgotten."[65] Cherubini, though still alive, was past his prime. Spontini, seen by Bellaigue as an intermediary between Gluck and Méhul on the one hand and grand opera on the other, was still popular but was regarded by many as antiquated.[66] Indeed, although his *Fernand Cortez* (1809) marks a turn toward historical subject matter and pageantry that was to be exploited in grand opera of the 1830s, Spontini's major works of the early decades of the century—*La Vestale* (1807) and *Olympie* (1819)—were within a tradition which was definitely declining during the Restoration. Audiences no longer cared for themes from classical antiquity represented by these operas, and theatres remained nearly empty during performances of the traditional fare, much to the dismay of the young Berlioz, who arrived in Paris in 1821.[67]

Nor was the Opéra's lack of popularity with the theatre-going public solely the result of its repertoire. The great singers who had first created the roles of the classic figures were either dead or on the verge of retirement. Others, less famous, remained with the company beyond the years when their voices could contribute anything to the success of a work. In short, the stage of the Opéra was populated by superannuated and mediocre singers, and Sophie Leo reported:

> . . . I was really distressed by the affected style in which those divine works [by Gluck], Armida, Alcestis, and the two Iphigenias, were offered us by the old company; one enjoyed and suffered at the same moment.[68]

A combination of factors, then, worked against the Opéra in its attempts to achieve public success, and it found itself in a situation similar to that of the Théâtre-Français. Musically, wrote Joseph d'Ortigue, the times were comparable to those of the literary world at the time of Voltaire. Then, young writers were still imitating the older school, writing imitations of classical tragedy at a time when public admiration for it was nearly dead. So too did young composers in the first decades of the nineteenth century continue to follow the models of Cherubini, Spontini, Méhul and others of that generation without a chance of surpassing them in the styles and genres they had created.[69] As Sophie Leo remarked:

> For the Opéra it had become a question of perishing altogether or, by adopting a form more in keeping with the spirit of the times, of obtaining a new lease on life.[70]

With this d'Ortigue agreed. The French operatic stage needed not new works but a new genre, created by a composer "who could be understood at once, without the need to study him; . . . in a word, a Rossini was needed."[71] Gioacchino Rossini, the toast of all Europe, thus arrived in Paris at a critical time in the history of French opera. Before he ended his career there in 1829 he had affected everything in French opera, from musical style down to the make-up and performing technique of the company.

Jean-François Gail, writing in 1832, admitted that Rossinian style and performance standards had greatly modified national taste during the preceding ten years, stating that French opera owed to him "a kind of material regeneration."[72] Rossini fever in Paris was a gradual development, beginning quite tentatively in 1817 with the first full performance of a Rossini opera, *L'Italiana in Algeri*, at the Salle Favart before small audiences.[73] About a dozen of Rossini's operas were performed by the Italian company between 1817 and the composer's first arrival in Paris late in 1823, and these had aroused increasing public enthusiasm as well as a flood of polemics from the critics. Having made known while passing through Paris on his way to London that he would be pleased to stay on and work in the former city provided the terms were right, Rossini signed a contract the following year and returned to Paris in 1824 to conduct at the Théâtre-Italien and to compose Italian and French operas. His effect on operatic production in Paris was electric. Not only were French composers now directly exposed to the musical influence of the famed Italian, but the musical stage itself underwent some basic changes. With the premiere of Rossini's first French opera, *Le Siège de Corinthe* (1826, revised from his earlier Italian work *Maometto II*), the French singers found themselves confronted with a vocal style for which most of them were totally unprepared. The necessity that the French vocalists retrain their voices in the Italian image for the works of Rossini and his French imitators helped effect a much-needed improvement in the level of vocal performance at the Opéra and elsewhere. Moreover, the freshness of style and subject matter of Rossini's operas provided a much-needed shot in the arm for the Opéra, making composers and librettists alike more willing to turn from the French classic tradition to music and libretti more in keeping with the times. Gradually the prospects for opera began to take a turn for the better, and Sophie Leo observed:

> Though at the time of my arrival [1817-18] all three opera houses were deteriorating, a very few years sufficed for their rehabilitation. By this I do not mean to imply that there was any improvement in the compositions that were provided for the two French theatres; it was rather that the standard of singing, the personnel, the costumes and the buildings themselves, were improved and that the whole was given a fresher and more inviting appearance.[74]

Even more basic, however, was Rossini's effect on the character of opera as a whole. Although easily grasped by the listener, Rossini's music was far from simple and required first rate performers even to begin to perform it effectively. Each member of the cast was important, and more than ever the way in which the opera was staged and performed was of supreme importance, rivaling that of the music itself, in the success of the work. Just as some dramatic poetry cannot be spoiled no matter who reads it, observed d'Ortigue, some music in opera can be performed and staged indifferently and yet be appreciated for its intrinsic beauty as long as a certain level of competence is reached. Not so with Rossini who, like Voltaire, is better "played" than "read."[75] The same observation could be made of the works of many composers of French opera influenced by Rossini, particularly those of grand opera. Indeed, one of the reasons commonly put forth for the oblivion into which Meyerbeer's masterpieces have fallen is that these operas require resources not normally possessed by any single opera company: a huge cast, elaborate scenic resources, and—above all else—superlative performers in every role. Even in the 1830s the medium was at least half the message, and this development is both a direct and an indirect result of the phenomenon called Rossini.

Rossini wrote only a few more operas for the French stage: *Moïse*, a revision of his Italian *Mosè in Egitto*, in 1827; *Le Comte Ory* in 1828; and his last opera, *Guillaume Tell*, in 1829. Yet whether through direct influence or by means of reaction against him, Rossini exercised great power in the French musical world.

As Mme. Leo mentions, there was seemingly no sudden improvement in the fare offered the public by either the Opéra or the Opéra-Comique. Yet just as tragedy gave way to drama in the spoken theatre, classicistic subjects in opera gave way to those from modern history, largely under the influence of the popular—and especially the romantic—theatre. Scribe above all was responsible for these changes, for he brought to opera the best, or at least the most typical, features of romantic drama and to opéra comique the traits of the *comédie-vaudeville*, both at a time when change was desired and, indeed, necessary.

Although elements of French grand opera as well as of a more serious or "romantic" type of opéra comique can be traced back to the musical stage of the postrevolutionary era, the phases of both forms of opera showing a definite, deliberate move in a new direction can be dated from the productions of Boieldieu's *La Dame blanche* at the Opéra-Comique in 1825 and of Auber's *La Muette de Portici* at the Opera in 1828. These two works represent on the one hand the culmination of various trends in musical style, stage design, subject matter, and dramatic structure; and on the other hand the beginning of a new era, one which coincides with the rise of the French bourgeoisie to a position of power and influence.

Grand opera was, according to Lang, "a necessity, a logical outcome of the trends of French literature," in that it partook of the historical atmosphere created by romantic literature and particularly by romantic drama.[76] French opera needed a change. It could not compete with Rossini on his own ground, and in looking for a new basis found in historical subjects a substitute for the dramatic distance previously provided by mythology. As Hugo's *Burgraves* is less a picture of medieval Germany than of Napoleonic France; as Scribe's own *Bertrand et Raton* is less concerned with seventeenth century Denmark than with conditions in France of the 1830s; so *La Muette de Portici*, although externally dealing with a revolution in Naples, is actually outlining conditions that could—and eventually did—lead to revolt in Auber's Paris. The dramatic distance provided by the cover of history thus granted perspective to the thoughtful observer, but more than that it made necessary the concentration on local color. As Lang has put it:

> This history-created distance . . . seemed not only much more conscious than its predecessors, but it semed less firm and required the assistance of facts, of 'historical truth.'[77]

Yet just as one cannot attribute the creation of grand opera to any single cause, one cannot ascribe merely to the demand for historical truth the emphasis on lavish and exact depiction of time and place typical of this form of opera as early as *La Muette*, an emphasis which derives in turn from the historical development of melodrama into romantic drama. While grand opera begins in 1828, its real triumph comes in the 1830s. This coincides with the rise and final triumph of the bourgeoisie which involved, among other things, a gradual increase in ostentatious, often tasteless display of wealth by members of this class. It should come as no surprise that these arbiters of Parisian social life were also the prime consumers of theatrical and, more specifically, operatic entertainment, and that they should demand in such entertainment those things on which they placed most value in life. Thus, as one kind of dramatic distance gives way to another in the replacement of mythological themes by historical, so one kind of spectacle yields to another having greater horsepower and more modern design.

> Forced to suppress its Olympus, a bit antiquated [the Opéra], locked up in its storehouses with regret the passé rose tricot of Venus, the soft goddess, and the green-scaled armor of the warrior Pallas. But, at least, it has not fallen lower than prince and princess.[78]

In addition to Scribe, the men most responsible for the creation and cultivation of French grand opera were the manager Louis Véron, who was in charge of the Opéra from 1831 to 1835; the composer Giacomo Meyerbeer, who brought all features of the genre to their highest point of musical development; the stage director Duponchel, later to become full manager of the company; and scene designers Ciceri and Séchan. Together they practiced what Jean-Francois Gail, among others, preached: that "the principal end of the arts is to please."[79] And what pleased the French opera-going public, however much it seemed to celebrate Rossini, was, according to Gail, a work that appealed not merely to the senses but to the intellect as well. Something more than Rossini's lovely vocalism and insignificant action was required. The first condition was fulfilled by Meyerbeer, who brought to the stage a musical style that combined elements of Italian lyricism with Germanic seriousness and at times intellectualism, underscoring the whole with a development of the art of operatic orchestration unknown in his own day and influential on future composers. The second requirement, "an action follow[ing] an uninterrupted course," free of improbable or forced situations,[80] was met in the well-ordered libretti of Scribe. Emphasis on exact local color for the historical settings of grand opera's romantically-tinged plots was seconded by a desire for great scenic spectacle which had always been an important element in French opera. One critic has made the following comparison.

> In the last analysis, it surely seems that the *mise en scène* or the spectacle, in our national grand opera, is the equivalent of the dialogue in our opéra comique, this other equally French genre. The two elements play the same role and have the same advantage: that of distracting us from the music and of diverting us from it.[81]

The enterprising Louis Véron not only best personifies the domination of the theatre by the middle class but is largely responsible for making French grand opera "an art *and* a business."[82] A journalist and physician of some means, Véron carried out a plan to invest his own funds in the opera—which had up to this point been owned, managed, and subsidized by the state—and to turn this theatre into a profit-making venture. Like Scribe, Véron reasoned that he could turn political events and the temper of the times to his own good uses.

> The July Revolution is the triumph of the bourgeoisie: this victorious bourgeoisie will want to lord it over everything, to be amused; the Opéra will become their Versailles, they will run there in a crowd to take the places of the grand *seigneurs* and the exiled court. This project to render the Opéra at the same time brilliant and popular seemed to me to have great chances of success after the July Revolution.[83]

In a contract signed February 28, 1831, Véron was called upon to manage the Opéra for six years "at his own risk, peril, and fortune," thus bringing to a satisfactory solution—from the government's point of view—the problem of declining revenues plaguing the Opéra during most of the Restoration.[84] Although some subsidy from the state was to be provided, it was to grow smaller over a period of years. In return for the privilege of risking his fortune in this venture Véron had to agree to maintain the theatre in a style suitable to the established position of this national enterprise and to present a certain number of new works each year.[85] Very corporation-minded, Véron proceeded to surround himself with the best talents available for the various tasks involved in production and to manage the whole with a businesslike efficiency of which the bureaucratic government ministries would have been incapable. The years of his directorship set the tone for the development of French grand opera, and the methods of operation he established lingered on long after he had ceased to head the company. Thus, to Lang's statement that "grand opera has its foundations not in nature, but in the nature of Meyerbeer and Scribe"[86] should be added the phrase: "and Véron." Such was the state of the operatic stage when Scribe first became an active participant and began to increase his position to that of the most important and sought-after librettist of his age.

As with opera, opéra comique was going through a lesser but nevertheless important crisis in its history at the time Scribe began to write libretti in this genre. Romanticism, or at least melodrama, had entered the opéra comique during the postrevolutionary era in the works of such composers as Méhul, Cherubini and Lesueur. There thus arose a division between such *drames lyriques* and the more traditional opéras comiques cultivated by such composers as Dalayrac, Gaveaux, Isouard, and the young Boieldieu. The latter works, whether sentimental or farcical, were of a lighter nature. In addition to this difference of subject matter between the two branches of opéra comique, there were also differences of length and style. The more serious opéra comique was generally a three-act work in which musical scenes played an important role, whereas works of a lighter, more comical nature were more often in one act and relied less on the music than on the spoken dialogue for the depiction of characters and for the main elements of dramatic effect.

The vogue for rescue opera declined during the first decades of the nineteenth century, and although Dalayrac and Isouard continued to write—the latter until the 1820s—their best work was of the eighteenth century in time as well as in style. Boieldieu had left Paris for St. Petersburg in 1803 and did not return until 1811, after which date his best and most influential works were produced. In addition, the Opéra-Comique was poorly managed during part of the Restoration, and government bureaucracy got in the way of just and efficient administration.[87] Thus, this "eminently national genre,"[88] like the more serious spectacles at the Opéra, was decaying and slipping into a rut of mediocrity.

It should go without saying that opéra comique as a genre has a literary as well as a musical history. As was mentioned earlier, the eighteenth century opéra comique relied more on spoken dialogue than on music for its effect, to the extent that Longyear is of the opinion many eighteenth century libretti could be performed just as well without the music as with it.[89] Although one cannot make such a statement with regard to the libretti of Scribe, there were writers within the older tradition who served in one way or another as his predecessors, among them Louis Benoît Picard, playwright and librettist of Devienne's *Les Visitandines* (1792) and *Les Comédiens ambulans* (1798). In a preface to one of his plays, *Les Marionettes ou les Ricochets*, Picard mentions "a principle which sounds familiar, 'Les petits causes amènent souvent de grands effects' [*sic*],"[90] a sentiment echoed, among other places, in Scribe's *La Figurante*, Act III, iii, when the Duke of Lemos remarks: "Il faut souvent si peu de chose pour occasionner de grands malheurs." Yet the order of the day in libretti for the lighter forms of opéra comique was not similar to that in Scribe's works. The subjects of earlier libretti, while having "a certain feeling of plausibility," were not real.[91]

> The plots often dealt with an idealized peasantry, with a naive heroine (usually a shepherdess) in love with a manly youth (the *ténor amoreux*) but oppressed by a wicked noble who was eventually confounded by the intervention of the magnanimous prince.[92]

Although the turn toward rescue opera in the later eighteenth century added seriousness and melodramatic quality to the old formula and often made use of more sophisticated characters, the connection with actual life was at best symbolic.

> The medieval settings [when such were used] were not intended to be historically accurate, and the characters therein were those of Watteau, Boucher, and the Dresden china factories.[93]

In general, structural aspects of opéra comique libretti in the late eighteenth century and first decades of the nineteenth were also quite different from those of Scribe. These differences derived not only from the comparative lack of importance of the music but also from a turn from a one-act structure toward more two- and three-act libretti after 1810. This change caused problems in the parceling out of the action into the various act and scene divisions.

Two events, more or less simultaneous, led to the rejuvenation of the opéra comique in the mid-1820s. The first, which affected the musical side of the genre, was the growing enthusiasm for Rossini. The second, which helped revolutionize the art of libretto writing, was the development by Scribe of the *comédie-vaudeville.*

The effect of Rossini's success on opéra comique was two-sided. On the one side composers, among them the young Auber, found in the sprightly and lyrical style of the Italian an antidote to the musical lethargy of the *petite musique agréable* represented by the successors of Gaveaux and Dalayrac. Although Auber by no means became simply an imitator of Rossini, he and others found the Italian style useful for specific characters and scenes, and this in turn helped increase the importance of the music in the whole production. Ensembles and finales became longer and arias more frequent and more florid. On the other side, however, many fought against the encroachment of Italian style on French music, among them Boieldieu, to whom "is due the merit of having upheld the national French comic opera almost singlehanded for a long time against the blandishments of the Italian opera of Rossini."[94] This too strengthened the position of music in opéra comique, and together Boieldieu and Auber led the genre out of decline and into the so-called "classic phase" of its development exemplified by Boieldieu's *La Dame blanche* and Auber's *Fra Diavolo* and *Le Domino noir.*

Scribe's development of the *comédie-vaudeville* had its effect on his opéra comique libretti in several ways. First, the structural devices of the well-made play, many of which apply in modified form to Scribe's libretti, were first cultivated in the plays given at the Gymnase. Second, in these plays Scribe creates real characters—not in the sense that they are fully human and three-dimensional figures, but in the sense that they typify the best and the worst features of Parisian society of the 1820s.

When he carries these people and the situations in which they find themselves over into opéra comique he not only revitalizes the genre dramatically but brings to it the kinds of characters who are enhanced by musical development and the kinds of situations that go hand in hand with the modern musical styles. Thus by 1832 Gail can speak of opéra comique as "a literary fiction, which is vaudeville perfected," in full recognition of the transferences and transformations effected by Scribe during the previous decade.[95]

Along with the revolution in musical composition brought about by Rossinian influences, the gradual replacement of the old company and the elimination of dead wood in the orchestra also helped opéra comique toward rejuvenation in the mid-1820s. New, young, skilled performers, often from the Conservatoire, brought a fresh approach and greater enthusiasm to the stage of the Opéra-Comique.[96]

Between 1825 and 1850, 216 new opéras comiques were produced in Paris, twenty-three of which remained in the repertoire for ten or more years after their premieres.[97] From the textual and musical regeneration of the genre in the mid-1820s opéra comique increased in popularity once more, largely due to the work of Scribe and his musical collaborators. It grew to a point that Cauchie could call the reign of Louis-Philippe "the most glorious era for *opéra-comique*."[98]

Yet as Longyear has rightly observed, "*Opéra comique* . . . was part of the bourgeois world to which the Romantics were opposed."[99] Regardless of how grand an opéra comique became in subject, setting, or music, its characters were still people from the society of Paris who did not even have the elegance of bearing to sing to one another rather than to speak as ordinary mortals. The opinion of critic Théophile Gautier is often quoted.

> For our part, we have no tenderness for the virtues of opéra comique, a bastard and mesquin genre, a mixture of two incompatible modes of expression, in which the actors play badly on the pretext that they are singers and sing badly on the pretext that they are actors.[100]

However, it was this bourgeois world that was supporting the theatre in all its forms during the 1830s, as Scribe's annual accounts so aptly show, and the fact that romanticists profited somewhat less from that support than did the opéra comique is enough to make one suspect the presence of the proverbial sour grapes in their judgments of the genre.

Longyear has summarized the general characteristics of opera comique from 1825 to 1850, its "classical phase," as follows.

> (1) Spoken dialogue alternated with specially-composed music. This distinguished opéra comique from French grand opera or Italian opera, in which the music was continuous throughout, and from the comédie-vaudeville, which used pre-existent tunes. . . .
>
> (2) The plot was, as a rule, not meant to be taken seriously. . . .
>
> (3) The dominant character in *opéra comique* was a certain type of soprano called *première chanteuse de roulades.* In all but a few scores the most important male character, the *ténor léger,* is ancillary to the principal female role. . . .
>
> (4) Opera was intended to appeal to the aristocracy, the *haute bourgeoisie* (after 1830), and the intellectuals; *opéra comique,* in contrast, was essentially a petit bourgeois entertainment.
>
> (5) A happy ending was obligatory.[101]

It was this type of opéra comique for which Scribe was in large part responsible and which continued with relatively few changes until the end of the July Monarchy. However, there were within the tradition the seeds of another division similar to but not so great as the one which occurred before 1800. Scribe wrote libretti for Auber, Boieldieu, Hérold, Carafa, and others, but he also wrote for Adolphe Adam, a composer whose style tended more toward the *petite musique agréable* of former days. He was the first and most important composer to turn from the rather more serious style of his contemporaries and to pave the way for the comical operettas of Offenbach. Scribe thus plays an important role in the major changes in the history of opéra comique in the first half of the nineteenth century: that from the declining eighteenth century style to the "classic" style of Auber, Boieldieu, Hérold, and later the more serious *opéra lyrique* of the second half of the century; and that from this "classical" style to the lighter entertainments of Adam and his successors.

In the final category of Parisian theatres, those devoted to farce and extravaganza, one particularly deserves mention for the influence it exercised on scenery and stage effects in the musical theatres: the Cirque Olympique. Managed by the Franconi family, the Cirque Olympique specialized in pantomimes and mimodramas *à spectacle,* taking themes from current events, contemporary literature, history and fantasy, and employed as scenic designers a number of the pupils of Cicéri.[102] One illustration of the influence this theatre had on the musical stage is to be found in Castil-Blaze's coining of the phrase *Opéra-Franconi* to refer to the costly and lavish scenes used at the Opéra after the later 1820s.

The total number of theatrical companies active in Paris at any one time during the first half of the nineteenth century was not particularly large, but the types of entertainment available were varied nonetheless. From classic French tragedy to melodrama, from grand opera to the simpest vaudeville using popular tunes, there was something for every taste. It was Scribe's good fortune to have entrance to a variety of theatres, to have the intelligence and creative foresight to use what he needed from every theatrical form, and to have as collaborators composers and technicians who embodied the best, or at least the most renowned, styles and devices of their time.

## SCRIBE AND THE LIBRETTO: PERSPECTIVE

Scribe's work dominated the musical stages of Paris for several decades, leading critics then as now to the frequent allegation that the reason for this domination was that the better poets and dramatists had no desire to cultivate the operatic genre and deliberately left the Opéra and the Opéra-Comique to second-rate writers. Theophile Gautier, for example, once observed: "Every true poet flees collaboration with a composer like the plague."[1] Yet Gautier encouraged activity in the operatic medium by the first-rate poets, and wrote in a review of Germain Delavigne's libretto for *L'Apparition*:

> The greatest poets of our times, Lamartine, Victor Hugo, Alfred de Musset, de Vigny, ought . . . to work for the Opera, their natural place and center: they alone are lyrical. . . . If France lacked poets or even versifiers, it would then be necessary to resign ourselves to libretti such as they are singing to us; but never have verses been so well turned as today, and Paris numbers more than three hundred people who know all the secrets of rhyme, rhythm, and prosody. Anyone, now, could write lines as bad as those of M. Scribe or M. Germain Delavigne if he wished.[2]

Gautier saw several factors as the causes for his plaints: one, the contention of some that a libretto, being "a programme of words," had no need of "naturalness, interest, grace, terror, love, and especially style," that it was "a question not of a poem or of verse";[3] another, what he assumed to be a fear on the part of the poets that their verses, when sung, would be unintelligible and therefore as good as nothing.[4]

Another writer blamed what he considered to be the low state of libretto writing on the composers, stating that in their willingness to accept Scribe's poems they

> did not seem to ask themselves whether a beautiful poem could or ought to be essential in the complete success of their work. They did not seem to want to follow the advice of George Sand, for example, who invited them to look for their librettos in Shakespeare, Byron, Dante, Aeschylus, Euripides, and even in the genius of contemporaries, such as Vigny, Musset, Lamartine, and the others.[5]

These observations are based on two assumptions: that it is a desirable thing that the best writers create operas; and that the best writers could create operas if only they would. Indeed, the former assumption is still present today, as is demonstrated by Douglas Moore's recent statement of satisfaction that:

> We now have operas, or operas in the making, with librettos based on plays by Arthur Miller, Eugene O'Neill, Tennessee Williams, Archibald MacLeish, William Saroyan, Pirandello and Brecht, and new librettos by such men as Thornton Wilder, Stephen Vincent Benet and Paul Horgan. Until recently it has been difficult to persuade successful authors to collaborate or even to allow adaptations of their works. The fact that they will do so now is an indication of the increasing prestige of American opera.[6]

Yet there is ample evidence now as then that the person needed to write a successful opera libretto is not just a fine poet or a fine playwright, but rather a dramatist who understands the stage and who has a good concept of how the music, text, plot, and staging will best fit together in the creation of a fine production. For the task of creating a libretto, then, poetic talent is quite as much beside the point as is experience in the spoken theatre. Neither quality is requisite, and its presence or absence does not guarantee a good opera any more than it determines a bad one. In fact, it is even possible that fine poetic lyricism could at times get in the way of the composer and thus account for an opera's failure. Castil-Blaze recognizes this problem when he writes:

> Nevertheless, excepting the sections of dialogue and that which, in an ensemble, relates directly to the theatrical action, the words are nothing and ought to be nothing; and if, instead of repeating them twenty times in succession, each musical motive introduces a new verse, the attention is necessarily fixed on two different things; and the mind, too much occupied, will find work where it looked for entertainment.[7]

He concludes that perhaps poetic richness is often more of a hindrance than a help, since poetry can move more quickly than music and can expose a number of images in a short time span, thus creating a disparity between the rates at which music and text can be comprehended. Furthermore, Castil-Blaze believes, the poet should leave the painting of images to the composer and not attempt to be too original in his own right. "What does it matter if the same words serve the poet for indicating the same sentiments? All their variety of expression is reserved for the talent of the musician."[8] Summing up his discontent with the French libretto as opposed to the Italian (which he considers far more musical), he observes:

> Italian music is in verse.
> French music is in prose.[9]

His meaning is clear: Italian libretto verse, banal though it be at times, is nevertheless regular in length of lines, stanza form, and above all, in rhythm; whereas in French libretti the accents of the text are less strong and tend to be less regularly placed within the lines, making musical setting more difficult. That this problem is the frequent cause of a conflict between musical and textual accent is demonstrated in any one of a number of examples by Auber, Adam, Boieldieu, and Halévy, who do no better in this regard than the foreigners Carafa and Meyerbeer.

Perhaps Castil-Blaze goes too far in his limitation of the role of true poetry in an opera libretto. Yet no less a man than Lamartine opposed a union of music and poetry on the grounds that their natures were too diverse and that the poet would be held down and limited by the composer in what he could accomplish;[10] and Lasserre, no admirer of Scribe, remarked:

> In view of the very dominant part that music plays in opera, it is hardly to be expected that many librettists will be found who combine disinterested enthusiasm with the power to create anything equivalent to the accepted masterpieces of literature. If this combination should be found, so much the better; but all one can expect, or rather all one ought to exact, from the poet of an opera is that he should contribute . . . good sense, a delicate and sure taste, a certain grace and a good style.
>
> . . . The essential thing is that music should find certain poetic elaboration completed and ready to her hand.[11]

The notion that the best French writers of the time could have written fine libretti if they had wished is also a false assumption. Evidence that most French writers, even some of those who wrote libretti, were not comfortable with music is sufficient to enable Lang to state that some

> were utterly uninformed when musical problems were involved. In their language they could not select or vary their rhythms; they abused the alexandrines and filled their airs with decasyllabic verse which contributed a great deal to the monotony and *carrure bourgeois* of the art of the Empire. Still, most of these authors attended the performances of the *Théâtre des Italiens* where they must have noticed that when verses were scanned symmetrically, half of the composer's labor was saved.[12]

Nor was a lack of ease when writing for music the greatest of their problems. Contrary to common opinion, many of the first-rank authors, Alexandre Dumas *père*, Heinrich Heine, and Gérard de Nerval among them were willing and even eager to provide libretti. Nerval, however, had some rather strange ideas on the content of a libretto and offered Meyerbeer one *Queen of Sheba* for which he did research in "the Bible . . . the Talmud, the Babylonian Berosus, Hermes, and Herbelot de Molainville's *Bibliothèque Orientale* (especially the articles on Sabi, Soliman, Adam, Cain, Enoch, Hermes)."[13] Although Meyerbeer at first expressed some interest in the project, other commitments and a subsequent falling out between himself and the poet caused him to decline the offered scenario and to return to Scribe. According to Berlioz, Victor Hugo offered to write a libretto for him in 1835,[14] and later delivered *La Esmeralda*, an adaptation of his novel *Notre Dame de Paris*, to Louise Bertin. This work, first performed on November 14, 1836, was a failure.[15]

Perhaps a third assumption should be added to the two already discussed: namely, that Scribe was not a good writer. Of this there can scarcely be a doubt, for his writing was subject to flaws in grammar, versification, scansion, and even in linguistic inventiveness. For example, in *Le Drapier*, set by Halévy (1840), "the verb *je t'aime*, accompanied by the rhyme *suprême* or *moi-même*, is repeated twenty-seven times in three acts. . . ."[16] Often the same text phrases appear in libretto after libretto in similar but not strictly comparable situations. "Quel est donc ce mystère?" as an ensemble reaction to an unexplained event or word appears in *Leicester*, Act II, v; *La Neige*, Act II, iv; *Le Maçon*, Act I, v; *La Dame blanche*, Act II finale; *Le Fils du prince*, Act II finale; and elsewhere. Other favored reactions include "O surprise nouvelle," "La force m'abandonne," and "O bonheur extrême."[17]

In view of the facts already stated that the best writers were often not capable of coming to terms with the requirements of the musical stage and that some persons believe good poetry to be an impediment to the success of an opera, one must ask whether Scribe's lack of poetic sensibility or even of refined writing skill is of any importance in a consideration of him as a successful librettist. There is overwhelming evidence that it is not, for the fact remains that his work was in demand by any composer who aspired to operatic success in Paris. One does not reach such a position in the literary world by means of total incompetence; thus, there must be more involved in successful libretto writing than the creation of euphonious lyrical poetry. Yet how can it be that a writer capable of leaving uncorrected noticeable grammatical errors, not to mention repetitious wording and gauche imagery, can stand as one of the best representatives of the art of libretto writing for half a century? The answer lies in a consideration of one idea underlying all the questions under discussion.

The problems behind the stating of such assumptions as those just mentioned have to do with a central misconception: namely, that opera is drama; or, stated another way, that the principles in operation in a good spoken drama are the same as those behind a successful opera libretto. It seems that librettists themselves have at times shared this view. Zeno and his contemporaries, in reforming the style and content of the opera libretti of their day, had in mind the achievement of "both popular and literary success through libretti which could be both staged and read."[18] Their successor Metastasio took pride in the fact that "in Italy, [my libretti] were more popular with actors than with singers,"[19] thus pointing up the fact that he too considered his libretti to be dramas as well as foundations for musical setting.

> [Metastasio] made no differentiation between the writing of dramas and that of libretti and was proud that his so very successful libretti also won success as spoken tragedies. Such a double usage of the libretto was only possible in the realization of a type of opera in which the drama and music stood widely separated from each other. The drama-loving public could thus enjoy the elegant performance of the action and the refined intrigue without reference to the music, while the opera-goer found satisfaction in the enjoyment of arias with sonorous, pathos-filled verses without having to concern himself with the action. As soon as the music invaded the core of the action, however, . . . the latter could no longer be taken and judged on its own merits. . . .[20]

As early as the mid-eighteenth century, such critics as Algarotti realized that even in such "pure tragedies" as the libretti of Metastasio there were certain basic differences between opera and drama. First, Zeno, Metastasio, and others rid the libretto of all nonessential dramatic accessories, elements which would be necessary to any but the most highly stylized dramas, and their libretti became primarily the exposition of a single moral idea or conflict. Second, opera and drama parted company in the cultivation of one important dramatic element, the marvelous. "It is within the realm of the marvelous that so many of the intrinsic, inalienable characteristics of opera are to be found."[21]

In French opera, however, the differentiation of opera and tragedy was not as much of an issue as in Italian opera, not because the librettists equated the two in the manner of Metastasio but because the two arose like twin stars out of the same era and to some extent out of the same pens. The rise of French opera coincided with the flowering of

French classical tragedy in the seventeenth century, and Philippe Quinault, who set the standards for all French libretti from the latter half of the seventeenth century to the time of the Revolution, had already made a name for himself as a writer of tragedy before turning to opera. The mythological subjects and characters of his libretti, along with their poetic style, were similar to those of his tragedies, and the marvelous, although cultivated to a greater degree in opera, was nevertheless a component of tragedy as well. Along with the living art of tragedy, the contemporary ballet also provided a strong influence on the make-up and character of French opera. Furthermore, French opera was less dependent than Italian opera on public taste for its approach and was reinforced in its traditional aspects by a spoken theatre which also preserved and cultivated the best in drama and acting style. Thus in France the desires of the general public were only a limited factor in changing styles and trends of *tragédie-lyrique*, coming more to the fore in the rise and development of opéra comique in the last half of the eighteenth century. Because of the early equation of opera with classical tragedy and the preservation of the Quinault tradition, although it gradually lost its exclusive or dominant position, for over a century, no less a figure than Theophile Gautier could still aver in the nineteenth century: "Opera is of course Greek tragedy with choruses, recitatives, hymns, and all its harmonic development. One cannot have beautiful enough verses for that."[22]

At about the same time "L. de M." remarked in the *Revue et Gazette Musicale de Paris* that:

> An opera is a sung drama; that is all. . . . The drama of the Opéra and the drama of the Comédie-Française are brothers. The same rigorous laws are imposed on both; and if one side has more difficulties, one cannot deny, it is the Opéra, for besides the natural conditions it ought to satisfy there are others, numerous ones, which music brings with it and which must be accepted.

Among these conditions he mentions the laws of regular rhythm imposed on certain portions of a libretto by the demands of musical setting.[23]

If the traditional equation of opera and tragedy in France was slow to die, it was nevertheless dying. The Revolutionary years brought a turn away from the old courtly basis of opera and a widening of the audience went hand in hand with a widening of the concept of proper subjects for the musical stage. Alongside the more traditional mythological topics in *tragédie-lyrique* and the more commonplace topics of opéra comique, librettists and composers turned to the pseudo-historical "rescue" or "horror" opera (e.g., Cheubini's *Lodoïska* or *Les deux Journées*, Lesueur's *La Caverne*), topical opera (e.g., Gossec's *L'Offrande à la liberté*), exotic themes (Lesueur's *Ossian*), or historical episodes (Spontini's *Fernand Cortez*). A mixing of genres and purposes was also taking place at about this time, and it brought new seriousness to one type of opéra comique and new romantic elements to libretto and music. Most of the works on "rescue" or "horror" themes were opéras comiques, thus closer by nature to spoken drama because of their use of speech in place of recitative. Besides their serious subjects, these "comic" operas began to make use of large-scale musical scenes of a kind previously cultivated mainly in *tragédie-lyrique.* At the same time, composers of these works did not abandon the simpler forms and musical styles still prevalent in opéras comiques in a lighter vein. Scenic effects of the type developed primarily in spoken melodrama made their influence felt on the stage of the Opéra-Comique. Yet despite evidence of change during these years, the fact remains that "Quinault's dynasty had fallen, but no other had been established in its place and none was installed until the advent of Scribe."[24]

The difference between opera and tragedy, particularly in matters of increased emphasis on the marvelous and, along with this, of scenes of dance and spectacle, had been apparent from the first. However, with the demise of the Quinault tradition and the attendant breakdown in the relatively close relationship between the spoken and the musical stage, the question of whether opera is or is not drama becomes increasingly important, particularly when considered in connection with the establishment by Scribe of a new order in libretto writing. This final divorce of opera from tragedy is well illustrated by a letter in which Boieldieu rejects a particular librettist proposed to him.

> I have heard tell of M. Licquet. I know that he has written several tragedies which have obtained the commendation of the most distinguished men of letters. But we do not lack examples [which can be] cited to prove that the person who writes a tragedy well may perhaps write an opera very badly, especially such an opera as is necessary today to attain great success. In this genre one needs a piquant subject, capable of being treated without the help of developments which, with the place the music ought to occupy, would lead to the slowing down of the action so fatal in this genre. Finally, one needs musical situations; one needs airs, duos, ensembles, finales for each act; one needs gradation and contrasts in the effects. M. Licquet is convinced of these verities, I am sure; and if, with the taste that he has for the more elevated genre, he wants to confine himself to making only an outline destined to be filled in with color by the composer, I do not doubt that he will succeed; the whole thing is to find a suitable subject.[25]

Here Boieldieu has summarized several points more true of the new libretto than the old. Earlier, particularly in opera without spoken dialogue, subjects and formal variety were of less importance. In traditional French opera the same mythological figures appear again and again in the stylized poetic forms. Even in the Italian libretti of Metastasio the same characters appear over and over again under different names and a stylization of scene and act structure betrays a lack of concern for variety in the overall form of the piece. Now, the older and more consistent tradition dead or dying, one must have above all a "piquant subject," and it must be laid out with an eye to proper distribution of the "musical situations" and without unnecessary involvements in character development or subplots. Quinault's writing was admired for its fine poetry, but Boieldieu says not a word about literary style, demanding only that the librettist trace out "an outline destined to be filled with color by the composer." Here indeed is one point at which opera divorces itself from literary romanticism. The work of Hugo, for example, is very rich in the language it employs, in its expressions and imagery. Yet, as Blanchard observed:

> Lyric poetry has two quite distinct meanings: poetry which carries its lyricism in itself, which is rebel to music, repulses it, is sufficient in itself by its expansive and varied phrasing, its numerous periods; and poetry which calls for music, [poetry] of which the movement is regular, the ideas clear and expressed in two or four verses. . . .[26]

Thus, if one cannot find verses beautiful enough for Gautier's "Greek tragedy," one can nevertheless find verses too beautiful for modern opera. Literary drama and opera are definitely separate by the time Scribe reaches the height of his popularity, to the point where the practical Reicha can offer the following down-to-earth advice to the would-be librettist.

> 1) Any good comedy or tragedy which has a true basis of interest to captivate the listener can serve [as the basis] for an opera.
>
> 2) To convert this comedy or tragedy into a good opera subject one must slow down the action and the succession [of events], suppressing all unnecessary scenes, and shortening as much as possible the dialogue and the monologues.
>
> 3) [In opéra comique] everything that is most interesting in these plays must be set to music and not left in dialogue. . . .

> 4) The poet must introduce ensembles and choruses as often as he can.
>
> 5) The scenes in which the actor is alone but in an interesting situation must be set in accompanied recitative followed by an air.
>
> 6) The scenes in which several actors are involved must be terminated most often by an ensemble, and the last scenes that close an important act must be set to music throughout in order to create a noteworthy and glowing finale in which most of the singers take part.[27]

Nowhere in this advice is there the hint of an emphasis on literary quality, good poetry, or even good drama. The points to be remembered are a strong subject and the structural details by which this subject becomes an opera. Deprived of language as an expressive means, the librettist must place at least partial reliance upon

> auxiliaries such as are generally avoided by the dramatists. . . . Scenic mounting, which with the spec[tacular] element it involves [,] becomes a feature of tragedy. The librettist does not hesitate to bring before the eyes of his audience pictures or events which, in the classical tragedy, were described by recitation, such as scenes in nature, movements of a crowd, combats, cataclysms, etc.[28]

Although reliance on spectacle as an important component of opera dates from the seventeenth century, at no time was it more highly cultivated than in the nineteenth century, a time when connections with the literary theatre existed only superficially. Subject, structure, spectacle, and song: more and more these became the bywords as opera went through the transition from more or less strong ties with the classical French theatre to a point at which these ties had been broken completely. Indeed, Auber, upon reading the libretto of *Gustave III*, worried that the subject was "perhaps too dramatic to be musical."[29] Opéra comique too was changing from a work in which the drama was primary and the music secondary to one in which the two elements enjoyed equal status. Throughout the transition, however, and in whatever form of opera, the importance of the libretto to the enjoyment and success of an opera in France was never questioned. In fact, Reicha states without qualification: "The success of an opera depends most often on the worth and interest of the poem, especially in France";[30] and Spohr, visiting Paris in 1820, observes that this very emphasis on the libretto has caused him to change his mind about trying to write for the Parisian stage, since "in the end I should find, although I might have written good music, its success would be uncertain, as that depends . . . almost wholly on the theatrical piece."[31] Castil-Blaze, commenting on the practice in the 1830s of performing only portions of Rossini's *Moïse* and *Guillaume Tell*, cites this practice as:

> a sad consequence of the phenomenal stupidity of the libretti of these operas. Remember that the Paris public, scarcely understanding anything but the words of a sung drama, is excited first of all by the libretto. When a work has neither tail nor head, one can without inconvenience stage the middle, the beginning, or the end of it.[32]

In a similar statement Gautier observed: "We stress the libretto a great deal, for we do not believe that one can write good music to a disorderly collection of words without sense and without harmony. . . ."[33] Nor was this desire for a strong and interesting libretto a new one, for it can be traced back to the time of Quinault, whose operatic poetry was respected as literature. Opera-goers and critics of the nineteenth century still placed great importance on the libretto, but now they were looking for different things: a subject that could hold the spectator's attention, carefully developed to utilize in the best possible way the talents of the composer, stage designer, costumer, and ballet master. Véron was more specific in this matter.

> . . . For a long time people have thought that nothing was easier to compose than a poem for opera; [what a] huge literary error. An opera in five acts can only come alive by means of a very dramatic action bringing into play the grand passions of the human heart and strong historical interest. This dramatic action, however, ought to be able to be comprehended by the eye like the action of a ballet. It is necessary that the chorus play an impassioned role in it and be so to speak one of the interesting characters of the play. Each act ought to offer contrasts in settings, costumes, and above all in ably prepared situations. *La Muette, Robert-le-Diable, Gustave, La Juive, Les Huguenots, Le Prophète* by M. Scribe offer this abundance of ideas, these dramatic situations, and fulfill all the conditions for variety of *mise en scène* that the poetics of an opera in five acts demands. When one has at one's disposal the most vast theatre . . . an orchestra of more than eighty musicians, nearly eighty chorus members, male and female, eighty supernumeraries, not counting children, a company of sixty stage hands [*machinistes*] for moving sets, the public listens and expects great things from you. You fail in your mission if so many resources only serve you to put on opéras comiques or vaudevilles.[341]

No simple matter was it, then, to dispose of all these forces in the most advantageous way. This being the case, it is impossible to agree with Lang that opera's "most characteristic component and its greatest weakness is its text, the *bassesse littéraire* of its text, . . . "[35] for the text is only part of the libretto. There being so many other things to consider, as Reicha rightly points out, almost anything could account for the success or failure of a work: the subject, the music, the acting or singing talents of the star performers, even the contributions of the scenery or costumes. "But," concludes Reicha, "we do not know of a single production in the musical theatre in our time that has succeeded solely by the regularity and beauty of its verses."[36]

Over and over, then, we find the same themes: opera is not tragedy or even drama, an opera libretto is not poetry, and the simultaneous development of literary theatre and opera such as existed in the days of Quinault and his successors is a thing of the past. However, the connection of opera to all spoken theatre has not been severed. What Scribe does is not so much to overturn an older concept of "opera-equals-sung-tragedy" as to incorporate into opera dramatic elements not of the classical or literary theatre but of the rising popular or bourgeois theatre, thus creating new associations—and new differences—between opera and drama.

# THE OPERA COMIQUE LIBRETTO BEFORE SCRIBE

In the course of discussions of the Paris theatres and of the general situation in which French opera found itself before the time of Scribe many general statements have been made regarding the nature, subjects, and traditions of opéra comique during that time. The present chapter will deal primarily with the more technical aspects of these opéras comiques, using as specific examples a number of successful late eighteenth and early nineteenth century works: Grétry's *Zémire et Azor* (1771) and *Richard Coeur-de-Lion* (1784), Lesueur's *La Caverne* (1793), and Boieldieu's *Béniowski* (1800). Of course, this list is highly selective and omits many important works and composers, which necessarily would limit its usefulness were the discussion not combined with the aforementioned general comments on pre-Scribe opéra comique. Nevertheless, consideration of a few important works can be very helpful in assessing the contributions Scribe made to libretto writing and the unique lasting influence he had on later writers.

All the pieces to be discussed are three-act works except for *Zémire*, which has four acts. This is in keeping with the usual custom of the time to use the three-act structure for the more serious *drames lyriques*, reserving a one-act form for the lighter opéras comiques, especially those written during the years after the Revolution. The less well developed story line of the latter was not the sole reason for their retaining the one-act format, however. Money for the production of new operas was relatively scarce during the postrevolutionary years and directors thus encouraged composers to produce single-act works. Also, although many such works were written by established composers, they were often the only way many beginners could break into the operatic scene.[1] After ca. 1810, two- and three-act works became the norm.

The dialogue in most cases was more important to the total work than the music, in that there was often more of it than in Scribe's libretti and especially in that the musical numbers were largely nondramatic, contrasting with the abundance of dramatic ensembles and the purposeful solos engineered by Scribe. Thus the action, including the important turning points and climaxes, was more often part of the spoken dialogue in pre-Scribe libretti. However, rescue operas and other, more serious opéras comiques made greater and greater use of music to enhance the dramatic high points, although frequently their techniques were different from those used later by Scribe. Techniques of harmony and orchestration, and general compositional devices, such as the early use of reminiscence motives and *leitmotifs*, contributed to the more "romantic" cast of the music in some works of this period, especially the rescue operas of Méhul, Lesueur, and Cherubini. However, simpler music was still used in rescue operas and found its greatest favor in the more lighthearted sentimental comedies and *bouffons.*

With these few general observations in mind, let us turn now to some specific works to observe the particular techniques used in their libretti.

## Grétry's *Zémire et Azor*

The libretto for *Zémire et Azor* was written by J. F. Marmontel, who based it on a comedy by P. C. Nivelle de la Chaussée entitled *Amour par Amour* (1742). It is essentially the same in structure and incidents as Spohr's opera of the same name produced in 1819. First performed privately, Grétry's work gained great public success after its public premiere at the Comédie-Italienne on December 16, 1771. Given regularly in Paris until 1836, it was revived in 1846 in a version revised by Adam and was performed again as late as 1862. In its time it was an international favorite.[2]

*Zémire et Azor* centers around the adventures of Sander, father of Zémire and of two other daughters. Once a wealthy man, Sander has just lost his fortune because a shipwreck has destroyed valuable cargo in which he invested. Now, caught in a storm, he and his servant Ali take refuge in a lavish palace, where they are provided comfort, food, and some sort of hospitality—although the castle seems deserted and their wants are supplied by some invisible magic force. When Sander picks a rose to take to his daughter Zémire, the monster Azor appears, reprimands Sander for repaying hospitality by destruction, and demands that Sander send one of his daughters to the palace to live or face death himself. A magic cloud then carries Sander and Ali to their home, where the disappointed daughters learn of their father's financial ruin. Sander cannot bring himself to tell them of Azor or the conditions on which he was allowed to return home, but Zémire soon learns the truth from Ali and resolves to give her own life to save her father. Taking Ali with her, she departs for Azor's palace.

Azor, alone, explains that he once was a handsome prince but was forced to assume this ugly aspect as punishment for his vanity. The charm can be broken only if a girl falls in love with him as he is now. Zémire arrives and finds that Azor, through his magical powers, has arranged a room for her, has furnished it with all the things of which she is fond, and has arranged a royal welcome for her from a group of genies. All is well until Azor appears in person and frightens her, but his kindness and generosity gradually win her over. Seeing in a vision that her father is very unhappy at having lost his daughter, Zémire asks to return home to reassure him. Once home, Zémire listens to Sander's pleas that she not return to Azor, but she believes in Azor and is not afraid. When she arrives again at Azor's palace she breaks the magic spell by declaring her love, and Azor becomes a handsome man once more. Sander is finally convinced that Zémire will come to no harm and gives his blessing to her marriage.

The following chart outlines the structure of the *Zémire et Azor* libretto.

Key to abbrevbiations:

| | | |
|---|---|---|
| A | - | Ali |
| Az | - | Azor |
| S | - | Sander |
| Z | - | Zémire |

| **Scene** | **Technique or form** | **Action involved** |
|---|---|---|
| | | **ACT I** |
| i | Dialogue: S, A. | S & A take refuge in seemingly uninhabited palace. A concludes lavish setting must be dream & is afraid of what the mysterious owner might do if he finds them. S resolves to wait out storm regardless of possible magic spells. |
| | Air: A (aba′ form) | Tries to endourage S to leave. |
| | Dialogue: S, A. | Storm grows worse but A still wants to leave. S still wishes to stay until dawn. |
| | Air: S (rondo form) | Misfortune has made him insensitive to fear, since his cargo has been lost. |
| | Dialogue: S, A. | A still afraid, but S encourages him to rest. A mentions hunger; a full table appears & S eats. A finally joins him & is impressed by wine. |
| | Air: A (aba′ form) | A praises magic spirits he had feared, lauds quality of food & drink. |
| | Dialogue: S, A. | Now A, no longer afraid, wants to sleep. |

| | | |
|---|---|---|
| | Duo: S, A. | Storm abating, S wants to leave. A, now comfortable, wants to rest. |
| | Dialogue: S, A. | S decides to leave, picks rose. |
| ii | Dialogue: S, A, Az. | Az reprimands S & threatens him with death. S explains how he lost ship & how 2 daughters, thinking he would return rich, asked for valuable gifts, but how Z wanted only a rose. |
| | Air: S. | S pleads that no one tell Z her rose was cause of his death. |
| | Dialogue: S, A, Az. | Az will release S if 1 daughter will return in his place. A urges acceptance of condition. S decides to return home, promises either to send daughter or to return to take his punishment. Az agrees. |
| | Air: Az (aba′ form) | Az warns S that his magic power extends over whole earth, but he will be merciful & return S's fortune if bargain is kept. Az calls for magic cloud to take S & A home. A is afraid but soon consents to ride on it. |

"Symphonie qui exprime le vol du nuage" [Symphony that represents the cloud's flight]. Instrumental.

**ACT II**

| | | |
|---|---|---|
| i | Trio: Z, sisters | Girls waiting for father's return & promised gifts. Sisters ridicule Z's choice of a rose. |
| ii | Dialogue: S, A, Z, sisters. | After welcome, S tells of losses. Sisters cry but Z consoles S. He gives her the rose. |
| | Air: Z | Z praises rose's beauty, shows it to sisters. |
| | Dialogue: S, Z, A, sisters. | Sisters go off to sleep. |
| iii | Dialogue: S, A, Z. | Z asks why S is so sad, but he will not tell. S leaves. Z follows. |
| iv | Monologue: A. | Moralizing. |

| | | |
|---|---|---|
| | Air: A. | He will go on no more voyages, will take root like a plant. Travel on land or sea is all right, but clouds are out of the question. |
| v | Dialogue: Z, A. | Z asks A for information. A begins to tell of adventure but S interrupts. A promises to tell Z later. |
| vi | Dialogue: S, A. | S forbids A to tell daughters about adventure. He has decided to return to Az alone, asks A to bring writing desk, then to leave. |
| vii | Recitative: S. | S writes he is going on long voyage, encourages girls to trust in heaven, lead good lives, love one another. |
| viii | Duo: Z, A. | Backstage A has told Z the whole story. Z wants to go to Az's palace, persuades A to accompany her. |
| | Entr'acte | Instrumental; binary form. |

ACT III

| | | |
|---|---|---|
| i | Monologue: Az. | Explains the magic spell on him, conditions for its removal. |
| | Air: Az (aba′ form) | Torment of not being loved, of inspiring only terror. |
| | Monologue: Az. | Wonders whether S will send daughter, whether girl will love him. Sees Z and A coming & hides to observe Z. |
| ii | Dialogue: Z, A. | A, fearful, wants to leave, but finds door locked. Now denies he told Z that Az is ugly & says instead that Z will be sure to like him. Z finds room, furnishings & accessories to her liking. |
| | Duo: Z, A. | Z urges A to return & tell S she is all right, but A wonders how to get out. |
| | Dialogue: Z, A, Az. | Az appears long enough to order A away & open doors. Z doesn't see him. |
| iii | Monologue: Z. | Z happy that S is now safe & sure heaven will protect her. |

"Entrée des Génies qui rendent hommage à Zémire" [Entrance (dance) of Genies who pay homage to Zémire]. Instrumental.

| | | |
|---|---|---|
| iv | Monologue: Z. | Z impressed with reception & throne of flowers offered her. |
| | Air de ballet. | 3 short dances; instrumental. |
| v | Dialogue: Z, Az. | Az frightens Z, but he explains magic spell & reassures her. Z is about to send him away but gradually he wins her over. |
| | Air: Az. | He is more afraid than she, but assures her he won't harm her. |
| | Dialogue: Z, Az. | Z, reassured, says she is no longer afraid. Az says she may have anything she wants & promises to restore S's fortune. |
| | Air: Z. | "Echo song," virtuosic, sung to entertain Az. |
| | Dialogue: Z, Az. | Seeing Z is still sad, Az agrees to let her see S & sisters in magic tableau but warns they will vanish if she approaches them. |
| vi | Dialogue: Az, A, S, sisters. | Az agrees to let Z hear what S & sisters are saying even though he fears she will then want to leave him. |
| | Trio: S, sisters. | S weeps for Z while sisters try to console him. All wish for her return. |
| | Dialogue: Z, Az, S, sisters. | Z approaches tableau; figures vanish. |
| vii | Dialogue: Z, Az. | Z wants to leave, but Az says she will die if she goes. He finally agrees to let her leave, but she must swear to return by sundown or he will die. |
| | Entr'acte. | Instrumental piece; aba form. |

ACT IV

| | | |
|---|---|---|
| i | Dialogue: S, A. | A has seen something approaching through the air. |

| | | |
|---|---|---|
| | Air: A. | Description of object: a moving chariot or cloud or something unknown, drawn by flying serpents. A is afraid it will land here . . . but perhaps it doesn't even exist. When one is afraid, he doesn't see very well. |
| | Dialogue: S, A. | S asks what all this has to do with him. |
| ii | Dialogue: S, A, Z, sisters. | Z says she can only stay a short time & has come to assure all that she is happy. S wants Z to remain, but she protests she must return, that Az is really kind & not the monster he seems to be. S says she has been deceived by magic, but Z points to her present visit as example of Az's kindness. |
| | Duo and quartet: S, Z, sisters. | S pleads with Z not to return but Z is resolved. Sisters offer to go in her place but she refuses. |
| | Dialogue: S, A, Z, sisters. | Z invokes Az's magic & disappears. S announces he is going to Az. |
| iii | Recit & air: Az. | Az believes Z will not return & despairs of life. |
| | Monologue: Az. | Without Z there is nothing left but to die. (He falls.) |
| iv | Air: Z. | Z returns, calls for Az, but can't find him. She announces she loves him. |
| | [Scene changes to an enchanted palace, with Az as handsome ruler.] | |
| v | Dialogue: Z, Az. | Az explains Z has broken spell. Z asks for father, sisters, who appear. |
| vi | Dialogue: A, Az, S, Z, sisters. | S gives blessing to marriage of Z and Az. |
| | Finale: all principals, chorus. | General reflection on the trials of true love. |

Several items of importance emerge in a study of this libretto. First, both dialogue and musical texts are in verse, a custom which did not survive in later opéras comiques. Second, the plot involves a single relatively simple action with no subplots or other complicating intrigues. The plot proceeds logically from the early meeting of Sander and Ali with Azor to the eventual marriage of the Prince and Zémire. However, there are some incidents unnecessary to the development of this plot line which are included merely as effective stage pieces: Ali's constant comical and cowardly sputterings, exploited in his air in Act I, v, and especially in his solo scene (Act I, iv); or Sander's letter scene (Act II, vii), the only extended recitative in the work and the only musical number without metrical and/or formal regularity. These scenes are dramatically unnecessary because none contributes to the main action, and Ali's numbers are pure comic relief. The letter scene provides a good example to the contrast between this work and Scribe's later libretti, for with Scribe such devices as letters and messages, usually placed in the wrong hands, often serve as the basis for developments and misunderstandings central to the plot. Here, Sander's letter is never heard of again; thus no dramatic use is made of it.

The way in which the action proceeds is another noteworthy feature of *Zémire et Azor.* Because of the prevailing operatic customs and tastes of Grétry's time, we assume from the beginning that the ending of the opera will be happy one for all concerned, save any villain who might be involved. Yet until near the end of the first act we are not really aware of the basis for the action. Thereafter, the plot progresses gradually in steps, so that while nothing that happens is totally unexpected, neither is it so carefully prepared as to be the only logical outcome of all previous developments. There is relatively little suspense, and this aspect of the plot is not deliberately heightened or emphasized. The only exception to this occurs in relation to Zémire's return journey to her home, when the audience must really wonder whether she will keep her promise to Azor.

In keeping with this sort of logical but not inevitable progress of the action, the individual acts proceed in a low-keyed manner. Even in Act IV there is no real sense of climax, no sense that each act is ending with a dramatic *coup* which is the logical outcome of earlier developments but which leaves the spectator anticipating events to follow. In Act I the high point comes with Azor's ultimatum to Sander and its acceptance, but the effect of this scene is dulled by subsequent events which are scenically desirable but dramatically and musically unnecessary. Similarly, the real climax of Act IV comes with the transformation of Azor and his palace. The break for dialogue and additional action before the finale dulls the effect of this spectacle, although not to such a degree as in Act I. Acts II and III present a slightly different picture. In Act II there is a kind of double climax: the pathos-filled scene of Sander's farewell letter to his daughters, and the more dramatically significant scene between Zémire and Ali. Act III ends strongly in the dramatic sense, for suspense over whether Zémire will return to Azor begins here and the audience is left with a sense of expectancy that carries over into the fourth act and is resolved only when Azor is transformed. However, this dramatic *coup* is in dialogue, following the largest and most dramatic vocal number in the act; thus it also has the effect of dulling a high point in the act.

Only the climax of Act II is set to music throughout, while those in the other acts are either set in dialogue or in music interrupted by speech. This illustrates the place of music in Grétry's opera: decorative, but usually nondramatic. Most of the solo numbers reiterate and/or elaborate upon statements already made in speech. For example, Ali's first air continues his attempts to persuade Sander to leave the enchanted palace, and Azor's air in Act III, i, elaborates upon plaints voiced in his spoken monologue. Some ensembles also fit into the category of musical numbers that elaborate on spoken dialogue: the Sander-Ali duo near the end of Act I, i, or the duo and quartet in Act IV, ii. Some musical numbers are pure decoration, excuses for music: Ali's comic monologue (Act II, iv), Sander's recitative (Act II, vii), Zémire's "Echo Song" (Act III, v), the fourth act finale, and all the ballets. Only exceptionally does a musical number involve any dramatic action. The best example of this type of number is the Zémire-Ali duo which closes Act II. Thus nearly all the important turning points or climaxes in the opera are related in speech, not in song.

The musical style of *Zémire et Azor* is for the most part relatively simple, although such popular forms as *couplets*, *romances*, and other strophic numbers are not used. True dramatic ensemble techniques comparable to those cultivated by Italian composers and later by Mozart are seldom used and are rudimentary at best. Some products of earlier French operatic tradition remain in the use of descriptive orchestral interludes and the moralizing finale.

Character development is a particularly strong feature of *Zémire et Azor*. Although there is no great amount of psychological depth to them, the figures take on their own distinctive character traits as portrayed in their speeches and actions. The depiction of Zémire and of Azor and the growing warmth in their relationship is well done and provides the audience with superior examples of sympathetic characters.

Many of the traits of *Zémire et Azor* die out or are modified in the later years of the eighteenth century, but others remain typical of the opéra comique libretto before the time of Scribe, as will be illustrated by further examples.

## Grétry's *Richard Coeur-de-Lion*

Quite different in plot, setting, and general orientation from Grétry's *Zémire et Azor* is his *Richard Coeur-de-Lion*, on a text by Sedaine, produced at the Comédie-Italienne on October 21, 1784.[3] Whereas *Zémire* is a fairy opera which capitalizes on the oriental setting and magical characters to introduce spectacular mechanical effects, dancing genies in exotic costumes, and unusual scenery, *Richard* has a historical theme which makes an appeal to patriotic sentiment and to a closeness to "the people" through its story of a nobleman saved by the diligence of a man of inferior social status and its introduction of peasants as soloists, chorus, and dancers. Yet its libretto shows many of the same characteristics as that of *Zémire* and the function of many of the musical numbers within the work is similar. A French favorite into the twentieth century, *Richard* was also an international success and was performed in English, Italian, German, Danish, Dutch, Swedish, Polish, Spanish, and Russian in the course of the first thirty years of its history.[4] Although its popularity alone would entitle *Richard* to be named among the landmarks of opéra comique, the work is also imporant as one of the earliest rescue operas.

*Richard Coeur-de-Lion* deals with the rescue of King Richard by Blondel, a troubadour who had served under him and had accompanied him to Palestine during the Crusades. Set in Germany, the opera begins with a chorus of peasants anticipating Mathurin's golden wedding anniversary, which will be celebrated by a remarriage of the elderly couple. Blondel, pretending to be blind, is led by Antonio, whom he sends to find shelter for the night. Meanwhile Blondel surveys the area, especially the fort where he thinks Richard may be imprisoned.

Williams, originally from Wales, has fled to Germany after avenging the murder of his father by a Welsh nobleman for having shot a rabbit on the noble's property. Williams too had been in one of Richard's companies in Palestine and is still loyal to the king. He now enters, reprimanding his daughter Laurette for having received a secret love letter from Florestan, the governor of the fort. Antonio reads the note for Williams—and Blondel—in which Florestan mentions that he must guard his prisoner during the day but could come to see Laurette at night if she would name a convenient hour. Later, Laurette admits to Blondel that she returns Florestan's love. When Blondel requests shelter for the night at the Williams home, Laurette reveals that a noblewoman and her company have rented the house for the evening and that she can admit no one else without the lady's permission.

The lady is none other than Marguerite, a countess still in love with Richard. She agrees to admit Blondel to the house after he plays on his violin a tune that Richard composed. This tune will return several times at important turning points in the action.

Act II takes place at the fort, with the stage set in such a way that the audience can see Blondel outside on the parapet but Richard, inside the fort, cannot. Richard laments the fact of his imprisonment. Soon Blondel and Antonio arrive and the former sings Richard's tune to attract the king's attention—if the prisoner inside the fort is indeed Richard. Blondel's plan succeeds, for Richard recognizes the troubadour's voice and sings the second stanza of the song in reply. Soldiers, arriving with Florestan to shut Richard up for the night, seize Blondel and question him. Blondel claims to be a messenger from Laurette and tells Florestan that there will be a party at Williams' house this evening, during which Florestan will be able to steal in among the guests and meet the girl. Florestan sets Blondel free and the "blind" man is led off by Antonio.

Act III takes place in Williams' house. Marguerite announces that she is leaving to enter a convent but Blondel, now suddenly no longer blind, stops her with the news that Richard is in the fort. With Williams and the nobles, Blondel sets his already-conceived plan in motion. Preparations are made for a celebration and Williams sends for the forewarned peasants to help celebrate Mathurin's anniversary. When Florestan arrives to find Laurette, the nobles seize him, then storm the fort and rescue Richard. The king pardons Florestan, who will now marry Laurette, and all give thanks to Blondel for his heroism.

The following chart will outline in more detail the positions and functions of the dialogue and musical numbers in Sedaine's libretto.

Key to abbreviations:

| | | | | | |
|---|---|---|---|---|---|
| Mat | - | Mathurin | G | - | Guillot, a peasant |
| Bl | - | Blondel | P | - | a peasant (anonymous) |
| A | - | Antonio | L | - | Laurette |
| W | - | Williams | M | - | Marguerite |
| Fl | - | Florestan | B | - | Beatrix, a lady-in-waiting |

| Scene | Technique or form | Action involved |
|---|---|---|
| | | **ACT I** |
| i | Peasants' chorus | Peasants look forward to celebration of Mat's golden wedding anniversary. |

| | | |
|---|---|---|
| | Dialogue: Bl, A. | Bl pretends to be blind. A describes scene to him. A says he can't lead Bl tomorrow because Mat, his grandfather, is being remarried & A's older brother will be married. A asks Bl to play violin for dancing at festival. |
| | Couplets: A. | 3 stanzas. A doesn't like dancing *per se*, but likes being near Nicholas' daughter & sings her praises. |
| ii | Monologue: Bl. | Bl sends A to look for lodging, then observes surroundings & says he hopes to gain entrance to fort by pretending to be blind. |
| | Air: Bl ("O Richard, ô mon roi") | Bl intends to save R from prison although rest of world forsakes him. Advises rulers to cultivate friends not only among noble but among lower classes too, since their services are likely to be given without thought of self-interest. |
| iii | Dialogue: Bl, W, L, G. | W threatens G with punishment for bringing letters to L. |
| | Trio: Bl, W, G. | G protests letter is from Fl, but W replies that L is not made to amuse the governor. Bl tries to smooth quarrel. |
| | [G is replaced by L.] | W warns L he will punish her if she yields to such a seducer. L promises to follow W's orders. Bl tries to smooth quarrel. |
| iv | Dialogue: W, Bl. | W wants to know contents of letter but Bl can't read it because Saracens blinded him. Bl calls A to read. |
| v | Dialogue: W, Bl, A. | A reads that L told Fl she loves him, that Fl wants to see her but can only come at night because he must guard prisoner. W tells Bl about his background, flight from Wales. |
| vi | Dialogue: A, Bl, L. | Bl reports to L that W knows contents of letter & is angry. L can't tell Bl identity of Fl's prisoner. |
| | Air: L. | About L's love for Fl, his advances to her. |

| | | |
|---|---|---|
| | Dialogue: L, Bl. | L admits she loves Fl. Bl warns her about nobles who try to deceive girls of inferior station. L replies she too is noble, although no longer rich. Bl teaches her a song to sing to Fl. |
| | Couplet: Bl, L. | Love is never more mischievous than when it is blind. |
| | Dialogue: Bl, L. | Bl asks for shelter for night, but L replies they must get permission from noblewoman who has rented house. |
| vii | Dialogue: Bl, M. | Bl recognizes M as Countess of Flanders & Artois, beloved of R. He plays tune R composed. M recognizes it & agrees to let Bl stay at W's house. |
| | Instrumental: variations on R's song. | During variations, servants bring table & prepare supper. In return for wine Bl entertains them. |
| | *Chanson*: Bl, with choral refrain. | Drinking song dealing with Sultan, Richard, Crusades. |

ACT II

| | | |
|---|---|---|
| | Entr'acte. | Instrumental. |
| i | Dialogue: R. Fl. | R tries to convince Fl he is a traitor, but Fl won't listen. |
| ii | Monologue: R. | R laments having been cut off at height of career by imprisonment. |
| | Air: R. | R reflects his glory is worth nothing if he is forced to stay here. Thoughts of M. If all is lost, he wants to die. |
| iii | Dialogue: R, Bl, A. | Bl & A arrive at fort. Bl sends A to buy food. |
| iv | Dialogue: R, Bl. | R complains he has been imprisoned 1 year & has no hope of freedom. Bl plays R's tune on violin, thinking R will hear if he's in fort. |
| | *Romance*: Bl, R. | Bl sings 1 stanza, R replies with 2nd, both sing 3rd. Bl plays tune & dances. Fl & |

| | | |
|---|---|---|
| | | soldiers arrive, lock R up, seize Bl & bring him into fort. |
| v | Chorus of soldiers, with soli. | Soldiers question Bl whether he knows who answered his song. Bl pretends to have message for Fl & asks to see him alone. Soldiers announce Fl's return. |
| vi | Dialogue: Bl, Fl. | Bl invents message from L that Fl should mingle with guests at (as yet fictional) party in order to see her. To cover this "mission" Bl urges Fl to reprimand him, send him away. |
| | Continuation of chorus with soli. | Soldiers & Fl rebuke Bl. A returns & defends Bl. Both are sent away. |

**ACT III**

**(Williams' house.)**

| | | |
|---|---|---|
| i | Trio: Bl, 2 of M's men. | Bl tries to convince men to let him see M but they refuse until he bribes them. |
| ii | Dialogue: M, W, knights, seneschal. | M prepares to leave, announces she will enter a convent. |
| iii | Dialogue: the same, B. | B announces that Bl, no longer blind, wants to see M. |
| iv | Dialogue: the same, Bl. | Bl states he is no longer blind, that he has recognized M, that he is Bl, & that R is prisoner in fort. |
| | *Morceau d'ensemble*: soloists, chorus. | Bl announces to M's knights that R is in fort. All glad to see Bl again, want to plan R's rescue. |
| v | Dialogue: same. | M asks knights, Bl, W to draw up plan to free R. |
| vi | Dialogue: W, Bl, 2 knights, seneschal. | Bl learns from W that Fl will be brave & can't be bribed, but will come to see L. Bl asks W to follow through on Bl's earlier message to Fl & prepare a party for peasants, who have been forewarned. |
| vii | Monologue: Bl. | If friendship & ardor were ever strong enough to accomplish anything, this is the time. |

| | | |
|---|---|---|
| viii | Dialogue: W, L, domestics. | Preparations for party. |
| ix | Trio: W, L, Bl. | Bl tells L that Fl loves her, will come to see her during party. |
| x | *Couplets:* P, chorus. | Rustic song about shepherds, followed by peasant dance during which Fl appears & is surrounded by W & knights. |
| | Dialogue: W, Fl. | W arrests Fl. |
| | Chorus: knights, Fl. | Men demand Fl release R. He refuses. |
| [xi] | Instrumental piece ending with brief "Vive Richard" by chorus. | Scene changes to fort, where knights assault & take building. Bl saves R from 3 armed men. Crowd yells, "Vive Richard." |
| | Finale: all principals, chorus. | |
| | March (orchestra) | M faints at sight of R. R forgives Fl, returns his sword. |
| | Vocal | M revived by R. Both thank Bl for his bravery.<br>Fl & L get permission to marry.<br>General rejoicing. |

In many respects Sedaine's libretto is more modern in outlook than is the book for *Zémire et Azor*, for *Richard* has a clear over-all structure, some carefully prepared moments of suspense, and act structures which set the spectator and the curtain down simultaneously. Act I consists almost entirely of exposition. We meet most of the main characters, learn Blondel's purpose, are given valuable background information on Williams, Florestan, and Laurette so that we anticipate how each will act or react later in the face of Blondel's discovery of Richard's presence in the fort. In the remaining acts action which is to some extent prepared in Act I is carried out. Each act ends with a large scene. Although those of Acts I and III are definitely anticlimactic, the size of their performing forces and the length of the numbers give them the appearance of a dramatic *coup.* At the same time there is much in Sedaine's libretto that marks it as very much of its time: for example, the rescue plot and the spectacular scene of siege near the end of Act III. The latter, of course, was a type of scene common not only in later rescue operas but repeated with cast-of-thousands splendor in later grand operas as well.

Despite its basic clarity, many elements of the work are handled in ways which are also very much of their time and in some cases seem illogical and even clumsy, especially when compared to techniques later used by Scribe. Like Marmontel before him, Sedaine allows the action of *Richard* to unfold gradually, and events are often unexpected, unprepared, and even unexplained despite the fact that the overall course of action is set up by events in Act I. For example, the opening peasants' scene provides the excuse for the feigned celebration at Williams' house in Act III, but in the meantime the peasants have no place in the opera, not even as moving scenery. Similarly, there are many explicit politically-oriented statements near the beginning of the work—e.g., the middle section of "O Richard, O mon roi!"—which are not carried through the remainder of the work and seem strangely out of place, as if the librettist were making his nod to the coming Revolution before getting down to business. A third example of unprepared action is Blondel's spur-of-the-moment plot to trap Florestan ouside the fort. Until Blondel delivers his message, he does not even know how he is going to escape Florestan and the soldiers, much less how he will eventually free Richard.

Some events in *Richard* simply happen for no reason at all. We are given no hint as to the cause of Richard's imprisonment, an event upon which all the rest of the action is based. True, Richard mentions that Florestan is a traitor, but why should the German governor of a fort holding the English king, who will be rescued by a French troubadour, a Welsh noble, and knights in the service of a Flemish countess, be a traitor? The audience perhaps knew history, but a librettist like Scribe would have left no such important background information go by in this fashion. Also unexplained is the series of coincidences leading to Blondel's discovery of Richard and the latter's final deliverance. Blondel has no particular reason for believing Richard is in the fort, other than observing that the building "is suitable only for keeping prisoners of state." No reason is given for Marguerite's arrival with her knights, nor for her having wanted to rent a private home to spend the night. Williams' Welsh origins and his loyalty to Richard, his former commander, however, are coincidences worthy of Scribe were they not linked to such a chain of absurdities as exists in the rest of the libretto. Finally, when Blondel appears in Act III to reveal news of Richard, Beatrix simply announces to Marguerite—in a dependent clause and without further details—that Blondel is no longer blind, a change Blondel himself does nothing further to explain. All of this reveals a certain carelessness with dramatic detail that is ever present in the opera.

Sedaine, like Marmontel, also made use of offstage action that is merely narrated to the audience. The "restoration" of Blondel's sight may or may not be an example of this. One important and well-defined instance, however, is in Blondel's plan to trap Florestan, when Blondel announces that he has already told the peasants they will be invited to a celebration.

Sedaine's main characters, Blondel and Richard, are well developed as operatic characters go. Their personalities are formed gradually and the audience's impression of them is gained primarily through observations of their deeds and thoughts rather than by what they or others say about their personalities. Other characters, however, are not so fortunate. Florestan is quite an ambiguous figure, for one is never sure whether he is a villain, a representative of the corrupt noble class, a patriot, a man merely doing his duty, a rather naive young lover or any combination of these. Except for Williams and Antonio, the rest of the personae are human cyphers. Moreover, Sedaine gives prominent if isolated positions to characters who do not deserve such emphasis. This is particularly noticeable because it occurs in musical numbers. Mathurin, the supposed reason for the peasants' celebrations, has a short solo and is never heard from again; Guillot, a mere messenger, has a prominent part in half of a dramatic trio; two of Marguerite's servants spar verbally with Blondel in another trio; and an unnamed peasant sings a rustic song and leads the chorus in the refrain. This sort of looseness in leading the characters through their paces could result in some confusion before the audience realized that they need not carry this excess dramatic baggage any further than the final cadence of a given number.

*Richard Coeur-de-Lion* centers on a single theme, that of Blondel's rescue of Richard, but the action is more complex than in *Zémire et Azor* because of two weakly developed subplots. The first, dealing with Mathurin's anniversary celebration, provides the excuse for an opening chorus, Antonio's *couplets*, and Williams' celebration in Act III, but has little real function within the main action. The second, the love interest between Laurette and Florestan, is more important to the plot because it provides the excuse for Blondel's escape from the fort and for Florestan's arrest. The plot could have survived without the peasants' activities, although the opera would have been less colorful visually and less interesting musically, but it could not have withstood elimination of the Laurette-Florestan subplot. Marguerite also provides a kind of diversionary action, if not an actual subplot, in her unexplained arrival and her decision to enter a convent. As a character she is dramatically necessary to provide the expected love interest for Richard; she is musically necessary to provide a vocal contrast to the young, light soprano of Laurette, but as an element in the main plot she is not needed at all.

Two particular devices used by Sedaine will also become favorites of Scribe: a letter falling into the wrong hands is the key to some central point or event; and a song is repeated at various points in the opera. *Fra Diavolo* and *Zanetta* contain illustrations of the letter device, which Scribe also uses frequently in his spoken dramas, and *La Barcarolle* and *Le Maçon* are examples of works in which a song returns at intervals for a dramatic purpose.

The function of the music in *Richard* is often purely decorative, as was the case in *Zémire et Azor.* This is particularly evident in such a piece as Antonio's *couplets*, the songs Blondel sings to entertain the company, and the Peasant's song. Even the ensembles, which ordinarily carried action in the works of such composers as Auber, are often nonfunctional because action they involve is discussed either before or after the number. Yet some of the musical numbers do have dramatic importance in that they elaborate upon a character's state of mind or carry some action not otherwise presented or explained: for example, Richard's air in Act II or the trio which begins Act III. It is noteworthy that Florestan in Beethoven's *Fidelio* sings an aria similar in structure, sentiments, and even the order in which those sentiments are expressed, when he finds himself in a situation like that of Grétry's Richard. The French tradition of descriptive instrumental music to cover stage action is preserved here in the battle scene.

In sum, Sedaine's libretto for Grétry combines elements of an older structural and musical practice with more modern ideas of subject, preparation of important actions, and greater complexity of plot. That some devices succeed better than others is to be expected in any opera, particularly one which enjoyed the pathbreaking status of *Richard Coeur-de Lion.*

## Lesueur's *La Caverne*

*La Caverne* by Jean-François Lesueur (1760-1837) was first performed on February 16, 1793, at the Feydeau Theatre in Paris. The libretto by P. Dercy was based on an episode in Lesage's *Gil Blas* and was one of the earliest "bandit" operas, a type which was to be cultivated in the nineteenth century as well.[5] Scribe himself used the romantic bandit as the hero of such operas as *Fra Diavolo, La Sirène,* and *Marco Spada.* However, the contention of some writers that *Fra Diavolo* is based on *La Caverne* is not true, as is apparent in even a superficial comparison of the two works.[6] The setting for the opera aroused some comment, for it consisted of an underground cavern the roof of which formed the ground of a forest. Thus action could take place on either or both levels and characters hidden from each other could be seen simultaneously by the audience.

Lamy has given a concise summary of the plot of *La Caverne.*

> It is a story of brigands. Captain Rolando, their leader, is one of these *sympathiques malfaiteurs* who had a long vogue in the theatre and of whom the first in date as well as in importance was Schiller's Karl Moor. Like the latter, Dercy's hero is of noble family and good education, gifted with the finest qualities and the most generous sentiments, somewhat obliterated by the mistakes of his youth, since from one downfall to another he has become the captain of a troop of very brave men who are not very noble [a play on words in French: 'Gens très braves' who are not 'braves gens'] . . . On one of their expeditions they bring back to the cavern in triumph a beautiful and innocent young woman for whom Rolando soon conceives a love as deep as it is respectful. He defends her against the brutality of his companions and virtually proposes a proper marriage to her. However, he first learns that she is married, then that she is his own sister; third that his crimes have caused the despair and death of his elderly father. Touched by repentance, he decides to abandon and atone for his criminal life, and everything comes out for the best except, however, for the brigands, who are killed by Rolando, now become Don Juan again, aided by his brother-in-law and by a sort of good thief sent there by convenient chance.[7]

A chart will provide a convenient outline of the structure of *La Caverne.*

Key to abbreviations:

| | | |
|---|---|---|
| S | - | Seraphine |
| L | - | Leonarde (an old woman, servant of the bandits) |
| G | - | Gilblas |
| Rol | - | Rolando |
| Rou | - | Roustan |
| A | - | Don Alphonse |

| Scene | Technique or form | Action involved |
|---|---|---|
| | | **ACT I** |
| i | Acc. recit.: L, G, S. | L & G discuss S, who sobs in the background. S reveals they have kidnapped her from her husband but she has faith she |

| | | |
|---|---|---|
| | | will be rescued. G, aside, says he is looking for a way to help S escape. |
| | Dialogue: L, G, S. | L tells S not to fear, since Rol loves her & will protect her even though other bandits are villains. |
| ii | Dialogue: G, S. | G reveals he too is a prisoner & only goes out with bandits to try to find some way to escape. S knows bandits wounded her husband (A) & fears him dead. G, former servant of S's father-in-law, is not too encouraging about chances for escape, but |
| | Air: G. | encourages S to be hopeful, since Rol is a good man & won't let others harm her. |
| iii | Dialogue: S, G, L. | G has found former entrance to cavern, hopes to open it when he goes out with bandits. |
| | *Chanson:* L. | Song to cheer S. |
| iv | Dialogue: Rol, G, S, L, bandits.<br>Chorus: bandits. | Rol reproaches bandits for having been too cruel to victims. |
| v-vi | Dialogue: S, G, L, Rol, Rou, bandits | Rol defends S against Rou's advances. |
| vii | Dialogue; S, Rol.<br>Duo: S, Rol. | Rol declares his love, but S refuses to consider this from one who may have killed her husband. |
| viii | Finale: all principals, double chorus. | A enters forest above cavern, searching for S. |

ACT II

| | | |
|---|---|---|
| i | Recit. & air: S. | Alone & frightened, S wonders how everything will end & longs to join A in death. |
| ii | Dialogue: S, L. | L comforts S, agrees to help protect her against Rol's attentions. |
| | Air: L. | L explains that she stays with bandits because she feels there is some good in them. |

| | | |
|---|---|---|
| iii | Dialogue: S, L, A, Rol, bandits. | L brings in blind man (A in disguise) to sing for S. |
| | *Romance*: A | Entertainment. |
| | Dialogue: same. | A tells bandits he went blind weeping over loss of wife. |
| | Air: A. | Same subject. |
| iv | Dialogue: S, Rol, A. | S recognizes A's voice & asks that he be removed from cavern because his presence saddens her, but Rou declares once in the cave no one can leave. Rol promises A will not be harmed. |
| v | Dialogue: S, Rol, A, more bandits. | Bandits announce G's escape & band goes off to confer. |
| vi | Duo: S, A. | Happy reunion. |
| | Dialogue: S, A. | A tells how he was left for dead, then disguised himself to gain entrance to cavern. S reveals Rol loves her but is too well-bred to harm her. A has friends outside who will attack cavern at night. S adds that G also works in their behalf. |
| vii | Dialogue: S, A, L. | S introduces A to L. L now fears for their lives but promises to help them. |
| | Air: L. | L sings to accompaniment of A's guitar to divert returning bandits' attention. |
| viii-x | Dialogue: S, A, L, Rou, Rol, bandits. | Rou carries S off while others hold A & L, defies Rol to stop him. |
| | Finale: all principals, chorus. | Rol stops Rou, but many others take sides against Rol in favor of Rou. Rol wins out. |

ACT III

| | | |
|---|---|---|
| i | Chorus: bandits. | Angry, swear revenge on Rol. |
| ii | Dialogue: L, Rou, bandits. | L overhears bandits' plans to take over, kill Rol & A, replace Rol with Rou. |
| | Chorus: bandits. | More on plans. |
| iii | Dialogue: L, Rol. | L warns Rol, who is worried about S & plans to attempt an escape for himself, S, A, & L. |

| | | |
|---|---|---|
| iv | *Récitatif obligé*: Rol. | Rol doesn't know what to do. Repents having left family for bandit life, resolves to lead good life now, to save S but not to expect her to return his love. |
| v | Dialogue: Rol, S, A, L. | Rol tells S not to fear him now. S moved by his generosity. Rol warns of danger. A reveals his identity. Rol happy A didn't die, tells story of his remorse, his family & early life. |
| | Ensemble: Rol, S, A. | Rol discovers S is his sister & that father is dead. S persuades Rol to return home, but first they must escape. |
| vi-vii | Air: S. | S is afraid. |
| viii | Dialogue: S, L. | L announces Rol & A have beaten half the bandits & imprisoned them. |
| ix-xii | Finale: all principals, chorus. | Rest of bandits return. G & A's friends converge on cavern & win. |
| | Dialogue: all principals. | Everyone reunited, all is explained, & everyone is happy except the bandits. |
| | Chorus with soli. | General rejoicing. |

In many respects the libretto of *La Caverne* represents a decided change in style and technique from those of the Grétry works. The primary difference is that more of the dramatic high points are set to music, leaving only the main expository material for the spoken dialogue. Thus most of the musical numbers have some function in the plot as well. Yet one reminder of older practice remains in the structure of the third act finale. Music carries the action for a time, but when the important recognition scene occurs the music stops and spoken dialogue is used. After the major conflicts of the plot are resolved, a chorus of rejoicing closes the opera. The acts are more tightly constructed so that there are fewer purely decorative musical numbers and so that each act ends at a dramatic high point. Thus at the end of Act I we have a very successful scenic and dramatic tableau: in the cavern, the relationship between Rolando and Seraphine becomes more complex, while above, in the forest, Seraphine's husband searches for her. Suspense is built into this scene, for we are left wondering whether Alphonse will find Seraphine in time; how he will extricate her from the cavern if he does find her; and whether Seraphine will eventually fall in love with Rolando. All these items must be resolved in subsequent acts, and the way in which Dercy ends the act leaves the audience with a feeling of anticipation, not of finality. Similarly, the bandits' revolt at the end of Act II raises speculation regarding the possible effects of the incident on Rolando's position of leadership, hence on the safety of Seraphine and Alphonse.

Several characteristics of *La Caverne's* libretto, however, are similar to those of the Grétry examples. Like the latter, *La Caverne* begins *in medias res*, after Seraphine has been captured and her husband wounded, and the action develops gradually, in steps. The plot centers around the tale of Seraphine's rescue by her husband, assisted by Gilblas and Rolando. However, *La Caverne* includes two lesser actions which are not really important enough to qualify as subplots but which do have some independence: Roustan's rivalry with Rolando for leadership of the bandits, and Rolando's conversion from a life of crime. Thus the plot line is somewhat more complex than in *Zémire*, if not in *Richard*.

Although we assume that Seraphine will escape from the bandits somehow, the story of her liberation involves both expected and unexpected events. Early in the opera Gilblas is portrayed as friendly to Seraphine's cause, but deciding whose part Rolando will take is problematical for some time and the discovery that he is Seraphine's brother comes like the proverbial bolt from the blue. Also, until the end of Act I the audience may well believe with Seraphine that Alphonse is dead. When he does appear, his plans and purposes are uncertain, and the whole story of his adventures does not come out until the middle of Act II.

Another suspense-giving element is the use of offstage action. In *Zémire et Azor*, Ali told Zémire the story of Sander's bargain with Azor while offstage, and only the outcome—Zémire's decision to go to Azor—is presented to the audience. Similarly, such central actions as Alphonse's search for Seraphine and the defeat of some of the bandits by Rolando and Alphonse take place offstage and are only related in spoken dialogue to the other characters and to the audience.

Throughout the libretto some events are carefully prepared while others—the greater number—come as unexpected but usually welcome surprises. This goes hand in hand with the librettist's art of character development. Like Grétry's librettists, Dercy does not present his characters as known quantities from the first, but allows them to develop through their own words and deeds. His best portrayal is that of Rolando, at first the active leader of bandits, then gradually turning away from this life until the discovery that Seraphine is his sister and that his father has died causes him to break with the criminals and actively oppose them.

*La Caverne* shows some development from the type of libretto used in the Grétry works, particularly in the increased dramatic importance of the music and the greater complexity of the plot. Nevertheless, certain basic structures and procedures of the older libretti remain and will continue to be cultivated in later works.

### Boieldieu's *Béniowski*

*Béniowski*, a three-act work, was first presented at the Opéra-Comique on June 8, 1800. The libretto was by A. Duval, who based it on a play by Kotzebue. The work remained in the repertoire of the Opéra-Comique until 1828, although after 1824 in a revised version.[8] Another rescue opera, *Béniowski* is rather unusual in that it includes only one major female character who, along with her attendants and the women of the chorus, makes her appearance only in the second and third acts. Thus the entire first act and large sections of the two remaining acts feature only male voices, the highest of which is the male alto or *haut-contre*.[9] Another unusual feature is a conspiracy scene in Act I, iii, which is somewhat similar to the famed "Blessing of the Daggers" in the fourth act of *Les Huguenots* and may have been one of the many influences on Meyerbeer's scene. The libretto of *Béniowski* also features a wealth of specific references to topics of patriotism and individual liberty, designed to appeal to the heart of every true Frenchman and—more to the point—to the government. In technique and general story line *Béniowski* continues the tradition of which *La Caverne* is an earlier representative.

Béniowski, one of a number of political prisoners serving as slaves in Russia, has succeeded in gaining the governor's favor and has risen to a trusted position in the latter's household. He has also fallen in love with Aphanasie, the governor's niece, who returns his love and has persuaded her guardian to allow them to marry. Yet Béniowski is also the mastermind of a revolutionary conspiracy among the slaves. Although he believes the revolution to be right and necessary, he has come to respect the governor as an honest man who often must carry out harsh orders from the central government even though he does not favor them. Stéphanow, another slave, is jealous of Béniowski on two counts: he is also in love with Aphanasie, and he feels that his abilities and former rank entitle him to lead the conspiracy. Stéphanow therefore tries to plant doubts in the minds of the other prisoners as to Béniowski's continued loyalty to their cause.

Hearing of a slave uprising in a camp in Siberia, the governor asks Béniowski to lead a force against the approaching prisoners, promising him freedom and Aphanasie's hand in marriage as rewards. Stéphanow has overheard this and now tries to use it as evidence to turn the other conspirators against Béniowski. The latter, however, proposes to begin the rebellion at once, using his inside information from the governor to help the plans succeed. In return the prisoners consent to Béniowski's marriage. At this, Stéphanow himself goes to the governor and, although disturbed that his desire for personal revenge could cost the lives of 600 prisoners, tells him of a conspiracy led by Béniowski. When the governor confronts Béniowski with this knowledge, however, the latter does not confess and the governor decides he has insufficient evidence to do anything but imprison Béniowski unti he can get further testimony. Béniowski escapes and returns to the prison camp to find that the slaves now believe he has betrayed them. Torn with guilt and remorse, Stéphanow finally confesses his crime. Meanwhile the slaves capture the governor's palace. Béniowski saves the lives of Aphanasie and the governor, then prepares to lead out of the country his fellow slaves and the newly arrived prisoners from Siberia.

The structure of the libretto and distribution of the musical numbers in *Béniowski* are outlined below.

Key to abbreviations:

| | | |
|---|---|---|
| S | - | Stéphanow |
| B | - | Béniowski |
| G | - | Géslin |
| P | - | Panow |
| Gov | - | Governor |
| A | - | Aphanasie |
| Cho | - | Chorus |

| **Scene** | **Technique or form** | **Action involved** |
|---|---|---|
| | | ACT I |
| i | Acc. recit. & air: S. | S complains he has lost A to a rival, the last in a series of misfortunes. He wishes to die, fears his jealousy will cause him to do something drastic. |
| | Monologue: S. | S is jealous of B's position with Gov, his winning A, & his leadership of conspiracy. |

| | | |
|---|---|---|
| ii | Dialogue: S, G. | G tries to cheer S, make the best of things even in misfortune. |
| | Recit. & air: G. | G looks forward to happier times after revolution. |
| | Duo: G, S. | G has hope, but S is gloomy. |
| | Dialogue: G, S. | S casts doubt on B's loyalty to conspiracy, but G defends B, pointing out his fine leadership qualities & technical knowledge necessary to make revolt succeed. S feels he deserves a position of leadership but has none. |
| iii | Dialogue: G, S, B, P, rest of exiles.<br>Ensemble with cho. | Prisoners discuss political crimes for which they have been exiled. All swear loyalty to cause of revolution. When Russian officer approaches, exiles pretend to be playing cards, etc. |
| iv | Dialogue: officer. | Officer announces Gov is coming to see B. |
| | Ensemble with cho. | Exiles wonder why, but continue to feign innocent activities until officer leaves. |
| v | Dialogue: S, G, B, P, exiles. | B is sure plans have not been discovered. S hides to eavesdrop. |
| vi | Dialogue: G, B, exiles. | B promises to report to friends on Gov's business. |
| vii | Monologue: B. | B torn between loyalty to conspiracy & respect for Gov, whose niece he loves. |
| | Acc. recit. & air: B. | Elaboration on this conflict. |
| viii | Dialogue: Gov, B. | Gov observes there has been no talk of revolt since B became leader of prisoners. B replies this is because Gov is just ruler. Gov appoints B to lead force against escaped Siberian prisoners, gives B freedom & promise of marriage to A, asks B's help to discover any conspiracies that may arise among his own prisoners. |
| ix | Monologue: S. | S decides to try to turn other prisoners |

| | | |
|---|---|---|
| | | against B & force him to renounce Gov's favors. |
| x | Dialogue: S, G, P, exiles | S reports to prisoners but G defends B. |
| xi | Dialogue: same, B. | Prisoners demand answers from B, who promises to lead them to freedom that night. B points out advantages of his position with Gov, asks consent of friends to marry. |
| | Finale: ensemble, cho. | All agree to B's marriage, but S mutters angrily in background. |
| | | **ACT II** |
| i | Chorus | Ladies help A prepare for wedding. All wish her happiness. |
| | Recit. & air: A. | Reflections on happiness, love for B. |
| | Dialogue: A, ladies. | Ladies announce arrival of guests, beginning of festivities. |
| ii | Dialogue: A, B, Gov. | Gov asks that B & A stay near him after marriage to cheer his old age. B agrees, unless extradordinary circumstances interfere. |
| | Trio: A, B, Gov. | Elaboration on preceding dialogue. |
| iii | Dialogue: A, B, Gov, officer. | Officer announces a prisoner wants to see Gov alone. Gov takes B to meet some guests, promises to return soon to meet prisoner. |
| iv | Dialogue: S, officer. | Officer tells S that B & A are now married. |
| v | Monologue: S. | Seems that everything works in B's favor, making S want revenge even more. Still torn between desire for revenge & knowledge it could cost 600 lives. |
| | Cho. | Wedding cho as at beginning of act. B & A pass by stage front. |
| | Monologue: S. | Seeing them makes S decide in favor of revenge. |

| | | |
|---|---|---|
| vi | Dialogue: S, Gov. | S first demands amnesty for conspirators & gets Gov's word to punish only the leader. S reveals plans but refuses Gov's offer of freedom because he is still loyal to exiles & has only become informer for personal reasons. His reward will be B's death. |
| vii | Monologue: Gov. | Gov decides to pretend ignorance of conspiracy & see what develops. |
| viii | Ensemble with cho. | Wedding celebration continues. A & B sense change in Gov's attitude. Gov sends all but B away. |
| ix | Dialogue: Gov, B, 2 officers. | Gov dictates order for B's execution, naming S as B's accuser, but B doesn't confess & Gov decides to put B under house arrest until he has more evidence. |
| x | Monologue: B. | B knows how to escape, but is torn between love for A, respect for Gov., loyalty to friends. |
| xi | Dialogue: B, A. | A urges B to escape, since Gov would not be solely responsible for B's fate & other officials would demand execution. |
| | Finale: B, A, Gov, cho. | B escapes through window as A watches & prays for his safety. A hears gunshots, fears B may have been killed. Soldiers enter, searching for B. Gov orders them to follow B. |

**ACT III**

| | | |
|---|---|---|
| i-ii | Pantomime, melodrama, soli with cho: S, P, G, exiles. | Armed exiles fight ferocious bears in wilderness. S filled with guilt. P fears danger because they have been separated from rest of men. All hear someone approach, hide in rocks & prepare for ambush. G enters with rest of men, reveals that B has betrayed them. Exiles feel hopeless. |
| iii | Dialogue: S, P. G, exiles. | At sound of shots, exiles fled & now meet among rocks to defend themselves. Situation looks hopeless, but S agrees to take over as leader & G leaves to search for Siberian escapees to serve as reinforcements. |

| | | |
|---|---|---|
| iv | Dialogue: S, P, exiles. | S orders P to take detachment to village & capture women & children as hostages, sends others to watch Gov's palace & report on developments there. Rest are to return to camp & prepare for battle. |
| v | Monologue: S. | S hopes to atone for guilt by leading exiles to victory. |
| vi | Duo: S, B. | B, exhausted, enters, faints. |
| | Dialogue: S, B. | S revives B, then realizes B's testimony to others would unmask S. B, his sight failing, doesn't recognize S & reveals he plans to denounce S to others. S cannot murder a defenseless man. S reveals his identity & B calls for help. |
| vii-viii | Dialogue: S, B. | Prisoners want to kill B, but S defends him & confesses. B forgives S & all reenter camp to prepare to fight Gov's men. |
| ix-xi | Dialogue: P, S, exiles, women, children. | In camp, P has brought A among hostages & will not allow S to free her. |
| | Ensemble with cho., some pantomime. | Women & children, fearful, are told they will die. Gov, B, troops arrive & battle exiles in word & deed. G arrives with reinforcements, declares victory, & announces capture of Gov's palace. |
| | Dialogue: all principals, cho. | B, reunited with A & Gov, thanks G for sparing Gov. B proposes to take ships & lead all prisoners out of the country. |
| | *Choeur final.* | All agree to follow B & make good their escape. |

Like *La Caverne*, *Béniowski* begins *in medias res*, after Béniowski has inspired Stéphanow's jealousy for a variety of reasons but before the major events of the conspiracy take place. The action unfolds gradually, but events are more carefully prepared than in *La Caverne* so that few events are thoroughly unexpected. However, Duval has left himself room for some subtleties in characterization and a great deal of suspense. For example, Stéphanow's course of action is never irrevocably set, but could go in either of two directions at any one of several points in the story. Similarly, Béniowski's reactions to any one development or revelation are often open to question until he states them.

In *Béniowski* there is no reliance on offstage action to cover major turning points in the plot. Béniowski's escape, for example, takes place offstage, but he described his route in detail to Aphanasie, and her coments in the Act II finale keep the audience informed of his progress. Similarly, the hostages who appear in the final scenes of Act III are expected because of Stéphanow's order for their capture. These dramatic procedures are quite unlike the "messenger" technique used in *La Caverne* and have more in common with Scribe's writing than those of the earlier work.

Like *La Caverne, Béniowski* also utilizes large-scale musico-dramatic *coups* to end each act, but here again the *Béniowski* libretto shows the effect of more careful preparation for subsequent events in the plot. The story line is relatively simple and centers around Stéphanow's efforts to discredit Béniowski and to gain for himself the favors his rival enjoys. There are no subplots or major diversions from this. Yet each act has within itself a kind of substructure to the main plot in that it deals with a single major portion or step in that plot. At the beginning of Act I Stéphanow declares his intention of turning the exiles against Béniowski, but by the end of the act this aim has been thwarted temporarily. Act II emphasizes Béniowski's relationship to the governor and the ruling circle. Beginning with preparations for the marriage of Béniowski and Aphanasie, the act ends with the latter's encouraging Béniowski to escape and fulfill his mission. At the beginning of Act III Stéphanow reveals his remorse and his willingness to atone for his deeds. By the end of the act he has done so and has contributed to the success of the revolution. Thus each act is a miniature drama and illustrates a dramatic procedure cultivated in a much more systematized fashion by Scribe.

*Béniowski* also contains at least one good example of a device used to extreme by Scribe: the contrived entrance or exit. In Act II, iii, Duval creates a pretext to move Béniowski off the stage before he sees Stéphanow and becomes suspicious, and to move Stéphanow onstage for a monologue before the governor's return.

*Béniowski* resembles *La Caverne* in the importance and dramatic substance given the musical numbers. Some merely elaborate on ideas presented in the spoken dialogue, but most—especially the larger ensemble and choral scenes—have some dramatic significance in themselves and even carry parts of the action. As in *La Caverne*, important turning points in the plot are often reserved exclusively for spoken portions of the libretto but are rather more likely than earlier in the century to be worked out as suspenseful, slowly unfolding musical scenes. One still finds, however, that the finale is broken for a spoken "recognition scene," a technique common to a large number of libretti of this period and carried over even into Scribe's early works.

*Béniowski* preserves many of the older rescue opera traditions in libretto writing. Nevertheless, it comes closest of any opéra comique yet discussed to the well-made libretti of Eugène Scribe.

## A SURVEY OF SCRIBE'S OPERAS COMIQUES

There are two main reasons for considering Scribe's opéra comique libretti before dealing with those of the many successful works he wrote for the Opéra. First, they afford the best comparison of Scribe the dramatist—a role for which he is best known in literary history—with Scribe the librettist, thus giving the opportunity to compare and contrast techniques of spoken drama with those of the musical theatre. Second, they reflect in the broadest sense an intermediate stage between Scribe's spoken dramas and his opera libretti, thus yielding a kind of bird's-eye view of the nature and function of music in a dramatic work without having to consider the fuller range of musico-dramatic styles and media utilized in opera.

Scribe is particularly known for his development of the well-made play, a dramatic structure in which all elements fit together so well that not a single one is jarring or upsetting to the spectator and no loose ends are left over at the end of the play to become bases for post-curtain speculation. Steven S. Stanton describes the technique involved in Scribe's well-made plays as follows.

> . . . well-made plays have six structural features: (1) a delayed-action plot whose point of attack occurs at the climax of the story of which it is a part and whose central character struggles to overcome obstacles (usually to love and marriage); (2) a pattern of increasingly intense action and suspense, carefully prepared by exposition which establishes certain facts for the spectator and causes him to anticipate each significant event (this pattern is supported throughout the play by contrived exits and entrances, letters, and other devices for conveying these facts to certain characters while keeping them secret from others); (3) a teeter-totter arrangement of incidents to create successive ups and downs in the fortunes of the hero caused by his conflict with one or more opponents and leading to his ultimate triumph or failure; (4) the counterpunch of peripeteia or upset followed by *scène à faire* or obligatory scene, in which the hero is victorious because of the release to his opponent of the formerly withheld secrets (these have on the latter a devastating effect); (5) a central misunderstanding or *quiproquo*, made obvious to the spectator but withheld from the participants; and (6) the reproduction in miniature of the overall delayed-action pattern in the individual acts.[1]

Commenting on this technique, Stanton has observed that:

> This formula varies from play to play only in the smallest details. The structure remains constant in all major respects. Comedies of this type developing historically from classical comedy through

> Italian, Spanish, and French channels, have become known as *comédies d'intrigue*: they depend for their dramatic effect on incident rather than on ideas or psychological depth.[2]

In addition to this general description of Scribe's writing technique Stanton also mentions the device of *numérotage*, "sequentially ordered scenes which systematically prepare for each new development in the action."[3]

Because Scribe's opéra comique libretti are, externally, comic plays with music, consideration of them in relation to the well-made play is in order. In addition, of course, certain conventions of opéra comique enter into their structure. Because of these conventions a libretto and a spoken drama necessarily differ, but this does not rule out discussion of the opéras comiques in terms of the principles operating in Scribe's spoken dramas as well, for both sets of conventions are in operation in the majority of his mature libretti. A point-by-point consideration of the way in which the technique of the well-made play appears in the opéras comiques will be deferred until discussion of specific operas because of the desirability of having concrete examples at hand to substantiate assertions made. For the present, suffice it to say that the general character of the well-made play is preserved in Scribe's mature libretti and constitutes an unvarying structural framework for even the weakest works.

The application of the principles of the well-made play to libretto writing, however, was not something Scribe hit upon at once. Rather, it was the result of the author's experimentation and took some years to develop. Concurrent development of new musical styles and forms, particularly of Rossinian techniques of dramatic ensemble composition, made no small contribution to the transition Scribe effected from the older style of libretto as represented by *La Caverne* and especially *Béniowski* to the new style of bourgeois comedy founded as much on social changes as on his own development of the *comédie-vaudeville* in the 1820s.

Scribe's first libretto, *La Chambre à coucher ou une demi-heure de Richelieu* (April 29, 1813; music by Guénée), is a rather amusing but not at all outstanding example of the old style of light comedy cultivated in opéra comique for some time. In this one-act work Scribe definitely shows himself to be feeling his way into the genre and he makes some unmistakable errors. Scribe's aim in his plays was to make dramatic capital out of the social and political scene, and he attempts to do the same in this first offering for the musical stage. The result is a fast-moving, often witty comedy of manners in which, incidentally, the characters sing an occasional song or duo. However, the quick delivery and topical humor in the dialogue are not particularly congenial to the operatic medium, which requires relatively simple plots which can without harm unfold at an easy pace. Most of the musical numbers in *La Chambre à coucher* are loosely connected to the action but make no contribution to it other than to provide a pleasant interlude, and the work closes with an old-fashioned vaudeville in which the moral of the story is stated and the characters request that the critics not judge their efforts too harshly.

Some eight years later Scribe returned to the Opéra-Comique with a one-act work for Garcia, *La Meunière.* Also a comedy of manners, this work featured the type of finale used by Dercy and Duval: an ensemble broken by some spoken dialogue stating the moral of the story and reconciling opposing factions. The plot has some similarities to that of Scribe's later work, *Le Chalet. Le Paradis de Mahomet* (1822, music by Kreutzer and Kreubé) is again a wordy piece in which precise motivation and preparation for successive events are not as strong as in later works. Although Scribe takes greater care in placing musical numbers and in providing them with variety and dramatic purpose, his technique in this respect also remains rudimentary and the older ensemble finale broken by spoken dialogue is still used.

By the time of *Leicester* (1823, music by Auber), Scribe has arrived at most of the dramatic characteristics of the well-made libretto: carefully prepared action, delayed-action plot, contrived entrances and exits, ups and downs in the fortunes of the hero, and the like. He has also turned from the worlds of comedy of manners and fairy opera to a pseudo-historical world populated by contemporary figures whose speeches are concise and to the point, without topical humor and satirical barbs. Scribe's concept of the placement and function of musical numbers has also matured considerably, and his particular technique of writing ensemble texts appears in the form it will retain throughout the rest of his creative life. Specific examples of this technique will be given in connection with the individual operas discussed. Musical numbers are often dramatic, less frequently decorative, and Scribe shows more skill than earlier in placing the numbers and creating formal variety among them.

Yet it is not until *Léocadie* (1824, music by Auber), one of Scribe's better works, that he breaks with the practice of interrupting the musical finale for a spoken resolution of the dramatic loose ends, a development concurrent with Auber's assimilation of well-developed ensemble technique. Thereafter, Scribe only rarely returns to the earlier practice. Thus Scribe has taken over ten years to overcome the remnants of traditional libretto writing and to replace them with his own techniques derived from the well-made play. *Le Maçon*, the earliest work to be discussed below in detail, is among the first examples of Scribe's mature style in opéra comique, and represents the final stage in a long development and the beginning of a seldom-varied pattern of libretto writing.

In establishing the well-made libretto as a consistent, reliable, and influential technique, Scribe did more than merely change the libretto's format. All other aspects of the libretto are altered or varied from earlier practices as well. On the one hand, Scribe's plots are more complex than those of earlier writers and deal not just with a single, central story line but with any number of subplots as well. On the other hand, his characters are simplified, two-dimensional figures who appear fully formed at the beginning of a work and remain consistent to the end. Characterization is accomplished simply and directly: the character and/or someone associated with him states his position, character, and function in the drama. The audience becomes acquainted with a character not by observing his actions and forming judgments about his personality but by listening to and absorbing what the character or others say about his personality. Character development is rare and psychological depth is infrequent. *Fra Diavolo* provides good examples of these points. From the central tale of Lorenzo's eventual capture of Diavolo there are threads of plot involving the Lorenzo-Zerline romance and Lord Cokbourg's jealousy of Diavolo for the attention he pays to Lady Cokbourg. Each major character is identified and characterized verbally and none changes or develops in the course of the opera. Scribe's methods are thus quite different from those of earlier librettists discussed, who deal with a single, relatively simple plot and who allow characters to develop gradually and to impress their traits upon the observers by action and implication, not by specific statements regarding their own personalities.

All the earlier libretti discussed used some form of delayed-action plot, but Scribe is more systematic in his use of this technique. In most cases all major motivating forces necessary to the action of the opera have been established before the opera begins, and the audience sees only the culmination of events. In *Le Maçon*, for example, the following have taken place before the first act begins: Léon and Irma have met, fallen in love, and planned their escape; Abdallah had discovered their plans and has moved to stop them, while also carrying out his announced intention of leaving France; Roger has become financially able to marry and has just wed Henriette; Roger has saved Léon's life and has become his friend. Everything that happens in the opera is the result of culmination of one of these events. Among the earlier opéras comiques discussed, only *Bêniowski* approaches this degree of tightness in the relationship between pre-curtain and onstage happenings. Further, Scribe's repetition of the delayed-action pattern in miniature in each act is systematic and tightly organized. Again, only *Bêniowski* approaches the typical Scribe libretto in this respect.

Just as Scribe reduces dramatic structure to a science, so too he systematizes the placement of musical numbers and the use of specific musical forms in similar proportions in his libretti. The charts in Appendix A provide a complete list of the opéras comiques of Scribe with summary information about them. While subtleties are necessarily obscured in any such graphic presentation, profiles of each opera are readily discernible. There are several things, however, which the chart is not intended to show or could not show without becoming unnecessarily complex. One is the use of recitative in connection with the various set-numbers. Most large ensemble scenes, particularly Introductions and Finales, include sections of recitative or arioso, as do the majority of the smaller ensembles. Recitative is also frequently used before a solo air and occasionally before a strophic solo, but these have not been given a place on the chart. (In this connection it should be noted that Scribe most often precedes a strophic solo by a spoken monologue having a function similar to that of a recitative preceding an air.) Recitatives occurring as independent pieces, although infrequent, have been noted in appropriate columns according to the number of singers involved.

A second item not shown on the chart is that the strophic forms (*couplets, rondes, romances, légendes,* etc.) are not necessarily performed by a single soloist. Stanzas may be sung in turn by two or three solo voices, or interludes between stanzas may include commentary made by another character or characters. Some of the strophic pieces have choral refrains, and others are incorporated into larger ensemble scenes—e.g., Introductions. Thus these simple forms can be treated in a variety of ways. Reicha explains the reason behind much of this variety when he observes:

> When several actors are on the stage it is always advantageous to have them all sing rather than to isolate one. . . . Thus it is better, in this circumstance, to write an ensemble or a chorus or an air interrupted by or accompanied by the other voices than to [have a character] sing all alone, which usually gives a cold effect.[4]

Just as the *cavatines* have been specially designated in the category of *air*, so the *rondeau* forms, although not strophic, have been placed in the strophic category and given special designation to avoid unnecessary complexity in the chart.

The listings of number of characters are also somewhat simplified in that they do not show the distribution of male and female roles nor the types of choruses involved. In general, male characters outnumber female even though, as Longyear has observed, the heroine is very often the most important character in the work.[5] In an average cast of about eight characters, normally only two or three will be female. In addition, many operas have more than one chorus: e.g., *Fra Diavolo*, with its choruses of soldiers and villagers. A work may also include a large chorus made up of various groups of people—villagers, soldiers, servants, pirates, court attendants, etc.—which may sing together or separately. Lacking scores for all the operas listed, it was not possible to determine with accuracy how the latter choruses of two or more groups were treated; hence the abbreviation "cho." has been used in all cases.

Save for exceptional cases (e.g., the finale of *Manon Lescaut*), the relative length of the musical numbers has not been indicated. Again, this was impossible because scores of all works were not available.

The most striking thing revealed by the chart is not the differences between the various operas but rather their relative consistency in the course of more than forty years of Scribe's production. Solo songs, especially the strophic forms, continue to form the musical core of opéra comique, although libretti written after 1850 have a comparatively higher number of large ensemble scenes involving chorus and soloists or more than five solo singers. This is another instance of Scribe's riding with the times, for everywhere the shorter set-piece was giving way to more complex musical scene structures. However, in very few works does Scribe eliminate the traditional long ensemble, with or without chorus, as the closing number of the work. The tendency toward greater, more sensational dramatic climaxes in opera is reflected in the final scene of Scribe's *Marco Spada* (1852), in which the actual conclusion of the plot ends the work and there is no dramatic "cushion" provided by a final ensemble or chorus. Similarly, only a short chorus follows the death of the heroine at the end of *Manon Lescaut* (1856) and the action of *Yvonne* (1859) concludes with another such short chorus.

Choruses are used extensively in the opéras comiques, even in short works with small casts, but they are rarely used in numbers not also involving one or more soloists. Perhaps the reason for this is to be found in Reicha's observation that choruses are not particularly suitable for melodic writing because of the variety of expression necessary to reflect the sentiments of any large group of people. Some melodies, however, are best performed by the chorus: "national[istic] tunes; dance tunes accompanied by chorus; chansons; barcarolles; refrains; and songs which can be performed more *forte* than *piano*."[6] Indeed, precisely these kinds of music most often employ the chorus in Scribe's works. Similarly, ensembles larger than a quintet seldom occur without chorus except as Introductions or Finales, where they are designated by the latter terms. The exceptional sextet and septet have been noted on the chart in the column for large ensembles.

> It has been found that an ensemble or a chorus or both at the same time executed immediately after the overture open the scene of an opera most suitably. But since all opera subjects do not lend themselves to this sort of beginning the poet, in order to satisfy the composer and a portion of the public, finds himself with the necessity of drawing up an introduction whether he wants to or not. As a result this initial piece becomes a kind of appetizer; and since it precedes the exposition of the piece, one most often does not know its significance.[7]

Reicha published these comments in 1833, when Scribe had produced only about a third of his opéras comiques. However, the words might well be applied to Scribe, for the majority of his works do begin with the type of introductory ensemble Reicha describes. These Introductions, however, are seldom as purposeless as the hypothetical cases Reicha imagines. Although static pieces, they contain at least the illusion of action and—because of the delayed-action plots used by Scribe—sharpen the interest of the audience to learn more about the situation. Moreover, Scribe is not held to any formula, for over one-third of his opéras comiques do not begin with an Introduction. Of these, twenty-two open with spoken monologues or dialogues, ten begin with solo numbers with or without a preceding monologue or recitative, and three begin with a duo, while there are isolated examples beginning with a trio, a quintet, or a chorus. Opening with a large-scale introductory scene, then, was most common but was by no means the only way to set the drama in motion. Nor did the lack of such a large scene at the beginning necessarily damage the opera's chances for pleasing the public, all other things being equal. A case in point is Auber's very successful *Le Domino noir*, in which the first musical number, a trio, occurs in Scene iv. In fact, the total number of musical pieces in this work is rather small, but this is made up for by the skillful handling of drama and music and by the fact that some numbers, especially those at the ends of each act, are long and carefully planned for maximum effect.

Acts other than the first may begin in any number of ways. Most frequent is the solo, sometimes with chorus, but dialogues or introduction-like scenes are not uncommon. Ways to end an act are less varied. Except for the antiquated vaudeville of his first libretto, most of Scribe's opéras comiques end with large finales involving chorus and most, if not all, of the principal singers. Works without chorus or with smaller casts may end with smaller-scale but usually extended trios, quartets, quintets, etc. The ending of acts other than the last is less standardized, but Finales of similar character to those ending the opera predominate. In fact, the closing scene of the second act of a three-act work may have greater musical and dramatic weight than that ending the opera, e.g., in *La Dame blanche*, *Fra Diavolo*, or *Le Maçon*.

Whatever the kind of musical number used—whether a solo, duo, trio, quartet, or larger ensemble—Scribe makes sure that the important turning points and climaxes in the drama are set to music. This practice would have earned him Reicha's commendation, for the latter wrote:

> It is an unpardonable fault on the part of the composer and of the poet to place a piece of music outside the action, i.e., where an event of any importance has just ended. In this case a musical number can only annoy, for it needlessly slows down the course of the action and freezes it; thus it is the action itself which ought to be set to music.[8]

Many examples of the way in which Scribe uses musical setting to enhance dramatic action and suspense will be given in connection with the individual operas discussed. Because the music, particularly in long ensemble scenes, is intended to slow down and heighten the effect of the action, occasions when such scenes are broken by spoken dialogue are worthy of note. Examples of this practice are infrequent and occur in one of two contexts: 1) the insertion of a fairly long section of dialogue followed by a recapitulation of a chorus or other section from the preceding ensemble; 2) the insertion of a few lines of dialogue in the middle of an otherwise musical scene. The reasoning behind the first type of scene structure is quite simple: librettist and composer use this method to form a neat musico-dramatic package without wasting valuable musical time on information which might better be conveyed in speech. An example of this practice occurs in the first scene of *Haydée*. In the second case the effect desired is one of clarity and immediacy of effect: a point must be made unambiguously and suddenly. The delaying effect of music and its tendency to blur important text, unless the words are carefully prepared and/or repeated, make a lapse into speech necessary and desirable at such a point. An example of this can be found in the Finale of *Fra Diavolo.*

Many considerations evidently led to the selection of musical form and medium. Judging by the variety of forms contained in each opera and the consistency with which they appear regardless of the number of acts or the size of the cast, Scribe must have taken into account the composer's desire to display his talents in several ways and the audience's desire to hear conventionalized yet varied musical genres. These considerations in turn must have influenced Scribe's technique of *numérotage* as applied to the operatic medium, for the obvious reason that one cannot provide for a trio if one has no scene in which three characters appear onstage in a musical situation. By the same token, however, Scribe's skill in arranging scenes, entrances and exits, and combinations of characters made him an ideal librettist, for he practiced a similar *numérotage* in his spoken dramas.

Choice of musical medium also seems to have been done according to a kind of musical division of labor. Strophic forms are used for solos of a static, reflective, or general narrative nature (e.g., the numerous *ballades*), whereas airs are called for in situations in which the soloist has to trace out the progress of a single idea, a train of thought, or an emotional state. Small ensembles (a few soloists with or without chorus) generally chart the course of one idea or conflict as it unfolds or is resolved—whether satisfactorily or not—whereas larger ensembles take in a number of dramatic ideas or conflicts.

One of Scribe's most important contributions to libretto writing was the setting up of new conventions regarding the types of music chosen and the uses to which each type was put. In doing this he created more and larger musical scenes than had his predecessors and made the music more functional—and therefore more important—in relation to the drama. He tightened the dramatic structure by applying his well-made play formula to the libretto. This also gave increased importance to the music, for the numbers occurred at points in the work for which careful preparation had been made. Scribe's carefully planned and skillfully executed *coups de théâtre* coincided with the introduction of the musical numbers, and both profited from the partnership.

Scribe not only systematized the types of musical numbers and their placement within the libretto, but to some degree systematized the situations he used as well. Michael Kaufmann has classified various scenes and situations, a total of fifty-five, which may recur as many as twenty or twenty-five times in the spoken dramas of Scribe.[9] Similarly, the operas and opéras comiques of Scribe also make use of recurrent, stock situations. Although these are often very general situations and their recurrence is hardly unexpected in the work of a man whose output was so vast, their tabulation does point up—as does the entire definition of the well-made play—the triumph of craft over art in the works of Scribe. The table below enumerates a number of the recurrent situations in Scribe's opéra comique libretti. Titles in parentheses are those of works which contain variants of the situation described.

1. A man tries to gain (earn, inherit, etc.) enough money to marry the woman he loves.

*La Petite lampe merveilleuse* (1822)
*Le Maçon* (1825)
*Les Deux nuits* (1829)
*Fra Diavolo* (1830)
*Le Cheval de bronze* (1835)
*Le Fidèle berger* (1838)
*Le Shérif* (1839)
*Haydée* (1847)

2. Two lovers set out to make their fortunes so that they can be married.

*Le Concert à la cour* (1824)
*La Reine d'un jour* (1839)
*Le Main de fer* (1841)
*Manon Lescaut* (1856)

3. A girl loves (and/or may marry) a man who seems (but may not be) above her station.

*Léocadie* (1824)
*La Dame blanche* (1825)
*La Fiancée* (1829)
*Lestocq* (1834)
*Le Fils du prince* (1834)
*Le Cheval de bronze* (1835)
*Les Chaperons blancs* (1836)
*L'Ambassadrice* (1836)
*Manon Lescaut* (1856)
*Zanetta* (1840)
*La Part du diable* (1843)
*Le Puits d'amour* (1843)
*Lambert Simnel* (1844)
*Haydée* (1847)
*Giralda* (1850)
*Les Mystères d'Udolphe* (1852)
*Jenny Bell* (1855)

4. A man loves (and/or may marry) a girl who seems (but may not be) above his station.

*La Petite lampe merveilleuse* (1822)
(*Régine* [1839])

*Zanetta* (1840)
*Le Guitarrero* (1840)
*Le Ménétrier* (1845)
*La Charbonnière* (1845)
*La Dame de pique* (1850)

5. A man searches for and finds a girl with whom he has fallen in love. (In most cases he does not know her name until he finds her.)

*Leicester* (1823)
*La Dame blanche* (1825)
*Fiorella* (1826)
*Le Cheval de bronze* (1835)
*Le Portefaix* (1835)
*Le Domino noir* (1837)
*Le Duc d'Olonne* (1842)
*La Part du diable* (1843)
*Manon Lescaut* (1856)

6. A man sees a woman in a carriage or descending from it and falls in love with her.

*Le Portefaix* (1835)
*Le Guitarrero* (1840)
*La Barcarolle* (1845)

7. A girl searches for and finds a man she loves but whose identity she does not know.

*Le Paradis de Mahomet* (1822)
*Le Timide* (1826)
(*Le Mauvais-oeil* [1836])
*Les Chaperons blancs* (1836)
*La Figurante* (1838)
*Le Shérif* (1839)
*Le Duc d'Olonne* (1842)
*Le Code noir* (1842)
*La Part du diable* (1843)

8. Two friends love the same woman, but one eventually loses out and/or steps aside.

*Leicester* (1823)
*La Neige* (1823)
*Fiorella* (1826)
*Les Deux nuits* (1829)
*Le Domino noir* (1837)

*Les Diamants de la couronne* (1841)
*Le Puits d'amour* (1843)

9. Two women love the same man, but one loses out and/or steps aside.

*Lestocq* (1834)
*Cagliostro* (1844)

10. An impending marriage is broken up in favor of a rival for the hand of one of the partners.

*La Meuniére* (1821)
*Le Loup-garou* (1827
*Les Deux nuits* (1829)
*La Fiancée* (1829)
*Le Fils du prince* (1834)
*Le Mauvais-oeil* (1836)
*Jenny Bell* (1855)
*Les Diamants de la couronne (1841)*
*Le Duc d'Olonne* (1842)
*Cagliostro* (1844)
*Giralda* (1850)
*Les Mystères d'Udolphe* (1852)

11. Secret marriages are revealed.

*Leicester* (1823)
*Le Valet de chambre* (1823)
*La Neige* (1823)
*Le Fils du prince* (1834)
(*Régine* [1839])
*Le Main de fer* (1841)
*Cagliostro* (1844)
*Giralda* (1850; 2 secret marriages

12. Nobles appear unidentified or in disguises, usually as persons from a lower social class.

*Le Maçon* (1825)
(*La Vieille* [1826])
*Le Loup-garou* (1827)
*Fra Diavolo* (1830)
*La Prison d'Edimbourg* (1833)
*Le Fils du prince* (1834)
*Les Chaperons blancs* (1836)
*L'Ambassadrice* (1836)
*Le Domino noir* (1837)
*Les Diamants de la couronne* (1841)
*Le Puits d'amour* (1843)
*Le Ménétrier* (1845)
*L'Etoile du nord* (1854)
*Jenny Bell* (1855)

13. A character discovers he is of noble birth.

(*Léocadie* [1824])
*La Dame blanche* (1825)
*La Figurante* (1838)
(*Lambert Simnel* [1843])

*La Sirène* (1844)
(*Marco Spada* [1852])

14. A noble, once ruined, is saved or restored to titles and wealth, sometimes through the efforts of a member of a lower social class.

*Le Maçon* (1825)
(*La Dame blanche* [1825])
*Le Domino noir (1837)*
*Régine* (1839)
*La Barcarolle* (1845)
*Haydée* (1847)
*Giralda* (1850)
*La Dame de pique* (1850)
*Les Mystères d'Udolphe* (1852)

15. A performer becomes "respectable" but may not be happy about it.

*L'Ambassadrice* (1836)
*La Figurante* (1838)
*Polichinele* (1839)
*La Part du diable* (1843)

16. A soldier or sailor hopes to be killed in battle, usually because of an unhappy love affair.

*Marguerite* (1838)
*Régine* (1839)
*La Reine d'un jour* (1839)
*Le Duc d'Olonne* (1842)
*Haydée* (1847)

17. A character sings a ballad about a legend which has some bearing on the plot of the opera.

*La Dame blanche* (1825)
*Fra Diavolo* (1830)
*Le Puits d'amour* (1843)
*La Sirène* (1844)
*La Dame de pique* (1850)

18. A young page, usually played by a woman, is at a "girl crazy" age.

*Actéon* (1836)
*Le Puits d'amour* (1843)

19. A man imitates a woman's voice in the course of a musical number.

*Fra Diavolo* (1830)
*Les Chaperons blancs* (1836)
*Le Diable à l'ecole* (1842)

20. A foreign character's accent is deliberately written into his speeches.
*Le Concert à la cour* (1824)
*Fra Diavolo* (1830)
*L'Ambassadrice* (1836)

21. Characters conspire against a current government.
*Lestocq* (1834)
*Les Chaperons blancs* (1836)
*La Reine d'un jour* (1839)
*Lambert Simnel* (1843)

That these situations recur in two or more libretti is no indication of conscious self-borrowing on Scribe's part, but only an illustration of the degree to which Scribe's technique was systematized, the product of a facile and prolific pen.

During Scribe's time even serious literary dramatists often ignored the classical unities of time, place, and action, and Scribe was no exception. The only unity he preserves in his libretti with any degree of consistency is that of time, for the action of the majority of the opéras comiques and many of the operas takes place within a period of twenty-four hours or less. This is due to his custom of beginning the action at a point shortly before its culmination. Nevertheless, there are frequent exceptions to this practice. *La Prison d'Edimbourg*, *Les Deux nuits*, and *La Reine d'un jour* are examples of works the action of which takes place over several days. At times the action is spread over several months or even years, as in *L'Ambassadrice*, *Régine*, or *Manon Lescaut*. The demand for scenic display was not so great at the Opéra-Comique as at the Opéra, but such demand as existed undoubtedly influenced Scribe's usual lack of adherence to any sort of unity of place. Although the action of any opéra comique most often takes place in one generalized location—e.g., the Duke of X's palace, an estate in the vicinity of Y, etc.—it is unusual to find all acts of a work set in exactly the same place and it is not at all rare to find a different setting from each act. The alterations in setting can be simple changes to another room within the same house, more remote shifts from one area of a city or country to another, and still more remote moves from country to country. As for unity of action, Scribe's plots center on a single main theme or story line but usually include one or more subplots or other tangential activities, even in opéras comiques of one act.

While adhering to the same basic structural principles in all his opéra comique libretti, Scribe deals with a wide range of topics. Sentimental comedy predominates—as in *Le Chalet* or *La Barcarolle*—but there are also a number of works on exotic topics (*Le Paradis de Mahomet, Le Cheval de bronze*); plots that combine sentimental comedy with exoticism (*Fra Diavolo, Haydée*) or history (*La Dame blanche*); comedy bordering on farce (*Le Timide*); and pieces on more serious topics (*Léocadie, La Prison d'Edimbourg, Manon Lescaut*). From the romanticism of the marvelous in *La Dame blanche* to that of history in *Lambert Simnel*, from the middle-class world of *Le Maçon* to the Russia of *La Dame de pique* or *Lestocq*, there is a story for every interest or taste in Scribe's theatre. Considering this, it seems even more amazing that he subjected all topics, locales, characters, and situations to a uniform technique without depriving them of their freshness, their suitabililty for the musical stage, or their appeal—through the variety contained within them—for composers and audiences alike.

In a sense, the well-made libretto reflected life not so much as it was but as the patrons of the Opéra-Comique thought it should be. Scribe's work enjoyed a burst of popularity from *ca.* 1823-1829 and again after 1833—postrevolutionary eras in which people, tired of turmoil, wished for a life that would move in the stable, predictable manner of a well-made play. In reflecting political and social ideals on the musical stage Scribe served his age as well as his composers.

Yet Martin Cooper has observed that:

> After 1830 the opéra comique ceased to develop as a genre and went into a decline, marked by some of the most brilliant works of its history but with so little *raison d'être* that it was only a matter of time before a man of genius [Offenbach] should administer the *coup de grâce* and evolve a new comic genre, or revive in a new form one of the primitive species from which opéra comique had itself developed.[10]

The years of Scribe's greatest successes were thus years of an artistic status quo in which opéra comique's leading librettist, having found his formula, continued to apply it with a consistency illustrated by every aspect of his craft. France too was moving toward a showdown. Beginning in 1835 repressive laws were passed which resulted, among other things, in a reduction of freedom of the press and suppression of many revolutionary clubs, which were forced to go underground after their leaders were jailed or exiled. By 1840 the government's centralized control was of a nature that one historian could observe: "Louis Philippe, Guizot, and Duchâtel governed France as they believed the upper classes wished her to be governed."[11] A series of bad harvests beginning in 1845 resulted in high food prices, and less demand for manufactured goods put many out of work. Because of increased mechanization in large factories in the 1840s the lower bourgeoisie and shopkeepers also began to feel the economic pinch. There seemed to be no way these classes could gain a hearing in the government, and they became fertile soil for the growth of radical doctrines.[12] The breakthrough came in February of 1848, when the revolution brought to an end the July Monarchy. How these events affected the artistic scene in Paris is illustrated by Berlioz's observations in a letter to J. W. Davison dated July 26, 1848.

> . . . I am very sadly affected by the deplorable state in which I have found the music and musicians of Paris after my long absence. All the theatres are closed, all the artists ruined, all the professors idle, all the students in flight, poor pianists playing sonatas in the public squares, historical painters sweeping streets, architects employed in mixing mortar on public building sites. . . .[13]

Although Scribe's star did not fall immediately, its light was waning. By 1848 his greatest successes were behind him, and after the revolution a new operatic order arose to carry on the best of his practices while making contributions more in keeping with its own time.

> The year when the classical phase of *opera comique* formally ended was 1851, when the Théâtre-Lyrique opened its doors and all the small theatres began to mount operettas after the legislation restricting the number of singers and musicians permitted a given theatre was gradually being removed.[14]

All of Scribe's opera and opêra comique libretti to be discussed in detail were completed before 1848, during the years when his style and that of his musical collaborators was most timely. For purposes of surveying and evaluating Scribe's technique in the writing of opéra comique libretti a number of works from a twenty-year span has been chosen.[15] They are:

Auber's *Le Maçon* (May 3, 1825; text by Scribe and G. Delavigne);

Boieldieu's *La Dame blanche* (December 10, 1825; text by Scribe);

Auber's *Le Timide* (May 30, 1826; text by Scribe and Saintine);
Auber's *Fra Diavolo* (January 28, 1830; text by Scribe);
Carafa's *La Prison d 'Edimbourg* (July 20, 1833; text by Scribe and Planard);
Adam's *Le Chalet* (September 25, 1834; text by Scribe and Mélesville);
Auber's *La Baracarolle* (April 22, 1845; text by Scribe);
Auber's *Haydée* (December 28, 1847; text by Scribe).

A number of factors were considered in the selection of these works. It would have been tempting to consider only Scribe's most successful works, a number sufficiently large to yield a reasonable sample of the author's writing. Yet the larger purpose involved here spoke against a selection of work along these lines; for if one wishes to discover the ingredients making for success on the musical stage, one must also consider the failures. Thus the list above contains several brilliant successes (*Le Maçon, La Dame blanche, Fra Diavolo, Le Chalet, Haydée*), one moderately successful piece (*La Prison d'Edimbourg*), and two failures (*Le Timide, La Barcarolle*). It also contains, along with a number of works in the standard three-act structure, two one-act works (*Le Timide, Le Chalet*), the latter one of the most successful pieces in the list, the former the greatest failure.

However, there are still more reasons for selecting these works. Since the collaboration of Scribe and Auber was one of the most successful pairings of librettist and composer in the history of opera, the largest number of works on the list is by that team. Nevertheless, several other composers prominent in French opéra comique during the second quarter of the nineteenth century are also represented: Boieldieu, now at the end of a long and successful career; Carafa, an Italian known for operatic composition in his native land and language as well as for French opéra comique; Adam, whose music was lighter and less skillful technically than Auber's and who began the move toward operetta. Thus a group of different types, generations, and nationalities from among those composers who used Scribe's talents is represented here.

What makes an opera libretto an opera libretto? Viewing more or less with alarm the numerous and often unsupported statements of critics condemning the libretto for its lack of drama, lack of lyricism, lack of poetry, lack of intelligibility—the contradictory flaws presented are legion—and blaming it, whatever the basis, for the failure of a given opera, it was difficult to determine just what factors to consider in evaluating Scribe's technique. One solution to this problem was to choose for study libretti based on earlier literary models, thus providing a basis for comparison of the treatment of given material in two different ways, and to place these derivative libretti against freely composed works to determine the nature of the elements held constant between the two groups of libretti. As Holz has pointed out, dramatists often do not invent their own subjects—the works of Shakespeare being among the best proofs of this statement—and librettists are even more prone to work from some preexistent source.[16] Adding to this observation a reminder of Scribe's tendency to seek material everywhere, it is obvious that one must make some mental qualifications about the degree of originality of the three "freely composed" works, *Le Maçon*, *Le Timide*, and *Fra Diavolo*. The rest of the works to be discussed are adapted from literary models of different types: *La Baracarolle* from *La Chanson, ou l'intérieur d'un bureau*, a one-act vaudeville by Scribe and Varner; *Le Chalet* from Goethe's singspiel *Jery und Bätely*; *Haydée* from a short story by Merimée, "La Partie de tric-trac," with some elements from other sources; *La Prison d'Edimbourg* from a novel, Sir Walter Scott's *The Heart of Midlothian*; and *La Dame blanche* from Scott's *Guy Mannering* and *The Monastery*, with elements from the same author's *The Abbott* and his lengthy poem, "The Lady of the Lake." Scribe's basic style changes little in the course of the period under consideration. Therefore, the works will not be considered in chronological order but rather—with the exception of *Le Timide*—in the order just given.

## Auber's *Le Maçon*

*Le Maçon*, one of Auber's greatest successes,[17] was also among his earliest collaborations with Scribe. Although the libretto is a joint effort by Scribe and his long-time friend and associate Germain Delavigne, one cannot assign to the individual co-workers responsibility for specific elements or details. In general, it was not part of Scribe's nature to be original; therefore it is impossible to believe that the imaginative and adventrous stories involved in both *Le Maçon* and *Fra Diavolo* are truly of Scribe's own invention. Although considered here as freely composed libretti, *Le Maçon* is based on an English report of a supposedly true story,[18] while a subject similar to that of *Fra Diavolo* had been used in several works: *Le Brigand napolitain* at the Vaudeville, *Le Bandit* at the Variétés, and *Cartouche*, a comedy by Overnoy and Nézel.[19] In the absence of any single model or source for either work, however, one can consider them—with qualifications—freely composed.

*Le Maçon* takes place in Paris at an unspecified time in the recent past.[20] The people, largely middle-class craftsmen and small shopkeepers, are celebrating the marriage of Roger, a mason, to

Henriette, the sister of Baptiste the locksmith. This marriage has been made possible by Roger's rather sudden acquisition of an amount of money which Mme. Bertrand, a widow and semiprofessional busybody, suggests may have come to him by means of some sort of shady dealing. The mystery is cleared up by Léon, a nobleman whose true identity is as yet unknown to all save himself. He is on his way to a *rendez-vous* with Irma, a young Greek captive of Abdallah, a Turkish visitor in France who plans to return to his native land the next day and to marry Irma upon his arrival there. Irma, however, has fallen in love with Léon and the two are to meet this evening to effect her escape from the Turk's rented chateau. Before he can get to the chateau, however, Léon meets the wedding party and recognizes Roger, to whom he had given a sum of money in return for the latter's having saved his life. After wishing Roger and Henriette well, Léon leaves and Roger tries to persuade his bride to quit the célebration with him. However, Mme. Bertrand insists that tradition be kept and the guests escort Henriette to her new home, leaving Roger behind to wait a suitable length of time before following. Before he can leave, however, two mysterious strangers arrive and ask help in locating a mason and a locksmith. Finding that Roger is a mason, they kidnap him at knifepoint.

The strangers turn out to be Usbeck and Rica, slaves in the service of Abdallah, in whose chateau the second act takes place. As the act begins Irma tells her friend Zobéide of her plans to escape with Léon, revealing that two slaves—one of them Rica—know of the plot and are helping her. Irma, however, has been betrayed, the first slave has been killed, and Rica, along with Usbeck, has been given the duty of carrying out Abdallah's revenge. Roger and Baptiste, who has also been kidnapped and led, blindfolded, to Abdallah's chateau, are put to work walling up the exits to the garden and preparing locks and chains to secure Léon and Irma inside this prison once they are together. When Léon arrives, Rica warns the pair of the danger ahead and suggests a means of escape, but Baptiste unwittingly alerts Usbeck and the other slaves, and Rica's lot is cast with the unfortunate lovers.

Roger, outnumbered, is not able to help Léon and Irma while he is at work in the chateau and, once outside, has the double problem of finding a way to save the lovers and discovering where they are, for both he and Baptiste were taken from the chateau blindfolded. Meanwhile Mme. Bertrand, aware that Roger did not return home on his wedding night, arrives to "console" the despondent Henriette with news that Roger was seen entering Abdallah's chateau. Baptiste, during the same time, has discovered that the coat of arms on a sword he has taken from the mysterious chateau is that of the Mérinvilles, a wealthy Parisian family of which Léon is a member. When Henriette confronts Roger with what she believes to be incriminating evidence regarding his whereabouts on the previous night, Roger is overjoyed and rushes off to the now-deserted chateau to save Léon. After a brief but necessary explanation to Henriette, all concerned rejoice that the situation has ended happily.

## The Well-Made Libretto

The general characteristics of the well-made libretto have already been discussed. *Le Maçon* provides a clear example of a relatively early libretto by Scribe in which all these traits appear in a mature and well-developed form, and is therefore a good work to discuss in detail as a concrete illustration of these characteristics.

In its over-all structure the libretto of *Le Maçon* shows nearly all the traits of the well-made play as enumerated by Stanton. The opening is that of a delayed-action plot, for it occurs amid the marriage festivities, after Roger has met Léon and the latter has become involved with Irma. The scene as a whole provides much of the basis for later action. Character types are clearly outlined from the first. Mme. Bertrand is the busybody jealous of Henriette's success at winning Roger, and is thus the most likely person to be interested in Roger's whereabouts later and to want to "do her duty" by informing Henriette of her suspicions. Although Mme. Bertrand as a character is unnecessary to the main action of the work, her function in setting in motion certain essential elements of the plot make her indispensable. Roger, entertaining the company with "the rondelay of the good worker," not only establishes the main traits of his character—honesty, diligence, good humor, pride in his work—but sings the refrain that runs through the entire opera and at times provides valuable clues to the future course of the drama. Roger, newly married, can scarcely bear to be away from Henriette for a moment, a situation remarked upon with disapproval by Mme. Bertrand (Scene ii). When he disappears, therefore, the event takes on greater significance than would a brief stay away from home on the part of a long-married man. Somewhat later, in his conversation with Mme. Bertrand (Scene iii), Baptiste reveals his character traits: fear, suspicion, a healthy dose of avarice, and a disinclination to get involved, however slightly, in events which could cast a bad light on him. Henriette has little to do in the first scenes, but perhaps this is indicative of her character. Hers is the role of the sweet little wife, loving and not too noisy.

However, Scribe does not merely give us these general clues as to what will take place. He prepares specifically for each successive event, with the result that nothing that happens in the opera is really unexpected and every fact that is given out comes to rest properly and regularly in its own good time. Scribe plays on suspense, but it is a suspense of a special kind. Far from wondering what the outcome will be, the spectator knows the general direction in which each action will lead and only need find out when and precisely how the author will manage to tie events together.

In *Le Maçon* the action begins as if the participants were in a race. In Scene i—static save for the putting forth of some general character traits—principals and chorus crowd behind the starting gate; they talk among themselves, move around a bit, sing and dance, but dramatically remain quite stationary. In Scene ii the race begins: someone announces that persons inside the house are calling for the bride and groom, and all except Mme. Bertrand and Baptiste leave the stage. But if Scribe has designed a race, it is like that of the Olympic torch-bearers. Throughout the opera characters throw out bits of information sufficient to carry the action to a point further down the road; these actions are brought to their natural conclusions but form the basis for new actions which in turn carry the drama further. Over and above this are certain central dramatic movements of which all the details eventally form a part.

The torch is lit in Scene iii when Mme. Bertrand arouses Baptiste's suspicions about the source of Roger's sudden wealth, moves forward with the arrival of Léon in Scene iv, and come to a rest when it is annonced that the latter gave Roger the money some time before. Thus not only is one mystery solved, but a friendly connection is established between Léon and Roger that will be exploited later. At this point also an association is made between Roger's refrain (the *Ronde* of Scene i) and his saving Léon's life, since Léon heard Roger singing the tune just before he arrived to drive off the assailants. The subject of Léon's secret love is introduced as well. Thus we are not surprised when these items return later in the work. There are other elements of the Léon-Roger encounter that give the audience hints of things to come. Léon arrives in an expensive coach and later gives Henriette a valuable ring as a wedding gift; thus none is surprised when, in the third act, he is discovered to be a wealthy Parisian nobleman. Mme. Bertrand has already mentioned the mysterious Turk, preparing us for later events and persons associated with him. We are not particularly surprised that the kidnappers Usbeck and Rica are identified as the Turk's slaves, nor that Léon's secret love turns out to be Abdallah's unwilling fiancée.

Although details and complications are added gradually throughout the opera, the audience has all the basic information necessary to prepare for and understand the remainder of the work by the time Léon leaves the stage for his *rendez-vous* with Irma. Not unexpectedly, then, bride and groom are separated and Roger is abducted (prepared by his own announcement of his skill as a mason, the introduction of the mysterious strangers in Léon's tale and, a bit later, by their momentary appearance on the stage); he finds Léon again (prepared by Léon's: "And if we are ever separated, if I am never to see you again . . . But no, let us not think of that" [Act I, vi]) in another dangerous situation (Léon: "Know then that this evening, in a few moments, someone waits for me; and for such a *rendez-vous* I could sacrifice my fortune and my life" [Act I, vi]) and saves him (prepared by his earlier bravery on Léon's behalf). Also not surprising are the disclosures, already mentioned, of the various links connecting the mason with the Turkish ambassador; the identity of Léon; and Mme. Bertrand's role in solving the mystery. This is what Stanton refers to as the "exposition which establishes certain facts for the spectator and causes him to anticipate each significant event. . . ." The means are simple, clear, and—above all—most carefully contrived. We need only the details: how all these things will be accomplished. Like the exposition, the rest of the opera is carefully worked out to provide these details at the right times and in just the proper amounts. The torch is passed on.

First, since a wife, especially a new bride, would most definitely get in the way of the rest of the action, she must be disposed of in a convenient but logical manner. This Scribe does by inventing the traditional wedding custom mentioned in the synopsis. Roger can then be abducted quite easily. He must not know where he is being taken, but the audience needs this information. Hence the opening scene of Act II, in which Irma is introduced. By means of her song (a tale of a slave girl who refuses a Turk's proposal of marriage) and her conversation with Zobéide, we learn that she is a Greek captive of the Turk and that she intends to run off with a young Frenchman who will come for her that very night. The last bit of information makes definite the already-suspected identity of Léon's secret love. From Irma we also learn that Rica is one of her collaborators, so that it is no surprise when he offers the lovers help in escaping what seems to be certain death, nor when he indirectly (in a conversation with Usbeck) informs the audience that Irma's plans have been discovered.

In Scenes v and vi Roger and Baptiste are brought in and put to work. They make quite clear that they do not know where they are or why they have been ordered to perform the tasks with which they are occupied. From earlier information, however, the audience knows their whereabouts and can deduce that their handiwork is to be part of Abdallah's plan to punish the lovers. The conversation between the two workmen also brings into clearer focus Baptiste's cowardly character. We can be sure that when such a man later finds the pavillion in which he has been locked entered by two strange people—Léon and Irma attempting to escape—he, in his extreme fear, will somehow alert their captors in time to prevent the lovers from escaping. Yet we are left with some hope: the second act closes with Roger's refrain, a clever device both musically and dramatically, assuring us that somehow Roger will save the prisoners.

In the final act Scribe makes use of many ideas for which preparation was made as early as the first scenes of Act. I. Mme. Bertrand fulfills her function as a jealous gossip admirably. Far from breaking up the marriage of Henriette and Roger, however, Mme. Bertrand's gossip is the means contrived by Scribe to tell Roger the whereabouts of Léon. The first act also contained information that the Turkish entourage was to leave France on the very morning that Act III takes place, and this was reiterated by Irma in Act II. Thus there will be no one to stand in Roger's way once he learns where the prisoners are. Since we already know that Roger will succeed in rescuing the lovers, these details serve only to provide a logical method. In Act I Scribe also established the fact that Henriette was very much in love with her new husband. Now, not unexpectedly, we find her more confused than angry, and quite ready to forgive him even before she learns the entire story of his activity on the previous evening. In addition, Léon's actions in Act I made one suspect the identity that is confirmed in Act III. By the end of Act III, then no loose ends remain: Roger is reconciled with Henriette; Léon has succeeded in rescuing Irma from the Turk; Baptiste is satisfied that his sister has made a good, safe marriage; and Mme. Bertrand, while not completely happy with her lot, seems reconciled to it.

In order to effect this skillfully engineered plot, the entrances and exits of the characters have been carefully manipulated. In the first act, for example, it wold not do for Roger to be present when Mme. Bertrand confides to Baptiste her suspicions about the source of Roger's wealth; not only would the latter be able to clear up the matter at once, but the strength of this preparation for Léon's entrance would be lost. Scribe therefore has someone from inside the house call for the newlyweds; the crowd accompanies the pair indoors, and Mme. Bertrand

and Baptiste are left alone. Similarly, Roger cannot enter and recognize Léon before the latter has the chance to ask directions to the Turkish ambassador's chateau, for we need this information to prepare for later developments. When Roger is trying to persuade Henriette to leave the wedding guests and run off with him, Usbeck and Rica must enter momentarily to create suspense and to prepare the audience for their return; and Henriette must be carried off by the wedding party before Roger can be kidnapped.

Similar contrived entrances and exits occur in Acts II and III. A martial tune warns Irma and Zobéide of the arrival of Usbeck and Rica in time for them to leave the stage, where their presence during the ensuing discussion of Abdallah's discovery of Irma's plans would ruin the remainder of the plot and, later, would prevent Roger and Baptiste from setting to work. The latter pair are led away before Léon enters, delaying his recognition of Roger until he has had a chance to see Irma and establish his identity securely as that of her lover. Rica arrives in time to warn the lovers, but they attempt to escape before Baptiste is returned to the work site, thus ensuring that their flight will be discovered in time. In Act III Mme. Bertrand, rather than talk to Henriette onstage, takes the latter away to tell her part of what the audience already knows and to allow Roger to enter, converse with Baptiste, and discover Léon's true identity. As a result of her conversation with Mme. Bertrand, Henriette now can return to the stage to give Roger the last necessary clue needed to free Léon. Like parts in a machine, the personae have successfully met and avoided meeting each other for three full acts of carefully contrived and manipulated action, and the "pattern of increasingly intense action and suspense" of the well-made drama (Stanton's second point) has been carried out.

The third item Stanton mentions in his description of the technique of Scribe's well-made plays is "a teeter-totter arrangement of . . . successive ups and downs in the fortunes of the hero. . . ." The adventures of Roger in *Le Maçon* definitely reflect this sort of arrangement, although necessarily to a lesser degree than in a spoken drama. At first very happy over his marriage, Roger faces a future uncertain at best when he is kidnapped and forced to work for an unknown employer. Things look better, however, when it appears that he will be well paid for his labors, but his peace of mind—if not his fortunes—is disturbed when he finds Léon a prisoner and must discover a way to save him. Again, however, his fortunes rise with Henriette's revelation in Act III and climb still higher as all ends happily.

The last of the traits of the well-made play as described by Stanton—"the reproduction in miniature of the overall delayed-action pattern in the individual acts"—is also characteristic of the first and third acts of *Le Maçon* and is present but less apparent in the second. The first act begins in the middle of a wedding celebration, which is brought to a halt by the exit of Henriette and the abduction of Roger. Act III finds Henriette confused and saddened by Roger's mysterious disappearance, an explanation for which is completed in the final scene. Act II begins slowly: the Greek slave girls are amusing themselves by singing and listening to Irma's narrative *romance.* Only after most of the girls retire for the night does the real action begin, and then only indirectly, as Irma tells of her plans. However, the plans were made before the act began—and those plans end in a partial but unhappy solution by the end of the act. The same technique is used for the structure of each act: an action stated at the beginning is somehow resolved at the end. However, the resolutions of Acts I and II are not definite. In each case an action has been concluded, but the plot as a whole is propelled forward by this conclusion: we want to know where Roger is being taken, how Henriette will react to her husband's disappearance, and what means will be used to free Abdallah's captives. Graphically, then, the action proceeds:

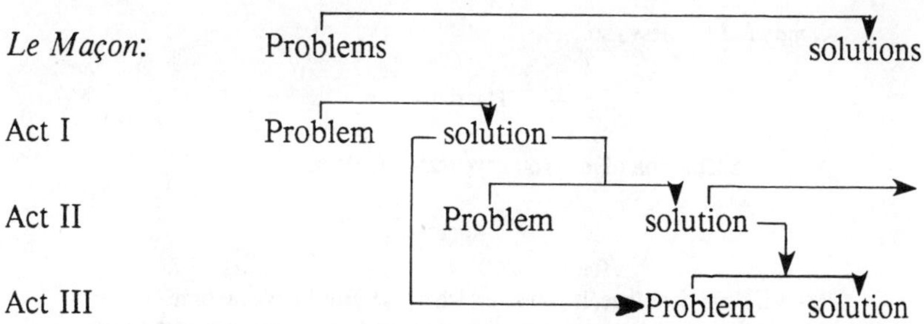


In a sense there is no real *scène à faire* in which the hero emerges victorious and the villain, defeated, slinks off to his just deserts. This is in part due to the fact that the actual villain, Abdallah, does not appear in the opera and that the substitute villain has already left the country before the last act begins. If one looks for a scene in which the effects of villainy are overcome, however, the tenth scene of Act III is the one in which "the hero is victorious. . . ." In this scene Henriette provides Roger with the final bit of necessary information.

**Henriette.**

[Telling the story] . . . But this is too much for me, and I cannot go on.

**Roger.**

O heavens! Henriette, I beg you, I implore you, continue: it is a matter of my life, of my happiness.

**Henriette.**

Of your happiness! Well, faithless one, since you force me, it is you she [Mme. Bertrand] saw get out of that coach; you were with the same persons [Usbeck and Rica], and you entered that luxurious and superb mansion that is occupied by the foreigners.

**Roger.**

What do I hear?

**Henriette.**

That Turkish gentleman's mansion.

**Roger (throwing himself at her knees).**

O *mon Dieu,* I bless you.

**Henriette.**

Yes, sir, ask pardon of me; you have reason to do so.

**Roger.**

My wife, my dear love, if you knew what joy! But I have no time. I love you, I adore you; I am going away. (Meeting Mme. Bertrand, who enters at the rear) My neighbor, here you are; stay with my wife; console her, talk to her; I shall return soon. (He exits at the rear, running.)

Although no real showdown is involved here, part of the function of the *scène à faire* is fulfilled by this exchange.

Similarly, there is no single element in *Le Maçon* that can be regarded as a "central misunderstanding or *quiproquo*," although the libretto does contain several small misunderstandings that must be resolved: the source of Roger's income, Roger's disappearance, Baptiste's failure to recognize Léon when the latter tries to escape through the pavillion, Rica's role as a kind of double agent, Léon's identity, his mysterious *rendez-vous*.

Implied in this discussion of the *Le Maçon* libretto in terms of the well-made play is the fact that to Scribe situations and actions were more important than characters. This is not to say that the figures in *Le Maçon* are without personality, but merely that they are without subtlety. Each person assumes all his traits of character at once; thus there is no wondering who is who or what side or position each character will assume as the action progresses. All are clearly two-dimensional figures, some of them type-characters, others merely personae created for the occasion, but all are ideal for opera since their traits are so clearly established from the beginning that they distract neither from the action nor from the music.

A comparison of Roger, the hero, with Usbeck, the substitute villain, reveals that although Scribe creates flat figures, his characters are not often either wholly "black" or wholly "white." Usbeck is not entirely and irrevocably evil, as shown in his efforts to save Rica from Abdallah's wrath when he first senses Rica's involvement in Irma's plan to escape. One slave is put to death for his part in the plot, but Usbeck's failure to admit his suspicions about Rica saves the latter from the same fate. Indeed, one major purpose served by the conversation between Usbeck and Rica in which this information is related is to make clear to the audience that Usbeck has a heart. If Usbeck is no thorough villain, neither is Roger a magnificent hero. His is not the role of the white knight dashing in to save his friend despite insurmountable odds and great personal danger. He is brave, but he is also reasonable and not one to take chances. When he rescues Léon he does it at no great personal sacrifice. Indeed, as Abert has pointed out in connection with Meyerbeer's grand operas, Scribe's heroes act in accordance with practical considerations for their own well-being, like the prosperous bourgeois of the time.[21] Thus pure heroes and pure villains are rare in Scribe's libretti.

Proofs of this statement abound in opera and opéra comique alike. In *La Dame blanche* neither Dickson nor Georges save the Avenel estate from Gaveston's grasping hands; both rely on the White Lady, who in turn relies on wealth hidden by the Avenels before their escape. Fra Diavolo is not an evil robber but a combination of Don Juan and Robin Hood, and he is not caught by Lorenzo but is trapped by the unwitting testimony of his own associates. Daniel in *Le Chalet* wins Bettly's hand because of the ingenious scheming of her brother Max. Robert the Devil is as weak and ineffectual when he attempts evil as when he tries to do good, and Bertram is better as a concerned father than as some evil genius. In *Les Huguenots* Raoul is not a hero but a coward or, at best, a man whose dedication to his cause is somewhat less than noble, whereas Saint-Bris and his associates are neither strong enough to be villains nor religious enough to be saints. In the end Masaniello (*La Muette de Portici*) cannot handle the people of whom he is the leader, and Alphonse comes running to him for protection like a hurt puppy. These people are neither black nor white; they are human but without depth, mortal but not immortal, part of the *juste milieu.*

The means Scribe uses to establish the essential personalities of his figures are always external and always consistent. Persons are good, bad, shy, noble, because they—or someone else in the cast—say so, not because of any impression that reaches the audience as a result of their behavior in the course of the drama. Roger is a good and willing worker; his *ronde* tells us that. Rica, so Irma informs us, is sympathetic, while Léon, Roger tells Henriette, is a truly good and noble person. Mme. Bertrand herself admits that she is jealous and gossipy. Usbeck informs us that, whatever he does, he is only following orders. And so it goes, in this and every other libretto Scribe writes. The motto is clarity, whether in plot or in characters.

As will be demonstrated later in a comparison of the libretto of *La Barcarolle* with the *comédie-vaudeville* from which it was derived, Scribe's well-made plays not only fit more accurately than his libretti the mold Stanton describes, but are more timely as well. Nevertheless, Scribe could hardly have abandoned completely a technique so carefully worked out in his spoken dramas when writing for a medium so closely related; his time was too valuable, his output too vast, and—most important—his technique too good. The craft of the well-made play in its essentials influences the structure of every opéra comique libretto under consideration.

**Words and Music**

Auber's score for *Le Maçon* is, from a purely musical point of view, not particularly distinguished. The influence of Rossini, except for a few short cadenzas, is completely absent and that of Boieldieu, who was soon to present his own masterpiece of the 1820s, is strongly felt in the simplicity of the melodic lines, with their frequent dependence on triadic outlines and dotted rhythms and their unobtrusive accompaniments. In addition, Longyear and Knepler have mentioned some similarities to the postrevolutionary rescue opera in the recurrent song, Roger's *ronde*, and in the finales of the first two acts, which "show most strongly the influence of the 'rescue opera' of Lesueur and Méhul."[22] Indeed, the similarities to earlier rescue opera are dramatic as well as musical, the most obvious comparison being Cherubini's internationally acclaimed *Les Deux journées.* In both operas a nobleman and his lady are rescued from an otherwise hopeless situation by the efforts of a lower middle-class laborer. In Cherubini's opera, however, the plot has more definite political overtones, whereas in *Le Maçon* the relationship between the nobleman and the worker is purely personal. There is also a musical parallel between Cherubini's famous opera and *Le Maçon,* for the refrain of Anton's air, "Un pauvre petit Savoyard," like that of Blondel's song in *Richard Coeur-de-Lion* and Roger's *ronde,* recurs at intervals throughout the opera.[23] Knepler, however, finds political overtones even in *Le Maçon.*

> Indeed, the air of '1788' [Knepler assumes this as the date of the action of *Le Macon*] was blowing again in Paris; a new revolution was coming to a head. In 1824 Charles X had ascended the throne of the Bourbons; he continued more strongly the politics of his predecessor, Louis XVIII, drawing to the court aristocrats of the old way of thinking and being aware of their influence. The opposition to these policies was taken up quickly under Charles X; it reached from the circles of the bourgeoisie deeply into the masses, where for many years revolutinary energies had been assembled. Auber appeared to have sympathized with this oppositional-revolutionary mood.[24]

However, in addition to the fact that the lower-class masses were too disorganized to have been concerned with any great deal of revolutionary activity—labor unions were illegal and even small clubs organized by lower middle-class craftsmen were often suspect and subject to vigorous persecution—one must take into account an influence that was undoubtedly far stronger in Auber's comfortably bourgeois artistic world than was the mood of the masses: that of Boieldieu's *La Dame blanche.* Although Boieldieu's work was not performed until some months after *Le Maçon,* the libretto had been prepared as early as 1821 and given to the composer, whose illness had forced him to put it aside. It is this very libretto that Knepler attacks for its emphasis on "an important message from the Reaction, . . . " that of Georges' reaquisition of feudal holdings and titles with the active support of faithful peasants.[25] Yet this work shows strong resemblances, both in music and in drama, to *Le Maçon.* Despite a seeming dissimilarity the situations in the two operas are more alike than different, for it is not until the end of the opera that the brave soldier Georges Brown learns that he is actually the nobleman in whose behalf he and the peasants were acting. Thus in both cases the nobleman owes his ultimate good fortune to the labors of a poor but honest man.

There are also more specific similarities between the two works: the happily married Roger and Henriette are comparable to Boieldieu's Dickson and Jenny; and Auber's Baptiste resembles Dickson in his extreme fear and skittishness at the slightest noise or unfamiliar situation. Indeed, *Le Maçon* even boasts of a white ghost, or at least of a person who appears so to Baptiste when he is locked in the dark pavillion (Act II, xiii).

**Baptiste.**

I was all sad and desolate
In that isolated pavillion
In which you had locked me,
When I heard, with hurried noise,
The door opening . . . and then, alas!
A large white phantom appeared.

Although the following cannot be documented, it would be possible to explain the similarities between the two operas quite logically, all within the day's work of everyone concerned. Perhaps the basic idea for *Le Maçon* came to Scribe by way of Germain Delavigne. Scribe, a busy librettist as well as a prolific dramatist, having recently finished the libretto to *La Dame blanche*, sets to work on the new idea and in the course of his labors uses a few ideas, consciously or unconsciously, which already have been incorporated into Boieldieu's libretto. Auber then begins to compose. He knows Boieldieu, knows his earlier works, and is necessarily influenced by this giant of French opéra comique. Perhaps he has even seen parts of the uncomplete score to *La Dame blanche*. Whatever the case, both librettist and composer arrive at products which resemble those of the Scribe-Boieldieu collaboration. In addition, as Longyear points out, Auber may have seen Castil-Blaze's version of Weber's *Der Freischütz* or otherwise have become acquainted with this score, "for Irma's scene in Act II shows Weber's influence."[26] The spirits and phantoms of German romantic opera as represented by *Der Freischütz* turn up in typically French dress in *La Dame blanche*. Undoubtedly a number of factors must be considered to explain the position of *Le Maçon* in the mainstream of opéra comique. Of these the influence of rescue opera is only one, others coming from various activities in which both composer and librettist were involved during the time in which *Le Maçon* was in preparation.

The preceding analysis has shown the relationship between Scribe's dramatic technique as a whole and the libretto of *Le Maçon*. If one believes that opera is merely another type of drama, this discussion is sufficient. But, in fact, an opera libretto—or rather a successful opera libretto—contains many forms and ideas that set it apart from ordinary drama. The nature of these differences has been suggested by Stanton as "the conception of musical situations which allowed the composer free expression."[27] Just what is a "musical situation"? One suggestion has been offered by Longyear.

> The principal distinction between the *livret bien fait* and the *comédie-drame*, from the standpoint of construction, is that in the former the musical numbers generally serve as points of rest, during which the action stops.[28]

Although he later qualifies this statement to the effect that many ensembles do in fact further the action, it seems that Longyear has missed the point of the musical scenes and the function of music within the opera by failing to distinguish between mere "excuses for music" and dramatically necessary or desirable musical interludes, and by failing to appreciate the skill which Scribe constructs those musical portions in which action unquestionably takes place.

In view of the vagueness of the concept of "musical situation," it would be well to look at the music used in *Le Maçon* and to determine its purpose and/or function in the opera as a whole. The following tabulation outlines the types of musical numbers and their position within the three acts.

**Musical Numbers in Le Maçon**

| Scene | Number | Characters and type of music involved |
|---|---|---|
| | | **ACT I** |
| (NB: numbers 1-3 occur without break between them.) | | |
| i | 1 | Chorus with incidental soli by Roger, Henriette, Mme. Bertrand, Baptiste. Short air for Baptiste, followed by some arioso dialogue between Roger and Mme. Bertrand. |
| | 2 | *Ronde.* Roger. 3 *couplets*, each with choral refrain. |
| | 3 | Recitative (Mme. Bertrand, Roger, Henriette, Baptiste); recap of opening chorus. |
| ii | 4 | *Couplets.* Mme. Bertrand. 2 stanzas. |
| v | 5 | Quartet. Roger, Léon, Mme. Bertrand, Baptiste. |

(NB: numbers 6 and 7 occur without break between them.)

| | | |
|---|---|---|
| viii | 6 | Duo. Roger, Henriette. |
| ix-xi | 7 | Finale. Roger, Henriette, Usbeck, Rica, Baptiste, Mme. Bertrand, chorus. Includes recitative, the actual end of No. 6, chorus, ensembles. |

ACT II

| | | |
|---|---|---|
| Entr'acte | 8 | Instrumental; similar to material in introduction to No. 9. |

(NB: numbers 9-11 occur without break between them.)

| | | |
|---|---|---|
| i | 9 | Chorus; solo by Zobéide; recap of chorus; recitative. |
| | 10 | *Romance.* Irma. Recitative introduction; 2 stanzas. |
| | 11 | Recitative. Zobéide, chorus. |
| ii | 12 | Air. Irma. |
| vi | 13 | Duo. Roger, Baptiste. |
| ix | 14 | *Romance.* Léon. 2 stanzas. |
| x | 15 | Duo. Léon, Irma. 4 measure recitative transition to: |
| xi-xiv | 16 | Finale. Rica, Irma, Léon, Usbeck, Roger, Baptiste, chorus. Includes recitative, ensembles, choruses. |

ACT III

| | | |
|---|---|---|
| Entr'acte | 17 | Instrumental; unrelated to No. 18. |
| i | 18 | Air. Henriette. |

(NB: numbers 19-20 occur without break between them.)

| | | |
|---|---|---|
| ii | 19 | Chorus. Includes short solo for Henriette. |
| | 20 | Duo. Henriette, Mme. Bertrand. Recap of part of chorus, No. 19. |
| vi | 21 | Air. Roger. |
| xii-xiii | 22 | Finale. All principals plus chorus. Includes recitative, choruses, ensembles. |

As can be seen from the table, the musical numbers are distributed quite evenly among the three acts, and there is a balance between the simpler forms—*couplets, romances, rondes*—and the more complex numbers—airs, large ensemble scenes—as well as between solo and ensemble sections. An example of each type of piece will suffice to illustrate the dramatic function of the musical numbers in an opéra comique and Auber's technique in dealing with them. The following will be used as examples: Roger's *ronde* (No. 2), the airs by Irma (No. 12) and Henriette (No 18), Léon's *romance* (No. 14), the finale to Act II (No. 16), and the duo between Mme. Bertrand and Henriette (No. 20).

Both Roger's *ronde* and Léon's *romance* are strophic forms presenting static situations. Of the two, the latter comes closest of any musical number in *Le Maçon* to being expendable, for its only function is to provide a solo for the young nobleman. Rica has just admitted him to Abdallah's chateau and he sings merely to entertain himself and the audience, and perhaps to provide a musical buffer between the lively duo by Roger and Baptiste in Scene vi and the more serious duet between himself and Irma in Scene x. The purest example of a point of rest, during which all action is suspended, it is also among the loveliest solos in the opera. It features a sustained, lyrical melody and the finely shaded colors of the woodwind choir (Example 1). If it has any dramatic function at all, it is merely that of putting into relief Léon's love for Irma, and of providing for a lapse of time between events in the drama.

**Example 1**

**Example 1 (continued)**

"Everyone knows the air, 'Du courage, à l'ouvrage,'" writes one nineteenth-century commentator.[29] Like Léon's *romance*, Roger's famed *ronde* also occurs at a static point: Mme. Bertrand requests a song, and Roger supplies it. Yet the effect of the *ronde* is different for a number of reasons: first, it is a static point in an otherwise mobile situation (the wedding celebration); second, it is as much a definition of Roger's character and station in life as it is an opportunity for him to sing a solo; third, it is important in past and future actions, and this importance is exploited to particular advantage in the second act finale. The musical and dramatic context of the *ronde* is outlined below.

| Characters | Action | Music | Keys |
|---|---|---|---|
| 1) Chorus, Baptiste, Roger, Henriette, Mme. Bertrand. | General celebration of the wedding | Chordal chorus with incidental soli | C to V/A |
| 2) Roger. | None. | *Ronde.* 3 stanzas with choral refrains. | A |
| 3) Same as | Bridal pair called into | Accompanied, mea- | C |

| Section 1 | the house; all leave but Mme. Bertrand and Baptiste. | sured recitative or arioso with closing chorus (repeat of opening of Section 1. |
|---|---|---|

Roger, as the central character of the scene and the hero of the opera, deserves to be brought into the foreground for something other than a part in the general dialogue. The audience wants and needs to know who he is, what kind of person he represents, what he does for a living—in short, all the things anyone would ask of an unknown but prominent person. The *ronde* answers those questions. As if to second what Scribe has provided in this text, Auber writes a simple, robust melody for Roger and emphasizes the all-important refrain with restatements by the chorus (melody in Example 2). Soon Léon will sing this refrain when identifying Roger as the man who saved his life, and Roger will sing it again at the end of Act II as a signal that he intends to repeat the favor.

**Example 2**

In Léon's *romance* and Roger's *ronde* we have two pieces of similar form and involving similar dramatic movement—or lack of it. How, then, would one define "musical situation" in relation to these two songs? Perhaps as follows: a musical situation is one in which, for a time, a single character is brought into the spotlight for any one of a number of reasons: to establish his character, to reflect upon a situation, to prepare for his part in later action, or merely to sing beautifully for the audience.

The airs sung by Irma and Henriette are quite another proposition, however, and fit the above definition of "musical situation" only in the most general way. Whereas *romances, couplets, rondes*, and the like are songlike, strophic forms, the designation *air* or *aria* in opéra comique is reserved for pieces of some length and usually of some formal and vocal complexity as well. Henriette's air at the beginning of Act III is such a piece and is among Auber's most dramatically successful numbers. The melodic line and key changes reflect Henriette's sorrow, confusion, and increasingly disturbed emotional state. The first half of the air is reproduced as Example 3. Beginning softly and somewhat hesitantly in *E* minor with a section in *abcc* form, Auber moves to C major, where a more sustained and lyrical melodic line reflects the content of the text (Roger's declarations of love). After a modulation to G, the section ends on the dominant of *E* minor, after which a portion of the opening section is brought back to emphasize the contrast between the actual situation and the world of pleasant memory. Becoming more agitated as she sings of the secret about which Roger told her in Act I, Henriette performs a more extended and intense version of the earlier C major - G major section, moving this time to *B* minor and G major and closing again on the dominant of *E* minor. A second restatement of the opening *E* minor section, again varied and given a coda, brings the air to a close. Like Léon's *romance*, this air is also reflective and to a certain extent occasioned by the desire or necessity to provide Henriette with a solo song. Yet it is not dramatically dispensable, for it contains action, although emotional rather than physical in nature, and it provides the basis for Henriette's less than angry reception of Roger when the latter returns.

Example 3

**Example 3 (continued)**

**Example 3 (continued)**

**Example 3 (continued)**

Like Henriette's air, that sung by Irma is a long and comparatively complex piece that traces the progress of an emotional state. Beginning with an arioso section (Example 4a) in which Irma tells that the image of Léon follows her everywhere, the piece moves to the more regularly melodic opening section of the air. In this lyrical and mildly virtuosic melody, lightly accompanied by soft, repeated chords, Irma gives voice to the mutual love between herself and the Frenchman (Example 4b).

**Example 4a**

## Example 4a (continued)

## Example 4b

Then, to more agitated music (*E* major, Example 4c) using shorter vocal phrases and note values, she tells that she expects Léon to come for her that night and is fearful lest something hinder their plans. Returning to the opening key of *A* major, the air concludes with a varied and extended version of its opening section. Irma's solo is different from that of Henriette in form and to some extent in musical style, having somewhat greater dignity and lyricism. However, the purpose of both numbers is the same: to consolidate into a single musical scene a number of successive, different thoughts or emotional states.

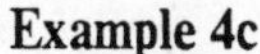

**Example 4c**

On the basis of this pair of scenes, the earlier definition of "musical situation" can be enlarged considerably. These airs not only bring a soloist into the spotlight but provide the opportunity for both composer and librettist to give expression to and valid dramatic framework for changing emotional states or a succession of thoughts. They are the musical equivalent of the dramatic soliloquy.

It is in the ensemble scenes, however, that the greatest amount of action, both physical and emotional, takes place. That it takes place slowly goes without saying, for music not only interferes with the intelligibility of text, often making repetitions necesary, but fixes the time dimension of the drama in accordance with its own laws and requirements. In order to reconcile the idea of a forward-moving drama with the relatively slow pace of music Scribe has devised a technique of ensemble writing which he uses in nearly all such scenes and of which both the Henriette-Mme. Bertrand duo and the finale of Act II are good examples. Since the chorus preceding the duo (No. 19) is both a dramatic and a musical part of the former scene, it will be included in the discussion.

Musically, the scene between Mme. Bertrand and Henriette is constructed as follows:

| Section | Musical style | Key |
|---|---|---|
| 1 | Women's chorus (soprano-alto) with one solo phrase for Henriette near the end. | G |
| 2 | Recitative: Henriette. | D |
| 3 | Measured rectiative or arioso: Mme. Bertrand and Henriette, conversation. | D |
| 4 | Duo: Mme. Bertrand and Henriette, alternating stanzas, then simultaneous lines. | D |
| 5 | Measured recitative or arioso: more conversation, similar to Section 3. | D |
| 6 | Duo: restatement of Section 4, but with order of entrances reversed and with coda. | D |
| 7 | Recitative: dialogue between chorus and Henriette. | D—G |
| 8 | Chorus: same as Section 1, but without Henriette's solo. | G |

Considering the length of both text and music, the real action of this scene is rather slight. Henriette's neighbors arrive with Mme. Bertand to bring good wishes, although Henriette admits in an aside to the audience that she dislikes Mme. Bertrand and is in no humor to deal with her. With mock innocence the latter begins to inquire about Roger. When Henriette pretends that Roger has gone out on business, Mme. Bertrand counters with her observations that he did not return home the previous evening. After some verbal sparring between herself and Mme. Bertand, Henriette thanks the neighbors for their visit and requests that they now leave her alone. They exit and the two principals are left to continue their conversation in spoken dialogue. In this scene, the longest single sections are those in which musical interest predominates over drama: the two choruses and the two duos (Sections 4 and 6 in the table). Nevertheless, the whole number is just as carefully worked out in terms of dramatic effect as is the libretto as a whole. Each major point of action is balanced by a point of repose in which the music takes over as the primary element in the piece. Dramatically, the scene has the following profile.

| Section | Subject | Function |
|---|---|---|
| 1 | Neighbors arrive to offer congratulations. | Physical action, musical repose. |
| 2 | Henriette admits disliking Mme. Bertrand. | Action. |
| 3 | Mme. Bertrand questions Henriette. | Action |
| 4 | Mme. Bertrand begs pardon for offending Henriette; the latter wonders what the former has in mind. | Reflection |
| 5 | Mme. Bertrand continues to question Henriette. | Action. |
| 6 | Similar to Section 4, but with roles reversed. | Reflection. |
| 7 | Henriette asks neighbors to leave. | Action. |
| 8 | Neighbors exit. | Physical action, musical repose. |

The whole scene is thus nothing more than a series of dramatic starts and stops. When action (Mme. Bertrand's questioning) is taking place the vocal lines assume a recitative-like style with short phrases, small range, syllabic declamation, and light orchestral accompaniment (see Example 5a). When this questioning reaches an important point—the revelation that Mme. Bertrand knows of Roger's seeming desertion—the characters and the audience need some time to reflect on the implications of the news; hence the relatively static and musically more interesting duo (Example 5b). The same alternation of action and reflection is repeated for the second half of the scene. Scribe has effected a compromise between drama and music. Auber seconds his efforts by means of musical contrasts and devices of musical form—key relationships, repetition of sections in a kind of arch form—which, like the alternation of action and reflection, help hold the scene together in all its dimensions.

**Example 5a**

**Example 5a (continued)**

**Example 5b**

**Example 5b (continued)**

In addition to being the best single musical number in *Le Maçon*, the finale of Act II is also an excellent example on a larger scale of the musico-dramatic principles in operation in the Mme. Bertrand-Henriette duo. Following a rather pale love duet and a short recitative, the finale proceeds as outlined below.

**Musical Outline**

| Section | Musical features and characters | Keys |
|---|---|---|
| 1 | Recitative/arioso: Rica, Léon, Irma. | a, C. |
| 2 | Prayer: Rica. | C. |
| 3 | Recitative/arioso: Usbeck, Rica, Roger. | F, B♭, D♭, B♭ minor. |
| 4 | Chorus with soli: Usbeck, Rica, slave. | B♭ minor. |
| 5 | Monologue: Baptiste. | F, d. |
| 6 | Chorus with soli: Léon, Usbeck, Roger, slaves. (Includes Roger's *ronde.*) | D♭, B♭. |

**Dramatic Outline**

| Section | Subject | Function |
|---|---|---|
| 1 | Rica warns Léon and Irma that they have been discovered and gives them the key to the pavillion. | Action. |
| 2 | Rica prays to Allah for help and forgiveness. | Repose. |

| | | |
|---|---|---|
| 3 | Usbeck brings in Roger and orders him back to work, then orders the slaves to find Léon and Irma. | Action. |
| 4 | Chorus of slaves agrees to Usbeck's order; Rica hopes Allah will help the lovers to escape. | Reflection. |
| 5 | Baptiste tells of his experience while locked in the pavillion. | Momentary action, then narration (static situation). |
| 6 | Irma and Léon, attempting to defend himself, are brought in. Usbeck and chorus swear to punish them. Roger offers encouragement by singing the refrain of his *ronde.* | Repose (dramatic tableau). |

This scene resembles the duo in that it is constructed of alternate sections of action and repose. Textually it is a kind of dramatic crescendo in which the periods of action become longer and more intense, the periods of repose more ambivalent. In order to differentiate between the functions of the various sections, Scribe has given each a distinctive literary cast: regular stanzas with short, balanced lines for sections of repose or reflection (see Example 6d, the text of section 4); poetry with longer lines, often broken by ellipses or divided among several characters, for sections of action (see Example 6e, the text of section 1).

In addition to these typically Scribean poetic structures, *Le Maçon* contains examples of the type of ensemble text Scribe ordinarily writes for sections of reflection or reaction in a musical number involving two or more characters. Example 6f, part of a quartet in Act I, v, illustrates Scribe's practice of writing text stanzas for each character which have the same structure and the same rhyme scheme. Although the stanzas are not alike in all details, they share text phrases and final words, something which makes the sentiments of the characters somewhat more intelligible than they would ordinarily be in an ensemble and thus helps the composer by rounding off textual rough edges that might detract from the smoothness of his musical setting. The relationships between the three stanzas in Example 6f are interlocking but varied. Mme. Bertrand and Baptiste share the same first line and the final word of their second lines, but at the end of the third line the word "prospère" occurs in stanzas for Roger, Léon, and Mme. Bertrand, while the final lines of all characters have only the "eur" rhyme in common. Similar interlocking devices are to be found in nearly all Scribe's ensemble texts covering static situations.

The dramatic crescendo of the number is reflected in Auber's setting by the gradual introduction of successively darker keys and by the skillful and extremely successful changes in the style of the text setting employed for the various scenes. Auber begins the finale in measured recitative (or arioso) in a small vocal range on a series of ascending monotones (Example 6a). As the pitch gets higher the notes become

**Example 6a**

longer, reflecting Rica's growing fear at the peril of his situation, while the pedal point and the constantly reiterated low E intensify the foreboding atmosphere. Rica's prayer is similar in style: a series of lightly-accompanied monotone phrases broken by rests. The chorus of slaves in Section 4 reinforces the dark mood with more singing on repeated single tones, the choral statements having no real melody. Baptiste's monologue (Example 6b) again makes use of repeated single tones, but in a new context. Baptiste has been badly frightened; hence his calls for help and his tale of horror are sung loudly and at the top of his range to an increasingly excited orchestral accompaniment. The tremolos and the ascending vocal line as the story reaches a high point are tried and true devices, but they are so precisely because they work. Neither Scribe nor Auber had any dreams of immortality.

**Example 6b**

**Example 6b (continued)**

The stroke of genius for both Scribe and Auber comes at the end of the scene (Example 6c): slaves and prisoners exit, Léon

**Example 6c**

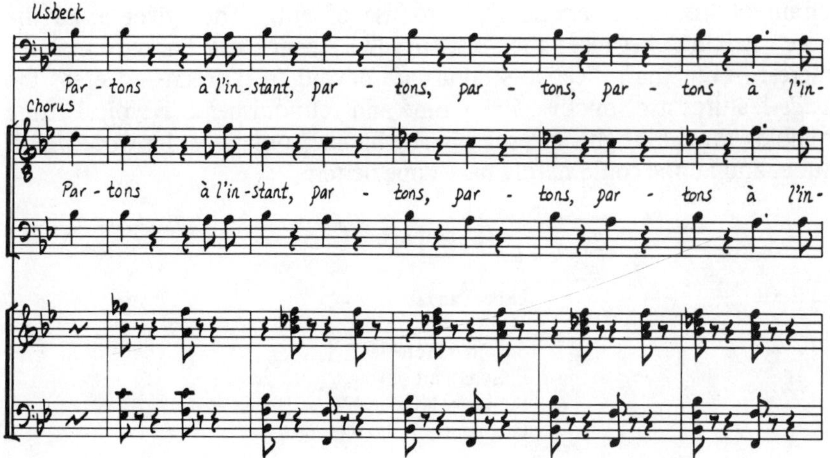

## Example 6c (continued)

protesting loudly to the end, leaving Roger alone on the stage singing the refrain of his *ronde*, an implied promise of aid. The effect is all the more striking because the rest of the scene has lacked melodic interest—even the reflective sections are devoid of lyricism—whereas the *ronde* features a distinctive, lively tune and relinquishes the typical string tremolos for the bright and sharply rhythmical sounds of the woodwinds. Auber and Scribe could hardly have done better.

## Example 6d

Act II, xii.

**Usbeck and slaves.**

Soyons inexorables,
Faisons notre devoir,
Punissons les coupables:
Oui, pour eux plus d'espoir.

**Rica.**

Daigne, Dieu favorable,
Seconder mon espoir.

[Translation:

**Usbeck and slaves.**

Let us be inexorable,
Let us do our duty,
Let us punish these guilty ones:
Yes, for them no more hope.

**Rica.**

Propitious God, deign
To support my hope.]

## Example 6e

Act II, xi.

**Rica.**

Malheureux! arrêtez! vous courez au trépas!

**Irma.**

O ciel!

**Léon.**

Il se pourrait!

**Rica.**

Silence! parlez bas!
Il y va de mes jours, mais la pitié l'emporte:
Abdallah savait tout; on vous aura trahis;
Tantôt votre billet en ses mains fut remis;
Et du piège fatal où vous fûtes conduits
Vous ne sortirez plus.
Là, près de cette porte,
Vingt esclaves au moins vous attendent.

**Léon.**

N'importe!
Je suis armè, marchons!

**Rica.**

Vous nous perdez tous trois;
Mais un autre moyen peut vous sauver, je crois.

[Translation: **Rica.**

Unfortunate ones! stop! You are running to your deaths!

**Irma.**

O heavens!

**Léon.**

Can it be!

**Rica.**

Silence! speak softly!
It could mean my life, but pity outweighs all:
Abdallah knew everything; someone must have betrayed you;
Earlier your letter was placed in his hands;
And from the fatal trap into which you were led
You will never escape.

There, near this door,
At least twenty slaves are waiting for you.

**Léon.**

That makes no difference!
I am armed. Let's go!

**Rica.**

You will be the ruin of all three of us;
But another means can save you, I believe.]

## Example 6f

Act I, v. **Roger et Léon.**

O hasard tutélaire!
Quel moment pour mon coeur!

Le ciel qui m'est prospère
Me rend mon bienfaiteur!

**Mme. Bertrand.**

Quel est donc ce mystère?
Il connaît ce seigneur.
Tout lui devient prospère,
Tout lui porte bonheur.

**Baptiste.**

Quel est donc ce mystère?
Quoi! ce jeune seigneur
Embrasse mon beau-frère;
Ah! pour nous quel honneur!

[Translation: **Roger and Léon.**

O kind fortune!
What a moment for my heart!
Heaven, which is favorable to me,
Returns my benefactor to me!

**Mme. Bertrand.**

What then is this mystery?
He knows this gentleman.
Everything turns out well for him,
Everything brings him good fortune.

**Baptiste.**

What then is this mystery?
What! this young gentleman
Embraces my brother-in-law;
Ah! what an honor for us!]

Two questions remain to be answered: 1) in what way are the ensembles in *Le Maçon* "musical situations"; 2) how do they differ from other sections of the libretto in which action is carried out—i.e., those sections in spoken dialogue? Ensembles in the opera occur under the following conditions.

| **Location** | **Nature** |
|---|---|
| I, i | Introduction, discussed above. |

| | |
|---|---|
| I, v | Roger and Léon recognize each other and tell the story of Roger's saving Léon's life to the curious and amazed guests. |
| I, viii | Roger tries to persuade Henriette to leave the party and go away with him. |
| I, ix-xi | Finale: Henriette is carried off by the wedding guests; Roger talks wth Usbeck and Rica and is kidnapped by them. |
| II, i | Irma, Zobéide, and slave girls sing of their servitude and their love of the freedom of France. |
| II, vi | Roger and Baptiste set to work and discuss the mystery surrounding their capture. |
| II, x | Léon calms Irma's fears; the lovers ask God's blessing on their vows of faithfulness. |
| II, xi-xiii | Finale, discussed above. |
| III, ii | Chorus and duo, discussed above. |
| III, xii-xiii | Roger returns with Léon and Irma; the lovers thank Roger; Henriette forgives him; all rejoice. |

All these situations have two things in common: they occur at important turning points in the action, and they are well suited to expansion in time because of the emotion which they generate: love, remorse, rage, happiness. To be sure, many other situations in the opera fit one or the other of these qualifications and perhaps could have been worked out as ensemble scenes but were not because the action they contained was of less significance or because the reactions of the characters involved could be expressed as well in spoken dialogue. In all the situations described above the interests or emotions of all participants are at a high pitch. Thus the emphasis and intensification given by means of a musical setting is most appropriate. The intense action-reaction cycles which occur—illustrated by the duo and the Act II finale—are ideal for a medium which slows down so decisive a point in time and allows it to unfold with maximum suspense and as much allowance as possible for the expression of individual views and reflections. As demonstrated above, such cycles are also ideal for the production of the calculated effects for which Scribe is well known (e.g., the end of Act II). Also, music adds new dimensions to expression via melody, harmony, orchestration, outstanding rhythms, any of which can serve to place a given character or moment in relief. The logic behind having chosen these particular points for musical treatment thus helps define—or expand—the concept of "musical situation": a situation involving a particular dramatic or emotional high point best expressed in a medium which demands a slowing down of the action and which can emphasize or intensify elements of the scene which otherwise seem of equal weight or occur simultaneously.

"Musical situations" also contain certain structures which are not found in spoken dialogue: namely, poetic forms. There is really no point in bringing up the relative merits of Scribe's poetic style, for it has already been observed that his verse is on the level of that in modern greeting cards, with all the good middle class sentiment of a French Edgar Guest. Yet poetry, with its regular rhythms and predictable verse lengths, is most suitable for music, whereas no good bourgeois could be imagined speaking in alexandrines. Thus the language of the spoken sections in *Le Maçon* is in as realistic a prose style as one could expect from the stage, and is filled with the usual Scribe-isms in praise of honor, freedom, friendship, and the French government. Favorite Scribe devices are the ellipsis, used to create suspense on a small scale, and the breaking up of otherwise lengthy speeches by one character with such phrases as "O ciel!", "Tu crois?", "C'est vrai," "Eh bien," and the like, appropriately salted and peppered across the page. Whereas the important climaxes of the opéra comique are set to music, large blocks of information for purposes of background, exposition, and tracing the progress of an event are conveyed by the spoken dialogue.

Clearly there is no single definition for the much tossed-about phrase, "musical situation." Such a situation can be one in which a given character holds the stage for an extended solo dealing with his character or his function in the action, or perhaps just provides a performer with a song to demonstrate his talents to the audience. It can be a soliloquy-like scene expressive of a character's inner mental or emotional turmoil. It can be a dramatic turning point played in slow motion through the medium of music. Whatever the case, the situation involved is one enhanced by the music, one in which the music expands the expressive or dramatic potential of its text. The variety of musical situations in *Le Maçon* testifies to the skill and stage sense of both librettist and composer.

## Auber's *Fra Diavolo*

The subject of *Fra Diavolo* had been used several times on the Frence stage before Scribe and Auber fashioned it into one of the most successful opéras comiques of the nineteenth century. In addition, Scribe and Auber themselves capitalized on the Italian bandit theme in two later opéras comiques, *La Sirène* (March 26, 1844) and *Marco Spada* (December 21, 1852). Although the latter has little in common with *Fra Diavolo, La Sirène* is somewhat similar. Scopetto, the hero of *La Sirène,* is in reality the disguised bandit and smuggler Marco Tempesta. He keeps his identity secret even from his sister Zerline by pretending to be the proprietor of a hotel in the mountains. The cast of *Fra Diavolo* also includes a Zerline, the daughter of an innkeeper, who is in love with Lorenzo, a young soldier who is offered a reward for the capture of Diavolo. In *La Sirène* the Duke comes to the mountains with his soldiers to attempt to capture Marco Tempesta, thus hoping to earn a reward and honor from the king; but unlike Lorenzo, the Duke does not succeed.

*Fra Diavolo* was first performed on January 28, 1830, and remained in the repertoire of the Opéra-Comique during the years 1830-40, 1844-52, 1858-66, and 1870-96. It was given there some 909 times until 1911.[30] An international favorite, it was performed in Brussels, Berlin, Vienna, Budapest, St. Petersburg, London, Copenhagen, Zagreb, Prague, Warsaw, and New York during its first year-and-a-half of life, and was sung not only in French, but also in German, Hungarian, Russian, Italian, English, Danish, and Czech. Made into a film in 1931, recorded in the 1950s, it is occasionally performed even today and is thus one of the few works from the French musical stage of its time to show such remarkable longevity, despite the now old-fashioned and overworked devices employed.

Scribe wrote *Fra Diavolo* without the assistance of a literary collaborator, yet it shows the same stytlistic characteristics as *Le Maçon.* Here the honest laborers of *Le Maçon* are replaced by the soldiers—those favorites of both Scribe and his bourgeois audience—and elements of exoticism are provided by the master bandit, the romantic Fra Diavolo. The scene is not Restoration Paris but Italy, and the time is unspecified but undoubtedly meant to be the recent past. Italian peasants replace the Parisian shopkeepers and laborers of *Le Maçon.* Yet the more things change, the more they are the same: the captain Lorenzo resembles Roger, Zerline is a more prominent Henriette, Matheo reminds one of Baptiste, and the local color is merely a change of costume and the addition of a *barcarolle* or two. Scribe is still Scribe; Auber, improved by experience, is still Auber; and the craft of the well-made libretto serves both to good effect.

The opera takes place in Italy, at a hotel in the vicinity of Terracina. Lorenzo and the soldiers are discussing the reward that will be theirs if they capture the notorious bandit, Fra Diavolo. Mathéo, the innkeeper, announces the approaching marriage of his daughter Zerline to a rich farmer, Francesco, and invites all to the wedding. Lorenzo, however, is in love with Zerline and, although poor, seeks some way to win her father's approval as a prospective son-in-law.

A flurry of unexpected activity accompanies the arrival of Lord Cokbourg and his wife, Paméla, who have just been robbed by Fra Diavolo and his band. Lorenzo and the soldiers go off in search of the bandit, while Mathéo departs for Francesco's house, leaving Zerline to tend to the guests at the inn. One of these guests, a latecomer, is a certain Marquis who has been following Lord and Lady Cokbourg around Italy and has been paying what the Lord regards as too much attention to Paméla. To entertain these guests Zerline sings the ballad of Fra Diavolo. In the next scene the Marquis, in conversation with two cohorts (Beppo and Giacomo) who have just arrived, reveals that he is really the famous bandit in disguise and that his purpose at the inn is to discover the hiding place of additional jewels and a large sum of money which Lord Cokbourg was supposed to have been carrying and which the bandits had not found during the earlier robbery.

The Marquis then pays court to Paméla in order to trick her into revealing the location of the money and the jewels. No sooner does he learn this secret than he hears the returning soldiers, who have found and killed a number of Fra Diavolo's band of followers. Lorenzo has recovered Paméla's jewel box, for which he is given a reward sufficient to enable him to ask for Zerline's hand when her father returns in the morning. In the midst of a victory celebration the Marquis, Giacomo, and Beppo begin to plan how they can get the jewels back and take the money as well. Lorenzo and the soldiers leave to renew their pursuit of the bandits.

As the second act begins Zerline is showing the Cokbourgs to their room. The Marquis enters, joined by Beppo and Giacomo, but the three are forced to hide in a closet when they hear Zerline returning. The closet turns out to be in Zerline's room, and the three men, now trapped, watch as Zerline prepares to retire. She is no sooner asleep than a loud knocking announces the return of the soldiers. A peasant has informed Lorenzo that Fra Diavolo was seen in a coach traveling toward Terracina, and Lorenzo has decided to stop at the inn for food before proceeding further. Zerline goes to prepare the meal, and Lord Cokbourg and Lorenzo are left alone. When Beppo knocks over a chair in Zerline's room the Marquis is forced to do some quick thinking. He comes out of the room and, in the course of questioning, tells Lorenzo that he had been awaiting a *rendez-vous* with Zerline, yet implies to Lord Cokbourg that he had really been waiting for Paméla. Although Lorenzo agrees not to expose what he believes to be his beloved's deceit, he challenges the Marquis to a duel to be fought the next morning.

At the beginning of the third act the Marquis reveals his plans. Having stationed some of his band to deal with Lorenzo when the latter arrives for the duel, he now proposes to go into hiding until the soldiers have gone and the villagers are away attending Zerline's wedding, lest Lorenzo's peasant informant identify him as Fra Diavolo. Leaving a note in a tree for Giacomo and Beppo, he departs. A chorus of villagers signals the arrival of Mathéo with Francesco, the proposed bridegroom, and Giacomo and Beppo join in the festivities. Although Zerline is puzzled at Lorenzo's actions when he seems unwilling to ask Mathéo for his daughter's hand, she is prevented from discussing it with him. Giacomo and Beppo, seeing Zerline, recall songs she sang the previous night in her room. When Zerline demands an explanation Lorenzo becomes suspicious. He finds and reads the letter left by the Marquis and tricks the latter into returning while the soldiers are still present. All discover the true identity of the Marquis, and a victory chorus closes the opera.

## The Well-Made Libretto Revisited

The characteristics of the well-made play have already been enumerated. The fact that this technique is more consistently and thoroughly applied in *Fra Diavolo* than in *Le Maçon* is perhaps an indication of the effects of collaboration on Scribe's libretti, although *Le Maçon* bears the unmistakable stamp of Scribe's style throughout. In *Le Maçon*, however, some elements of the well-made play were not fully exploited, whereas in *Fra Diavolo* the pattern is as near to perfect as one finds in Scribe's libretti.

The use of a delayed-action plot is obvious. As *Fra Diavolo* begins, the major conflicts worked out in the remainder of the work have already been set in motion: the soldiers are on the trail of Fra Diavolo; Lorenzo is threatened with the loss of Zerline if he does not acquire some money; Lady Cokbourg has met and been impressed by the Marquis de San-Marco; and the English pair have been robbed. The formal exposition of the play is accomplished to a large degree in the first three-and-one-half scenes, although Scribe combines more or less narrative revelation of background information with continuing action and leaves a few items of lesser importance (the introduction of Beppo and Giacomo and their positive identification of the Marquis as Fra Diavolo) until later in the act. By the middle of Scene iv the audience knows of Fra Diavolo; learns that Lorenzo and Zerline are in love but that Mathéo has refused to allow them to marry and has found a more suitable match for his daughter; and meets Lord and Lady Cokbourg, identified as wealthy English tourists and the most recent of Fra Diavolo's victims. They are also introduced to the Marquis and learn of his relationship to the Cokbourgs. The first hints of his true identity, however, come only in the last stanza of the *couplets* telling of the famed bandit (Scene v), when he sings:

> . . . perhaps also
> All that is taking place
> Is being observed by him [Fra Diavolo]?
> Often, when one accuses him,
> Near you a young man
> Steals incognito
> For some new piece of larceny.

Positive identification must await the Marquis' conversation with Beppo and Giacomo in Scene vii; but no one should be surprised at the revelation, for it has been prepared from the first statement of the bandit's name in Scene i.

As usual, Scribe's characterization is external, the personae acquiring personalities by means of descriptions by themselves or others. Lorenzo is brave, particularly so since he feels he has nothing to live for if Zerline marries another (Act I, ii). Zerline is sweet, young, in love, and hopeful (Act I, i, and especially iii). Paméla is young and flirtatious (Act I, iii), making her husband quite jealous (Act I, iii, *couplets*). Lord Cokbourg's nationality is emphasized, for Scribe has built an English accent into this character's speeches: e.g., "Je havais l'honneur d'être Anglais; je havais enlevé, selon l'usage, miss Paméla, une riche héritière qui je havais epousée par inclination" (Act I, ii). The Marquis is a ladies' man well practiced in courtly manners, including singing to the accompaniment of his guitar (Act I, iii), whereas his henchmen Giacomo and Beppo exhibit the standard proportions of brawn to brain common in most "thug" types in present-day television dramas (Act I, vi-vii) and Mathéo, whose part in the action is purely mechanical, is the mercenary father with little personality.

Throughout the libretto each revelation or turn of events can be anticipated, largely because of the information contained in the first scenes of Act I. No one is surprised when the soldiers recover the Cokbourg's stolen valuables, when the reward money Lorenzo thus earns is sufficient to assure his marriage to Zerline, or when the Marquis is identified as Fra Diavolo. The resolution of these questions provides the basis for further complications in the plot, which in turn are worked out in not unexpected ways. Diavolo's plans to complete the unsuccessful robbery lead to his downfall, and his successful attempt to arouse Lorenzo's jealousy contributes to the ease with which, when the situation is completely explained, the latter is able to identify and capture the bandit. The suspenseful atmosphere in which all this is carried out is assisted by the usual contrived entrances and exits (the best example of which occurs in Act II, from the time the bandits hide in Zerline's closet until the scene between the Marquis, Lorenzo, and Lord Cokbourg); letters (Diavolo's note to Giacomo and Beppo); and "other devices for conveying these facts to certain characters while keeping them secret from others"[31] (e.g., the Marquis' use of a *barcarolle* to signal Giacomo and Beppo).

Events in *Fra Diavolo* are also organized to provide successive ups and downs in the fortunes of the hero, Lorenzo. As the opera he is down—it seems that he is about to lose Zerline—but the reward from Lord Cokbourg erases that difficulty. His good luck seems to climb still higher when, in Act II, he receives further information on the whereabouts of Fra Diavolo. Before he can act on this information, however, he discovers the Marquis in Zerline's closet and the suspicions thus aroused plunge him into despair, whence he agrees to a duel from which he hopes not to emerge alive. Before the duel can take place, however, Lorenzo has become reconciled with Zerline and at the same time has discovered the secret of the Marquis' disguise. His rising fortunes are crowned in the important *scène à faire* (Act III, ix) where, with the unwilling assistance of Beppo and Giacomo and the positive identification by the unnamed peasant, Lorenzo exposes the Marquis for what he is.

**The Peasant.**

It is Diavolo!

**Lorenzo.**

What's that?!

**The Peasant.**

I swear it!

**Lord Cokbourg.**

It is the Marquis!

**Paméla.**

O dreadful error!
This gentleman . . .

**Lord Cokbourg.**

This courtier
Was nothing but a bandit!

Lorenzo captures the Marquis and, with all other affairs of the heart and the pocketbook properly settled, presumably lives happily ever after. By way of contrast, the fortunes of the Marquis do not really decline until his ultimate capture, for throughout the opera he has the means to secure his ends: a clever disguise, the presence of Lord and Lady Cokbourg at the inn, his relationship with Lady Cokbourg, and the assistance of two seemingly able assistants. Only the audience knows that Fra Diavolo will not succeed, whereas Lorenzo himself is always aware of the state of his own fortunes.

In *Le Maçon*, although several small misunderstandings occurred, there was no single misunderstanding that could be termed a *quiproquo*. In *Fra Diavolo*, however, one mystery is central to the entire plot: the dual identity of the Marquis. It is this Clark Kent – Superman existence that makes possible his carrying out the first robbery of Lord and Lady Cokbourg, his concealing himself from the bounty-hunting soldiers, his diversionary tactics while planning the second robbery, and his escaping detection until the end. The nature of the *quiproquo* is gradually unfolded to the audience in the course of the above-mentioned *couplets* and the subsequent conversation between the marquis and his two associates, but is kept secret from the rest of the principals until the very moment of detection in Act III, viii-ix.

The well-made play structure is used in miniature within each act. The major problem of the first act is that obstacles surround Lorenzo's marriage to Zerline. By the end of the act these obstacles are removed, but the major problem of the opera, the bandit Fra Diavolo, is yet unsolved. Like the first act the second opens *in medias res*: Zerline, having seen her father off on an overnight journey, is in the process of making the guests comfortable for the night. The problem arises when the three bandits are forced to hide in Zerline's closet, and is partially resolved when Diavolo diverts Lorenzo and Lord Cokbourg, thus allowing his associates to escape without arousing suspicion as to their real intent. However, several questions are left unanswered: that of the eventual success or failure of Diavolo's second robbery, of the outcome of both Lord Cokbourg's and Lorenzo's aroused jealousy, and of the central *quiproquo*.

Besides providing answers to these questions, Act III has its own structure. As it begins the Marquis, in an extended monologue, looks to the future. He has just seen his robber band and has hopes that the wealth of the Cokbourgs will soon be his and that he will again escape to lead his double existence in relative peace. By the end of the act, all these hopes dashed, Fra Diavolo and his band are the prisoners of Lorenzo. In the course of the act Scribe also finds ways to bring together Lord and Lady Cokbourg and Lorenzo and Zerline, and to convince Mathéo that the latter pair should be allowed to marry. By the end of the final scene there are no more loose ends to tie up, no further questions to answer. Graphically, the following represents the structure of *Fra Diavolo*.

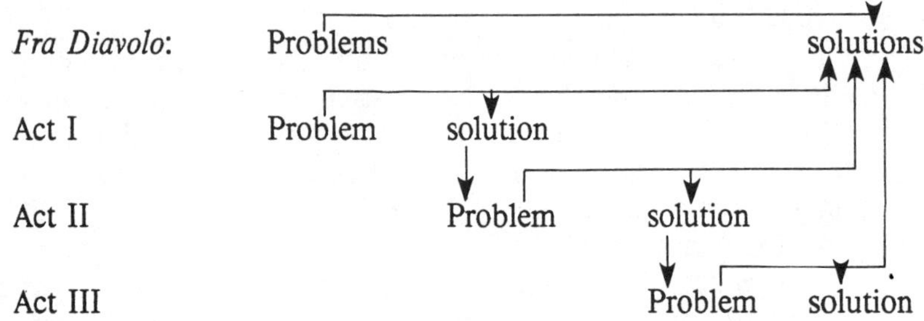


**Words and Music**

Whereas the music for *Le Maçon* is adequate if undistinguished, Auber's score for *Fra Diavolo* contains some of his best dramatic music in both solo and ensemble scenes. By now Auber is master of all techniques and media—recitative, simple song, air, solo ensembles, choral writing—to the point that even the simplest *couplets* have new freshness and distinction and the Rossinian cadenzas and coloratura passages are skillfully handled so that they blend with the Frenchman's less ornate writing in a unified style that gives off an aura of gaiety, high spirits, and robust good health. Again, the types of musical numbers are varied and the pieces evenly distributed throughout the acts, as the following tables will show.

Musical Numbers in *Fra Diavolo*

| Location | Number | Musical characteristics, persons |
|---|---|---|
| | | ACT I |
| i | 1 | Introduction: soldiers, Mathéo, Zerline, Lorenzo, Lord and Lady Cokbourg. Includes choruses, recitative, airs, ensembles. |
| iii | 2 | *Couplets.* Stanzas 1-2, Lord Cokbourg; stanza 3, Paméla. |
| iv | 3 | Quintet: Mathéo, Lord and Lady Cokbourg, Zerline, the Marquis. |
| v | 4 | *Couplets.* Stanzas 1-2, Zerline; stanza 3, the Marquis. |
| viii-ix | 5 | Duo: Lady Cokbourg, the Marquis. Trio: Lord and Lady Cokbourg, the Marquis. |
| ix-x | 6 | Finale: Lord and Lady Cokbourg, the Marquis, Beppo, Giacomo, Zerline, Lorenzo, the soldiers. Includes choruses, recitatives, airs, ensembles. |
| | | ACT II |
| i | 7 | [Recitative and] air: Zerline. |
| ii | 8 | Trio: Zerline, Lord and Lady Cokbourg. |
| iii | 9 | *Barcarolle*: Marquis. 2 stanzas. |
| v | 10 | Scene for Zerline, Beppo, Giacomo, the Marquis. Includes air with ensemble interludes, prayer, recitative and arioso. |
| vii-ix | 11 | Finale: Lorenzo, Lord and Lady Cokbourg, the Marquis, Beppo, Giacomo, Zerline. Includes recitiative, ensembles, airs. |
| | | ACT III |
| i | 12 | [Recitative and] air: the Marquis. |
| ii-iii | 13 | Chorus with solo interludes for Giacomo, Beppo, Mathéo. |
| v | 14 | *Romance*: Lorenzo. 2 stanzas. |
| vii | 15 | Finale: all principals, villagers, soldiers. Includes recitative, arioso, spoken segments, choruses, ensembles. |

Solo Numbers in *Fra Diavolo*

| Location | Characters | Subject | Keys |
|---|---|---|---|
| I, iii | Lord and Lady Cokbourg. | *Couplets*: the Lord's jealousy aroused by the Lady's flirtations. | A |
| I, v | Zerline, the Marquis. | *Couplets*: the story of Fra Diavolo. | G |
| II, i | Zerline. | Air: Zerline's happiness over her forthcoming marriage to Lorenzo. | G |
| II, iii | Marquis. | *Barcarolle*: song of a young girl awaiting her lover. | A |
| III, i | Marquis | [Recitative and] air: monologue on his life as a bandit. | E, B, E, e, D, d, D, G |
| III, v | Lorenzo. | *Romance*: unhappiness over Zerline's supposed unfaithfulness. | G |

Ensemble Numbers in *Fra Diavolo*

| Location | Characters | Subject | Keys |
|---|---|---|---|
| I, i | Soldiers, Lorenzo, Zerline, Mathéo Lord and Lady Cokbourg | Soldiers are going to search for Diavolo. Mathéo announces Zerline's engagement to Francesco but Zerline encourages Lorenzo not to lose hope. Lord and Lady Cokbourg arrive, tell of robbery. Lady Cokbourg complains of the hardships of traveling; others sympathize. | F<br>d<br>F |
| I, iv | Mathéo, Lord and Lady Cokbourg, Zerline, the Marquis. | The Marquis arrives and is greeted with surprise by the Cokbourgs. | B♭, E♭ |
| I, vii-ix | The Marquis, Lady Cokbourg. | Duo: the Marquis plays the cortier to discover the location of some valuables. | A |

| | | | |
|---|---|---|---|
| | The same, Lord Cokbourg. | Trio: Lord Cokbourg asks the Marquis to stop serenading the Lady. | A,E,A |
| I, ix-x | All principals but Mathéo, chorus of soldiers. | Soldiers have caught some members of Diavolo's band. Lorenzo takes reward from Paméla. Lorenzo and Zerline rejoice that they can be married. The Marquis, Giacomo, Beppo make plans to steal the reward money as well as the Cokbourgs' valuables. | $E^{\flat}$ |
| II, ii | Lord and Lady Cokbourg. | Lord Cokbourg is tired, but Paméla wishes not to retire. | C |
| | | The Lord discovers Paméla's locket is missing (she has given it to the Marquis). | G,C |
| | | Paméla avoids a quarrel by suddenly becoming tired. | C |
| II, v | Zerline, Beppo, Giacomo, the Marquis, soldiers. | Air: Zerline dreams of future happiness as she prepares to retire; the bandits comment on her song. | A,a,C<br>A |
| | | Zerline prays for good fortune and protection for herself and Lorenzo. | C |
| | | Marquis *et al.* plan to escape, think of killing Zerline. | A |
| | | Zerline repeats prayer in her sleep. | C |
| | | Soliders return, wish food prepared for them. | C |
| | | Bandits continue to plan escape. | A |
| II, vii-ix | All principals but Mathéo, soldiers. | Lorenzo hears a noise from closet, investigates. | E |
| | | Marquis steps out, deceives the Lord and Lorenzo about purpose of his hiding. | G<br>C |
| | | Lorenzo and Marquis agree to a duel. | |
| | | Ensemble: reflective | E |
| | | Paméla and Zerline are | G |

| | | | |
|---|---|---|---|
| | | accused of faithlessness. | |
| | | Ensemble: reflective. | E |
| III, ii-iii | Chorus, Beppo, Giacomo, Mathéo. | Chorus sings in celebration | F, B♭ |
| | | of Palm Sunday, prays | F |
| | | blessing of Virgin on them | |
| | | Giacomo and Beppo join in celebrations. | |
| III, vii | All principals, villagers, soldiers. | Soldiers prepare to continue search for Diavolo. | E♭ |
| | | Villagers arrive to celebrate Zerline's wedding. | E♭ |
| | | Giacomo and Beppo reveal they were with Marquis in Zerline's closet. Lorenzo becomes suspicious. | C, G |
| | | Mathéo finds note from Fra Diavolo. Lorenzo sets a trap. | |
| | | All pray for Lorenzo's success. | B♭ |
| | | Peasant identifies Fra Diavolo. | B♭, F, D, E♭, B♭ |
| | | General rejoicing. | E♭ |

From a dramatic point of view some of the musical numbers could be eliminated without harm to the plot. Among the solo pieces the Marquis' barcarolle in Act II and Lorenzo's romance in Act III are such numbers. The barcarolle is supposedly a signal to Giacomo and Beppo, but even in an opera such a purpose might have been served by such stock dramatic devices as lowering a curtain, opening a window, lighting a lamp, and the like. Lorenzo sings his romance to express his bitterness at the discovery of Zerline's alleged perfidy, something he has already expressed in speech and in song (Act II finale). It thus serves no dramatic purpose.

Yet a glance at the second table will reveal the reasons for these two numbers in the score. Lorenzo, although the hero of the opera and as such an important figure in all the central ensembles of the work, has no solo number which is not part of a larger piece. The *romance* gives him a chance to sing alone, to claim musically what he otherwise often holds dramatically: the center of the stage, the spotlight. There is still another reason for the existence of Lorenzo's *romance* which is easily seen when considering it in conjunction with the Marquis' *bacarolle.* The Marquis, while not a hero, is the central figure in the plot and as such is given a lengthy and skillfully composed monologue to open Act III. Why should he then have a second, dramatically insignificant and musically inferior solo number? Again, the table provides a clue to the answer. Auber's score abounds in a variety of ensembles, from duo to large scenes involving all members of the cast. By way of contrast, each act is provided with two—and only two—solo pieces, each balancing the other. In Act I the couplets each have the unusual feature that the first two stanzas are sung by one person, the last by a second. In No. 2 the first singer is male; in No. 4 the female vocalist sings first. The balance in Acts II and III is of a rather different sort. Each of these acts is opened by a relatively long and musically complex scene for a single character. The second solo number in each of these acts is of a simpler type: the strophic *barcarolle* and the romance. To eliminate either of the latter pieces would not only deprive some character of a chance to sing but would destroy the balance built into the two acts between solo numbers and ensemble scenes and between the types of solo numbers employed, thus indirectly damaging the dramatic outline and pacing of the work. In addition, the *barcarolle* and a similar one included in the duo of No. 5 provide a touch of local color for the Italian setting. The nonessential soli are necessary after all.

The same is true to a lesser extent of the dramatically unnecessary ensembles: the trio in Act I (second half of No. 5), the trio in Act II (No. 8), and the choral pageant scene of Act III (No. 13). No. 5 begins as a duo between the Marquis and Lady Cokbourg, the latter constantly fearful lest her husband find them together. In the course of the duo the Marquis takes from Paméla a locket as a token by which to remember her. He later uses this as evidence that his hiding in Zerline's closet is occasioned by an appointment with Paméla. Lord Cokbourg enters at the end of the duo and his wife explains that she and the Marquis were merely performing some music together. The Lord comments that he does not like music, after which a tableau-like trio closes the scene. The action of the second trio is described sufficiently in Table III. Both trios involve some dramatic action and both occur at minor turning points in the opera, but the action is neither so important nor the kernel of that action so central as to demand its emphasis by means of music. Equally important ideas are presented throughout the opera in the spoken dialogue. Clearly, the trios are included not primarily for dramatic purposes but for purely musical reasons: to balance the great number of large ensembles and to provide pieces for different vocal combinations: soprano and two tenors, two sopranos and tenor. Only one further extended trio occurs, that of Beppo, Giacomo, and the Marquis in No. 10, but this is used in conjunction with an air by Zerline and, later, with a male chorus.

Musical considerations are also responsible for the choral scene of Act III (No. 13). The action is slight and totally unnecesary to the plot. Furthermore, there is no good reason why Scribe should want the villagers to celebrate a religious holiday at this or any other point in the opera, for the townspeople have played no part in the action up to this point. Practicality, however, enters in. The sound of a mixed chorus is needed, particularly in the last finale, and soprano soldiers would be ridiculous even in a theatrical genre known for its lack of realism. It would not be economical to use so large a group of singers for a single number; hence the creation of a nondramatic scene in which the chorus plays a substantial part, one which also increases the variety of musical means employed in the opera. Moreover, the chorus is one of the loveliest numbers in *Fra Diavolo* and partakes of a number of current and traditional associations employed, no doubt, to insure warm reception (see Example 7).

> The chorus *Pâques fleuries* with its musical substance right out of Beethoven's *Pastorale* (also in F major) perpetuates the dignity of thanksgiving choruses glorified a quarter of a century before in Méhul's *Joseph*.[32]

The whole scene could be eliminated, but the opera would be the worse for having done so.

**Example 7**

### Example 7 (continued)

The solo numbers in *Fra Diavolo* serve functions similar to those in *Le Maçon*: to emphasize the personality traits or views of a particular character at a given moment; to trace the course of a train of thought or emotional state; or simply to allow the character to sing a solo. An example of the last type has already been discussed, and two further examples will illustrate the remaining points: No. 4, *couplets*, and No. 12, Fra Diavolo's monologue.

**Example 8a**

## Example 8a (continued)

"Voyez sur cette roche" (No. 4; stanza 1 given in Example 8a) is constructed in such a way and placed at such a point within the unfolding drama that it serves several purposes. The major function of the piece is narrative, to acquaint the listeners both onstage and off with the nature and adventures of Fra Diavolo, and as such it points the spotlight at a character who is deserving of the special emphasis that music provides. The narrative aspect of the song also serves the ends of the well-made libretto, first preparing the audience for the arrival of the bandit, then providing the first clear indication that Diavolo is indeed already present and is identical with the Marquis de San-Marco. In this function it is not just a static narration but at the same time a motivating force in the opera. This is emphasized musically by assigning the third stanza to the Marquis, even though it could have been sung by Zerline with no damage to dramatic logic. Other musical devices also contribute to the effect of this piece. At first glance it seems similar to any one of a number of such *couplets* appearing in opéras comiques of the day. It has strophic form, a simple yet catchy melody with regular four-bar phrases and predominantly conjunct motion, a text in evenly balanced lines set in a syllabic style, a recurrent refrain, and light orchestral accompaniment. Indeed, at some points the text is not particularly well served by the setting, as illustrated by the conflict of musical and textual rhythms of the first two lines.

Text: Vŏy / ēz sŭr cēttĕ / rōchĕ
Cĕ / brāve ă l'āir fiēr / ĕt hărdī.

Music: ∪/ > ∪ > ∪ / > >
∪/ > ∪ > ∪ / > ∪ >

Yet Auber's setting reflects the sense of the narrative and the drama in other ways, some hackneyed, some fresh and original. Among the devices in the former category are the tremolos, the mild chromaticism of the instrumental introduction and coda, the somewhat Schubertian shifts between major and parallel minor keys underlining the final statements of "Diavolo," and the logical change from major to minor at the refrain ("Tremblez . . ."). Opening the piece on a first inversion Eb major chord in an otherwise G major-minor piece is somewhat more original, although by no means unprecedented. However, the most striking device used by Auber to complement Scribe's dramatic purpose is rhythmic in nature: the repetition of the word "Diavolo" at the end of each *couplet*. The turn to minor mode, the change from medium to high vocal range, and the use of longer note values at "Tremblez" brings all possible change to the previously light-hearted piece. Perhaps there is something to fear after all. But no, there can be nothing so terrible about a bandit whose name can be reiterated in this staccato rhythm to the accompaniment of a motive from the first part of the tune. "Diavolo" as presented here has a certain puckish cast and suggests what the Marquis' monologue later confirms: that the bandit is gallant *au fond* and possesses to some degree the proverbial heart of gold. It is not he who wishes Zerline's death, and he wants from the Cokbourgs only a share of their undoubtedly plenteous wealth. The setting of "Diavolo" takes on a new importance in the third *couplet*, for the notes as sung by the Marquis are doubled in length and the rests between the statements are removed, although the accompaniment remains the same as in the first stanza (see Example 8b). These changes

**Example 8b**

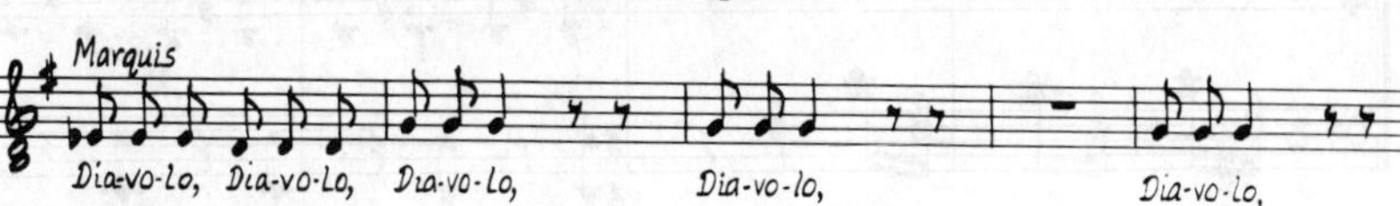


give greater weight to the Marquis' words and confirm musically the suspicions aroused by the text: the Marquis is indeed the bandit in disguise. In his final "Diavolo" the Marquis points with scorn and pride at his own cleverness.

In "Voyez sur cette roche" Auber provides an example of the narrative *ballade* or *romance* so common in nineteenth century opéra comique and also a conventional feature of many German romantic operas: e.g., Marschner's *Der Vampyr* or *Hans Heiling*. The tradition in France dates back to Cherubini's *Les Deux journées* (1800), in which Anton's song, "Un pauvre petit Savoyard," in Act I "is a forerunner of numberless romances and ballads in nineteenth century opera, including Senta's ballad in *The Flying Dutchman*, which has the same two-part structure and is even in the same key (G minor-major)."[33]

The impression of the Marquis' character provided by these *couplets* is seconded and more clearly defined in his monologue in Act III, a piece which traces the thought processes of the bandit Diavolo and gives a closer view of his personality. After an orchestral introduction in G major, the Marquis relates in accompanied recitative that his plans are about to be carried out. The E major aria that follows (Example 9a) is

## Example 9a

## Example 9b

**Example 9b (continued)**

in an ABA′ form and in a heroic style similar to that of many a military air in nineteenth century opera. In fact, it bears a striking resemblance to the tenor solo "Cujus animam" in Rossini's *Stabat Mater*, the first version of which was not written until 1831-32. (Compare Example 9a with Example 9f.) The virtuosic tendencies exhibited in the wide leaps, short runs and ornamental figures of "Je vois marcher" may suggest a kind of chain relationship.

General Rossini influences ________ Auber's "Je vois marcher" ________ Rossini's "Cujus animam"

Auber then turns to arioso as the text changes from static reflection to more direct narrative. In Example 9b Diavolo paints a picture of himself as a kind of Robin Hood, telling first how he would demand money from the wealthy banker, the haughty nobleman, a businessman for whom robbery is a form of justic (*E* minor, declamatory lines with chordal accompaniment); then how he would show kindness to the poor and provide them with money and food (*D* major, monotone declamation with orchestral melody). In the next section (Example 9c) the Marquis conducts a clever dialogue with himself to demonstrate how he will deal with frightened young girls. Beginning with a brief recitative announcing the subject of the dialogue, the bandit first acts the part of the woman confronted with a robber (*D* minor; *allegro*; aabb′ form). Returning to *D* major, in a slower tempo (Example (9d), he then reassures the audience in the most lyrical melody of the scene that: "We ask nothing of beautiful women: / It is the custom to spare them; / But we always receive from them / That which their hearts wish to give." The influence of Rossini is evident in the style of this melody. Summing up, Diavolo is quite happy with prospects for the future, but realizes that he must attend to present business if his daydreams are to become reality.

## Example 9c

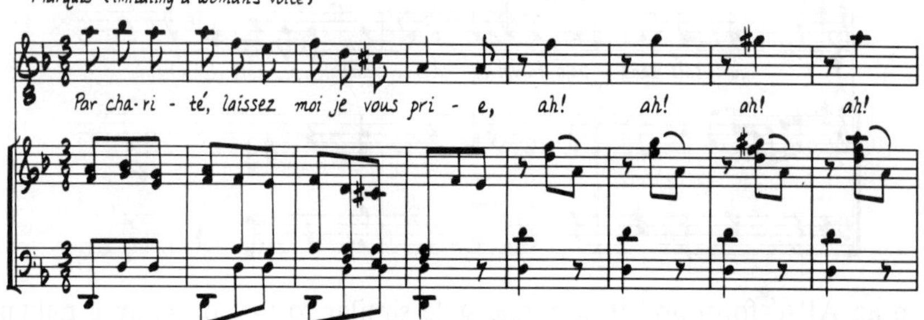


## Example 9d

## Example 9e

**Example 9e (continued)**

**Example 9f**

Coming out of his Rossinian reverie, he launches into a brisk air in *G* major and 6/8 meter (Example 9e; form: aba′b′ccb′ coda). The triadic melody and syllabic setting are more in keeping with the traditional (hence realistic) style of Boieldieu and French opéra comique. In terms of Fra Diavolo's character this scene is a dramatic high point. Never do we know him better than after this monologue, for both music and text provide a variety of moods the expression of which illustrates what all three men—librettist, composer and character—can do.

A similar glimpse into character portrayal as well as a fine example of the technique of ensemble writing is afforded by No. 10. (A general description is given in the third table above.) The first major section is built around an air by Zerline which is interspersed with commentary by the three bandits, much in the same way that the interludes of Donna Elvira's aria in Mozart's *Don Giovanni* are devoted to comments by Don Giovanni and Leporello. Zerline looks forward to her marriage on the next day (*A* major), vowing that hers will be a much more compatable match than that of Lord and Lady Cokbourg because Lorenzo is not the jealous type (*A* minor). The air is interrupted as Zerline pricks her finger with a pin and cries out. This occasions the first bit of commentary from Beppo, accompanied by a modulation to *B* major, thence to *C*, *A* minor and *E* in the space of nine measures.

Tonality becomes stable as Zerline resumes her air (*A* minor) and repeats the opening *A* major section. In a second *A* minor portion similar to the first, Zerline continues the train of thought begun there: she has not Paméla's elegance, but Lorenzo really has nothing to complain of for all that. With this she begins a contrasting section in 6/8 (*C* major) in which she enumerates her good qualities: for a servant girl she has quite a good figure, one with which she is quite content. This expression of vanity brings a second outburst from the closet and with it a second section of tonal instability (Example 10a). The bandits cannot help but be amused and their laughter is heard by Zerline. In recitative accompanied by only a few short orchestral figures between the vocal motives Zerline wonders whether something may be troubling the Lord and Lady. Satisfied that it is nothing, she returns to her air, a varied repetition of material from the *A* major section. The dramatically static air thus forms the musical framework around which this small amount of action is built. Sections of the air are tonally stable, changing key as they change subject, whereas the ensemble's interruptions are modulatory.

Outline of No. 10, Section 1

Air a - *A* major
Air b - *A* minor
Interruption 1 - modulatory
Air b continued - *A* minor
Air a′ - *A* major
Air b′ - *A* minor
Air c - *C* major
Interruption 2 - modulatory (Example 10a)
Air a" - *A* major

**Example 10a**

## Example 10a (continued)

Immediately the stability of key and form are broken as the orchestra introduces a new, romantically lyrical melody in *F* major in the oboe, continued into *D* minor by the bassoon in a progression not unworthy of Chopin (Example 10b).

Example 10b

A dramatic pause, then Auber plunges into *C* major for Zerline's prayer (Example 10c). Again somehow romantic in its simplicity, it "anticipates those subtle harmonic and coloristic inflections that suggest a similar atmosphere in Verdi's later creations."[34] As Zerline rises from

Example 10c

Example 10c (continued)

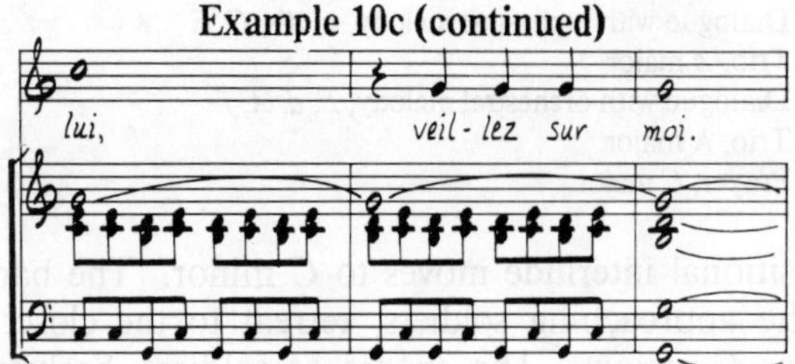


her prayer, the orchestra brings back a hint of livelier music and, momentarily, the keys of the earlier aria (*A*, *G*, then *C*, but minor rather than major). The orchestra retains the melodic interest as the girl intones a good-night to her absent fiancé. The prayer is repeated, but before Zerline can finish it she falls asleep. After a pause and a monophonic orchestral line of ambiguous tonality, the key of *A* major is strongly restated as the Marquis and his men prepare to leave their hiding place. A robust trip featuring strong martial rhythms leads into a modulatory section with dominant orchestral melody moving from *A* minor to *A♭*, *G*, *E* (V/*A*) as the bandits discuss their plans. The previous *A* major trio is repeated, followed again by a tonally unstable section (*F*, *D* minor, *A*, *F* minor ending with a half-cadence on *C♯*) in which the men try to decide Zerline's fate. After determining to kill her they repeat the *A* major trio, ending with a transitional modulation similar to that which led into the two earlier modulatory sections of dialogue under orchestral melody. According to the bandits' plans and expectations, this should be the point at which Zerline is murdered. The audience has been led to expect this in both text and music, yet somehow one knows that Zerline will not die. This feeling of hope stems from the earlier prayer and it is this prayer which, not unexpectedly, Zerline repeats in her sleep, just in time to save her life. This concludes the second large section of the number. More complex dramatically, featuring larger and more important parts of the action, it is also more complex musically. The underlying conflict between the innocent girl and the bandits finds expression not just in text but in musical form, for this section has two focal ideas, points of tonal and musical stability, around which the scene is organized: Zerline's prayer and the recurrent *A* major trio.

Outline of No. 10, Section 2

| | |
|---|---|
| a | Prayer, *C* major |
| b | Interlude, *C* minor |
| a′ | Prayer, *C* major |
| c | Trio, *A* major |

| | |
|---|---|
| d | Dialogue with orchestral melody, *a, A♭, G, E* |
| c′ | Trio, *A* major |
| d′ | Dialogue with orchestral melody, *F, d, A, f* |
| c | Trio, A major |
| a | Prayer, *C* major |

A transitional interlude moves to *C* minor. The bandits, hearing the noise of the approaching soldiers, retreat to the closet and Zerline awakens (arioso, *C* major). The chorus of soldiers, backstage, calls out (*C* major), causing Beppo and Giacomo to fear discovery (*A* minor). At a summons from Lorenzo (*E* [V/*A*]) Zerline leaves to admit the troops to the inn and the three men, left alone, decide to wait in silence to see what develops (*A* major). In these sections the action involving Zerline and the bandits is brought to a close and a new action begins with the arrival of the soldiers. Sections are relatively short, keys are successively stable, and no single musical idea binds the whole together just as no single dramatic idea pervades this portion of the number.

Outline of No. 10, Sections 3 and 4

| | |
|---|---|
| Interlude. | Dialogue - *C* minor |
| Section 3. | Zerline awakens - *C* major |
| | Soldiers' chorus - *C* major |
| | Beppo's fear - *A* minor |
| | Lorenzo's call - *E* major |
| Section 4. | Trio: Marquis, Beppo Giacomo - *A* major |

In this scene music and text are perfectly matched. The librettist has provided for alternating sections of action and repose/reaction in the text which have been accommodated by Auber using all the musical means at his disposal. Dramatic situations which are static exhibit tonal stability and a predominance of voice(s) over accompaniment; points at which action occurs are accompanied by tonal instability and most often the use of dominant orchestral melody or motivic work against which the singers act and react. In the course of the scene Auber also makes some attempt to paint the expressive content of the text in the music, the best example of this being Zerline's prayer and the orchestral transition leading into it. Thus musical form is built into the libretto and dramatic form is reflected in the music.

Considering this scene in combination with No. 12, the Marquis' aria, one can easily see the ways in which Scribe and Auber were ideally suited to one another, how they complemented each other. Scribe's characterization is always external. Similarly, Auber's musical characterization deals in externals. He is capable of providing relatively realistic pictures of the various moods and thoughts expressed by any given character (e.g., the Marquis in No. 12, Zerline in No. 10) but does not trouble himself to provide consistent musical characterization throughout the opera. This may be one reason for his dependence on clichés and stock devices, however skillfully he may handle them. In ensemble writing Scribe's texts are musical in the sense that most already provide for a musically valid form through the repetition of sections of text and the provision for action and reaction contained in their layout. His writing technique is more or less standard whatever the ensemble; hence again discouraging his musical collaborator from any great amount of originality while at the same time encouraging a craftsmanlike handling of the dramatic situation.

Except for the brief choral statement near the end, No. 10 is on a small scale in that Auber makes use of only four solo voices (or five, if one counts Lorenzo's short solo). The largest ensemble scenes occur in the introduction and in the act finales, in which Auber uses all or nearly all the solo characters and one or two choruses. The finales are particularly action-filled and one, that of the second act, is considered by Gerald Abraham to be one of Auber's finest technical feats.[35] The finale to Act III is also a fine piece of work and is perhaps even more interesting because it includes a great amount of action (e.g., the reconciliation of Zerline and Lorenzo and the *scène à faire*) and a great range of musical means (solos, ensembles, choruses, speaking). In music, action, and staging the scene is built up as a crescendo and, as in No. 10, all the musical materials contribute to the intensification of the drama by reinforcing forms, ideas, and stage movements suggested in the text. Although a general description of the scene has already been given in the third table above, a more specific chart of the course of events is necessary and is given below.

**FINALE, ACT III**

| Section | Action | Style | Key |
|---|---|---|---|
| 1 | Soldiers wish to leave to continue search for Diavolo. | Chordal TTBB chorus. | E♭ |
| 2 | Lorenzo, leaving for duel, tells sergeant to take command if he does not return soon.<br>Beppo, Giacomo, Zerline make side comments. | Arioso; chordal accompaniment. | c, E♭, f, G, c |

| | | | |
|---|---|---|---|
| 3 | Double chorus: villagers and soldiers. Soldiers sing same text as in Sec. 1; villagers celebrate arrival of Francesco. | Mixed chorus, chordal | E♭ |
| 4a | Mathéo announces Francesco and Zerline will soon be wed. | Arioso; chordal accompaniment. | E♭ |
| b | Zerline pleads with Lorenzo for explanation of his actions.<br>Lorenzo accuses her of faithlessness.<br>She is dumfounded. | | B♭<br>G♭<br>G♭ a |
| c | Giacomo and Beppo recognize Zerline as the girl on whom they spied. | | a, V/C |
| d | They taunt her by mockingly quoting the first part of her air. | | C |
| e | Zerline is puzzled | | c |
| 5 | Repeat double chorus as in Sec. 3. | | E♭ |
| 6a | Zerline wishes to speak, | | E♭, c |
| b | Orchestral interlude. | | 11 bars of V/C |
| c | Zerline declares she was alone in her room yet Giacomo and Beppo have just quoted words she said then. Lorenzo decides to investigate. | Spoken | |
| 7a | Soldiers seize Giacomo and Beppo. | Male chorus, chordal. | C M/m |
| b | Lorenzo recognizes them as bandits, but the peasant cannot identify them.<br>Mathéo sees the note. | Arioso | C<br>C, B, e,<br>D, G |

| | | | |
|---|---|---|---|
| c | Lorenzo reads the note. | Spoken | |
| d | The Cokbourgs are frightened. | Arioso | C M/m |
| e | Lorenzo lays a trap for Fra Diavolo. | Arioso | C, d |
| 8 | Chorus prays for success. Bits of sung dialogue inserted between choral phrases as characters watch for Diavolo's arrival. | Chordal mixed chorus with arioso dialogue under orchestral melody. | B♭ |
| 9 | Marquis arrives: the *scène à faire*. | Arioso dialogue under orchestral melody. | B♭ |
| 10 | Victory chorus. | Mixed chorus, chordal. | E♭ |
| 11 | Ensemble of soloists: triumph. | Chordal, using melody of No. 4 *couplets*. | G |
| 12 | General rejoicing. | Soli with choruses, chordal. | E♭ |

Since the action here is continuous and involves a succession of several important events, rather than being centered around only two or three items, there are no central musical forms around which the various sections of the finale are organized. Nevertheless, the piece contains a well-defined alternation of tension (action, dialogue) and relaxation (reflection or reaction) as in all Scribe's ensembles.

| | | | |
|---|---|---|---|
| Section | 1 | - | static situation |
| | 2 | - | action |
| | 3 | - | static situation |
| | 4 | - | action |
| | 5 | - | static situation |
| | 6 | - | action |
| | 7 | - | action |
| | 8 | - | choral tableau with inserted action |
| | 9 | - | action |
| | 10-12 | - | reaction |

As the action becomes more intense the periods of relaxation become less frequent (e.g., in Sections 6-9), but this midsection of snowballing events is anchored at either end by the opening choruses in *E♭* (Sections 1, 3, 5) and the lengthy closing tableau (Sections 10-12).

Key relationships help define the dramatic motion, since key centers move farther away from the tonic *E♭* as suspense builds up, then gradually return as Lorenzo plans and executes the capture of the bandit. The turning point in Section 7 is followed by a long section in *B♭*, the most extended period of tonal stability in the finale except for the closing portions of the scene. This is resolved to *E♭*, thus a V - I relationship, when the mystery itself is concluded with what amounts to a fourth stanza of "Voyez sur cette roche" (No. 4).

Scribe uses several methods with which to convey important information, action, and reaction. Two items are central to solve the whole mystery and bring the adventures of Lorenzo to a happy conclusion: that Lorenzo be assured of Zerline's faithfulness despite evidence to the contrary, and that he discover some central clue to enable him to capture Fra Diavolo. To clear up matters on both accounts Scribe resorts to spoken dialogue in the midst of an otherwise musical scene in order to insure that nothing will interfere with the audience's understanding of the material involved. Like the rest of the spoken portions of the opera these central segments are in prose, another insurance against possible lack of clarity (see Example 11a).

Static or reflective sections of the scene are given regularly rhymed poetry set in lines of regular length and in simply constructed stanzas: for example, the opening chorus (Example 11b).

Except for the two brief spoken passages the action is carried out in measured arioso soli and dialogue, which may or may not be complemented by orchestral melodies. These sections use longer poetic lines which are often divided up among several characters to good effect: for example, in the section of dialogue immediately following Lorenzo's reading of the letter (Example 11c).

## Example 11a

Text of Section 6c, finale Act III (Act III, viii)

**Zerline.**

I do not know what gave birth to the suspicions of which I am the object, and I seek in vain to explain it to myself, but I do know that last evening I was alone in my room, yes, alone! I was thinking of persons who are dear to me and I recall having uttered aloud words meant for the ears of God alone, and yet someone has just now repeated them within my presence.

**Lorenzo.**

And who might that be?

**Zerline.**

These two men whom I do not know. Therefore, they must have been nearby last night! Without my knowledge.

**Lorenzo.**

With what purpose? What intention? We must find out.

Text of Section 7c.

**Lorenzo.**

As soon as the soldiers and the wedding guests have left, signal me by sounding the bell at the hermitage; I will then come with a few henchmen and take care of the Lord and Lady.

## Example 11b

Allons, allons, mon capitaine,
Allons, allons, il faut partir;
Voici le jour qui nous ramène
Et les combats et le plaisir.

[Come on, come on, my captain,
Come on, come on, we must go;
This is the day that brings us back
Both to combat and to pleasure.]

## Example 11c

**Lord and Lady Cokbourg.**

It is a conspiracy against us.

What does it mean?

**Lorenzo.**

We shall find out.

**Lord Cokbourg.**

I tremble . . .

For you.

**Lady Cokbourg.**

For you.

**Lord Cokbourg.**
No, for both of us.

May love . . .

**Lady Cokbourg.**
Or at least fear bring us together.

**Lorenzo.**

Go, arrange yourselves as I have told you.
You, go up to the hermitage with him; if he hesitates,
May he fall instantaneously under your blows.
You, my friends, hide quickly
Behind these thick bushes.
As for you [Beppo], you alone stay here, stay!
And if, to betray us, you make the slightest move . . .
Remember that I am over there! You understand?

**Beppo.**
Too well.

**Lorenzo.**
Quiet!

The types of texts and the way in which Scribe uses them in *Fra Diavolo* are thus similar to those in *Le Maçon.* He is consistent not only in over-all structure of ensembles but also in the devices used to carry out that structure and the scheme of the work as a whole. This is far less a matter of artistry or originality than it is consideration for the clearest, most easily intelligible means of making the audience understand precisely what is happening on the stage and why it occurs in the way presented.

As an opera *Fra Diavolo* has a far greater impact, interest, and musical personality than *Le Maçon.* Its subject is more inviting, its music more varied and colorful. Important changes have taken place, particularly in the work of Auber as a composer, but more important for present purposes are the elements that remain constant: the dramatic structure of libretto, the distribution of the musical numbers, the situations in which music is required and used, the types of music involved. These are elements which, as will be pointed out again, recur consistently in Scribe's opéras comiques, and they are items that set the pace and the conventions for opéra comique during Scribe's productive life.

## Vaudeville Into Libretto: Auber's *La Barcarolle*

Though neither *Fra Diavolo* nor *Le Maçon* were based on original stories, the absence of a sole model made possible their consideration as freely-composed libretti. In many other cases the models for Scribe's libretti are known, and it is to some of these works that we now turn. The questions to be answered are two: how does an author transfer a work from another literary genre onto the operatic stage?; and does the nature of the original work have any effect on Scribe's end product? In the course of the discussion, aspects of Scribe's technique of adaptation will come to light and, when the operas are viewed as a group, will be shown to be very consistent from work to work.

Sources of the opéras comiques to be discussed range from an unpretentious one-act vaudeville to a trio of long, adventure-filled novels, and even include one opera libretto. Yet Scribe applied similar writing styles, techniques, and devices of dramatic structures to all. A survey of these and others of Scribe's libretti provides a clear illustration of the skill and consistency with which this writer approached his craft.

The subject of Auber's *La Barcarolle* was provided by a one-act *comédie-vaudeville, L'Intérieur d'un bureau.* This small work was written by Scribe in collaboration with Ymbert and Varner and was first performed at the Gymnase on February 25, 1823.[36] Its action takes place in nineteenth century France at the office of a ministry, and the characters, with the exception of the heroine, are all government employees. In this vaudeville Scribe shows his talent for mirroring his own society in his writings, for seizing on the foibles and shortcomings of its people and satirizing them in a bourgeois equivalent of high comedy.

Victor, a young man who writes songs in his spare time, has arrived very early at the office in order to escape his creditors. The latter, he remarks, have been arriving so early at his doorstep that he has been forced to come to work at dawn to escape them. When elderly Belle-Main, a secretary and copyist of letters, arrives, Victor sings for him a new piece he has written, a satire on the insecurity of government appointments and the dangers of being replaced by someone else on the list of favorites. Belle-Main, at age fifty-two, reveals that he has been awaiting a raise promised him some five years ealier so that he and his thirty-six-year-old fiancée Charlotte finally can be married. Victor in turn tells that he is in love with Eugénie, a wealthy young woman and daughter of the *chef de division*, but is prevented by poverty and debts from marrying her. Yet since Eugénie loves him, he has not yet lost hope of winning her.

After Victor leaves, Belle-Main receives M. de Valcour, the *chef de division*, and Eugénie. The present minister, according to Valcour's inside information, has just submitted his resignation, and the man who is certain to be his replacement is fond of topical, witty chansons. When Dumont, the office manager, shows Valcour a satirical verse he believes to be by Belle-Main but which is really by Victor, Valcour—taking it to be by Dumont himself—believes it will be just the thing to amuse the new minister and to get into the latter's good graces. While Valcour is copying the poem, Belle-Main, whom Dumont had just dismissed for writing verses against the minister, enters, briefcase in hand, ready to leave. He is pleasantly surprised to find that Dumont has changed his mind and goes off to shop for a wedding suit on the basis of Dumont's promise of a raise.

Valcour has a reputation as an amateur poet and is touching up Dumont's supposed verses when Victor returns. When Valcour asks Victor's opinion of the poem, which he now passes off as his own, Victor recognizes the lyric for which he had been searching all morning lest the less than laudatory comments fall into official hands. He therefore utters a very favorable opinion of the song and agrees to sing it at a party to be given by Valcour that evening.

Eugénie returns from the minister's office with the news that the present minister's resignation has not been accepted, but that he has been retained and his powers strengthened. Hearing this, Valcour snatches the poem from Victor and hints that the latter's secrecy about the whole matter could be handsomely rewarded. Victor thinks of Eugénie and leaves happily.

When Dumont returns, Valcour finds that the former has already circulated copies of the chanson and decides that the only honorable way out is to go to the minister himself and admit his guilt, come what may. Dumont in turn dismisses Belle-Main once more, but the latter determines to take his case to Valcour. Finally the confusion is cleared up, for Victor admits his authorship of the original verses, thus saving Belle-Main's job, and a messenger arrives to tell Valcour that the minister has received the poem favorably as an honest expression of truth and wants to meet the author. The play ends happily as Belle-Main is given a raise and Valcour promises Victor the hand of Eugénie in marriage.

There are certain similarities between Scribe's well-made plays and his opéra comique libretti with regard to structure, characters, and situations. In addition, the *comédie-vaudeville*, like the opéra comique, makes use of spoken dialogue with interpolated musical numbers, some of them serving a slight dramatic function. This music, however, is much simpler than that in opéra comique and uses popular melodies or tunes from various composed sources, such as earlier opéras comiques. Nevertheless, the adaptation of a *comédie-vaudeville* of this type as an opéra comique presents certain very difficult problems. There is, first of all, the difficulty of expanding the original single act of *L'Intérieur d'un bureau* into the three acts of *La Barcarolle.* The rather complex and compact intrigue of the vaudeville must necessarily be somewhat simplified for opera, and this very complexity of the plot makes its expansion less difficult than it might be otherwise. The solution of a second problem, that of expanding the muscial portion of the production to include more and larger muscial numbers, affects that of the enlargement of the material, since the music does occupy an important position in the opéra comique and does slow down the forward motion of the plot.

A third problem in adapting vaudeville to opéra comique stems from the nature of the former as a timely comedy of manners. Scribe's opéra comique libretti are very much of their time in that, whatever the setting, characters and situations are usually reflections of the lives of the French bourgeoisie of the nineteenth century. Yet the vaudevilles are much more specific in their references and in the satirical barbs included in the dialogue. Good examples of this point are to be found in Victor's songs and in the character of Belle-Main, an old government functionary who only copies the letters he is given but never reads them, a quality which has given him "a reputation with the administration as *homme discret,* which has its useful side."[37] Belle-Main prefers a raise in salary to a promotion because:

> Since that time [twenty years ago], assistant managers, managers, and ministers, how many I have seen enter and depart . . . ; everything has been changed, everything turned around, everything, except my chair which, despite these continual oscillations, is still on its legs, as I on mine. It is always there, fixed to the floor, stationary, immobile, and I do likewise; I do not advance, but I remain in place, as always.[38]

When he believes he was been dismissed he comments, "This is the first time in fifteen years that I have left the office before 4:00."[39]

These and other passing barbs at the French bureaucracy included in *L'Intérieur d'un bureau* have no place in an opéra comique. Not only do they go by too quickly in a drama otherwise relying on rather slow-paced action, but they tend to distract one's attention from the central plot line and the music, both of which are far more important in an opéra comique than in the miniature comedies of manners created by Scribe in his one-act *comédies-vaudevilles.* Thus when Scribe fashioned *La Barcarolle* he eliminated the topicality of the orginal vaudeville by transfering the scene to Parma, the action taking place in a musician's studio and in the palace of the Marquis de Felino. He also substituted for his government employees somewhat more remote and therefore more musical figures: royalty, high government officials, musicians.

The dramatic distance must be greater for opera than for other dramatic genres because the very nature of the form necessarily restricts it on several counts: number of characters, amount of action, complexity of plot, and the fact that the characters sing. Thus Scribe had to simplify the action of his vaudeville, take his characters out of their office, and remove the witty jibes at the follies of the French.

Yet this whole process must be seen in perspective, and perhaps a distinction made between realistic and contemporary in terms of what actually goes on the stage. Only quite recently has absolute realism in any art form been a deliberate objective, and selectivity and exaggeration still go on in the name of realism. There are few if any equivalents in daily life of Roth's Jewish mothers, Leonard Bernstein's Puerto Ricans, Arthur Miller's salesmen, Edward Albee's college professors, Menotti's Bleecker Street residents, Penderecki's monks and nuns. Rather, these characters are composites having traits taken from or alluding to contemporary life. As such they seem realistic but are not real. So too in Scribe's writings. The personae of *L'Intérieur d'un bureau* are no more real than the figures in any comedy of manners, yet they are contemporary and undoubtedly more realistic than the dukes, counts, musicians, and seamstresses who inhabit the Italy of *La Barcarolle.* Going one step further, however, the opera's characters, in embodying middle class ideals, values, and aspirations, and in presenting a cross-section of contemporary society, are more realistic than, say, Cherubini's Medea or Spontini's Julia. In addition, the taste for historical settings and local color also contributes to making *La Barcarolle* contemporary if not real. Some of Scribe's libretti do present more accurate pictures of bourgeois society–*Le Maçon, La Fiancée, Le Fidèle berger,* and *Marguerite,* for example–and some, such as Le *Cheval de bronze* or *La Petite lampe merveilleuse,* picture the more exotic world of fantasy, yet the characters are always of the same stylized bourgeois cut as in *La Barcarolle.* Sufficiently realistic to gain the empathy of the middle class audience, sufficiently stylized and simplified to be effective in a musical situation, they represent the operatic version of idealized composite characters out of Scribe's nineteenth century world. Scribe's change of scene and characters are symptomatic of the way in which he uses the material from the *comédie-vaudeville.* The plot is totally rearranged and the incidents are added and subtracted at will. Yet despite this major overhauling every main character and incident has its roots in *L'Intérieur d'un bureau* and is in some way an elaboration of or a variation upon the given theme.

*La Barcarolle* opens in the garret studio of Fabio, a struggling young musician who is hoping to gain fame as a composer of opera. The Count de Fiesque who, unknown to the other characters, is Fabio's brother, has come to ask the latter to orchestrate a love song he has written for Clélia, daughter of his enemy the Marquis de Felino. While he is waiting he catches Gina, a young seamstress and niece of Cafarini, Fabio's teacher, in the act of leaving some money on Fabio's table. She swears the Count to secrecy, then leaves.

When Fabio enters he reveals that he is in love with a lady of the court whose life he once saved, and that love for her has caused him to pursue seriously the study of music in order to make a name for himself. During the time spent as Cafarini's student, Fabio has received money from an unknown benefactor whom he now believes to be the lady in question but whom the Count knows to be Gina. Now Fabio has written an opera, and the Count offers to help him arrange a performance by speaking to his friends at court and by introducing Fabio to the right people. In return, he asks Fabio to correct and orchestrate the *barcarolle* he has brought. This Fabio agrees to do.

After the Count leaves, Cafarini enters, demanding the rent for Fabio's studio. Fabio is at a loss until he finds the money on the table. A messenger arrives to invite Fabio to a reception at the Marquis' palace, and Fabio goes out to buy suitable clothes, counting on his brother's generosity to pay for them. The Marquis arrives to find Cafarini in Fabio's studio and tells him of a plan he has to further his desire to imitate Cardinal Richelieu in things political. As prime minister, the Marquis is playing this role by paying court to the Grand Duchess in the same way that Richelieu courted Anne of Austria. He wishes to send the Duchess a love song of his own composition. For this purpose Cafarini appropriates the Count's barcarolle, which he believes to be by Fabio, and agrees to allow the Marquis to send it to the Duchess as his own composition.

The second act finds Gina in the Marquis' palace awaiting the latter's daughter Clélia. While she waits, the Marquis tells her uncle, Cafarini, that he has hidden a copy of the barcarolle in the Duchess' needlework basket, where she is sure to find it when she picks up her embroidery. Clélia arrives and relates that the Grand Duke himself has found the song accidentally and has flown into a jealous rage, vowing to punish its author. When Clélia leaves, the Marquis, now in trouble, points out to Cafarini that the copy was in the latter's handwriting, but Cafarini retorts that he has saved the copy made by the Marquis when in Fabio's studio. A confrontation between the two is prevented by the arrival of Fabio who, believing Clélia to be his unknown benefactress, sings for her the Count's *barcarolle.* The air is recognized by the Marquis and Cafarini, who ask the composer's name. When Fabio pronounces the name of the Count de Fiesque he meets with an unexpected reaction. Clélia, in love with the Count, now believes him to be faithless, whereas her father sees the opportunity to implicate his enemy as the object of the Grand Duke's jealousy.

Meanwhile the Count, although already an outlaw, has arrived at the palace, and Gina hides him until Clélia can return. In the dim light Fabio, entering, mistakes Gina for Clélia and declares his love. Furious when he learns that Clélia does not love him after all, he vows to denounce her real lover and is shocked to find that it is his own brother whom he delivers into the hands of the returning Marquis.

Fabio, disconsolate and with only a partial knowledge of the reasons for the Count's arrest, now seeks some way to deliver his brother from prison. Hidden, he overhears Cafarini propose to Gina, whereupon Gina admits that she loves Fabio, that it was she and not Clélia whose life he saved, and that she has been providing the necessary money for his studies. Cafarini, furious, convinces the Marquis to have Fabio imprisoned, then blackmails the Marquis into appointing him to a court position. Fabio does not know the significance of the paper they discuss, but realizes that its possession could help his brother. When Clélia shows him the copy of the *barcarolle* sent to the Duchess, Fabio recognizes Cafarini's handwriting and realizes that it must be the paper mentioned by the latter and the Marquis. Fabio is refused admittance to the ball at which the Marquis is in attendance, but gains the latter's attention by giving the court musicians parts to the orchestrated version of the *barcarolle.* When the Marquis enters in a rage, Fabio, showing him the paper, implies that he knows the whole story and offers to take the Count's place in prison if the latter is freed. The Marquis agrees, and the Grand Duke has the Count reinstated and his powers strengthened. Finally the mystery of the *barcarolle* is unraveled, the Count is given the hand of Clélia in marriage, and Fabio is betrothed to Gina. In addition, the Grand Duke has been persuaded to have Fabio's opera performed at court. The opera closes with an ensemble and chorus singing the *barcarolle.*

Some of the relationships between the libretto of *La Barcarolle* and *L'Intérieur d'un bureau* are obvious, but more often they are obscured by changes in the story. Victor of the vaudeville becomes the Count de Fiesque, an amateur poet-composer, while Fabio, although totally different in character, takes on the dramatic functions of old Belle-Main. It is Fabio who, like Belle-Main, innocently makes it appear that the song is his own, whereupon the song is appropriated by Cafarini (Dumont), revised by the Marquis (Valcour), and inadvertently brought to the attention of a person—the Grand Duke (the minister)—in whose hands it could cause harm to its authors. Clélia is, of course, the opera's equivalent of Eugénie, whereas Gina has no real opposite number in *L'Intérieur d'un bureau* unless it be Charlotte, the fiancée of Belle-Main. Once these equations of characters are established many of the events of the plot of *La Barcarolle* fall into place as having originated in the *comédie-vaudeville.* If Fabio is a younger, more imaginative Belle-Main, then the money he receives from Gina in order to continue his studies and thus become famous enough to win the hand of a noble lady is the equivalent of Belle-Main's long awaited raise, necessary to provide for his marriage to Charlotte; and Belle-Main's shopping for his wedding suit on the basis of Dumont's promise is the source for Fabio's buying new clothes in the expectation that his brother will provide the money.

Many other incidents in the opera originate in the vaudeville. The *barcarolle*, to be sure, is different in nature: in the vaudeville it is a topical satire, in the opera a love song. Yet in both cases the song's major effect is political. Both Valcour and the Marquis use a song as a way to curry favor with higher authority, and in both cases their schemes backfire. In both cases the original song is revised and "improved" by the person who appropriates it as his own, and in both cases the chain of authorship begins with lower-class characters and gradually ascends. At one point in *L'Intérieur d'un bureau* the minister's wife asks to see Eugénie, who later returns to complain that she has spent two hours in the company of the former while waiting for Valcour to come for her. This serves as the basis for two incidents in *La Barcarolle.* First, Clélia sends for Gina but the latter is forbidden to go unless her uncle, Cafarini, accompanies her. Having waited some time, Gina returns to complain that the uncle is taking too long discussing business with the Marquis and has kept Clélia waiting. Later, Clélia returns from waiting on the Grand Duchess and complains, as does her counterpart Eugénie, that such duties bore her. She then apologizes for having kept Gina waiting some two hours.

From these few examples one can see that while in many cases specific references or actions are different in *La Barcarolle*, the roots of these actions are to be found in *L'Intérieur d'un bureau.* Their transformation gives evidence of Scribe's skill in working out commonplace or second-hand details in contexts totally different from the original yet unmistakably related to it.

Since Scribe's libretto style is based on the technique of the well-made play developed in the *comédie-vaudeville,* one would expect *La Barcarolle* to retain all the characteristics of the well-made libretto as defined and illustrated by *Le Maçon* and *Fra Diavolo,* written fifteen to twenty years earlier. As the delayed-action plot, a standard feature, begins, the Count has already written the troublesome *barcarolle*; Fabio has saved the life of someone he believes to be a noblewoman and has fallen in love with her; Gina has assisted Fabio financially to obtain his musical training; and the Marquis has begun his political life on the model of Richelieu and has become the Count's enemy. Events are always carefully prepared and are carried out by means of contrived entrances and exits (for example, those of the Count, Gina, Fabio, Cafarini, and the Marquis, each of whom enters and leaves Fabio's studio during the first half of Act I without encountering another person or persons in the group who could hinder his or her plans); and such stock devices as letters (in this case replaced by copies of the *barcarolle*), mistaken identity (Fabio's mistaking Clélia for Gina), and overheard conversations are utilized. The ups and downs in the fortunes of co-heroes Fabio and the Count de Fiesque become quite complex, particularly after the latter is imprisoned, but nevertheless are a prominent feature of the plot.

Act III, Scene vii contains the crucial *scène à faire.* Here the Marquis, enraged at hearing the infamous *barcarolle* performed by the orchestra, comes out of the ballroom and is confronted by Fabio with the incriminating copy of the song. This has a "devastating effect" on the latter, who grants freedom from arrest and banishment to Fabio and full pardon and restitution to the Count. This done, nothing remains for Fabio but to explain the matter to Clélia, who is reconciled with the Count, and to marry Gina. The troublesome *barcarolle,* the authorship of which provides the central *quiproquo* of the action, ends the opera.

The delayed-action pattern of the main plot is reproduced on a smaller scale in all acts. As Act I opens Fabio has completed his muscial training and is seeking ways to become known as a composer. By the end of the act he has gained entrance to the house of a possible patron through the influence of his brother, the Count. At the beginning of Act II Gina, who has been in love with Fabio for some time, sings of her wish that this secret love be brought out into the open. At act's end this simple matter not only is unresolved but is more complicated than ever:

Fabio has declared his love, but only when he mistakes Gina for Clélia; the Marquis' plans have backfired; the Count is estranged from Clélia and imprisoned; and Cafarini plans to marry Gina himself. This situtation has not become any clearer by the first scene of Act III, when Fabio tries to think of a way to save his brother, but beginning with the *scène à faire* all problems are resolved as one would expect them to be by the end of the opera.

## *La Barcarolle*: The Portrait Of A Failure

First performed in 1845, *La Barcarolle* was unsuccessful, enjoying only twenty-seven performances.[40] In discussing the reasons for the failure of "such a charming and delightful score," Longyear conjectures, perhaps with tongue in cheek, that it was not the fault of Scribe's libretto but rather "because the hero is a musician, and the events of a musician's life are seldom interesting to an audience."[41] Although this is a possible contributory factor, it certainly cannot bear the entire blame for the opera's failure, for there are a great many things about *La Barcarolle* that may have worked against it. One of these has nothing to do with the opera itself. The years immediately preceding the Revolution of 1848 were troubled ones in which so frivolous a tale may have found no response, particularly when part of the joke was made at the expense of power-hungry politicians, something with which the public had quite enough first-hand experience. Furthermore, whereas the years from 1840 to 1844 were ones of comparative prosperity, 1845 began a period of economic slump which was "relevant to [the] 1848 revolution, though indirectly."[42]

In comparing the libretto with its vaudeville model it was apparent that the latter emphasized timely satire of contemporary life, whereas such things were deemphasized in the libretto because of the quickness of delivery necessary to bring them off successfully. However, traces of topical humor remain in the dialogue and even in some of the muscial portions, thus creating a curious duality between the more generalized and simplified libretto style and the fast repartee of the *comédie-vaudeville*. The shift of mental direction from a lesser to a greater degree of reality may have contributed to the opera's failure to find acceptance among its audiences. For example, in Act I, iii, Fabio remarks to the Count: "He [Cafarini] has never been able to compose anything but church music . . . and I, I have written an opera . . . . *The Guardian Angel*," a direct commentary on the status of musical genres in nineteenth century Paris. Later, Fabio evaluates the talents of the amateur musician, the Count, at the same time mildly poking fun at "gentleman amateurs" as a group (Act I, iv): "Despite his modesty, these words are no worse than any others . . . and the melody is very good . . . for a nobelman!"

The first part of No. 4 (Scenes iv-v) is a thoroughly topical bit of satire, using musical gimmickry to lampoon the customary orchestration of contemporary opera and the unyielding conservative sentimentality of the church musician. Fabio begins to orchestrate the *barcarolle,* imitating the sounds and sterotyped effects of the various instruments as he works (Example 12a). This disturbs Cafarini, who simultaneously scolds Fabio and carries the satire further by repeating Fabio's melody a fourth lower. Fabio points out that Cafarini, after all, is to blame for the noise, since the latter was his teacher. The master, however, replies that his teaching was not for this purpose but to the end of enhancing church music. He then provides a sample of the more serious, conservative style of that genre (Example 12b). The argument ends in a stalemate and Cafarini goes on to discuss more pertinent matters: Fabio's unpaid rent. Thus the first part of the duo scene, while amusing, is thoroughly unnecessary, and one must shift from topical satire to the dramatic reality of the opera's plot in the middle of the number. Furthermore, the device of musical satire is not even particularly original. Paër had used the voice to sing instrumental effects in *Le Maître de chapelle* (1821) and Donizetti did the same in his *Il Fortunato inganno* (1823) and *Le Convenienze ed inconvenienze teatrali* (1827).[43] However, these last two works could have been unknown to Auber, since he rarely left Paris.

**Example 12a**

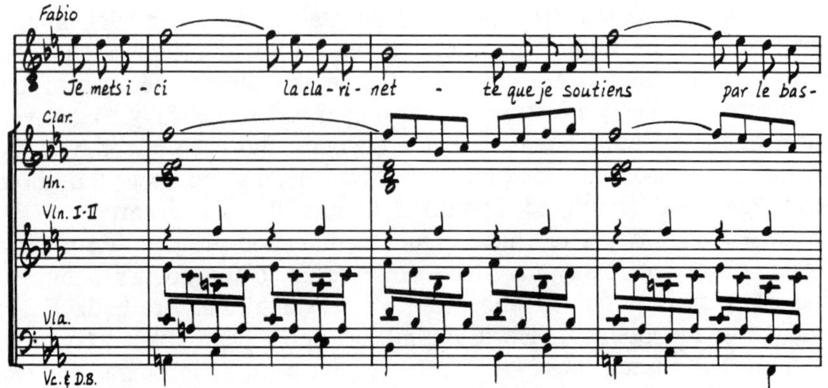

## Example 12a (continued)

Example 12a (continued)

Example 12b

Example 12b (continued)

A further example of timely satire in a musical number occurs in the middle of No. 5, a duo for Cafarini and the Marquis. The two are trying to think of a song to send to the Grand Duchess and utter a prayer to the god of fine arts (Example 13). Here Auber uses light counterpoint and a mocking imitation of ecclesiastical chant, both of which satirize contemporary church music. Such satire not only causes a shift of attention from the world of operatic fantasy to that of everyday life, but weakens the characters as well. Cafarini is supposed to be an inferior composer scheming for a court appointment, while the Marquis is the Count's enemy and the villain of the piece. Here, however, they appear as two perfect clowns, exaggerated to the point of lampoon. In the case of the Marquis this section merely reinforces his aim, stated earlier in the scene, of imitating Richelieu in his handling of governmental affairs. He says (Act I, x):

> The Cardinal governed his master . . . mine thinks only through me or else he does not think at all . . . The Cardinal made himself hated by the entire court . . . I think I have succeeded there . . . The Cardinal wrote verses, and I manage this rather well!

After playing the fool throughout his first big scene, even to the point of convincing himself that the verses Cafarini dictates are his own invention (Example 14), the Marquis can hardly be taken seriously as a villain, and his intrigues to imprison the Count and exile Fabio seem curiously out of context.

## Example 13

## Example 14

Example 14 (continued)

Other examples of satirical dialogue and/or music could be mentioned. All would illustrate the same points: that the transformation of vaudeville into libretto is incomplete, and that the changes of outlook represented by these remnants of the original work endanger the continuity of the opera and the very nature of the medium onto which they have been grafted.

The lack of the conventional and, at the same time, the overuse of the conventional may have caused adverse reactions to the opera. An opéra comique of this time ordinarily opened with music, usually a chorus with a few incidental soli. In *La Barcarolle*, however, two of the three acts begin with spoken monologues, which plunge the audience directly into the action without the comfort or warm-up provided by a large-scale, more or less static musical number. Only one act—the second—opens with music, but this too is a monologue, a scene for Gina. Although the situation is static enough, the number is hardly on a large scale. In fact, the use of the chorus is kept to the barest minimum, perhaps an indirect effect of the state of the national economy, for there are only two choruses, both at the end of the final act (Nos. 15 and 16).

Another unconventional aspect of *La Barcarolle* is the over-all plan of the musical numbers. The table below outlines the first act's music.

| Scene | Number | Characters and nature of music |
|---|---|---|
| i | 1 | Gina: recitative and multisectional air. |
| iii | 2 | Fabio, the Count: duo; several sections, some repeated or recapitulated. |
| iii | 3 | Fabio, the Count: duo; several sections, including the *barcarolle.* |
| iv | 4 | Fabio, Cafarini: duo; several sections (discussed above). |
| x | 5 | Cafarini, the Marquis: duo; several sections, including the *barcarolle* text. |
| xi | 6 | Fabio, Cafarini: "Duo final"; several sections, including the *barcarolle* tune and text. |

This table presents a totally different profile from that of acts in operas already discussed. Of the six numbers five are duos, all for male voices. Moreover, they are not distributed evenly throughout the act but occur in early or final scenes. In addition, three of the five duos contain the *barcarolle* itself, while all but No. 4 make extensive use of 6/8 meter and *barcarolle*-like rhythms. Indeed, this meter pervades the entire score. Monotony reigns supreme in music and in performing forces. Some of the individual numbers are delightful, but the collective effect is less than charming.

Although later acts include greater variety in the make-up of ensembles, the actual music again presents a monochromatic picture. Textures are not imaginatively worked out and polytextual chordal writing predominates in ensembles. As for the solo numbers, they too present a curious situation. Act I contains one air (No. 1), for Gina, and a *cavatine* for Cafarini included as part of No. 6; Act II begins with another air for Gina (in 6/8!) and includes an air for Fabio (No. 10) which leads directly to a duo (No. 11); in Act III the musical numbers are all ensembles. Thus we are faced with an opera in which there are no solo numbers for the co-hero or co-heroine (the Count and Clélia) nor for the villain; and in which the only trace of the familiar *couplets*, the mainstay of soloists in opéra comique, is to be found in the *barcarolle* (Example 15a), itself introduced as part of a duo scene. A contemporary reviewer criticizes the music for lacking "freshness and distinction" and for being quite old-fashioned, commenting that "anyone could have composed [the *barcarolle*] thirty years ago. . . ."[44] Realizing all this, one wonders how singers were prevailed upon to create such ungrateful roles, but one no longer wonders why the work was not a success.

The overall musical monotony is reinforced by a number of single pieces in which ideas that could otherwise be quite engaging or effective are carried to extremes. One such piece is No. 15, in which through Fabio's contrivance the *barcarolle* is played by the court musicians. Perhaps taking a cue from Mozart's *Don Giovanni*, Auber has the tune played first by an onstage brass band (Example 15b), then repeated by another onstage band, this one made up of woodwinds, bass drum, and cymbals, while the Marquis complains in the background (Example 15c). A third statement of the tune follows, the *a cappella* chorus accompanying side comments by Fabio and the Marquis (Example 15d). At midpoint the vocalists are joined first by the brass band (Example 15d, measure 8), then by the wind (Example 15d measure 12). The little *barcarolle*, rather frail in any event, has been bludgeoned to death in what might otherwise have been quite an effective number. As if to secure the deed Auber closes No. 16, the finale, with a tutti rendition of the *barcarolle*, in memoriam.

**Example 15a**

**Example 15a (continued)**

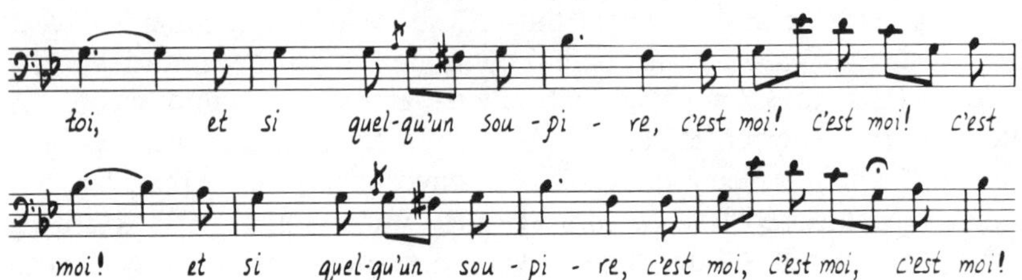


**Example 15b**

**Example 15c**

Two specific details in the libretto of *la Barcarolle* will serves as examples of the use of second-hand ideas. The first is the *barcarolle* itself (Example 15). Repeated throughout the work as a kind of hackneyed unity device, it resembles nothing so much in function as the famed song of Blondel in Grétry's *Richard Coeur-de-Lion.* Adam's reorchestrated version of the Grétry work for the Opéra-Comique had been performed in 1841; thus it was a recent memory to the Parisian public.[45] Auber's *Le Maçon* and *La Sirène* also use a recurrent tune, but in a more dramatic way than does *La Barcarolle.*

## Example 15d

Marquis
A d'au- tres maintenant! cerné
Sopranos
O toi dont l'oeil ray-on - ne de mil- le traits vain-queurs, sans scep- te ni cou-
Tenors
O toi dont (etc.). . . .
Basses
O toi dont (etc.). . . .
Fabio
Grâce à mon strata - gê - me,
de tous cotés! cou- rez, courez donc à l'in-stant! Sur eux tous a-na - thê - me!
ron - ne tu rè - gnes sur les coeurs! Oui, je t'ai- me sans le di - re, mais é-
Cornet à pistons
Trombones

Example 15d (continued)

Another example of a second-hand idea is to be found in Act II, x. Fabio, waiting in a darkened room for Clélia to appear, sings of his happy anticipation. This scene is quite clearly modeled on the famed "Viens, gentille dame" sung by Georges Brown in *La Dame blanche* as he waits by the fireside for the appearance of the supposed ghost. The first part of Fabio's air, "Asile où règne le silence" (Example 16a), corresponds to the opening section of Boieldieu's "Viens, gentille dame," for both are lyrical and reflective and both express the hope that the young woman spoken of will soon arrive. In Boieldieu's aria there follows a section in 5/4 meter in which the singer speaks of the advancing hour and of his impatience; the accompaniment is simple repeated chords in an eighth-note rhythm. Auber's second section is similar, although in a simple 4/4 meter: to the accompaniment of tremolo chords in the strings Fabio sings, "O moment séduisant del'attente, tourment pour nous" (Example 16b). Finally, like Georges Brown, Fabio calls to the lady to appear (Example 16c) but, since she does not enter immediately, he repeats "O moment séduisant" before a two-measure instrumental transition leads into a duo for himself and Gina. In Boieldieu's aria the White Lady appears to the sound of a harp and also sings a duet with the hero, but only after some spoken dialogue. It was always Scribe's belief that there was no shame in reusing successful ideas, hence the structure of the well-made play. In this case he was correct, for Fabio's air and Gina's solo scenes are among the most successful numbers in the opera.

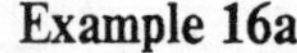

**Example 16a**

**Example 16b**

Example 16b (continued)

Example 16c

In may respects to accuse Scribe of overusing convention is to elucidate the obvious. Indeed, Gautier is not far from wrong when he writes:

> Aren't the pieces always the same? And, moreover, why change? . . . *La Barcarolle* causes no intellectual flounderings. From the first word you know the last, and [the work] moves on wheels in a soaped groove, without a shock, without a jerk. It is charming! One does not fear these horrible anxieties with which the daring authors may inspire one. . . . M. Scribe's horses never take death in their teeth. They go along, downcast, in a gentle trot and take merrily to its destination the subject one confides to them, provided, however, that there are no more than three stops; for beyond that they begin to be out of breath.[46]

A later author is in general agreement, stating: "Here the librettist has perhaps abused a bit too much his ability in the art of distributing the details, of creating incidents, of giving birth to situations and words centered around a theme insufficient in itself to be conducted regularly and to justify the complete development of a dramatic action."[47] At a time when Scribe' career has passed its peak, one could conclude from these statements that people had seen enough of well-made libretti to make them receptive only to the best of them. If, as is generally agreed, *La Dame blanche* represents the best, then *La Barcarolle*, although amusing, is not up to earlier standards.

The only deviation from the usual dramatic plan of the Scribean libretto to be found in *La Barcarolle* occurs in Act II, when the situation stated at the beginning of the act, far from being even partially resolved, is even more complex at the end. This points up one further problem of this libretto that may have contributed to the opera's failure. The entanglements are very complex and require a great deal of attention by the spectator in order to be comprehended. Although the plots of *Le Maçon* and *Fra Diavolo* are not particularly simple, they are easily grasped without a great deal of mental involvement. In *La Barcarolle* events are just as carefully and logically prepared, but the steps toward solution of all entanglements are often so small that an audience depending on the opera for light entertainment could soon become tired or bored trying to follow the slow progress of all the characters, not to mention that of the ever-present *barcarolle*. For example, in Act III Fabio, hidden, overhears everything that happens on the main part of the stage. However, he must listen to and piece together a number of conversations, the precise details of which he does not fully understand until they are explained to him at the end of the opera. Thus his solution to the problem of his brother's imprisonment is based on partial information and may not work. The spectator, ordinarily sure of the outcome of any action, is left to wonder whether Fabio can carry out his plan with sufficient boldness to make it work, and must follow every word carefully in order to find out. Even with the help of the printed page and the advantage of being able to go over the text several times at one's own pace, this act is a difficult one and may have annoyed an audience ordinarily receptive to Scribe-Auber products.

There was no single reason for the failure of *La Barcarolle.* Rather, the fault lay in a combination of factors to which composer, librettist, and extra-theatrical matters contributed. The combination of too much topicality and too little clarity marred the libretto; monotony and old-fashioned styles and devices destroyed some of the appeal of the music; and adverse political conditions may well have affected the minds of the normally receptive listeners and turned them away from this work. The fact remains, however, that the Scribe-Auber collaboration itself was a success, for whatever errors the writer committed were reinforced in kind by the composer.

## Libretto Into Libretto: Adam's *Le Chalet*

*Le Chalet*, a one-act opera in eighteen scenes, was first performed on September 25, 1834, and is considered to be the best opéra comique by composer Adolphe Adam.[48] The libretto is by Scribe in collaboration with A. H. J. Mélesville, but like all such collaborations it bears the unmistakable stamp of Scribe's style and technique. Concerning the work Adam wrote:

> I accepted the play eagerly because it seemed musical to me, but I was far from sensing its value and from predicting the success that it would one day have. Already people had tried several times to bring this subject, which stems from Goethe, to the theatre, and they had never succeeded. By a singular circumstance, the first air I had composed for the theatre had been written for a vaudeville, staged unsuccessfully at the Gymnase, on the same subject as *Le Chalet.* A bad memory of it remained, and I did not understand in reading [the libretto] the extreme ability with which Scribe had averted the pitfalls of the situation. In Goethe's play it is a rebuffed lover who installs himself at the home of the young lady and who stops at nothing to make her understand the dangers of isolation. In making of the lover the young lady's brother, Scribe succeeded in allaying the scruples of the French public.[49]

The Goethe work in question is a singspiel, also in one act, entitled *Jery und Bätely.* This work was first produced with music (by C.

S. von Seckendorff) at Weimar in 1780 and subsequently set by Peter von Winter (1790), Schaum (1795), Reichardt (1801), Conradin Kreutzer (1803), Bierey (1803), Frey (1810), and Julius Rietz (*ca.* 1825).[50] Thus, its success and stageworthiness as an opera libretto was unquestioned, at least by German composers of Goethe's generation.

Judging by the comments just quoted, Adam was not familiar with Goethe's original but probably relied for his knowledge of the plot on the ill-fated vaudeville adaptation, for he reveals no accurate evaluation of the changes Scribe has made. Nor does Paul Henry Lang, when he writes:

> Goethe's *Jery und Boately* [*sic*] served as source for an opera-libretto which Scribe rebaptized *Le Chalet.* The story discusses a young girl living in seclusion, who finally yields to the persuasion of a young man and gives up her isolation. Scribe, very complacently, changed the lover into a brother, killing the sense of the play but satisfying the chaste bourgeois.[51]

Actually, Scribe does nothing of the kind, for the simple reason that Goethe's story has none of the immoral implications suggested by Lang's comment. Scribe's changes are made for one of two reasons: to pare down the cast to its essentials, a particular necessity in so light a piece as Adam's work; and to make those elements that are retained as stageworthy and as dramatically vital as possible. This will become apparent in a comparison of the two works.

*Jery und Bätely* is set in the Swiss Alps, where Bätely and her father live in a isolated country dwelling. We meet the central characters immediately: Bätely, a young milkmaid in love with country life and the out-of-doors; her father, a genial old man who prefers sleeping late in the morning and keeping company with the tavern-goers in the evening to hard work; and Jery, described by Bätely and her father as a well-to-do but unwelcome suitor for the girl's hand in marriage. The father is concerned that Bätely refuses to marry, since he is aging and is worried about her future should he die. Bätely, however, is quite happy as she is and enjoys the freedom afforded her by her single state and the secluded location of her country home.

When Jery arrives at the cottage Bätely rejects his proposal and urges him to try to find someone else, but he cares only for her. Bätely leaves Jery, who is then joined by Thomas, a fellow countryman and friend who has been away on a tour of duty with the army. Thomas tells of the joys of soldier life and explains that now, since he has been discharged, he is engaged in a livestock venture and is taking a herd of oxen to Milan to be sold. After some good-natured advice to the lovelorn, Thomas listens as Jery relates Bätely's rejection of him and of several other young men from the village, actions which have caused the neighbors to become irritated with her for what appears to be snobbishness. In the end Thomas proposes that he try to convince Bätely to marry Jery. The latter leaves with hope renewed.

Bätely emerges from the house and Thomas asks her for food and drink, which she is willing to provide until he takes her hand as he attempts to speak to her. Bätely flees into the cottage where, from an open window, she informs Thomas that her home is not an inn. The latter, however, has a plan. He calls upon one of his helpers to drive the herd of oxen into the meadow belonging to Bätely and her father. This done, Bätely finds that she is powerless to prevent this and her father runs off to seek assistance from some of the neighbors. Thomas, left alone with Bätely, tries to kiss her. She runs back into the house and he, attempting to enter, breaks some window panes. He leaves just as the father returns. The latter has been refused help by all the neighbors, who still feel offended by Bätely's superior attitude. While father and daughter despair at their situation, Jery enters and, after having been informed of the problem, offers to help. Thomas returns and Jery, before giving him a chance to explain, begins to fight. Jery is beaten by Thomas, who then leaves, but not before reminding Bätely that Jery has sustained injury on her account. When Bätely goes into the cottage to get bandages for Jery, Thomas returns and admonishes him to take advantage of the situation to propose again to Bätely. However, he has little need to do so, for Bätely has seen the light, begs Jery's forgiveness, and declares that she will be his forever. Thomas, meanwhile, has roused the neighbors and villagers. They arrive and find to their surprise that Bätely has agreed to marry Jery. The work ends with a chorus of rejoicing.

A comparison of Goethe's libretto with the adaptation of it made by Scribe in *Le Chalet* will reveal that, although Scribe has altered the plot and reduced the number of characters, the story remains essentially the same. As *Le Chalet* opens, the chorus is preparing to leave for the village after a day in the country. They reveal that they have sent a letter to Daniel, a wealthy and handsome young man, purporting to be from Bettly, a country girl Daniel has loved for some time but who has always refused his proposals of marriage. On the basis of the forged letter, which contains the welcome news that Bettly finally has decided to marry him, Daniel has ordered preparations for a wedding celebration and has had a marriage contract drawn up. Now the chorus, observing that their joke is proceeding as planned, leave Daniel and return to town to take advantage of the lavish party in preparation. Daniel rejoices over what he believes to be his good fortune. However, his happiness is soon ended when Bettly, informed of the letter, reveals that she could not possibly have written it since she does not know how to read or write. Furthermore, she is still determined to retain her freedom. Keeping some hope alive, however, she declares that she is fond of Daniel and that if she did wish to marry, he would be her choice.

Bettly then asks Daniel's assistance. She has received a letter from her brother Max, who left home fifteen years earlier to join the army, and is unable to read it. As he reads aloud, Daniel is pleasantly surprised to find that Max is his ally, for the letter urges Bettly to marry "a worthy young man from the area from whom I have received a request [for your hand] in marriage." The young man in questions is, of course, Daniel, who admits having written to Max some two months earlier. The letter also reveals that Max has plans to return home soon for a visit.

Daniel, unhappy over Bettly's latest rejection of him, sees a troop of soldiers approaching and resolves to join them. They enter, Max at their head, and Daniel asks to be enrolled, telling Max of his desire to escape the futility of his love for Bettly. Max, without revealing his identity, sends Daniel away to get his birth certificate and other necessary papers, then decides to resolve the conflict by tricking Bettly into marrying her forlorn lover. Accordingly, he orders his soldiers to take over Bettly's chalet and to eat, drink, and revel at her expense.

When Bettly returns she is confronted not only with the military take-over of her house and supplies but also with the unwelcome attentions of Max, whom she does not recognize. As she is trying to find a way to solve her problem, Daniel returns and reveals that he is joining the regiment. Bettly, seeing in him a means to avoid being left alone with the soldiers, asks him to stay with her—but just as a friend. Daniel, grateful for crumbs, remains, but he is not the brave gallant who rescues the fair maiden. In fact, he promptly falls asleep in an easy chair, leaving Bettly to fend for herself. Her cries for help awaken Daniel who, although obviously fearful of the soldier Max, displays what little courage he has in defending Bettly, at first verbally, then by agreeing to a duel. Max goes off after promising to meet Daniel in the woods in a quarter of an hour.[52]

Bettly has heard all this and begins to regret her rejection of Daniel, something which now may cause his injury or even death. She is not yet willing to go so far as to agree to marry him, but she determines to make him forget the time so that he will not keep the appointment with Max. The latter, however, returns when Daniel does not appear. In order to save Daniel, Bettly tells Max that she and Daniel are married and produces the marriage contract Daniel had drawn up earlier. Daniel is surprised to see the girl's signature on the contract, but she tells him in an aside that this is just a ruse to trick Max, since the contract would require her brother's signature in order to be valid. At that Max steps over to the table, signs the contract, and admits that he is Bettly's brother, "who tricked both of you in order to force you to be happy." The opera ends in a chorus of rejoicing that the joke which began the opera has ended happily.

As is evident from both summaries, most of what both Adam and Lang say concerning the original material and its adaptation is either misleading or false. Goethe's Jery does not "install himself" at Bätely's home, nor is he one who "stops at nothing to make her understand the dangers of isolation." Scribe does not change "the lover [Jery] into a brother [Max]," but merely renames him. Nor is there anything about Goethe's play that would justify considering it risqué. Scribe has not radically altered the plot lines of Goethe's work at all, but he has made the original more stageworthy and more musical by means of several strategic changes.

The action in Goethe's libretto begins slowly: Bätely returns from her morning chores, her father arises, they discuss Jery until the latter arrives and is again rejected. Only when Thomas arrives does the drama begin to move. In contrast, Scribe plunges directly into the action: the chorus has already set the trap that will start the plot moving (the typical delayed-action plot). Although this specific incident does not occur in Goethe's original, Scribe has fashioned it not merely to motivate what follows but to set up the main dramatic conflict and to prepare for the end of the work. When Daniel comes on the scene he has already drawn up a marriage contract and has made plans for a celebration, acting upon Bettly's promise of marriage in the forged letter. The contract saves the day for Daniel and makes Max's plan easier to effect, while the celebration ends the opera. The opening of Scribe's piece thus displays its greater dramatic strength via its immediate action and its function as preparation for later events.

Many other changes made by Scribe strengthen the dramatic structure of the piece. In Goethe's work specific actions take place as if by chance. Thomas, driving his oxen into Bätely's meadow, acts on impulse. Jery's attack on him is equally impulsive, and Bätely's repentance is so sudden and so complete as to be unbelievable. Unlike Goethe, Scribe carefully provides motivation for every action. After the opening scene Bettly's admission that she cannot read or write causes Daniel to read aloud Max's letter, which in turn prepares not only for Max's arrival but for his later action on Daniel's behalf. The troop of soldiers accompanying Max provides the force and rationale for the invasion of Bettly's chalet, which in turn provides the excuse for Bettly to turn to Daniel for help and, finally, to be tricked into marrying him. When Bettly begins to show signs of changing her mind about Daniel and his proposal of marriage, her conversion is gradual and never complete, a course of events much more realistic than that which is found in Goethe's libretto.

Scribe's characters are also better than Goethe's. First, Scribe combines the functions of two of Goethe's characters into one, the father and ex-soldier Thomas becoming Max: soldier, relative to Bettly, and friend to Daniel. At the same time Scribe provides a reason for Max's appearance (a visit to his sister), whereas Goethe provides no motivation for the appearance of Thomas. In a sense Goethe's characters are more human in that they reveal the small inconsistencies of human nature. Yet although Scribe was never known for portraying strong, three-dimensional characters, the outlines of his two-dimensional people are much more distinct than are Goethe's. All, to be sure, are stereotypes: Bettly, the virtuous and independent maiden; Daniel, the rather timid but honorable (and rich) lover; Max, the brave soldier. Yet the traits of each are depicted with such clarity and consistency that they seem to live much more in reality than do Jery, Bätely, and Thomas. Here, it seems, the greater artifice leads to the greater truth.

A further strength in Scribe's libretto, at least from the point of view of the Parisian public, is its exposition of middle class morality. Regarding the matter of marriage Scribe is explicit. Daniel has written Max regarding his desire to marry Bettly because, as he explains, "it seemed to me that, when one loves honorably, it is first of all to the family that one ought to address himself." In his lettter Max replies with a practical view typical of Scribe's ideas on a proper marriage: "This [proposal] seems to me to be a good thing: he is of a good family, he is rich, he loves you to distraction. . . . He seems to be a bit of a fool. . . , but that, on the contrary, is no reason to refuse him!" Bettly's demand that Daniel not visit her chalet again also smacks of middle class morality, for her reasons have nothing to do with an aversion to Daniel but rather stem from her belief that his constant presence will cause gossip among the villagers and damage her reputation. In the end bourgeois philosophy triumphs. Bettly, so fiercely independent as to refuse a good marriage, is tamed through trickery and Scribe assures us that, despite the ruses involved, she will be happy.

Music is not an important part of Goethe's singspiel. In fact, except for three ensemble scenes—a trio when Bätely and her father discover what Thomas has done, a duo when Jery enters and begins to attack Thomas, and an extended musical scene at the end of the work for the four soloists and chorus—the music in *Jery und Bätely* is nondramatic and incidental.[53] Scribe, however, is adept at creating musical situations, and the music in *Le Chalet* is important, essential, and dramatic. The inclusion of a company of soldiers not only provides the means to disturb Bettly's chalet directly (the oxen in *Jery und Bätely* are only mentioned, not seen), but also provides the excuse for lusty soldiers' choruses of a type favored by Scribe and many of his musical collaborators. In a similar vein, the opening exposition gives rise to one of the popular choruses of villagers. Daniel's decision to join the army, while helping to soften Bettly's heart, also leads to the long duo in Scene xi and to Daniel's leave-taking *romance* in Scene xiv. The suspense built up in the final scenes demands the kind of slowing down of the action the music provides and gives rise to an extended ensemble in which the action unfolds to its inevitable conclusion. Thus, whereas Goethe's use of music is largely nondramatic and the music itself rather unimportant to the whole production, Scribe has provided ways to increase music's importance and dramatic function. In addition, the distribution of the musical numbers is more consistent in *Le Chalet* than in *Jery und Bätely*, with the larger numbers and dramatic ensembles occuring at well defined and regular intervals.

There are few dramatic ideas in *Le Chalet* that do not stem from *Jery und Bätely*. The characters are Goethe's and most events are to be found in the German source. Yet Scribe's superior sense of theatre and his remarkable sense of musical timing and necessity make of *Le Chalet* a far stronger libretto than that of the original singspiel, proving that even another libretto may well lack the essential qualities needed for adaptation to Scribe's musical stage.

Although it consists of a single act, *Le Chalet* uses all the techniques of the well-made libretto. Some of these have already been mentioned: the delayed-action plot and the careful preparation for each successive event. There is also the usual teeter-totter motion in the fortunes of the hero. Daniel is elated at Bettly's supposed acceptance of his proposal, disheartened when he learns that she did not write the letter, hopeful when he learns that Max is on his side, yet unhappy enough to want to join the army. The adventures taking place after Max's arrival are accompanied by a gradual rise in Daniel's fortunes, concluding in the usual happy ending. The *scène à faire* occurs near the end of Scene xvii when Max signs the marriage contract, thus revealing the truth about the opera's central misunderstanding (*quiproquo*): the fact that he is Bettly's brother. The repetition of the delayed-action pattern in miniature cannot occur, of course, since the work has only one act. Nevertheless, *Le Chalet* stands as a valid example of the well-made libretto and in dong so illustrates once more the consistency with which Scribe used his tried-and-true formulas. Goethe has influenced his choice of subject but not his dramatic technique.

**Words and Music: Scribe and Adam**

According to Adam, Scribe proposed the story of *Le Chalet* to him after the librettist had attended a performance of Adam's *Une Bonne fortune.* Mélesville was against entrusting Adam with the opera (the reasons for this opposition are unknown) but finally agreed to Scribe's choice when Adam consented to take less than the composer's usual share of the proceeds for the little work.[54] As usual, Scribe knew what he was doing, for the libretto is tailored to a composer of Adam's genial but modest talents. Adam's gift is for the composition of light, simple melodies with piquant rhythms and easily singable lines, whereas he does not excel in the realms of harmony and orchestration nor is he particularly skilled at writing long, dramatically complex ensembles. Moreover, his music, at first fresh and alive, tends toward a certain sameness which gives little satisfaction to even a casual listener after a certain point. For Adam, *Le Chalet* is the ideal work. It is a short, light drama using small forces in musical numbers that do not require the sustaining power, expressive style or musical technique of an Auber, yet are well situated within the work to give the best effect, the greatest variety, and the largest amount of dramatic mileage possible under the circumstances. The musical numbers are outlined below.

| Scene | Number | Type of piece |
|---|---|---|
| i-ii | 1a | Introduction. Includes choruses, recitative. |
| | 1b | Air: Daniel. ABA′B′ form. |
| | 1c | Similar to 1a. |
| iii | 2 | *Couplets*: Bettly. Two stanzas. |
| vi | 3 | [Recitative and] Air: Max. |
| viii | 4a | Duo with chorus: Max, Bettly, soldiers. Includes recitative/arioso, male choruses. |
| | 4b | *Couplets*: Max. Two stanzas. |
| | 4c | Duo with chorus: Max, Bettly, soldiers. |
| xi | 5 | Duo: Bettly, Daniel. |
| xiii | 6 | Duo: Max, Daniel. |
| xiv | 7 | *Romance*: Daniel. Two stanzas. Between stanzas, arioso for Bettly. Short duo at end. |

| | | |
|---|---|---|
| xvii | 8a | Trio: Bettly, Daniel, Max. |
| | Finale: | |
| xviii | 8b | Air, arioso, chorus: all principals, soldiers, villagers. |

The numbers are evenly distributed throughout the work, occuring every second or third scene. Solo numbers predominate, evenly divided among the principals and equally divided between simple strophic pieces and longer, more complex numbers. Ensembles of soloists, primarily duos, come next in frequency, followed by large-scale scenes involving one or two choruses. Of the latter, however, both Introduction and Finale are formally simple and can be divided into two distinct sections: a chorus and an air in No. 1, a trio and a chorus in No. 8. Neither is so complex as the larger ensembles or finales of, say, *Fra Diavolo.* As for the choruses, groups of villagers and military men were so common on the operatic stage that it must not have been a difficult matter for an experienced and observant composer like Adam to write a chorus for one or the other group.

Subject and musical numbers in *Le Chalet* are thus formed with Adam's style in mind. Yet he apparently had some difficulty getting started on the work, for he wrote:

> 'Come on!' I said to myself. 'try again. Leaf through things already composed that are not known in Paris; perhaps you will find something there.' My glance then fell on the manuscript of my ballet *Faust.* A dance of demons could be fitting for a *choeur d'orgie* [Scene vii]. I tried to adapt the music to the words, [but] they would not work. I wrote others and I composed these two infamous verses for which people have reproached Scribe so much:
>
> Du vin, du rhum, et puis du rac,
> Ca fait du bien à l'estomac.
>
> I found in my scene of *Ariane* fragments of my introduction. From that moment everything worked as if by magic. . . . The next day, thanks to the remembrance of some national airs I recalled from Switzerland, I wrote the introduction to the overture and the *couplets* 'Dans ce modeste et simple asile' [No. 2]. My imagination was fired by this and I no longer needed to look into my past, forgotten, or unknown works; and on the fifteenth day my score was finished and sent to the copyist.[55]

Adam's melodic style is one which relies on regular, balanced phrases; triadic outlines and scale passages within a relatively small range (an octave or less); consistent, often dotted rhythms; and frequent repetition of melodic figures or whole phrases. A good example is

Daniel's air in No. 1 (Example 17). The piece is made up of three main phrases which are repeated and slightly varied throughout the stanza. Within these phrases the rhythm 𝅘𝅥𝅯𝅘𝅥𝅮.𝅘𝅥𝅯 is most prominent and the melodic motion is primarily conjunct or centered around the main tones

**Example 17**

of an accompanying triad. Perhaps one would expect that a tune like that of No. 2, which Adam admits is not original, would show traits different from the composer's own style. However, most composers generally choose to adapt material that fits their own values and purposes, and this is the case with Adam as well. The refrain of the *couplets* in question (Example 18) is in a style like that of Daniel's air, with a few stock phrases or figures, emphasis on triadic outlines and conjunct melodic motion; rhythmic consistency (the figure ♫ ♪ or ♫ ♩ is very prominent); and a range of slightly over an octave (there are some higher notes, but the body of the melody falls within the f′-f″ octave, a meduim range for a soprano). Combined with the light orchestral work that normally accompanies such tunes, the result could well be tedious if listened to for any length of time. Fortunately, the musical numbers are interspersed with spoken dialogue and provide sufficient variety in forces and situations from one piece to the next that monotony is not so great a problem as it might be.

**Example 18**

By far the best solo number in the opera is Max's recitative and air "Chant de nos montagnes" which, according to one source, became "a classic air" for the bass voice.[56] Well written for the voice and dramatically successful, it nevertheless partakes of some of the more hackneyed devices of Adam's style: an over-abundance of triadic outlines and a dependence on certain specific, oft-used rhythmic figures (e.g., in Example 19, after the double bar). The whole scene is outlined below.

| Section | Content and style | Keys |
|---|---|---|
| 1 | Max, returning home after a long absence, stops to gaze at the scenery (recitative). | E♭ |
| 2 | He sings a patriotic air (*aabbccd* form, 6/8 meter, typical Adam melodic style). | E♭ |
| 3 | He hears a folklike melody sounding in the distance (orchestral melody with vocal arioso) and sings a sentimental song about his homeland (form: *aba'c* - recapitualtion of Section 2 - *ab*; some coloratura writing). | E♭<br>E♭, B♭, E♭ |

### Example 19

Example 19 (continued)

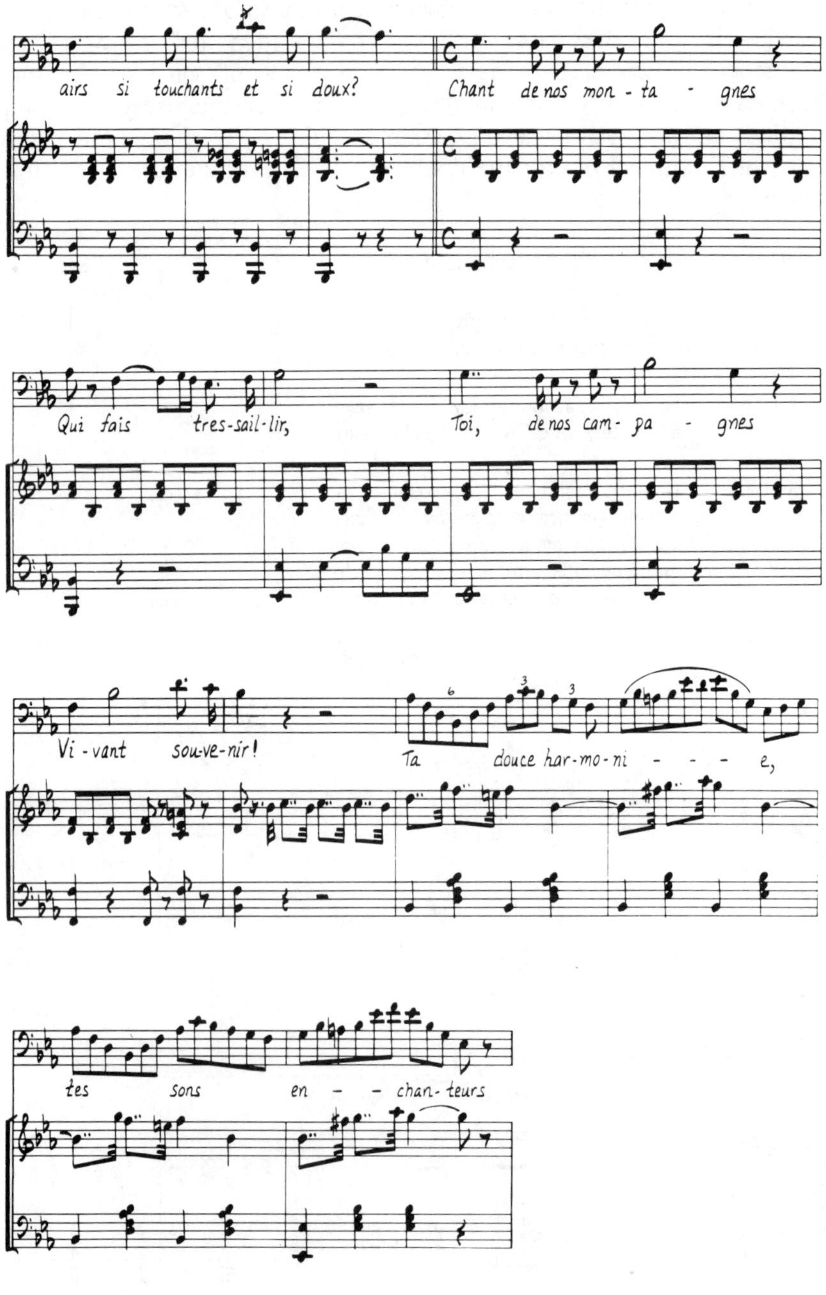
airs si touchants et si doux? Chant de nos mon - ta - gnes
Qui fais tres-sail-lir, Toi, de nos cam- pa - gnes
Vi - vant sou-ve-nir! Ta douce har-mo-ni - - - e,
tes sons en - - chan- teurs

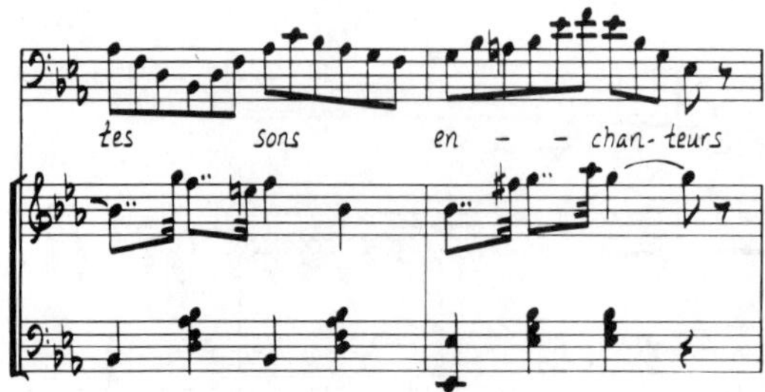

Section 3 and the first part of 4 are particularly well written (Example 19). Adam makes very effective use of the device of orchestral melody as Max hears the distant folk tune, which continues as a kind of obbligato to the singer's *fiorature* near the end of the example.[57] Although not particularly original, the folk tune nevertheless adds a colorful and thoroughly scenic touch to the aria.

Among the ensembles two are particularly worthy of attention: the Introduction and the Max-Daniel duo (No. 6). The structure of the introduction parallels that of the introductory scenes of *Le Maçon, La Prison d'Edimbourg,* and *La Dame blanche,* and in so doing points toward a pattern, perhaps even a convention, in keeping with Scribe's over-all *modus operandi.* After a chorus of villagers, various members of the chorus speak of the joke they have played on Daniel. The latter enters and expresses his happiness in an air (Example 17), after which the chorus leaves. Similarly, *Le Maçon* begins with a chorus of villagers, Baptiste and Mme. Bertrand identify the occasion for the revelry, and Roger sings his *ronde.* In *La Prison d'Edimbourg* the chorus of villagers has gathered after the harvest and sings as Jenny arrives to pay them for their labors. The latter and her sister Effie discuss in song their father's illness, and Jenny sings some *couplets* relating to the harvest festival. The inevitable villagers' chorus which begins *La Dame blanche* is interrupted by the arrival of Georges, who asks for food and drink and entertains the crowd with his well known air, "Ah, quel plaisir d'être soldat." The pattern of *Le Maçon*'s opening scene is thus repeated in other introductions. Since all works mentioned here were indeed successful, one might conclude that getting off to a good—and predictable—start contributed to the ease with which the operas were accepted by the audience. The fact that this convention is missing in two of Auber's worst failures, *La Barcarolle* and the one-act *Le Timide,* would tend to reinforce this claim, although the absence of this opening pattern in both *Fra Diavolo* and *Haydée* suggests also that a truly outstanding work had no need for scrupulous adherence to convention so long as the spirit of expectation prevailed.[58]

The duo "Il faut me céder ta maîtrese" (No. 6) is a fine piece of dramatic writing, suitably constructed to provide for the usual action-repose alternation in the Scribean ensemble, yet parceled out in such a way that Adam's talents are well served.

| Section | Subject | Style | Keys |
|---|---|---|---|
| 1 | Daniel refuses to step aside and allow Max to court Bettly; Max challenges Daniel to a duel, yet notices Daniel's fear as he accepts the challenge. | Air-like melodic phrases in dialogue, using Adam's usual vocal style. | B♭ |
| 2 | Reaction: Daniel is frightened; Max is amused by Daniel's feigned courage. | Duo with lines of contrasting character. A *duo bouffe* style of text setting. | B♭ |
| 3 | Daniel explains that love makes him brave. | Arioso dialogue; orchestra plays melodic material derived from Section 1. | B♭<br>d,C,F |
| 4 | Same as Section 2. | | B♭ |
| 5 | Max proposes a time and place for the duel. Daniel prays for courage. | Air-like melodies in dialogue, ending in cadenzas for both singers. | G♭ |
| 6 | Max and Daniel agree to meet at the appointed spot and Max prepares to leave. | Arioso dialogue under orchestral melody. | Sequence of diminished chords leading to V/B♭ |
| 7 | Duo: Daniel has renewed courage, which Max observes in Daniel's altered bearing. | Mainly parallel thirds. ABA form. | B♭ |

The amount of action involved here is small and each "action" section (1, 3, 5a, 6) presents no new developments but is merely a continuation of the previous action. Since Adam has no great gift for picturing contrasting moods nor for reflecting strong passions, this arrangement justifies his use of the melodic and rhythmic consistencies so prominent a part of his style. Material from the short orchestral introduction precedes Section 3 and music from the vocal lines at the beginning of the duo recurs in the orchestra immediately thereafter. Section 1 builds to a climax as the two men agree to a duel, at which point Adam introduces an octave-leap motive (Example 20a) which

**Example 20a**

recurs at the comparable climactic point in Section 3. Scribe now gives Adam the opportunity to do that for which he is best suited: to write solo melodies. The only major key change of the scene is effected, although for no particular dramatic reason, and both Max and Daniel sing brief airs in *G*♭ major. Fortunately for Adam, the soli are not long—Scribe undoubtedly knew that excessive length would destroy a situation only slightly dramatic in the first place—and inch the plot forward while at the same time providing a diversion from the quicker action of Sections 1 and 3. Returning to *B*♭, Adam closes the ensemble with a long, resolute duo (Example 20b). The action has neither been so intense as to trouble the composer nor the sections of repose so long as to trouble the listener. For this we must thank Eugène Scribe.

## Example 20b

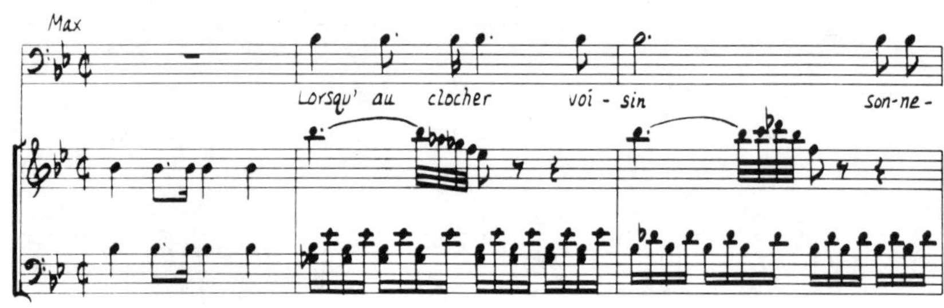
Max
Lorsqu' au clocher voi - sin sonne -

Daniel
J'i - rai, j'i -
ra la de - mi - - - - e je se - rai là!

rai! j'i - rai, j'i - rai!
Je se - rai là! Je t'at-

Example 20b (continued)

## Short Story Into Libretto: Auber's *Haydee*

Auber's *Haydée* was first performed on December 28, 1847, at the Opéra-Comique. An immediate success, it remained in the Paris repertoire until 1894 and received 499 performances during these years.[59] Longyear has observed:

> The plot is one of Scribe's most hastily written, but the music includes some of Auber's most dramatic and powerful work. Later writers have united in considering *Haydée*, along with *Fra Diavolo* and *Le Domino noir*, as Auber's three best compositions.[60]

The action of *Haydée* takes place in the sixteenth century: the first act in Dalmatia, the second on the sea, and the third in Venice. The opera opens with a festive scene in "a rich apartment in the palace of the governer of Zara in Dalmatia." The sailors and officers, among them Captain Malipieri, are preparing to indulge in an evening of gambling and drinking before departing for Venice the next morning. The admiral, Lorédan, is moody and, having some objections to carousing on the night before what promises to be an important battle, does not join them. Haydée, a captured Cypriot serving as a slave in Loredan's household, announces that Rafaëla, Lorédan's ward, wishes to speak to him, and Lorédan leaves. The rest of the company goes into another room to continue the revelry.

Left alone, Haydée and Domenico, a sailor in Lorédan's company, discuss their master, bringing out not only his major character traits but information about Haydée, Domenico, and Rafaëla. They break off their conversation as Malipieri, whom they consider an enemy, enters and sends Domenico for refreshments for the sailors. Alone with Haydée, Malipieri reveals his anger that Lorédan forced him to sell Haydée, even though he, Malipieri, had captured her in battle. He then tries to discover any secret information that Lorédan may have told Haydée, but is unsuccessful.

Andréa enters and asks to join Malipieri's company, but the latter rejects him. Haydée whispers that Andréa should return later and that she will see that he speaks to the admiral. Lorédan returns and asks Haydée to get him pen and paper. Malipieri asks Lorédan for his consent to marry Rafaëla, but Lorédan declares he has other plans for his ward. Haydée, entering in time to overhear this, agrees with Lorédan's decision, since Malipieri does not love Rafaëla and is also the admiral's enemy. Lorédan then reveals that he plans to marry Rafaëla himself, but that he has not told her of this yet. Rafaëla, coming onstage, responds favorably to the proposal until she sees Andréa at the door. On Haydée's recommendation, Lorédan admits the young man to the company and promises him the first ship he captures as a reward for his services. After Andréa leaves, Lorédan begins to write furiously as Haydée, Rafaëla, and Domenico look on and comment. After singing a *barcarolle* to lull Lorédan to sleep, Rafaëla and Haydée retire and Domenico goes off to join the sailors.

Malipieri enters, finds Lorédan asleep, and observes him reenact a scene from his youth. In the scene Lorédan has been gambling with a Venetian senator, Donato, and has lost nearly his entire fortune. By changing the dice to read six and four while the senator's back is turned, Lorédan wins back all his worldly goods and those of his adversary as well. Because of this loss the senator commits suicide. Out of remorse Lorédan has since adopted Donato's niece Rafaëla, who had been Donato's ward, and has searched unsuccessfully for the latter's long lost son. In his dream Lorédan also reveals that he has resolved to divide his own fortune between this son and Rafaëla and that he has written the whole story in a letter to be delivered to the son. Malipieri takes the letter and keeps it for later use.

As the second act begins Lorédan's company is celebrating a victory over the Turkish fleet. A single remaining vessel is sighted and taken. During this scene Lorédan reveals in asides that he was hoping to be killed in battle. The company proposes throwing dice for the prize of a barrel of rum. When Lorédan forbids this, Malipieri mentions the numbers six and four, and Lorédan becomes agitated. Rafaëla and Haydée enter, the latter expressing concern for Lorédan's safety, the former for Andréa's. Domenico reports that Andréa earlier set out in a small boat with about ten other sailors. After the company goes below to celebrate the victory, Rafaëla tells Haydée that she has recognized Andréa as her cousin and the childhood sweetheart with whom she is still in love. The company returns bearing the barrel of rum and Haydée entertains them with a sea song.

Domenico sights a Turkish ship with Andréa on board and the sailors run to investigate. Haydée comments that Andréa is now a worthy match for Rafaëla. Malipieri tries to claim Andréa's ship on the grounds that the sailors who assisted in its capture were from his company, but Lorédan awards the ship to Andréa as he promised earlier. Malipieri, left alone with Lorédan, threatens him: he knows the secret and has the letter as proof. However, this is not enough to convince Lorédan to go back on his word, and Malipieri vows revenge once they reach Venice. In the meantime Andréa reveals that he is of noble blood; that his father killed himself after a heavy gambling loss; that he,

Andréa, has spent the past years paying his father's debts and redeeming the family name; and that his last name is Donato. Lorédan gives the Turkish ship to Andréa before the assembled company just as Venice is sighted, and the act ends amid general rejoicing.

The third act takes place in Venice. As it opens Haydée reflects on her love for Lorédan, who really should be her enemy, since the Venetians conquered her people. Rafaëla enters, troubled because Lorédan has made arrangements to marry her that afternoon. Andréa informs them that Lorédan, presently reporting to the Venetian senate, has sent him on a secret mission. As Rafaëla goes to the window to watch after Andréa, Domenico tells Haydée that the former Doge has died and that another is to be chosen soon. Lorédan arrives in triumph with the senators and a large number of others, all of whom sing his praises for having defeated the Turks.

While awaiting Andréa's return, Lorédan reveals that Haydée is really a princess, that Cyprus is now a part of the Republic of Venice, and that Haydée is therefore a free citizen. Andréa arrives to tell Lorédan that Malipieri has refused the admiral's challenge to a duel because the Venetian law against it carries the death penalty. Instead, Malipieri has hopes of marrying Rafaëla. However, when Haydée reports that Rafaëla loves Andréa, Lorédan gives the couple his permission to marry and divides all his worldly goods between them.

Lorédan, alone, reflects on the past and resolves to leave Venice. Haydée enters and, after having told him of her love, vows to find out his secret and to save him. Malipieri arrives and threatens to tell everything to the senate unless he can marry Rafaëla, but Lorédan gives orders to prepare for Rafaëla's marriage to Andrea and challenges Malipieri to go to the senate. Having overheard all this, Haydee offers herself as Malipieri's bride in order to save Lorédan's honor. Malipieri accepts but, before he can marry the princess, Andréa kills him in a duel. In the meantime Lorédan has been elected Doge and uses his power to pardon Andréa. The opera ends in a chorus of general rejoicing.

Despite its dramatic shortcomings—or perhaps rather because of them—*Haydée* provides an excellent example of the craft of Eugène Scribe. As in the libretti discussed earlier, the first act provides all the background necessary to the opera in the usual manner of the delayed-action plot. Scribe starts slowly at first, but even the opening *couplets* with chorus establish the fact that the singers are a group of Venetian sailors who are fighting the Turks. In the conversation that follows, the characters of Malipieri and Lorédan are first given some definition: Malipieri, the lover of pleasure, and Lorédan, a more serious man who is particularly opposed to gambling. The motif of gambling and dice, along with the numbers six and four, are two of several which recur throughout the opera, giving the libretto some additional dramatic unity and serving to increase suspense as the audience puzzles over their meaning. Other such motifs are those of Lorédan's secret (the *quiproquo*) and Venice, held up throughout the work as the place where everything, whether of great or little importance, will come to a head.

Scene ii presents good examples of the contrived entrances and exits to be found in Scribe's libretti. Haydée has come to tell Lorédan that Rafaëla wishes to see him, yet later in the act (Scenes vi-vii), when Lorédan presents Rafaëla with his proposal of marriage, it is as if the two were meeting for the first time since the opera began. Also, no reason is given for Rafaëla's request. It simply provides the means to move Lorédan offstage so that some information about him can be filled in by other characters. Before he leaves, Lorédan prepares his return by making an appointment with Malipieri for later in the evening. The departure of the sailors has already been prepared by the discussion of a night of gambling. Thus the purposes of the second scene are purely mechanical: to move Haydée onstage, to move the rest of the cast offstage, and to provide a reason for Lorédan's return.

Haydée's entrance in Scene ii is preceded by a remark of Malipieri identifying her as "the Greek slave who belonged to us and who was taken from us," another example of Scribe's method of characterization by verbal identification. This method is also particularly well illustrated in Scene iii. In this scene Haydée and Domenico discuss themselves, their backgrounds, and various past and future events. Throughout the opera Domenico is a foil for other characters. He is the one who conveys necessary information, fills in details, makes announcements, serves as a sounding board. Although Scribe justifies his presence by manufacturing a love involvement between him and Haydée, this is never really developed and thus requires no wrapping up at the end of the work when all other conflicts are resolved.

The third scene contains descriptions of events which occurred as many as six years earlier and which are now coming to a head. Domenico is a source of information for the audience. From him we learn that Haydée was captured on Cyprus by Malipieri during a horrible massacre and that Lorédan exchanged for her all the booty he had gained. Other bits of information about Haydée's origins are added later to create an aura of suspense around her identity. Domenico also tells how Rafaëla became Lorédan's ward, and adds some tales of his master's youthful adventures. He says that he has seen Lorédan seem to roll dice and talk in his sleep, uttering the words "six and four" (the gambling motif elaborated). After having told how Haydée nursed Lorédan back to health, Domenico announces that he has an idea which he will reveal when they reach Venice (introduction of the Venice motif). In the first part of the speech three ideas come together very compactly: Haydée's present situation in life, Domenico's pride in Venice, and a suggestion of his love for Haydée.

> . . . Since that time [when you nursed Lorédan back to health], although you are only a poor Greek, a slave, I, Domenico, who have the honor of being a sailor and citizen of Venice, have conceived an esteem for you which has given me ideas, or rather a project about which I shall tell you. . . .[61]

Throughout the scene various statements are made which picture Lorédan as "glorious," "grand," "rich," "esteemed by the senate, adored by the people," a person who "will be Doge one day" (a prophecy to be fulfilled at the end of the opera), and there is more than one suggestion that Haydée is in love with him.

The third scene, then, provides major background information, principal motifs and motivation of the drama, and characterization (always verbal, explicit), all very compactly within the space of five short pages of spoken dialogue. From this point almost every new fact is a building block to be fit into place over this foundation. In Scene iv, for example, we learn that, when captured, Haydée was wearing diamonds, something which heightens the aura of mystery surrounding her, and that Lorédan has a secret which Malipieri would like to learn. This last has already been prepared for as early as the first scene, in the apparent lack of friendship between the two men, and elaborated upon in Domenico's tale of Lorédan's mysterious actions during a dream. Haydée's song also adds to what has come before, establishing Lorédan as a truly virtuous and noble man.[62]

In Scene v Scribe adds something new in the person of Andréa, yet leaves himself room to build by having Malipieri reject the young man. This makes a meeting between Lorédan and Andréa necessary and establishes animosity between Andréa and Malipieri. A third element, the definite prospect of Lorédan's return, has already been presented. Thus it is no surprise when Malipieri keeps his appointment with Lorédan (Scene vi) nor when Andréa returns and is accepted by the admiral (Scene ix). But the web is more complex than that, for besides these connections to later scenes, other events occur which in turn carry the drama further.

Before speaking to Malipieri, Lorédan sends Haydée for writing materials, preparation for the letter-writing in Scene x, which in turn creates suspense as to the letter's contents. Malipieri's request for the hand of Rafaëla reveals in passing that the captain has lost most of his fortune and has not received a desired promotion. These factors are essential to motivate his major actions later in the opera: his attempts to acquire the Turkish ship, his repeated attempt to gain Rafaëla for himself, and his acceptance of the rich princess Haydée as a prospective wife. In dealing with Malipieri's request, Lorédan first says that he has other plans for Rafaëla which he will make public in Venice, and later (Scene vii) tells Haydée that he has plans to marry his ward. In revealing his plan he has resolved one item of suspense only to provide the basis for another, for the fact that there is some connection between Rafaëla and Andréa is strongly suggested in Scenes ix and x. In addition, Lorédan's promise that Andréa shall have the first ship he captures is given in Scene ix, and Scene xi contains another reminder of Lorédan's seemingly overly severe attitude toward gambling.

**Domenico.**

> They are capable of staying there all night! They are drinking and gambling too. . . .

**Lorédan (brusquely).**

> Gambling! Tell them that we leave tomorrow and that it is time to get some rest. . . .

Here again Domenico's function is that of a foil, for his only reason for entering at this point is to give Lorédan an excuse to remind us of the gambling motif.

So far there have been many good illustrations of the pattern of action carried out via contrived entrances and exits, letters, conversations adding essential information for characterization and motivation, and the reiteration of a number of key motifs. In the final scene of Act I, Lorédan's dream, all these elements come together as Lorédan's fortunes descend for the first time and the action proper commences. Although this scene is the most dramatic point in the act and its effect is enhanced by musical setting throughout, nothing in it is really unexpected. Because of Malipieri's animosity toward Lorédan, we anticipate his desire to seek some means of revenge. Because of Domenico's account of Lorédan's strange dream, we are not surprised that the latter is again dreaming "out loud" and that the dream concerns gambling. The recurrent gambling motif is accompanied in this scene by that of Venice (Lorédan's song) and the explanation of the mysterious "six and four," while the nature of the previously written letter and the true reason for his adoption of Rafaëla are also revealed. In resolving several mysteries, however, Scribe has created a situation that is but one stone in the dramatic edifice, upon which subsequent action will rest.

Because the first act is so important as the exposition and foundation of the drama it has been discussed in detail. Although the second act contains a great deal more action *per se*, an extensive analysis would only yield further examples to support points already made in connection with Act I and with the general nature of the well-made libretto. A few comments, however, are in order.

The gambling motif, along with Lorédan's attitude toward gambling and the numbers six and four, is recalled immediately as a dispute over a barrel of rum gives Scribe the excuse to introduce it. (Indeed, even the barrel of rum returns in later scenes [Scenes iii and v], almost as if to justify its inclusion here.) The development of the character of Andréa is accomplished by means of his exploits and partial revelation of his identity by Rafaëla, who also makes explicit her love for the young Donato. Haydée's attempts to discover Lorédan's secret now have some further motivation when she learns of this love. The inimical relationship between Andréa and Malipieri, along with Lorédan's promise to Andréa from Act I, come together in the affair of the ship. In addition, the Venice motif recurs at various points: for example, in Domenico's report of his "project" to be accomplished in the city, to which Lorédan's reaction provides the first clue that he returns Haydée's love; or in Malipieri's threat to make public the truth about Lorédan once they reach Venice. This motif builds to a climax as the sailors sight the city at the end of Act II. Throughout the act Lorédan's fortunes continue to rise and fall, from the heights of a glorious victory to the low point that comes with Malipieri's revelation of his knowledge. By the end of Act II, as was the case at the end of Act I, certain items have been at least partially resolved, yet we are left with further expectations of the last act because of the preparation made here.

At the beginning of Act III Haydée sings, "I am in his palace, at Venice . . . his home!" This first line of the act not only sets the scene but also serves to put the audience on guard for the conclusion of all business connected with the Venice motif. Indeed, all the questions and mysteries of the story are resolved here, some more successfully than others, so that there are no loose ends remaining, no questions left unanswered and, above all, nothing that is in any way unexpected.

The first secret to be disclosed is that of Haydée's identity (Scene v), to which Scribe adds her automatically acquired Venetian citizenship. He thus erases any conflicts that could arise between her and Lorédan over the fact that her Venetian conquerors ought ordinarily to be considered her enemies. Next, the question of Rafaëla and Andréa is resolved (Scene vi) by Lorédan's giving them his blessing and his fortune. Haydée is then free to tell Lorédan of her love for him without causing a conflict between the latter's sense of duty to Rafaëla and his real love for Haydée.

Scene xii is the important *scene à faire.* Although Lorédan gains final victory over Malipieri only when the latter is killed, the hero's moral victory is certainly contained in this scene, particularly in Lorédan's final speech.

> And I do not hesitate! (To a valet who appears) Get everything ready for the marriage of Rafaëla, my ward, to Andréa Donato, to whom I leave all my fortune! (To Malipieri, who makes an angry gesture) You may go to the senate. (He exits by the door on the left.)

As frequently happens in Scribe's comedies, this *scene à faire* is followed by events which for a moment cause the hero's fortunes to decline more or less unexpectedly. Haydée's offer to marry Malipieri in exchange for the letter fulfills this function. In order to resolve this situation Andréa must kill the villain in a duel and, having broken the law, must be arrested. Not unexpectedly, however, Lorédan has become Doge and thus has the power to pardon Andréa.

The repetition of the over-all dramatic structure within the acts themselves in quite obvious. The first act begins in the midst of a feast held before the trip to Venice; the second opens near the end of an important battle fought on the way to Venice; and the third takes place after arrival in the city, before the activities there have taken place. Each act shows the careful preparation of each new event; the contrivance of entrances, exits, and even whole characters; and the ups and downs of the hero's fortunes. Yet each is merely one floor in the dramatic edifice, the roof of which is provided by the *scene à faire* and the final wrap-up scenes.

There is no doubt that the libretto contains some serious dramatic weaknesses, particularly when seen in light of Scribe's usually masterful technique. Some of the major flaws have already been mentioned: for example, Domenico's transparent *raison d'être.* There are also some examples of poor or inadequate motivation despite the general care taken in preparation of each situation or event. For example, Lorédan leads the joyous drinking chorus at the opening of the opera, yet later claims to be displeased by the carousing. Also, Lorédan's reason for writing the letter to Donato's son is never made clear. This action is particularly confusing since the admiral states that he does not know where the son is or whether he is even alive. The one reason given—that he wishes to give it to Rafaëla to keep for young Donato—can scarcely be reconciled with his intentions to marry the girl. Indeed, the only obvious excuse for the letter is to give Malipieri and the audience some explicit information, since the dream is only strongly suggestive, and to provide the villain with a product for barter. Other glaring weaknesses are the explanation of Rafaëla's love for Andréa (she was only twelve years old when they separated), the fact that Haydée never really does find out Lorédan's secret (although she nearly marries Malipieri to protect it), and the overly contrived *dénouement* (Malipieri's death). Yet these weaknesses actually point up the strength of a technique that works so well that the libretto survives and even succeeds in spite of them.

### The Adaptation

According to Soubies and Malherbe, the libretto of *Haydée* was adapted from a Russian *nouvelle* translated by Prosper Merimée.[63] Longyear goes further, stating that "Scribe obtained the central anecdote of the plot from one of Prosper Merimée's short stories, 'Six et quatre,' written in 1830."[64] Both, however, are mistaken. Merimée was indeed active in translations from the Russian of short stories by Pushkin, Turgeniev, Gogol, and others, and wrote critical essays on the lives and works of these authors. However, he did not begin to learn Russian until 1847 and began his first translations in 1848, one year after the premiere of Auber's *Haydée*.[65] Perhaps Soubies and Malherbe based their statement on a passing allusion to Byron's Haidee in Merimée's essay on Pushkin.[66]

Longyear's is a somewhat less serious error. Although Merimée never wrote a story entitled "Six et quatre," he did publish a tale on which portions of the plot of *Haydée* are based. It was "La Partie de trictrac," a short story which first appeared in the *Revue de Paris* in June 1830 and was reprinted in the 1833 collection *Mosaïque*. Although no written source exists for this story, one scholar has suggested that it may have been told Merimée by his cousin, a naval officer who visited Paris in 1828 and 1829.[67] Since Merimée also was acquainted with various Russian authors visiting or living in Paris at about this time, it is not impossible that some anecdote told him by one of them could have provided the basis for "La Partie de trictrac." However, there is no basis for designating the work a translation of any kind.

"La Partie de trictrac" is a tale within a tale, a story told by a ship's captain to members of his crew during a voyage. It concerns one

Lieutenant Roger, the illegitimate son of a rich father. The father's generous allowance becomes insufficient for his son's needs when the latter takes as his mistress a capricious French actress, Gabrielle. When a Dutch frigate docks at the harbor Roger, normally not a gambler, begins playing backgammon for very high stakes with a lieutenant and loses all the money he and Gabrielle have. When the Dutchman's attention wanders for a moment, Roger changes his dice to read six and four, thus winning that throw. This marks a change in Roger's fortunes and he continues to win throughout the evening. The next morning he learns that the Dutchman, despondent over his losses, has committed suicide. Gabrielle is ready to enjoy the money but soon discovers that Roger cheated to win it. Roger becomes increasingly depressed until he himself begins to think of suicide. One night, the captain relates,

> . . . seeing his light burning, I went in to borrow a book. I found him busy, writing. He did not disturb himself, and scarcely seemed to notice my presence in the room. . . . All at once I noticed a letter already sealed on his desk, addressed to myself. I immediately opened it. In it Roger announced to me his intention to put an end to himself, and gave me various instructions to carry out. While I read this, he went on writing the whole time without noticing me. He was bidding farewell to Gabrielle.[68]

When questioned, Roger relates the story of the Dutchman. The captain and Gabrielle stand by him, however, and dissuade him from killing himself. Soon thereafter Roger is assigned to a new ship which becomes engaged in battle with an English frigate. Roger is wounded. Before the captain can finish the tale, however, one of the members of his own crew spots a whale and the rest go off to investigate. Roger's fate remains unknown.

The tale of Lieutenant Roger provides Scribe with certain of the essentials in the plot of *Haydée*: the dice game that forms the central part of Lorédan's secret, and the letter-writing scene. Yet what of Haydée, Rafaëla, Andréa, Malipieri? What of the totally different conclusion given the story by Scribe? Where did he find these characters, these details?

In 1845 Alexandre Dumas published what was to become one of the most popular adventure novels of all time, *The Count of Monte Cristo*. Widely read and much acclaimed, it could not have escaped Scribe's notice. It was the kind of tale that would appeal to him, for the intrigues were complex yet carefully worked out, the suspense was ever present yet climaxes were carefully prepared and outcomes never unexpected. The characters were also to his taste: flat, two-dimensional figures with strongly outlined profiles who inhabited the world of the middle class and minor nobility and had about them a certain vitality and currency. More specifically, the novel contained the models from which Scribe drew his Haydée, his Rafaëla, his Andréa, his villainous Malipieri, even Lorédan himself. For Lorédan is not Lieutenant Roger grown older, but Monte Cristo himself—a benevolent Edmond Dantès engaged in settling his accounts with the world.

Dumas' Haidée is a Greek princess purchased by Monte Cristo as a slave after the girl's father was betrayed by a trusted French soldier. Once in Paris, Monte Cristo announces to her that she is free under French law, but she prefers to stay with him. She later recognizes in the Comte de Morcerf the former Fernand Mondego, the soldier who betrayed her father. When the latter's treachery is revealed to the Paris public, his son Albert challenges Monte Cristo to a duel, charging that the Count is responsible for having awakened the long forgotten or unknown past. The duel never takes place, and Fernand later commits suicide. Albert, feeling the shame of his father's disgrace, leaves Paris to make his own way in the world and to try to recapture honor for his name.

All these events and personae become a part of Scribe's *Haydée.* Like the original Haidée, Scribe's heroine is also a Greek slave who is sold to Lorédan (Monte Cristo) by a villainous soldier, Malipieri (Fernand). She also owes something to Byron's Haidee, for like the latter she nurses a man back to health, then falls in love with him. Once in Venice (Paris) Haydée is free and can reveal both her royal ancestry and her love for her master. Andréa (in this case Albert) has spent some years paying his father's debts and bringing respect to his dishonored family name. He finally kills Malipieri in a duel (a combination of the Albert-Monte Cristo duel and Fernand's suicide) and is pardoned for his offense.

Although Scribe's Andréa resembles Dumas' Albert de Morcerf in some respects, he is really more closely modeled on young Maximilian Morrel, the son of the employer of the youthful Edmond Dantès. Just as the latter rewards Maximilian by befriending him, saving the life of his beloved Valentine, and settling on him a large fortune, so too Lorédan sees merit in Andréa, son of the unfortunate Donato, and becomes his protector. Finding that the young man is indeed a Donato and is in love with Rafaëla, Lorédan allows the couple to marry and gives them his fortune. Then, just as Monte Cristo and Haidée set sail together to enjoy a presumably happy life, so Lorédan and Haydée are united with all promises of a bright future.

Malipieri is basically the opera's equivalent of Dumas' Fernand. Yet certain elements of his character are taken from other sources within the novel. His constant seeking for revenge is not unlike that of Monte Cristo, who appears in Paris for the sole purpose of punishing the three men—Fernand, Danglars, and Villefort—who caused his unjust imprisonment some twenty years earlier. In his desire to marry first Rafaëla, then Haydée, to avoid imminent financial ruin Malipieri resembles Danglars, who tries to arrange a marriage between his daughter Eugénie and the supposed Count Andrea Cavalcanti in order to gain the latter's fortune and thus offset a number of recent investment losses. Coincidentally, there is even some similarity between the fates of Danglars and Fernand and that of the elder Donato. Like Danglars, Donato faces financial ruin because of the villainy of another man (Monte Cristo, Lorédan) and solves his problem as does Fernand, by killing himself.

The problem of adapting earlier literary models for the musical stage can be viewed here from two angles: that of expanding a short story having few characters and a single theme; or that of contracting a complex and wide-ranging novel. Both problems undoubtedly contribute to *Haydée's* defects, for Scribe had to add enough of Dumas' material to flesh out Merimée's *nouvelle* and to make the dependence of Dumas' popular novel clear to the audience, a factor which probably contributed to the immediate success of the opera. Yet Scribe also had to retain and emphasize something as a focal point, and this was contributed by the tale of Lieutenant Roger. Hence the prominent position of the secret, the recurrent motifs, the strength of the dream scene, the use of a stock device—the letter—to build suspense. Yet it must be admitted that Scribe distracts from his main point with the introduction of a second *quiproquo* (Haydée's identity) and the various entanglements in which Andréa finds himself because of the librettist's need to do something about Malipieri and Rafaëla once they have served their purposes.

Scribe's craft is strong enough to carry him through this rough situation, but not without a few scars. These scars are the direct result of the literary sources he used and the haste with which he combined them. Nevertheless, Scribe's technique of adaptation from large-scale models is illustrated here and is carried out even more skillfully in *La Prison d'Edimbourg.* He does not take items in order, does not recreate a previously told tale. Rather, he invents a new work using extant material and weaving together action from here, a character from there, the traits of several personae from somewhere else, until he has created a piece which, although it shares common theme elements with its model or models, is totally different from them. The process is not so much analogous to Bach's organ transcriptions of Vivaldi's concerti as it is to Handel's use of themes from various earlier work in his *Israel in Egypt*. This process will be illustrated further in discussions of *La Prison d'Edimbourg* and *La Dame blanche*.

## Words and Music

Auber's score to *Haydée* is among his best achievements and is his last major successful effort in the field of opéra comique. The effect of long years of collaboration is nowhere illustrated so well as in this opera, for Scribe and Auber work together and complement each other perfectly. Drama and music progess equally: as the drama is heightened Auber works into more serious and well-wrought pieces of music, beginning with the dream scene in the finale of Act I. Yet the opera shows no stylistic changes from earlier offerings by Auber. The melodic style, harmonic adventurousness or lack of it, ensemble technique, handling of the orchestra, are all essentially the same as they have been throughout his mature years as a composer. In fact, *Haydée* shows a direct connection to its immediate predecessor in the list of Scribe-Auber collaborations, *La Barcarolle*, in that it is set in Italy and makes prominent use of *barcarolles* (Nos. 5 and 13) and other pieces in 6/8 meter (Nos. 1 and 3, parts of No. 6, Nos. 7, and 14), this time with more success than in the earlier work.

The musical numbers in *Haydée* are listed in the following table.

| Scene | Number | Type of piece; characters |
|---|---|---|
| | | ACT I |
| i | 1 | *Couplets.* Lorédan, Malipieri, chorus. Two stanzas with choral refrain. |
| ii | la | Recapitulation of choral refrain of No. 1. |
| iv | 2 | *Romance.* Haydée. Two stanzas. |
| vi | 3 | *Romance.* Malipieri. Two stanzas. |
| vi | 3 | *Romance.* Malipieri. Two stanzas. |
| vii-ix | 4 | Quartet. Lorédan, Rafaëla, Haydée, Andréa; includes accompanied recitative, arioso, ensembles, *couplets* for Andréa. |
| xii | 5 | *Barcarolle.* Haydée, Rafaëla. Two stanzas. |
| xiii | 6 | Finale. Lorédan, Malipieri; includes airs, accompanied recitative and arioso, duos. |

ACT II

| | | |
|---|---|---|
| i-ii | 7 | Introduction. Chorus, Domenico, Lorédan, Malipieri; includes choruses, airs, accompanied recitative and arioso, ensemble with chorus. |
| iv | 8 | Air. Rafaëla. |
| v | 9 | *Couplets.* Haydée. Two stanzas. |
| ix | 10 | Duo. Lorédan, Malipieri. |
| x-xi | 11 | Finale. Lorédan, Andréa, Haydée, Malipieri, Domenico, Rafaëla, chorus; includes air, accompanied recitative and arioso, choruses, ensembles. |

ACT III

| | | |
|---|---|---|
| i | 12 | [Recitative and] air. Haydée. |
| iii | 13 | *Barcarolle.* Andréa. Two stanzas. |
| v | 14 | Chorus with incidental solo for Lorédan. |

(NB: no break for dialogue between Nos. 15-17.)

| | | |
|---|---|---|
| vii | 15 | Accompanied recitative-arioso. Andréa, Haydée, Lorédan, Rafaëla. |
| viii | 16 | *Romance* with backstage chorus. Lorédan. Two stanzas. |
| ix | 17 | Duo. Haydée, Lorédan. |
| xii-xiv | 18 | Finale. All principals except Malipieri, chorus. Includes accompanied recitative and arioso, ensembles, choruses. |
| xv | 19 | Final chorus. |

As is evident in the table, the musical numbers are quite evenly distributed through the work, with the first act having slightly fewer because of the necessity for clear (i.e., spoken) exposition. There is something of a balance between the simple forms (*couplets, barcarolles, romances*) and the more complex forms (airs, ensemble scenes). In *Haydée* slightly more weight is given to the more sophisticated and colorful strophic forms of *barcarolle* and *romance* than to the simpler *couplets.* Among the major characters Haydée, Rafaëla, and Lorédan are assigned the more serious and musically complex airs, while Malipieri's role includes some lengthy monologues within longer ensembles which serve the same function as the airs (e.g., the opening of the Act I finale). Andréa alone has no air to sing, but is given *couplets* and a *barcarolle.*

Curiously, there is no real love duet in the opera, for No. 17 deals mainly with Haydée's attempts to learn Lorédan's secret, and Rafaëla and Andréa sing together only in larger ensembles. Also unusual, Scribe chooses to end the first act not with a large ensemble scene but with a duo. Fortunately the scene—the aforementioned dream sequence—is one of the strongest in the work, a dramatic *tour de force* for both composer and librettist which makes up in suspense and high dramatic tension for what it lacks in performing forces.

Another unusual feature of the opera is the comparative lack of variety in the ensembles. Besides duos (nos. 5, 6, 10, 17) and large-scale ensembles (Nos. 1, 7, 11, 14, 18, 19), there are only two quartets: No. 4 and No. 15, a relatively short scene of musical dialogue, not a fully organized musical number. This lack of variety in smaller ensembles is further emphasized by unusual reliance on the chorus. Although they serve primarily as "scenery," the groups of sailors, soldiers, senators, and citizens are often treated in an imaginative fashion. They engage in dialogue with solo characters, make announcements, and react to situations in which the various figures are involved. Thus their presence is somewhat more than a mere convenience or convention, though somewhat less than a clearly defined dramatic necessity.

All of the long ensembles in *Haydée* further the action in some way. Among the finest of these, and one which will serve as an illustration of various points applicable to other ensembles as well, is the scene between Lorédan and Malipieri at the end of Act I. Musically the scene is constructed as follows:

| Section | Action; musical style | Keys |
|---|---|---|
| 1 | Monologue for Malipieri: measured recitative and arioso followed by grand air. | A♭,g,G, |
| 2 | Lorédan: drinking song; between stanzas he recreates pieces of gambling scene in measured recitative-arioso (Example 21a; note the similarity to the gambling scene in Act I of *Robert le Diable*). | A, C |
| 3 | Malipieri: commentary in measured recitative-arioso on Lorédan's motions and expressions | A♭ |
| 4 | Lorédan: ending of gambling scene; varied recapitulation of drinking song with melody in orchestra and new harmonization (Example 21b) | B♭,E♭,A♭<br>D♭,C/A♭ |

| | | |
|---|---|---|
| 5 | Lorédan takes out letter; Malipieri seizes it and reads; measured recitative and speech | e,a, modulatory |
| 6 | Lorédan: recapitulation of drinking song, varied. | C |

Considering both the textual and musical length, the real action here is rather slight: Malipieri discovers Lorédan's secret and takes the letter for future use. The longest single sections are those most concerned with music rather than with action: Malipieri's monologue and the portions of Lorédan's part given over to the drinking song. As is usual in Scribe's ensembles, each major point of action is balanced by a point of dramatic repose. Dramatically, the scene is constructed as follows:

| **Section** | **Action** | **Function** |
|---|---|---|
| 1a | Malipieri enters and finds Lorédan asleep. | action |
| 1b | Malipieri's monologue (air). | repose |
| 1c | Malipieri thinks Lorédan is waking. | action |
| 2a | Lorédan sings drinking song. | repose |
| 2b | Lorédan begins to recreate gambling scene and to lose for the first time; Malipieri looks on, astonished. | action |
| | Repeat drinking song. | repose |
| 3 | Malipieri comments that Lorédan's attitude is changing | action |
| 4 | Lorédan recreates end of gambling scene, including his cheating and his remorse. | action |
| | Repeat drinking song, partial. | repose, but not complete |
| 5 | Lorédan tells of letter and produces it; | action |
| | Malipieri takes it and reads. | action |
| 6 | Repeat drinking song. | repose |

Textually the scene is constructed as a kind of crescendo in which the periods of action become longer and more intense, the periods of repose shorter and finally, before the climax of the scene, incomplete. In order to distinguish between the sections of different function, Scribe has given each its customary literary cast: poetry in regular stanzas with short, balanced lines for the sections of repose; poetry with longer lines made up of short phrases often separated by ellipses for the sections of action; and prose for the spoken lines.

## Example 21a

Lorédan
Ah que la nuit est belle, et quels ac-cents joy-eux, mon pa-
lais é - tin-cel - le ce soir de mil - le feux.
Loin de nous les pro-fa - nes; a- mis, ver-sez tou-jours. Je
bois à vos sul-ta - nes, je bois à vos a- mours. Je bois à vos sul-

Example 21a (continued)

**Example 21a (continued)**

This gradual intensification of the drama is reflected in Auber's setting by the ambiguous harmonization of the drinking song in its penultimate appearance. Here the orchestra is given the melody and Lorédan, a beaten man, sings in an arioso style (Example 21b). Whereas the high point in Lorédan's part is reached at the climax of the gambling scene, the high point in Malipieri's role does not occur until he has a tangible weapon, the letter, to hold over Lorédan. Since Auber has reached the musical climax of the scene in the resetting of the drinking song and can go no farther without detracting from it, Malipieri's victory must have a different sort of impact. Thus Malipieri's reading of the letter, the only prose in the scene, is spoken before the final statement of the drinking song helps bring the situation to a formal close.

The points of repose in the scene serve a calculated dramatic function even though they are not dramatic in themselves. In contrasting with each other (Malipieri's monologue *v.* the drinking song) they add the possibility for musical variety that goes beyond that of mere recitative and aria contrast. The very nature of these static moments serves a double purpose: that of providing room for the expansion of an idea

## Example 21b

Lorédan
Ah, pour lui six et trois
il me faudrait six et quatre.
Je perds!
ô
Plus lent
ciel! il ne re-gar-de pas il est à ramas-ser son or.
Ah, six et quatre!
Oui, je gagne! ô honte, j'ai ga-
Malipieri
Quel my - stè - - - - re!

**Example 21b (continued)**

(Malipieri's hate, the pleasures of Venice) before going on to the next; and that of giving the audience a dramatic resting point so that the action can be absorbed fully. More important, however, is the deliberately calculated placement of the points of repose within the scene. Malipieri's expression of hate has a more immediate effect when sung in the presence of his sleeping enemy than it would have were Malipieri alone on the stage. Similarly, the placement of the drinking song within the scene is calculated for maximum effect: first, to make the transition from Malipieri to Lorédan as the center of attention; second, to give a hopeful cast to the revelation of Lorédan's first loss; third, with new harmonization and mood, to break the gambling story after its climax, to reflect the mood it has produced, and to help make the transition from past to present and set off the information about the letter. The appearance of the song at the end of the scene has a calming effect, a gentle descent after the double climax.

A true dramatic function can be demonstrated for nearly all the solo numbers in *Haydée.* The opening *couplets* with chorus not only set the mood of the evening's festivities but also yield some information: that the singers are sailors and that they are fighting against the Turks. In this and other solo songs one of Auber's particular traits in text setting is illustrated. Auber at his best has a sharp sense of the delineation of a mood, a type of person or a situation; and his simple conjunct melodies, tuneful and well-balanced phrases, most often are highly appropriate. However, once having captured the atmosphere, Auber tends to overlook the smaller details of text setting, the proper accentuation of the words, or the emphasis placed on key words in a given phrase. In this opening song the refrain (Example 22), while tuneful and in the spirit of the occasion, shows little regard for proper accentuation. A similar quality is found in Haydée's *couplets* (Act I, iv; Example 23). Here, although text accents are not grossly transgressed, the emphasis placed on certain words and the passing over of others work against the music's expressive quality. For example, the words "la vertu, la gloire et l'honneur" are passed over very quickly and are placed at one of the weakest points in the phrase. Later in the song even the text accents are misplaced (Example 24). Thus, while the general meaning of the text phrase—"Sing always, sing gaily, but do not talk about it"—is conveyed in the music, no special attention is given to the individual words.

Example 22

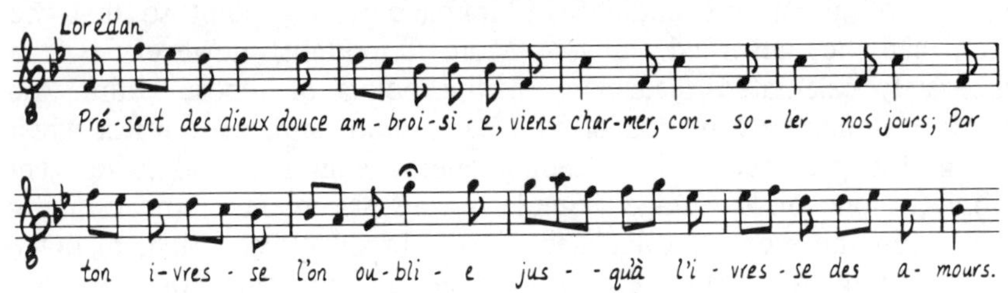


Example 23

Example 24

Both Auber and Scribe have a tendency to develop characters through the cumulative effect of single impressions or effects rather than by consistent, psychologically-oriented means. Because of this, few of the static solo numbers in the opera are without significance in some aspect of the drama. In her *couplets*, Haydée establishes herself as a major character, someone who is strong enough to act independently to overcome major obstacles. Her song has text showing her to be at once naive and clever. Set to a piquant, memorable melody and sung in reply to a character (Malipieri) who has already begun to show his villainy, her song establishes this impression of her at once. Similar claims and observations can be made for the dramatic functions of Andréa's *couplets* in Scene ix.

Malipieri's *romance* (Scene vi) has a slightly different purpose, that of expanding upon a lyrical moment: his proposal to marry Rafaëla. As such it seems on the borderline between solo numbers which help deepen drama and those which are music for its own sake. The *romance* is also one of Scribe's mistakes, for the apparent sincerity of the sentimental text blurs the outlines of Malipieri's character. However, it does give him a solo number in the opera, a necessity for both performer and audience. There are certain additional advantages to setting Malipieri's proposal to music, not the least of which is to center the audience's attention on Malipieri's aim to marry a rich woman, an aim which has important consequences in the last act.

The solo numbers in the first act, then, fall into four general categories: 1) those centering attention on an individual for purposes of characterization; 2) those contributing to the establishment of an over-all setting; 3) those expanding upon a lyrical moment but within the main stream of the action; 4) those which only provide muscial diversion. The solo numbers in the rest of the work also fit into these categories. That the musical situations found in *Haydée* are comparable to those in *Le Maçon* illustrates the consistency of opéra comique tradition for over twenty years during the central period of Scribe's creative life.

## Novel Into Libretto: Carafa's *La Prison D'Edimbourg*

Although Carafa, the composer of *La Prison d'Edimbourg*, was prolific and internationally known in his own day, his fame has all but disappeared in the nearly one hundred years since his death and his name is scarcely mentioned even by historians. This being the case, it would perhaps not be out of place to include a brief biography of him here.

Michel-Henry-François-Louis-Vincent-Paul Carafa de Colobrano was born in Milan on November 17 or 18, 1787, the second son of Giovanni, Prince of Colobrano and Duke of Alvito. Although he received musical training as a youth, studying with Fenaroli and Zingarelli at Naples[69] and Cherubini at Paris,[70] he spent the first years of his career as a successful military officer. As aide to Joachim Murat he fought in Calabria, Apulia, and even in Russia, where he distinguished himself in battle and received the cross of the Legion of Honor. After 1815 he returned to private life and was able to devote more time to composition.

Although he did not settle in Paris permanently until 1827, he returned to that city in 1818 and enjoyed increasing success there. During these years he was also engaged in writing Italian operas, which were performed at the best theatres in Italy: La Scala in Milan and San Carlo in Naples, for example. Evaluation of the success of these operas differs. While Borrel states that they were "successful even at a time when Rossini, Paër, and Mayr dominated all stages,"[71] Loewenberg says:

> Of these Italian works 'Gabriella di Vergy' (Naples, 1816) had some success; most of the others, although performed at the first Italian stages, . . . hardly ever lasted for more than one season; 'Abufar, ossia La famiglia araba,' which he wrote for Vienna in 1823, was also a failure.[72]

Clément's comments on Carafa hold a kind of middle ground. Carafa, he says, was a very talented composer who did not win as great success as his abilities merited primarily "because a fatal coincidence caused him to be born a contemporary of Rossini and of M. Auber, and because he had the occasional misfortune of setting the same subjects as these illustrious men, something which was to expose him to dangerous comparisons."[73]

Whatever the case, all three sources agree that Carafa enjoyed significant successes in France, citing *Le Solitaire* (1822), *Le Valet de Chambre* (1823), *Masaniello* (1827, considered his masterpiece), and *La Prison d'Edimbourg* (1833) as his most significant and popular works. Although he wrote about twenty Italian operas and seventeen French operas or opéras comiques, two in collaboration with other composers, only five are listed in Loewenberg's *Annals of Opera*. His other works include two ballets, Italian and French songs and duos, pieces for military band, and sacred choral works.

Carafa's French successes did not go unnoticed. In 1838 he was named director of the Gymnase Musical Militaire, a training school for directors of military music, and in 1840 he succeeded Lesueur as Professor of Composition at the Conservatoire. In 1847 he became an officer in the French Legion of Honor, and was also honored by membership in several foreign academies. He died in Paris on July 27, 1872.

Borrel gives the following evaluation of Carafa's position in operatic history.

> Carafa can be viewed as one of the best representatives of the Italian school of his time; he has its merits and its defects: melodies (almost always banal) and coloratura passages bring the singing voice into prominence, [while] little value is placed on harmonic or orchestral beauty [and] the libretti are laughable or insignificant. Even the above-mentioned operas, which had such success in Paris, are forgotten today.[74]

That Carafa was definitely a representative of the Italian school of his time is illustrated by a great deal of the music of *La Prison d'Edimbourg.* However, it cannot be denied that he also absorbed something of the character and the forms typical of the more serious opéra comique compositions of his time, and that the music in *La Prison d'Edimbourg* combines many features of both schools.[75]

**The Libretto**

*La Prison d'Edimbourg,* adapted by Scribe and Planard from Sir Walter Scott's novel *The Heart of Midlothian,* takes place in eighteenth century Scotland.[76] It is evening. As the first act opens the harvesters have finished their work and Jenny Jackins is settling accounts with them. Her sister Effie, apparently troubled by something, returns from a walk around the farm and Jenny tries to cheer her. After Effie leaves to attend to her sick father, Jenny is surprised by the appearance of Patrice, an alderman from Edinburgh, and informs him that Effie has returned home this very morning from that city in the company of the village miller. Suspicious, Patrice goes off to question the miller. Before Jenny has time to reflect on such strange happenings Sarah, the local madwoman, appears to beg for food. Jenny learns from Sarah that she and her mother, now dead, had been hiding an apparent pirate, George, with whom Sarah fell in love and who left with the pirates when the police came in search of him. Left alone on the stage, Sarah is attracted by the roses surrounding a small pavillion, then forces her way into the edifice when she hears someone coming.

Tom and George enter from different directions. Tom, a pirate, has been looking for George, but the latter declares that he has some business at the Jackins farm and asks Tom to act as a lookout in case the excise men from Edinburgh, whom George has seen on the road, approach looking for them. During this conversation Sarah is seen leaving the pavillion with an object under her cloak. After Tom leaves,

Effie comes out of the house, intending to go to the pavillion, and recognizes her lover George. He tells her that after the pirates helped him escape the police, he went to Edinburgh to try to find her and discovered that she had left, intending to go to her father's farm. Although he went to the farm at once, he has now waited for ten days for her to appear. Effie explains that she spent the time hiding in the mountains at the cabin of Sarah and her mother and that in this time she gave birth to a son of whom George is the father. She tells him that she has hidden the child in the pavillion.

Tom interrupts to announce that a search party is on its way. He also relates that he has overhead a courier tell the party of the arrival of English troops under the command of the Duke of Argyle, who has been sent to pacify Scotland. The Duke's name brings a strong reaction from George, after which he and Tom run off.

As it happens, however, the party is not coming for George, but for Effie. Patrice, at the head of the group, reveals that he has questioned the miller and has found that Effie did not arrive with him. This, in addition to other information he has, is enough for him to order Effie's arrest on a charge of infanticide. Effie runs to the pavillion to get the baby and thus disprove the charge, but finds that the child has disappeared. Patrice arrests her and takes her off to Edinburgh prison.

The second act takes place in a room of the royal palace at Edinburgh, where the Duke Of Argyle declares his intention of uniting his homeland in peace once again. Patrice has just come from putting down a prison revolt in which the jailer has been killed. The Duke asks him to find a replacement before the day is over, but Patrice is preoccupied with the case of a young man who was banished for his part in the civil war and who now requests pardon. The young man is George, the Duke's own son, who now enters and is reconciled with his father. After George leaves to exchange his pirate attire for more suitable clothing, the soldiers enter with Effie and Jenny. Jenny reminds the Duke that her father had once been wounded while saving the Duke's life, and asks that he intercede in Effie's behalf. Although angered to discover that George has wronged Effie, the Duke promises to do all he can for her. However, he forbids George to go before the court for fear that the revelation of his part in the affair might touch off a reaction among the people.

Meanwhile, the soldiers have arrested Tom and bring him into the room where George is waiting. George offers Tom the post of jailer in return for his silence, and the latter accepts. Sarah, who has been responsible for leading the soldiers to the pirates, is brought in time to observe the unhappy scene after the trial, at which Effie has been condemned to death. In the course of her disconnected rantings she makes references to an infant for whom she has been caring, but those involved with Effie and her fate pay little attention to these statements. Although the Duke believes in Effie's innocence, he has no powers in civil matters. Effie must go to prison.

Most of Act III takes place inside the prison. Tom has become jailer, but refuses to compromise himself by helping any of his former friends and fellow pirates to escape. Although he dislikes the task, he is charged with informing Effie that she is to be hanged within the hour, the execution to be held at night out of consideration for the family. Effie recognizes Tom as George's friend and asks him to allow Jenny to visit her. Before Tom admits Jenny he gives to her the task of informing Effie of the execution.

Jenny brings little hopeful news. Although George has been searching for the child during the three days' stay of execution which the Duke was able to obtain, he has found nothing. Tom returns, bringing Sarah into prison for stealing milk, straw, a basket, and a silk curtain. Thinking that Sarah's ravings will disturb Effie, Tom sends the sisters to another part of the jail. George then arrives and learns from Sarah that she knows something of the child. In order to get more information George embraces her and suggests that he is in love with her, but at that moment Effie and Jenny leave their cell and observe the scene. Effie, in despair, is led away, but George and Sarah are not aware that anyone has passed through the room. The cries of the crowd outside convince Sarah that the people are going to take the baby from her, and a fire set by the prisoners makes it possible for her to run off in search of the child.

The final scene takes place outside the jail. While the building burns in the background, Effie approaches the gallows. Suddenly the crowd sees Sarah on the prison roof. The madwoman withdraws the baby, asleep in the stolen basket, from a bell tower and lowers him on a rope. While the chorus reacts in surprise and terror, Effie joyously recovers her son and Sarah perishes in the flames.

Although the plot of *La Prison d'Edimbourg* has more than its share of absurdities, the libretto exhibits many qualities typical of the well-made drama. The first act is given over to exposition, including necessary background information and introduction of the opera's main characters. The delayed-action plot begins just after Effie's sudden homecoming, after she has become involved with George and has given birth to his son, but before the actions of her trial, sentence, and ultimate vindication have taken place. In the first scene the chorus, serving as vocal stage furniture, helps set the scene, indicating the prosperity of the farm and introducing Jenny as "the head of the household." Scene ii provides more information. We learn that Effie is secretly troubled, that she has returned after an absence of six months, and that her (and Jenny's) father is ill. His illness has no real significance in the action, but does add an additional touch of pathos to an already unhappy situation after Effie is arrested. The information also prepares for Jenny's appeal to the Duke of Argyle in Act II. The father's awakening at the end of this scene serves as a convenient way to move Effie off the stage and thus avoid a premature encounter with Patrice.

Jenny's dialogue with Patrice contains further background information. Most important for the immediate action are the details, or what Jenny believes to be the details, of Effie's arrival at the farm. The scene also contains references to crazy Sarah, whose madness has frequently caused her imprisonment, and to the fact that Jenny's father, now a farmer, was once an officer in the military. Information concerning the nature of the pavillion is also given: it had been built so that Effie, whose education was supervised by a noblewoman, could have a quiet place to study, and is thus her private sanctuary.

The fifth scene brings in one of Scribe's most interesting and strangely attractive characters, crazy Sarah. (Carafa's music is, of course, a distinctive and necessary contribution to her memorable quality.) So that the initial effect of her entrance will not be lost, Jenny identifies her at the end of the previous scene.

> Who is coming now? It is poor Sarah!
> Unfortunate one, O sad life!
> She sings in her madness.
> Her reason is gone, and love troubles her.

Knowing that it will be difficult for the audience to determine exactly what part of Sarah's raving to believe, Scribe takes the first opportunity to establish the fact that not all she says comes from her imagination, while at the same time preserving the picture of madness he has already drawn. This opportunity comes when Sarah interjects into her song comments about her mother's recent death which Jenny takes seriously. Immediately thereafter, however, Sarah insists that Jenny sing with her, and returns to her mad state. Later in the scene Scribe adds the following.

> Sarah.
>
> They say that I am crazy; but I know well that I am not. Goodbye, I am going away now.

Jenny.

And where will you go, poor girl, if your mother is dead?

Sarah.

My mother? Ah, yes. I carried her out yesterday evening. . . . But it does not make any difference; I am not alone in the world. The image of George is with me.

Jenny.

And who then is this George who has decided your fate?

Sarah.

No one knows him; but he told me when he was hiding in our cabin. . . . George left with our friends, with the pirates. . . . He embraced me! Since that time my reason, my heart, all my existence. . . . O Jenny, you will see if you fall in love some day.

When a man who has been a pirate appears, it is not surprising that his name chances to be George. Still later in the opera Scribe capitalizes on Sarah's love for George, first in the happiness she shows when Effie is found guilty, then in the use George makes of this love to discover the location of the baby. Thus, although Sarah's speeches are often disconnected and leap from one topic to another, Scribe has established from the beginning that when Sarah is speaking of definite people and events her information can be believed and is relevant to the drama. When Sarah, hearing Tom and George approach, forces her way into a pavillion we know is Effie's own retreat, and when she is seen leaving with something hidden under her cloak, we can assume that she will be involved in some mysterious event concerning Effie. The nature of that event, however, is made clear only when the main body of the action begins at the end of the first act.

Because the stage is empty after Sarah's exit, Tom and George must introduce themselves. In Tom's case, this is partially accomplished by means of a song, the text of which indicates that he is a seaman of some sort. Further details come out in the conversation with George: the hidden ship and the fear of excise men point to the profession of pirate. In addition, we learn that George has been away from the ship for some time and that he urgently wishes to see someone who lives in the Jackins farmhouse. Effie, the object of his search, comes out of the house almost at once—a good example of Scribe's contrived entrances—

and, after a duo, informs George that his son is hidden in the pavillion. The timing of this information is important, for it must come at a point near enough to Sarah's departure that the audience can make the connection between the child and the madwoman, yet before Effie's arrest, so that the latter scene is not overloaded with action and so that the discovery of the child's disappearance does not come as a great surprise to the audience.

The interruption between the revelation of the baby's hiding place and the arrest is provided by the contrivance of Tom's having left the stage to stand watch. Tom also serves to convey news of the arrival of the Duke, who otherwise would be unidentified at his first appearance in Act II. Act I, x-xi provide an excellent example of the dramatic craft employed by Scribe in turning out an orderly and easy-to-follow libretto.

The exposition over, Scribe begins the real action in the final scenes of Act I with Effie's arrest. In doing so he also resolves a few items which need not be carried further into the drama: Jenny is informed of the conditions surrounding her sister's return, and the audience's suspicion that Sarah has stolen Effie's child now becomes a stated reality. However, the central mysteries remain to be solved: Effie's situation, George's identity, and the location of the child. As before, the illness of Philippe Jackins is not a factor in the drama, but merely an element introduced to heighten the pathos of the situation.

The opening of the second act is also a delayed-action affair. The Duke, already arrived and settled, introduces himself and his purpose by means of a song. After introducing an expected addition to the cast and the item about the jailer, a contrivance which will become important later, Scribe again cleverly arranges the course of the action in a kind of "first things first" manner. So that the scenes between George and Effie and between George and Tom can be effective yet not overloaded, the first step is to establish George as the Duke's son and to arrange a reconciliation. In order to give the audience a more sympathetic understanding of George and the reasons for this estrangement from his father, Scribe gives additional important information: that George fought on the side opposite that of his father during a recent civil war, that he has been banished under an assumed name, and that he has spent the intervening time on the sea. The fact also comes out that the Duke has power to pardon "in matters of political revolts, but that is all; and I can do nothing with regard to the city franchises and the jurisdiction of the people." It is important that we know this from the beginning, lest we expect a magnanimous pardon for Effie as the solution to her problem.

The interview between the Jackins sisters and the Duke provides the means of telling the whole story of Effie's child, details which fit in logically with Sarah's tale in the first act.

> In the mountains, at the home of an old woman whom I did not know, I gave birth to my child; she hid me from all eyes; but the day before yesterday, in the morning, I heard moans. I came out of my retreat, and I found this woman on the ground, still holding a bottle of gin and dying in the most hideous convulsions. I put down my child, I ran through the countryside to look for help! But there was no one! A desert! I came back. Imagine my surprise: the dead woman had disappeared. I was afraid; I lost my head; I carried my child away! I passed the night looking throughout the area for my father's house. I arrived there: everyone was still asleep. I hid my child in a pavillion to which I had the key. I went away for a while. O misfortune! This child, my sole possession, I could not find; someone had stolen him from me!

We now have two items connecting Sarah with the missing child: that she has stolen it and that it was evidently born in her mother's cabin.

George, now identified as the Duke's son, appears and for the first time learns of Effie's arrest. Although the motivation behind the Duke's forbidding George to enter the courtroom is not too convincing, the fact that there is little if anything that George's appearance could do for Effie makes this an acceptable excuse. It is also a convenient one, for when the others depart for the court, George has the chance to talk privately with Tom before anyone else can learn of their association. Here the question of the new jailer is resolved, and Tom is placed in a position advantageous to the rest of the characters and to the story as well.

Sarah's appearance clears up another mystery, although its solution is not really surprising. Since we already know (Act I, ix) that Sarah's mother had given shelter to George, and since Sarah had spoken of someone named George with whom she was in love (Act I, v), all that remains is that these associations with the Duke's son become more clearly defined. Conveniently, anything Sarah says can be refuted on the grounds that she is insane, although the audience knows that she can be taken seriously. It is only when George discovers what the audience already knows about Sarah's ravings that the fortunes of hero and heroine begin to rise from their lowest point in the opera.

In Act I the final scenes marked both an end and a beginning: the exposition was over, and the forward motion of the plot had begun by means of a single decisive action, Effie's arrest. What happens at the end of the second act is analogous. The action begun by Effie's arrest has been concluded by her conviction, yet some decisive action—Sarah's references to the baby and her lulling him to sleep in imaginary gestures during the final ensemble—provides the basis for Act III and holds out the hope that the child is still alive and somehow will be found.

As one might expect, Tom meets some of his former associates in prison during his first day in his new post. That he chooses to remain neutral whatever their plans might be makes him a more effective foil for the action of the third act. He becomes a piece of human stage machinery functioning as giver of information and sympathetic friend to Effie. His neutral position makes it impossible for him to disclose information concerning the proposed burning of the prison. Since a prison revolt led to Tom's appointment as jailor, it is not really surprising that the prisoners are again planning some way to escape. The function of the opening scene of Act III is simply to make clear that such a second attempt is in the offing. The prisoners' plans already exist before Tom enters the scene, another illustration of the delayed-action technique used within each act.

Reference to the earlier prison revolt is also made in Scene ii when Tom tells Effie that he has searched out all avenues of escape from the prison and found them guarded by soldiers to prevent a second uprising. The single possibility, he says, involves a nearly impassable route over the rooftop. "Nevertheless, the mad woman from the mountain has set up her nest there," Tom observes, "there, under the big bell." Though the reference does not suggest that the child may be hidden in so unlikely a place as the bell tower, it does prepare for Sarah's appearance on the rooftops during the last scene and for the discovery that the baby is indeed hidden in the tower.

The idea of having Effie executed at night out of consideration for the family is again a clever contrivance, this time a scenic one. Surely the spectacle of the crowd with torches and that of the burning prison would be more effective in a nocturnal setting.

Sarah's entrance into the jail is accompanied by a number of not-so-veiled references to the missing child, built up in a crescendo fashion. First she is accused of stealing items which suggest the needs of a baby for food, clothing, and a bed. Sarah then tells of preparations in the church; since she denies the possibility of a wedding, the logical conclusion is that she has planned to have the baby baptized. Finally, Sarah's reactions to George's entrance leave little doubt that the child to be baptised is his and, therefore, Effie's. George's realization of conclusions the audience has long since reached leads to the most suspenseful and dramatic scene of the opera, that in which he attempts with near success to persuade Sarah to tell him where the child is hidden.

**Sarah.**

Where are you going? It is not that way. Come. Oh, you will see how handsome he is! I have made him a cradle with a basket and green curtains! And I shall call him George! And when his father returns I shall tell him: 'Look here, see how I have taken care of the little angel you sent to my mother's cabin.'

**George.**

What do I hear? In your mother's cabin! Really! Effie said . . . O God! What misfortunes are attached to shadow of a hope!

**Sarah.**

Silence! Speak softly! . . . if they take me away again! . . . Yes, yes! they stole him from me; but I found him again, I took back my child!

**George.**

Ah, take me to him! O, if only I could see him too! Sarah! Remember me! A flash of reason! I am George, a friend! Remember me, please!

**Sarah.**

Leave me alone! Leave me alone! You have an evil appearance! You want to fool me . . . you are George, you? With these beautiful clothes? Oh, what a difference! Leave me alone! Leave me alone!

. . . . . . . . . . . . . . . . . . . . . . . . . . . . . . . . .

I love him too much to mistake him;
You do not have his sweet appearance;
You do not have that voice so tender
That said: 'Sarah, do you love me?'

**George.**

Just for an instant hear me!
Remember those days so sweet

When your friend, in a tender voice,
Said to you: 'Sarah, do you love me?'

**Sarah.**

Ah!

**George.**

Do you love me?

**Sarah.**

I thought I heard him!

**George.**

Listen to me.

**Sarah.**

That tender voice.

**George.**

Look at me.

**Sarah.**

These sweet features!

**George.**

Ah, Sarah, Sarah, do you love me?

(Sarah utters a cry and falls into George's arms. At that moment Effie comes out of her cell with her sister and the soldiers. . . . The group exits quickly by the door at the left. George and Sarah see nothing of their passage and their departure. The duo continues.)

. . . . . . . . . . . . . . . . . . . . . . . . . . .

**George.**

And now?

**Sarah.**

Supreme happiness!

**George.**

Deign to hear me.

**Sarah.**

Ah, how much I love you!

**George.**

Listen to me, I beg you
Listen to me. It concerns my life.

**Sarah.**

What are you saying? Your life? And how?

**George.**

Tell me again about that child
To whom your faithfulness . . .

**Sarah.**

Be quiet! It is true . . . I remember . . .

**George.**

Yes?

**Sarah.**

Ah, do not trouble me . . .

**People.**

Make way, make way! [etc.]

. . . . . . . . . . . . . . . . . . . . . . . . . . . . . .

**George.**

What cries!

**Sarah.**

Do you hear them down there? The child! They want to snatch him from my arms.

**George.**

Her delirium returns!

**Sarah.**

They want to take him from me again. Look, hide him well and think of a way to protect him.

The announcement of the prison fire makes this unnecessary, for Sarah runs off to find the baby and to bring the opera to its melodramatic end.

The libretto of *La Prison d'Edimbourg* features many of the devices of the well-made libretto. A *quiproquo* is provided in the mystery of the child and his disappearance; the delayed-action plot and the construction of each act as a miniature of the over-all delayed-action idea also are used. In addition, *La Prison d'Edimbourg* shows a seesaw effect in the fortunes of the hero, along with the usual contrived entrances, exits, and logical ordering of scenes that normally accompany this effect. However, this libretto contains a kind of double seesaw, for the fortunes of the heroine, Effie, are just as important as those of George, and the high and low points in her story do not necessarily coincide with those in his. For example, George's reconciliation with his father is a high point for him but involves Effie only indirectly. On the other hand, Effie's conviction and sentence to death is a low point for both characters, but not in the same way: Effie is destined to remain in prison until her execution, whereas George is free and has hope of coming up with a solution. Structurally, a balance is effected between Acts II and III via the introduction of new characters in the opening scenes of both acts. The *scene à faire* is provided by the dialogue and duo between George and Sarah quoted above, and is capped by a brief but melodramatic recognition scene when the lost child is recovered. The careful structuring of the action, the patterns of entrances and exits, the use of a dramatic seesaw, the presence of a *quiproquo*, the delayed-action plot, and other less important details of style and structure all mark this work as belonging among the typical examples of Scribe's dramatic practice.

**Novel into Libretto**

There is no disputing that the art of the novelist is far different from that of the dramatist, even as that of the dramatist differs from that of the librettist. Whereas the novelist can work in as extended a time span as he chooses, introduce an unlimited number of characters—some of whom may be totally insignificant to the work as a whole—and shape his material into a narrative of any size taking place in any number of settings, the dramatist for either the spoken or the musical stage must limit his work to some extent in all these areas. The librettist is further limited in his choice of characters by the size of the company and the stage; and in his choice of situations to those which are most "musical," i.e., those which are capable of being sustained over as long a period of time as the musical setting may require. The librettist is further restricted by certain operatic conventions which may call for an opening chorus where a spoken drama would envision no such large group, or for an ensemble where the novelist would have each character go off by himself to think or act as he would in response to a given situation.

Scott's *The Heart of Midlothian* is an expansive novel. The action takes place over a total period of some thirty-five years, although the major part of the novel covers only half that time. The characters are legion, ranging from unimportant messengers and shopkeepers to half a dozen major characters and another half-dozen or more minor ones; and the settings cover the distance from the Scottish farm of David Deans to Edinburgh to London and back to Scotland once more. Yet there are in the tale a great many possibilities for musical situations. Needless to say, the story must of necessity be telescoped with respect to time, place, and characters. The ingenious way in which Scribe combines elements of different characters and different times into one is worthy of study.

The novel concerns the arrest of Effie Deans on a charge of infanticide and the efforts of her sister Jeanie to obtain a pardon. During the period with which the novel deals the law stated that if an unmarried mother told no one of her pregnancy and if no child could be found, she was automatically assumed to have murdered the baby and charges could be brought against her for this crime without absolute proof that such a crime had been committed. Such is the case with Effie Deans, whose child was stolen from her shortly after his birth, while Effie is delirious with fever. Although George, a black-sheep nobleman who later marries Effie, demands that Jeanie save her sister's life by testifying that Effie had told her of the pregnancy, Jeanie cannot bring herself to lie while under oath because of her strong Presbyterian upbringing. Without Jeanie's testimony, Effie is found guilty and sentenced to death. Jeanie, however, determines to go to London to seek a royal pardon for her sister from the King. By means of various chance happenings and general good fortune Jeanie travels to London and presents her case to the Duke of Argyle. Although the situation is far from hopeful, the Duke arranges a secret meeting for Jeanie with Queen Caroline, who in turn recommends Effie's pardon to the King.

In granting the pardon, the King stipulates that Effie should leave the country for some years. Effie, however, simply elopes with her lover and goes off to the Continent. In the meantime the Duke awards Jeanie's father, David Deans, the custody of one of his farms and Jeanie is married to her childhood sweetheart Reuben Butler, a Presbyterian minister. In the course of the years Effie, now Lady George Staunton, returns to England, educated, well dressed, and the toast of London Society. Disturbed over the fact that they can have no more children, the Stauntons begin a search for Effie's firstborn. They discover that the infant was stolen by the mad daughter of the woman with whom Effie was staying when he was born and that, having passed through the care of several guardians, the boy has joined a band of young thieves living in the area where Jeanie and her husband now live. While approaching Jeanie's house, George Staunton is set upon by this robber band and murdered. Although the youths are arrested, Effie's son escapes and is eventually sold into slavery in America, from whence he escapes with a band of Indians. Effie, as Lady Staunton, later rejoins London society and Jeanie lives, proverbially, happily ever after. In addition to this main story line there are several events of lesser importance which are not central to the plot and have therefore been omitted here.

If this brief summary of the novel is compared with that of the opera it will become apparent that, although the main reason for most of the action—the story of Effie—is the same in both novel and libretto, many of the details of the story are quite different in Scribe's version. Yet there is scarcely a personal characteristic or an event in the opera that does not have some basis in the novel. At the beginning of the opera two ideas are presented which do not occur until quite late in the novel. The Jackins' (Deans') farm, which was a reward for Jackins' having saved the Duke's life, is based on David Deans' management of the Duke of Argyle's farm and an incident involving a relative of Jeanie's fiancé Reuben Butler.

> 'Havena I heard you say, that your grandfather . . . did some gude langsyne to the forbear of this MacCallummore [the Duke of Argyle], when he was Lord of Lorn?' 'He did so,' said Butler, eagerly, 'and I can prove it.'[77]

The second idea, that of the differences in upbringing of the two sisters, is also a combination of elements. In the novel both are simple country girls, but Effie is prettier and more taken with what her father terms "secular pleasures," while Jeanie is simple, plain, and devout. Effie is sent as a housemaid to a middle class relative in Edinburgh, where she continues an involvement with one George Robinson, supposedly a thief and smuggler but actually the headstrong son of an English Lord. Only later, after she and George are married, does Effie acquire the education which, in the opera, she supposedly was given throughout her childhood. The visit to an Edinburgh relative, however, is preserved by Scribe as a dramatic convenience. Scribe makes Effie and George the central characters in the opera, eliminating any love interest for Jenny and greatly diminishing her importance, largely by reducing the outcome of Effie's predicament to the short scene with which the opera ends.

Although there is no exact equivalent in the novel to the opera's Patrice, there are persons who contribute various elements to his character. From Captain Porteous, head of the Edinburgh city guard who is hanged by a mob, Patrice takes a suggestion of his name and his position. From the incidental character of Mr. Middleburgh, a magistrate of Edinburgh who is responsible for bringing to Jeanie the summons to court, Scribe takes another element of Patrice's position and the visits he makes to the Jackins farm.

Sarah and her mother find equivalents in the novel's Meg Murdockson and her daughter, popularly known as Madge Wildfire. Meg has a hideout in the hills to which Effie comes to bear her child. Meg's house also serves as a hiding place and meeting hall for a group of thieves and pirates, among them George Robinson and one Thomas Tuck, from whom Scribe's Tom takes his name if not his character. In the novel Meg's daughter Madge also has an illegimate child which her mother takes from her and kills in order to protect Madge's reputation. This action causes Madge's madness and gives her reason to steal Effie's baby. Meg is finally convicted of various crimes involving thievery and is hung, after which the mob causes Madge's death. Whereas in the opera it is Sarah's evidence that causes Tom's arrest, in the novel the character called Tom is responsible for turning Meg over to the authorities. In creating Sarah and her mother Scribe combines many aspects of Scott's characters with new associations that keep their actions closely connected with those of the characters he has chosen for his libretto. Thus Sarah's mother, although she is never seen, serves as midwife for Effie and provides a hideout for Tom and George. No longer dramatically necessary, she dies of more or less natural causes.

Sarah herself has much in common with Scott's Madge Wildfire. Like Madge, Sarah has not completely lost touch with reality and is constantly singing. Some specific incidents involving Sarah also have their roots in Scott's story. Her begging for food is mentioned.

> These words recalled to Jeanie's recollection, that, in fact, she had been one morning much frightened by meeting a crazy young woman near her father's house at an early hour, and that, as she appeared to be harmless, her apprehension had changed into pity, and she had relieved the unhappy wanderer with some food, which she devoured with the haste of a famished person.[78]

Sarah's supposed love for George, which she says has been the cause of her madness, is nothing more than a reworking of the incidents involving Madge's child, here rewritten along more moral lines and associated with George rather than with the nobleman who was Madge's seducer. Sarah's song about a vain girl named Emmy who sees and admires her own reflection in the water (Act III) pictures a situation similar to that in which Madge finds herself during the time that she is unknowingly helping Jeanie to escape from Meg Murdockson's cabin.

> [Jeanie] sate herself down, therefore, at the foot of an oak, and by the assistance of a placid fountain, which had been dammed up for the use of the villagers, and which served her as a natural mirror, she began . . . to arrange her toilette in the open air. . . .
>
> . . . Madge Wildfire, who, among other indications of insanity, had a most overweening opinion of those charms to which, in fact, she had owed her misery, . . . no sooner beheld Jeanie begin to arrange her hair, place her bonnet in order, rub the dust from her shoes and clothes, adjust her neck-handkerchief and mittans [*sic*], and so forth, than with imitative zeal she began to bedizen and trick herself out with shreds and remnants of beggarly finery, which she took out of a little bundle, and which, when disposed around her person, made her appearance ten times more fantastic and apish than it had been before.[79]

Although Sarah's death in the prison fire is a product of Scribe's imagination, the prison fire itself is not. Early in Scott's novel a mob storms the Edinburgh jail to find Captain Porteous, whose sentence to hang for the unnecessary shooting of some spectators at an execution has been commuted. Finding the door too difficult to break through, the members of the mob decide to burn it down. In the course of subsequent action many of the prisoners escape, although the only part of the prison to be damaged is the door itself.

One prisoner who chooses not to escape is James Ratcliffe, the model for Scribe's Tom. Like Tom, Ratcliffe has been the head of a large network of thieves, smugglers, and pirates, and has been sentenced to death for his crimes. He is a clever, witty fellow with a blustery way with words, and his purpose in remaining in prison when he might have escaped is that he might be rewarded with the position of turnkey. To support his application Ratcliffe reasons just as Tom does in the opera's third act.

> 'But,' continued the magistrate, 'how do you think you can be trusted with a charge in the prison, when you have broken at your own hand half the jails in Scotland?'
>
> 'Wi' your honour's leave,' said Ratcliffe, 'if I kend sae weel how to wun out mysell, it's like I was be a' the better a hand to keep other folk in.'[80]
>
> Altrec.
>
> What the devil saved you?
>
> Tom.
>
> My merit, I have so much of it! They thought that in order to be a good jailer, in order to guard such skilled and tricky rascals, they needed someone who knew the game, and they gave me this honorable post.[81]

Like Tom, Ratcliffe also is in sympathy with Effie and tries to make her stay in jail as comfortable as possible; but unlike Tom, Ratcliffe has no further direct connection with George after Effie's trial until he almost recognizes in Lord George Staunton his old collaborator in crime. Thus Ratcliffe never learns the truth of George's noble birth.

Scott's George Staunton, alias George Robinson, is without doubt the most immoral character in the novel, with the possible exception of Meg Murdockson. Son of a titled lady and a respected military man turned Episcopal rector, George has all the characteristics of the willful, indulged black sheep of the family. The life of thievery and piracy he leads before his marriage to Effie, a life which involves the ruining of more than one young woman, is entered into by choice, not—as is the case with Scribe's George—out of the necessity to escape dangerous pursuers. Far from being reconciled with his father, George Staunton openly defies his parent even when the latter is most willing to forgive him, and is finally disowned after his elopement. Throughout his later life George Staunton remains a moody, generally unfriendly character who nevertheless treats his wife well, if a bit sternly. Although Scribe has created in Effie a character as close to moral "gray" as normally exists in his works, the original George Staunton is too much for him. Taking some ideas from Scott's character, under the necessity to simplify and reduce as much as possible the number of characters and their relationships to each other and to make of George a worthy hero (there being no equivalent of Reuben Butler in the opera to stand for the side of morality), Scribe creates a George who does indeed lead a pirate's life and who is also a noble son estranged from his father. However, this George enters a brief life of crime out of necessity, and proves the model of the dutiful son by humbly requesting his father's pardon and obeying the Duke's request to keep secret his temporary occupation and his revolutionary activities. Making of him the son of the Duke of Argyle—and disregarding the fact that the real Duke had only daughters—at once solves the problem of establishing George's noble blood and of eliminating a character, the elder Staunton, who is otherwise unnecessary to Scribe's story. Incidentally, Scribe does make use of the name of Robinson, George Staunton's alias, in a totally different connection in the following bit of banter between Tom and one of his prisoner friends.

**Altrec.**

> . . . Also, out of prudence, I sold myself [he is sentenced to hang] this morning to Doctor Robinson, the foremost surgeon in Edinburgh.

**Gilby.**

> Yes, the doctor bought him for one guinea. . . .

**Tom.**

> One guinea? You were never worth that much.

**Gilby.**

> Alive, perhaps, but afterwards. . . .

The novel also suggested to Scribe other incidents involving George. During the first act of the opera Tom acts as a lookout for George and later warns him of the approach of some officers. The model for this is provided in Scott's Chapter 14. George has asked Jeanie to meet him after nightfall at some deserted ruins, where he demands that she testify in her sister's favor. The officials, however, have been informed of the proposed meeting and charge Tom Ratcliffe with leading a search party. Tom, still loyal to his fellow thief, arranges to have Madge Wildfire guide the party, saying that she is the only one who can find her way to the appointed spot in the darkness. Knowing Madge's habit of singing at the least suggestion, Tom uses her loud performance of the song quoted below to warn George, who makes good his escape.

When the glede's in the blue cloud,
The lavrock lies still;
When the hound's in the green-wood,
The hind keeps the hill.

O sleep ye sound, Sir James, she said,
When ye suld rise and ride;
There's twenty men, wi' bow and blade,
Are seeking where ye hide.[82]

Although the means are rather different and the woman speaking to George in the novel is Jeanie, not Effie, there are definite parallels between the situation as it appears in the novel and the version in the libretto.

If the novel can be said to have a hero, it is the Reverend Reuben Butler. Since this character has been eliminated from the opera, it is not surprising that certain of his traits and actions turn up in George's role. For example, Butler's efforts to help Effie and to try to find the child or information about him are comparable to George's own efforts toward the same end.

Although the Duke of Argyle and Effie are similar in the opera to the analogous figures in the novel, little remains in the character of Jenny Jackins of the original figure of Jeanie Deans. Whereas in the novel she is the central figure and her heroic deeds the central action of the tale, Scribe reduces her role to that of the sympathetic older sister. We know little about her other than that she is a country girl and that she has been managing the prosperous Jackins farm during her father's illness. There is, however, one puzzling speech in the opera that is at least partly inspired by the sentiments of Jeanie Deans. In Act III, v, Jenny says:

> My sister! Take pity on the little strength that remains in me! I have had enough! Poor girl that I am, I must think of my father, must still live for him, so that he many find in me alone both my cares for him and yours! Ah, believe me, when such misfortunes strike a family, those who leave this life are not the ones to be mourned the most. Your son calls you to the rest of angels! In order to be near him, pray that God who chastens us yet grants grace to the penitent! Our separation is frightening, but it will not be a long one! Sadness will soon fill our unhappy days, and soon, I hope, we will meet again in a better world.

That this outburst should come from Jenny Jackins as Scribe has portrayed her up to this time is surprising, to say the least. Yet its roots do not lie in the character of Jenny at all, but in several speeches or situations involving Scott's Jeanie Deans. The scene between the two sisters which takes place in the prison before the trial suggests at times the condition under which a similar speech might have been uttered by Jeanie had she expanded upon her thoughts.

> 'O Effie,' said her elder sister, 'how could you conceal you situation from me? O woman, had I deserved this at your hand?—had ye spoke but ae word—sorry we might hae been, and shamed we might hae been, but this awfu' dispensation had never come ower us.'[83]
>
> 'I do believe,' said Jeanie, 'that ye are as innocent of sic a purpose as the new-born babe itsell.'
>
> 'I am glad ye do me that justice,' said Effie, haughtily; 'it's whiles the faut of very good folk like you, Jeanie, that they think a' the rest of the world are as bad as the warst temptations can make them.'
>
> 'I didna deserve this frae ye, Effie,' said her sister, sobbing, and feeling at once the injustice of the reproach, and compassion for the state of mind which dictated it.[84]

In addition, Jeanie makes numerous references to the family disgrace, particularly in connection with her intention to break off her engagement to Reuben Butler because of it. These and other similar passages also contain a grain of the sense and sentiment of Jenny's unexpected speech, but they are nearly all that remain of Jeanie Deans in Scribe's libretto.

Very little of major significance occurs in *La Prison d'Edimbourg* that is not found somewhere in Scott's *The Heart of Midlothian.*[85] Yet the libretto, while using some of the same techniques of contrivance and coincidence as the novel, as quite different from it not just in such obvious matters as time span and number of characters, but in emphasis as well. Scott, basing his tale on a supposedly true account, has neither intention nor need to whitewash any of his characters or situations. Rather, he presents a picture of eighteenth century life which contains all the types and stations of people one might expect given this society and period. Scribe, on the contrary, reveals in his selection of materials and manner of adaptation not just the exigencies of the operatic stage but the desire to entertain and edify, to appeal to a distinctly middle class audience on its own terms. Hence the lack of characterization in depth, pointed up particularly in Scribe's pictures of George and Effie, and the miraculous rewarding of innocence with absolution in the final scene. It is also apparent that while the libretto owes nearly all its action and characters to the novel, many elements have been spliced together or juxtaposed in a way that little short of free association can explain. The use made of the name Robinson is the furthest fetched example of this. The character of Effie is another, more extended instance, since in the novel she acquires the traits she is said to possess at the beginning of the opera at widely divergent times and places. More obviously, the person of Patrice combines position, character traits, and a name which are taken from diverse times, places, and people in the novel.

Although Scribe's usual dramatic techniques, the careful arrangement of scenes, the contrived entrances and exits, the use of superficial characterization by means of verbal references rather than actual deeds or psychologically based means, the complex yet logical action, and all the rest of his dramatic machinery are present in the libretto of *La Prison d'Edimbourg,* there are certain elements which are somewhat atypical for Scribe. First, there is the seriousness of the action itself. Despite the appellation "opéra comique," it would be impossible to consider such libretti as *La Dame blanche* and *Haydée* as comical works in the usual sense of the word. Yet there is about them a certain light-heartedness, a certain sense that even the characters most disturbed or in the most distressing circumstances will fare well in the end, that the function as entertainment is never lost. *La Prison d'Edimbourg,* on the contrary, recalls in its more melodramatic aspects the opéras comiques of the 1790s by Méhul, Cherubini and others. There is in this subject a certain immediacy to the situations with which its characters must contend and this gives the opera a problematical quality. Although there is something truly human—in the idealistic bourgeois sense—in such characters as Georges Brown, Anna, Lorédan, Haydée, and others, the spectator is nevertheless separated from them by the knowledge that he could never find himself in a similar situation. The combination of the real with the improbable creates distance between audience and players, allowing the former to move sympathetically with the latter and to be entertained at the same time.

The same is not true of *La Prison d'Edimbourg*. Tom, the only humorous character, is almost out of place stylistically even though he is necessary dramatically. Of course, a Frenchman of the 1830s would never expect to be troubled with the same situations, but the distance between his own actual experiences and those of some of the opera's characters is really not so great. Surely everyone knew—or knew of—a young girl in a situation similar to that of Effie, though the events be never so romantically woven in real life. It is precisely in this character and her story that the problems lie, for she, unlike any of the others, is in danger of becoming a "gray" character. Scribe generally works with absolutes: *the* soldier, *the* virtuous young maiden, *the* clever servant, *the* good-hearted thief, *the* noble lord. Effie, however, is a character who has trangressed bourgeois standards of morality by bearing a child out of wedlock, and yet must appear as the pure, guiltless heroine. Faced with this problem, Scribe has wisely emphasized the dilemma of proving her innocent of murder, while de-emphasizing the fact that the child is illegitimate. In fact, the only pointed reference he makes to the immorality of Effie's actions comes in a short speech by Effie to the Duke of Argyle.

> Milord, wrong neither my lover nor myself! And if God alone received our vows, are they less sacred and less solemn because of that?

This is clearly a modern approach to morality that Scribe, of all writers, did not care to advocate. Yet the problem is there nonetheless, and it is perhaps more than usually fitting that the libretto should have been set by an Italian, to whom the expression of actual, as opposed to merely verbalized, passion is more natural. It should be recalled that some of Auber's weakest musical numbers were his love duets.

In addition, the opera contains an element of anti-clericalism and an even stronger portion of pro-royalist sentiment. The anti-clericalism is very slight, to be sure, yet it is built up into a large-scale and effective satirical piece: the mock prayer of the thieves at the beginning of Act

III. The lyrical, Italianate melody and sustained, mock serious quality of this prayer emphasizes Scribe's satire against a spiritual institution (Example 25). The pro-royalist sentiment, however, runs like a red thread through the opera, becoming stronger particularly in the second act with the appearance of the Duke of Argyle. First, the Duke is portrayed as a benevolent, reasonable man, a good father, and a kindly ruler, one who wishes to keep the peace and who declares the breaking up of families a "dreadful effect of civil wars!" There are, however, more direct references to the advisability of a royal government as opposed to a democracy; for example:

**Tom.**

> No, and the three days [of Effie's stay of execution] have expired. And the cursed bourgeoisie who have condemned you are so jealous of their prerogatives! The Duke has no rights over their jurisdiction.[86]

**Example 25**

**Jenny.**

. . . the Duke of Argyle can only mourn with us. . . .

. . . . . . . . . . . . . . . . . . . . . . . . . . . . . . .

Yes, I was afraid in the square! The cries of the people! . . . They recognized me and followed me with their torches.[87]

It is difficult to escape the conclusion that Scribe's political views do more here than merely follow the suggestion given in Scott's novel that the Duke, pictured as the finest of men, was a ruler preferable to those in power, for in Scott's version of the story the objectionable governing body was that of the English royalty and Parliament, not the bourgeoisie of Edinburgh.

Another irregular feature of the libretto is corrections and additions. In settings by French composers—Auber, for example—the items included in the score have been, with few exceptions, those indicated in the libretto as it appears in the complete edition of Scribe's works. Minor corrections, omissions of a line or two, and infrequent additions are hardly worth mentioning. In the score of *La Prison d'Edimbourg* as it was published soon after the first performance, there are numerous and extensive additions to the musical portions of the opera, particularly to ensembles, which do not appear in the printed libretto. The longest of these occurs in the finale of the second act. Beginning near the end of Act II, xii, a relatively short ensemble is added in the middle of what appears originally as a song for Sarah. Later, a more extensive ensemble is included at the end of Scene xiv. Where the present edition in Scribe's complete works gives this ensemble as it appears in Example 26 below, the score gives the ensemble as in Example 27.

**Example 26**

**Tous, excepté Sarah.**

O sort fatal! arrêt terrible!
De la loi quelle est la rigueur!
Faut-il qu'elle soit inflexible
Pour la jeunesse et le malheur!

**Sarah**, dans son coin, comme si elle berçait un enfant.

Il me sourit! Il est sensible
A tous mes soins, à mon malheur!
Dors d'un sommeil doux et paisible,
Dors, mon enfant, dors sur mon coeur.

[Translaton: **All, except Sarah**.

O fatal fortune! terrible judgement!
What is the rigor of the law!
Must it be inflexible
For youth and misfortune!

**Sarah**, in her corner, as if she were lulling a child to sleep.

He smiles at me! He is aware
Of all my care, of my unhappiness!
Sleep with a sleep sweet and peaceful,
Sleep, my child, sleep on my heart.]

## Example 27

**Jenny**.

C'en est fait; le destin funeste
Sur nous épuise sa rigueur,
Et désormais il ne me reste
Que la honte et le déshonneur.

**George**.

C'en est fait; le destin funeste
Sur nous épuise sa rigueur,
Et désormais il ne me reste
Que remords et la douleur.

**Duc d'Argyle**.

O sort fatal, destin funeste!
Mais des lois tell est la rigueur.
Ah, je deplore, je l'atteste,
Et sa jeunesse et son malheur.

**Tom et le choeur**.

O sort fatal, destin funeste!
Des lois quelle est donc la rigueur.

Ah, je déplore, je l'atteste,
Et sa jeunesse et son malheur.

**Patrice.**

C'en est fait; le destin funeste
Sur nous épuise sa regueur.
Ah, je déplore, je l'atteste,
Et sa jeunesse et son malheur.

**Sarah.**

Sur mon sein voilà qu'il repose.
Berçons, berçons-le doucement,
Clos tes yeux, tes lèvres de rose;
Dors près de moi, mon bel enfant.

[Translation:

**Jenny.**

It is done; terrible destiny
Exhausts its rigor on us,
And henceforth there remains for me
Only shame and dishonor.

**George.**

It is done; terrible destiny
Exhausts its rigor on us,
And henceforth there remains for me
Only remorse and sadness.

**Duke of Argyle.**

O fatal fortune, terrible destiny!
But such is the rigor of the laws.
Ah, I lament, I swear,
Both her youth and her misfortune.

**Patrice.**

It is done; terrible destiny
Exhausts its rigor on us.
Ah, I lament, I swear,
Both her youth and her misfortune.

**Sarah.**

On my breast see how he is resting.
Let us lull him, lull him sweetly.

Close your eyes, your rosy lips;
Sleep near me, my lovely child.]

The same ensemble is repeated at the end of the act, with the addition of a part for Effie (given below, Example 28) and of some new lines for an extension of the ensemble in all parts (Example 29).

### Example 28

**Effie.**

Mon coeur de son destin funeste
N'a point mérité sa rigueur;
Et le ciel, qu'en mourant j'atteste,
Qui, bientôt deviendra mon vengeur.

[Translation:

**Effie.**

Of its terrible fate my heart
Has not deserved its rigor;
And heaven, which in dying I call to witness,
Yes, soon will become my avenger.]

### Example 29

**Duc d'Argyle.**

Oui, ma douleur, comme la sienne, est grande.
Je voudrais épargner son sang.
Hélas! ce que son coeur demande,
La justice me le defend.
Quittons, quittons ces lieux,
Et détournons nos yeux
De ce spectacle affreux.

**Jenny et George.**

Répondez à nos voeux.
Suspendez en ces lieux
Cet arrêt rigoreux.

**Tom et le choeur.**

C'est vraiment malheureux.
Oui, détournons nos yeux
De ce spectale affreux.

**Effie.**

Amis trop généreux,
Recevrez tous mes voeux
Et mes derniers adieux.

**Sarah.**

Que mon coeur est joyeux.
Pour moi quel jour heureux.
Oui, de mon coeur joyeux
Il comble tous les voeux.

[Translation:

**Duke of Argyle.**

Yes, my sadness, like hers, is great.
I would have wished to save her blood.
Alas! that which her heart asks
Justice forbids me do.
Let us leave, let us leave this place,
And turn our eyes away
From this fearful spectacle.

**Jenny and George.**

Respond to our prayers.
Suspend in this place
This fearful judgment.

**Tom and chorus.**

It is truly unfortunate.
Yes, let us turn our eyes away
From this fearful spectacle.

**Effie.**

Too noble friends,
You will receive all my prayers
And my last farewells.

**Sarah.**

How joyous my heart is.
For me what a happy day.
Yes, from my joyous heart
All prayers are fulfilled.]

In both cases cited the ensembles are worked out into lengthy pieces containing numerous textual and musical repetitions.

Although this example is the most extended of the interpolations, there are numerous shorter additions and recapitulations of sections of solo numbers or ensembles, all of which point up the comparatively large amount of music in this opera brought about by additional musical texts and the extension of numbers already in the libretto. The end result is quite different from that in the normally concise, well balanced works of Auber. The fact that Auber shares Scribe's essential sense of equilibrium between points of tension and those of release and that apparently Carafa does not points up the vital sympathy between composer and librettist that existed between Scribe and Auber, a sympathy essential to a continued successful partnership.

## Words and Music

The extent to which the comparatively extended additions to the printed libretto disturb any concept of a balance between music and drama in *La Prison d'Edimbourg* is a point which must be investigated. If some sort of balance is upset, the degree to which this is or is not detrimental to the success of the opera must also be determined. For if the extensions are detrimental, what then can account for the success apparently enjoyed by the opera? And if they are not, why not? At what point would they become disturbing? These are questions the answers to which provide valuable insight into Scribe's libretto technique.

The musical numbers in *La Prison d'Edimbourg* are the following.

| Scene | Number | Characters, type of music |
|---|---|---|
| | | ACT I |
| i-ii | 1 | Introduction. Jenny, Effie, chorus. Includes choruses, arioso, *couplets* for Jenny. |
| iv | 2a | Accompanied recitative: Jenny. |
| v | 2b | Duo: Sarah, Jenny. |
| vii | 3 | *Couplets*: Tom. Two stanzas. |
| ix | 4a | Accompanied recitative: George. |
| x | 4b | Duo: George, Effie. |
| xi-xiii | 5 | Finale: all principals except Duke. Includes recitative, arioso, ensembles, choruses. |

ACT II

Entr'acte: instrumental. March.

| | | |
|---|---|---|
| i | 6 | Chorus and air: Duke of Argyle, people. |
| iii | 7 | Trio: Duke, George, Patrice. |
| v | 8 | *Romance*: Effie. Two stanzas. |
| xi | 9 | Duo: George, Tom. |
| xii-xv | 10 | Finale: all principals, soldiers, villagers. Includes recitative, arioso, air, ensemble, chorus. |

ACT III

Entr'acte: instrumental.

| | | |
|---|---|---|
| i | 11 | Chorus of thieves; includes incidental soli for Gilby. |
| ii | 12 | *Couplets*: Tom. Two stanzas with choral refrains. |
| v | 13 | *Romance*: one stanza each for Jenny and Effie, respectively. |
| vii | 14 | [Recitative and] *Rondeau*: Sarah. |
| viii-xi | 15 | Finale: all principals, soldiers, villagers. Includes recitative, arioso, air, ensemble, choruses. |

One particularly notable difference between *La Prison d'Edimbourg* and most other operas discussed thus far is the comparative lack of variety in the musical numbers, particularly those for single soloists. There are no airs in the opera and the only nonstrophic solo number, Sarah's *rondeau* (No. 14), is in a form closely related to strophic. However, there is no lack of solo singing, for the opening scenes of Acts II and III involve solo-chorus combinations, and many ensembles include outstanding sections of solo vocalism for one or more characters: for example, the formula-ridden coloratura lines for Sarah in the finale to Act II (Example 30). Moreover, there is in Carafa's score somewhat

**Example 30**

Example 30 (continued)

more recitative and/or arioso than is usual for an opéra comique of, say, Auber or Boieldieu, probably due to his Italian training and composition experience. Each major character has at least one solo number, but those given more than one are not the hero and heroine but rather the more colorful figures of Tom and Sarah. Indeed, the latter has the most prominent role in the opera, since she is mad, since she provides the key to the resolution of nearly every mystery in the plot, and since her part contains by far the showiest and most taxing vocalism in the score. Thus the opera lacks balance from a musical standpoint, in that ensembles far outweigh solo numbers and in that the supposed principal characters are outshone by supporting figures. However, it must be noted that the balance is swung in favor of those elements most deliberately calculated for success: colorful roles, coloratura singing, and ensemble scenes (lusty soli with chorus or ensembles emphasizing a small number of solo voices) which feature fine singing against the best possible scenic background.

The balance between action and repose in Scribe's ensemble scenes has already been discussed. Since it is in the ensemble scenes that the longest and most consistent textual additions occur, they are the best scenes in which to study the effects of extension. The first act, containing examples of various types of additions, will serve as a point of departure for conclusions reached on the basis of the work as a whole.

The first ensemble having lengthy additions is that between George and Effie (No. 4b). As it stands in the printed libretto the scene is organized as follows:

| | | |
|---|---|---|
| 1. | Effie enters; George recognizes her; they are happy to be reunited. | Action |
| 2. | Duo: "All the sorrows of absence are forgotten in this day." | Repose |

To this has been added:

| | | |
|---|---|---|
| 3. | Musical dialogue dealing with George's adventures. | Action |
| 4. | Recapitulation of duo (Section 2). | Repose |

Clearly, although the amount of music *per se* is necessarily increased because of the added text, the balance between action and repose in the ensemble has not been disturbed. In fact, the information provided in the additional dialogue improves the libretto, for it gives further details about George's exile and his penitence, thus providing clearer and stronger motivation for his reconciliation with his father.

The additions to the ensemble of Scene xi seem at first glance to be dramatically illogical. Tom having arrived with news of the approaching officers, the need for a hasty departure is not served by adding text. However, the audience has had to take in and sort out a great deal of information: the imminent arrival of the search party, the announcement of the Duke of Argyle's landing, and George's unexpectedly strong reaction to this news. It could be that while dramatic logic is not served by extending the ensemble, lengthening of this static moment does allow the mind to catch up.

Additions to the final scenes of Act I are most extensive, yet they serve in some cases to enhance the balance between action and repose rather than to destroy it. Scenes xii and xiii form a musical unit, with no break between them. In Scene xii Patrice and the soldiers arrive, to the consternation of the villagers, and arrest Effie. Immediately thereafter, in the printed libretto, Jenny enters and the musical dialogue continues. In the score, however, an ensemble with chorus is inserted between Effie's arrest and Jenny's entrance, the chorus a varied version of that which opened the scene. In view of Scribe's usual technique, this ensemble is well placed, for it gives time to react to the all-important event that has just occurred. However, after Jenny has uttered but four lines, and not particularly important lines at that, Carafa repeats the same ensemble, adding a part for Jenny. Although this could be viewed as a dramatic delaying tactic calculated to increase the suspense of the situation, there is little reason for it at this point. The only justification for Jenny's having entered at all is to save some other character the trouble of informing her of the circumstances of her sister's arrest and the charges involved. The rest of the action could have taken place just as well without her. Thus, although the introduction of the ensemble is dramatically justifiable, its repetition some four lines later is not and, in fact, detracts from the balance Scribe generally writes into such scenes.

The next addition of text is that to the dialogue in Scene xii. Here the interpolated lines add to the dramatic effect by keeping up the suspense to the point at which Patrice's accusation is made, thus allowing the spectator more time to take this all in. They also have the effect of shifting the emphasis of the scene to Jenny's point of view: a spectator who truly does not know what is happening. The members of the audience are in a sense in the same position as Jenny, although the events are not nearly so unexpected to them as to her. Thus she serves partly as a guide for or personification of the audience in her reactions to events, and the slowing down of the action via additional dialogue helps in defining her—hence the audience's—reactions.

Although the scene has been made quite long already, the enlargement of the closing ensemble with chorus is nevertheless a good move dramatically. A great deal has taken place in this scene and there is a definite need for a musical anchor before the curtain. Originally Scribe provided but two lines of text for the closing number, but he was reckoning without the addition of an extended ensemble at the beginning of the scene. It is essential that the closing ensemble not be anticlimactic. The composer, of course, could have repeated the two short lines as often as necessary, but surely his task would be easier were he provided with additional text. In practice, the shorter text was completely replaced by a new four-line stanza for each character or group of characters. This provides a much better picture of the reactions involved. However, it must be admitted that the composer, who has already overplayed his part, goes completely beyond bounds at this point. After the first statement of the ensemble Jenny reminds the soldiers that her father is not well and they, in another stanza added to the printed text, promise to leave promptly—but not without repeating the previous ensemble in varied form. The weight is too much even for so momentous a scene, but this is not so much due to the addition of text *per se* as to the uses to which the composer has put this text.

Judging by comments made in nineteenth century French opera criticism, the French audience valued the libretto as much as the music in an opera and demanded that both be of high quality within their own spheres. This being the case, one could assume an equal interest in both story and music. In works in which one overbalances the other to an excessive degree the result is unsuccessful. Furthermore, when some progress occurs in the drama, then a balancing section of repose can take on dimensions proportionate to the amount of action and the time desired to allow the audience to digest information and to react to it. The problem is to decide when the limits have been reached.

Carafa's background as a composer of Italian operas and his significance as a typical representative of that school account for a great deal with respect to *La Prison d'Edimbourg.* All the cliches of Italian melodic style occur in profusion. Particularly good examples can be found in the coloratura role of Sarah and the lyrical melody of the *romance* in Act II (Example 31a), which reminded at least one writer of Rossini's famous "Di tanti palpiti" from *Tancredi* (Example 31b).[88] Undoubtedly this experience in Italian opera makes Carafa want the music to reign supreme even in a genre in which most of the lines in the libretto are spoken. Hence the extended ensembles, which both enhance and detract from the work as a whole depending on their placement and length.

**Example 31a**

**Example 31b**

Yet this opera was one of Carafa's greater successes, and it is worthwhile to consider why the weight of the music at several key points did not ruin the work. Although Rossini's popularity was undoubtedly still great, this master had ceased composing operas some four years earlier, and it is safe to assume that "Rossini fever," having reached its peak, was now declining somewhat. Thus, although the Rossini vogue might account for some of Carafa's success, it surely cannot claim all the credit.

For the answer to this question one must turn to Scribe's libretto. Italianate though the music might be, the libretto itself is a fine example of Scribe's French handiwork. The action proceeds in logical steps, the story is complex but easily followed, and the key scenes are so arranged as to sustain interest from beginning to end. If Scribe can be said to have a dramatic canvas, it is surely permanent-press canvas. It can be bent, folded, spindled, stapled, even mildly mutilated, yet the fabric itself has such resiliency that it comes through the process fresh and undamaged. There are points in the opera, such as the first act finale, in which potential dangers present themselves because of the composer's lack of sensitivity to the opéra comique genre and/or to Scribe's dramatic logic. Yet the action is so structured that even such temporary cross purposes of composer and librettist need not spell doom for the opera. Whether repeated problems of this sort would have killed the work is a question that cannot be answered at present, for one would then have to take into consideration the skill of the performers and stage designers as well as the tastes and temperament of the times.

In subject matter, setting, and details of characterization Scribe's *La Prison d'Edimbourg* relies on Scott's novel, yet his craft and technique remain consistent and in force as if unaffected by the model from which the libretto is drawn. The sources for all the operatic adaptations discussed up to this point have been relatively short literary works: a vaudeville, a libretto, a short story with sections of a novel added. In its greater expansiveness *The Heart of Midlothian* surely provided greater problems to its adaptors. Yet perhaps the clue to the success with which this adaptation has been accomplished lies in the novel itself. Viewed as a group, the novels Scribe chose to use in the libretti under discussion —*The Heart of Midlothian, The Monastery, The Abbot, Guy Mannering,* and *The Count of Monte Cristo*—have one major characteristic in common: they are technically similar, within their own genre, to Scribe's plays and libretti. All rely a great deal, sometimes even to excess, on careful preparation of suspenseful events, on contrived entrances and departures of key characters, on coincidence, on tying the loose ends of the narrative up as neatly as possible by the end of the tale. In short, all might conceivably be termed "well-made novels." Whether consciously or subconsciously Scribe, no mean judge of dramatic material, must have been aware of this, must somehow have felt that he surely could make these novels work on the stage of the Opéra-Comique. He was not mistaken.

## Several Novels Into Libretto: Boieldieu's *La Dame Blanche*

On December 16, 1862, at the thousandth performance of *La Dame blanche*, the following verses were recited during one of the *entr'actes.*

> C'est que Scribe a donné tout ce que le poète
> Peut inventer de mieux pour la lyre interprète;
> Et le maître inspiré prodigua tout à tour
> Le charme que les mots n'ont jamais su decrire,
> L'accent qui fait rêver, l'accent qui fait sourire,
> La gaîté de l'esprit, l'extase de l'amour.[89]

The credit which Scribe reaps here is not the result of his having produced a great lyrical masterpiece himself, but of his providing the dramatic scaffolding upon which the interpreter, Boieldieu, could create a variety of moods, "the charm which words have never known how to express." This landmark in the history of opéra comique, a model for what Longyear terms its "classical phase,"[90] enjoyed 300 consecutive performances, of which nearly 150 had taken place during the first year of its history.[91] Boieldieu's masterpiece remained constantly in the repertoire for nearly a century,[92] and its popularity was not confined to France. A glance at the listing in Loewenberg demonstrates its worldwide favor and particularly its popularity in Germany.[93]

The scene opens at a Scottish farmhouse in the year 1759. Peasants are celebrating the projected baptism of the infant son of Dickson and Jenny when Dickson enters to inform them that the sheriff, who was to be the child's godfather, has taken ill. The discussion ends with the arrival of Georges Brown, a sublieutenant from the British army, who comes to the village to seek food and shelter. He sings of the pleasures of being a soldier and impresses Jenny as the ideal replacement for the sheriff as her baby's godfather. Georges accepts the honor and Jenny runs off to find the minister. While waiting for Jenny's return Georges tells Dickson a bit about himself. He remembers little of his childhood, although he has faint memories of servants, a girl with whom he was brought up, and an old woman who sang Scottish songs to him.

He was taken away by one Duncan, who sold him into naval service. After having escaped from this he enlisted in the army, was wounded in battle, and was nursed back to health by an anonymous young woman with whom he fell in love. Although he has been searching for her he has had little success, but he did come upon Duncan, old and ill, in the course of his travels.

At this point Jenny returns to report that the baptism cannot take place until much later, and Georges volunteers to stay until the ceremony can be held. To pass the time, he asks about the local landmarks and is told of the Avenel chateau, which is to be sold at auction the next day. Dickson and Jenny tell about the Avenels, forced to go into political exile some years earlier, and about Gaveston, who hopes to buy the estate and the title of Lord Avenel that goes with it. Jenny is sure Gaveston will not succeed, for their farmhand Gabriel has seen the White Lady, ghostly protectress of the Avenel fortunes. At Georges' urging, Jenny sings the ballad of the White Lady. Gabriel arrives to tell Dickson that the farmers have come to confer with him regarding the means to block Gaveston's purchase of the estate, and the other peasants go off to meet with them.

When they have gone, Dickson asks Georges for advice. Thirteen years earlier the White Lady provided Dickson enough money to save his farm and to pay some outstanding debts. In return for this favor he promised to serve her and is fearful now, but does not say why. Jenny is upset and, after Dickson goes to speak to the farmers, she tells Georges that Dickson seems to be afraid constantly. Georges reassures her, saying that any man with such a pretty wife would be afraid. A minor flirtation scene follows, after which Dickson returns to tell the two that the farmers have pooled resources and have instructed him, as deputy, to bid up to 200,000 Scottish pounds for the Avenel estate. He also relates that a dwarf has given him a message from the White Lady, telling him to come to the Avenel chateau that evening. Seeing Dickson's fear and Jenny's unwillingness to allow him to go, Georges volunteers to go instead, despite the fact that a storm is brewing.

The second act takes place in a large room in the gothic chateau of the Avenels. Marguerite sings a spinning song, then muses to herself about Anna, an orphan brought up by the Avenels; Gaveston, now Anna's guardian; and Julien, the lost Avenel heir. She hears someone and thinks perhaps it is the White Lady appearing to announce the return or the death of Julien, but it is only Anna. She has just been touring the ruins of the old estate and is troubled at not being able to enter one of the buildings. Marguerite tells her that the seals on the locks will be removed only after tomorrow's sale, then asks of her adventures during the time she was away from the estate and of the fate of the Avenels. Anna reports that to her knowledge Julien, her childhood friend, simply disappeared and that his father died in exile. Lady Avenel, whom Anna had accompanied, died some eight years after leaving the estate, giving Anna over to the custody of Gaveston. Anna relates that while Gaveston was away on a journey she nursed a young soldier back to health because he reminded her of Julien and that she fell in love with him. Even though she once loved Julien, she feels that he is now above her station. Hearing Gaveston return, Anna tells Marguerite that a man will come to ask for lodging in the name of St. Julien of Avenel and that she should admit him to this room. Marguerite agrees and leaves.

Gaveston enters and, in the course of the conversation, reminds Anna of how moved she seemed at the story of Dickson and the White Lady which Marguerite told them earlier. Anna, however, knows the story is true, for it was Lord Avenel himself who provided the money. Gaveston has just returned from dining with MacIrton, the justice of the peace, and has made arrangements for the auction. He declares his intention of buying the estate and the title of Lord Avenel to gain status. He then asks Anna what became of a large sum of money the previous Lord Avenel had gained from the sale of some lands in England. Anna replies that it was used in the service of the Pretender, but Gaveston doubts this and states his belief that a paper given Anna by Lady Avenel contained information about this money. Since Anna has sworn not to reveal the paper's contents, Gaveston can get no further information from her.

At this point the tower bell sounds and Marguerite enters to tell Anna and Gaveston that a traveler has asked for shelter from the storm. Anna persuades Gaveston to allow the man to stay by promising that she will reveal the contents of the mysterious paper the next day. After sending Anna to her room, Gaveston admits Georges. In the ensuing conversation Georges reveals that he has come to the chateau because he has a *rendez-vous* with the White Lady. Gaveston and Marguerite leave and Georges makes himself comfortable in an armchair. In a song he calls for the White Lady and Anna, disguised, enters through a secret panel in the wall. Although disturbed at first that Dickson has sent a substitute, she elicits from Georges a promise to follow whatever orders he is given the next day, in return for which she promises that he will see again the girl who saved his life.

After Anna leaves, Gaveston comes to announce that it is dawn and Georges relates that he has become "a knight of the White Lady." The White Lady, says Georges, is guarding the fortunes of the Avenels, whereupon Gaveston repeats his determinaton to buy the estate, all the time becoming more convinced that Georges is mad.

The farmers arrive, along with Dickson, Jenny, MacIrton and other justices. As the auction opens, Dickson bids against Gaveston and soon reaches the limit of the pooled funds. Just as Gaveston begins to gloat over his victory, Anna arrives and orders Georges to bid for the estate. He outbids Gaveston, but before the act ends MacIrton warns him that he must pay the price by noon or go to prison. The people rejoice that Georges is now their new ruler.

The third act takes place in the main building of the Avenel estate. Anna tells Marguerite that Georges has no money but is counting on her (Anna) to provide it. She asks Marguerite about the statue of the White Lady which used to be in the reception hall and despairs when Marguerite relates that she saw the statue leave when the Avenels went into exile. Anna had planned to use the money from Lord Avenel's sale of his English lands, which is hidden in the statue, to pay MacIrton. She asks Marguerite to show her a certain secret passage and the women exit.

Georges and the peasants arrive to celebrate. The peasants sing a Scottish tune which Georges recognizes, although he is not sure where he learned it. Alone again, he muses that he also feels sure he has been in the house before. His reflections are interrupted by the arrival of Gaveston, who is surprised to learn that Georges has no money. MacIrton enters as Georges is leaving and, soon after, Anna appears. The latter, seeing MacIrton and Gaveston in conversation, hides in a secret passage and listens. MacIrton has come to tell Gaveston that old Duncan, before his death in London, signed a statement to the effect that Julien Avenel was serving in the army under the name of Georges Brown. Since Georges has no money, Gaveston proposes that they merely wait until noon, when he (Gaveston) will buy the estate and Georges'
identity will make no difference.

When the two men leave Anna comes from her hiding place, in conflict now over whether to tell Georges of his identity and—since his social position would then be far above her own—to lose him as a sweetheart, or to let him remain ignorant of his birth. Marguerite runs in to say that she is sure Julien will appear soon because she has seen the White Lady appear in a chapel on the estate. Thus informed as to the location of the statue, Anna decides to give the money to Georges, then leave the estate. Jenny's news that MacIrton and the lawyers have arrived sends Anna running toward the chapel.

Georges and Dickson arrive. The latter is angry that Georges and not he had the privilege of buying the estate simply because Georges kept the appointment with the White Lady. Georges now offers to let Dickson take his place, but when MacIrton enters to demand payment, Dickson shrinks from what he thought to be a high position. A harp arpeggio announces the arrival of the White Lady (Anna in disguise), who gives Georges the money and tells him his true identity. Gaveston, furious, tears off Anna's veil. Upon recognizing her all agree with Georges that she is worthy, because of her noble actions, to become the next Lady Avenel. The opera closes with a chorus of rejoicing.

## The Adaptation

Not surprisingly, a landmark such as *La Dame blanche* was not produced overnight. In 1821 Scribe had given Boieldieu the libretto of a three-act opéra comique entitled *La Dame d'Avenel*, a work inspired by the writings of Scott.[94] The sources of the work are not merely *Guy Mannering* and *The Monastery*, as Loewenberg and Cooper state.[95] The libretto also contains elements of the *The Abbot* and "The Lady of the Lake," both by Scott, and of a successful novel in the same vein by Desirée de Castera entitled *La Fantôme blanc ou le protecteur mystérieux* first published in 1810 and given a second edition in 1823.[96] Favre also cites as a source a tale told to Boieldieu by a French emigré in St. Petersburg. The latter had regained his paternal estate by a means similar to that planned but not carried out by Dickson and the farmers in *La Dame blanche*: his servants bought the estate and held it until he could return from exile.[97]

Since 1816, when the first translation of his works appeared in France, Scott had enjoyed a great vogue, and the growth of the romantic movement in general made almost inevitable the appearance of his themes or subjects similar to them in opera. In England, Bishop had written musical adaptations of *The Lady of the Lake* (1811, produced as *The Knight of Snowdoun*), *Guy Mannering* (1816), *The Heart of Midlothian* (1819), and others, while Italy had seen Rossini's *La Donna del lago* in 1819.[98] Catel's *Wallace, ou le ménestrel écossais* (1817) can be considered a part of this trend, which also included Auber's *Leicester, ou le château de Kenilworth* (1823, libretto by Scribe and Mêlesville); *Ivanhoe*, a pasticcio with music by Rossini (1826, libretto by E. Deschamps and G. de Wailly); Louise Bertin's *Guy Mannering* (performed privately, before 1827);[99] and Carafa's *La Prison d'Edimbourg* (1833, libretto by Scribe and Planard); as well as other works based on local color themes inspired at least indirectly by Scott's material. Thus Scribe, in 1821, was in the forefront of the movement in France. However, Boieldieu, because of illness, did not finish the opera until quite late in 1825. Once completed, according to a contemporary report, it was copied, approved, rehearsed, and performed in the space of twenty-eight days. Catel's *Wallace*, the first of France's Scott-inspired operas, was an indirect influence here, for Longyear reports: "The staging [for *La Dame blanche*] was inexpensive, since the costumes and scenery used were those left over from Catel's unsuccessful *Wallace* (1817)."[100]

Indeed, the music itself partook of some leftovers, for Georges Brown's "Ah! quel plaisir d'être soldat" was taken from Boieldieu's score to *Les Trois genres* and was originally a bass air, "La belle chose qu'un tournoi," while the 5/4 portion of the impressive "Viens, gentille dame" was taken from his *La Dame invisible*, a one-act opera performed in St. Petersburg in 1808 which "seems to be the first idea for *La Dame blanche*."[101] The Scotch tune which Georges recognizes in Act III was a popular Scottish song, "Robin Adair."[102]

Although no collaborator is listed with Scribe as librettist, Adam reveals that Boieldieu himself was responsible for suggesting the important scene in the third act in which Georges recognizes and finishes a Scotch tune sung by the chorus. According to Adam, Boieldieu had been working on Bouilly's libretto for *Les Deux nuits* when the leading performer for this opera left the company and Boieldieu returned to the text of *La Dame blanche*.

> Boieldieu, imprisoned for more than a year by the laborious and antimusical rhymes of Bouilly, found himself at once completely at ease with the collaboration of Scribe, who understands the exigencies of musicians just as do the musicians themselves and who tailors the pieces with such felicity that we consider them ready-made as soon as we read the words; thus music was never composed so easily. Labarre, having made several journeys to England as a harpist, furnished Boieldieu with all the Scotch themes which are used in *La Dame blanche*, such as those of the air in the third act, the motives of . . ."Vous le verrez le verre en main," etc., etc. This third act greatly frightened Boieldieu. He found no [focal] situation in it, and one day I went to see him and found him working in his room, which he left only for about three or four hours a day, very preoccupied with this third act.
>
> 'Do you understand,' he told me, 'that after two acts so full of music, I have nothing in the third act but an air for a woman, a little unimportant chorus, a short duo for women, and a finale without a development? I need there a large-scale piece for effect, and I have nothing but a little chorus of villagers, "Vive, vive Monseigneur!" Scribe has made a note to me: "Peasants throwing their hats in the air"—proof that this ought to be an animated and short piece. They cannot throw their hats into the air for a quarter

> of an hour. However, last night an idea came to me which will perhaps be good. I read in Walter Scott that an individual who returned to his country recognized an air that he had heard in his childhood.[103] If, instead of a *vivat* chorus, the vassals sang to Georges an old Scotch ballad which he recalled enough to be able to continue it himself, do you not think that this situation would be musical?'
>
> 'Certainly,' I replied, 'it would be charming, and it would fill up your third act perfectly.'
>
> 'Yes,' he answered, 'but I do not have words for it.'
>
> 'M. Scribe is nearby.'
>
> 'I cannot go there, sick as I am.'
>
> 'But I am in splendid health, and I shall be there in five minutes.' And without waiting for his response I ran to Scribe's house. . . . Scribe received the idea that I related to him even more favorably.
>
> 'Return to Boieldieu's house,' he told me. 'Tell him that this is excellent; that there is in it a sure success; that the third act is saved, and that he will have his words in a quarter of an hour.'
>
> I ran to bring the news to Boieldieu, and the next day he had me hear in its entirety this delightful piece which did not make the success of *La Dame blanche* but which added to and brought to an apogee that which the first two acts had received.[104]

The main elements of Scribe's libretto are taken from Scott's *Guy Mannering* and occur some thirty pages near the beginning of the book and in a few chapters near the end. Scott begins his novel with about a hundred pages of background information, much of which is brought into the libretto after the typical delayed-action beginning. In this section of the novel the young colonel Guy Mannering stops at the Ellangowan estate for shelter on the night that Henry Bertram, eventual heir to the estate, is born. An amateur astrologer, Mannering draws up a horoscope for the child in which he predicts that some unfavorable event will occur when the boy is five years old. On Henry's fifth birthday he is captured by Dutch pirates, led by one Dirk Hatteraick, and taken to the Netherlands, where he takes the name Vanbeest Brown after the merchant with whom he is housed. Bertram-Brown later becomes a junior officer in the army under Colonel Mannering. When the two fight a duel, Mannering is led to believe that he has killed the young man.

Meanwhile, the fortunes of the Bertram family decline rapidly. At her father's death, Henry's sister Lucy is forced to leave her home and the estate is put up for sale. Here the opera picks up the thread of Scott's plot. One Glossin, an intelligent but devious lawyer, wishes to buy the estate and assume the title of Lord of Ellangowan. For sentimental reasons Guy Mannering, having returned to Scotland with his daughter Julia, also takes an interest in the property. However, the Mannering bid arrives too late for the auction and Glossin purchases the estate. Mannering buys another piece of property nearby and moves in with Julia, Lucy Bertram, and the latter's tutor, Dominie Sampson.

The parallels between this part of Scott's novel and *La Dame blanche* are quite clear. Henry Bertram is renamed Julien Avenel-Georges Brown, and Henry's adventures correspond to Duncan's selling Julien into service on a ship and the latter's life as the soldier Georges Brown. Colonel Mannering corresponds roughly to Georges Brown's beloved superior officer in the opera, and the wound by Colonel Mannering from which Bertram recovers has an equivalent in Brown's battle wound, which heals with the help of Anna's care.

Although the actual person and name of Marguerite are taken from Scott's "The Lady of the Lake," there is much in Scribe's libretto to suggest that his character is borrowed not so much from that of the woman in the narrative poem as from the character of Dominie Sampson, the awkward but lovable parson. It is the Dominie to whom the elder Bertram entrusts the education of the children Henry and Lucy. An interesting comparison can be made between Scott's version of Brown's recollections of his childhood and Scribe's adaptation, for here the Dominie is definitely replaced by Marguerite.

> 'Do you remember nothing of your early life before you left Scotland?'
>
> 'Very imperfectly; yet I have a strong idea, perhaps more deeply impressed upon my by subequent hard usage, that I was during my childhood the object of much solicitude and affection. I have an indistinct remembrance of a good-looking man whom I used to call papa, and of a lady who was infirm in health, and who, I think, must have been my mother; but it is an imperfect and confused recollection. I remember, too, a tall, thin, kind-tempered man in black who used to teach me my letters and walk out with me; and I think the very last time. . . .'
>
> . . . . . . . . . . . . . . . . . . . . . . . . . . . . . . . .
>
> [He tells of the kidnapping.]
> ' . . . The rest is all confusion and dread, . . . In short, it is all a blank from my memory, until I recollect myself first an ill-used and

> half-starved cabin-boy aboard a sloop, and then a school-boy in Holland under the protection of an old merchant who had taken some fancy to me.
>
> ' . . . I went out to India to be a clerk in a Dutch house; their affairs fell into confusion. I betook myself to the military profession, and, I trust, as yet I have not disgraced it.'[105]
>
> . . . Except for some vague and confused recollections, my memory recounts to me nothing of my childhood or my family. I have some idea of grand servants in lace-trimmed clothing who carried me in their arms, of a lovely little girl with whom I was brought up, of an old woman who sang Scotch songs to me. But suddenly, and I know not how, I was transported on board a ship, under the orders of a man named Duncan, a first mate who called himself my uncle and whom I shall never forget, for he rudely taught me naval service! At the end of some years of slavery and of mistreatment, I succeeded in escaping, and I disembarked without a shilling in my pocket.
>
> ' . . . I signed up as a soldier to King George. . . . From that moment I have been the happiest of men. . . .'[106]

The "lovely little girl" mentioned is, of course, Anna, who bears some similarity to Julia Mannering. Like Scribe's Georges Brown, Vanbeest Brown falls in love with Julia (Anna) while serving in the army and comes to Scotland to seek her. Julia, of course, is not beneath his station; in fact, the reverse seems to be true until Brown is revealed to be Henry Bertram, of noble blood.

The creation of Anna, however, is one more character for whom Scribe goes outside *Guy Mannering* to find material. In this case he goes to *The Monastery*, another tale of the decline and partial restitution of an ancient Scottish family. In this novel, war deprives the Avenel house of its Lord, and Lady Avenel flees with her young daughter to the home of some farmers, the Glendinnings, with her faithful servants Tibb and Martin in attendance. This couple provides Scribe with a partial model for Dickson and Jenny. The child, Mary Avenel, is brought up in the farm household in the company of two brothers, Halbert and Edward Glendinning. Lady Avenel dies, and the orphaned girl eventually falls in love with Halbert, who is assisted by the White Lady of Avenel to gain his ends.[107] At the end of *The Monastery* Mary Avenel marries Halbert Glendinning and the two return to the Avenel estate. Although their roles are reversed in rank, Scribe's Julien Avenel and Anna have a relationship similar to that of Halbert and Mary. In character, however, Julien resembles Henry Bertram, while Anna is more like Mary Avenel.

The Lady Avenel of the novel suggests the equivalent character in the opera, although nothing can be said about the personality of the latter; and a message left in a Bible by Scott's Lady Avenel may have suggested to Scribe the mysterious paper his Lady Avenel gives to Anna.

A situation similar to that in *The Monastery* exists in Scott's *The Abbot*, another novel which influenced *La Dame blanche. The Abbot* is the story of Roland Graeme, who is unaware of his true identity but knows he is of noble blood. Graeme is sent by the Earl of Murray to be a page to Queen Mary Stuart, imprisoned on an island estate. Before he enters this service, however, he is introduced to Catherine Seyton, a young noblewoman, and agrees to follow her instructions whenever they might be given in the future. Catherine appears later as a lady-in-waiting to Queen Mary and turns up in what seem to Roland to be numerous clever disguises to give him orders regarding the part he is to play in the conspiracy to effect the Queen's escape and her restitution to the throne. Roland falls in love with Catherine, yet believes her to be above his station until he learns that he is the son of Julian Avenel, the late uncle of Mary Avenel. Since the latter has no children, Roland is heir to the Avenel estate. The question of Catherine's disguised appearances is cleared up when Roland learns that the girl has a twin brother who also has a hand in the conspiracy. Despite the failure of this conspiracy the novel ends with the prospect of marriage of Catherine and Roland and of the latter's inheritance of a noble estate and position.

The relationship of Roland Graeme to Catherine Seyton in *The Abbot* is similar to that between Halbert Glendinning and Mary Avenel in *The Monastery.* Thus either pair could have served as models for Georges Brown and Anna, although the latter's character is more like that of Mary than of Catherine. One aspect of Catherine's role, however, appears in that of Anna: her function as a behind-the-scenes conspirator for the restitution of a ruling noble. Like Anna, Catherine helps plan the course of events and relays orders which others must obey in order to carry out the scheme. Just as Roland finds the "disguised" Catherine, who also relays orders, to be the girl's brother, so Georges discovers that the White Lady is none other than Anna in disguise. Like Roland, the brave page with a military background, Georges too finds that his is an Avenel.

Scribe's libretto takes into account the supernatural elements in German romantic opera by introducing the White Lady. However, by showing her to be merely a disguised mortal he rids the opera of truly supernatural or mystical qualities and thus of the aesthetic and philosophical outlook which is central to an appreciation of the German operas. So, too, he eliminates the core from Scott's novels by concentrating on the persons of the hero, heroine, villain, and all their accessories. It must be remembered that although the Waverley novels, which include the three in question, feature prominent heroes, heroines, villains, love affairs, and numerous subsidiary characters, none of these represents the novels' true focus. Each of Scott's tales has at its center the depiction of the decline of the old Scotch nobility and the rebirth of these noble families under altered circumstances which necessitate changes in the whole concept of hereditary nobility. Thus Scott's focus is primarily a political-historical-analytical one and the major characters in his novels serve only to bring these historical changes down to a personal level. Except for the fact that it reflects the general socio-political background of his own time, Scribe's *La Dame blanche* ignores completely Scott's backdrop of history.

Yet Scribe has included in the opera very few events or characters not based in some way on ideas provided in one of the Scott sources or on unique combinations of those ideas. In choosing carefully the details he wished to use in his libretto Scribe proved his understanding of the medium in which he was working. It was not possible to convey on the stage of the Opéra-Comique the vast historical panorama of the Waverley novels, for time was too short and the issues too confused. In addition, clarity was very important to Scribe in any dramatic medium. Scribe himself recognized this when he wrote to Charles Duveyrier concerning the proposed addition of a melodramatic and mildly philosophical complication to his libretto for Verdi's *Les Vêpres siciliennes.*

> This [situation] is very Sicilian. It would be perfect in a drama. I do not know if at the Opéra, where everything ought to be simple, this would not complicate the action too much.[108]

The fact that opera and opéra comique provided him less opportunity than spoken drama for complexities of plot and characters or for lengthy involvements of any kind made absolutely necessary the reshaping of his literary models along lines that conformed to the operatic medium's requirements. This he did in a first-rate manner, in a way that far outshines the adaptation made of his own vaudeville for *La Barcarolle.*

## The Libretto: Structure and Significance

> [*La Dame blanche*] marks a date in the history of the theatre as well as in that of music, for librettist and musician have both found what Sarcey called *un monde nouveau.* There is nothing in the repertoire

> of Favart, Sedaine, or Marmontel in just this genre. 'La Dame blanche' is romantic opera. The sombre, mysterious, and poetic features of Sir Walter Scott's novel have given place to a modernized, humanized charm; the hero is a real Frenchman, an intrepid, heedless lieutenant of the Empire; and yet Scribe was too clever not to keep the local Scotch color that was to contribute so much to the success of the play.[109]

In discussing this *monde nouveau* Favre, Boieldieu's biographer, has commented upon the skill with which Scribe put together the various sources of his libretto, in addition to the realistically handled romanticism of the book, "sufficient qualities to justify the astonishing success that it won and the fascination that it exercised on the public."[110] That Scribe, master of the well-made play and mirror of public taste, should be able to do these things is not at all surprising. There are a great many elements of this libretto that reflect Scribe's craft, starting with such items as role distribution and the handling of conventions. Cooper has observed:

> The combination of the traditional popular background and many of the traditional roles (the *ingénue* couple and the amorous and enterprising *jeune premier* tenor) of the old opéra comique with the mysterious and the hair-raising scenes of the White Lady in the deserted castle of Avenel, the novelty of putting an auction on the stage and the ingenious postponement of the—purely naturalistic—*dénouement* until the last moment were enough to make the work popular even without Boieldieu's music.[111]

Indeed, some of these items are an integral part of Scribe's writing technique whether in this libretto or any other.

Scribe's usual delayed-action plot is combined at the beginning of *La Dame blanche* with what was by now an established convention of opéra comique, the opening chorus-ensemble. Preparations for the baptism of the son of Dickson and Jenny have already been made; George has met and fallen in love with Anna; Anna and Gaveston have returned to the Avenel estate; Gaveston has planned to buy the estate at an auction; the farmers and villagers have begun to think of a plan to defeat Gaveston's purpose; and Anna has her own plan, based on the local belief in the White Lady and her knowledge of past events involving the Lady and Dickson.

The actual exposition begins in Scene iv, in which Georges begins to relate the story of his life and his reasons for being in the area. From his reference to servants and to an old woman who sang Scotch songs to him we can assume he started life as the son of a wealthy Scotch family. It only remains for Scribe to fill in the details, which he does near the end of Act III. The references to a young girl and to a man named Duncan are among those details to be filed for future reference and recalled later, when the puzzle's pieces have been fitted together. The information Georges gives about his participation in the army is included partly for the same reason as Georges' earlier song: to characterize the young officer. As always, Scribe's identification and characterization of his personae are done externally.

Along with the mystery of Georges' birth, Scribe has included in this scene a second suspense-giving item: the identity of a young woman for whom Georges is searching. Later in the act another mystery person is added: the White Lady of Avenel. Arvin's contention that the "dramatic mainsprings" of the opera are "the amusement excited by the Highlanders' terror of the White Lady of Avenel, and the spectators' desire to know whether she really exists and just who she is" is quite an oversimplification of the situation, although a great deal of the action does hinge upon this character.[112] She is discussed in increasing detail in Scenes v, vi, and viii. The elaborate contrivance which surrounds the gradual revelation of this character is already prepared in Scene iv, however, in the following bit of dialogue.

Dickson.

She [the unknown girl] was perhaps your good angel, some *démon familier* as exist so often in the country.

Georges.

Truly, that is just like you Scotchmen.

This simple reference to belief in ghosts prepares for Jenny's statement (Scene v) that Gabriel has seen the White Lady and for the ballade, which in turn paves the way for further discussion of the phantom. This line of development reaches a climax when Georges volunteers to keep Dickson's appointment with her because he feels he must meet her himself.

Georges concludes the story of his wanderings by mentioning that he gave money to Duncan, whom he found on the verge of death, and that Duncan had stated that this act would bring Georges good fortune. When, in Act III, Duncan's testimony establishes Georges' identity, the truth of this statement is confirmed.

Before going on to more detailed information about the White Lady, Dickson and Jenny tell Georges of the Avenels and the coming auction. This information includes identification of Gaveston as the villain (instant characterization) and gives in concise form all the preparation and motivation for most of the second act. In addition, Scribe provides another piece of motivation for Georges' taking Dickson's place at the Avenel chateau: Dickson's "well known fear." Perhaps because this is one of the weakest motifs in the libretto it is interesting to note that Scribe builds it up as carefully as any of the stronger elements in the plot. Indeed, the only reason that it is such a weak link is that it is totally unnecessary, Scribe having provided enough motivation for Georges in the story of the White Lady and in Georges' character itself. Nevertheless, Gabriel's entrance brings another reference to this fear—

**Dickson.**

. . . He always comes when one is fearful.

**Gabriel.**

. . . That is just because you are always fearful when someone arrives.

and the whole of Scene vii is devoted to a discussion of it by Georges and Jenny.

**Jenny.**

Indeed, he is always this way:
I always see my husband trembling.
At the least noise in the village
He is afraid.

**Georges.**

He is afraid?

**Jenny.**

The minute he hears a storm coming
He is afraid.

**Georges.**

He is afraid?

This sort of dialogue is extended over an entire duo scene to the point that it appears nonsensical. Yet nothing is developed to this extent in Scribe unless it is to have significance for later events, and the fact that a reader might conclude that the drama could function quite well without it is no good indication that Scribe shares this judgment.

Since Dickson had declared himself a sworn servant of the White Lady (Scene vi), it is no surprise when, in Scene viii, he reveals that she has just called upon him to fulfill his promise. For reasons already given, it is also no surprise when Georges volunteers to go to the chateau in Dickson's place. As is usual with Scribe, it is this final scene of the first act that marks the beginning of some real action.

One unusual feature of the libretto is that three major characters (Gaveston, Anna, and Marguerite) and one minor character (MacIrton) have not yet appeared. Although it is possible that Scribe has delayed their entrances "in order to contribute to the tightening of the intrigue and cater to the 'fashionable lateness' of many opera goers," as Longyear has suggested,[113] the author's technique is so predictable as to give reason to doubt this. Since exposition for the entire opera is contained in the first act, any consideration for "fashionable lateness" is definitely out of the question. Although the delayed appearance of the villain and the heroine do "contribute to the tightening of the intrigue," the reason for this is to be found in the carefully considered cause and effect relationships basic to Scribe's craft. Among the missing characters Gaveston has already been described and his motivation outlined, and MacIrton is just a piece of machinery necessary to carry out an auction about which we already know. Yet nothing in a Scribe libretto is totally unexpected. Marguerite has already been mentioned as an anonymous woman who sang Scottish folk songs to Georges during his childhood; thus, when a woman answering that description turns up at the beginning of Act II the audience, knowing Scribe's customs, might logically conclude that she will have some significance when the secret of Georges' identity is revealed. In Anna's case the situation is similar. Since much has been made of a young woman for whom Georges is searching, we anticipate the eventual appearance of such a woman. However, because her identity and origins are important to subsequent action, Act II, ii, is the vehicle for additional exposition. Although this is a rather unusual technique for the master of the well-made play, its use does not harm the logic in the sequence of events. Something similar occurs in *La Prison d'Edimbourg*, where George's father does not appear until Act II but is prepared for in Act I.

The second scene of Act II, which takes place at the Avenel estate, also contains further information on the Avenel family which will become important to later developments in the opera. At this point all we know about them is that they went into political exile and that they were good masters (Act I, v). Now Anna, a more likely source of information than any of the characters yet introduced, adds news of the eventual deaths of Lord and Lady Avenel and the disappearance of their son Julien. She also tells of a young soldier she nursed back to health, who can be none other than Georges. His eventual discovery of Anna can come as no surprise to the audience. So that one is not left with the impression that Anna is fickle, Scribe reconciles what at first appears to be a conflict between her devotion to Julien and her love for the unknown soldier by informing us that Julien is socially far above an orphan girl like Anna. However, Scribe leaves open to question the soldier's identity in the following speech.

**Anna.**

> The war had just broken out, they were fighting at the very gates of the estate where we were staying, and a young soldier dangerously wounded . . . it was one of our soldiers, a compatriot. How could I refuse to help him? And then, I swear, in spite of myself, I thought of Julien; Julien would have been about his age, and I said to myself, 'Perhaps my master's son is just as unfortunate and without aid.'

Combining this speech with the information given by Georges about himself, the audience can now formulate the question of Georges' identity. Is he just Georges Brown, a soldier in search of his benefactress Anna? Or is he Julien Avenel? The concrete information already given points toward the first solution, yet hints at the second. While leaving the answer in suspense, Scribe gives enough clues that neither solution would be unexpected.

Act II, ii also includes clues that Gaveston's designs on the Avenel estate will be thwarted, for there is no reason to suppose that Anna knows of the farmers' plan to pool resources and bid for the estate. Thus, when Anna declares that she has hope of saving Julien's heritage, Scribe is really hinting that she is to be part of a double-barreled attack on Gaveston.

Scene iii also contains a great deal of information in a small space. First the tale of Dickson and the White Lady, contrived initially to call the farmer, then Georges, into the Avenel affair, is now no longer necessary and must yield place to mysteries more central to the action. Anna's realistic explanation thus disposes of unnecessary dramatic baggage but at the same time provides the first definite clue that Anna is to be involved in the mystery of the White Lady. Since Anna alone, of all persons yet alive, knows the truth, she is the only one in any position to take advantage of it. (There is also the possibility that Marguerite might know, but Scribe disposes of this by making clear throughout the opera that she, like the superstitious farmers, sincerely believes in the White Lady's existence.)

The second bit of information is mere machinery introduced in keeping with Scribe's desire that nothing be unexpected. MacIrton and his function in the drama are mentioned by Gaveston so that we anticipate his appearance later.

Finally, we meet with a typical Scribe device: the secret letter. It is linked in conversation with a large sum of money, and one is not amazed to discover later that this money actually exists. In addition, Anna's character is fixed in ths scene in Gaveston's statement that "beneath your sweet and timid air you hide more courage and resolution than I would have suspected." Clearly, strong, faithful, virtuous Anna is a girl to be trusted.

So far, Act II has been concerned with exposition. The action begins near the end of Scene iii when the bell announces Georges' arrival. The secret letter here serves a practical dramatic purpose, for it is Anna's promise to reveal its contents that induces Gaveston to admit Georges to the house. A further contrivance, Scribe arranges that Anna leave the room so that she does not find out until the proper moment that the man she believes to be Dickson is really her soldier, Georges. Gaveston, however, remains for good purpose, since he must be informed that the White Lady is to appear and that she and Georges are likely to be allies.

In Scene vii, the first meeting between Georges and the White Lady, Scribe again clears up one of the minor mysteries of the plot, one no longer needed to sustain the action, and replaces it with another. It is dramatically unnecessary to delay further a positive identification of Georges as the soldier of whom Anna has spoken. Indeed, to do so would be to strain the point and to leave too many things to be resolved at the last minute. Yet clearing up at least half the mystery now gives Scribe another one on which to build. To maintain suspense, then, Anna promises to appear undisguised on the morrow, bearing the White Lady's instructions, instructions which will mean defeat for Gaveston. One further point: that the audience has been made aware of Anna's disguise in some way cannot be doubted, for her identification of Georges and her surprise, expressed in asides, at seeing him again would make no sense otherwise. Thus statements made by both Arvin and Favre[114] that the key conflicts in the plot revolve around the identity and reality of the

White Lady cannot be supported. The audience is already aware of her identity, and whether a real ghost exists in addition is immaterial.

In the next scene Georges declares to Gaveston that he is now a servant of the White Lady and that Gaveston will be defeated. The lines are clearly drawn: black (Gaveston) *v.* white (Lady). Although the situations are completely different, this conflict is similar to that in *Haydée*, Act III, xii, when Scribe pits Malipieri against Haydée in the battle for Lorédan.

Needless to say, Georges emerges victorious at the end of the act, but suspense is maintained and the finale still leaves something upon which Scribe can build Act III. First earlier threads of the plot are pulled together. Dickson and the farmers are defeated, after which Anna's appearance and recognition by Georges resolves this mystery entirely and provides the follow-through on the part of the White Lady. Once her instructions are carried out, Gaveston's predicted defeat brings to a clear close the action begun in Scene vii. Before the final ensemble Gaveston requests that MacIrton read the law—

> The same day, at noon, the price of this sale
> Shall be paid in full to our hands; if not,
> And lacking sufficient security,
> The aforementioned buyer will be placed in prison.

—and Georges emphasizes his own position:

> Georges Brown, sublieutenant;
> Two hundred francs
> Fixed salary.

Here again the battle lines are drawn.

As Act III opens Anna is searching for the statue of the White Lady and, in her explanation to Marguerite, resolves the question of Lady Avenel's secret letter. Marguerite's mentioning a secret passage in connection with the disappearance of the statue is another contrivance: to be used first as a hiding place where Anna can listen to the conversation of MacIrton and Gaveston, then as a spot from which she can emerge, disguised, to identify Georges and to present him with the hidden money. Later, when Marguerite's superstitious mind turns the statue into a real ghost seen hidden in a chapel, this is all the information Anna needs to find the money

The first hints at Georges' identity came near the beginning of the second act: first in the appearance of two people Georges himself described; second in the statement that the soldier Georges had reminded Anna of Julien Avenel. Although these bits of information are not conclusive, they begin to take on new significance beginning in Act II, iii. Here Georges recognizes and sings a national song identified with the Avenels, after which he reflects that "many times in my imagination I have dreamed of a gothic castle like this one, a gallery like that." To increase the suspense, however, other characters (Gaveston, MacIrton, Anna) discover and act upon the fact of Georges' identity before it is revealed to him. In any event, the build-up to the solution of this central mystery (the *quiproquo*) is gradual, logical, and in keeping with Scribe's technique.

The fact, revealed in Act III, v, that Georges has no money of his own is combined with Gaveston's secret knowledge of Georges' identity to produce the lowest point in the hero's fortunes. Georges' first appearance in the opera came at a low point: he was hungry and had no success in his search for Anna. Gradually his fortunes have been rising until, at the end of Act II, he has found Anna and defeated Gaveston. Now, with Gaveston's intention to withhold from Georges his identity and to have him imprisoned, the low point has been reached. As in *Haydée*, this sudden decline in the hero's fortunes follows the *scène à faire*, in which Gaveston learns the truth about his adversary. In the usual recognition scene the remaining loose ends of the plot are brought together. Anna, because of her courage and faithfulness, is deemed worthy to marry her "soldier" after all; Marguerite rejoices that the lost boy has been returned to her; and Dickson and Jenny reap the only rewards they wished at the beginning of the opera: a good master and a fine godfather for their son.

One of Scribe's more outstanding qualities as a writer is the way in which he faithfully reflects the taste and temper of his middle class French audience. By the 1820s the extremes of revolutionary thought and of Napoleon had simmered down and a more conservative element, sympathetic to the monarchy, had come to the fore. In *La Dame blanche* this pro-royalty reaction is central to whatever message the opera may have, for the basis of the action is the return of the Avenel estate to its rightful owners. This message, of course, is not as elaborate as in Scott's novels, for reasons already given. Despite the fact that the supposed setting is during a revolutionary period in Scotland, the royalist sentiment is prominent and is made explicit in such speeches as these.

**Dickson.**

> . . . [the estate] belonged to the former Lords of Avenel, brave men whom everyone in the countryside still holds dear; but they were supporters of the Stuarts, and after the battle of Culloden the Lord of Avenel, who had

been banished, fled with part of his family to France, where he is said to have died.

**Jenny.**

Now, during this time this Mr. Gaveston has so ruined the business affairs of the Lord, whose agent he was, that in order to pay the creditors they are going to sell this beautiful domain tomorrow.

**Dickson.**

And what's more, they say that Gaveston, who has become rich, wants to purchase the chateau himself and in this way to become Lord Avenel. . . . I ask you, a coxcomb of a trustee who wants to become our ruler! No sir! This we shall not suffer!

These royalist ideas also permeate the speeches of Georges, soldier and servant of the state, and others in the opera; for example:

Act I, iv

**Dickson.**

Perhaps that would not be agreeable to you.

**Georges.**

By no means! What else does an officer on leave have to do? He can be a godfather as well as anything else. That uses his time; it is also an indirect service that he renders to the state.

Act I, iv

**Georges.**

. . . I enlisted as a soldier of King George. Forward, march! the pack on your back! . . . Since that moment I have been the happiest of men; everything has succeeded for me; it seems as if fortune is leading me by the hand. . . . My brave colonel! He was like a father to me, a friend! He took a liking to me, took upon himself my education, my advancement. Six months ago, in Hanover—I had just been named sublieutenant—I found myself beside him in the face of an armed charge. 'Georges!' he cried to me, 'go back!' and he tried to place himself in front of me. You can well believe that I rushed to the forefront of the battle, but in vain. We both fell, and he was never to rise again.

**Dickson.**

He died?

**Georges.**

Yes, on the field of honor! The death of a hero! (Removing his hat) May he pray in heaven that the same happens to me!

Act II, ii

**Marguerite.**

It seemed to me that you only loved Julien, at least that was my impression, and many times I dreamed of your marriage.

**Anna.**

What are you daring to say! He, heir of the Lords of Avenel, and I, a poor orphan, without fortune, high birth; is it thus that I should repay the goodness of my benefactors?! . . . No, Marguerite, Julien, once my friend, my brother, is now my ruler, my master; it is as such that we ought to respect him, serve him, and sacrifice ourselves, if necessary, to save his heritage.

Knepler, out to prove his own Marxist points, undoubtedly goes too far when he comments:

> There is no questions that Boieldieu's opera strikes at the heart of a wide circle: without pretentions and pleasing in form and character, cleverly supporting the political advances of the Reaction and introducing in their lack of principles the new era of bourgeois society.[115]

Yet the political bent of the opera is no mere byproduct of the story, and it is no accident that Favre notes: "The greatest eulogies on Scribe [with regard to *La Dame blanche*] are found, in general, in the journals devoted to the monarchy."[116]

## Words and Music

Just as the libretto of *La Dame blanche* achieves classic stature in Scribe's opéra comique production, so the music of Boieldieu itself represents a model of its kind and presents the highest development of this composer's style. Except in Anna's role the music avoids direct Rossinian influence, yet is more serious, therefore more able to be taken seriously, than many of Boieldieu's earlier, lighter works in the opéra comique vein. Some of the simplicity of his earlier style remains, however, in the predominance of triadic outlines or conjunct motion in his melodies and the reliance on dotted rhythms in a great many tunes. Longyear has observed in his work "a virtual 'language of intervals'; for instance, ascending chromatic steps represent effort or ardor, descending chromatic steps represent suffering; a series of ascending perfect fourths depicts great élan, descending perfect fourths roughness; and diminished fourths great melancholy."[117] His harmonic style is straightforward and rather limited both in its long- and short-range aspects, and modulation for dramatic purposes is relatively infrequent and not particularly adventurous or original. It is a style on which composers as different as Adam and Auber can build, for its simplicity and melodic qualities are carried on by Adam, while Auber takes from it the seriousness of purpose and some technical features which he fuses with more Rossinian traits, especially a highly developed technique of dramatic ensemble writing. Boieldieu's music, in its straightforwardness, matches the clarity of Scribe's libretto to form a unified work.

Some good examples of Boieldieu's melodic style occur in Georges' air, "Ah! quel plair d'être sòldat" (No. 2), and in Jenny's ballade, "D'ici voyez ce beau domaine" (No. 5) (Examples 32 and 33, respectively).

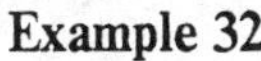

**Example 32**

Example 33

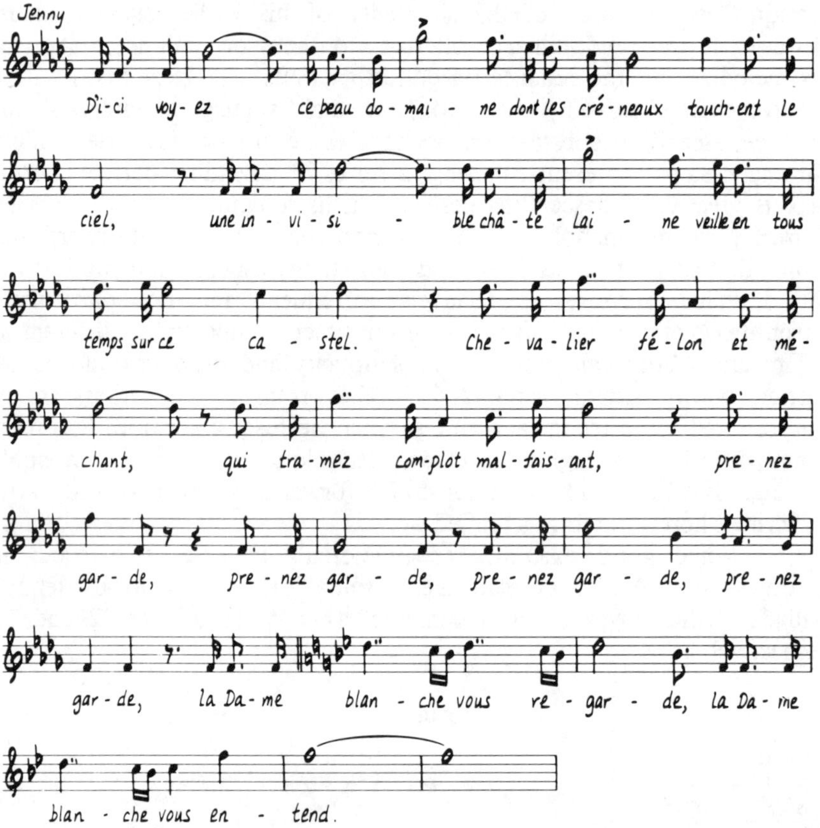
Jenny
D'i-ci voy-ez ce beau do-mai - ne dont les cré-neaux touch-ent le
ciel, une in - vi - si - ble châ - te - lai - ne veille en tous
temps sur ce ca - stel. Che - va - lier fé - lon et mé -
chant, qui tra - mez com-plot mal - fais - ant, pre - nez
gar - de, pre - nez gar - de, pre - nez gar - de, pre - nez
gar - de, la Da - me blan - che vous re - gar - de, la Da - me
blan - che vous en - tend.

Both tunes feature prominent dotted rhythms and a great reliance on the notes of accompanying triads, features which also typify the two Scottish songs used in the work: the drinking song in No. 3 (Example 34) and the tune recognized by Georges in Act III (No. 16; Example 35).

Example 34

Georges
Vous me ver - rez le verre en main, vous me ver - rez le
verre en main, tou - jours, tou-jours chan - tant, chan - tant quel-que re - frain.

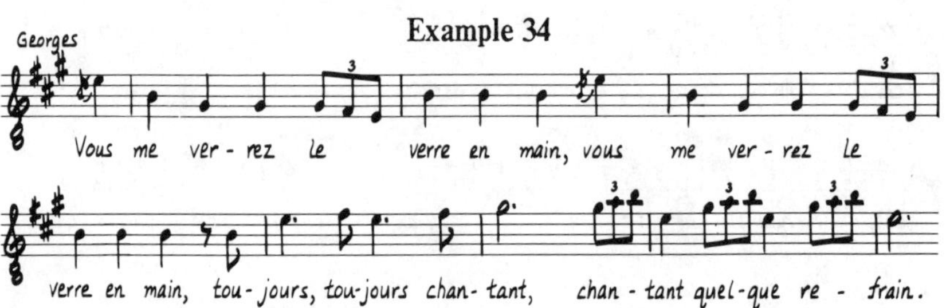

**Example 35**

Thus there is no disparity between the style of the composed melodies and the borrowed material. In a more ornamented vein, an air for Anna ("Enfin je vous revois," No. 14) imitates Rossini in form and in melodic style. Like many Rossinian arias (for example, the well-known "Una voce poco fa" from *The Barber of Seville*), "Enfin je vous revois" begins with a slow section featuring a sustained, lyrical melody decorated at times with short, rapid scale passages (Example 36a). This is followed

**Example 36a**

by a more highly ornamented *allegretto* in ABA′ form, the last section of which is particularly well adorned with virtuosic vocal writing (Example 36b). Since Anna's is the only role which consistently uses this type of vocal writing, it becomes an element of characterization, external yet clearly defined and thoroughly in keeping with the mode of the librettist.

**Example 36b**

Examples given thus far have displayed a certain energy and warmth without conveying great depth of emotion regardless of the circumstances. This is in keeping with the orientation of the librettist: his superficial characterization, his lack of subtlety in engineering the succession of scenes and events, and his apparent trust in honesty and goodness. However, Boieldieu was able to depict deeper emotional conflicts when the occasion demanded, just as Scribe was able to design important emotional climaxes in his libretti. By far the most personal conflict in the opera is between Anna's love for Georges and her desire to restore the rightful heir to the house of Avenel. This conflict is brought to a head in a brief soliloquy in Act III, viii, just after Anna has learned Georges' identity. An emotional high point in the libretto, it is set as the longest and most impassioned accompanied recitative in the work (Example 37).

**Example 37**

Anna
Mal-heu - reu - - - - se!
Recit.
Que fai - re, et que viens-je d'ap - pren-dre? Ce-lui que j'ose ai -
mer est Ju-lien d'A-ve - nel! son rang et ses tré - sors, que je voulais lui
ren-dre, vont mettre en-tre nous deux un obstacle é-ter - nel!
Allegro maestoso

Indeed, although a general description of the musical style employed by Boieldieu in *La Dame blanche* would seem to suggest a certain sameness, this quality does not in fact dominate the score. As the table below shows, Scribe provides a great deal of variety written in the musical situations, which in turn inspire the composer to create different forms and styles of writing. Solo numbers range from the simple strophic forms in Jenny's *ballade* (No. 5) and Marguerite's *romance* (No. 9) to the more complex rondo-like forms of Georges' two airs (Nos. 2 and 11) and Anna's scene (No. 14). Ensembles are varied: there are duos and trios for a number of different combinations of characters—hence voices—as well as larger ensemble scenes for soloists and chorus. The chorus plays a more prominent role than usual in that it takes an active part in dramatic dialogue in addition to providing the popular but non-dramatic choruses of happy villagers. Some examples of the best of these numbers will be discussed below.

**Musical Numbers in *La Dame blanche***

| Scene | Number | Characters and types of music |
|---|---|---|
| | | ACT I |
| i-iii | 1 | (NB: Nos. 1-3 occur without break between them.) Introduction: Dickson, Jenny, villagers. Includes chorus, recitative-arioso, ensemble with chorus. |
| iii | 2 | Air with chorus: Georges Brown ("Ah! quel plaisir d'être soldat"). |
| iii | 3 | Trio with chorus: Jenny, Dickson, Georges. Includes recitative-arioso, ensembles with chorus, recapitulation of opening chorus of No. 1. |
| v | 4 | Trio with chorus: Jenny, Dickson, Georges. Includes ensemble, drinking chorus. |
| v | 5 | *Ballade* with chorus: Jenny ("D'ici voyez ce beau domaine"). Three *couplets* with choral refrain after each; short ensemble after final refrain. |
| vi | 6 | Duo: Georges, Jenny. Alternating dialogue phrases with recurrent refrain in ensemble style for both voices simultaneously. |
| viii | 7 | Finale: Jenny, Georges, Dickson. Ensemble. |

ACT II

| | | |
|---|---|---|
| | 8 | *Entr'acte.* Orchestral, ending on the dominant of E (the key of No. 9). |
| i | 9 | *Romance*: Marguerite. Two stanzas, each ending with the same refrain. |
| iii | 10 | Trio: Anna, Marguerite, Gaveston. |
| vi | 11 | *Cavatine*: Georges ("Viens, gentille dame"). Modified rondo form. |
| vii | 12 | Duo: Anna, Georges. |
| ix | 13 | Finale: Anna, Marguerite, Jenny, Dickson, Georges, Gaveston, MacIrton, chorus. Includes choruses, recitative-arioso, ensembles with chorus. |

ACT III

| | | |
|---|---|---|
| i | 14 | *Entr'acte* and air: Anna ("Enfin je vous revois"). Extended solo scene; main portion in ABA′ form. |
| iii | 15 | (NB: Nos. 15 and 16 occur without break between them.) Chorus and air: Georges, villagers. The "air" is almost entirely in the style of accompanied recitative or arioso. |
| iii | 16 | *Air National-Ecossais*: Georges, villagers. recognition of a Scottish folk song by Georges. |
| viii-ix | 17 | Recitative and duo: Anna, Marguerite. Accompanied recitative and ensemble. |
| xiv | 18 | Finale: all principals, chorus. Includes ensembles with chorus, recitative-arioso, recapitulation of Scottish song (No. 16) for all soli with chorus. |

Like his librettist, Boieldieu is the master of well-calculated effects. This talent is particularly noteworthy in two numbers involving Georges: "Viens, gentille dame" (No. 11) and the *Air National-Ecossais* (No. 16). In No. 11, opening with a memorable lyrical tune, Georges invokes the White Lady, asking that she keep her word (Example 38a).

**Example 38a**

As the music moves from *E♭* first to *C♭*, then to *V/E♭*, *C* minor, *F*, and *B♭*, Georges comments on the setting—the mysterious castle and the dark night illuminated only by the fire—but declares that he is not afraid. Returning to *E♭*, Georges repeats the opening theme, ornamented. This is followed by the often-cited section in 5/4 meter (Example 38b). The fact that the meter is an extraordinary one is empahsized by the superscription, "Conduct one measure of three and one of two beats." This perfectly reflects Georges' growing impatience to see the ghost. Changing to 3/4, the music becomes faster and faster until, at the climax of Georges' excitement, the sound of harp arpeggios announces the arrival of the White Lady (Example 38c) and Georges, now in wonder, repeats softly and slowly the opening phrases of the *cavatine*. The gradual build-up of expectation of an event every spectator knows will occur corresponds perfectly to Scribe's technique of *numérotage*, with all details arranged to insure the ordered effects of the drama.

Example 38b

Example 38c

**Example 38c (continued)**

Viens, gen - til - le da - me, viens, gen-til - le da - me,

viens, gen - til - le da - me, viens, je t'at - tends!

The structure and effect of No. 16 are similar to those of Georges' *cavatine.* The villagers sing a folk tune associated with the Avenel clan (Example 35), after which Georges inquires about the song's origin and urges them to sing it again. As they begin the refrain, however, he stops them, declaring that he believes he can sing the rest himself (Example 39). As Georges finishes the tune the villagers remark, "He is sensitive to our melodies, to the old songs of our country." Although neither Georges nor the villagers are aware of the specific significance of this event, the audience has been prepared for it since Act I and its effect is to resolve the pent-up suspense over another not unexpected outcome.

## Example 39

Georges
At-ten-dez, at-ten-dez, at-ten-
Soprano
chan- tez la guer - re, beau mé - ne - strel.
Tenor
chan- tez la guer - re, beau mé - ne - strel.
Bass
dez, j'a-che - ve-rais je crois... La, la, la, la, la, la, la,
la, la, la, la, la, la, la, la, la, la, la,

Example 39 (continued)

"He is sensitive to our melodies, to the old songs of our country." Although neither Georges nor the villagers are aware of the specific significance of this event, the audience has been prepared for it since Act I and its effect is to resolve the pent-up suspense over another not unexpected outcome.

In a letter to Pixérécourt written early in 1825 Boieldieu reported: "I am a bit ill, for the finale of the second act has tired me extremely. . . . This finale is the longest I have ever written."[118] He was referring to the most skillful and dramatic ensemble in the opera, the auction scene (No. 13).[119] Filled with action and suspense, carried out by the largest number of singers to be onstage in the opera up to this point, it is a number constructed on the principles of action and repose seen in so many ensembles of Scribe's devising. The tables below outline the action and music of the scene, and the dramatic functions of each section.

**Finale of Act II**

| Measures | Characters and events | Musical style | Keys |
|---|---|---|---|
| 1-28 | Chorus: villagers and farmers arrive for the auction. | SSTTB chorus, chordal. | C |

| | | | |
|---|---|---|---|
| 29-67 | Marguerite, Jenny, Dickson, Georges; the last three discuss events of the previous night. | Ensemble. | C, G |
| 68-86 | Farmers and Dickson discuss plans. | Ensemble with chordal chorus. | C |
| 87-110 | MacIrton announces beginning of auction. | Accompanied recitative and arioso. | E♭ |
| 111-151 | Auction begins. Dickson bids against Gaveston. Chorus encourages Dickson. | Short phrases in arioso over orchestral motivic work; chordal interjections for chorus. | E♭ |
| 152-159 | Gaveston (aside) resolves to succeed. | Accompanied recitative and arioso. | a, F, d, G |
| 160-171 | Farmers and Dickson begin to lose courage. | Ensemble with chorus. | V/C |
| 172-177a | Gaveston outbids the farmers. | Accompanied recitative and arioso. | C |
| 177b-190a | Farmers are despondent. | Ensemble with chorus. | D♭ |
| 190b-212a | Gaveston chides Georges for his earlier confidence. Georges is angry. | Arioso. | D♭, C |
| 212b-234 | Anna appears and orders Georges to bid for the estate. He makes his first offer. | Arioso. | V/C |
| 235-302 | All are astonished. | Extended ensemble with chorus. | A♭ |
| 303-359a | Auction continues: bidding between Gaveston and Georges, with brief side comments by other characters and chorus. | Short arioso phrases over orchestral motivic work; chordal interjections for chorus. | C, E, F, A, C♯, A, B♭, C |
| 359b-383a | Gaveston asks MacIrton to read the law governing auctions; he does. | Accompanied recitative and arioso. | d, A M/m |
| 383b-400a | Georges makes high bid. | Arioso (Example 40). | C |
| 400b-414a | Gaveston admits defeat. | | |
| 414b-421 | Georges admits he is only a sublieutenant. | | a, C |
| 422-end | All express pleasure or displeasure at outcome of auction. | Extended ensemble with chorus. | C |

Finale of Act II, Dramatic Functions

| Measures | **Function** |
|---|---|
| 1-28 | Introductory; static. |
| 29-67 | Slight action, preparatory. |
| 68-86 | More pertinent action, preparatory. |
| 87-110 | Still more pertinent action, preparatory. |
| 111-151 | Action proper begins. |
| 152-171 | Reaction. |
| 172-177a | Conclusion of action begun in m. 111. |
| 177b-212a | Reaction. |
| 212b-234 | New action begins. |
| 235-302 | Reaction. |
| 303-359a | Action continues. |
| 359b-383a | Action held up; static, expository. |
| 383b-421 | Conclusion of action begun in m. 212b. |
| 422-end | Reaction. |

Here again one can see the mastery of calculated effects on the part of both librettist and composer. The distribution of the action is built into the text: the forward motion gains momentum, rises to a high point (mm. 172-177a), declines somewhat, then rises to yet a higher point, at which it concludes. These traits are taken into account in the music. Beginning with a stable choral number, Boieldieu introduces first the ensemble of soloists, then an ensemble in which the chorus takes a active part. Action is suspended and the mystery enhanced in the monotone recitative of MacIrton, which brings with it the introduction of a new key. Boieldieu reinforces the suspense in the text by inserting phrases of encouragement from the onlookers, thus preventing the action from moving forward at too swift a pace. Before this part of the auction ends, Boieldieu writes a relatively long solo for Gaveston, a reflective ensemble for the others. Then, like a bolt of lightning, Gaveston wins and all action ceases. Time is suspended in the longest static section since the beginning of the scene, centered largely around the tonic key. When Anna appears on the scene a build-up in dramatic momentum even more gradual than the first is accompanied by the second major change of tonality in the scene. The length of the ensemble in mm. 235-302 has the effect of increasing suspense, which rises further as the bidding resumes. In a suspension of action paralleling that in mm. 87-110 MacIrton's monotone is heard reciting the law. The *coup* in mm. 383b-400a (Example 40) is as sudden as that in mm. 172-177a and is also accompanied by a return of the tonic key. The action reaches another plateau (mm. 400b-421) paralleling a similar earlier situation (mm. 190b-212a), after which an extended ensemble concludes the scene and anchors it in place.

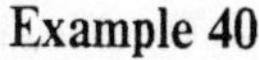

## Example 40

Jenny & Marguerite

Cinq cent mille é - cus!

Anna

C'est

Georges

À cinq cent mille é - cus!

Dickson

Cinq cent mille é - cus!

Gaveston & MacIrton

Sopranos & Tenors

Cinq cent mille é - cus!

Basses

(Anna)

bien, c'est bien, je suis con- ten- te, c'est bien, c'est bien, je suis con-ten-te

MacIrton

Cinq

**Example 40 (continued)**

Boieldieu's modulations in the course of the finale are not particularly adventurous, and Auber can readily be awarded top honors for designing key schemes to underscore the course of events in similar musical numbers. However, the key scheme does help define major sections of the finale: actions begin and end in *C*, while the two large sections of the auction are centered around *Eb* and *Ab*, with numerous sections of successive, short range modulations to accommodate much of the actual bidding. Modulations become more frequent during the second half of the scene and underline the growing excitement of the drama.

*La Dame blanche* is indeed a classic. Musically it presents a tasteful synthesis of the lightness and simplicity of French *couplets*, Rossinian melodic style, dramatic ensemble writing, a variety of vocal forms, borrowed and newly composed material. Dramatically it combines elements of three novels and a narrative poem, all of foreign origin, with a touch of German romanticism and the contemporary characters and outlooks so appealing to the French middle class, all fitted neatly within the framework of the well-made libretto. Librettist and composer complement each other at every turn, reflecting an ideal of collaboration equaled only by that of Scribe and Auber.

## How Operas Fail:
## The Case Of Auber's *Le Timide*

Although pieces in three acts are by far the most common among Scribe's opéras comiques, nearly one-fourth of his libretti are one-act works. *Le Chalet,* one of the most successful of these, has already been discussed. Taking his material from Goethe's singspiel, Scribe refashioned *Le Chalet* in keeping with his own highly developed techniques of the well-made libretto and made of it a more up-to-date and stageworthy piece.

*Le Timide,* another one-act work, presents the opposite side of the dramatic coin. So little information is available about the opera that it is impossible to say whether Scribe had a literary model in mind when he wrote the libretto. However, the nature of the work, the types of characters, and the situations presented make the use of a model seem likely. Some work of the *comedie-vaudeville* type would bc a probable candidate. Now that Scribe's techniques of structure, the creation of musical situations, and the way in which these situations occur in opéras comiques have been discussed, perhaps the reasons for the complete failure of such a seemingly pleasant work will be clearer.

> Auber ended his first period with *Le Timide,* given 30 May 1826, which failed to the accompaniment of boos and whistles. The libretto is merely a *comédie-vaudeville,* and the music is Auber at his dullest. After fourteen performances, the work was withdrawn.[120]

This one-act work is so insignificant as to be omitted from Loewenberg's listings. However, it is not really the libretto by Scribe and Saintine nor the mere dullness of Auber's music, but a combination of factors that was responsible for its lack of success. Not the least of these factors was one Auber himself mentioned: "Although *Le Timide* was a weak work, it would have been performed more often except for a pregnancy which took from the stage one of my actresses [Jenny Colon, a very popular soprano at the Opéra-Comique]."[121]

A comedy of manners, the opera takes place some time in the 1820s in a chateau thirty leagues from Paris. Mme. d'Hérancy, the owner of the chateau and a young and attractive widow, has brought her younger sister Amélie from Paris to the country for a vacation. Amélie and Adrienne, the chambermaid, are bored and Amélie is particularly anxious to return to Paris because of a young man she met at a ball.

Although she has only spoken to him once, Amélie reports that she has seen him watching her at the theatre and at the Tuileries and has been favorably impressed by his sweet, timid disposition. Now, having left so abruptly for the country, she fears she will never see him again or that he will forget her.

A valet announces the arrival of M. de Sauvré, Mme. d'Hérancy's tutor. In their conversation Mme. d'Hérancy reveals that on the previous evening a young man, his post-chaise having broken down, was given shelter in the chateau. St.-Ernest, a colonel from a regiment quartered in the nearby village, arrives to visit Mme. d'Hérancy. He is the nephew of de Sauvré's old friend, General Valmont. When de Sauvré questions St.-Ernest about his reputation as a lover, the latter counters that it is not he but another nephew about whom de Sauvré is speaking. Embarrassed by the discussion of this cousin's amorous exploits, Amélie leaves. Just then the door opens to admit young Valmont, who is St.-Ernest's cousin and also the timid young man of whom Amélie has become fond. By the time Amélie returns, the rest of the company is convinced that Valmont is the notorious seducer and Mme. d'Hérancy begins her attempts to separate the two young people.

When the rest leave, Valmont tells St.-Ernest that he is in love with Amélie but has been too timid to approach her. St.-Ernest advises him to get the others on his side—especially the chambermaid. Then St.-Ernest, determined to carry out the ruse he has begun, warns Mme. d'Hérancy of Valmont's intentions to speak to her. He will pretend to be timid, says St.-Ernest, but is up to no good. St.-Ernest then declares his love for Mme. d'Hérancy, but she gets from him a promise not to speak to her again of such matters.

Adrienne and Amélie enter to report that during breakfast Valmont has said not a word, but has been looking at Amélie as if he wished to do so. St.-Ernest denounces this timidity as a ruse, predicting that Valmont's entire approach will change when he talks to Adrienne. When Valmont and Adrienne are alone this prediction comes true, for he speaks to her in a way that admits of double meanings and she believes he is trying to seduce her. This impression is secured when he, trying to win her over to his side, offers her money. Adrienne's calls for help bring de Sauvré who, after Adrienne leaves, asks Valmont's assistance in composing a love letter to Mme. d'Hérancy. While de Sauvré is off writing a draft of the letter, Mme. d'Hérancy enters. When the former, on his return, finds Valmont and Mme. d'Hérancy together, he concludes that Valmont has betrayed him. In the meantime, Mme. d'Hérancy herself has misunderstood Valmont's words and believes his declaration of love was meant for her. Thinking to take revenge, de Sauvré tries to force Valmont to declare his love to Amélie before the entire company, but Valmont can only stammer. Finally de Sauvré challenges him either to marry Amélie or to face a duel. Naturally, Valmont is overjoyed to accept the former, but Mme. d'Hérancy objects and in her objections reveals that St.-Ernest has told them of Valmont's reputation as a rake. When accounts are finally set right, Valmont wins Amélie and Mme. d'Hérancy consents to marry St.-Ernest despite his deserved reputation.

Granting that its plot is too slight for anything but a one-act opera, *Le Timide* shows logical progression in its action, with the usual contrived entrances and exits of Scribe's longer libretti. There are times, however, when even the technical logic breaks down, and this is one of the contributory factors to the weakness of the work.

The major ingredients of the action are contained in the first four scenes. The plot is of the delayed-action type and begins after a great many events important to the action have already occurred: Amélie and Valmont have met, St.-Ernest has been in town long enough to have become acquainted with Mme. d'Hérancy, and Valmont has arrived unexpectedly at the chateau. In the first scene, external circumstances and verbal references serve purposes of exposition and characterization. The conflicting attitudes of the three women regarding their stay in the country and Amélie's observations on the character of the young man she has met delineate the personalities of these figures immediately, and the relating of circumstances surrounding the departure from Paris helps fill in background information.

The appearance of M. de Sauvré, identified before his entrance as the young ladies' tutor, serves rather little dramatic purpose at this point except to move him onstage and to fix his character and identity for the audience. Except for points relating to these items, the only elements of any importance here are found in the information given in one of de Sauvré's speeches (quoted below) and the statement by Mme. d'Hérancy that de Sauvré often seems jealous.

> Someone wanted to marry you [Mme. d'Hérancy]; it was not my idea, it was yours, and although this party disappointed me on every point, I did not hazard an objection. . . . You become a widow, you want to take your young sister, who is still under my care, with you; I quickly consent to it, I cede to you all my rights; I only reserve one, that of coming to see you from time to time in order to ask your wishes and to bring you my signature [of approval]. . . .

This finished, however, the plot continues as Mme. d'Hérancy tells of the young man to whom she has given hospitality, followed directly by the entrance of St.-Ernest, identified beforehand as a colonel garrisoned nearby. When he turns out to be the nephew of de Sauvré's old friend, the conversation logically turns to St.-Ernest's reputation and thence to the *quiproquo*: St.-Ernest's assigning this reputation to his cousin.

Since it would be inconvenient to have to deal with a meeting of Amélie and Valmont before we know, or at least guess, his identity, Amélie leaves before the young man enters. All the characters have now been introduced and we know what will happen to them. Two young men have already been mentioned in some detail: a timid one with who Amélie is in love, and a cousin to whom St.-Ernest has shifted his own reputation. Scribe skillfully handles the equation of both men with the character of Valmont by first having him recognized as the cousin, then (Scene v) as the sweetheart. Although the arrival of both men in one character is in the category of pleasant coincidences, Valmont's arrival *per se* has been carefully prepared and the audience knows as much about him as is necessary for the rest of the opera. The delight for the spectator comes not in seeing what Scribe will do, but only how he will do it.

By this point we already know too that St.-Ernest is interested in Mme. d'Hérancy, and we suspect de Sauvré's interest as well because of the reference to his apparent jealousy. We also know that anyone with Valmont's supposed reputation should try to take advantage of three lovely and unattached ladies. Yet knowing that the reputation is not his, we expect some comic misunderstandings and a final unraveling of the entire mix-up.

Although the plot of the opera is too slight for a longer work, the anticipated action is perhaps too much. Rather than creating a complex plot the threads of which are interwoven and brought to a conclusion at whatever point beyond which they are no longer necessary, Scribe here has only one main theme—the mistaken identity—and must embroider that by means of unnecessary characters and repetitious actions. Adrienne, for example, could be eliminated and de Sauvré's part cut considerably. At the same time St.-Ernest's predictions of his cousin's conduct, followed immediately by the expected behavior, or Valmont's misunderstood conversations with both Adrienne and Mme. d'Hérancy are too much of an amusing thing; one example of each would make the point. In view of what we know by Scenes iv-v to be the theme of the opera, even the logic of introducing some of the later scenes is questionable. Except for Mme. d'Hérancy's comment concerning de Sauvré's jealousy and the hints given in the latter's comments on the arrival of St.-Ernest, there is no good reason why the love letter scene (Scene xii) should be introduced at all. While not unexpected, it is also not necessary as the resolution of any major questions raised earlier in the opera and is quite peripheral to the action itself. Also, there is no reason for de Sauvré to insist that Valmont declare his love for Amélie before everyone except to give the occasion for a rather comical scene and ensemble.

As can be seen from this overview, there is something in this libretto that is atypical for Scribe's technique in this genre. The fact is that the work displays too many of the characteristics of the comedy of manners and too few of the essential simplified, logical structural elements typical of the best of Scribe's opéras comiques. Numerous speeches in the opening scenes, which normally contain information essential to exposition, background and characterization, are included, as are some entire scenes, merely for effect, for a satire of contemporary society in a high comic vein which is not essential to the opera's main theme. For example, the first scene contains the following bit of sung dialogue.

**Amélie.**

I would have spoken to him . . . But suddenly, what a shame!
My sister left for the country, and here one sees
Spectacles . . . only in the countryside . .

**Mme. d'Hérancy.**

Concerts only in the woods.

**Adrienne.**

And love only in novels!

Further examples of this sort of social judgment are to be found in the following illustrations.

Scene ii.

**Adrienne.**

We [chambermaids] always know, but I did not speak of it for fear of annoying madame . . . because madame knows as well as I that post-chaises breaking down, bewildered travelers, all adventures begin like that . . . at least all that I have read.

Scene iii.

**Mme. d'Hérancy.**

Perhaps Monsieur comes also to have lunch with us?

. . . . . . . . . . . . . . . . . . . . . . . . . . . .

**St.-Ernest.**

I would not dare to take that liberty. I only come to inform myself of your health . . . and to remain with you for dinner.

**de Sauvré.**

What, colonel, you who do not dare . . .

**St.-Ernest.**

It is quite different, monsieur: dinner is without consequence . . . it is an affair of etiquette, of ceremony . . . it is a meal by invitation. . .

**de Sauvré.**

Not always, from what I can see.

**St.-Ernest.**

Nowadays one dines for business purposes, and one lunches for pleasure! In the afternoon one receives at his table the persons one must . . . in the morning one admits there the people one likes . . . and it is because of this that I ate before I left . . . I do myself justice, my ladies, and have not yet such self-esteem to aspire to the honors of a cup of chocolate.

Scene vi.

**Valmont.**

I know nothing more absurd and more annoying than timidity . . . it is the calling of a dupe.

**St.-Ernest.**

Especially in this day and age when there never was a rarer defect.

**Valmont.**

So much so that I am the only one of my species; I am like a lost being in the civilized world; I have the appearance of a foreigner who does not

> understand the language of the country! Women mock you, fools always believe you stand in admiration before their merits, and intelligent men take you for a beast . . . I am sure that people here already have that opinion of me.

Extended speeches of this sort serve no dramatic function. Since they are similar to one another they do little to further characterization, which, in any event, is accomplished through external, descriptive means in most cases. They present, further, or resolve no action, present no clues, hide no mysteries. Thus in the ordinary opéra comique by Scribe they would never have been included, for they distract the audience from consideration of the main theme and the actions central to its development. Since one does not know at the time they occur whether these speeches contain important motifs or ideas, one must carry in one's mind a great deal of excess dramatic baggage. When this is combined with unnecessary or overworked scenes, characters, and situations, the overload is more than so slight a comedy can bear, and the structure collapses. The parallel to *La Barcarolle* is obvious. There too Scribe has included too much topical humor, has drawn up a plot of far too great complexity, and has created a failure.

Comparison of *Le Timide* to *Le Chalet* is both easy and difficult: easy because the scope of the two works is similar, difficult because the dramatic logic and appropriateness of every element of *Le Chalet* is in direct opposition to everything in *Le Timide.* In Adam's work no time or motion is wasted and there is no extraneous material. Each event leads logically to the next, each development is carefully prepared and resolved, yet the quality of logic is never strained. The opposite is true of *Le Timide*: the libretto is filled with verbal padding and the dramatic engineering is so mechnical as to be computerized, without regard for the artful naturalness usually present in Scribe's better works. Even the contrivances are overly contrived.

The seesaw effect in the fortunes of the hero and the *scène à faire,* those usual members of the well-made libretto, are blunted in their effect by the ineptness of the writing in *Le Timide.* Valmont's fortunes neither rise nor fall in the course of the work but remain on the same hopeless level until circumstances and misunderstanding bring him his heart's desire, marriage to Amélie. Never is Valmont in control of his own fate; thus he is totally unable to overcome the obstacles facing him. In *Le Chalet* chance also has a hand in bringing about the marriage of Daniel and Bettly, but there is a difference in the way the entire course of action is handled. First, Daniel tries to help himself to gain his own goals. Only when he can do no more on his own does Max come to his aid. Second, each stage in Max's plan is carefully enacted, whereas de

Sauvré's demand that Valmont marry Amélie comes like the proverbial bolt out of the blue. Lacking logical motivation, it resolves nothing but is only the purest artifice. Following this "solution" to Valmont's problems, the *scène à faire* seems ridiculously anticlimactic and even inept. The mistaken identity problem is brought to a satisfactory conclusion, but instead of being punished, the villain in the piece—St.-Ernest—is rewarded with a promise of marriage to the rich, attractive widow. In the context of Scribe's usual morality the rewarding of such a rake with the hand of the most puritanical member of the cast is illogical at best.

**Words and Music**

There is more to Auber's failure in *Le Timide* than the mere "dullness" of which Longyear speaks, and for this failure the libretto is partly responsible. The best examples for study are the ensemble scenes, for it is here that Scribe's usual dramatic logic and acute sense for the placement of moments of tension and release normally come into play with good results. The best—or rather, the worst—example of Scribe's failure in this respect is the ensemble in Scene xvi, in which de Sauvré tries to force Valmont into a declaration of love for Amélie. Although for reasons mentioned earlier the scene has little *raison d'être* other than to enhance the comedy of manners aspect of the opera, it is definitely a musical situation. The action proceeds slowly in music, allowing full scope for the expression of all its elements and adding suspense as to its outcome. As usual, Scribe has constructed the text as a series of moments in which the action moves forward alternating with some sections of reflection or repose. Valmont stammers to a halt; a static ensemble follows; then another bit of stammering and a repetition of the earlier ensemble. Although quite an extended scene, it does not contain enough drama to justify the scope of the music. We are given a point of repose when there has been so little action, so little new information revealed, that we have no need of it. The action between the two ensemble sections is still shorter and repetitious at that. The effect is that of one long, static piece containing sections of greater and lesser repose. Even the best music could do little with such a scene.

In addition, there is little in the opera to illustrate the quality for which Auber was most often praised, his talent for writing delightful, piquant melodies. Solo songs are few: a rondo for St.-Ernest (Scene iii), *couplets* for Valmont (Scene xiii). The remaining musical numbers are scenes involving sung dialogue and ensemble work betwen two or more characters and a final chorus, which is merely a convenience. A glance at one of the solos, St.-Ernest's rondo, is sufficient to show that Auber did not waste his greatest gifts on this opera (Example 41). The melody is quite undistinguished, overburdened with triadic outlines and having none of the outstanding vital rhythmic qualilties which are apparent immediately in Auber's best tunes. The lack of melodic goal and the use of too wide a variety of undistinguished rhythmic figures characterize this and other melodies in the opera and account for the musical lethargy found throughout the score.

**Example 41**

The great variety of musical forms and their treatment in *Le Chalet* presents a sharp contrast to those in *Le Timide.* The use of a chorus in *Le Chalet* is a definite advantage, for it widens the range of musical possibilities and heightens the effect of Introduction and Finale.

The musical profile of *Le Timide* is pale by comparison, particularly at the end of the work. The largest ensemble in the piece, the quintet described above, is nondramatic and occurs at the beginning of the final scene. It is followed by three pages of spoken dialogue containing the *scène à faire*, after which the opera closes with a four-line chorus for all characters. Not only does the placement of the quintet make what follows it anticlimactic, but its own lack of dramatic activity or significance dulls rather than sharpens one's appetite for the conclusion of the opera. In comparison, the gradual increase in intensity in the final scenes of *Le Chalet* is masterful and holds the listener's interest in the opera until the final ensemble and chorus provide an anchor for the long and logical ascent of the hero's good fortunes.

There is no single reason for the failure of *Le Timide*, for no one thing went wrong. Rather, everything was at fault, from the orientation of the drama to the lack of musical variety or interest. An opéra comique could survive without truly great music, as is illustrated by *Le Maçon.* It could succeed without consistent realism or naturalness in the exposition, development, and resolution of the drama, as is illustrated by *Haydée.* Without both, however, and with the added liability of comedy of manners qualities antithetical to the opéra comique genre, *Le Timide* was doomed.

## POST-SCRIBE: MEILHAC AND HALEVY

Eugène Scribe died in 1861, but his world died some time earlier. In opéra comique the 1850s saw the beginnings of a more serious genre, the lyric opera, and a more frivolous one, eventually known as *opéra-bouffe* or operetta. Lyric opera, "a more intimate counterpoise to the grandiose operas of Meyerbeer,"[1] developed in quantity and quality to such an extent that by the 1870s the Opéra-Comique and the Théâtre-Lyrique led the Opéra in the production of the most significant, progressive, and popular musical dramas. Many of these works, set by Gounod, Massenet, Thomas and others, retained little of their "comique" origins except the spoken dialogue, and by the end of the century this too was often eliminated in favor of recitative.[2] In a lighter vein, *opéra-bouffe* was popularized, although not created, by Jacques Offenbach in the Paris of the 1860s.[3] The difference between *opéra-bouffe* or operetta and opéra comique has been summarized by Grout.

> . . . in the opéra comique the audience is expected to lend a certain amount of credence and sympathy to the story; some appeal is made to the feelings of the spectators, some trace of sentiment exists. In the operetta and similar genres . . . the aim is simply to amuse, and the means are wit, parody, and satire.[4]

In the best examples of this fast-moving and popular form, the works of Offenbach, some critics even saw "the only new species of dramatic art produced during the second half of the nineteenth century, the first half having evolved the romantic drama."[5]

The roots of both lyric opera and *opéra-bouffe* are to be found in the works of Scribe and his musical collaborators. Some of his later opéras comiques do show a change in the direction of lyric opera (for example, Auber's *Jenny Bell*). He even provided a quite inferior and ridiculous libretto, *Barkouf*, for Offenbach. Yet Scribe was old; he had spent the better part of his life creating, remolding, and producing in great quantities all the dramatic genres of his day. In the face of advancing age and a changing theatre, Scribe's production declined. While providing the basis for change in opéra comique, Scribe himself could not or would not effect that change.

Times had also changed, for in 1852 Louis-Napoleon Bonaparte, since 1848 president of the French Republic, made himself Emperor Napoleon III, eventually earning what one historian designates "the dubious title of the first modern dictator. . . ."[6] Once again the people of France, tired of revolutionary turmoil, longed for order and stability, and Louis-Napoleon appealed to the people on these grounds. An authoritarian ruler who allowed little political freedom, he became "a leader in a great march toward material progress."[7] Thus while riding into power on a wave of public approval, he at the same time moved to crush public disapproval, or at least the means to express it. Newspapers were carefully censored and public positions thought to be influential were carefully regulated. Yet all was not somber even though it could easily have been so under such a form of government, however intelligently run. The Emperor set up a luxurious and gay court and hired noted city planners and architects to rebuild and redecorate Paris. Prosperity was everywhere in a state of becoming, and external appearance was important to citizens and outsiders alike.

By the time of Scribe's death, however, even this new and seemingly prosperous government was in trouble at home and abroad. Longing for peace, France had no peace: ". . . war is after all the supreme pageantry (or was then); France was the strongest country in Europe, and the emperor's name was Napoleon."[8] The Crimean War was soon followed by war with Italy, then with Mexico, and finally an unnecessary war with Prussia brought an end to the Second Empire. The people's anxiety over an almost constant state of war was heightened in the 1860s by their growing fear of Bismarck's Prussia. Merimée, writing to Madame de Montijo in the Spring of 1867, observed:

> Because no one has any really clear idea of the danger, everybody is frightened. M. de Bismarck has become the universal bogey-man. His words are weighed and reweighed, and people think he wants to swallow us whole. . . . If you could see the way our poor country is split, the lack of patriotism, the love of money and high living, you would not recognize the French of the past and you would dread a war for them, even against an enemy of inferior strength.[9]

Into this milieu stepped a team of librettists destined to provide texts to the best and most popular composers of their day and to picture society in their writings in the same way as Scribe had some twenty-five years before. Henri Meilhac (1831-1897) and Ludovic Halévy (1834-1908), like Scribe, both came out of the active Parisian middle class and were known in their own day as dramatists as well as librettists. Meilhac started his working life as a bookseller and journalist, writing humorous contributions to the *Journal pour rire* and *La Vie parisienne.* In 1855 he turned to the theatre, but his first vaudevilles were, like Scribe's, failures. In 1856 his third play, *La Sarabande du cardinal,* played successfully at the Gymnase, the scene of over a hundred Scribe premieres in the 1820s and 1830s. He later tried his hand at a five-act comedy but was unsuccessful.

In 1860 Meilhac began a collaboration with Halévy that was to last for over twenty years and was to encompass all theatrical genres: drama, comedy, vaudeville, farce, opera, opéra comique, *opéra-bouffe*, and ballet. Like Meilhac, Ludovic Halévy, nephew of composer Jacques-Fromental-Elie Halévy, also first earned his living in a nontheatrical profession. Until 1858 he was a civil servant, although he had begun early in life to write dramas. Even before he left government service to devote all his time to the theatre he had met one of his chief musical collaborators, Jacques Offenbach, for whom he wrote his first libretto, *Ba-Ta-Clan*, in 1855. After Halévy joined pens with Meilhac, the two produced many such spirited farces for this composer, beginning with *La Belle Hélène* in 1864. Other successful collaborations of the two writers and Offenbach included *Barbe-bleue* (1866), *La Vie parisienne* (1866), *La Grande-duchesse de Gérolstein* (1867), *La Perichole* (1868), *and Les Brigands* (1868), all among Offenbach's most popular works. Yet Meilhac and Halévy are known to us perhaps less for all these works than for thc masterful libretto of Bizet's *Carmen*.[10]

The collaboration was a successful one not merely because of cooperation but because these writers brought to the partnership different but complementary talents. Meilhac is said to have had a stronger and more individual style, while Halévy was "a clever French dramatist of the more conventional pattern."[11] According to one source, Meilhac was ordinarily responsible for the "planning of the plot and the writing of the prose dialogue. . . . His greatest gift was for humorous characterizations."[12] Such a talent would be put to good use in any work for Offenbach and is evident in the creation of the comical smugglers of *Carmen*. Toning down and polishing the work would thus normally fall to Halévy, who created the largest proportion of the lyrics for music as well. Together, Meilhac, Halévy, and Offenbach established a genre, the *opéra-bouffe*, and prepared the way for numerous less skillful imitators in the field of operetta. In a totally different vein, nearly ten years after the success of *La Belle Hélène*, Meilhac, Halévy, and Bizet began preparing their musical and dramatic bombshell for the Opéra-Comique, *Carmen*. With this work, the violent ending of which was a first for the Opéra-Comique, realism in plot and characters was introduced into the genre, replacing Scribe's realism the bourgeois audience wished to exist with "lifelike, working-class characters ruled only by their passions. . . ."[13] The first important realistic opera in France, *Carmen* paved the way for Italian *verismo* later in the century.[14]

Because Meilhac and Halévy are similar to Scribe in their background, in the genres they cultivate, and in the orientation of their works toward middle-class audiences, it would be unnatural if the heritage of Scribe should not influence their work. This heritage is evident primarily in the *opéra-bouffe*, a genre which shows its derivation from the popular theatre and a definite orientation toward the language and manners of the boulevard. Primarily a vehicle for satire and parody, the *opéra-bouffe* thrived on lively action and animated, timely dialogue peppered with puns, word plays of other types, and verbal barbs directed at classes or situations rather than individuals. Musically, *opéra-bouffe* tended to use the more conventional forms already typical of opéra comique, with frequent use of popular or *café-concert* styles shown in the straightforward, tuneful melodies with their lively dance rhythms. The chart in Appendix B lists the musical numbers in the works selected as illustrations of Meilhac's and Halévy's libretto style: Offenbach's *La Belle Hélène*, *Barbe-bleue*, and *La Grande-duchesse de Gérolstein*; and Bizet's *Carmen*.

The last-named work is, of course, not in the same category with those of Offenbach, and the differences between them show up in their musical profiles. *Carmen* contains a large number of scenes involving ensembles with or without chorus, which would imply that a relatively large amount of action is carried out within the musical numbers. In the Offenbach works, however, the largest single category of musical numbers is that of strophic forms, the traditional *couplets*, *ballades*, *chansons*, and *rondes* of opéra comique. Often these strophic solo numbers have choral refrains after each stanza and appear within the course of a longer musical scene, e.g., an Introduction or a Finale. Thus not only are there fewer ensemble scenes in the Offenbach works than in *Carmen* or in any typical work by Auber, but these ensemble scenes are more often taken up by static solo numbers. Compared to *Carmen* or to a typical Scribe work, then, relatively little dramatic action is carried on within a musical number and more importance is placed on the spoken dialogue. Nevertheless, the chart clearly shows that an *opéra-bouffe* of Meilhac and Halévy included the same types of music as did an opéra comique of Scribe, even to the conventional forms of opening and closing an act.

Meilhac, Halévy, and Offenbach include in their works two new but not unprecedented categories of music: *mélodrame* and reprise. A *mélodrame* is not necessarily the equivalent of earlier operatic melodrama. While it may involve spoken dialogue over an instrumental accompaniment, an Offenbach *mélodrame* may also consist simply of short instrumental interludes to cover stage action, such as the entrance or exit of a large number of characters. The music for a *mélodrame* may be reused later in the work or may be an instrumental reprise of a previously sung refrain or coda to an earlier number. In nature and function such pieces thus resemble the ritornelli and sinfonie of Italian baroque opera.

The vocal reprise is also not without precedent, for Scribe himself used the device in the same way as Meilhac and Halévy. Normally the reprise is a refrain, often choral, of a previous musical number which is sung after an intervening interlude of spoken dialogue. It usually covers the entrance or exit of a character or group of characters and serves to round off the scene musically. Scribe used the technique in the same way, although he was more likely to write a section with this sort of structure to be set to music throughout. It hardly need be mentioned that reprises should not be confused or even associated with reminiscence motives or *leitmotifs* used in more serious operas of Offenbach's time and earlier.

Among the three examples of Meilhac's and Halévy's *opéra-bouffe* style, *La Grande-duchesse de Gérolstein* is the best candidate for more detailed examination. It not only contains good illustrations of Meilhac's and Halévy's technique but is relevant to its social, musical, and dramatic milieu. The work, first performed at the Variétés on April 12, 1867, was one of Offenbach's greatest successes. Only six years after its premiere it was said to have been performed on sixty-five stages in France and one-hundred-seventeen stages in foreign lands, and had been given in English, German, Swedish, Portugese, Norwegian, Spanish, Catalan, Polish, and Czech translations.[15] The international success of the work was undoubtedly furthered by the presence in its audience not only of Emperor Napoleon III, Thiers, and Bismarck, but of the Princess of Wales, the Duke of Edinburgh, the Tsar, and the Kings of Bavaria, Portugal, and Sweden, all in Paris to attend the Exposition of 1867.[16] Its favorable acceptance by the audience was further insured by the excellent performance of Hortense Schneider as the Grand Duchess.[17] However, another significant factor in the public's ready acceptance of the work lay quite outside the intrinsic merits of libretto or score, in the political overtones of the satire. The atmosphere in Paris, described above by Merimée as one of fear, was emphasized by the presence of Bismarck. For the French, the *Grande-Duchesse* had an effect similar to that of comic scenes in an otherwise serious drama, serving as a "distraction and purge".

> In the imaginary Grand Duchy of Gerolstein there was no threatening exhibit of Herr Krupp's inventiveness, blatantly in evidence at the Exposition. Here the hero was Genral Boum, a

> parody of the ineffectual, bombastic commander, eager for war, no matter what the cause, and incapable of planning a campaign or achieving a victory. He delighted the audience as the *reductio ad absurdum* of a figure familiar in real life, and for the time being dispelled their fright. Bismarck, too, enjoyed the spectacle, both for itself and as evidence of the weakness of the French.[18]

Yet one should not mistake the intention of the authors, for the *Grande-duchesse* provides a good example of the non-specific nature of their satire. True, Meilhac and Halévy poked fun at the military and at the nature of war, but they could hardly foresee that three years later the Emperor would declare war on Prussia on grounds nearly as trivial as those for which Gérolstein's soldiers are sent off to fight, nor were they fully aware of the capricious nature of their sovereign nor of the weakness of the French army at this point. The satire was not directed specifically at "the absolute power of the Kaiser and the already declared war,"[19] since the war was not yet declared, but at war in general, as Halévy himself remarked.

> This time it is war we are making fun of, . . . and war is at our gates. . . . People look for and find allusions to absolute power and the military mind. Events are giving our jokes a significance and violence that we had not intended.[20]

That it was possible for contemporary audiences to find specific allusions in the libretto of *La Grande-duchesse de Gérolstein* illustrates only how much its authors were in tune with their times, as was Scribe in his *comédies-vaudevilles* and dramas thirty or forty years earlier.

*Le Grande-duchesse de Gérolstein* is set in eighteenth-century Germany. As the opera begins, the soldiers of Gérolstein are amusing themselves dancing and drinking with the young ladies of the village before going off to the recently declared war. Fritz says goodbye to his fiancée Wanda, but General Boum interrupts the party and sends the girls away. The General then singles out Fritz for reprimand, but the latter remarks that the sole reason he is always the object of Boum's anger is the the General is in love with Wanda and is jealous. Népomuc announces that the Grand Duchess will soon arrive to see the army pass in review and the General, after assigning Fritz to guard duty, goes off to take care of last minute arrangements. Wanda returns to sing a humorous love duet with Fritz, after which General Boum enters, reprimands Fritz, and admits that he left the soldier alone only to trap him disobeying orders. Fritz remarks that this is the first of the General's manoeuvres ever to succeed.

The sound of gunfire offstage announces the arrival of Baron Puck, who is shot at by a sentry for neglecting to give the password. Puck informs Boum that he has taught the Grand Duchess the regimental song so that she can sing it with the soldiers and help raise their morale before they leave for battle. The reason for the war is also brought out in this conversation. The Grand Duchess has been content until now to lead a life of pleasure and to leave the affairs of the state to Baron Puck and his confederates. Now, however, she is twenty years old and has become bored with her former life. Even Prince Paul, chosen as a husband for her, has failed to make an impression, and she has refused even to see Baron Grog, the ambassador sent by Paul's father to conclude arrangements for the marriage. Perhaps a little war will be just the thing to cure her boredom and make her decide to marry Paul after all. If the war game fails, Puck and Boum fear the Duchess may look to other amusements, choose a favorite, and restrict their own powers and influence. Hence the war, a diversion for their youthful sovereign. As a drum roll announces the arrival of the Grand Duchess, Puck and Boum agree on their strategy: today they will charm her with the regimental song, next week with a military victory; then they will return home to share the power of state.

The Grand Duchess, watching the army pass in review, notices the handsome Fritz and has him called forward. As she becomes more and more infatuated with him she promotes him successively to corporal and sergeant. Finding that he hopes to marry Wanda, she then promotes him to captain in order to place him above the station of a mere peasant girl. After singing the regimental song, the Grand Duchess prepares to discuss battle plans, but is interrupted by the arrival of Prince Paul. The Prince is disturbed that the Grand Duchess has postponed their marriage for so long that he is being ridiculed in all the courts of Europe and even in the gossip column of a Dutch newspaper, but the Duchess is in no hurry and promises she will marry him when she has some time to spare. General Boum begins his explanation of the battle plans. Fritz ridicules them but Baron Puck silences him, saying that he is not allowed to speak at a conference unless he is a superior officer and a noble. Hearing this, the Grand Duchess makes Fritz a baron and a general and orders Boum to carry out Fritz's plan. When Boum refuses, Fritz is given full command of the army. Baron Puck, Boum, and Prince Paul begin a conspiracy against Fritz.

The second act begins shortly before the soldiers are to return. Fritz has won a great victory over the enemy and all the ladies look forward to the army's return. Prince Paul, still unwed, enters with Baron Grog. The Grand Duchess still refuses to see the ambassador and has one of her servants divert him by showing him out the wrong door. The Grand Duchess then greets Fritz, who explains that he won the war by allowing the enemy to capture a large liquor supply and drink themselves into a bloodless defeat. Alone with Fritz, the Grand Duchess uses the hackneyed lovers' ruse of pretending that a friend of hers, a noblewoman, has asked her to intercede with Fritz and to tell him of her secret love. Fritz remains refreshingly obtuse throughout the whole affair and, in an aside, renews his decision to ask the Grand Duchess' permission to marry Wanda.

General Boum, Baron Puck, and Prince Paul arrive in time to overhear Népomuc state that Fritz is to be housed in the right wing of the palace. The General and Puck know that there is a secret passage to Fritz's room through which, years before, an ancestor of the Grand Duchess would pass to meet her lover. They persuade Prince Paul to join them in conspiring to murder Fritz, entering his room through the passage. The Grand Duchess overhears their plans. She has just granted Fritz's request to marry Wanda and is furious that he would prefer a peasant girl to her. In a surprise move the Grand Duchess asks to join the conspiracy.

Fritz and Wanda are married and still at the wedding celebration when, at the beginning of Act III, the Grand Duchess and General Boum prepare for the assassination. The Grand Duchess asks only that the men not stab Fritz in the face, since he is so handsome. She then notices Baron Grog, who has joined the conspiracy to keep from getting bored while waiting to see her, and is attracted to the handsome ambassador immediately. When they are alone the Grand Duchess promises Baron Grog a higher position in her court than he ever had at home, but the Baron says that unless she and Paul marry he will have to leave. The Grand Duchess, realizing that she has no more interest in Fritz's murder, orders the other conspirators to leave but does give General Boum permission to play a practical joke on the intended victim instead. Then, in another surprise move, the Grand Duchess tells Prince Paul that they will be married in two hours.

The wedding party escorts Fritz and Wanda to Fritz's quarters in the palace, but before the couple even has a chance to sing a love duet General Boum and a crowd of people return twice to serenade them. Finally the General breaks into the room to tell Fritz that he must go at once, since the enemy is poised for attack. The unhappy bridegroom dons his uniform, straps on his sabre, and departs.

As Act IV begins, guests are celebrating the marriage of the Grand Duchess and Prince Paul. The Grand Duchess asks about Fritz and General Boum tells of the joke he has played on his enemy. The

General, having been warned by his mistress that her husband was becoming suspicious and was planning to wait in ambush for him that night, has sent Fritz on a military wild goose chase down the road where the husband and his friends were to be waiting. At the end of this explanation Fritz returns, beaten, bruised, and bloody. The Grand Duchess accuses him of being a home-wrecker, removes his titles one by one, and confers them on Baron Grog, her new favorite. The Baron thanks her on behalf of his wife and four children, whom he is sure will be overjoyed at his success. Hearing this, the Grand Duchess takes back all the titles and honors and returns the power of state to the hands of Boum and Puck. As a final gesture she allows Fritz to ask one favor. Fritz replies that he wishes to be appointed village schoolmaster, since he has always wanted to learn to read and write. The Duchess grants his request. All characters express their pleasure at the way events have been resolved, and the Grand Duchess resigns herself to a fate that is "unexpected but moral."

There is much in this libretto that reflects the influence of Scribe. The delayed-action plot is of the type Scribe habitually used, for the stage acton shows only the culmination of events which had been set up previously. Before the curtain rises the war has already been planned; the Grand Duchess has learned the regimental song; Fritz and Wanda have fallen in love; Wanda has caught the eye of General Boum, who then punishes Fritz out of jealousy; Prince Paul has been waiting patiently for a marriage that was announced months before; and Paul's father has dispatched Baron Grog, whose attempts to see the Grand Duchess have already been rebuffed several times, to the court in Gérolstein. In the course of the opera the fortunes of the hero, Fritz, rise and fall until, at the end, he is back where he started socially but has married the girl he loves. If there is a *quiproquo* it is to be found in Fritz's failure to understand the reasons behind the favor shown him by the Grand Duchess. Characters enter and exit in ways and for reasons often more contrived than any Scribe might have invented.

Throughout the opera, most events are carefully prepared by the authors. For example, the picture of Fritz's witty verbal sparring with the General Boum over the latter's jealousy makes Fritz's attempts to overrule Boum in the discussion of battle plans a logical action. Because Boum and Puck express their fear that the Grand Duchess might be inclined to choose a favorite and deprive them of their influence, we are not surprised when she does so. News of Fritz's victory in Act II and of his beating in Act IV precede his arrival. The only major actions that are unexpected are those of the Grand Duchess herself. However, one is immediately made aware of her capricious nature by the conversation of

Boum and Puck and by the extreme speed with which she promotes Fritz from simpler soldier to commander-in-chief. Thus she is expected to do the unexpected, and she fulfills this promise by turning her affections to Baron Grog, the career diplomat whose practiced noncommital attitude makes one suspect that he may well be hiding something up his sleeve. That this something turns out to be a wife and four children is all to the good, for the revelation of these facts precedes the expected return to power of General Boum and Baron Puck.

Some elements of characterization are also quite Scribean. Characters are talked about before they enter, thus establishing their identities for the audience. However, Meilhac's and Halévy's major characters have much more individuality if not humanity. As in any good parody, these figures are caricatures and thus show extremes in personality that make them quite unlike most of Scribe's rather bland bourgeois characters.

Anyone looking to the plot summary for the spate of pointed satire he has been led to believe exists in *La Grande-duchesse de Gérolstein* must be sadly disappointed. Apart from the reasoning behind the declaration of war, the plot itself is quite an ordinary little comedy of manners and intrigue. The fact is that the point of this *opéra-bouffe* lies not entirely in its plot but in the finer elements of its execution: dialogue, word plays, puns, characterization, activities or actions not essential to the plot, and musical parody.

Meilhac, Halévy, and Offenbach himself show their fondness for word play in the frequent use of musical numbers the humorous effect of which relies on the repetition of nonsense syllables, onomatopoetic words or phrases, or verbal constructions which carry in themselves the possibilities for amusing musical setting. Such a number is the *trio bouffe* in Act II, x-xi (No. 11), which occurs during the conspiracy of Paul, Boum, and Puck against Fritz. Part of the text is reproduced below.

**Boum.**

Maintenant nous comprenez-vous?

**Paul.**

e vous comprends . . . mais c'est horrible.

**Puck.**

Il faut qu'il tombe sous nos coups!

**Paul.**

Le croyez-vous? . . . c'est bien possible . . .

**Puck et Boum.**

Il faut qu'il tombe sous nos coups!

**Boum.**

Logeons-le donc, et dès ce soir,
Dans la chambre au bout du couloir!
Logeons-le donc, ce mirliflor,
Là-bas au fond du corridor!

[All repeat the above stanza.]

**Paul.**

Ce soir quand il se fera tard,
Ecoute, dans ta folle ivresse,
Si tu n'entends pas, par hasard,
Le pas léger de ta maîtresse!

**Boum.**

Ce pas,
Ce pas,
Ce joli pas,
Ce pas,
Ce pas
Ce petit pas!

**Tous.**

Tu n'l'entrendras pas, Nicolas!

[All repeat "Ce pas" stanza.]

[All repeat "Logeons-le donc" stanza.]

**Boum.**

Quand faisant des rêves de gloire,
Tu te dis, 'Je serai Grand Duc!'

Voici venir, dans la nuit noire,
Voici venir Paul, Boum, et Puck.

**Paul.**

Voici venir Paul!

**Boum.**

Voici venir Boum!

**Puck.**

Voici venir Puck!

**Tous.**

Oui, Paul, Boum, Puck!

[All repeat "Logeons-le donc" stanza.]

[Translation:

**Boum.**

Now do you understand us?

**Paul.**

I understand you . . . but this is horrible.

**Puck.**

He must fall beneath our blows!

**Paul.**

Do you think so? . . . that is certainly possible. . .

**Puck and Boum.**

He must fall beneath our blows!

**Boum.**

Let us install him, then, this evening,
In the room at the end of the passageway!
Let us install him, this dandy,

Down there at the bottom end of the corridor!

**Paul.**

This evening when it is getting late,
Listen, in your mad rapture,
If you do not hear, perchance,
The light footstep of your mistress!

**Boum.**

This step,
This step,
This lovely step,
This step,
This step,
This little step!

**All.**

You will not hear it, Nicolas!

**Boum.**

When in dreams of glory,
You say to yourself, 'I shall be Grand Duke!'
Here come, in the black of night,
Here come Paul, Boum, and Puck.

**Paul.**

Here comes Paul!

**Boum.**

Here comes Boum!

**Puck.**

Here comes Puck!

All.

Yes, Paul, Boum, Puck!]

This text is organized in the manner of a Scribe ensemble, with periods of action or dialogue alternating with the static refrain of "Logeons-le donc." However, the verses contain within them possibilities for word play in the musical setting. The various repetitions *à 3* of the stanza beginning "Ce pas" results in the creation of a musical setting humorous in and of itself for its sound alone. A better example of this is the quasi-onomatopoetic development of a play on the names of Paul, Boum, and Puck, which gives the effect of a vocalized imitation of a percussion section (Example 42).

**Example 42**

**Example 42 (continued)**

Other types of word play in which the librettists frequently indulge are puns and witty conversation. In Act I, ii, for example, Fritz immediately establishes his attitude toward General Boum when he observes, as Boum enters, "Voilà le gêneur" (intruder, spoilsport) instead of, "Voilà le général." Later, when explaining how he won the war (Act II, iv), Fritz refers to the battlefield as the "champ de bouteilles" (bottlefield), a pun on the customary "champ de batailles" (battlefield). Witty conversations abound and often serve as a means of characterization. In the following exchange between General Boum and Baron Puck (Act I, vii), the authors have given a picture of the unreasoning military mind.

**Puck.**

Ah! my dear Boum!

**Boum.**

What happened?

**Puck.**

Someone asked me for the password . . . absorbed as I was by the high-level mechanations of politics, I neglected to answer, and then. . . .

**Boum.**

Pan, pan, ratapan!

**Puck.**

Pan, pan, ratapan! . . . They drew [on me]. . .

**Boum.**

That was their duty.

**Puck.**

Fortunately, they missed me. . .

**Boum.**

They will be punished for that. . .

**Puck**

What are you saying?

**Boum.**

I say that they should not have missed you.

**Puck.**

Then you would have wished. . . ?

**Boum.**

As a general, certainly! . . . but I would have been grieved as your friend.

At other times topical observations are directed outward at the contemporary world rather than at any character or situation directly involved in the action. Such is Prince Paul's observation on the gossip about his engagement in the Dutch newspaper (Act I, x).

> My heaven, yes . . . they dared to talk of me. . . . Some time ago there appeared a race of men which has given itself the mission of talking about everything, of writing about everything, to the end of amusing the public. . . . People call them journalists. . . . They dare to enter into one's private life, something which is monstrous, and, what is still more monstrous, is that they dare to enter *my* private life!

For purposes of characterization the various figures often perform actions that have no direct bearing on the plot. Thus General Boum, eager for war, prepares to charge forth against the enemy whenever he hears the least suspicious sound from backstage, and Fritz and the General taunt each other with cries of "Disgraceful soldier!" throughout the opera.

In sum, the way in which the action is carried out, with all the puns, word plays, satirical jibes at this character or that institution, make of the *opéra-bouffe* a comedy of manners with music. The question then arises: if Scribe's inclusion of comedy of manners characteristics in such libretti as *La Barcarolle* contributed to their failure, how can Meilhac and Halévy go even further in this direction and succeed? The answer lies in the nature of opéra comique as opposed to *opéra-bouffe* and is implied in Grout's differentiation of the two forms. The *opéra-bouffe* was meant as a vehicle for social satire. Thus the inclusion of topical humor and allusions to circumstances and figures from contemporary Parisian society was expected and even anticipated. This was not true of opéra comique, and the inclusion of such humor or references in the pseudo-realistic world of Scribe's libretti would be jarring in that it would for an instant transport the spectator from the world of the opera stage to the world of everyday life.

The music of Offenbach contributed to the comedy of manners atmosphere created by Meilhac and Halévy. In addition to the musical parodies and tonal play illustrated by Example 42, Offenbach used current musical fashions, particularly the rhythms and styles of popular dances, as the basis for his satire. Setting a mock-serious text in a *galop* rhythm could not help but be perceived as a mocking of the values or sentiments contained in the text. His solid technique, masterful orchestration, and awareness of the practical problems involved in staging and conducting any given work, along with this use of fashionable musical styles and a gift for musical humor, made Offenbach an ideal collaborator for the librettists at this stage of their careers.

Meilhac and Halévy continued to write for Offenbach and were responsible for the majority of his most successful works. Yet, according to Mina Curtiss, ". . . after the presence of Bismarck and Moltke at a performance of *La Grande-duchesse de Gérolstein* during the Exposition of 1867 gave that operetta a significance not intended by the authors, Meilhac and Halévy sensed that the era of frivolity, of parody, of *opéra-bouffe*, was drawing to a close."[21] The team turned toward more serious subjects in their dramas, as illustrated by *Froufrou* (1869), the story of a frivolous and unthinking young woman who leaves her husband and young son to go off with a lover, then repents and devotes herself to charity work among the poor until she falls victim to disease and returns to her husband to ask his pardon before dying. "In permitting a prodigal wife to expiate the sin of infidelity by dying on the stage at a popular boulevard theatre, Meilhac and Halévy had shown their determination to break with the past."[22] Yet "a popular boulevard theatre" is not the Opéra-Comique, and even Meilhac and Halévy had doubts about the advisability of bringing reality to this conservative theatre in their treatment of Merimée's story, *Carmen*.

The plot of *Carmen* is too well-known to require summarization here, and the relative merits of the original version of the work and that usually performed today have been discussed by Winton Dean and Ernest Newman, among others.[23] The present consideration will therefore concentrate only on the new elements in the libretto as they relate to techniques of the past, primarily those of Scribe.

In *opéra-bouffe*, Meilhac and Halévy's works show a similarity to and probable derivation from the techniques of their prolific predecessor. Indeed, they could hardly help but do so, since it was Scribe who was largely responsible for creating and establishing the ruling operatic conventions during the period of his greatest activity. Yet the plot of *Carmen* was so unconventional for opéra comique of its time that one would expect some evidence of a break in the continuity of libretto technique as well. Despite such evidence, there are also elements of *Carmen* that are conventional, proof enough of the durability of the techniques perfected by Eugène Scribe.

According to Halévy, "It was Bizet who, in 1873, had the idea of extracting an opera libretto from the admirable novella of Merimée." As might be expected, the administrators of the Opéra-Comique, particularly de Leuven, objected to the subject on moral grounds, for one could not have real bandits, gypsies, girls working in a cigarette factory, and a wanton woman who is killed by her lover presented on the stage of a "family theatre." Halévy reassured the director, saying that his would be:

> . . . a toned-down softened *Carmen*, and that we had introduced some characters perfectly in keeping with the style of the *opéra comique*, especially a young girl of great chastity and innocence [Micaëla]. . . . Carmen's death . . . would be sneaked in somehow at the conclusion of a lively and brilliant act, in broad daylight, on a holiday filled with processions, dances, and gay fanfares.

Although de Leuven finally consented, he still requested that the librettists find a way to keep Carmen alive at the end of the work.[24] Fortunately, they did not.

To some extent Scribe and his musical collaborators had provided the basis for *Carmen*. As Halévy has indicated, the character of Micaëla, intended as a foil to Carmen, was meant as a typical opéra comique role of a type seen in numerous opéras comiques of Scribe. She is chaste, innocent, long-suffering, and rather colorless compared to her opposite number in the opera. Her most obvious counterpart in Scribe's works is Alice in *Robert le Diable*, originally planned as an opéra comique. Like Alice, Micaëla brings the opera's hero a letter from his mother containing advice he intends to follow. Indeed, the opening scenes of *Carmen* are very similar to those of *Robert le Diable*: in both, the innocent girl bearing a letter is terrified by the unruly group of men with whom she is forced to deal in her search for the hero.

Also from the portfolio of typical opéra comique characters are the comical smugglers Le Dancaire and Le Remendado, here portrayed with more genuine wit than one would ordinarily find in any of Scribe's numerous operatic bandits; and the soldiers, who begin the opera with a chorus of devil-may-care military life somewhat more colorful but nonetheless of the same tradition as the numerous soldiers' choruses that begin Scribe's opéras comiques. At first Don Jose appears to be just another in a series of opéra comique heroes who desert their virtuous childhood sweethearts for more attractive women, later to return in time for the wedding celebration written in as a fitting close to the piece. Some of the general characteristics of the musical numbers are also based on tradition: in addition to the opening soldiers' chorus, the form of the introduction, the frequent use of strophic song forms with choral refrains, and the numbers chosen to begin and end all acts except the last could be mentioned. To be sure, Bizet enlarges the scope and dramatic impact of the musical numbers, particularly the ensemble scenes, and imparts to the music an unprecedented amount of local color for an opéra comique, but the basis in tradition is still evident.

Even the most revolutionary elements of the *Carmen* plot have some basis in Scribe. The heroines of *Léocadie* and *La Prison d'Edimbourg* are not the most virtuous of women by conventional standards, and Scribe implies that Jenny Bell's life affords at least the opportunities for the accumulation of a number of lovers. The title character of *Fiorella* is rejected by her lover when he learns that she lived for some years with a man to whom she believed she was not married, although this belief later turned out to be false. Indeed, the death of a principal character at the end of a work is not even unprecedented, for the title characters of *Marco Spada* and *Manon Lescaut* both expire in the final scenes of theses operas. Yet in many respects these works and characters of Scribe provided the habitués of the Opéra-Comique no preparation at all for what they found in *Carmen.* If some of Scribe's heroines were not models of virtue, they either had the good sense to be ashamed of their sinful conduct or to try to mend their ways and live good lives. Carmen did not fit in this picture, for she was neither ashamed nor determined to reform. Manon Lescaut dies a relatively peaceful death in the arms of her lover, and the audience can hardly help but feel sympathy for her as she is presented by Scribe. Marco Spada dies a violent death, but he is a man and loses his life in a fair fight. Furthermore, he dies after telling a lie that will insure his daughter's happiness and thus ends his life a virtuous man. The reason Carmen's death was so shocking was that it lacked any similar redeeming features. It was a realistically portrayed crime of passion committed against a sinful woman with whom members of the audience could not sympathize, for they had nothing in common with her. Although specific events of the ending of *Carmen* were not unprecedented, their manner of presentation gave the audience a completely new and perhaps unpleasant experience.

The realism of *Carmen* is reflected not only in the creation of characters and their emotional conflicts but in the libretto technique as well. Gone is the delayed-action plot and carefully planned and interlocking sequence of events typical of Scribe's writing. In its place Meilhac and Halévy present the major events of the plot as they occur in time. The only events of any significance to the opera that occur before the curtain rises have to do with Don José's background, his coming to the vicinity of Seville with his mother and Micaëla, and his enlistment in the army. From this point the entire story, not just its climax, unfolds before the eyes of the audience.

It is interesting to speculate just how Scribe would have handled the same material. Before the beginning of the opera, Don José would probably have met Carmen, perhaps even have run off with her. The opera would open with a triple chorus of soldiers, bullfighters, and factory girls, after which Escamillo, in response to popular demand, would sing his Toreador Song to entertain the company. Carmen, who had already met Escamillo, would be among those applauding his performance, thus arousing Don José's jealousy. The rest of the opera would consist of a carefully worked out sequence of events resolving the love triangles of the plot, which would have been presented and discussed in the opening scenes of the first act. In the end, Don José would probably marry Micaëla and Carmen would be paired with Escamillo. How different is the drama created by Meilhac and Halévy.

This is not to say that all events in *Carmen* are unexpected or not carefully prepared. Micaëla comes looking for Don José long before they actually meet for their duet, thus giving the librettists an excuse to have Don José tell something of his history. The soldiers talk about the factory girls and Carmen before they appear, and Carmen warns about the dangers of loving her before she chooses Don José as her next victim. The conversation between Zuniga and Carmen at Lillas Pastia's inn at the beginning of the second act prepares for the later entrance of Don José and his "accidental" meeting with his superior officer later in the evening. Dialogue between Carmen and Escamillo at the inn flashes a warning that the bullfighter will become Carmen's next lover and that Don José will be cast aside. Don José's desertion to join the band of smugglers is rather precipitous and to some extent outside his control, but is nevertheless the logical outcome of facts the audience already knows about the expected return of Zuniga and about Carmen's nature.

Yet many of these events are not so carefully prepared that they are inevitable. Carmen could just as easily have chosen Zuniga, yet fascinated Don José sufficiently to cause a conflict between him and the officer; Carmen could just have been indulging in a mild flirtation with Escamillo; and Don José could have obeyed Zuniga at the inn. Meilhac and Halévy set up situations in advance, but there is often the possibility that fate might intervene and events might take a totally unexpected turn. In Scribe's libretti such ambiguity often characterizes the course of action as the players see it, but normally does not affect the audience's point of view, since the spectator has as much information as possible at his disposal to predict the outcome of any given event. Nevertheless, some sort of preparation, ambiguous or no, had become such a strong convention of opera that Saint-Saëns could complain:

> The *preparation*! This was at that time [*ca.* 1860] a dogma, as were the three unities in bygone times. When the Opéra obstinately refused to produce 'Samson et Dalila' I requested an influential person to give me his support. He replied that my work was not playable, because the character of Dalila was not *prepared*.[25]

Because of Scribe's dominant role in nineteenth-century opera it would not be too much to assume that his was a decisive influence on the formation of the sort of mind-set described by Saint-Saëns.

In both music and text the violent outcome of Don José's involvement with Carmen is seemingly the most carefully prepared action in the opera. From the *habanera* to the final duo the tragedy is foretold, first in general terms, then more specifically as Carmen sees in the cards that she will be killed, finally in the warning from Frasquita and Mercedès that Don José has come to the bullfight looking for Carmen. Musically, Bizet seconds these warnings in the repetition at various points in the opera of the so-called "fate" motif. Yet just how unambiguous is the librettists' preparation for the opera's dénouement? To the modern audience the warnings are very clear, but to those attending the Opéra-Comique on that opening night in 1875 they may not have been so obvious. These people had not yet become accustomed to having the hero or heroine meet violent death at the end of an opera, particularly under circumstances in which neither librettists nor composer provided them with an emotional cushion after the event. Furthermore, the libretto had contained numerous ambiguities in the course of the first three acts. Perhaps Carmen could be wrong about her fate; perhaps Don José would try to kill her but fail or be captured before he could complete the murder; perhaps he would plan the crime, then not be able to bring himself to carry it out; perhaps Micaëla would intervene.

Because of the way events earlier in the opera had been presented, people may not have believed even Carmen's clearest premonitions of her own death. There is no doubt that the final scene of *Carmen* was a shock to its earliest audiences and even to some of the original performers and others connected with the production. It is impossible to say whether this shock resulted from so general a consideration as the presentation of an unprecedented conclusion to an opéra comique or whether it was simply the result of dramatic techniques and structure, but the latter must have been a definite contributory factor.

The more realistic dramatic structure and preparation of events seen in *Carmen* is symptomatic of the major differences between the Meilhac-Halévy team and Scribe. With Scribe, events and their sequence were of prime importance, and drama was equated with physical activity, with stage action. The inner conflicts and turmoil of individual characters was expressed only if it contributed something to furthering this action, and characters therefore tended to be flat, two-dimensional figures with a certain sameness from work to work. In Carmen and Don José Bizet's librettists present concentrated character studies, in the transformation of Don José from dutiful son to murderer and in the vivid portrayal of an amoral gypsy. Psychology has entered opera to a degree not possible given Scribe's technique.

With *Carmen*, Meilhac and Halévy broke away from the heritage of Scribe so long dominant in the production of opéras comiques. While remnants of the earlier tradition remained in both text and music, the orientation of this work is toward the future, not the past. Yet there is a curious paradox here, for this monumental break of opéra comique from the actual life of the major part of its middle class audience was caused by the advent of realism on the operatic stage.

# THE FRENCH OPERA LIBRETTO BEFORE SCRIBE

Eugène Scribe's greatest contribution to the history of French dramatic music was in the area of opéra comique. This is true not only because of the numbers of libretti he wrote nor the number of years during which he was the primary source of libretti for the Opéra-Comique, but because he truly transformed the opéra comique text from an older to a more modern style by bringing the technique of the well-made play to bear on this musical form. At the Opéra Scribe also effected a revolution no less important in its ultimate outcome. However, the type of change involved here was not so much the derivation of a new technique for a new genre as it was the adaptation of techniques already fully formed to a genre in the process of modernization. This modernization affected all aspects of the Opéra, artistic as well as managerial, and resulted in the creation of that unique form of bourgeois entertainment, French grand opera.

To help gain perspective on the changes taking place in French opera after 1828, changes in which Scribe played a major role, a few representative operas from the generation before Scribe have been chosen to exemplify techniques in libretto writing then in practice. Two of the examples, Grétry's *Le Caravane du Caire* (1783) and Catel's *Les Bayadères* (1810), are based on the exotic themes so long favored by the French, while Cherubini's *Démofoon* (1788) and Catel's *Sémiramis* (1802) deal with the topics from classical antiquity and Spontini's *La Vestale* (1807) takes its theme from ancient Rome. While a study of these works provides a by no means exhaustive survey of opera before Scribe, it does yield sufficient material to establish trends and to provide a basis for comparison.

## Grétry's *Le Caravane du Caire*

*Le Caravane du Caire*, an opera in three acts, was first performed publicly on January 15, 1784, but this performance followed by some two-and-one-half months the private premiere of the work at Fontainebleau on October 30, 1783. A popular work, it was performed more than five hundred times at the Paris Opéra until 1829[1] and was still well enough liked in the 1850s to make publication of a piano-vocal score potentially profitable. The libretto was by E. Morel de Chédeville, but a member of the royal family is said to have had a hand in its creation.[2]

As the title suggests, the opera capitalizes on the perennial French taste for exotic settings. At the beginning of the opera a caravan of travelers and captives arrives at Cairo. Among the captives are a Frenchman, Saint-Phar, and his bride Zélime, the daughter of an eastern nabab. Saint-Phar had hoped to take Zélime back to France to receive his father's blessing on their marriage, but Husca, the leader of the caravan, has noted Zélime's beauty and believes he can sell her as a slave for a good price. Although Saint-Phar's father has powerful friends in Cairo who might be able to prevent this, there seems to be little chance that the Frenchman will be able to escape Husca and get their assistance. Suddenly the Arabs attack and Saint-Phar wins his freedom by fighting alongside Husca and others to defeat them. Saint-Phar asks that Husca free Zélime instead, but the slave trader refuses and the act ends in conflict.

Act II takes place in the slave market in Cairo. The Pasha has rejected his former favorite Almaide, although she still loves him, and comes to look over Husca's newest offerings. Naturally, his choice is Zélime. Despite Saint-Phar's pleas he buys her and takes her away to his harem. Saint-Phar vows to find a way to rescue his wife.

At the beginning of Act III Florestan and Surville, two Frenchmen, come to say goodbye to the Pasha before leaving for France. Florestan is sad, for he fears his only son, for whom he has been searching, is dead. After the two enter the Pasha's chambers, Almaide and Osmin, a palace guard, join forces with Saint-Phar to free Zélime. Just as Florestan and Surville are saying their last farewells to the Pasha, a chorus announces that Zélime is being kidnapped. The palace guards give chase and return with Zélime and Saint-Phar in chains. Florestan recognizes the latter as his long-lost son and the Pasha, moved by pleas from all sides, frees Zélime and restores her to her husband.

The following chart shows the arrangement and distribution of the musical numbers.

Key to abrreviations:

SP — Saint-Phar
Z — Zélime
H — Husca
P — Pasha
T — Tamourin

F — Florestan
S — Surville
O — Osmin
A — Almaide

| Number | Technique or form | Action |
|---|---|---|
| | | **ACT I** |
| 1 | Introduction | |
| | A. Double Chorus. | Travelers happy to arrive at Cairo but captives unhappy. |
| | B. Dance. | Instrumental. |
| | C. *Cavatine:* a Frenchwoman. | She should be sad because she is a captive, yet cannot repress her natural French gaiety. |
| | Repeat double chorus. | |
| 2 | Recit: SP, Z. | SP sees end to his plan to take Z to France. |
| | Duo: SP, Z. | Both vow to be faithful despite impending separation. SP vows to fight against separation. |
| 3 | Recit: H, SP, Z. | H announces SP and Z must part and Z be sold into slavery. |
| | *Cavatine:* H. | SP should not try to save Z, for she will bring high price and H is determined to sell her. |
| 4 | Recit: H, SP, Z. | SP's father has powerful friends in Cairo, but H says SP has little hope of escaping to get their aid. |
| | Trio: H, SP, Z. | SP and Z beg for mercy. H refuses. |
| 5 | *Morceau d'ensemble:* soli, triple chorus. | Soldiers offstage announce attack by Arabs. SP and H go off to fight. Z and women pray for victory. H says they have won because of SP's leadership. All rejoice. |
| 6 | Recit: SP, H. | SP asks that Z be freed in his place. H refuses. |
| | Finale: SP, H, Z, chorus. | Argument in which chorus joins on SP's side. H refuses to give in. |
| | | **ACT II** |
| 7 | Recit: H, T. | T offers to act as agent between P and H to insure that P will buy slaves from H. |
| | Air: H | H describes women he has brought. |
| 8 | Recit: T, H, P. | H asks P to prepare feast for Frenchman who helped defeat Arabs. T seconds this, saying F will be glad to see one of his countrymen. P agrees. |
| 9 | Recit: T, P, A. | T announces A, but P says he is bored with her. A has brought girls from harem who have prepared entertainment for the Frenchman and wants P's approval. |

| | | |
|---|---|---|
| | *Divertissement* | |
| | A. Chorus with dance. | A and girls hope dance will please. |
| | B. Dances. | Instrumental. |
| 10 | Recit: P, T. | P agrees to allow dance as entertainment for Frenchman, but such things no longer amuse him. |
| | *Ariette*: T. | P needs some variety in his life to banish monotony, cheer him up. |
| 11 | Recit: P, T. | P believes nothing can cheer him, but T tells of H's stock of beautiful slaves. |
| | *Cavatine:* P. | P tells T his advice would lead to inconstancy, something which has caused his ruin. |
| 12 | Recit: P, T. | P wants a companion, not just more slaves. T suggests a European woman. |
| | Trio: P, T, H. | T brings in H, who has some European women in stock. P prefers French women. All agree he has made best choice. |
| 13 | Recit: P, H, T. | P wants to see slaves and goes off to bazaar. Instrumental interlude. |
| | *Divertissement* | |
| | Cairo. | |
| | B. March (P and train). | |
| | C. Slaves presented to P. | |
| | D. Air: a Frenchwoman. | Everyone is born a slave to something, whether captive or king. |
| | E. Minuet. | Instrumental. |
| | F. *Air Italienne*: an Italian woman. | Coloratura aria in Italian. |
| | G. *Pas de deux*: Italian man and woman. | Instrumental. |
| | H. *Pas de deux*: English man and woman. | |
| | I. German song and dance with chorus. | Song in French but sung by supposed German woman. Instrumental dance. Chorus repeats part of song. |
| | J. *Pas de trois:* ladies of different nationalities. | Instrumental. |
| 14 | Recit: P, H, Z, SP. | P purchases Z. SP arrives, pleads for Z's return. P refuses, leaves. Instrumental march. |
| | Air: SP. | Vows to free Z or die trying. |

ACT III

| | | |
|---|---|---|
| 15 | Recit: F, S. | About to leave for France, will say farewell to P first. F has no hope of seeing son again, but S has faith. |
| | Acc. recit: F. | Sadness over loss of son for whom he has been searching. |
| | Air: F. | Wonders how son died, hopes death was honorable and in service of his country. |
| 16 | Recit: T, F, S. | T takes F and S to see P. |
| | Air: A. | Vows to win back P's favors. |
| 17 | Recit: A, O. | A agrees to join with O and SP for release of Z. |
| | *Cavatine;* A. | No longer jealous, A hopes to return Z to SP and regain favors and empire she has lost to Z. |
| 18 | Recit: A, P. | P assures A she is still queen despite Z's presence, but A admits she will feel better when Z is gone. |
| | *Cavatine:* P. | A tries in vain to win him back, for he loves Z. |
| 19 | Recit: O. | O announces F. |
| | March. | Instrumental. Scene change to reception room prepared for celebration. |
| | Recit: F, P. | F thanks P for having helped repair F's ships, damaged in storm. |
| | *Morceau d'ensemble*: F, P, double chorus. | Elaboration of recit. P pays tribute to French bravery. |
| 20 | Recit: P, F. | P invites F to celebration. |
| | Finale: All principals, Chorus. | Chorus, offstage, announces Z's kidnapping. F, hearing a Frenchman is to blame, wants him severely punished. Z and SP are led in, chained. Z pleads for mercy for SP. F recognizes SP as his son. P restores Z to SP. General rejoicing. |
| 21 | Final *divertissement*. | Instrumental. |

The most striking element of *Le Caravane du Caire* is the amount of time and energy taken up with the items having nothing whatever to do with the drama. These include not only the *divertissements* but also the prominent airs by characters having no role in the story and the lengthy dissertations on the virtues of France by all and sundry. The second act consists almost entirely of such numbers and is the sort of thing that must have set precedents for similar acts in later grand operas. All the operas to be considered in the present chapter contain *divertissements* of one sort or another, but only in those on exotic themes does this element play so large a role.

The structural characteristics of the *Caravane* libretto are similar to those of Grétry's opéras comiques discussed earlier, particularly to that of *Richard Coeur-de-Lion.* The action begins *in medias res* but does not show the Scribe type of delayed-action plot. Rather, any information necessary to one's understanding of the action is presented directly or worked into the opera. Some events are prepared, but most preparation is not realized as such until after the action has taken place. For example, Saint-Phar mentions his father in Act I, and Florestan discusses a lost son in Act III; but since no names are mentioned the audience is not aware until the final recognition scene that the two men are related, and the sense of expectation created by Scribe in comparable situations is absent. A better prepared sequence of events is that leading up to Zélime's attempted escape. Here the librettist has even included a contrived entrance of the guilty pair before the Pasha in order to precipitate the reunion of father and son.

One element that interferes with even the clearest preparation of events is the constant interruption of the drama for distractions of a verbal or scenic nature. *Le Caravane*'s use of nonessential characters is particularly problematical and at times confusing to the spectator, who must sort of out in his own mind the important and unimportant figures. Character development in *La Caravane* is similar to that in opéras comiques of the same period. Most characters are rather flat, but do develop through their own actions.

The musical numbers are for the most part conventional and nondramatic, with a few notable exceptions. The best among the latter are the *morceau d'ensemble* No. 5 and the third act finale, for both carry a certain amount of dramatic action of a type that benefits from unfolding at the slow, suspenseful pace necessitated by music. Among the other numbers, most are for single solo voices. They are skillfully composed but not extraordinary or adventurous from either a formal or a technical point of view. The musical divisions are also quite conventional, with no attempt to create larger scene complexes out of smaller forms or to go beyond the usual bounds of recitative and aria forms. Even some of the larger numbers, such as the Introduction or the *morceau d'ensemble* of Act I, end their various sections with definite cadences and are thus not all of a piece.

*Le Caravane* has a relatively simple plot, but nevertheless includes two subplots: the attempts of Almaide to win back the Pasha's affections (one is reminded somewhat of Rossini's *L'Italiana in Algeri*) and the search of Florestan for his lost son. The first is very well integrated into the main plot and does not distract from it. The second, involving one of those happy coincidences so frequently found in opera, is somewhat distracting in the rather abrupt way the two Frenchmen are introduced at the beginning of Act III. The only preparation the librettist gives the spectator is in briefly mentioning Florestan's name early in Act II. Saint-Phar's comments regarding his father's influence in Cairo are so nebulous as to be all but forgotten by the time Florestan appears. Once the initial awkwardness of his appearance has been dissipated, however, this subplot also works quite well within the main plot.

The structures of the individual acts in *Le Caravane* are more modern than were those of Grétry's opéras comiques. While forming part of the whole, each is a miniature drama in itself. At the beginning of Act I both Saint-Phar and Zélime are captives, but by the end of the act the former has earned his freedom and one has hope that he will be able to free his wife as well. Act II begins with a discussion of the slave bazaar and ends with the sale of Zélime to the Pasha. In Act III we meet Florestan who, before the act is over, is reunited with his son. Each of the first two acts ends with some degree of finality in that a problem or situation posed at the beginning of the act is at least partially resolved. Yet suspense is maintained because the conflicts are either only partially resolved or, in being resolved, set up new problems. This technique is one worthy of Scribe.

Seen as a whole, the libretto of *Le Caravane du Caire* has quite a modern orientation. Nevertheless, certain of its conventions mark it as a product of its time: the extensive use of all varieties of nonessential material, the strict division of the music into recitative and set-numbers, the ending with a *divertissement*, and the use of semiprogrammatic instrumental numbers. *Le Caravane*'s pattern will be seen again in Catel's *Les Bayadères*.

### Cherubini's *Démofoon*

*Démofoon*, Cherubini's first French opera, was premiered on December 5, 1788, at the Paris Opéra. Its libretto, by J. F. Marmontel, is based on Metastasio's work of the same name and still bears some of the traits commonly associated with that librettist: statue-like characters, two pairs of lovers, and the magnanimous tyrant. Although *Démofoon* was not a particularly successful opera, its librettist was a writer of note and a popular librettist in the last decades of the eighteenth century. In addition to the the libretto for Grétry's *Zémire et Azor* discussed above, Marmontel wrote several other pieces for Grétry and was responsible for the text of Piccini's most successful French opera, *Didon* (1783), and of two debut operas: Zingarelli's *Antigone* (1790) and Cherubini's

*Démofoon.*[3] Many other operas were based on his novels, tales, and libretti. Thus his work in *Démofoon* can serve as a good example of libretto style for his generation of writers. *Le Caravane du Caire* exemplified the recurrent exotic themes and settings of French opera. *Démofoon* represents another popular type of opera, the *tragédie-lyrique* based on a subject from Greek or Roman antiquity.

The story of *Démofoon* centers around the character of Osmide, oldest son of Demophon, King of Thrace, and Dircé, to whom Osmide is secretly married. Astor, Dirce's father, refuses to allow the name of his only daughter to be placed in the urn from which the name of a victim for sacrifice to Apollo will be drawn because Demophon, believing himself above the law, has not entered the names of his daughters. Denouncing this injustice, Astor has aroused Demophon's anger and is preparing to flee with Dircé. Meanwhile, Osmide has returned home from battle to find that Demophon has arranged a politically sound marriage between his son and Ircile, daughter of the King of Phrygia. Ircile arrives accompanied by Osmide's younger brother Néade, who has served as Demophon's emissary to Phrygia and has fallen in love with Ircile. When Osmide tells Ircile and Néade of his marriage and says that he will renounce all claim to the throne in Néade's favor if the couple will help him, Ircile agrees at once to refuse to marry Osmide. Yet all are afraid to tell the stern Demophon of Osmide's secret marriage, particularly since the king has announced that he will choose the sacrificial victim personally rather than have a name drawn out of the urn. Dircé, as the daughter of an enemy, would be even more likely a choice for Demophon if he wishes to punish her as the person responsible for preventing the desired alliance between Thrace and Phrygia.

Despite pleas from Osmide, Néade, and Ircile, Demophon chooses Dircé and has her prepared for the sacrifice. At the last moment Osmide reveals to Demophon and the people assembled at the temple that Dircé is his wife and that they have a son. After much pleading by all present, the king relents and grants the couple pardon. At this the people rejoice, for the requirement of an annual sacrifice to Apollo was to be lifted "when strength yields to weakness, when the pride of the fierce lion is tamed, when the torrent is seen to stop in its course. . . ."[4] Ircile and Néade are united, and all celebrate the triumph of nature and love over the strict rule of law.

The table to follow will make clearer the course of action and the way in which this action is set to music.

Key to abbreviations:

| | | |
|---|---|---|
| Dem | — | Démofoon |
| O | — | Osmide |
| N | — | Néade |
| As | — | Astor |
| Ad | — | Adraste (captain of the guards) |
| L | — | Lygdame (the high priest) |
| Dir | — | Dircé |
| I | — | Ircile |
| Cho | — | chorus |

NB: All recitatives are accompanied; the designation "recit" refers to this style. "Arioso" refers to a more lyrical, regularly measured solo that has the same function as recitative—conveying information—but is less expansive than an air and without a clearly defined musical form. A broken line across the page indicates that a final cadence occurs at the end of the preceding number or scene.

| Scene | Form or technique | Action |
|---|---|---|
| | | ACT I |
| i | Double cho: People of Thrace. | Prayer to Apollo for relief from requirement of annual sacrifice. |
| - - - | - - - | - - - |
| ii | Recit: people, L, Oracle. | L announces Apollo has answered prayer. Oracle relates answer (quoted above). |
| - - - | - - - | - - - |
| iii | Chorus | People continue plaints, as conditions announced by Oracle seem impossible. |
| | Recit: As, Dir, L. | As objects to having to place Dir's name in the urn when Dem's daughters are in safety. |
| | Air: As. | As wants daughters of Dem to share this fate. |
| | Recit: As. | As will confront Dem. |
| - - - | - - - | - - - |
| iv | Recit: Dir. | Dir reveals she is secretly married to O, has a son. Fears what could happen if Dem learns of it. |
| | Air: Dir. | She fears nothing for herself but would not want to be taken from those she loves. |
| | Recit: Dir. | She will go to visit her son. |
| v | Recit: Dir, O. | Dem has called O back from battlefield unexpectedly, but O does not know why. O wants to tell Dem about secret marriage. |
| | Arioso: O. | Love and nature will win Dem's heart and knowledge of O's victories will make him more receptive. |
| | Recit: O, Dir. | O wants to see son, but Dir wants to wait until danger is past; she describes son as looking like O. |

| | | |
|---|---|---|
| | Duo: O, Dir. | O promises to remain faithful. Dir feels hopeful that all will end well. O promises to protect Dir and son. |
| vi | Recit: O. | Who is worthy of me if not Dir? |
| vii | Recit: O, Ad. | Ad announces arrival of ships and Dem's call for O. |
| viii | Recit: Dem, As. | As threatens drastic action at the temple because of Dem's refusal to yield. Dem vows to punish As for insolence. |
| ix | Recit: Dem. | Dem announces he will choose the victim for sacrifice. |
| x | Triple Chorus: people, girls. | People rejoice as girls, candidates for sacrifice, return to their parents. |
| xi | Recit: Dem, O. | Dem has plans for O's future. |
| | Arioso: Dem. | Seeing kingdom flourish again after war makes Dem happy. |
| | Recit: Dem, O. | Dem has arranged marriage for O to I, does not believe O's feelings should interfere. O wonders what to do now. |
| | March (orchestral). | Ship arrives, N, I, attendants descend. |
| xii | Recit: Dem. | Marriage of O and I will unite Thrace and Asia. |
| | *Choeur et danse* | Celebration of peace, praise of love. |

## ACT II

| | | |
|---|---|---|
| i | Recit: I, N. | I wonders why Dem seems so angry with O, but N does not know. |
| | Arioso: I. | I wonders why N now seems so cold, since they became good friends earlier. |
| | Recit: I, N. | N finally admits unhappiness that I is to marry someone else. |
| | Arioso: N. | N asks for sympathy. |
| | Recit: N, I. | N tells how friendship grew to love. |
| | Air: N. | N believes I loves him. |
| | Duo: N, I. | I tells N to go away, that she must marry O. N threatens suicide. Both curse fate and duty that interfere with their feelings. |
| ii | Recit: O, I, N. | O wants I's help, confides he is married and fears punishment for Dir and son. |
| | Arioso: O. | O pleads for help. |
| | Recit: O, N. | O asks that I tell Dem she is offended by O's coolness but would marry N instead. O promises to renounce rights to throne. |

| | | |
|---|---|---|
| | Air: O. | O tells I and N how good their lives will be if they accept his offer and help him. |
| | Recit: O, I, N. | O tells them to go and live happily. I and N are hopeful. |
| iii | Recit: O, Dir, As. | As has decided to take Dir far away. |
| | Air: Dir. | Dir does not want to leave, asks where they will go. |
| | Recit: O, Dir, As. | O tries to reassure As that Dem will not punish Dir out of anger at As, but As says Dir has already been named victim. O promises to save her. |
| | Arioso: As, | As will go as far as Caucasus if necessary. |
| | Recit: As, Dir, O. | As leaves Dir in O's care while he goes to prepare for journey. |
| iv | Recit: O, Dir. | O thinks he should tell Dem of marriage, but Dir believes this will make matters worse. |
| | Duo: O, Dir. | Dir wants to yield to fate and trust heaven to help them. O agrees; heaven will help, and they will be faithful. |
| - - - | - - - | - - - |
| | Recit: Dir, O. | Dir will place son in O's care. O assures her they will be reunited soon. |
| v | Recit: As, Dir, O. | As has prepared boat. |
| vi | Recit: As, Dir, O, Ad, guards. | Ad orders guards to seize Dir, warns O not to go against king's law. As swears vengeance. |
| vii | Air: O. | Rage aria. |
| - - - | - - - | - - - |

### ACT III

| | | |
|---|---|---|
| i | Recit: Dem, O. | O pleads with Dem for Dir's life, but Dem wants to punish As and will force O to obey. O reminds Dem that As was O's tutor. |
| | Air: O. | O asks that Dir's life be saved as reward for As' past service; he recounts As' bravery in battle. |
| | Recit: O, Dem. | Dem suspects O must have another reason: love for Dir. O asks what consequences would be if this were true. |
| | Air: Dem. | Dem promises punishment, no mercy, separation from Dir. |
| | Recit: O, Dem. | O asks if Dir will die. |
| ii | Recit: O, Dem, I. | I pleads with Dem, says she opposes marriage to O and wants to leave. Dem says N will replace O as bridegroom and will succeed to throne. O agrees to step aside without struggle, swearing this as N enters. |
| iii | Recit: add N. | Dem thinks O is being agreeable to appease him, which makes him angrier. O agrees to leave, but warns Dem that he (O) will die with Dir. |

| | | |
|---|---|---|
| iv | Recit: Dem, I, N. | Dem thinks O wanted Dir to be queen and that this crime is worthy of punishment. I and N try to change his mind. |
| - - - | - - - | - - - |
| | Trio: Dem, I, N. | N and I speak in favor of O, plead with Dem to change his mind, but Dem is firm. |
| v | Recit: I, N. | N hopes gods will somehow reconcile Dem and O. I tells N to go after O while she waits for Dir. |
| - - - | - - - | - - - |
| vi | March: Dir, guards, priestesses of Apollo. | Orchestral. Procession to temple. |
| | Recit: I, Dir. | I tells Dir her only hope is to allow I to reveal secret marriage. Dir fears for O and tells I to try to reconcile O and Dem. |
| | Arioso, air: Dir. | Dir asks I to be a mother to her and O's son. |
| | Recit: priestess. | Priestess calls for Dir. |
| | Recap, part of above air (Dir). | |
| | Recap march. | Orchestral. |
| - - - | - - - | - - - |
| vii | Cho: priests. | Even the best blood will be shed if the gods demand it. |
| - - - | - - - | - - - |
| | Cho, offstage: priestesses. | Victim should submit gladly to fate. |
| viii | Cho continues onstage as priestesses enter with Dir. | |
| ix | Recit: O. | O stops ceremony, threatens priests. |
| x | Recit: O | O threatens to kill any soldier who tries to stop him. |
| xi | Recit: Dem, O | Dem angry. O announces he and Dir are married. |
| xii | Recit: Dir, Dem, O. | Dir, O, son kneel before Dem, ask mercy. |
| | Ensemble with cho. | I, N, people urge Dem to relent. |
| | Arioso: Dem. | Dem agrees. |
| | Cho: people. | Rejoicing that Oracle's requirements are fulfilled. |
| | Ensemble with cho: all principals, people. | General rejoicing. |
| - - - | - - - | - - - |

From the relative infrequency of final cadences at the ends of numbers or scenes it would appear that Cherubini and his librettist are already quite advanced in the tendency to vary the usual numbers opera scheme by organizing smaller forms into large scene complexes, but closer examination of the score shows that this is not really the case. Cherubini camouflages the musical divisions by such devices as writing the cadence of a recitative as part of the first measure of an air, writing very short instrumental introductions to airs, duos, etc., and making the instrumental postlude of a number do double service as an introduction or transition to the following number. The musical seams are apparent throughout the work. The only series of numbers that shows a significant tendency toward the musical cohesivesness typical of later scene complexes is that in Act III, vi, in which recurrent musical ideas set off the sections of recitatives in a single large-scale form of March - Recitative - Arioso - Air - Recitative - Air - March. The last scene of this act also has a degree of musical cohesiveness because of the cumulative effect of the accompanying action, even though a clear formal outline is missing.

The reverse of this practice is also true. Many scenes that would have been set by a later composer as continuous musical numbers using such devices as orchestral melody and arioso to relate the action or conversation are set here in separate sections or numbers. For example, Act I, v, includes recitative, arioso, and a duo. A later composer might have eliminated at least the second recitative section and minimized the break between active and static situations by using musical ideas from the duo in an orchestral counterpoint to regularly measured arioso dialogue.

*Démofoon* contains a considerable amount of recitative, and almost all of the important events are set in this way, making of the musical numbers static set pieces. Cherubini often treats recitatives as imaginatively or at least as musically as he can without losing the sense of the text. Long sections of recitative, such as Act III, ii-iii, are held together by the use of a set of motives repeated at various points in the scene. Others may be broken by interpolating arioso passages of varying lengths to emphasize a particular point or an especially strong emotion. Examples of this practice are easily found in the table above.

*Démofoon* features a delayed-action plot, since every conflict that is resolved in the opera began some time earlier. Annual sacrifices to Apollo had been taking place for a long enough time that the people felt their burden very strongly. Osmide and Dircé were married before Osmide went off to war and have been married long enough for Dircé to have had a son. Néade and Ircile fell in love while Néade was arranging for Ircile's marriage to Osmide. Demophon evidently had always been a stern, legalistic, proud ruler and had already aroused the anger of Astor because of his manner of dealing with subordinates. The audience therefore must be informed of this pre-curtain activity before it can follow the action. Marmontel chooses to give this information out in small pieces and to allow the effect to accumulate. First we learn of the sacrifice, then of Astor's anger, Dircé's secret marriage and her son, and Demophon's plans for Osmide. Only in Act II do we learn that Néade and Ircile are in love. Throughout the work the pictures of Demophon are painted in bold, unshaded strokes.

Each act begins *in medias res* and ends with a conclusive event which is unrelated to that with which the act opened in all cases but Act III. As Act I begins the people are voicing their complaints about the sacrifice; as it ends, they are helping to welcome Ircile. Act II begins with the revelation that Néade and Ircile are in love and ends with Osmide's reaction to Dircé's arrest. Act III begins and ends with the matter of saving Dircé's life.

Individual scenes are constructed as free alternations of recitative and more formal musical numbers. A scene containing an air is most often linked to the following scene by a recitative "tag" leading the action away from the topic just covered toward events to come. In such scenes the airs seldom have final cadences but instead feature orchestral transitions to the recitative. Although this technique helps keep the action moving at a more consistent pace than would otherwise be possible, it also dulls any strong effect the air might otherwise have produced. This is only partly the fault of the librettist, since another composer might have handled the musical setting differently. However, there is a limit to how far a composer can deviate from this sort of peak-to-plateau arrangement of musical numbers and recitatives, an arrangement to a large extent inherited from the Quinault tradition of libretto writing.

Save for events which occur before the beginning of the opera, the action of *Démofoon* takes place on the stage. Although the argument between Astor and Demophon might be considered an exception to this, the conclusion and outcome of the behind-the-scenes action is played before the audience. Thus none but the pre-curtain happenings are merely reported. This is not to say that the audience is always given distinct clues as to the outcome of each conflict in the plot, for some events occur unexpectedly. For example, the audience has no direct warning that Demophon has arranged a marriage for Osmide until the king announces it to the people near the end of Act I, and the love of Néade for Ircile also comes as a surprise. Any opera-goer of the time might have anticipated these events from past experience with operatic plots, but the librettist gives no direct information. Some events, however, are quite carefully prepared. A good example is the choice of Dircé as the sacrificial victim, for a long chain of events moving from the general to the specific leads up to it. First the people complain about the annual sacrifice; then Astor brings the complaint to focus on individuals and in so doing breaks with the king. Demophon narrows the circle of action still further by taking the element of chance out of the selection of the victim, and everything points to Dircé as his eventual choice. Another example of careful preparation of an event is Demophon's eventual pardoning of Dircé and Osmide, although this preparation is not as clear. Throughout the opera Demophon's stern character remains unchanged, and his yielding to pleas for mercy seems unexpected. Yet the Oracle's prediction in the first scene is fulfilled at the end of the opera, and an action which began the work concludes it as well.

There are examples of contrived entrances and exits in *Démofoon*, most of them not very subtle, but such conventional operatic contrivances as eavesdropping, accidentally overheard conversations, misunderstandings of a single event by each of several characters, wayward letters, and the like are omitted from the opera and the action itself is played out in quite a straightforward fashion.

Like the action, the spectacular elements of *Démofoon* are neither very ornate nor very involved. They consist of the usual processions, a conventional sacrifice-in-the-temple scene, and a single dance. Although large, these scenes are not particularly colorful. The scenery is also monumental but conventional, featuring the usual palaces and temples common in operas on antique themes.

Neither the characters nor their problems are particularly interesting in and of themselves. The young lovers are all alike in their emotions and the effect these have on their reason, sense of duty, etc. Demophon is a marble king. Even Astor's outpourings of fatherly concern for Dircé's life seem to spring less from love than from his concept of what government should be. Thus neither the personae as individuals nor the situation in the opera seem of prime interest to the librettist. Yet he is obviously not deemphasizing them in favor of stage spectacle. The fact is that Marmontel has subordinated these elements of opera to the exposition of the more generalized moral conflict of law (or duty) and nature (or love), with events heavily weighted on the side of the latter. In such a concept of opera specific individuals or situations are not especially important and may indeed get in the way. If the spectator's attention is fixed on the psychological development and subtleties of reaction in the character or is caught up in a fast-moving, suspenseful plot, he may miss the moral. In *Démofoon* there is little chance this will occur.

Although the action is presented in a straightforward manner, the dialogue itself is not. The libretto is in rhymed verse and at times seems overly poetic, especially at points where the recitative breaks into arioso. Thus characters often take a long time to do or say very little, or say things in more or less obscure ways rather than simply stating a point.

They are also prone to off-the-cuff moralizing that has no direct effect on the action and, indeed, stops it abruptly for a time. Examples of these points are not difficult to find. In Act II, i, after Ircile has asked Néade several times and in various ways why his attitude toward her seems changed, we find the following dialogue.

**Ircile.**

Leave me alone,
Or tell me, cruel one, who has caused you to change?

**Néade.**

Well then, you force me to it,
I must cede to you;
But once again,
What do you want to know?

**Ircile.**

I want to know what is the cause of the vexation that obsesses you?

**Néade.**

It arises from my misfortune, from my duty,
From the horrible torment of seeing
That another than me possesses you;
From a desperate love.

Somewhere in the first few sentences any suspense remaining in this scene could well give place to annoyance.

The final scene of the opera provides a good example of Marmontel's tendency toward less-than-direct statements and moralizing. When everyone pleads with Demophon to pardon Osmide and Dircé, they focus not on the individuals involved but on the moral value behind such a decision.

Yield, great king,
Nature triumphs,
Do not resist its voice.

The king replies:

Yes! Nature is strongest;
I feel that everything yields to its laws.

The crowd's reaction again focuses on a general object rather than the individuals involved in it when the people sing:

The Oracle is fulfilled,
Apollo pardons us.
Divine son of Latona,
Our hope is realized.

A good example of spontaneous moralizing occurs at the end of Act I, iii, when Astor remarks:

Despite the brightness of the diadem,
Equals before the gods,
Nature is the same
In the heart of a subject
And in the soul of a king.

Astor is stating a political-moral belief and in so doing is telling the audience directly how to react, not merely suggesting it by his own actions.

Marmontel's *Démofoon* is an example of the older tradition of libretto writing handed down from the *tragédie-lyrique* of Quinault. In subject, scene and act structure, presentation of the action, characterization, and language it shows this tradition well, but it is a tradition from which Scribe will break.

## Catel's *Sémiramis*

Like Cherubini's *Démofoon*, Catel's *Sémiramis* is based on a pre-existent literary work, this time a drama of the same name by Voltaire. Librettist P. Desriaux writes in his preface that it is modeled on the work of "the authors of two *Iphigénies*, of *Hypermnestre*, of *Phèdre*, of *Oedipe*, etc."[5] It therefore is part of the Gluck tradition and to some extent a descendent of the Quinault tradition. First presented in 1802, *Sémiramis* was considerably revised for a production two years later and became a stronger work dramatically as a result. The present discussion will deal with the original version.

The plot is the oft used story of Sémiramis, undoubtedly familiar to the French of 1802 through Voltaire's writings. Azéma, a princess descended from the line of the demigod Belus, loves Arzace, a military hero who is returning victorious to present his conquests at the feet of Queen Sémiramis. Arzace, however, has a rival in Assur, who wishes to marry Azéma and rule the world. Since Assur secretly murdered the queen's husband Ninus at the former's request, and since Sémiramis' only son is believed dead, an alliance of Azéma and Assur could quite easily threaten the queen's power. Azéma, however, detests Assur and refuses his proposal, whereupon the latter swears to kill his rival.

Sémiramis enters, complaining of having been haunted by a ghost and praying Belus to lift this torment from her. Oroës, the High Priest, announces to the people that Ninus' blood must be avenged before the gods will favor them again. A military march in the distance announces the arrival of Arzace. After the people praise the hero, Arzace gives Oroës a letter from the former's now dead father. The priest promises to reveal its contents to Arzace later.

At the beginning of Act II Azéma and Arzace speak of their coming marriage, but Azéma fears what Assur may do. Arzace reassures her. When Assur arrives, Arzace announces his intention to marry Azéma, but Assur does not believe Arzace is good enough for such a princess and threatens him. After Arzace leaves, Sémiramis tells Assur that she has a plan to comply with the people's urgings that she provide them with an heir to the throne, and sends him to assemble the people. She then tells Otane, her confidante, that she will marry Arzace and put him on the throne. After the people are assembled, Oroës announces that the queen is to reveal her choice of a husband and the people agree to abide by her decision. Sémiramis' revelation that she has chosen Arzace produces a surprised reaction from the crowd. After the queen and her attendants have left, Assur and a number of co-conspirators begin to plot her death.

Act III is set in the garden near Ninus' tomb. Azéma is angry that Arzace seems unwilling to oppose Sémiramis, but Arzace seems to believe the situation is hopeless, since he has learned that Ninias, son of Sémiramis and the late king, is alive and will probably return to claim the throne. A chorus and ballet begin the celebration of Sémiramis' approaching marriage, but as the preliminary ceremony begins, the ghost of Ninus appears and calls for Arzace to make a sacrifice in the tomb. A chorus of terrified spectators ends the act.

As Act IV begins, Oroës is telling Arzace what the letter from the latter's father contains: that Arzace is really Ninias and should not fear the ghost of Ninus, since he is guilty of no crime. The priest then gives Arzace a sword with which he is to punish the person guilty of Ninus' murder, whose identity is revealed in the letter. When Sémiramis arrives, Arzace still cannot bring himself to tell her she is his mother, but the queen senses his change of mood and wishes to see the letter he has been reading. When she learns its contents she demands that he fulfill his destiny and punish her, but he says he must first visit Ninus' tomb.

Azéma rushes in to warn Sémiramis that Assur and his men plan to violate Ninus' tomb and kill Arzace. Sémiramis runs to the tomb to save her son and Azéma calls in soldiers to surround the tomb. Arzace emerges. He has wounded Sémiramis, he says, but could not kill her. Oroës reveals that Arzace is king, whereupon the latter orders the guards to arrest Assur. Sémiramis, wounded, emerges from the tomb to demand that her son avenge her assassin. When Arzace reveals he is the man, Sémiramis pardons him and dies. A final chorus laments the cruel course of fate.

Because the changes made in the work between the publication of the 1802 libretto and the 1804 score, the only one available for study, are so great, it is not possible to draw up a clear, concise table outlining the action and its musical setting. Description will therefore have to suffice in this instance.

Although Desriaux attempted to follow Voltaire's tragedy quite closely, the result was not a strong opera libretto but rather a weakened drama. There are two major flaws in the libretto: first, that the author assumes, perhaps rightly, a great familiarity on the part of the audience with the earlier drama or at least with the general course of the story; and second, that the author seemingly has not taken into account the differences between opera and drama that must necessarily result from the addition of music, this despite the fact that he deliberately changed Voltaire's alexandrines to lines more suitable for music and created new scenes to condense the action or provide new areas for the deployment of spectacle.[6] Desriaux's assumption of the spectator's foreknowledge of the story is evident in the fact that Ninus is mentioned early in Act I but not specifically identified until much later; that the details of his murder must be pieced together bit by bit during the course of the work; and that Assur's conspiracy is also rather vaguely outlined.[7] Without knowledge of the original story, the appearance of Ninus' ghost seems not well motivated, and Ninias' actions after he learns his true identity are strange indeed, even for a person in a disturbed state of mind.

The second point, the author's lack of awareness of the differences between a drama and an opera libretto, is in some ways bound up with the first. Desriaux seemingly did not realize how much music would actually slow down and distract the spectator from the action. Many ideas are put forth that serve as preparations for later action, e.g., Sémiramis' belief that she has seen Ninus' ghost or that Arzace's arrival will somehow bring her suffering to an end. Yet the eventual outcome of these and other events occurs so much later in the libretto and the connection between preparation and event is made so inexplicit that it is difficult for any but the most perceptive and informed spectator to see. Meanwhile, anyone less informed in these areas may well have become involved in the music, the processions, the ballets, the beautiful costumes or settings, or any one of a number of other possible distractions. It would not be hazardous to speculate that even in 1802 an audience would contain more persons of the latter type than of the former, traditional French attention to the quality of the libretto notwithstanding.

Yet on some occasions Desriaux has made some points altogether too explicit. For example, in Act II Sémiramis first tells Assur she has a plan regarding the royal succession, then tells her confidante what the plan is. After a procession, Oroës announces that the queen has an announcement to make, and Sémiramis reveals what the audience has known for some time. Such extensive preparation dulls rather than increases the suspense, for the crowd's reaction is inevitable, not merely anticipated.

Under the circumstances described above, it almost goes without saying that the action of *Sémiramis* unfolds gradually and without a great deal of prefatory material to establish a background of events. The plot is delayed-action in that the events with which it deals are the outcome of a crime committed fifteen years earlier, but it is not carried out as Scribe would have done. Because of the gradual unfolding of the action and the frequent lack of explicit motivation, events are often unexpected to anyone who is not familiar with Voltaire's tragedy.

To have based an opera libretto directly on a drama, with as few changes as Desriaux made, would have seemed absurd to Scribe, to whom preexistent ideas were a stimulus to his own imagination, sense of order, awareness of the exigencies of the musical stage, and desire to be up to date. Desriaux's work shows a respect for the preservation of a revered but unsuitable style and form not atypical for his time but quite unlike those of Scribe.

Desriaux's lack of awareness of differences between opera and drama shows up in two other aspects of the libretto: the style of poetry used for the musical texts and the designation of certain parts of the libretto for recitative or arioso, others for elaboration as set numbers. The recitative texts are in long, regular, rhymed couplets which are often quite beautiful poetically but which thereby lose the directness and edge necessary for intelligibility in a musical context. For example, in Act I, ii, Azéma sings:

> Mais d'ou vient que la paix qui règne dans mon coeur
> Ne répand que sur moi son charme et sa douceur?
> Hélas! Sémiramis, à ses douleurs livrée,
> Sème ici les chagrins dont elle est dévorée.
> L'horreur qui l'epouvante est dans tous les esprits;
> Tantôt remplissant l'air de ses lugubres cris,
> Tantôt mourne, abattue, égarée, interdite,
> De quelque dieu vengeur évitant la poursuite,
> Elle tombe à genoux verse ces lieux retirés,
> A la nuit, au silence, à la mort consacrés.

[Translation:

> But why does the peace that reigns in my heart
> Pour out only on me its charm and its sweetness?
> Alas! Sémiramis, given over to her sadness,
> Sows here the griefs by which she is devoured.
> The horror that fear [causes] is in all minds;
> Now filling the air with her mournful cries,
> Now mournful, dejected, distracted, confounded,
> Evading the pursuit of some vengeful god,
> She falls on her knees in these secluded places,
> Consecrated to night, to silence, to death.]

This recitative contains some lovely lines worthy of a dramatic soliloquy, and capitalizes on such typical poetic devices as repetitive description or elaboration of a single item or idea, word inversion, and quite introspective reflection on a psychological state. Such subtleties not only tend to become lost when sung from the operatic stage but seem somehow too beautiful for setting as a recitative and too lyrical in themselves for setting as an air.

The lines in texts for airs or other set-numbers are shorter than those for recitatives and are not necessarily arranged in couplets. Rhyme schemes in such texts are varied. Despite the fairly extensive use of large-scale numbers including choruses, the set-numbers are almost entirely nondramatic. Thus all the important events take place in recitative and the techniques of dramatic ensemble writings are less well developed in this respect than in an opéra comique like *Béniowski*.

The individual acts are not strong structures in themselves and act endings are particularly weak. Desriaux has attempted to create a suspenseful situation at the end of each act, but unfortunately the forces and activities involved in each case are not presented as dramatic *coups* and seem dulled by the scenes preceding them. In Act I the triumphal entry of Arzace with his army near the end of the act is a large scene involving chorus, processions, and huge forces on the stage. Immediately thereafter Arzace presents the letter to Oroës, who promises to disclose its contents to Arzace that evening. Surely this is more important to what follows in the opera than in Arzace's entry, yet it is placed in such a position and set in such a way (recitative, musically less attractive than any other style) that it seems unimportant and anticlimactic by comparison. Similarly, the dramatic climax of Act II comes when Sémiramis announces she will marry Arzace. After this, Assur and his friends begin to plan their conspiracy. This scene is very important to what occurs in Act IV but again is placed in such a position that it seems less important and weakens the end of the act. Act III ends not with the spectacular appearance of Ninus' ghost but with Sémiramis' reassurance to the people that the ghost seems to be approving, not disapproving, her actions. Throughout the work there is no systematic attempt to make each act a dramatic entity by posing a problem at the beginning of the act that comes to some sort of head at the end.

Characters in *Sémiramis* are statue figures of a type Calzabigi might well have created for Gluck. Their emotions are real and human, not the stylized affections or passions one would find in Metastasian texts, but for the most part they lack psychological depth or development. Here again, opéra comique of the same era seems more modern in this respect than does the *tragédie-lyrique.*

*Sémiramis* contains many elements typical of operas of its time. Its subject, based on ancient history, is of a type traditional to French opera, as are the character types and their presentation. The exploitation of the marvelous in the appearance of Ninus' ghost and the emphasis on spectacle in the ballet featuring dances in various national costumes and in the procession before Sémiramis' announcement of her choice of husband are also the products of tradition. The chorus is treated as a scenic mass, not as a character, another feature typical of earlier and contemporary opera which was to be changed by Scribe and his collaborators.

The libretto of *Sémiramis* is a weak one even in comparison to others of its genre and vintage. However, in fairness to Desriaux and Catel it must be admitted that the 1804 revision was made much stronger dramatically and many of the flaws mentioned in this discussion were corrected. The order of some scenes was changed, some scenes or parts of scenes were added or omitted to make the structure of the plot and the motivation of the characters clearer. In the later version, act structure was considerably strengthened by the rearrangement of several earlier scenes to different places in the work. With these changes the acts came closer to being miniature dramas in themselves and the work thus took on a more modern outlook.

## Etienne de Jouy: *La Vestale* and *Les Bayadères*

The name of V. J. Etienne de Jouy is an important one in libretto history. Not only is he responsible for a large number of libretti, among them those for Spontini's famed *La Vestale* and Catel's greatest success, *Les Bayadères*, but he collaborated on the libretto for Rossini's *Guillaume Tell*, one of the early landmarks in the history of French grand opera. His work on *La Vestale* has been cited by Grout as "brilliant," for it was not only a theatrically effective piece but "combined the old rescue motif and a passionate love story with the solemnity of the tragédie lyrique on a huge scale, adding a strong touch of the melodramatic."[8] Similar comments could be made of *Les Bayadères*, which combines many of the structural and scenic traits already seen in Grétry's *Le Caravane du Caire* with a heavy dose of melodrama and larger performing forces.

The story of *La Vestale* is similar to that of Bellini's *Norma*. The opera opens with a scene between the military hero Licinius and his friend Cinna. The latter cannot understand why Licinius seems so unhappy, since his recent victories have been rewarded with suitable honors and public adulation. Licinius finally confesses that he is in love with Julia, a vestal virgin who had once been promised him as a bride. At that time, however, Julia's father would not consent to the marriage because Licinius had no name or fortune, and by the time the latter returned victorious from foreign wars Julia had already been consecrated for service in the temple of the goddess Vesta. Even though Licinius risks punishment by the gods, Cinna agrees to stand by him and to help all he can.

The High Priestess of Vesta, Julia, and the other vestal virgins enter to pray that Vesta will preserve the eternal flame in the hands of the faithful. The High Priestess issues a general warning that the flame will be extinguished if any of the young ladies is guilty of a crime and Julia, in an aside, voices her fear of discovery. The ladies then enter the temple to prepare for a victory ceremony in honor of the returned warriors. The High Priestess warns Julia against the temptations of human love and the possibility of disgracing her holy calling, then tells her that she must guard the eternal flame and crown the hero, Licinius.

Alone, Julia recalls her love for Licinius but nevertheless determines to be faithful to her religious vows.

After a large victory chorus and procession during which Licinius is honored, the High Priestess announces that Julia will guard the eternal flame that night. Licinius observes to Cinna that Julia will therefore be alone in the temple. The ceremony continues with a ballet in honor of the hero and closes as the people march into the temple to make sacrifice to the gods.

The second act takes place in the temple of Vesta, where Julia is left to guard the flame. She is still torn between her love for Licinius and fear of the gods should she break her vows. Licinius arrives and tries to persuade Julia to run away with him. She finally consents, but before they can leave the eternal flame is extinguished and Cinna warns that a crowd is approaching the temple. Licinius does not want to leave Julia alone but knows that if she is discovered trying to escape she will be killed. The two men leave just before the priests and priestesses enter and discover that the flame has gone out. Julia confesses her crime but will not name her lover. The High Priest sentences her to death.

The third act is set at a place of execution outside the walls of Rome. Licinius and Cinna have come with a few friends to save Julia from death, but first Licinius tries to persuade the High Priest to intercede with the gods on Julia's behalf. This failing, Licinius warns the high priest that he, Julia's lover, will attempt to save her. A procession escorts Julia to the place of execution and the High Priest places her veil on the altar, saying that if Vesta is willing to forgive this crime she will send down a flame to consume the veil. When this does not happen the High Priest decrees Julia must die. Licinius enters with his soldiers to stop the execution, but Julia denies that he is her lover in order to protect him from punishment. Just as things are about to come to a head among these opposing forces, lightning descends and ignites the veil on the altar. The High Priest announces that the sacred flame has been rekindled, issues a pardon for Julia, Licinius, and his associates, and releases Julia from her religious vows. The scene changes to the temple of Venus, where the people celebrate the marriage of Julia and Licinius. A ballet ends the opera.

The libretto of *La Vestale* presents a more modern structural plan and dramatic effectiveness combined with many traditional elements and older operatic conventions, something represented already by the revised version of Catel's *Sémiramis.*The subject is one of the opera's more traditional aspects. Although it is not from mythology, its ancient Roman setting and its character types (priests, priestesses, military heroes) belong among those of *tragédie-lyrique*. *La Vestale* also includes the very conventional situation of the returning hero who discovers that for one reason or another the course of his true love is not to run smoothly; and the hero-confidant pair.

The use of the chorus in *La Vestale* is based on the Gluck line of French operatic tradition, for the singers are treated as a mass of movable human scenery. They turn small scenes into mammoth spectacles, react *en masse* and on cue, but have no independent life or identity. They are not "the people" pictured by Scribe in *La Dame blanche* or *La Muette de Portici.*

The way in which spectacle and mass scenes are used is also well within the conventions of earlier *tragédie-lyrique.* The thunder and lightning, the igniting of Julia's veil on the altar, the restoration of the sacred flame are from the gods, not from men; they are *merveilleux.* The large processions into, out of, and around the temples are also conventional scenic spectacles, and the ending of the opera with a ballet is an old custom soon to become outdated.

Certain of Jouy's comments in his preface to the *Vestale* libretto show him to be more aware than was the author of *Sémiramis* of the need for an opera and a tragedy to move according to their own requirements. Of Julia's perhaps illogical but nevertheless spectacular reprieve he writes:

> . . . historic truth demanded that the guilty Vestale should suffer the death to which her sin had exposed her; but was this fearful catastrophe—which might have been introduced by means of a narrative in regular tragedy—of such a nature that it could be consummated before the eyes of the spectator? I do not think so.[9]

Messenger scenes and offstage action of a violent nature were to continue to be a part of French opera even through the time of *La Muette de Portici.* However, the gradual but inevitable separation of opera from classical tragedy is somehow forecast in these words. By the time of *Gustave III, Les Huguenots,* and *La Juive* such a spectacle could indeed "be consummated before the eyes of the spectator"—and was.

The most outstanding new element in *La Vestale* is the modern construction of the libretto. In fact, in many respects *La Vestale* is more forward-looking in its structure than is *Guillaume Tell,* although the latter is not produced until more than twenty years later. The plot of *La Vestale* is quite simple and contains nothing that could be considered a subplot. Structurally, however, it is arranged in a manner worthy of Scribe. Its delayed-action plot does begin near the culmination of events. Thus the libretto is more like Scribe's than are *Le Caravane du Caire,*

*Démofoon*, and *Sémiramis*, with their modest bows to the delayed-action device. In *La Vestale*, all important events necessary to motivate the action have taken place before the curtain rises: Julia and Licinius have fallen in love, Licinius has become a military hero, and Julia has taken religious vows. The conflict thus already posed, the opera can proceed in a suspenseful unfolding of events to its *dénouement*.

Each event in *La Vestale* is carefully and clearly prepared so that actions are never totally unexpected when they occur. The first part of Act I is primarily exposition and spectacle, with the actual action beginning in the finale. In fact, little really happens in the opera until Act II, but then every event is anticipated. The significance of the sacred flame has already been explained, and Julia's conflict between her love for Licinius and duty to the goddess has been set up. Licinius has already revealed his plan to meet Julia in the temple and Cinna has sworn to stand by and help his friend. The attitude of the priests and priestesses toward any profanation of their religious laws has been stated clearly. Everything that happens in Act II is prepared for by one or more of these factors and is their logical outcome. The action of Act III is prepared to a lesser degree, for the *deus ex machina* solution to the conflict is something that could be anticipated only with knowledge of operatic conventions of the time, not from any statements or activities the librettist has written into his text. For the most part the course of action is smooth and the succession of scenes tight and logical.

The structures of individual acts show that the piece was written at a transitional stage of libretto history. The second act and the third act up to the change of scene are miniature dramas in which a problem posed at the beginning of the act reaches some sort of conclusion by the end. The same is true of Act I to a certain degree: at the beginning of the act Licinius reveals his love for Julia, and by the end of the act he has found a way to meet her. Yet there is so little action in this act, and this line of plot development is so frequently interrupted by a procession or a change of subject, that it does not constitute the major driving force of the act. Furthermore, both Acts I and III have cast-of-thousands finales that dull the dramatic effect of the strongest scenes in each act: the tense crowning of the hero in Act I and the pardoning of Julia in Act III. This sort of conclusion is more retrospective than progressive, and only the second act ends with a strong dramatic *coup*.

The characters of *La Vestale* are neither the statue-like figures of *Démofoon* or *Sémiramis* nor the more modern but two-dimensional figures created later by Scribe. If anything, they are more like certain of the leading characters in *Béniowski* in that they are truly human and do not develop in emotional poses or series of affections. Jouy has presented his characters with great care and attention to individual reactions and the portrayal of geniune emotional states. This focus on real emotional depth goes hand in hand with another noteworthy feature of *La Vestale*: its emphasis on personal confrontation and conflict between the characters. The High Priestess does not simply announce the significance of the eternal flame to all the vestal virgins; she also speaks personally to Julia, an individual about whom she is genuinely concerned. Act II deals almost entirely with interpersonal relationships and individual soul-baring. In Act III Licinius confronts not the impersonal gods but the majestic High Priest himself, and the High Priestess weeps for Julia, not for the disgrace she has brought to her sacred calling.

Musically *La Vestale* is somewhat more progressive than *Sémiramis* in that more action is set as lyrical arioso rather than recitative and more of the important turning points in the action are worked into large scene complexes rather than being carried out in relatively simple accompanied recitative. Although dividing lines between recitatives and set-numbers are still apparent, Spontini is more likely to join them with a transition than to end the recitative with a final cadence before continuing with the musical number. Thus real breaks in the music are infrequent and many of the larger scenes depart from traditional formal conventions.

Like *Le Carvane du Caire*, *Les Bayadères* is on an exotic theme and is set in an eastern land, this time India. The event forming one of the major turning points in the action—when the rajah Démaly pretends to be dying in order to convince Laméa, a bayadère, to marry him—is taken from the same tale that forms the basis of Scribe's *Le Dieu et la bayadère.*[10] The theme as a whole is somewhat like that of *La Vestale:* the rajah loves a bayadère (a young woman consecrated to service in the temple of the Indian gods) and finally convinces her to renounce her vows and marry him. However, *Les Bayadères*, although basically a serious opera, is carried out on a less passionate and dramatic level than *La Vestale.* Premiered on August 8, 1810, it was Catel's most popular opera, reaching 100 performances by 1818 and remaining in the repertoire into the 1820s.[11]

As Act I begins, Rustan, the intendant of the harem, is urging the women there to take extra care with their appearances, since this is the day Démaly, the rajah, will choose his wife from among them. The rajah arrives and is welcomed, but asks to be left alone for a time in order to make a decision. He does not really want to choose one of the women from the harem, however, for he loves Laméa, a bayadère, who cannot or will not marry him. He is also concerned about a war being waged by Olkar, a general from Meerut, against them. His ministers advise Démaly not to worry about Olkar and remind him that this day has been fixed by sacred law to be that on which he must choose a bride. If he does not abide by this law and pass on the sacred diadem, the city will no longer be favored by the gods. Nevertheless, Démaly has a feeling he and the people should be doing something about the war threat instead of preparing a marriage feast.

Laméa and the bayadères enter and entertain the people assembled for Démaly's wedding. Everyone is gay and heedless except Laméa, who warns of the danger from Olkar's army. The ministers silence her and demand that the rajah announce his choice of a bride and comply with the sacred law. Just as Démaly is about to declare his love for Laméa, an officer announces that Olkar's forces are at the gates and the people fall into disorder.

As Act II begins Laméa is conferring with some Indian officers. Oklar has won the city and has imprisoned Démaly, but Laméa thinks they may have a chance against the enemy. She proposes to trick Olkar, who has fallen in love with her, and the officers agree to help carry out her plans. Olkar particularly wants to carry off the sacred diadem of Vishnu, but is aware that only Démaly knows where it is kept. Laméa pretends to help Olkar by agreeing to try to get the information from Démaly, but when left alone with the rajah she reveals that she has been able to gather secret forces and that she and the bayadères will distract Olkar's army while Démaly's men try to retake the city and free their ruler. Démaly is returned to prison.

When Olkar returns, Laméa tells him a false location of the diadem. She recommends that he not stir up the people by violating so sacred a place but rather that he hold a large victory celebration during which she can steal the sacred object from its hiding place without being noticed. He agrees even though Salem, his confidant, fears the effect the bayadères will have on the soldiers and senses conspiracy in the air.

The scene changes to a public square where, during a long series of choruses, songs, and dances. Laméa carries out her plans. Finally Olkar begins to suspect something, but by this time Démaly has been freed from prison and has left with his forces to seek reinforcements. Olkar calls his troops together to give chase.

Démaly has reconquered his city, and Act II opens with a chorus in his honor. The rajah announces his intention of rewarding Laméa, but before she can be summoned Rustan tells Démaly that some people believe him to be wounded. Démaly asks that Rustan calm them and keep them away for a time. Laméa arrives but will not yield to his pleas that she renounce her vows and marry him, even though she now admits that she loves him. After she leaves, Démaly tells Rustan he has a plan to overcome her objections and goes off to carry it out.

The ladies from the harem enter, discussing Démaly's victory and the possibility that one of them will be chosen to marry him. Each claims to love the rajah very much until Rustan returns to announce that Démaly is indeed seriously wounded and will therefore not select a bride but will marry the woman who loves him most. A brahmin reminds the people that sacred law demands that Démaly fulfill the will of the gods or lose their favor, but Rustan also reminds them of the Indian custom that a widow be burned to death on her husband's funeral pyre. Finally Laméa agrees to marry Démaly in order to fulfill the law and in order that she can at least be near him in death. The brahmins prepare Laméa for her fate. The scene then changes to the throne room where Démaly, very much alive, receives his bride. The chorus wishes them happiness and a long ballet ends the opera.

The libretto of *Les Bayadères* is as unwieldy and as old-fashioned as its predecessor *La Vestale* is clearly organized and modern. The delayed-action plot is of an earlier type, in which only a minimum of preliminary action has taken place before the curtain rises, and the plot unfolds gradually. During the opera some actions are prepared—e.g., Laméa's plan to defeat Olkar—while others occur more or less on the spur of the moment—e.g., Démaly's plan to win Laméa. Even those events for which preparation is most explicit are carried out clumsily in comparison to actions in *La Vestale*. The best example of comparatively careful preparation is found in the requirement that Démaly choose a bride at a particular time. Once we learn, early in the opera, that he loves Laméa, no one should be surprised that he succeeds in marrying her. Yet the law covering this situation is repeated so many times in different ways and by different characters that it is difficult to sustain even such suspense as exists.

Spectacle is definitely the god called upon to resurrect the drama of *Les Baydères*, and the opera must indeed have been colorful. Yet the scene of the bayadères and the soldiers in Act II, if cleverly conceived, is interminable and quite as distracting from the drama as the bazaar scene in *Le Caravane du Caire*, regardless of the fact that the former involves actions essential to the plot. Like *Le Caravane* and *Sémiramis*, *Les Bayadères* closes with a ballet, again colorful but again weakening any dramatic edge the last scene might have had. The ending of the last act is thus typical for its time but does not present a tradition to be carried on in the later libretti of Scribe.

The structure of the individual acts is forward-looking if a bit clumsily handled. Only in the last act does an anticlimactic final scene dull the effect of a dramatic point made in the act. Each act presents a minature drama in which a problem is worked out, to be concluded in a strong finale. Part of the clumsiness in handling this structure lies in the distribution of the various events in the plot. Act I is loaded with a somewhat confusing array of material: the immediate fact of Démaly's having to choose a wife, the threat of war, the conflict between the rajah's love for Laméa and the sacred laws of his country, the ambivalent attitude of Démaly's ministers, and the necessity to include sufficient background in the narrative to set most of these events or attitudes in perspective and in proper relationship to one another. In addition, the comic aspect provided at the beginning of the act by Rustan and the ladies of the harem immediately confuses the spectator as to the nature of the opera's main plot. Finally, the action is interlaced with a large amount of spectacle which could be distracting in an act already so loosely structured. Act II is less filled with dramatic detail, but its length and the proportion of the act given over to musical and choreographic diversions contribute to structural looseness. Only in Act III is the action arranged with anything near the tightness of that in *La Vestale,* and this tightness collapses as Démaly sets in motion his clever but unanticipated plan to win Laméa.

Two additional factors contribute to the rather clumsy handling of the act structure. The first, a remnant from older French operatic conventions, is the use of major offstage actions and of messengers to relate them to the audience. All military activity occurs offstage, and the major battles take place between acts. This is not to suggest that the already unwieldy libretto would be improved by a staged battle or two, but merely to point out that the librettist has handled these violent scenes in a classicistic manner. Second, the relatively simple central idea of *Les Bayadères* has been burdened—perhaps overburdened—with subplots and subsidiary actions that may or may not turn out to be important. Besides the problem of Démaly and Laméa, the opera must deal not merely with a war but with both a defeat and a victory; with Olkar's interest in both Laméa and the sacred diadem; and with the comic distraction provided by the ladies of the harem. In addition, the spectator is faced with the possibility that Démaly's seemingly heedless advisers may in fact be traitors (they are not) and must try to comprehend the character of Rustan. Is he counsellor, confidant, or clown? Whatever the case, he is too unimportant to any aspect of the opera to have the librettist focus this much attention on him by his failure to give him clear definition.

In general, however, the characters in *Les Bayadères* are quite clearly defined by means of their own actions. Olkar swaggers, the harem ladies are as catty as rival actresses, the bayadères swirl gracefully and sing of pleasure, the ministers of state fumble. Démaly and Laméa are presented particularly well. At first the rajah seems a hopeless romantic and just a bit inept as a ruler, but adversity makes him strong and necessity makes him clever. Laméa's role as a truly heroic figure seems incongruous in view of her position as a bayadère, yet she is strangely appealing in her development from a somewhat confused, lovesick girl to a self-sacrificing, almost tragic heroine. The portrait contains just a bit of Alceste, and the gradual emergence of Laméa's strength of purpose constitutes the librettist's only claim to the creation of psychological depth among his characters.

The text style and language in *Les Bayadères* are similar to those in *La Vestale* and quite different from those in *Sémiramis*. Jouy's style is more direct, less poetic than that of Desriaux, and he wastes few words elaborating on even the most tender sentiments. For example, in Act II Laméa express her determination to save Démaly:

> Without turning my eyes
> From the trifling dangers to which I expose myself,
> Let me march forward toward the glorious goal
> Which my heart has in view.
> Dear Démaly, in your misfortunes,
> I enjoy this [much] good fortune
> To be able to say to myself:
> Alone today, in the universe,
> I watch over the one I love.

The expression here is simple and to the point, stripped of flowery adjectives and poetic restatements or descriptions of states of the soul.

Recitative texts, like those for the set-numbers, are in rhymed verse but are not arranged in any set patterns. Gone are the regular lines and rhymed couplets of Desriaux. In their place Jouy writes lines of irregular length, usually but not necessarily longer than those of the aria texts, with varied rhyme schemes. Once again, Jouy's straightforward expression is an outstanding feature.

*Les Bayadères* shows the same musical trends represented by *La Vestale:* a tendency to get away from strong divisions between recitatives and set-numbers and to create larger scene complexes. Catel, however, is less successful in this area than is Spontini and there are more actual breaks, represented by final cadences, between the various musical sections. In general, Catel's set-numbers are less adventurous than Spontini's and fall more readily within the traditional categories for such pieces.

Etienne de Jouy's writing in *La Vestale* and *Les Bayadères* represents both the most progressive and most conventional features of libretti of his time. The subjects are within the French tradition, yet each work contains new features, especially in the treatment of the heroines. The best and worst features of the old tradition of drama and setting are included. In its good features as in its less successful moments, Jouy's writing best represents the state of libretto style before Scribe. His style will present even more of a contrast to that of the creator of the well-made libretto when seen in the context of the rise of grand opera in the late 1820s.

## THE BIRTH OF GRAND OPERA

A general survey of the conditions surrounding the rise of French grand opera in the nineteenth century and the people involved in this development has already been given in the introductory chapters and has been elaborated upon in analyses of specific works written before Scribe became principal librettist at the Opéra. With this background in mind, we may now go further into detail, for the phenomenon of French grand opera is one that is intimately tied up not only with the situation of the French musical theatre but also with the personality and technique of Scribe and the social milieu in which he found himself in the late 1820s.

What was grand opera? It was many things: a theatrical form based primarily on plots from recent European history; a stage spectacle, the scene designer's dream, the machinist's delight; a musical form involving large ensemble-choral scene complexes and stunning ballets alongside the usual recitatives, airs, duos, etc., of traditional opera; a social necessity, a place to see and be seen for the bourgeoisie; a business run by individuals, with governmental assistance, to make a great deal of money; the musical stage's response to literary and musical romanticism. Librettists, composers, scene designers, ballet masters vied for a place on the Opéra's stage, for nowhere else was that unique combination of fame and fortune to be found in the Parisian musical world.[1]

Taken element by element, however, grand opera seems on the surface to have been an overblown extension of French opera traditions long since established or at least tried. Although themes from classical antiquity were most common in French opera until the 1820s, recent European history had provided the plots or backgrounds for many an opéra comique of the Revolutionary period and had given an added touch of novelty to such operas as Spontini's *Fernand Cortez* (1809). However, as Longyear has remarked, many of the seemingly historical operas before Scribe "were stories of Metastasian antiquity brought up to date," while those of Scribe and his contemporaries "were given a strong sense of immediacy and vitality which most probably derived from the historical novels of Sir Walter Scott."[2] The romanticism of Lesueur's *Ossian* (1804) could also be mentioned as one of the signs of the coming change in operatic subjects. Since the time of Lully stage spectacle and ballet had been integral parts of any new opera. The nineteenth century, then, was merely carrying out the base of French taste to the second power in these matters. The difference between grand opera and what came before it was to some extent a matter of degree, and the unique elements of grand opera thus would seem to lie primarily in social and business areas. Yet there is more to the often strikingly new quality presented by this form of opera. Both the unique elements of grand opera and its unique combination of elements can be traced to and in the libretti of Eugène Scribe.

In the seventeenth century Quinault set standards for the French opera libretto that remained in force to a greater or lesser degree into the first decades of the nineteenth century. In making this momentous contribution to operatic history in France, Quinault took elements of classical tragedy (subjects, verse forms, some scene structures), combined them with ideas already developed in French ballet (the dance itself, stage spectacle, the nature of *divertissement* scenes) and with the spectacle inherent in dramatic treatment of "marvelous" subject matter. His audience was both the general public and the aristocracy, and he worked accordingly in choosing plots, creating the poetic text, and making room for spectacle and dance, all to suit their tastes.

What Scribe did for grand opera was of a similar nature, but times and people had changed and new formulas had to be devised. Like Quinault, Scribe too derived basic elements of his libretto technique from a theatrical source. Now, however, it was not the artistically more respectable Comédie-Française to which the librettist turned, but to the popular theatre—more specifically, to the popular theatre of his own making. The techniques and to a lesser extent the subjects and characters Scribe developed in his *comédies-vaudevilles* he adapted first to opéra comique, then—by way of opéra comique—to grand opera. It is significant that Scribe's first grand opera to be performed—indeed, the first modern grand opera by anyone—was produced in 1828, after he had carefully developed his mature style of opéra comique writing.

It is also significant that this work, *La Muette de Portici*, has as its heroine a dancer. Only one year before, Scribe had begun to write ballet scenarios, producing with Aumer the ballet-pantomime *La Somnambule*, later the basis of Bellini's opera. The creation of a dancing heroine in *La Muette* was to a large extent an accident. However, Scribe did not allow accidents to remain in his works unless he was reasonably certain they would prove stageworthy in the end. Like Quinault before him, Scribe capitalized on the French love of ballet not only in creating Fenella but in continuing the use of *divertissements* in his operas. However, it was a different ballet tradition that Scribe called upon to assist him in creating his operatic spectacles. A new style in ballet was being born, a style in which Scribe played a significant role. In the rise of romantic ballet the popular theatre was a decisive influence.[3]

Although the more or less formal beginning of romantic ballet dates from the appearance in 1832 of Marie Taglioni in *La Sylphide*, events leading up to this landmark in ballet history had occurred gradually during the previous ten years. The romantic ballet was characterized on the one hand by the employment of supernatural themes involving fairies, gnomes, sylphs, and the like; and on the other hand by subjects emphasizing local color in the exotic settings of Spain, the mid-East, and the Slavic countries. In any event, ballet gradually developed a new freedom in all aspects of its production. Scribe's *La Somnambule* (1827), set in Scotland, introduced the element of local color into ballet, and Marie Taglioni's debut at the Opéra that same year showed the public a freer, more graceful style of dancing than that of the classical ballet to which they had become accustomed. Scribe's ballet also marks the debut of the ballet scenarist as distinct from the choreographer. Everywhere, features of the popular theatre began to invade ballet.

> Many dancers and choreographers who were to play a part in shaping Romantic ballet worked on these stages [of the popular theatres]. . . . Here there were no conventions to be observed, no effects to be scorned as below the dignity of art; here a more broadly based public demanded to be amused.[4]

This influence from the popular theatre coincided with increasing efforts to emphasize local color and to make ballet more expressive. Gradually a dancer's acting ability became just as important as his learning in classical ballet techniques. This combination of a well-developed mimed action with more formally organized dances—a kind of physical recitative-aria relationship—was a particular feature of ballets at the Porte-Saint-Martin theatre in the early 1820s, some years before these ideas invaded the stage of the Opéra.

In this move toward freer dancing styles and greater expressivity Scribe's contributions were great. Not only was he the first ballet scenarist for the Paris Opéra, but with *La Muette* he helped further changes in the prevailing dance style. In his ballet on *Manon Lescaut* (1830) he made the first real attempt to recreate a historical setting in ballet, and with the ballet of the nuns in *Robert le Diable*, admittedly not his own idea, he used effects taken from German romanticism: the setting, lighting, and general aura of the supernatural and mysterious.[5] Perhaps it would not be too much to speculate that the reason traits of German romanticism never really invaded opera in France was that the French found a better and more nationalistic outlet in romantic ballet, an equally escapist medium. Whatever the merits of this speculation, one thing remains clear: the great influence of the popular theatre on nineteenth century ballet. Since the popular theatre, especially through the works of Scribe, had influenced other stage forms as well, the Parisian theatre saw a complex interaction of dramatic genres during the decade of the 1820s. This interaction can be shown graphically as follows:

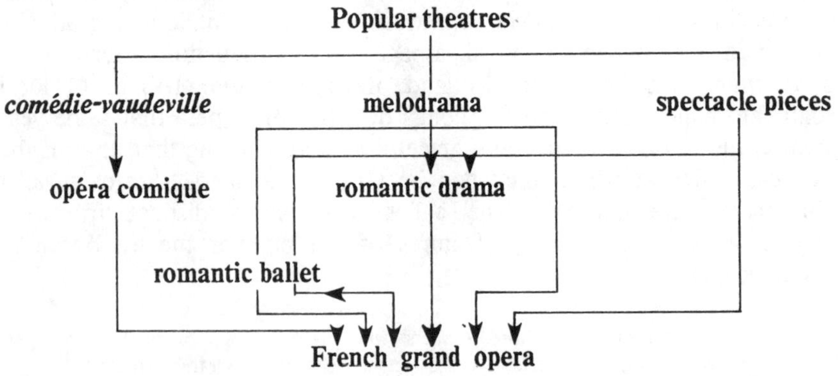


This presentation is not meant to suggest that French grand opera was the culmination of all previous or contemporaneous developments, but only that it combined elements of a great number of theatrical forms, all of which derive to a greater or lesser extent from the popular theatres.

Scribe, like Véron, recognized that the bourgeoisie would be the chief patrons of opera after 1830, and must have seen their growing influence in the last years of Charles' reign. For the ideas he promoted in grand opera, ideas which he himself did not perfect until as late as 1833, were drawn from forms cultivated by this class. The popular theatres provided models for historical plots and spectacular, realistic settings before the more literary romantic dramatists made them distinguishing traits of their works. The popular theatres—first the Gymnase, then the Opéra-Comique—provided dramatic techniques, characters, poetic forms, and actions. Finally, the ballet continued to play its traditional role in a new milieu and a new style. Like Quinault, Scribe carved grand opera out of the theatre of his own time. The audience, however, had changed. Quinault chose from styles and forms admired by the aristocracy to create works for their entertainment. Scribe did the same for the bourgeoisie.

However, Crosten's statement that Scribe's work in opera "from the start . . . was firm and settled in its outlines"[6] is not entirely correct.

*La Muette de Portici* was Scribe's first opera to be produced, but a later effort, *Robert le Diable*, was begun in 1827 as an opéra comique. *La Muette* is also essentially an opéra comique of the type represented by *Leicester, Léocadie*, or *La Dame banche.* Although it has been given a tragic ending and is dressed in all the spectacular trappings and local color of later grand opera, its overall form, the musical styles used, the characters, and the situations resemble those of the more serious of Scribe's opéra comique efforts. Like *Leicester* and *La Dame blanche* it has a historical background, and like the latter it includes an example of a nobleman being saved by persons of a lower social class. Along with this stock stiuation from opéra comique, *La Muette* includes a case of a woman falling in love with a man whose name she does not know and of her loving a man above her station, both common ideas in Scribe's opéras comiques. Like *Léocadie*, *La Muette* deals with a girl who is deceived by a nobleman. Like all three opéras comiques mentioned, *La Muette* contains the popular strophic vocal numbers in addition to the airs and ensembles commonly found in Scribe's more serious opéras comiques. Indeed, even the often cited use of the chorus as a vital character in *La Muette* has a precedent in *La Dame blanche.*

Thus, while it is true that "no preliminary fumbling was necessary when [Scribe] applied himself to serious opera,"[7] this is true in *La Muette de Portici* largely because he based his work on a style developed previously in opéra comique, eliminating the customary happy ending and turning to the popular theatre's stage effects and local color to add a new dimension in scenic concerns; and to the popular ballet to provide a new kind of character portrayal and the expected *divertissements.* *La Muette de Portici* was not so much the beginning of a new genre, then, as it was the synthesis of the concepts of traditional French opera with Scribe's techniques of opéra comique writing, also in part the result of traditions.

That this is so can be demonstrated in three ways: first, in an overview of Scribe's development as an opera librettist; second, in a comparison of *La Muette de Portici* with the next grand opera to come on the scene, Rossini's *Guillaume Tell;* and third, in a discussion of the first and second versions of *Robert le Diable.*

## SCRIBE'S OPERAS: AN OVERVIEW

Scribe's operas are not all of the "grand" variety but can be divided into three general categories: grand operas (such as *La Muette, Les Huguenots, La Juive*, etc.); lighter, usually comic operas (*Le Comte Ory, Le Serment, Le Philtre*, etc.); and operas on exotic subjects *(Le Dieu et la bayadère, Ali Baba, Le Lac des fées*, etc.). Grand operas, normally in five acts, exhibit most or all the characteristics outlined above for this genre and often have tragic or melodramatic endings. The lighter operas, like most of Scribe's opéras comiques, are usually in two or three acts, deal with comic subjects or at least less momentous serious topics than in grand opera, have characters of the types normally employed in opéra comique—a mixture of noblemen, middle class businessmen and women, villagers, peasants, servants, students, and the like—and have happy endings. The solo numbers are ordinarily in forms also cultivated in opéra comique—e.g., *couplets, romances*, airs—and the musical style is lighter than in grand opera and concentrated in less grandiose scene complexes. The operas on exotic themes deal with magical, fanciful, or exotic topics involving supernatural characters or situations often set against the backdrop of the Middle East. Opportunities for stage spectacle are especially plentiful in this type of opera.

Although Scribe's first opera was a grand opera, it was not until 1831, when he produced *Robert le Diable*, that he again attempted anything of the same type. However, *Robert* was a revised version of an earlier opéra comique libretto, the character of which will be discussed below. Thus of his earliest grand opera libretti the first bears marked resemblances to opéras comiques immediately preceding it and the second starts its life as an opéra comique of which it still shows traces. That Scribe soon recognized a change in the concept he had of grand opera—or, perhaps better, a solidification of ideas and techniques he had been developing—is evident not in *Robert le Diable* but in *Gustave III*, which was premiered over a year after *Robert*.[1] For this opera Scribe uses a designation he repeats for no other work: *opéra historique*.

Scribe's style in grand opera was therefore not fully developed until quite a long time after the supposed first example of a perfected technique. If viewed in this way, Scribe's process of development of a grand opera style is similar to that discussed in connection with opéra comique, for he worked from the familiar and built upon concepts he had developed earlier in connection with another theatrical form, opéra comique. A survey of the operas between *La Muette de Portici* and *Gustave III* reveals three significant facts: first, that all except two

(*Alcibiade* and *Le Dieu et la bayadère*) are related in plot, structure, music, and characters to opéra comique; second, that of the two exceptions, one (*Alcibiade*) is an example of an older type of opera on a theme from classical antiquity and the second is an *opéra-ballet*; third, that of the seven ballets-pantomimes and two *opéra-ballets* Scribe wrote, all but four fall between 1827 and 1831. Of the four exceptions the last two—the ballet-pantomime *Marco Spada* and the *ópera-ballet Le Cheval de bronze*—appear in 1857 and are adaptations of earlier opéras comiques by Auber.

All these points are important to illustrate that Scribe's grand opera style was not fully formed from the first. The opéra comique basis of *La Muette de Portici* and *Robert le Diable* has already been mentioned. That of *Le Comte Ory, Le Philtre*, and *Le Serment* is evident even from such external characteristics as their comic plots with happy endings and the prominence in all but *Le Comte Ory* of bourgeois or lower class characters.

Le Serment is a special case in point, for it strongly resembles the very successful Fra Diavolo, produced two years earlier. The music to both operas was composed by Auber. Like Fra Diavolo, Le Serment takes place in a hotel. Andiol, the hotel keeper, will not allow his daughter Marie to marry Edmond because the latter has no money. Instead he arranges a marriage between Marie and Captain Jean, the head of a band of counterfeiters whose activity Edmond discovers and stops, even though Jean himself escapes. This general situation parallels that in which Lorenzo and Zerline find themselves, except that Zerline is never engaged to marry Jean's counterpart, Fra Diavolo. Unlike Lorenzo, Edmond is not a soldier when the opera begins, but he is drafted and wins the honors and promotions in battle which, together with his disclosure of Jean's identity, entitle him to marry Marie. At one point in Le Serment the counterfeiters enter Edmond's room at the hotel while the latter, asleep, recalls in his dreams sections of an air he sang earlier, the text of which deals with his hopes for future happinesss. The counterfeiters want to kill Edmond, but Jean convinces them to spare his life. The scene is comparable to that in Act II of Fra Diavolo in which Diavolo and his henchmen are hidden in Zerline's room.

That such a close relationship can be demonstrated between an opera and an opéra comique illustrates the derivation of techniques of one kind of opera libretto from those of opéra comique. Internal analysis of the libretti of Le Comte Ory, Le Philtre, and Le Serment shows the use of the same techniques of the well-made libretto employed by Scribe in his opéras comiques. Indeed, there is very good reason to consider these and other similar operas in Scribe's output to some extent as opéras comiques of which the dialogue is sung and to which ballet scenes have sometimes been added to take full advantage of the Opéra's performing forces. Once perfected in the medium of lighter opera, these techniques could be applied first to the revision of an opéra comique as a grand opera—Robert—and then to the creation or solidification of something more distinctive in the full grand opera style of *Gustave III.*

That Scribe was "practicing" to write opera libretti during the first years he wrote in this medium is indicated not only by the noticeable relationship between many of the early operas to opéra comique, but also by the two exceptional libretti produced before 1833. Of all his operas, *Alcibiade* surely deserves to be considered the worst subject with which Scribe ever had to deal. The plot concerns Alcibiade, who returns victorious to Athens and is feted by the citizens. He has brought back as a prisoner Sophronie, whom he loves and wishes to marry, but she rejects the splendor and pleasures of his court while uttering plaint after plaint about the loss of her freedom. Once Alcibiade frees her, she admits she is in love with a painter, Protogène, who has refused the Athenians' commission to paint a portrait of Alcibiade in honor of his victory. Vowing revenge, Alcibiade has the freedom-loving Protogène taken prisoner and tempted with all manner of delicacies and samples of the good life of luxury until he finally agrees to paint the portrait. At that Alcibiade awards Sophronie to Protegène. The latter now feels he can serve Alcibiade with honor because although the ruler is a despot, he is a just and benevolent despot. Considering the effect a performance of Scribe's own *La Muette de Portici* had in sparking the revolution in Brussels in 1830, it is interesting to see the sentiments he expresses in this libretto written specifically for that city just one year earlier. The antique subject is old-fashioned and is treated in a static, almost Calzabigi-like manner, with large place given to choruses and *divertissements.* Scribe never wrote a similar piece.

*Le Dieu et la bayadère*, an *opéra-ballet*, to some extent resulted from the success of *La Muette de Portici.* Its heroine also dances rather than sings, although for a different reason: she is from a foreign country and has not yet learned to speak the language, although she understands it when it is spoken to her. The years 1827-1831 also saw the production of four of Scribe's ballets: *La Somnambule*, with music by Hérold (1827); *La Belle au bois dormant*, a *ballet-pantomime-féerie* also written with Aumer and Hérold (1829); *Manon Lescaut*, another ballet-pantomime written with Aumer and set by Halévy (1830); and *L'Orgie*, a ballet-pantomime in collaboration with Coralli, with music by Carafa (1831). That Scribe should have written several ballets and one *opéra-ballet* during these years is important, for this was the time during which he was also completing the new synthesis of popular theatre, spoken and musical, with long used operatic procedures and the traditional ballet to produce his own technique of grand opera writing. These ballets are his longest and most significant works in this genre, whereas the later ballets were less popular.

The great variety in his early opera production suggests that Scribe was indeed experimenting to find both a formula for grand opera and for an intermediate form between grand opera and opéra comique. Specific examples illustrative of this development will be discussed below in greater detail, after a general survey of Scribe's opera libretti.

The chart in Appendix C provides summary information about the musical numbers in each of Scribe's opera libretti. In addition to the limitations necessarily present in such an outline and discussed in connection with similar charts of the opéras comiques, there are those limitations imposed by the fact that musical numbers are not always clearly designated and labeled in the libretti. This is complicated further by the tendency of composers in this period to organize numbers into large scene complexes which may or may not be clearly divided into subsections. In the absence of scores for all the operas, certain assumptions had to be made in connection with many of these larger scenes, based on a knowledge of Scribe's libretto technique and how various types of text were set in operas for which scores were available.

The following principles have been followed in the chart. First, any number specifically labeled "air," "duo," "cavatine," etc., in the libretto has been cited as such on the chart. Most such set-numbers are preceded by at least a line or two of text which must have been set as acccompanied recitative or arioso. Because this occurs so often, these text sections have not been included in the recitative column on the chart. The latter column shows only those sections of the libretto specifically designated *récitatif* or relatively long sections of text which can be presumed by their style to have been set in some sort of recitative or arioso. Second, a number of special labels occur for single numbers in an opera, labels which seldom or never recur. These numbers and a brief description of their nature are listed in the "Misc." column. Third, many long scene complexes involving solos, choruses, and ensembles of various kinds are obvious from the text structure but are not given a specific designation in the libretto. These are listed in the "Ens.-Cho." column, and italicized numbers in this column denote pieces bearing no label in the libretto. Fourth, an italicized listing in any column indicates that the designation is that of the present writer, not of the librettist, and is based on considerations of text structure and the relationship of the section to surrounding passages of text. Such italicized numbers occur most frequently in the recitative column, where they indicate passages of sung dialogue having no musical form inherent in the text. These passages are written in the long lines customary for recitative and are usually placed between two clearly defined musical numbers.

As in the chart on opéras comiques, the outline in Appendix C cannot indicate which of the solo numbers occur as separate pieces and which are included as parts of larger scènes (e.g., within an Introduction). The terms Introduction and Finale, as before, designate scenes normally involving a number of solo characters and chorus and carrying some dramatic action. Only numbers performed exclusively by a chorus or involving chorus with very short incidental soli have been listed in the "chorus" column. All other choruses are parts of Introductions, Finales, or ensemble-chorus scenes. Special categories of airs—*rondeaux, cavatines*, nonstrophic *romances, prières*—have been listed in the column for airs but are labeled to set them apart.

The designation "cho." in any column may at times refer to double or even triple choruses, since the larger operas ordinarily involve at least two different groups of people in the course of the action (nobles, moors, villagers, bandits, soldiers, etc.). Some operas include a dancer as a principal character. It would be impossible to indicate all the occasions on which such characters appear without complicating the chart unnecessarily. Therefore, only long solo pantomime dance scenes and formal ballets are listed in the tallies.

Two of the operas—*La Tempête* (Halévy, 1850) and *Florinde* (Thalberg, 1851), both written for London—appear in the complete edition of Scribe's works only in the form of scenarios, prose summaries in French of the Italian texts used by the composers. In these cases the set-numbers as designated in the scenarios have been listed in appropriate columns, but no assumptions have been made as to how the rest of the text was set, since its formal characteristics cannot be determined from prose.

The development of specific aspects of Scribe's style in opera libretti will be discussed in later sections, but some general points should be made here. The first is that even a superficial study of the chart leads to the challenging of several commonly held assumptions or generalizations about French opera of the nineteenth century that are not necessarily true. The two quotations below are examples of such statements.

> Grand opera must have five acts, no longer three; it must include all the sensational features of operatic theatricality—especially the ballet. . . . It must, in a fixed order, display a romance or a ballade, a few cavatinas or arias for the female and male leads, a passionate

> duet, and moving scenic effects at the conclusion of at least two acts, to the accompaniment of all available sources of musical power: soloists, chorus, and orchestra.[2]

> [Scribe's grand opera libretti] were to be given five acts—with a ballet or chief scenic attraction in Act II and the sentimental *clou* in Act IV, which must culminate in one of the monster *morceaux d'ensemble*, with chorus added—such as the blessing of the daggers before the Saint Bartholomew massacre in the *Huguenots*, or the coronation of the prophet John in Munster Cathedral in *Le Prophète.* Act V brings the dênouement, with retribution for the guilty and a death or quasi-apotheosis for the virtuous, and probably a transformation-scene, a spectacular and edifying death or a *deus ex machina*, as in *Les Huguenots.*[3]

Disregarding the obvious errors here (e.g., the Blessing of the Daggers does not end Act IV of *Les Huguenots* nor does the end of this or any other opera by Scribe represent a *deus ex machina* type) items will be discussed in the order mentioned.

First, although most of Scribe's grand operas have five acts, not all works having five acts can be considered grand operas, nor is every grand opera in five acts. *Le Lac des fées*, a five-act work, is in no sense a grand opera, while *Les Martyrs* and *La Favorite*, although in four acts, should surely be considered grand operas. Second, there is no fixed order or even a reasonably predictable order in which the various solo numbers occur. The first and last acts of most of Scribe's operas, grand operas or not, ordinarily begin and end with large scenes featuring soloists with one or more choruses. More often then not, inner acts will also begin and/or end in this way. As for solo numbers, strophic forms such as *couplets*, *ballades*, etc., gradually disappear or receive less emphasis, while the more complex and freely constructed airs increase in importance throughout Scribe's productive years. Over and above this, one finds comparatively fewer solo numbers and more ensembles or large-scale solo-chorus scenes that eventually all but do away with the need for separate recitative sections. It should be remembered that of the solo numbers enumerated on the chart, at least one-third occur in the course of such large scenes.

One type of musical number exploited to good effect is the choral *prière*. Modeled on Rossini's "Dal tuo stellato" in *Mosè*, these *prières* also had ancestors in the works Rossini produced in Paris.[4] From the prayers of the Sicilians in *La Muette de Portici* to those of the Indians in *L'Africaine*, the *prière* enjoyed a long life in the hands of Scribe and his musical collaborators.

The chart in Appendix C reveals a general tendency on the part of either Scribe or his composers—or both—to create unusual numbers to fit particular scenes or dramatic needs. From the "Valse infernale" in *Robert le Diable* to various sermons, legends, complaints, curfews, and processions of later works, Scribe's work displays new uses of convention in creating forms familiar enough to be understood, yet individual enough to make the spectator feel he was seeing or hearing them for the first time in history.

Many writers have commented on tenor Adolphe Nourrit's unconventional suggestions that the fourth act of *La Juive* be ended with an air and that of *Les Huguenots* with a duo.[5] It is interesting that these suggestions were made regarding the fourth act which, as "the sentimental *clou*," had the greatest need of something extraordinary. That Nourrit's suggestions were indeed unusual can be demonstrated by the chart. Even after 1836, rarely did any act end with a piece so small in terms of number of characters on the stage.

There can be no doubt that the scenic attractions and ballets played a large part in the success of a grand opera, but their appearance was not quite so conventionalized as the writers quoted above would have one believe. A ballet was an expected component of a grand opera, but many not-so-grand operas included ballets as well. Furthermore, the placement of the ballet or *divertissement* scenes was rather more varied than one would be led to believe. In five-act works the ballet most often occurred in the second or third act. However, three operas have ballets in the first or fifth acts, and two late works—*La Nonne sanglante* and *L'Africaine*—feature fourth act ballets. In four-act works ballets never appear in Act I, but three works have ballets in Act II, one has a ballet in Act III, and two have ballets in the last act. The one three-act work to contain a ballet places it in the final act. In works having two acts, two have ballets in Act I and one in Act II. Nine operas contain two ballets apiece.

Cooper's remark on apotheosis scenes or spectacular deaths ending an opera is particularly apt, for the majority of Scribe's grand operas do end in this way. As in his opéras comiques, Scribe uses and reuses certain stock situations. Of the samples listed below, the first eleven also occur in opéra comique, but the last eight occur exclusively in the operas. Parentheses around a title indicate that the work contains a variant of the situation listed.

1. A man tries to gain (earn, inherit, etc.) enough money to marry the woman he loves.

*Le Philtre* (1831)
(*Robert le Diable* [1831])
*Le Serment* (1832)
*Ali-Baba* (1833)
*La Xacarilla* (1839)
*La Favorite* (1840)
*Carmagnola* (1841)
*Le Cheval de bronze* (1857)

2. A girl loves (and may marry) a man who seems (but may not be) above her station.

*La Muette de Portici* (1828)
*Le Dieu et la bayadère* (1830)
(*La Juive* [1835])

3. A man loves (or may marry) a woman who seems (but may not be) above his station.

*Guido et Ginevra* (1838)
*Le Drapier* (1840)
*La Favorite* (1840)
*Zerline* (1851)
*Le Juif errant* (1852)
*Les Vêpres siciliennes* (1855)

4. A man searches for and finds a girl with whom he has fallen in love. (In most cases he does not know her name until he finds her.)

*Les Huguenots* (1836)
*Guido et Ginevra* (1838)
*La Favorite* (1840)

5. A woman falls in love with a man whose name or identity she does not know.

*Le Muette de Portici* (1828)
*La Juive* (1835)
*Les Huguenots* (1836)
*Carmagnola* (1841)
*Jeanne la folle* (1848)

6. An impending marriage is broken up in favor of a rival for the hand of one of the partners.

*Alcibiade* (1829)
*Le Philtre* (1831)
*Le Serment* (1832)
*Ali-Baba* (1833)
*Le Lac des fées* (1839)
*La Xacarilla* (1839)
*Le Drapier* (1840)
*Le Juif errant* (1852)

7. Nobles appear unidentified or disguised.

*La Muette de Portici* (1828)
*Le Comte Ory* (1828)
(*Le Dieu et la bayadère* [1830])
*La Juive* (1835)
*Carmagnola* (1841)
*Jeanne la folle* (1848)
*L'Africaine* (1865)

8. A character discovers he is of noble birth.

*Le Juif errant* (1852)
*Les Vêpres siciliennes* (1855)

9. A character sings a ballad about a legend which has some bearing on the plot.

*Le Philtre* (1831)
*Robert le Diable* (1831)
*Le Serment* (1832)
*Le Juif errant (1852)*
*La Nonne sanglante* (1854)
*L'Africaine* (1865)

10. A young page, usually played by a woman, is at a "girl crazy" stage.

(*Le Comte Ory* [1828])
*Gustave III* (1833)
*Les Huguenots* (1836)
*La Nonne sanglante* (1854)

11. Characters conspire against a current government.

*Le Muette de Portici* (1828)
*Gustave III* (1833)
(*Les Huguenots* [1836])

*Le Drapier* (1840)
(*Les Martyrs* [1840])
*Dom Sébastien* (1843)
*Le Prophète* (1849)
*Les Vêpres siciliennes* (1855)

12. A character agrees to withhold some information provided the person to whom it would be damaging will allow this character to marry the person he/she loves.
*Le Serment* (1832)
*La Xacarilla* (1839)
*Le Drapier* (1840)
(*Zerline* [1851])

13. A woman agrees to marry a man to save the life and/or honor of the man she really loves.
*Le Dieu et la bayadère* (1830)
*Le Lac des fées* (1839)
*Dom Sébastien* (1843)
*L'Africaine* (1865)

14. A marriage is planned to cement warring factions.
*Les Huguenots* (1836)
*La Nonne sanglante* (1854)
*Les Vêpres siciliennes* (1855)
(*L'Africaine* [1865])

15. A dancer is a central character in the opera.
*La Muette de Portici* (1828)
*Le Dieu et la bayadère* (1830)
*Robert le Diable* (1831)
*La Tempête* (1850)
*L'Enfant prodigue* (1850)

16. Curfew scenes.
*Les Huguenots* (1836)
*Les Vêpres siciliennes* (1855)

17. Masked balls cover a planned conspiracy.
*Gustave III* (1833)
*Les Vêpres siciliennes* (1855)

(In opéra comique *Le Domino* noir features a masked ball, but not in connection with a conspiracy.)

18. An apotheosis scene ends the opera.
*Robert le Diable* (1831)
(*Guido et Ginevra* [1838])
*Le Juif errant* (1852)
*La Nonne sanglante* (1854)
*L'Africaine* (1865)

19. A leading character or characters die at the end of the opera.
*La Muette de Portici* (1828)
*Gustave III* (1833)
*La Juive* (1835)
*Les Huguenots* (1836)
*Les Martyrs* (1840)
*La Favorite* (1840)
*Dom Sébastian* (1843)
*Jeanne la folle* (1848)
*Le Prophète* (1849)
*La Nonne sanglante* (1854)
*Les Vêpres siciliennes* (1855)
*L'Africaine* (1865)

Along with these stock situations Scribe also uses many of the familiar standard reactions to new information, and we find again the usual: "Quel est donc ce mystère?", "O surprise nouvelle!","O bonheur! ô ivresse!" and many more.

One striking difference between Scribe's operas and his opéras comiques is that relatively few of the former are based directly on a literary model, whereas the majority of the latter take some story, novel, or drama as their foundation. This is not to say that the plots of the operas are original with Scribe or any one of his many collaborators, but rather that they are freely developed from suggestions, historical facts, and the like. To Scribe,

> a reference in an historical work sufficed to make the brook of his abundant fancy overflow. . . . He took from the reading of newspapers, stage pieces, short stories, novels, and historical works only suggestions which stimulated his creative fantasy.[6]

The fact that the libretti of many of the history-based operas include footnotes explaining the source of the story or various of its incidents and characters demonstrates that Scribe did indeed study his sources. Yet there is in the nature of such opera a good reason why Scribe should not want too strict a guide for his plot. Opéra comique emphasized action and music more or less equally; thus a strong, well constructed, and adventure-filled plot was vital and it was both desirable and possible to follow a literary model. In grand opera action shared more of the honors not just with music but with stage spectacle and dance as well. Since the librettist had to think of ways to work in or around these visual attractions, the presence of too clearly outlined a literary model for his opera could well have been more of a hindrance than a help. A suggestion sufficed, for a suggestion in this case was better than a volume.

## AUBER'S *LA MUETTE DE PORTICI* AND OPERA COMIQUE

That Scribe derived the style used in his first grand opera libretto from the techniques he had perfected in opéra comique can be demonstrated by an analysis of this work, *La Muette de Portici*, set by Auber and first performed on February 29, 1828. The libretto was the result of a collaboration between Scribe and Germain Delvaigne, his frequent co-worker in comédies-vaudevilles and a long-time friend. Rehearsed under the title *Masaniello, La Muette* won instant success and remained in the regular repertoire of the Opéra until 1852. Thereafter it was performed frequently but irregularly and reached its five-hundredth performance in 1880. At times single acts or pairs of acts were also performed separately.[1]

The subject of the opera is a historical event, a revolt led by Thommaso Aniello (known as Masaniello), a Neapolitan fisherman, in July 1647 against the unpopular Spanish government that had ruled Naples for over a hundred years. The only serious threat to their rule, Masaniello and his followers were at first successful, but later events "led to extremism and confusion, in the midst of which Masaniello was murdered."[2] Auber's opera was not the first based on this story. Already in 1706 Reinhard Keiser wrote an opera, *Masagniello furioso*, the music and libretto of which are preserved. The year 1825 saw the production of the first nineteenth century *Masaniello*, an unsuccessful work by Sir Henry Bishop based on Samuel Croxall's *Memoirs of a Most Remarkable Révolution in Naples.* Two years later Raimond de Moirmoiron's *Memoires sur la revolution de Naples de 1647* inspired two French works: an opéra comique by Carafa with libretto by Moreau and Lafortelle (1827) and Auber's *La Muette.*[3]

Scribe probably did study the story of the opera as historians presented it, if the case of *Les Vêpres siciliennes* is any model of his method for writing historical opera. In a letter to Charles Duveyrier, his collaborator for the Verdi opera, Scribe wrote: "I have read all the authors (and there are only Italian authors) who speak of the massacre of Sicily. . . ." After relating to Duveyrier a summary of what he had found, Scribe concludes: "I tell you this to put you at ease and to give you some latitude."[4] The fact that *La Muette de Portici* is not particularly accurate as history should not be surprising, given this testimony and the evidence of how Scribe adapted other sources—plays, novels, short stories—for the musical stage. Crosten has summarized concisely the details of Scribe's embellishments of history.

> . . . [Scribe] utilized the historical fact that there was such a man as Masaniello who led the popular forces of Naples in revolution, but embellished it with the legend concerning his poisoning by a beverage which is supposed to have affected his reason. Furthermore, both history and legend were supplemented by a tale of pure imagination: the tragic story of Masaniello's sister Fenella, a mute who was deceived and deserted by Alfonso, son of the Spanish Viceroy. Fiction and fact were joined in the one work, but it is obvious that the former occupied larger place.[5]

Little wonder. The workings of history are often very slow, and for every colorful leader there are hundreds of colorless minor figures. Neither of these properties will do for opera. Historical or even geographical accuracy would spoil the work, particularly the spectacular ending when Fenella throws herself into the erupting volcano Vesuvius, which is eight or nine miles from Naples. Yet even in his deliberate inaccuracies Scribe was showing the influence of the popular theatre of which he was a part. The melodrama, a favorite dramatic genre at the boulevard theatres and the only form to make extensive use of historical themes and local color before the advent of romantic drama, was generally no more concerned with true history than was Scribe himself. Rather, the authors used the historical setting in the traditional French manner also typical of many other dramas and even of opera: as a background against which current political, philosophical, or moral questions could be discussed in a meaningful but indirect manner. In the same way Scribe's libretto for *La Muette de Portici* is less a history of the Neapolitan revolt than an exposition of problems being faced by the French, problems that could bring on the same disastrous result if they were not resolved.

One should not think, however, that *La Muette* is an indication that Scribe or his collaborators favored revolutionary ideas. Indeed, Scribe's own remarks on the adverse effects of the events of 1830 point to precisely the opposite conclusion, as Stanton has rightly observed.

> . . . Scribe does not attempt to paint an idealistic view of revolutions. On the contrary, he finds everything connected with them repulsive and low. The victors he discovers to be hard-headed rationalists, who know the secret of keeping themselves detached, who, in their own interest, capitalize on the sins and weaknesses of others.[6]

This sort of picture of revolutions is surely a more realistic one than that prevailing in the rescue operas of the 1790s, when virtuous but oppressed persons from the lower classes were seen overthrowing some thoroughly evil and unjust ruler. It reflects the point of view of the bourgeoisie, whose well-being was more directly affected by revolution than was that of any other class. More numerous than the nobility, more affected by change than the already miserable and poor workers, the bourgeoisie required stable surroundings to pursue their businesses and prosper. The 1820s found them tired of fighting, longing for a peaceful, congenial atmosphere, and Scribe's "plague on both your houses" attitude was—and is today—a thoroughly modern view that pervades the pictures of revolution he paints. If the Catholics are oversensitive and treacherous in *Les Huguenots*, the Prostestants are self-righteous and gullible. In *Le Prophète* the three Anabaptist conspirators are just as wicked as the nobles against whom they are fighting. So too in *La Muette*, fanatics take over an originally idealistic revolution against a tyrannical ruler. In all cases, the losers are not primarily the leaders but rather the masses of people who have been taken advantage of by both sides. The mood of the times dictated the content of *La Muette de Portici*, and its warning was there for all who had ears to hear.

## *La Muette de Portici* and the Well-Made Libretto

The opera begins on the wedding day of Elvire and Alphonse, son of the Spanish Viceroy in Naples. The people wish Alphonse joy, but he is troubled and remorseful over the fate of Fenella, a mute peasant girl whom he has seduced and abandoned and whom his friend Lorenzo has not been able to find since she escaped from Alphonse one month earlier. Although Alphonse fears that Fenella may be dead, Lorenzo suggests that perhaps the Viceroy, known for his strict rule over his subjects and his son, has taken her away somewhere. After the two friends leave to prepare for the wedding, Elvire enters with her attendants, joyous over the coming nuptials. Elvire asks for some entertainment from those who have accompanied her on her journey from Spain, and they oblige her with a ballet. At the end of this *divertissement* Fenella, fleeing the solders, enters and, in pantomime, begs Elvire to protect her. Selva, one of the Viceroy's soldiers, identifies Fanella as one who has just escaped from the royal prison. In gestures Fenella tells Elvire that she was deceived by a man whose name she does not know; that she was then imprisoned for no crime of which she is aware; and that she has escaped and wishes Elvire's help. The latter agrees to assist her.

The wedding procession enters the the church while soldiers keep the crowds from advancing. Fenella recognizes Alphonse as her seducer but is prevented from entering the church to stop the wedding. When Elvire later presents Fenella to Alphonse as a girl deserving of justice, she learns the identity of the mute girl's seducer. As Fenella disappears in the crowd, Elvire and Alphonse mourn their lost happiness.

At the beginning of the second act Masaniello, Borella, and the fishermen are preparing to set sail at dawn. Although worried that his friend Pietro has not returned, Masaniello feigns cheerfulness and sings a *barcarolle* to enterain his crew. At the end of the song Pietro, the only person to whom Masaniello has confided his concern for his sister Fenella's safety, returns to report that he has learned nothing of the girl's whereabouts. He suggests she may have become the prey of some seducer. At this Masaniello becomes angry and swears vengeance against the oppressive government of Naples. Pietro agrees to join him.

Fenella appears. In gestures she tells Masaniello her adventures of the first act, but she will not reveal the identity of her seducer other than to indicate that he is a Spaniard. Masaniello's anger will not be appeased, however, and he calls the people to urge them to revolt against their Spanish rulers. Pietro enters to announce that soldiers are blocking the road into Naples, but Masaniello knows how to throw them off their guard. After telling the people to hide their weapons among the fishing nets and baskets of fruits and flowers, Masaniello leads them in a gay *barcarolle*.

The third act opens with a long scene between Alphonse and Elvire in which the latter admits she still loves Alphonse and forgives him. However, she also requests that Fenella be brought back to the palace and placed under her protection. Alphonse orders Selva and the soldiers to find the girl.

The scene changes to the marketplace in Naples, where the fishermen and other peasants are trying to sell their wares. Fenella is also there but takes no part in the festivities and looks around anxiously for her brother. After a peasant dance, Selva and the soldiers appear and seize Fenella without explanation. As they are about to leave, Masaniello and Pietro arrive with the other fishermen and attack the soldiers. At this, other peasants reveal their hidden weapons, surround and disarm the soldiers. After a prayer for victory the people rush off toward the Viceroy's palace.

The first scene of Act IV takes place in Masaniello's hut, where the leading officials of Naples have come to beg the fisherman to see that the revolutionaries' atrocities are stopped. Masaniello agrees to spare the lives of the officials, and after they have left he reflects on the unexpected and undesirably violent turn the revolt has taken. Nevertheless, the Viceroy is still safe in his palace and the revolution will not be a success until he has been captured. Fenella rushes in and, in mime, tells of new violence in the city, but Masaniello is helpless to prevent it. To calm his sister, Masaniello sings a lullaby and Fenella falls asleep, but she awakens when Pietro and the fishermen enter to demand permission to kill Alphonse when they capture him. Masaniello, however, believes there has been enough violence already. Thinking Fenella asleep, the men enter another room in the house to discuss matters further.

While they are gone, Alphonse and Elvire arrive to ask for shelter. Alphonse is disturbed to find that the girl whom he has wronged agrees to help them. Masaniello returns and promises to shelter the couple without knowing who they are, but Pietro recognizes the Viceroy's son. Alphonse moves to defend himself, and Fenella and Masaniello intercede on his behalf. This angers Pietro and the others, who turn against Masaniello. As the back of the cabin opens to reveal the citizens of Naples arriving to deliver the keys of the city to Masaniello, Pietro and the other fishermen conspire against their former leader.

Between stanzas of the *barcarolle* that opens Act V, Pietro reveals that he has poisoned Masaniello and that the latter will soon be dead. Borella rushes in with a call to arms, for Alphonse's forces have regrouped and are poised for attack. Moreover, the imminent eruption of Vesuvius has frightened the people and diverted their attention from the revolution. The people call for Masaniello to help them, but Borella reports that their former leader has lost his reason. The crowd threatens Pietro's life should Masaniello die, and the conspirators now try to bring the crazed Masaniello to his senses. Masaniello, however, sings his Act II *barcarolle* while Vesuvius and the Viceroy's army rumble ominously in the distance. Finally realizing to some extent what is happening, Masaniello goes off at the head of the rebels to fight against the army, leaving Fenella alone on the stage. Elvire finds her and warns of the danger from the approaching soldiers. Alphonse soon follows, reporting that the people, seeing Masaniello defend Elvire against them, turned upon him and killed him, but that the army has driven off the mob. Fenella, in despair, throws herself into the erupting volcano and perishes.

Many traits of the well-made libretto formula, by this time a staple of Scribe's opéras comiques, are in evidence in *La Muette de Portici.* The delayed-action plot begins after Alfonso has seduced Fenella and the Viceroy has imprisoned her; after Elvire has come to Naples to be married to Alphonse; and after Masaniello has begun to dream of revolting against the Spanish. The early scenes of Act I and to some degree Act II are expository, relating background information to the audience and carefully preparing for future events. In his aria and subsequent conversation with Lorenzo, Alphonse gives information about his relationship to Fenella; the fact that she is the mute daughter of a fisherman; that she has been missing for some time; and that during that time he has fallen in love with a noblewoman, Elvire, whom he will marry today. Lorenzo in turn suggests that Fenella may have been imprisioned and gives the first hints that the ruler is stern and oppressive. Thus no one is surprised when, in Scene iv, a girl enters who fits Alphonse's description of Fenella and who has indeed been imprisoned. The confrontation between Alphonse and Fenella is thus made inevitable, and the scene which ends Act I is the logical conclusion of events which began the act. Yet, as in his opéras comiques, Scribe has concluded a single action while at the same time leaving the plot as a whole in a state of suspense. The spectator is left to wonder what will become of Fenella and how the problem she has caused between the newly married couple will be resolved. This last must wait until the beginning of Act III, but the whereabouts of Fenella are not kept secret for long.

*La Muette* is like some of Scribe's opéras comiques, notably *La Dame blanche*, in having a split exposition, each section of which deals with a different but related set of characters. In *La Dame blanche*, the expository sections of Act I centered around the character of Georges, while those of Act II, prepared for by information given in Act I, centered around Anna and the Avenels. So too in *La Muette*, the first act deals with the noble characters, while the fishermen mentioned in that act and represented by the figure of Fenella appear only in Act II. The acts begin in a parallel manner: in Act I Alfonso, after an aria, converses with Lorenzo; in Act II Masaniello, after a *barcarolle*, discusses Fenella's fate with his friend Pietro. As in Act I, the beginning of Act II provides important preparatory material. Masaniello is the leader of the fishermen who promises to become the leader of a revolution at the drop of a suggestion. Since the Viceroy's iron rule has already been commented upon, some opposition is not unexpected. Pietro, for no apparent reason, suggests that Fenella may have been seduced, and Masaniello's reaction to this provides the first suggestion that Fenella's experiences will be the cause of a revolt. Masaniello's and Pietro's famed duo, "Armour sacré de la patrie," not only points ahead to the actual revolution but gives a glimpse of the forces which motivate each singer to his extreme course. Masaniello sings, "Think of my sister, torn from my arms," whereas Pietro sings, "Think of the power, the abuse of which oppresses us." Fenella's return brings an end to speculation over what has happened to her and over whether a revolution will actually take place. An act beginning with questions about Fenella ends with those questions resolved but presents a new problem: the revolution.

Since Alphonse and Elvire make quite clear in Act I that they are truly in love, that Alphonse is genuinely remorseful, and that Elvire is kind and willing to help Fenella, the events at the beginning of Act III are not surprising. Nor are those in the marketplace. We know the peasants are carrying concealed weapons; we know that Selva has orders to bring Fenella to the palace; and we know from past experience that he is not likely to be gentle or courteous in carrying out those orders. We also know that any threat to Fenella by a Spaniard will provoke instant response from Masaniello. Thus, not unexpectedly, the chain of events that closes Act III touches off a full-fledged revolution.

Masaniello's pardoning the Naples officials and his deploring the violence his followers have caused are ample preparation for his willingness to help Alphonse and Elvire in Act IV. Since the royal couple have already proved themselves deserving in the audience's eyes, a possible conflict or surprise is eliminated here. The reactions of Pietro and his friends to Masaniello's first refusal to grant them permission for Alphonse's execution insures the rumblings of discontent and eventual conspiracy against the revolutionary leader.

Just as all threads of the plot are pulled together at the end of an opéra comique, with a happy or at least deserved outcome for all concerned, so in *La Muette* all elements are resolved in the final scenes, but now the outcome is tragic. Masaniello, as expected, dies at the hands of his own followers. The ruthless soldiers put down the dissidents. News presented earlier in the act of an imminent volcanic eruption helps prepare for Fenella's suicide, which is not totally unexpected since she had planned to kill herself once before, at the beginning of Act II. The revolution has been put down, and of all the principal characters only Alphonse and Elvire, the good nobles, remain.

Throughout the opera contrived entrances and exits are carried out with as much precision as in any opéra comique. One good example is the opening of Act IV. First Fenella enters and falls asleep so that she can awaken in time to hear Pietro's plans to kill Alphonse. Then the men go to another room so that they will not see Alphonse and Elvire arrive. Finally, Masaniello returns to the room before the other men and promises the couple protection before he has to face an immediate challenge from Pietro, who stays offstage until a few minutes later.

The typical seesaw in the fortunes of the hero is characteristic of this libretto as it is of Scribe's opéras comiques. However, there does not seem to be any single central misunderstanding or *quiproquo* unless it be Alphonse's ignorance of the fact that Fenella is the sister of Masaniello, the future leader of the revolt, and that his actions toward her will touch off that revolt. There is a kind of reverse *scène à faire*, for the hero does not triumph but becomes the victim of the events he set in motion.

Although *La Muette de Portici* has five acts, compared to the normal two or three of opéra comique, there are not as many dramatic events contained in each act and the total amount of action in the opera as a whole is no greater than that in an opéra comique. The fact that recitative takes longer to perform than does spoken dialogue and the inclusion of two long ballets limit the possible length of the individual acts in *La Muette.* Nevertheless, Scribe has taken care to construct the acts in such a way that each ends with a dramatic *coup* that is the logical outcome of the action which begins the act. Thus, despite the relatively small amount of action they contain, none of the acts leaves the spectator with a feeling that it is somehow incomplete.

All in all, "*La Muette* proved to Scribe (and to other librettists, including Boito and Wagner) that the form of the *pièce bien fait[e]* could successfully be applied to grand opera. . . ."[7] Indeed, Wagner could still write admiringly of *La Muette* as late as the 1860s, perhaps because his own first successful opera, *Rienzi*, had a similar setting, design, plot, and characters.

Not only is the overall dramatic structure of *La Muette* modeled on that used many times before by Scribe in his opéras comiques, but many smaller details of style, form, and usage were not novelties even in their own day. The much-praised use of the chorus as a vital character in the action, although new to the Opéra, was a prominent feature of *La Dame blanche* some years before. Arvin mentions another previously used feature of *La Muette.*

> It is . . . rather curious to find at the very beginning of the first modern French opera the last of the confidantes of classical tragedy. 'De Fenella quel est le sort?' ['What is Fenella's fate?'] the prince asks his companion; and the latter replies, as Arcas, Théramene, or Corosmin might have done:
>
> Seigneur, je l'ignore, et mon zèle
> Pour découvrir sa trace a fait un vain effort.
> [My lord, I do not know, and my zeal
> to discover any trace of her has been a vain
> effort.][8]

One might also cite the parallel between Jason's marriage in Cherubini's *Médée* and that of Alphonse in *La Muette.* In *Médée* Jason is marred offstage while a chorus sings. Meanwhile action is taking place onstage which revolves around Medea, whose love Jason has spurned. After the wedding the chorus and wedding party march onstage, just as the participants in the ceremony come out of the church after Alphonse and Elvire are married.

Another detail carried over from classicistic opera is the use of a messenger to report on violent events that take place out of sight of the audience. The entire scene of the death of Masaniello and the dispersal of the mob is related by persons who flee the scene and rush onstage to comment. Later, perhaps emboldened by the violence of romantic drama or influenced by one successful transference of a melodramatic theme to the operatic stage, Scribe did away with most such messengers, as is shown in the bloody final scenes of *Gustave III, La Juive*, and *Les Huguenots.*

**Words and Music**

If there was little really new in the dramatic structure of *La Muette* there was just as little novelty in the music.[9] One can point to the more extensive and expressive use of the orchestra growing out of the necessity to provide background music for Fenella's miming, but this is one of the few extraordinary elements of the score and can be linked to earlier melodrama and to the French tradition of programme music. The extensive use of chorus has been seen by some modern scholars as a logical outgrowth of the choral writing by such earlier composers as Gluck, Spontini, Méhul, and Cherubini.[10] Hanslick also finds the influence of Spontini in the Masaniello-Pietro duet, "Amour sacré de la patrie."[11] The strongest influence of all, however, was that of opéra comique, found in the strophic *barcarolles*, the clear textual and musical lines of the ensembles, even the structures of Introductions and Finales. Recognition of this influence is implicit in Wagner's later observation that Auber was able to write so great an opera "through his seizing by its roots that remarkable product of our civilization, the *Parisian*, and raising it thence to its highest possible glory. . . . "[12]

If one compares *La Muette de Portici* to later grand operas one will see that the later tendency to build up large-scale, clearly organized scene complexes is much less in evidence here. The libretto of the early acts of *La Muette* reads like opéra comique in which recitative has been substituted for spoken dialogue. The same sorts of musical texts occur and their organization is based on the ordinary set-numbers or ensemble scenes of opéra comique. In later works Scribe learned how to organize larger scenes in order to eliminate obvious long stretches of recitative or arioso. In *La Muette*, however, the only really good examples of this later tendency are No. 14 (Act IV) and the finale of Act V, both of which are definitely of a piece, with a high degree of textual and musical continuity.

The following chart of the musical numbers in *La Muette* shows a profile comparable to that of opéra comique. A broken line across the page indicates that the piece preceding it ends with a full cadence rather than a transition to the next number. All recitatives are accompanied but often are written in the vocal style of secco recitative.

| Scene | Number | Type of music, characters |
|---|---|---|
| | | **ACT I** |
| i | 1 [a] | Introduction: Chorus, "Du prince, objet de notre amour." Arioso and air, "O toi, jeune victime," with chorus (Alphonse). |
| ii | [b] | Recit. (Alphonse, Lorenzo). |
| - - - | - - - | - - - |
| iii | 2 | Chorus (repeat "Du prince . . ."). |
| - - - | - - - | - - - |
| | 3 [a] | Recit. and air, "O moment enchanteur" (Elvire). |
| | [b] | Recit. (Elvire). |
| - - - | - - - | - - - |
| | Ballet | The *Guaracha;* the *Bolero.* |
| - - - | - - - | - - - |
| iv | 4 [a] | Recit. [and pantomime] (Elvire, Fenella, Selva, Lorenzo). |
| - - - | - - - | - - - |
| | [b] | Chorus (backstage chorus - prayer "O Dieu puissant"; onstage chorus of soldiers and people). |
| - - - | - - - | - - - |
| v | 5 | Finale: includes chorus, arioso, ensembles, pantomime (Elvire, Alphonse, Fenella, Lorenzo, Selva, people, soldiers, wedding attendants, and guests). |
| - - - | - - - | - - - |
| | | **ACT II** |
| i | 6 [a] | Chorus of Fishermen, "Amis, le soleil va paraître." |
| | [b] | Recit. (Masaniello, Borella). |
| | 7 [a] | *Barcarolle,* "Amis, la matinée est belle" (Masaniello, fishermen). |
| - - - | - - - | - - - |
| ii | [b] | Recit. (Masaniello, Pietro). |
| - - - | - - - | - - - |

| | | |
|---|---|---|
| | 8 [a] | Duo, "Mieux va mourir" - "Amour sacré de la patrie" (Masaniello, Pietro). |
| iii-iv | [b] | Recit. and pantomime (Masaniello, Fenella). |
| v | 9 | Finale: includes chorus, arioso, ensembles (Masaniello, Fenella, Pietro, Borella, fishermen, villagers). |
| | | **ACT III** |
| i | 10 [a] | Recit. and duo, "Ecoutez-moi" (Alphonse, Elvire). |
| | [b] | Recit. (Alphonse, Elvire). |
| ii | 11 | *Choeur du Marché*, "Au marché qui vient de s'ouvrir." |
| | Ballet | *Tarantella.* |
| iii-iv | 12 | Finale: includes arioso, choruses (including a choral *prière*), ensembles (Selva, Masaniello, Borella, Fenella, soldiers, people). |
| | | **ACT IV** |
| [i | Omitted from | piano-vocal score.] |
| ii | 13 [a] | Recit. and air, "O Dieu! toi qui m'as destiné" (Masaniello). |
| | [b] | Recit. (Masaniello). |
| iii | [c] | Recit. and pantomime (Masaniello, Fenella). |
| | [d] | *Air du sommeil*, "Du pauvre seul ami fidèle" (Masaniello). |
| iv-vi | 14 | *Morceau d'ensemble*: includes arioso, air, ensembles, pantomime, chorus (Masaniello, Pietro, Fenella, Alphonse, Elvire, fishermen). |
| vii | 15 [a] | Recit. and pantomime (Masaniello, Fenella, Alphonse, Elvire). |
| viii | [b] | Quartet with chorus, "Par le peuple conduits" (Masaniello, Alphonse, Elvire, Pietro). |
| | 16 | *Marche et choeur*, "Honneur, honneur et gloire!" (all soloists, double chorus). |

ACT V

| | | |
|---|---|---|
| i | 17 | *Barcarolle,* "Voyez du haut de ces rivages" (Pietro, chorus). |
| ii-vii | 18 | Finale: includes pantomimes, arioso, ensemble, chorus (all soloists, chorus). |

In general, the musical differences between *La Muette* and Auber's opéras comiques is one of degree rather than of kind. Ensembles take up a larger portion, simple solo numbers a smaller portion of the score. Yet the frequency of final cadences indicated on the outline demonstrates against Longyear's statement that: "The set-numbers were not blocked off into applause-fetching compartments, but moved imperceptibly from one number to the next, and often were connected by a highly dramatic accompanied recitative."[13]

The chorus is everywhere present, two ballets take their place alongside the vocal numbers, and pantomime replaces recitative and air in Fenella's role. Yet the ensemble scenes are constructed in patterns by now familiar to both Scribe and Auber: alternating periods of action and repose, the latter frequently in the form of repeated ensemble sections such as those in the duo "Amour sacré de la patrie" (No. 8). Recitative and arioso texts are written in long, irregular lines of rhymed verse, while short, regular, rhymed verses are used for solo songs and airs, choruses, and static sections of ensembles. These traits of text and music construction have already been seen in contemporaneous opéras comiques.

To be sure, *La Muette de Portici* contains some exceptional musical numbers. The most genuinely progressive and deeply emotional piece in the work is the finale of the fifth act, which takes in roughly two-thirds of the act. Between the stanzas of the *barcarolle* which begins the act, Pietro prepares for the beginning of this finale by telling a friend that he has put poison in Masaniello's food. Similar inclusion of sung dialogue between stanzas of a strophic number is not at all uncommon in Scribe's opéras comiques. The finale begins after the second stanza of the song and is outlined below.

Key to abbreviations:

P - Pietro
B - Borella
M - Masaniello
F - Fenella
E - Elvire
A - Alphonse

Act V Finale

| Section | Characters and action | Musical style | Keys |
|---|---|---|---|
| 1 | B informs P and the fishermen that A's soldiers are coming and that Vesuvius is about to erupt. | Arioso | f, A♭ |
| 2 | People call for M to save them. | Chordal choral statements | f,c |
| 3 | B and P tell them M has gone mad; P describes his state. | Arioso | f |
| 4 | People threaten P, but he silences them as M enters. | Arioso and chordal choral statements | A♭, modulatory |
| 5 | M's mad scene. | Reprises of fragments of earlier numbers. | D♭, B♭ |
| 6 | All plead with M to lead them against A. M replies by quoting *barcarolle* (No. 7) while Vesuvius threatens in the background. | Soli and chorus, declamatory | D♭,f# A |
| | People continue to plead. | | a, V/f |
| 7 | F, unaware of M's state, runs in to report on army's threat. | Pantomime | f |
| 8 | F realizes M's condition. People continue to call him. | Chordal choral statements | A♭ |
| 9 | M regains sanity in response to F, calls people to arms. | Arioso | modulatory, c |
| 10 | People predict victory. | Ensemble with chorus | F |
| 11 | F prays for M, then contemplates a scarf A gave her. | Pantomime | D♭ |
| 12 | E reports on destruction and that M saved her life. | Arioso | F |
| | B thinks M must have won and is returning. | Arioso | d |
| 13 | A reports that M has been killed by people because he saved E and that soldiers have dispersed the mob. | Arioso | bb, moduatory, C, F |
| 14 | F throws herself into Vesuvius. | Pantomime | d |
| 15 | People pray for mercy for their crime. | Chordal choral statements | |
| | Orchestral postlude. | | d |

In this finale the usual clearly defined sections of action and repose are, if not completely absent, at least minimized and camouflaged in a course of action that gradually gains momentum until it reaches a climax in Fenella's suicide. No ensemble texts are repeated for musical unity, and some of the sections that could be considered static are so short and presented in such a free, declamatory manner that the spirit of action and implied forward motion will not allow for musical or dramatic repose. Examples of this occur in the choral statements in the first part of the scene. Here the people sing what amounts to a choral arioso, acting and reacting in the manner of a single character (Example 43).

**Example 43**

## Example 43 (continued)

In a sense Masaniello's mad scene could be considered a section of repose, since it presents a static portrait of the man to which all listen in stunned silence (Example 44). Yet there is again an undercurrent of drama in the reminiscences of melodies which bring to mind memories of the more hopeful conditions under which they were first sung. The distortion of Masaniello's call to arms, first heard at the beginning of the second act finale, is particularly striking, and the madman's refusal to leave off the *barcarolle* tune despite his followers' pleading is an effective musical *coup*.

**Example 44**

## Example 44 (continued)

The tension of the situation increases with the entrance of Fenella and is not released until Masaniello, his sanity returned, agrees to lead the people once more. Finally, the long, dramatic ascent which began as early as the arioso between the stanzas of Pietro's *barcarolle* reaches a plateau in the victory chorus (section 10), the only long, static section in the finale.

As the people go off to battle, tranquility is temporarily restored. Yet Fenella's pantomime contains a presentiment of things to come, for she thinks again of Alphonse and realizes the hopelessness of the situation. This hopelessness increases as Elvire and Alphonse make their reports, and climaxes in Fenella's suicide. Again, the undercurrent of drama is such that there are no real points of repose and the scene propels itself forward, gaining momentum gradually. Nevertheless, progressive as the structure of text and music are in this finale, one cannot but notice that Fenella throws herself into the erupting volcano to the accompaniment of a rather simple chromatic passage (Example 45). This striking simplicity in even an exceptional number illustrates the truth of Crosten's statement that of all major elements of grand opera, music was the last to receive definition, for it had to wait for the arrival of Meyerbeer.[14]

**Example 45**

## Dance and Spectacle

One of the features of *La Muette de Portici* most remarked upon at its premiere was the use of a mute character as the heroine. Indeed, the addition of pantomime to the standard vocal components of opera produced a striking effect, one in keeping with the tendency in ballets of the same time for expressive dancing. Yet even this was scarcely a novelty. As early as the 1790s *Coelina ou l'Enfant de mystère*, a melodrama by Pixérécourt, featured a mute protagonist, Francisque Humbert, who turns out to be the heroine's father. This story was drawn from a still earlier novel by Ducray-Duminil.[15] At the Opéra-Comique, Dalayrac's *Deux mots* featured a mute heroine.[16] Dumesnil takes note that in Weber's *Silvana* (1810) a girl who is forbidden to speak to strangers is forced to express herself in gestures to an orchestral accompaniment.[17] On the stage of the Opéra itself it was common to adapt earlier opéras comiques as dramatic ballets, the dancers miming the roles to the accompaniment of the familiar music. In ballets freely composed or adapted from novels or short stories, composers would often use familiar tunes to provide clues as to what the dancer was supposed to be "saying."[18] Thus there were several precedents and sources from which Scribe and Auber might have developed the idea of using a dancing heroine and the way in which this character could be fit into the opera.

Despite this, however, it seems that the decision to use a mute heroine was not made until the authors had concluded, after Mme. Branchu left the Opéra, that no dramatic soprano in the company could play opposite the Elvire of Mme. Damoreau-Cinti.[19] Thus decided, composer and librettist had in Fenella enough of a novelty to arouse the interest of the audience, yet not so unusual a feature to detract from the rest of the work. The mute role was so successful an experiment that it was repeated in *Le Dieu et la bayadère* by the same authors.

Among the many noteworthy developments in French opera introduced or exploited in *La Muette de Portici*, the *mise en scène* is very significant, for it set standards for the employment of mechanical stage effects and local color in sets and costumes in French grand opera. The importance of the scenic spectacle became so great in grand opera that Camille Bellaigue remarked:

> In the last analysis, it surely seems that the *mise en scène* or the spectacle in our national grand opera is the equivalent of the dialogue in our opéra comique, this other equally French genre.

> The two elements play the same role and have the same advantage: that of distracting us from the music and of granting us some relief from it.[20]

Settings and costumes for *La Muette* were lavish and varied. No two acts took place in the same location, and in some acts two *tableaux* were used. One particularly striking effect was the eruption of Vesuvius in the fifth act. While not wholly original, it was nevertheless skillfully worked out and sufficiently awe-inspiring to produce the desired audience reaction. In 1827 Daguerre had presented a similar scene at his Diorama, which in turn influenced the designs of Cicéri for Carafa's *Masaniello* and Auber's *La Muette de Portici.*[21] In addition to his study of Daguerre, Cicéri went to Italy to observe a similar mechanical effect in Pacini's *Ultimo giorno di Pompeia,* presented at La Scala in 1827.[22] Pictures of Alessandro Sanquirico's setting for the volcanic eruption in Pacini's opera and that by Cicéri show essentially the same scene: in the foreground a large building with columns, through the courtyard of which a volcano is seen erupting. For the eruption Sanquirico perfected special machinery which Cicéri copied the next year at the Paris Opéra and which was described in the scenic libretto published at the time of the performance.[23]

The settings and costumes of *La Muette* were extraordinarily spectacular and realistic for an opera. However, like Cicéri himself, they were a product of the popular theatres of Paris and had only to be transferred to the more aristocratic stage of the Académie de Musique. It remained for Véron to guide the authors and designers of the Opéra in the direction of bigger and better spectacle, carrying this to such a degree that Heine could observe: "The name Véron will live forever in the annals of music; he has adorned the temple of the goddess, but she herself [has been] turned out of doors."[24] This great emphasis on spectacle was to affect the nature of grand opera to such an extent that *La Muette* is little more than a sample, for:

> As the scene itself gained extension, magnificence, and specific content it drew the other elements of the lyric theatre into its orbit. The first result was that music and drama took on the spectacular character of the settings, but the second and more important consequence was that they tended also to assume a formal shape which in essentials was a complement of the décors. The massive, colorful tableaux that were conceived in the popular theatre as purely visual spectacles were transferred to the Opéra where they were clothed in music and given dramatic substance.[25]

These musical and dramatic effects of scenic spectacle will be well illustrated by the works of Scribe and Meyerbeer.

Few of the elements of *La Muette de Portici* were new. The libretto's style and structure, much of the musical style, and the use of lower class characters were taken over from opèra comique. The historical subject and the way in which it was used were suggested by the melodrama, and the local color was a product of melodrama already tested in opèra comique. Extensive use of the chorus was a prominent feature of *La Dame blanche.* Suggestions leading to the creation of a mute heroine occur in plays, operas, and ballets; and the use of the orchestra to express emotional states was already a feature of ballet and musical melodrama. Although the extent to which scenic spectacle was carried out started an important trend, some specific ideas had already been used. The true novelty of this first grand opera therefore does not consist in the absolute newness of its elements but in the unique combination of these elements and in their presentation on the conservative stage of the Opéra. The revolutionary theme was a timely one. Yet even more timely was the fact that many of the components of the opera were carried over or transformed from the popular theatre. *La Muette de Portici,* a herald of a new operatic genre, was also a herald of the triumph of the bourgeoisie.

## *LA MUETTE* AND *GUILLAUME TELL*

Rossini's *Guillaume Tell*, the next French grand opera to be presented, was premiered on August 3, 1829. The libretto, based on Schiller's drama, was by V. J. Etienne de Jouy and H. L. F. Bis. Jouy, some of whose works have already been discussed, had been an active librettist since the early years of the century. With Dieulafoy he had written a one-act *fait historique*, *Milton*, for Spontini in 1805, and alone was responsible for the same composer's *La Vestale* (1807) and Catel's *Les Bayadères* (1810) and *Les Aubergistes de qualité* (1812). In 1809 he collaborated with J. A. Esménard to produce the libretto of Spontini's *Fernand Cortez*. Cherubini's *Les Abencérages* (1813) and the French version of Rossini's *Moïse* (1827) came wholly or in part from his pen.[1]

The story of *Guillaume Tell* is too well known to require summary here. In externals the opera appears as a successor to *La Muette de Portici*, for its historical subject deals with the same sort of theme: the revolt of an oppressed people against dictatorial foreign rulers. Yet it is not "a virtual sequel" to Auber's opera,[2] for its basis and derivation are quite different, a fact which probably accounts for its lack of immediate success. Nearly all elements of *La Muette de Portici* were strongly rooted in the popular theatre: *comédie-vaudeville*, opéra comique, melodrama and boulevard spectacles. *Guillaume Tell*, however, is rooted more in the styles and practices of Rossini's own *Siège de Corinthe* and *Moïse* and in the Spontinian tradition. Despite its timely subject, despite the extensive use of chorus and of characters from among the common people, *Guillaume Tell* lacked the popular basis of appeal that made the spectators take instantly to *La Muette de Portici*.

Of particular concern here are the libretto techniques, which preserve styles and forms from the past and contrast quite strongly with Scribe's fresher, more up-to-date approach to opera derived from *comédie-vaudeville* by way of opéra comique. The plot of *Guillaume Tell* is not delayed-action in the Scribean sense but is comparable to the plots of such earlier operas as Jouy's own *Les Bayadères*. Some important events have already occurred: the plans for a revolt against Gesler and the Austrian government, and the love between Arnold and Matilde. Yet most of the action unfolds gradually before the eyes of the spectator and with a minimum of explicit preparation. The tightly knit structure of Scribe's libretti is absent and a certain looseness in the ordering of events is apparent in the shifting of scenes and emphasis and in the lack of attention toward making each act an entity with its own beginning, middle, and end.

The structure of the plot is made even looser by including too much diversity in the main plot and using a subplot which has little justification or necessity. Scribe's much maligned technique of small causes producing large historical effects can be viewed as a virtue when the effects of the opposite treatment of a historical subject are seen in *Guillaume Tell.* Jouy and Bis portray the cumulative effect of political oppression as a cause of revolution: first the affair with Leuthold, then the murder of Melcthal, finally the scene at Gesler's palace and the imprisonment of Tell. It is a realistic succession of events building to the formal outbreak of the revolution in the last finale. In *La Muette de Portici,* one must assume that Masaniello's revolution was in the planning stages long before the second act of the opera, but Scribe uses only one event to touch it off: the revelation by Fenella that she has been seduced by an as yet unnamed Spaniard. The effect of this news is sudden and electrifying, whereas the gradual build-up in revolutionary fervor seen in *Guillaume Tell* makes the battle itself seem almost anticlimatic. Opera libretti are not subtle dramatic forms, and necessity makes a virtue of simplicity. The approach to revolution in *Guillaume Tell* may be more realistic, but Scribe's revolution is more arresting.

Furthermore, Jouy's and Bis's revolution is of a type pictured in many rescue operas. The thoroughly wicked ruler will perish; the noble peasants will triumph. This view is a direct contrast with Scribe's message on the effects of revolution, which is more modern and undoubtedly more realistic.

In *Guillaume Tell* the spectator must constantly change his perspective and sort out the important from the unimportant characters and actions, as in many of the earlier operas discussed above. Leuthold, for example, is the cause of a dramatic moment in the opera, but is otherwise unimportant to the work either musically or dramatically. Even the scene of Tell shooting the apple from his son's head is to some extent irrelevant, although it could be made less so if it were the cause of some immediate reaction. As it stands in the opera, however, it is merely the last in a long series of outrages against the Swiss people. It would be stronger in the cause-and-effect relationship of events were it the only such outrage shown.

In this connection one must take care to differentiate between distraction and diversion in an opera. The scenes just mentioned, along with the quite irrelevant subplot of Arnold and Matilde, are distractions in that they promise to be important to the main course of action but are not. At the opposite pole are such diversions as the ballets and festival choruses. These and similar numbers make no pretense of being relevant to the action. They are purely diversionary and are perceived as such by the audience. In *La Muette de Portici* the function of each number and each event in the totality of the work is clear. This is not the case in *Guillaume Tell*; thus the work is not a modern product of a new movement but a recostumed remnant of an older tradition.

The musical numbers in *Guillaume Tell* are generally longer than Auber's and show more fully developed the tendency to write large-scale pieces with many subsections. At times these long scene complexes are more static than need be, especially in Act III, and in this they contrast quite distinctly with even the longest scenes created by Scribe and Auber. The lack of any strong connection with the popular theatre is illustrated by the fact that there are no strophic songs or melodies in popular style in this opera. Precisely this greater length and seriousness of the musical numbers is responsible for the importance of *Guillaume Tell* to the history of grand opera. Its libretto is in an old style, and even its settings lack the obvious spectacle of *La Muette*, although it contains elements of local color and pageantry. Yet Rossini's music is grand and points ahead far better than does Auber's toward the final definition of grand opera style by Meyerbeer.

In this connection one scene is of particular interest: that of the vows-taking which ends Act II. Here Tell lines out an oath to which all the revolutionaries swear and which is set in a responsorial style (Example 46). This device has a long and interesting history. Meyerbeer's *Il Crociato*, first performed in Venice in 1824, had so impressed Rossini that he helped arrange a performance of the work in Paris the following year. This opera, "the first work which gave a definite intimation of what its composer was to become,"[3] deals with the religious conflicts arising out of the secret marriage of a Crusader to the daughter of a sultan. In Act II Meyerbeer has written a conspirators' chorus in which the imprisioned Crusaders resolve to overcome their enemies (Example 47) and, at the end, break their swords so that they will never be used by pagans. The situation is similar to that in the fourth act of *Les Huguenots*, when Nevers breaks his sword rather than join in the conspiracy planned by Saint-Bris and his associates. Musically, the scene in *Il Crociato* is similar to that of *Les Huguenots* (Example 48) except that the former is antiphonal rather than responsorial and involves no specific oath-taking.

The effect of this scene in *Il Crociato* was not lost on Rossini, who may already have been revising his earlier Italian opera *Maometto II* (1820) for performance as *Le Siège de Corinthe* (1826). The latter became not merely an opera in translation but a genuine recomposition, for Rossini added a great deal of music, changed the structure from two acts to three, and changed the names and activities of some of the

## Example 46

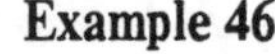
Tell
Ju - rons, ju-rons par nos dan-
Tell
gers,
Arnold
Walter
Ju - rons, ju-rons par nos dan-gers,
Men of Underwald
Ju - rons, ju-rons par nos dan-gers,
Men of Schwitz
Ju - rons. ju-rons par nos dan-gers,
Men of Uri
Ju - rons, ju-rons par nos dan - gers,

## Example 47

Tenor
Nel si - len - - zio fra l'or-ror,
Basses
Nel si - len - - - zio fra l'or-

cir-con-diam il tra-di-tor.
ror,
cir-con-diam il tra-di-tor.

### Example 48

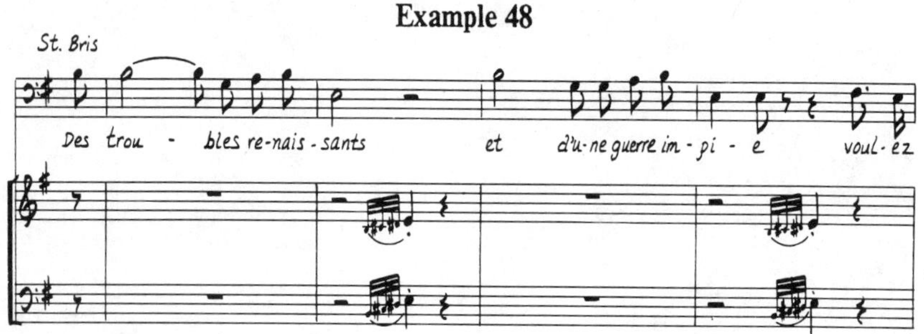
St. Bris
Des trou - bles re-nais-sants et d'u-ne guerre im - pi - e voul-ez

vous, com-me moi, dé - li - vrer le pa - ys?

Tenors
Nous som-mes prêts!
4 Noblemen
Basses

## Example 49

Iero
Sian chiu-si i vo-stri cuo-ri al duo - lo, al pian-to?
Soprani, Ismene, Pamira
Sì,
Tenori, Neocle, Cleomene
Sì,
Bassi
Sì,

sì, noi lo giu - riam.
sì, noi lo giu - riam.
sì. noi lo giu - riam.

Example 50

characters. Indeed, Adam saw the opera as "the signal for the immense revolution which has been effected at this theatre [the Opéra] . . . ."[4] One of the new pieces was a Blessing of the Standards scene in Act III (Example 49) in which the responsorial style of the later *Guillaume Tell* second act finale is used. This style and the tone and motivation of the scene are similar to those in Meyerbeer's earlier conspirators' chorus and look ahead past *Guillaume Tell* not only to the Blessing of the Daggers scene of *Les Huguenots* (Example 48) but to the finale of Act II of this same opera (Example 50).[5] It is not impossible that Rossini may also have been influenced to write his Blessing of the Standards scene and the *Guillaume Tell* number by a choral scene in Boieldieu's *Béniowski* in which the prisoners swear to work together to gain their freedom and overthrow the governor.

Interestingly enough, the plot of *Le Siège de Corinthe* revolves around a love conflict similar to that of Raoul and Valentine in *Les Huguenots*, Palmide and Armando in *Il Crociato*, and to some extent Arnold and Matilde in *Guillaume Tell*. Palmira, daughter of a Corinthian general, is in love with Mahomet II, leader of the Turkish army which eventually succeeds in destroying Corinth. However, she gives up her love for Mahomet in favor of love for her country and dies with the Greeks as the Turks set the city afire.[6]

There is at least one more chain linking Rossini's *Siège de Corinthe* to *Guillaume Tell* and *Les Huguenots.* As the standards are to be blessed in *Le Siège* the Greeks gather around an honored old man, Gerone, who blesses the flags and predicts independence for their country.

> God himself commands my agitated senses
> And reveals to my eyes the future of Greece.
> Before dying, listen!

The character of Gerone has descendants in Melcthal of *Guillaume Tell* and Marcel of *Les Huguenots,* and the latter's vision of the future in Act V is similar in kind to that of Gerone.

*Maometto II,* the first (Italian) version of *Le Siège de Corinthe,* marks a turning point in Rossini's career toward pieces conceived on a larger scale, using more novel harmonies, "strength and truth of expression."[7] Meyerbeer's *Il Crociato* represents a furthering of this Rossinian style, which the latter himself carries forward in a work, *Le Siège,* which shows specific evidence of Meyerbeer's influence. *Guillaume Tell* goes a step beyond *Le Siège* and along with the latter work provides some of the musical and dramatic foundations for *Les Huguenots.* In this specific chain reaction Auber's *La Muette de Portici* plays no part.

Although influential in the same development toward full-fledged grand opera, *La Muette de Portici* and *Guillaume Tell* are not of the same lineage and each contributes different elements to the genre. *La Muette* brings the popular theatre to the operatic stage, making some strides toward a new dignity, pomp, and display. *Guillaume Tell* is in a sense a response to this, for it uses older techniques of libretto writing and musical styles prepared for by Spontini, Meyerbeer, and Rossini himself, while at the same time seeming by its theme and setting to carry further the popular orientation. The battle lines at the Opéra are thus clearly drawn: grand opera can emerge through an updating of older techniques in conformity with modern trends, or the popular threatre can completely revolutionize the tradition-bound Académie Royale de Musique. In the end neither trend gained absolute mastery. Scribe, by his new libretto style, retained certain traits of the popular theatre in his operas. Yet he was too observant not to notice what *Guillaume Tell* had accomplished. Given a composer of Meyerbeer's tastes and abilities, he went beyond *La Muette,* beyond the "opéra comique with recitatives" style, to something larger and more distinctive yet in *Robert le Diable*. *Robert*, like *La Muette*, was an overgrown opéra comique, but one in which the spectacle and the breadth of conception of the musical numbers far outreached Auber's work. This mixture of the grandeur of the old with the spirit of the new became complete in the libretto of *Gustave III* and the totality of *Les Huguenots*.

## THE TRANSFORMATION OF A GENRE: MEYERBEER'S *ROBERT LE DIABLE*

In 1823 Meyerbeer sent a letter to Levasseur, a bass at the Opéra who was to become the creator of the role of Bertram in *Robert le Diable*. In this letter Meyerbeer admitted that he wanted very much to write an opera for Paris, saying:

> Where besides Paris does one find the immense forces that the French Opera offers to an artist who wants to write truly dramatic music? Here [in Italy] we are absolutely lacking in good opera libretti, and the public enjoys only a single genre of music.
>
> At Paris there are excellent libretti, and I know that your public applauds without discrimination all genres of music if they are carried out with genius. You will perhaps ask me why, seeing things in this way, I have not tried to write for Paris. It is because here people represent the French Opera as a field covered with difficulties, where one must ordinarily wait for long years before getting performed, and that makes one afraid.[1]

By 1824 it looked as if Meyerbeer were about to get his wish and fulfill his own predictions about the difficulties of composing for the Paris stage. In this year he went to Paris, "determined to apply himself to the study of French opera and to conquer what was after all the cultural capital of Europe," and the following year his last Italian opera, *Il Crociato in Egitto*, was performed there with moderate success. By 1826 he already had a sketch of what was to become his first French opera, *Robert le Diable*.[2]

For various reasons, the work was not produced until November 21, 1831, but its immediate and continued success made it one of the most popular operas of its time. Thanks to the success of *Robert*, the Opéra was the only Parisian theatre to show a profit in 1831.[3] Within three years the work had reached its hundredth performance in Paris, and in slightly over thirty-five years it was given at the Opéra five hundred times. Also popular on foreign stages, *Robert* soon saw performances in Brussels, Berlin, Strasbourg, Dublin, London, Vienna, Copenhagen, New York, Budapest, Brünn, St. Petersburg, The Hague, Amsterdam, Prague, Bucharest, Basle, and Calcutta, among other places,[4] and in three years had "conquered seventy-seven stages in ten countries."[5] Its most recent revival was in 1968 in Florence.[6] *Robert le Diable* marked the birth of the phenomenon of Meyerbeer in French opera.

The reasons for so great a success are many and are to be found not only in the separate elements of the work and their peculiar combination, but in certain social, musical, and dramatic associations the work called up in the spectators. The libretto of *Robert le Diable* as a tale and a scaffolding for music is little worse and surely not better than many an offering from Scribe's pen. To be sure, many critics, among them one of Balzac's fictional characters,[7] found it a ridiculous story, primarily because of the great weakness of the central character, Robert. Yet it was a veritable recipe for success, for it had everything the public wanted.

> Romanticism, then in all the charm of its novelty, has inspired both author and composer: the infernal waltz, the appearance of the nuns and their ballet, are typically romantic scenes. By appealing especially to the intelligence of the public, by learning from Scribe the importance of accessories and the theory of small causes producing great results, by taking advantage of the religious idea, a source of endless meditation and perpetual conflicts of opinion, Meyerbeer succeeded in winning over the French public. Moreover, the Norman legend of Robert was skillfully chosen, for with its romantic coloring it appealed to popular taste and dramatized the eternal struggle between good and evil in the human soul.[8]

Furthermore, it was not a product merely of Scribe's ingenious and trained pen, nor the usual sort of collaboration between Scribe and another writer—in this case Germain Delavigne. By the time the curtains rose at the premiere the director of the Opéra, the scene designers, and the composer himself had contributed to the final libretto.

Beneath the surface many critics found great social significance in the work. Véron's appeal to the bourgeoisie on their own grounds was apparently working, for Heine observed:

> The July Revolution had . . . caused a great movement in heaven and on earth; stars and men, angels and kings, even dear God himself were torn from their peaceful existences, again had much to do, had to put order into a new era, had neither leisure nor extended inner repose to enjoy the melodies of private feelings, and only when the great choruses of *Robert le Diable* or even *Les Huguenots* harmoniously sobbed, did their hearts listen, and sob, rejoice, become angry in inspired unison.[9]

In the indecisive character of Robert, Heine saw "a true picture of the moral hesitancy of that time, a time which wavered so terribly restlessly between virtue and vice, which wore itself out in efforts and hindrances, and never had enough strength to withstand the attacks of Satan!"[10] More specifically, Heine remarks:

> . . . enthusiastic Meyerbeerians must forgive me when I express my belief that many are not merely drawn [to *Robert*] by the music, but also by the political significance of the opera. Robert the Devil, the son of a devil, who was as abominable as Philippe-Egalité, and a princess as pious as the daughter of Penthièvre, is influenced by the spirit of his father to evil, to the Revolution, and by the spirit of his mother to good, the old *régime*. Both these natures, which are his heritage from birth, struggle in his mind; he floats midway between two principles, is a 'middle-of-the-roader.' In vain the hellish voices of the wolf's gorge seek to draw him into the 'movement,' in vain the ghosts of the Convention, rising from their graves in the guise of Revolutionary nuns, try to seduce him; in vain Robespierre, in the shape of Mme. Taglioni, gives him the accolade—he withstands all temptations, all seductions, he is guided by his love for a princess of both the Sicilies, who is very pious, and he, too, grows pious, and finally we see him in the bosom of the Church, priests muttering around him, and befogged with incense.[11]

However farfetched this and any other attempt to find specific references in allegory may seem, the fact that someone could attempt it at all demonstrates that the opera was more than an entertainment. As Théophile Gautier remarked:

> Probably Meyerbeer, in writing his immortal scores, did not have the precise intention of including in them the symbols that we find there. But the genius, unknown to himself, sums up in his works the spirit of the age in which he works and says the word that the whole world murmurs. . . .[12]

In *Robert le Diable* the work and its music were the expressions of a communal spirit, not of individuality, and appealed to those emotions all men to some extent shared. Gambara remarks to his friend Andrea in Balzac's novel that "this music is made neither for the incredulous nor for those who do not love."[13] Surely credulity and love, alone or together, are universal emotions, and Gambara's categories exclude few. This character continues:

> If you have never felt in your life the vigorous blows of an evil spirit who upsets the goal [just] when you see it, who gives a sad ending to the most beautiful hopes; in a word, if you have never seen the devil's tail wagging in this world, the opera of Robert will be for you what the Apocalypse is for those who believe that everything ends with themselves.[14]

In a certain sense this passage illustrates a non-German concept of romanticism in that it approaches *Robert* from a realistic rather than an escapist standpoint. Where a German romantic wants to stop the world and try to get off, Balzac's character seeks a way to cope with the perplexing situations of a developing technology and the realities of war and revolution and sees in Robert his own image. Robert is a *Doppelgänger,* but he does not mock.

The nature of both music and libretto in *Robert* made it easy for the audience to identify with the characters, for to a large extent it is a derivative work. Meyerbeer's music was considered learned precisely because it reminded listeners of the styles of the best composers: Handel, Mozart, Beethoven, Rossini, Weber. In showing so many styles he well could have been accused, as was his librettist Scribe, of having no style at all. At times this seemed precisely the point. For example, Dorothy Hagan remarks that Raimbaut's ballade was:

> a composition without individual style. . . . Rather, it had the ability to create a public by means of the shared interests that were generated. In this instance, the interests were folk-associations. . . .[15]

Both libretto and music make the same bows to familiar sources, the most obvious of which are Weber's *Der Freischütz*, Goethe's *Faust*, and Mozart's *Don Giovanni.* The great success of his friend Weber's opera may well have prompted Meyerbeer to try his hand at something similar. The fact that *Robert* was originally conceived as an opéra comique surely points in this direction. Specifically, the Wolf's Glen scene from *Der Freischütz* provides the model for much of Act III of *Robert*, and the characters of Alice, Isabelle, and Bertram are roughly the equivalents of Weber's Aennchen, Agathe, and Caspar, respectively.

The similarities of *Robert* to *Faust* are particularly interesting in view of the fact that Goethe himself considered Meyerbeer a likely candidate to compose suitable music for his drama.[16] Also significant is the fact that at one point Meyerbeer took great interest in a Faust opera, one not based on Goethe, which was being composed by another friend, Ludwig Spohr. The latter reports that in 1813 Meyerbeer studied the parts of the opera then completed and was very enthusiastic about it. It may well have left its mark on him in more ways than one, for Spohr's scene before Aachen cathedral, with chorale-like music played backstage by three trombones, three basset horns, and two bassoons, is similar to that outside Palermo cathedral in *Robert.* Here Robert, aware that Isabelle is to be married in the cathedral, nevertheless is drawn toward religious thoughts when an *a cappella* chorus with organ interludes, also in a chorale-like style, sounds from within the church. Perhaps Spohr's efforts even influenced Meyerbeer to attempt a Faust opera of his own, for he did begin such a work sometime in the mid-1820s and incorporated some ideas from it in the final score of *Robert*.

> All that is known from the sketches [of the *Faust* opera] is a 'promenade' of Faust and Mephisto through Hell where they come to the Tree of Knowledge, which became the 'rameau venéré' by which Robert controls the spirits. The Valse Infernale in *Robert* was originally an air of Faust's, and Act V of *Robert* corresponds to the Easter scene in the sketches.[17]

In addition to the Easter scene from Goethe's drama, in which the hero has a change of heart because he hears some religious songs at a crucial point in his adventures, Scribe and Delavigne also incorporate into *Robert* the idea of a devil wanting a mortal to sign a pact.

The atmosphere and theme of *Don Giovanni* are found in *Robert le Diable.* In addition, there is a specific dramatic parallel to the opening scenes of Mozart's opera. In Act I, ii, Robert tells Alice that he had challenged Isabelle's father out of love for the princess and was beaten and nearly killed by some knights in the father's service. This is a to similar but not so severe situation to that taking place between Don Giovanni, Donna Anna, and the Commendatore.

Other works also come to mind as possible influences on *Robert. Zampa* has a similar hero, and *La Muette de Portici* has a mute character corresponding in type if not in nature to Héléna, the prioress. Scribe's libretto of *Le Loup-garou,* an opéra comique written for Louise Bertin, has characters named Raimbaud, Bertrand, and Alice, but they are not like the characters with similar names in *Robert.* Rossini's *Le Comte Ory*, on a libretto by Scribe, also contains a Raimbaud and an Alice. Although unlike *Robert le Diable* in its final form, *Le Comte Ory* is similar in some respects to the original legend of Robert the Devil. Like the legend's title character, Count Ory is also a high-living prankster whose father worries that he will never be a fit successor to him as a ruler. Coincidentally, *Le Comte Ory* is also based on a medieval legend.[18] One also must take into account the growing influence of the tales of E.T.A. Hoffmann, whose works were just being translated into French and creating a vogue among French writers for similar marvelous stories. Specifically, the tomb of Saint Rosalie in the cloister scene apparently finds its basis in Hoffmann's *Devil's Elixir.*[19]

The legend of Robert the Devil on which the opera is based dates from the fourteenth century and is preserved in two forms, a *dit* or rhymed tale, and a miracle play. A version of the latter, presented in 1350 under Philippe de Valois, was in the holdings of the Paris

Bibliothèque National since 1733, and was published for the first time in 1836.[20] Despite this late date of publication, Scribe may have known of the work in some version, since *Le Comte Ory* does have some similarities to it. Perhaps his knowledge came from one of the popular versions of the tale in the *Nouvelle bibliothèque bleue* of 1775.[21] Perhaps the material came to him by way of Meyerbeer, who may have known one of the German versions of the legend published in the early nineteenth century.[22] Perhaps a pantomime based on the story and produced by Franconi in 1815 was an inspiration.[23] Whatever the case, the legend served the librettists only as a point of departure and was connected far more loosely to the opera than were any of the literary sources discussed in connection with opéras comiques.

The original Robert, who is generally believed to have been developed from a historical figure, was a thoroughly evil and cruel young man whose specialties were robbing monasteries and torturing peasants or religious. Learning from his mother that his evil nature was the product of a pact she made with the devil, Robert went to Rome to seek absolution. After a long period of penance he was released from his sins and married a princess.[24] Little remains of this story in the opera except the marriage to the princess, which occurs not at all as in the legend. Thus for all practical purposes the libretto is freely composed, based on only a suggestion from the legend and incorporating features of many another popular tale.

Auber had been a made-to-order musical collaborator for Scribe in opéra comique because his qualities of mind and his musical style corresponded so closely to those features of clarity, economy, and organization which characterized Scribe's writing style. So too was Meyerbeer this kind of ideal collaborator. Although seemingly stronger-minded than his French counterpart and having pretensions to greatness, Meyerbeer also possessed certain of the same qualities as Auber. The latter, a native Frenchman whose birth outside Paris was by chance rather than by plan, rarely left his home city and only once, before he began his musical career, did he stay away from it for any length of time. He knew his public from long experience, a fact which undoubtedly accounted for much of his great success. Meyerbeer had no such advantage. Yet as he became Italian some years before, finding himself able during his stay in that country to "think Italian, feel and sense Italian,"[25] so now he set about to become French and succeeded in his own way in absorbing the qualities of a Parisian. He studied the French, their music, art, literature, history, philosophy, embracing nothing radical but absorbing all, until he became "as much a symbol of the middle of the road July Monarchy as Victor Cousin, the reigning philosopher of the new society, and he was suitably rewarded in the words chosen by his critics to describe him. He was *spirituel, aimable, plein d'instruction.*"[26] The same words, with very few changes, could have been used to describe Scribe, and Dumesnil found it "strange that people made of the musician [Meyerbeer] a genius and undervalued the librettist. . . ."[27]

Musically, Meyerbeer's compositions have often been described in terms that, if applied to drama, could have been used with reference to Scribe. To Dauriac, Meyerbeer "does not invent, he discovers or rediscovers." He is inspired by situations and has a ready vocabulary of musical ideas, mostly second-hand, to deal with them. He is a master of calculated effect, a theatrical genius.[28] To Abert, the main formal principle at work in Meyerbeer's music is "the greatest possible variety with the greatest possible ease in finding one's bearings. The listener will be continually stimulated, but never be very much troubled in his ability to comprehend."[29] Johannes Weber mentions Meyerbeer's own equivalent of Scribe's uniform local and historical color: "it was to characterize the personae, to express their sentiments and their passions, that Meyerbeer occupied himself, without worrying whether the action took place in the fourteenth century or in the eighteenth."[30]

Like Scribe, Meyerbeer too employed stock or recurrent situations in his music. Cooper mentions his use of "the evil chatter of the wood-wind, the tremolando strings or timpani roll, sudden fortissimo brass chords of the dominant seventh" to depict demonic, supernatural elements, and "the harp arpeggios, the organ in a blaze of what the Germans call 'Scheinkontrapunkt' and 'celestial' hymn-like four-part writing in the wood-wind as in Lohengrin," to represent the angelic or sacred.[31] Finally, like Scribe, Meyerbeer too refused to theorize about his work. When someone suggested that he write a treatise on aesthetics, the composer replied, "When I can no longer compose."[32]

Scribe and Meyerbeer seemed almost destined to work together, and the time, place, and action were right. With *Robert le Diable* they bridged the gap between the first tentative attempts at grand opera and the full development of a new genre.

## The Libretto

At the beginning of the opera Robert is gathered with Bertram and a number of noblemen under a canopy near the port of Palermo, where all are eating, drinking, and being merry. All have come to a tournament being held by the Duke of Messina and the winner is to be awarded the hand of the Duke's daughter Isabelle in marriage. Raimbaut, a visitor newly arrived from Robert's homeland, Normandy, entertains the company with the *ballade* of Robert the Devil, unaware that the subject of his song is listening. Robert becomes angry but, finding that Raimbaut has come with his fiancée, agrees to spare the singer and steal the fiancée instead. The latter, however, turns out to be Alice, Robert's foster-sister, who has brought him the testament of his mother, recently deceased, which he is to read when he feels worthy to do so. Since he does not yet feel worthy, he asks Alice to keep the letter for him.

Robert then tells Alice of his seemingly hopeless love for Isabelle. Earlier, wanting to elope with her, he had attacked her father and had been wounded by one of the latter's men. Although Bertram, whom he regards as his only friend, saved his life, he has been forbidden to see the princess. Alice advises him to write to Isabelle, saying that she will find a way to deliver the letter. In return she asks only that Robert arrange for a certain holy man to perform the marriage ceremony for her and Raimbaut, which Robert willingly agrees to do. The arrival of Bertram makes Alice fearful, for he reminds her of a picture of Satan in her home church, and she leaves quickly with Robert's letter.

Robert confesses to Bertram that although he is very grateful for the latter's friendship he somehow fears an evil influence coming over him. Bertram dismisses this as nonsense and urges Robert to forget his troubles by gambling with some of the other nobles. The nobles meet Robert's challenge eagerly and win from him all his money and possessions. Although Bertram tries to console him, Robert sees this as the last in a long line of misfortunes and falls into despair.

In the opening scene of Act II Isabelle, alone, laments the fact that her father is to choose a husband for her without regard for her wishes. Alice enters with a number of other young ladies and delivers Robert's letter, then signals Robert, who has been waiting outside, that she is sure Isabelle will receive him favorably. The lovers are reunited and Isabelle gives Robert armor to replace that which he lost gambling, enabling him to enter the tournament for her hand. Since people are already assembling, Isabelle urges Robert to leave. In the background Bertram enters, indicating Robert to the latter's arch rival, the Prince of Granada. The latter's herald brings Robert a challenge for a duel in place of the regular tournament. Robert agrees and the herald leads him off into the nearby forest. Bertram then steps forward out of the shadows to reveal that Robert is being sent on a wild goose chase of Bertram's devising so that he cannot compete for Isabelle.

Isabelle returns with her father, Alice, Raimbaut, nobles, and spectators. After a ballet, Isabelle's father orders her to grant her standard to the Prince of Granada. The party goes off to begin the tournament without Robert.

As the third act begins, Raimbaut is waiting outside the city for Alice, whom he is to marry that day. Bertram, thinking to have Alice for himself, gives Raimbaut a purse of gold and convinces him he should enjoy life and find a woman more worthy of him. Won over, Raimbaut goes off to the village to spend his new-found wealth. Bertram too has an appointment. In a nearby cavern a chorus of demons calls out to him and he goes to join them, singing that Robert, whom he acknowledges as his son, will not escape him now.

When Bertram has gone, Alice arrives looking for Raimbaut and is annoyed that he seems to be late. Hearing the chorus of demons call out the name of Robert, she looks in upon the infernal scene. It so frightens her that she faints beside a large wooden cross. Bertram emerges from the cavern, disturbed that the demons have given him only until midnight to win the soul of Robert for them. Finding Alice there, he threatens her and Raimbaut with damnation unless she remains silent about what she has seen.

Robert enters, totally dejected by the loss of Isabelle and thinking to find his only help in Bertram. Alice, frightened, runs off to keep herself from telling Robert what she has seen. Bertram persuades Robert that the only way to regain Isabelle is through the commission of a sacrilege.[33] Robert must go to the tomb of Saint Rosalie near a deserted cloister and get a branch of a magic bough. The scene changes to the cloister, surrounded by the graves of nuns who broke their religious vows. Bertram invokes the nuns and, when they rise from their graves, instructs them that they are to make certain Robert does not shrink from the sacrilege he has sworn to commit. In a ballet the nuns and Hélêna, the prioress, lead Robert on to steal the sacred branch and bring his soul one step closer to hell.

In Act IV preparations are being made for Isabelle's marriage to the Prince of Granada when Robert enters with the magic branch. Immediately all those in the room fall asleep and Robert approaches Isabelle. So impressed is he by her innocent beauty, however, that he awakens her rather than harm her. Yet Isabelle fears some infernal power has come over him and will not go away with him. Moved by her pleas, Robert breaks the magic branch and is at once surrounded and seized by Isabelle's attendants.

Act V takes place in the vestibule of the cathedral of Palermo, where monks are calling penitent sinners to receive forgiveness. Robert and Bertram enter, Robert seeking asylum at the cathedral after having escaped from his captors with Bertram's help and having been beaten in a duel with his rival, the Prince of Granada. Bertram tells Robert his only hope for vengeance now is to sign his soul over to the devil. Yet Robert hesitates, for he hears the monks singing religious songs his mother used to sing when she prayed for her son. Reminding Robert that this church will soon be the scene of Isabelle's marriage only stirs up his anger against Bertram. At Robert's questioning, Bertram tells him that everything in Raimbaut's song is true, that Robert is the son of a mortal woman and a devil, Bertram himself. The unhappy father confesses all the deeds he has performed to bring Robert to this point of despair, but only so that Robert would be willing to join him in hell. At this Robert's defenses fall away and he prepares to sign the pact. Alice enters with the news that the Prince of Granada and his party cannot enter the church and that Isabelle awaits Robert at the altar. Both Bertram and Alice try to persuade Robert to go with them, but the hero cannot decide. Alice then gives him the letter from his mother, which counsels him to "flee the bold counsels of the seducer who has condemned me." Still undecided, Robert hears the clock strike midnight. Bertram's time is up and hell reclaims him, but Robert is saved and joins Isabelle at the cathedral altar.

### Opéra Comique and Opera

*Robert le Diable*, first intended to be an opéra comique, was commissioned by Pixérécourt, then director of the Opéra-Comique, and was announced as early as 1827. The devil was then a popular figure on the boulevard stages and Pixérécourt wished to capitalize on this generally innocent form of deviltry.[34] Yet many things interfered with the work's completion. Meyerbeer's private life included a series of misfortunes. Besides the deaths of his father, of his friend Carl Maria von Weber, and of his first two children, reported disagreements with Scribe troubled the composer. In the meantime, Pixérécourt had ceased to be manager of the Opéra-Comique.[35] Having set the first act of the work, Meyerbeer began to realize that his creation was no longer suited to be an opéra comique. The lines were too bold, the music too difficult for the company at the Théâtre-Feydeau.[36] Composer and librettists therefore decided to rework the piece and present it as a grand opera, but by this time *La Muette de Portici* and *Guillaume Tell* had set a new tone and standards for that genre with which Meyerbeer and Scribe now had to deal.

The score of *Robert* was finished and submitted to Lubbert, then director of the Opéra, in May 1830, but the July Revolution interfered with its production at that time.[37] Then Lubbert was replaced by Véron, who according to some sources was less than willing to stake his large investment on a debut work by a foreign composer in a genre not yet familiar to the bourgeois audience. Berlioz was among those who reported that Meyerbeer had to pay Véron 60,000 francs to help cover the costs of staging before the latter would agree to do the work with any degree of commitment.[38] Yet Véron himself contradicts these reports when he writes:

> I was struck by the grandeur and the originality of the subject. All the roles seemed interesting to me, something which is always a good omen for the success of a dramatic work.[39]

Véron also cites a letter from Meyerbeer of February 9, 1854, in which the composer expresses the desire to use Véron's soon-to-be-published memoirs as the vehicle to silence once and for all rumors that the director had not been enthusiastic at the thought of producing *Robert*.[40] Whatever the case, Véron and his associates insisted on a number of changes in libretto and score during the five months of rehearsals. The role of Bertram was rewritten for a bass rather than a baritone; and the nuns' ballet was added to replace an olympian scene.[41] In short,

> . . . every kind of change was made during rehearsals—libretto, orchestration, the music itself was subjected to perpetual tinkering. In the interest of perfection none was too humble for Meyerbeer to consult: he even approached the 'clef de claque.'[42]

Indeed, as late as 1832 Meyerbeer complained to Count Redern, who wanted to perform *Robert* in Berlin, that he could not send him the complete score even then because "M. Scribe made so many changes in the piece during the rehearsals that they *par ricochet* extended to the score and what I had written down before was in part not to be used."[43]

The change in *Robert* that is of greatest importance to the history of grand opera, and hence to the development of generic traits for grand opera libretti, is that from opéra comique to opera. In 1879 Adolphe Jullien published a study of the scenario for the original *Robert le Diable*.[44] The chart below, derived and annotated from his study, with supplements by the present writer, shows in concise form how the two versions are alike and how they differ. Letter citations refer to items in the annotations which follow the chart.

| Opéra comique | Opera |
|---|---|
| Act I, i-iii:<br>Introduction; includes drinking chorus, Raimbaut's ballade, entrance of Alice. | Same. |
| Act I, iv-va:<br>dialogue (Robert, Alice). | Set as recitative with topical allusions[(a)] eliminated and a *romance* (two stanzas) added. |
| Act I, vb-vi:<br>*couplets* (Robert, Bertram). [(b)] | Omitted; replaced by gambling scene finale of Act I. |
| Act I, vii ff.:<br>Alice announces arrival of Isabelle.[(c)] | Varied; action of Act II begins. |
| *Couplets* (Alice), during which she gives Isabelle Robert's letter. | Varied, with chorus added, Act II, ii. |
| *Grand air* (Isabelle). | An air (probably not the same one), beginning of Act II |
| *Couplets* (Alice) in reply to Isabelle. | Omitted. |
| Duo (Robert, Isabelle). Tournament.[(d)] | Used as Act II, iii. Variation, Act II, iv: the challenge from the Prince of Granada (see plot summary); ballet; tournament. |
| Act II, i:<br>same setting and situation as III, i, but in spoken dialogue. | Act III, i:<br>Duo (Raimbaut, opera's Act Bertram). |
| Act II, ii;<br>spoken monologue (Bertram). | Bertram's (sung) monologue and *Valse infernale* scene with off stage chorus. |
| Act II, iii:<br>*couplets* (Alice) | Same as first part of Act III, iii. |

| | |
|---|---|
| Act II, iv:<br>dialogue (Alice, Bertram) | Equivalent of Act III, iv<br>(cross scene). |
| Act II, v: scene showing Raimbaut spending Bertram's money.[(e)] | Omitted. |
| Act II, vi:<br>quartet (Robert, Alice, Raimbaut, Bertram). | Becomes trio (Alice, Robert, Bertram) of Act III, v |
| Act II, vii-viii:<br>dialogue scene[(f)] (Bertram, Alice, Robert; Bertram, Robert). Robert receives the magic branch from Bertram. | Partially incorporated into trio, partially into Bertram-Robert duo scene, Act III, vi. Finale: scene of Bertram, then Robert at the cloister. |
| Finale:<br>Robert waves the branch and is transported to Isabelle's room. Musical numbers and sequence as in opera, but without Alice in the finale. | Act IV of opera, with opening scene added. |
| Act III, i (setting: a cottage):<br>scene between Alice and Bertram (dialogue, duo).[(g)] | Act V (setting: in front of Palermo cathedral). Omitted. Replaced by chorus of monks. |
| Act III, ii:<br>Dialogue (Robert, Alice, Raimbaut) and duo (Robert, Alice)[(h)] with a religious melody heard coming from a nearby chapel. | Information incorporated into Act V,ii (Robert-Bertram scene).<br>Becomes a chorus of monks in Act V, ii. |
| Dialogue (Robert, Bertram). | Equivalent of Act V, ii, with air "O mon fils" for Bertram. |
| Final trio (Robert, Alice, Bertram), the defeat of Bertram, apotheosis of Robert and Isabelle. | Same. |

## ANNOTATIONS

(a) "Here, a long dialogue scene between [Alice] and Robert who, to pay his debts, imagines nothing better than to write to Duchess Bertha, his mother, to levy a special tax on the bourgeoisie of Rouen. And when Alice protests, 'That certainly astonishes you,' he tells her; 'this is not the first time, however, that this has happened. . . . They love me so much that where I threaten them with my return, fear makes them generous. It is a tax like any other, a tax by fear.'"[45]

(b) "There, three couplets, of which the last alternates verse by verse between Robert and Bertram, on the various ways of knowing true happiness."[46]

(c) Isabelle, at first named Isoline, stops at the encampment, "like all the princesses of opéra comique, like that of *Jean de Paris* in the past and that of *Lalla Roukh* in the future. . . ."[47]

(d) "The battle takes place offstage and all the characters onstage follow the turns of fortune anxiously.[48] They call with loud cries to Robert, who does not answer. Alice runs terrified to his tent and finds him overcome by a lethargic slumber. Robert then awakens and asks for his arms, but at the moment he rushes forth to combat the cries of victory announcing the end of the tournament resound. Robert goes to kill himself under the eyes of Isabelle; he is prevented by the demon."[49]

(e) "Peasants, Sicilian girls, *lazzaroni*, invited by Raimbaut to come drink with him [using] *Seigneur* Bertram's money, descend from the mountains and fill the stage; songs and dances, giddiness of Raimbaut who plays at [being a] junior-grade Zampa, who takes the bass part to the girls and sings to them a galant *tarantella*; anxiety and jealousy of Alice, who follows this horseplay hidden in an arbor and who tries in vain to stop Raimbaut so caught up in the revelry."[50]

(f) ". . . Alice, going to point out to Robert his evil genius, is prevented by Bertram, who threatens to kill Raimbaut at once before her eyes. Then, when she has escaped by [promising] not to betray him, a long scene which will become the duo [for Robert and Bertram], 'Des chevaliers de ma patrie.' . . ."[51]

(g) "The third act takes place in a rundown cottage where Alice and Raimbaut have taken refuge; they await the judgment which is to be passed on Robert, guilty of having entered the princess' apartments without warning. Here, the scene and the obligatory comic duo between the *trial* and the *dugazon*. Alice, not wanting to keep any of Bertram's presents, forces her fiancé to throw his [Bertram's] money into the stream and [Raimbaut], completely crestfallen, throws out this final thought:

> What humiliating developments!
> My destiny, I have always said,
> Is to be ruined by women!"[52]

(h) "[Robert] has been taken from prison by Bertram, who advised him to find Raimbaut and especially not to challenge the Prince of Palermo [the opera's Prince of Granada] to a new combat. Robert promised, but he has not kept his promise. He went to challenge his rival, fought him in close combat, and has been beaten. He then calls Bertram to his aid. . . ."[53]

The column on the left of the chart outlines a conventional opéra comique libretto in Scribe's usual manner. The pairs of lovers involved are roughly comparable to those in *Le Maçon*, *La Fiancée*, or *Léocadie*, and the course of action reveals the expected traits of the well-made libretto: delayed-action plot, careful preparation of each successive event, contrived entrances and exits, a dramatic seesaw effect in the fortunes of the hero, a *quiproquo* (the fact that Bertram is Robert's father), a *scène à faire* (the first half of the final trio), and a secret letter the content of which has a decisive effect on the outcome of the plot. Act structures are microcosms of the structure of the entire libretto and have their own beginnings, middles, and ends. Musical numbers are those normally found in opéra comique: large scenes of carousing or peasant festivities, smaller dramatic duos, trios, quartets, and solo *couplets*, *romances*, and *airs*.

The opéra comique does have several unusual features, however. The first is an abundance of pageantry, although this is not so great as to be excessive. The second, more decisive feature is the presentation of supernatural events in the manner of German romanticism rather than that of the French: that is, the supernatural characters and events are "real" for the duration of the opera and do not result from a trick played by an ordinary mortal to carry out a plan as, for example, in *La Dame blanche* or *Le Loup-garou*. It is here that the influence is felt not only of such earlier operas as *Don Giovanni* and *Der Freischütz* but of the vogue for the fantastic and bizarre touched off by the appearance of the tales of E. T. A. Hoffmann in French translation.

To say that the opera's libretto is not without weaknesses is an understatement. However, with so strong and virtually unbreakable a structure to back him up, Scribe could let in a few small inconsistencies. For example, in Act V of the opera Bertram breaks the spell of the monks' chorus over Robert by reminding him that the church is being prepared for Isabelle's wedding. Yet when Alice arrives with the news that the Prince of Granada cannot enter the church, Robert replies, "I know." Scribe could even rely on a not unexpected but nevertheless clumsily introduced variation on the *deus ex machina* as he saves Robert by the bell of midnight tolling in defeat of Bertram and victory for his weak-kneed son. Despite the inconsistencies and outright blunders, however, the traits of the well-made libretto are unmistakable.

The first major difference between the opéra comique and the opera version of *Robert* lies in the nature of the characters. Two characters are extensively modified and one is somewhat changed. Raimbaut, originally a comic baritone, is all but eliminated and performs no useful function after singing his *ballade* in the first act. In the opéra comique he not only provided comedy but helped explain actions and told the audience what opinion they were to hold. For example, one of his speeches from the opening of the original third act gives information on what has happened since the end of the second act.

> I ask you if you have ever seen an outrage like this! . . . to steal into the chamber of a princess during the night, and on the eve of her wedding at that. . . . It is enough to make all the husbands in Sicily tremble. Tomorrow the council will assemble . . . severe judges, inexorable . . . all married men; but we must hope that with influence he will be let off with life in prison. . . .[54]

In the opera only the duo with Bertram that begins Act III reminds us of Raimbaut's original humorous naiveté. The rest of the role is incorporated into narrative sung by other characters or is made visual.

If the role of Raimbaut was cut considerably, that of Bertram was enlarged, particularly with the aid of such spectacular scenes as the "Valse infernale" and invocation of the nuns. In the opéra comique, Bertram was to be quite an ordinary devil charged, much as is Mephistopheles in Gounod's *Faust*, with winning the soul of a man by tempting him with earthly rewards which he must obtain in such a way as to endanger his salvation. The opera, particularly in Acts III and V, provides greater possibilities for expansion of this role, and the authors choose to enlarge that element of Bertram's character which critics ancient and modern have found most objectionable: his love for his son. As Lasserre has stated:

> . . . it was necessary to invent a tragic and moving devil, and give him a psychology, a double psychology as a devil and father, which any pen but Scribe's would have been afraid to portray. . . . We

> know the result. This devil displays to his son at once the tender protection of a father and the wickedness of a tempter; he passionately desires the happiness of his son and from sheer love strives desperately to damn his soul, so as not to be separated from him.[55]

Whether one agrees with Lasserre's judgments or not, one cannot deny that Bertram has become a more important figure in the work, one which would have no counterpart were it not for the enlargement of the role of Alice. The simple peasant girl of the opéra comique becomes a stronger, more dramatic figure in the opera. She battles directly with Bertram for Robert's soul and, when all else fails, unveils her secret weapon: the letter from Robert's mother. Seeing the new Alice, one realizes why the old Raimbaut had to be eliminated, for the girl is no longer a sweet coquette and he is no match for her.

The characters of Robert and Isabelle remain much as they had been planned in the opéra comique. They are above all else the noble lovers and they play their parts well. This is not to say that they are strong characters, for of all the personae only Alice comes close to vitality and conviction. All are Scribean characters of a type seen many times before. Certainly Isabelle has no purpose other than to provide Robert with a love interest and the composer with an excuse for writing a virtuosic soprano role; but the same could be said of Rossini's Matilde in *Guillaume Tell* or of Scribe's own Berthe (*Le Prophète*) or Gemma (*Zerline*). Robert is only one of a number of Scribe's faint-hearted leading men who become heroes in spite of themselves. He is preceded in grand opera by Alphonse (*La Muette*) and is succeeded by Raoul (*Les Huguenots*); Léopold (*La Juive*); and Jean (*Le Prophète*), whose pangs of conscience result in the deaths of the innocent as well as the guilty. *Robert's* characters are flat, often ridiculous figures who need music to be at all acceptable. Of course, one must also take into account that the roles were written with specific singers in mind and that each would be expected to give something of himself to the role.

A second major difference between the opera and the opéra comique plans of *Robert* lies in the element of spectacle. The last three acts particularly differ not only from the opéra comique but from the earlier portion of the opera itself in the increased emphasis on mechanical wonders, demonic elements, and pure sensationalism. This is not to say that some of the spectacle was not genuine, however stunning its external effect. For the Nuns' Ballet, Cicéri designed an exact replica of the ruins of the Montfort-l'Amaury cloister in Seine et Oise province, a historical monument dating from the sixteenth century.[56] An answer to the call of the romantic dramatists for exact local and historical color, the cloister also represented to the audience an example of the rather starry-eyed, idealized view of Catholic Christianity current in France during the first three decades of the nineteenth century.[57]

Again the popular theatre was the source of some elements of the stage settings. In the above-mentioned letter of Meyerbeer to Count Redern, the composer mentions the special lighting effects necessary for the cloister scene and the church scene (Act V), both of which are to have a "diorama-like effect."[58] Although the cloister scene, the most talked-about of the many effects in the work, was originally the idea of Duponchel, it was carried out in grand style by composer and librettist alike.

Many connoisseurs reacted adversely to the great emphasis on display. Mendelssohn speaks more kindly but no less sincerely than a number of other critics when he says of *Robert*:

> There is an expenditure of all possible means of producing stage effects that I never saw equalled. All who can sing, dance, or act in Paris, sing, dance, and act on this occasion. The *sujet* is romantic; that is, the devil appears in the piece (this is quite sufficient romance and imagination for the Parisians). It is very bad, however; and were it not for two brilliant scenes of seduction it would produce no effect whatever.[59]

Yet here, perhaps without realizing it, Mendelssohn hit upon not merely an important factor in the success of *Robert* but the decisive element in the transition from the opéra comique basis of Scribe's opera libretti to the formation of a peculiar genre of opera libretto, that of grand opera. The increased emphasis on the visual element in opera, whether functioning as diversion, distraction, or drama, affected all phases of operatic producation. It was not merely a matter of bigger and better stage machines, longer ballets, or more colorful sets and costumes, but of an emphasis on the tableau as a musico-dramatic unit. This leads the librettist to the creation of scenes that, regardless of their dramatic function, are oriented toward a particular stage setting or effect. Such an orientation was nothing new to Scribe, for his celebrated skill at *numérotage* had as its goal the building up of certain *coups de théâtre*; thus, all he needed do was shift literary gears to adapt his own long-practiced technique to a new genre.

## The Music

The advent of the tableau as a dramatic unit to be reckoned with, though not specifically new with the production of *Robert*, can be seen reflected not only in a changing libretto style but in the musical setting as well. This constitutes the third major difference between *Robert le Diable* as opéra comique and as opera. As the chart indicates, the first two acts of the opera and the beginning of the third remain much the same as they were planned in the opéra comique, except that sections originally intended to be spoken are set as recitative or arioso. The music for these acts is not especially adventurous from a formal point of view. Although Meyerbeer does write more dramatic and difficult vocal parts and includes many special orchestral effects of which an Auber or even a Rossini would not have dreamed, there is little in these acts save the recitative that could not also have been found in an opéra comique. The opening is a conventional introductory scene similar to that which begins *Le Maçon*, *La Dame blanche*, and numerous other works. It consists of:

a. opening chorus on a convential "wine, women, and song" text (F major);
b. the introduction of Raimbaut (arioso; modulatory);
c. Raimbaut's *ballade*, "Jadis régnait en Normandie" (three stanzas with choral refrains; C major-minor);
d. Robert's protests (arioso; modulatory);
e. recapitulation of opening chorus, varied (F major);
f. the introduction of Alice, who is protected by Robert from the other nobles (arioso, choral statements; A major-F major);
g. defiance from nobles, who swear to get even (ensemble and chorus, ending with a strong final cadence, F major).[60]

In an opéra comique the Introduction would probably not have extended beyond the recapitulation of the opening chorus, but the layout of the ensemble and the nature of its components would not be at all unusual in such a work. The alternation of sections containing action with those of a more static nature is an obvious feature.

This introduction is followed by an unpretentious recitative scene between Robert and Alice that is quite frankly a replacement of the earlier spoken dialogue leading up to Alice's *romance*, a simple, strophic piece decorated with some rather incongruous cadenzas. The piece is composed in a more lofty style than one would usually find in an opéra comique, but the musical type is found frequently in the latter genre.

A conventional section of recitative links this musical number to the next, the gambling scene, a number reminiscent of an opéra comique finale. The auction scene in *La Dame blanche* is an especially strong parallel, as is the dream scene written more than fifteen years later for *Haydée*. Again the arrangement of sections of action and repose is apparent, the refrain "Fortune, à ton caprice" alternating with the sections of the number in which Robert gambles and loses his money and goods. While the scope and arrangement of the scene is not unusual, one feature of the number deserves special mention: the greater importance given to the visual element. The actual throwing of the dice is done as a pantomime with orchestral accompaniment (Example 51). It is significant that the gambling scene, the first large scene in *Robert* to utilize visual means of expression, is also the first scene not based in some way on the original opéra comique plan.

**Example 51**

The opening number of Act II, Isabelle's recitative and air with chorus, represents a not particularly large step toward the creation of scene complexes to replace the more traditional operatic numbers. Isabelle sings the first part of her virtuosic air, after which the young ladies enter and Alice presents Robert's letter. Overjoyed at having a message from Robert, Isabelle continues her air over the sounds of the chorus. The duo following this is not of an unusual scope. Like the air, it too has a basis in the opéra comique version of the drama. The challenge from the Prince of Granada, set in recitative, moves Robert off the stage to make way for the nobles and tournament guests. Again the visual element plays a part in this change of action from the opéra comique, for we see Bertram, not the Prince, send the messenger to Robert.

The next scene of the opera, expanded and quite changed from the opéra comique, puts the accent heavily on visual elements and is, like the market chorus of *La Muette*, a diversion. This large musical and scenic tableau falls into several sections: a *choeur dansé* in praise of Isabelle; a *pas de cinq* consisting of several contrasting sections; and a recitative and finale. Even the last large ensemble, which contains some action, is essentially a static piece. At the beginning of the number the master of ceremonies announces that the Prince of Granada wishes to bear Isabelle's standard; then Bertram, in an aside, assures us that Robert will not return in time. The rest is purely scenic, nondramatic music. A chorus, first *a cappella*, sings the Prince's praises; Alice worries that Robert is not there, but Raimbaut reassures her; the tournament begins offstage and those on the stage cheer the combatants on. The scene is of large dimensions, but nothing new happens after the opening recitative. Musically the piece consists of repeated fanfare-like motifs in the chorus and a coloratura obbligato for Isabelle, with a few side comments by other solo characters made in a melodically uninteresting style. Thus both music and drama are less than gripping, and the value of the number is purely visual.

The part of the original *Robert* plan that became the opera's third act was largely spoken. Thus freed from the possibility of retaining set-numbers already planned, composer and librettists departed greatly from their original plan, and these departures were exclusively in the direction of the musical-scenic tableau. The Raimbaut-Bertram duo, an outgrowth of a spoken scene, is quite conventional in layout and function and need not concern us further. The expansion of what was to have been a simple monologue into the scene of the "Valse infernale," however, is of definite significance in the rise of spectacle and sensationalism to a place of prominence in French opera. This scene, modeled on the first part of the Wolf's Glen scene in Weber's *Der Freischütz*, is like the Finale of Act II in that its musical and dramatic value in an absolute sense is practically nonexistent. As in the earlier Finale, very little happens: Bertram is summoned by the demons, makes a few comments on his desire to win Robert's soul, and enters the cave. Musically, the offstage chorus of demons seems even less sinister to us than it must have to contemporaries who thought to peruse the score apart from the visual spectacle. The melody is very trite, all but mindless in its repetition without variation of the same rhythmic and melodic patterns (Example 52). As before, the effect is scenic: choral

**Example 52**

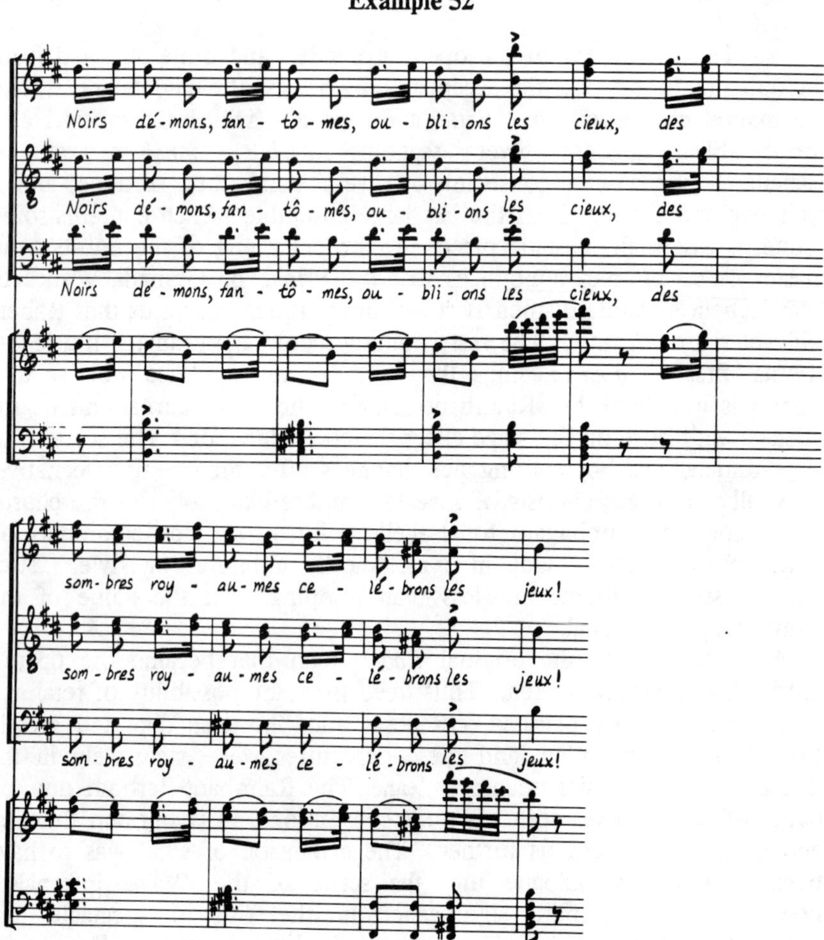

sounds come out of the deeps and thunder and flames burst forth from the cavern. This is enough to make anyone forget that neither composer nor librettist is going anywhere.

Alice's recitative and *romance* are suggested by or taken directly from the opéra comique plan, but the scene that follows is greatly expanded from a spoken dialogue to another tableau filled with spine-tingling effects. The action is slight: Alice hears the demons call Robert's name, learns Bertram's mission, and is threatened by the demon should she reveal this information. The music cannot stand by itself. It consists largely of recitative or arioso with the sparse orchestral accompaniment. Even the duo section lacks well developed melodies of form. The number must be seen, Alice's tentative steps toward the cave followed with anxious eyes, Bertram's slow advance toward the frightened girl observed with bated breath, before the piece makes its effect—an effect not of music, nor of drama, but of total theatre.

At Robert's entrance Meyerbeer has created an *a cappella* trio to replace the planned quartet (Example 53). The effect of an unaccompanied number following directly on the heels of so intense a

**Example 53**

### Example 53 (continued)

scene as that between Bertram and Alice is that of the proverbial calm before the storm. The ending, tapering off to a musical whimper, precedes an outburst by Alice (Example 54). At last someone is going to act—but no, she cannot, and she flees in fear.

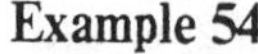

The duo between Robert and Bertram is again of a conventional cut, bringing relief to the audience before the last and greatest spectacle of all, the cloister scene. Here almost none of the action is verbalized. We already know what Robert's purpose will be when he arrives, and Bertram's "Evocation"—a declamatory arioso devoid of musical appeal—and recitative fill in the rest. The remainder of the scene, except for Robert's recitative, is pure pantomime and scenic spectacle taking up some twenty-five pages in the piano-vocal score. The sets, the special lighting, and the sight of dancing nuns seductively leading Robert little by little toward sin live only on the stage before the eyes of a hypnotized, receptive audience. Piling sensation upon sensation, a chorus of demons rushes on as soon as Robert has accomplished his crime and closes the act with a loud "Il est à nous!" and a wild dance of celebration.

Act IV of *Robert le Diable* is essentially the same in content as the last part of the original second act, except for the addition of an opening introduction-like scene for Alice, Isabelle, and the chorus. The way in which Meyerbeer reflects the effect of the magic branch on the chorus by writing in gradually diminishing dynamics, rallentandos, longer note values, and finally notes separated by rests is clever gimmickry but little more than that, and the finale is nothing more than a scene complex with obvious seams between the sections. It contains Isabelle's famous *cavatine*, "Robert, toi que j'aime," and finishes with an extended, static *morceau d'ensemble* for soloists and chorus.

In the last act the difference between the two *Roberts* most obvious immediately is the change of setting from a humble cottage to the cathedral of Palermo, where the visual effect of the massive edifice already demonstrates against the power of Bertram. Scenery thus serves a purpose similar to that of the words in Scribe's libretti and dramas: to warn the audience, to prepare them for the coming battle for Robert's soul. Apparently "il n'est pas à nous," at least not yet.

A simple religious tune from a nearby chapel (the original plan) is here transformed into a melody sung by a chorus of monks. The latter is similar in type to melodies in Rossini's *Stabat Mater* or that of "Anges pures" near the end of Gounod's *Faust* (Example 55). This is followed by an *a cappella* choral prayer. It is similar in kind to the prayer during the wedding of Elvire and Alphonse in *La Muette de Portici*, but the effect is heightened by the use of an organ prelude and postlude coming from inside the church. This prayer, with organ accompaniment, is repeated from inside the church at the height of Bertram's attempts to persuade Robert to sign over his soul to hell, and temporarily turns Robert toward God and heaven.

**Example 55**

Bringing Robert back to reality, Bertram reminds him that his rival is to marry Isabelle, then clinches the argument by telling Robert that he is Bertram's own son. At this point Scribe and Meyerbeer work well together, for Meyerbeer brings back the tune of Raimbaut's *ballade* in the orchestra to remind the audience of the story of Robert's life, heard some two or three hours earlier. Thus Bertram's revelation is not unexpected when it occurs.

The final trio is a conventional set-piece organized in Scribe's usual manner. It consists of alternating sections of action and repose and includes an ensemble section stated once, then repeated in varied form near the end of the number. The situation is more dramatic than that which usually ends one of Scribe's libretti, for a man's soul is at stake and Meyerbeer is more able than a composer like Auber to play up the emotional high points of the scene in a convincing manner. Like most of Meyerbeer's works, this trio passed for learned music, and one critic remarked of it:

> The music of Meyerbeer is the work of a musician of the first order, and also [that] of a thinker. At the same time that he has ideas, he also has the Idea.[62]

However conventional the trio may seem in perspective, the final tableau is pure spectacle. The earth opens to receive Bertram amid sounds of thunder, after which a succession of harp arpeggios accompanies a change of scene to the interior of the cathedral, where Isabelle leads Robert to the altar. Such striking contrasts of heaven and hell coming hard on the heels of a death struggle between good and evil in the persons of Alice and Bertram must have produced an electrifying effect, an effect possible only in the total theatre created by dramatic, musical, and scenic collaboration.

## Grand Opera and the Well-Made Libretto

Dorothy Hagan has written:

> Meyerbeer made a practice of contrasting the acts that carried an ideological burden with alternating ones that carried no burden at all. His critics, including Berlioz, made a practice of sidestepping the latter by blaming the librettist. 'What else can you do with pleasant gardens, fresh fountains, amorous waves and coquettry than fashion for them peaceful cantilenas, cavatinas, roulades and sweet choruses,' says Berlioz of the second act of *Huguenots*, and then he is off to the beauties of Act III.[63]

This statement gives a clear picture of the generic differences between the libretto of an opéra comique and that of an opera, differences which Scribe arrives at through experimentation in which *Robert le Diable* marks a decisive turning point. This turning point can be seen clearly by comparing the conception of *Robert le Diable* as opéra comique with that as opera.

In *Robert le Diable* some of the originally planned action has been telescoped, some characters have been made to serve the function of two of the original roles, and a great deal of spectacle has been added. However, when the ballets and pageantry are stripped away, when the dramatic changes are reconciled, what is left is a rather weak but nevertheless serviceable example of the well-made libretto. Thus the basic structural principles of the grand opera libretto are not those of contrast *per se*, whatever its nature, but of the well-made libretto interlarded with scenes of musical and scenic spectacle, ballets, and virtuosic singing. Because of this technique, the grand operas of Scribe seem to go from one scenic high point to another. When viewed in its original and final form, *Robert* becomes a transitional work, one which bridges the gap between the popular theatre and the Opêra by bringing together for the first time a modern libretto structure, already used in *La Muette*, with the grand musical style and tradition of earlier opera, by way of *Guillaume Tell*, all under the overriding influence of the scenic tableau. The last step in this transformation of the well-made libretto occurs in Auber's *Gustave III*.

In *Gustave III* the peasant characters of opéra comique and earlier grand opera are noticeably absent, as are any great numbers of the strophic solo songs they normally sing. The full-blown historical plot, spiced with intrigues, love affairs, blood and thunder, has none of the bourgeois supernatural aspects of *Robert*. To be sure, the supernatural element is present in the person of Arvedson, but even though she invokes Satan, she makes quite clear from her conversations that her fortune-telling is of the usual educated guess variety typical of modern soothsayers. The chorus is prominent as a character: the Swedish people, a role comparable to that of *La Muette's* Italians and *La Dame blanche's* Scotsmen. Scenic trappings, *divertissements*, processions, and the prominent masked ball provide the grand opera spectacle, as does the local color of such touches as Swedish national costumes at Gustave's court. With *Gustave III* Scribe also begins a practice he continues in his grand opera libretti, that of including footnotes in the printed text explaining references to historical events or characters occurring in the opera text itself. In neither *La Muette* nor *Robert* do similar footnotes apppear, but they are used quite consistently in grand operas after 1833. In *Gustave III* the full panorama of historical and local color bursts forth from Scribe's pen without obvious reliance on the framework of opéra comique. By the time of *Les Huguenots* both music and libretto have risen above their origins in the popular theatre and form a unique and specifically French *Gesamtkunstwerk* peculiar to the stage of the Opéra.

In addition to the revolution effected by *Robert le Diable* on the musical and dramatic profile of grand opera, its influences on other developments in opera were great. Among specific devices in the score that became common musical clichés later, Cooper mentions the gambling scene in which the "tremolando strings and pianissimo trombones hold the chord of the diminished seventh, there is a shrill wisp of a scale from the wood-wind, silence and then the strings pizzicato comment" as the source of similar passages in *Rigoletto* and *Carmen*. This gambling scene also influenced the dream scene in the finale of Act I of *Haydée*. Cooper also mentions the Chorus of Monks in Act V, on which Verdi models the chorus of priests condemning Rhadames in *Aida*; and the figure of Bertram, "the father of all operatic devils of the nineteenth century," as an influence on Berlioz, Gounod, and Liszt.[64] The ending of *Robert* is strictly paralleled in that of Gounod's *Faust*, and the influence of Alice on the character of Micaëla in *Carmen* has already been mentioned.

In Scribe's own work the story of *Robert* is to some extent repeated, but in a less serious vein, in a one-act opéra comique, *Le Diable a l'école* (1842), with music by E. Boulanger. In this work Stenio, a young merchant of Venice, signed a paper giving his soul to the devil after two years in exchange for the restoration of a fortune he had lost gambling. The opera concerns the attempts of Babylas, a friendly, bumbling sort of devil, to force Stenio to keep his part of the bargain and the efforts of Fiamma, Stenio's foster-sister, to prevent this. At one point in the opera Fiamma takes refuge from Babylas behind a statue of the Madonna, just as Alice clings to the cross when threatened by Bertram.

There are also striking parallels between *Robert le Diable* and another of Scribe's libretti, *La Nonne sanglante*, finally set by Gounod in 1854 after having been rejected by several composers, Berlioz among them. *La Nonne sanglante* is the only other opera libretto by Scribe to include a supernatural element that is not later explained away in perfectly logical terms or used as part of a genuine fairy tale—exotic background.[65] Like Hélèna, the prioress in *Robert le Diable*, Agnès, the Bleeding Nun, rises from the grave and at one point brings with her the ghosts of the hero's ancestors. The hero, Rodolphe, is nearly as indecisive as Robert. He swears to avenge the Nun's murder, then finds the murderer is his own father. Before he can decide whether to kill his father and thus be permitted by the Nun to marry the woman he loves, the father deliberately wanders into a trap meant for Rodolphe and is murdered. Thus avenged, the Nun goes to heaven and leaves Rodolphe and his fiancée in peace. Like *Robert, La Nonne sanglante* ends in an apotheosis scene.

*Robert* even exercised an external influence on the libretto of Verdi's *Les Vêpres siciliennes.* Both operas take place in the same locale, in or near Palermo, and Act II of the *Vêpres* contains a chapel of Saint Rosalie on the outskirts of the city. It is from the tomb of Saint Rosalie that the hero must steal the sacred branch in *Robert le Diable.*

"With *Robert*," writes Hermann Abert, "the new French romanticism took possession of the operatic stage."[66] Yet unlike German romanticism, French romanticism in opera did not long retain the supernatural element as it exists in *Robert.* The French had still another form of musical theatre, the wordless pantomime of the dramatic ballet. With *Robert le Diable* the supernatural entered the Opéra, whence it was transferred to the ballet in such works as *La Sylphide*, the prototype of the romantic ballet, *La Tentation*, and *Giselle.*[67] The ethereal figures of Marie Taglioni and Carlotta Grisi must have seemed to the French more divorced from reality, more purely romantic, than all the water sprites, mountain sylphs, and diabolical characters of German opera; and ballet, under the direct influence of *Robert*, became the primary vehicle for this phase of romanticism on the French stage.

## COMIC OPERA AND OPERA COMIQUE: AUBER'S *LE PHILTRE*

Now that the relationship between Scribe's opéras comiques and his grand opera style has been explored in some detail, it would be well to examine the opposite side of this musico-dramatic coin to see the expansion of opéra comique technique in quite a different way to serve the needs of comic opera. Auber's *Le Philtre* is a good example to consider, for not only is it the product of the same collaboration of composer and librettist that produced so many successful works at the Opéra-Comique, but it has a structure and plot similar to those of many a work produced at that theatre. Indeed, many critics considered the work to be little more than an opéra comique in which recitative replaced the usual spoken dialogue.[1] Although the transference of Scribe's opéra comique techniques to the comic opera genre is not really so simple as all that, the general orientation of these critics' opinions is quite correct.

First performed on June 20, 1831, *Le Philtre* was an immediate success and remained in the repertoire of the Opéra until 1862 with very few interruptions.[2] Scribe's libretto, based on an Italian story (Silvio Malaperta's *Il Filtro*, published in a French adaptation in the *Revue de Paris* by Stendhal in 1830), became the basis of Felice Romani's libretto for Donizetti's *L'Elisir d'amore* in 1832.[3] After the latter became very popular, "the inevitable happened: at St. Petersburg in 1836, music from the two operas was mixed in a *pasticcio*—which was sung in German."[4]

*Le Philtre* opens with one of the customary choruses of villagers enjoying some well-earned rest after their day's work. From the crowd Guillaume looks tenderly at Térézine, who is reading the story of Tristan and Isolda to the assembled workers. Guillaume wishes he could find such a love potion as Isolda's, for he sees no hope of Térézine's ever returning his love. The sound of military music offstage announces the arrival of Joli-coeur and his troops. The captain is in love with Térézine and tries to persuade her to marry him, but her answer is indefinite. She does offer refreshments to the soldiers, however, and the villagers accompany the troops to Térézine's farmhouse.

Alone with Térézine, Guillaume tries to convince her to return his love, but she urges him to forget her and tend to his sick uncle instead, since she is a hopeless coquette and has no intention of changing. Jeannette and the village girls tease Guillaume about his hopeless love, but they stop when Fontanarose, a charlatan vendor of patent medicines, arrives with his cart and a following of villagers. Hearing Fontanarose tell of his marvel-working medicines, Guillaume asks if he has any love potions. The charlatan produces a bottle of wine, which he sells to Guillaume with the understanding that it will not take effect for twenty-four hours—time enough for Fontanarose to have left town.

Now alone, Guillaume drinks the potion and finds himself feeling a good deal better about his prospects with Térézine. The latter, entering, finds that Guillaume is no longer the doting fool she rejected a few scenes earlier but that he actually seems indifferent to her now. This so infuriates her that she, hoping to make him jealous, agrees to marry Joli-coeur in one week. Still Guillaume seems untroubled, for he is certain Térézine will be in love with him at the end of twenty-four hours. When Joli-coeur receives a message that the troops must leave the next morning, he persuades Térézine to marry him that very evening. As Guillaume wonders what he should do now, the curtain falls.

Act II takes place some hours later. The villagers, led by Jeannette, are celebrating the approaching marriage of Térézine and Joli-coeur, and Fontanarose joins with Térézine in a duet to entertain the crowd. Térézine, however, is unhappy to find that Guillaume is not there, since her revenge will have no effect if he does not see it.

The villagers go off to Térézine's house, leaving Fontanarose alone on the stage. Guillaume, without hope, approaches Fontanarose asking for a love potion that will work at once. Guillaume, however, has spent all the money he had on the first potion and the charlatan refuses to extend credit. In order to get more money Guillaume joins Joli-coeur's regiment, for which he receives twenty *écus*. He quickly runs off in search of Fontanarose.

Meanwhile Jeannette and the village girls have discovered that Guillaume's uncle has died and left Guillaume all his money. When the latter, strongly under the influence of more love potion, emerges from Fontanarose's hotel, the girls all try to gain his attentions and he becomes convinced that the potion is working. Térézine, seeing how popular Guillaume has become, is very jealous. Fontanarose expresses surprise that his potion really works, and Térézine becomes increasingly distressed over Joli-coeur's news that Guillaume has enlisted and will soon be leaving with the troops. Fontanarose explains to her that Guillaume enlisted in order to gain enough money to buy the love potion. Now Térézine realizes how much Guillaume must love her and buys back his enlistment papers from Joli-coeur. Yet she still cannot bring herself to tell him she loves him and Guillaume gradually becomes disillusioned with Fontanarose's potion. Just as he is about to give up, Térézine gives in and agrees to marry him. When Joli-coeur returns, Térézine takes him aside to explain what has happened. Térézine and Guillaume then learn that the latter is rich. As the couple rejoices over their good fortune and prospects for happiness, Joli-coeur takes solace in the attentions of Jeannette and Fontanarose leaves town with honor and gratitude from all sides.

In matters of overall dramatic structure and musical style *Le Philtre* is similar to Scribe-Auber opéras comiques. Briefly, the work is constructed along the same general lines as the opéras comiques. The delayed-action plot begins at a crucial point in the course of Guillaume's seemingly hopeless pursuit of Térézine. Already Guillaume has become the laughing-stock of the village, and already Térézine has charmed Joli-coeur even though she is no more in love with him than she is with Guillaume. The sole character for whom no prehistory is immediately apparent is Fontanarose, but from the acclaim with which he is greeted when he arrives one would assume that he has been in the village before.

The two acts of *Le Philtre* show the delayed-action pattern in miniature, and each is a small drama in itself. By the end of Act I Guillaume seems to have found a solution to the problem with which he began the act, that of winning Térézine, only to find it thwarted through the conventional situation of a change in military orders. This ending is strong yet suspenseful, for one expects that Guillaume will want a stronger potion yet wonders how he will get it—since he has no money—and how it will work. The point of attack of Act II occurs after wedding preparations have been completed but before Guillaume has been able to think of a plan to win Térézine for himself. By the end of the opera this problem, in its larger form the basic one of the opera, has reached a satisfactory conclusion for all concerned.

As in Scribe's opéras comiques, the first act of *Le Philtre* is primarily expository: we meet the characters, learn who they are, what part they are to play in the story, and which of their pre-curtain activities are important to the plot of the opera. As usual, characterization is for the most part external, although Guillaume is presented with somewhat more subtlety than is usual for Scribe and is allowed a bit more leeway to develop his personality through his actions rather than by what he or someone else says about him. The real action of the opera starts only when Guillaume has taken the potion.

Throughout *Le Philtre* one sees the seesaw arrangement in the fortunes of the hero so common in Scribe's libretti. The opera also contains excellent examples of contrived entrances and exits: e.g., Fontanarose's entrance immediately after Guillaume has expressed a desire for a love potion or Térézine's entrance in time to see the other girls' reactions to Guillaume's newly acquired wealth. A *quiproquo* is also included: the alcoholic love potion. The liquid does have an effect on Térézine's attitude, but the nature of its power is comprehended differently by Guillaume and Fontanarose.

Throughout the libretto the action is tight and skillfully handled so that nothing is unexpected yet everything is suspenseful. For example, the death of Guillaume's rich uncle is forecast in Térézine's conversation with Guillaume in Act I when she mentions that the old man is ill; and Guillaume's change of personality after taking the elixir is not unexpected once the audience knows what the liquid really is.

The score of *Le Philtre* is uniformly good. The music represents some of Auber's best writing and is at a consistently high level, with no really weak numbers in the opera. Térézine's delightful *ballade* of Tristan and Isolda, the Act I airs for Joli-coeur and Fontanarose, and the second act duo "Je suis riche, vous êtes belle" for Fontanarose and Térézine are particularly attractive numbers. The work opens with an Introduction formally similar to many in Scribe's opéras comiques and the general nature of the musical numbers shows few real contrasts with Auber's opéra comique style.

*Le Philtre*, then, would appear to be just an opéra comique in operatic clothing, with larger choral and scenic effects and recitative instead of spoken dialogue. Yet there are some significant differences between this work and opéra comique that are worth noting, for they indicate that Scribe was aware that differences existed between the two genres regardless of whether his plot was comic or serious. The outline below gives a general sketch of the work's musical and dramatic profile. A broken line between numbers indicates that the preceding section ends with a final cadence.

Key to abbreviations:

G - Guillaume
Jo - Joli-coeur
F - Fontanarose
T - Térézine
Je - Jeannette
Cho - chorus
Ens - ensemble

| Number | Form or technique | Action involved |
|---|---|---|
| | **ACT I** | |
| 1 | Introduction:: T. G, Je, Cho. | Conventional situation, described in plot summary. |
| | Ballade: T, cho. | T tells story of Tristan and Isolda. |

- - - - - - - - - - - - - - - - - - - - - - - - - - - - - - - - - - - - - - - - - - - - - - - - - - - -

| | | |
|---|---|---|
| | Recit: G. | G wishes he could find a love potion. |
| 2 | Air: Jo. | Braggart air about his own skill as a soldier. |
| | Recit and cho: Jo, T, G, cho. | Jo asks T to marry him. T is vague, but offers soldiers refreshments. |
| | Recit: G, T. | T tells G to forget her. |
| 3 | Air: T. | She enjoys flirting and causing men to fall in love with her, but will never love anyone in return. |
| | Rec: G, Je. | Je advises G to find another girl. G asks if Je could fall in love with him. |
| 4 | Ens with cho: G, Je, girls. | Je and girls tease G. G is unhappy and angry. |
| | Recit: Je. | Je wonders who is approaching. |
| | 5 | Recit: Je. Je wonders who is approaching. |
| Air: F, cho. | F begins sales pitch. People express enthusiasm. | |
| | Recit: F, G, cho. | F continues sales pitch. G asks for love potion, buys it with his last three pieces of gold. F (aside) says potion is really wine and that during the 24 hours before it is to take effect he will leave town. Chorus praises F. |
| 6 | Air: G. | Praises potion, looks forward to how it will change his life. |
| | Recit: G. | G can feel effects already, begins to sing loudly and gaily a "tra-la-la" refrain. |
| 7 | Duo: G, T. | T expects G to be languishing, is shocked to discover him so confident and in high spirits, paying little attention to her. G reveals his belief that she will love him after one more day. |

| | | |
|---|---|---|
| 8 | *Trio et finale*: all principals, cho. | To make G jealous T promises to marry Jo in a week, but G still unpreturbed. Soldiers announce orders to move on. Jo persuades T to marry him later that evening. G is upset. |

ACT II

| | | |
|---|---|---|
| 9 | *Entr'acte* and ens with cho: T, Jo, Je, F, cho. | People come to celebrate marriage. |
| | *Couplets*: Je. | Wishing the couple happiness. |
| | Duo *(barcarolle)*: T, F. | Story of a girl who prefers love of poor gondolier to that of rich Venetian senator. |
| 10 | Recit: Jo, C, F, G, cho. | T upset that G is not there. Repeat celebration chorus. G asks F for more potion but has no money. |
| 11 | Duo: G, Jo. | Jo promises G money if he enlists, speaks of joys of army life. G agrees to join. |
| | Recit: G, Jo. | G signs paper, gets money. |
| 12 | *Morceau d'ensemble*: all principals, cho. | Je announces G's uncle is dead and G is heir to fortune. Girls surround G, who has just drunk more potion and thinks it is taking effect. F and T are amazed. |
| 13 | [Recit: T, F.] | F tells T about potion and that G bought it with money gained from enlistment. T now realizes how much G loves her. |
| | [Recit: T, G.] | G says all girls want to marry him but he is awaiting an unexpected miracle. |
| | Duo: T, G. | T has bought back G's enlistment papers. When she does not declare love G begins to doubt potion's effect, but T finally admits she loves him. |

| | | |
|---|---|---|
| 14 | Finale: all principals, cho. | T explains (silently) to Jo, who immediately looks to Je for consolation. F tells G he is rich. General rejoicing. |

The frequency of final cadences or of very thinly disguised transitions at the ends of sections indicates that Auber was not attempting any innovations in form even though he had been more adventurous in *La Muette de Portici.* In only two pieces, Nos. 9 and 12, does he attempt to work out forms that could be considered extraordinary.

All Auber's recitatives are accompanied by orchestra, but the voices usually sing in a *parlando* style accompanied only by a few light chords occurring once or twice a measure, sometimes even less frequently. Yet most of the sections in the outline specifically labeled recitative in the score are rather short. Were it true that *Le Philtre* is nothing more than an opéra comique with recitatives one would expect long stretches of recitative, particularly in view of the fact that Auber makes little attempt to write large-scale musical numbers. There are several reasons why this is not the case, and most of them have to do with the libretto.

First, *Le Philtre* contains less action and a simpler plot than is usual in most opéras comiques, although the structural elements of the libretto remain the same. Thus there is less need for recitative than would be the case were Scribe actually turning an opéra comique into an opera without major changes. Second, more of the action is incorporated into the musical numbers. Since there is less action than in an opéra comique, it can proceed at the slower pace necessitated by musical setting of the entire text. Since the plot is simpler than in opéra comique there is less chance that it will become confusing to the spectator when set to music throughout. Third, Auber sometimes resorts to recitative-like or arioso writing in the course of a musical number, thus increasing the amount of music in the opera having a recitative function. All three points show an awareness on the part of librettist and composer that their message is being told in a different medium.

Furthermore, Auber makes greater use of the more complex forms of music. Although no single number in *Le Philtre* would be out of place in an opéra comique context, there are relatively fewer strophic forms and more airs and ensembles, especially ensembles involving chorus, than in the usual opéra comique. Thus the librettist again shows his awareness that this comic opera is not after all an opéra comique.

Yet at the same time there can be no doubting the basis of techniques used in both libretto and music. The popular theatre, this time in a new mask, again visits the Opéra.

# THE TECHNIQUE OF GRAND OPERA AND THE TRANSFORMATION OF LITERARY MODELS: MEYERBEER'S *LES HUGUENOTS*

In March 1903 Meyerbeer's *Les Huguenots* saw its thousandth performance at the Paris Opéra.[1] Premiered on February 29, 1836, after an unusually long period of rehearsals, it became Meyerbeer's greatest success and, indeed, one of the most popular operas of the century. So great was the desire of opera-lovers outside France to hear the work, despite its daring use of a religious war as its theme, that numerous changes were made in the libretto to satisfy foreign censors. For example, in Vienna the Catholics and Protestants became Guelphs and Ghibellines,[2] and to satisfy the "pious souls of Munich" Charlotte Birch-Pfeiffer transformed them into Puritans and Anglicans, changing the setting to England.[3] Despite such revisions, however, the work was soon in the repertoires of opera companies throughout the Continent and in some cities of the United States.

Considering the instant success of *Les Huguenots*, the difficulties over its original production seem all the more amazing. Despite his good fortune with Meyerbeer's *Robert le Diable*, Véron was apparently not one to make exceptions either for genius or for the provider of healthy box-office receipts. When Meyerbeer had not finished his score for *Les Huguenots* by the contracted deadline, Véron demanded payment of the 30,000-franc indemnity specified in the agreement, 10,000 francs of which went to Scribe. The composer paid but was so angered that he determined never to allow Véron to produce the opera. When Véron was succeeded by Duponchel as manager of the Opéra, the latter refunded Meyerbeer's 20,000 francs and "thus secured the composer's sympathies and the *Huguenots* score."[4]

Once in rehearsal the opera went through an unbelievable number of changes. Even the libretto as it exists in the complete edition of Scribe's works, itself incorporating the majority of the changes from the original, is not exactly the same as the text Meyerbeer set; and Meyerbeer himself eliminated portions of the original score and added others, some of them before the first performance, some later.

The major changes in the libretto were made by Emile Deschamps. Deschamps had been very impressed with *Robert le Diable*, saying that it showed Meyerbeer to be to French romantic music what Delacroix was to painting and Hugo to literature, and had become a friend of the composer.[5] Meyerbeer, not Scribe, asked Deschamps to write texts for the corrections, additions, and changes to be made in the libretto. Thus the poet was in what could have been an unfortunate position, that of having to alter the basic work done by a major librettist and playwright, with or without the latter's consent or collaboration. Girard reports that in the one letter from Scribe preserved among Deschamps' papers the librettist appears to have been on good terms with both Meyerbeer and Deschamps. Since *Les Huguenots* was already well along in 1834, the date of the letter, Scribe was evidently not unhappy about the collaboration.[6] Additional evidence from the same year would substantiate this claim. Léon Halévy, whose brother was composing *La Juive* during 1834, reports that Scribe had little time to make the more or less minor changes in this libretto required by the composer and that he had no objection to Léon Halévy's taking this task upon himself.[7] With one exception, neither the work of Léon Halévy nor that of Deschamps could reasonably be considered basic to the structure or style of Scribe's libretti.

The exception is the fourth act of *Les Huguenots*. For this alteration, however, Deschamps was responsible only for the text, not for the idea. The latter came from tenor Adolphe Nourrit, "a true French singer, the singer of a people to whom musical emotions are not sufficient and who look for the interest of the poem and the display of the sets and costumes in an opera."[8] The first to play Masaniello in *La Muette de Portici*, Arnold in *Guillaume Tell*, Robert in *Robert le Diable*, and Eleazar in *La Juive*, Nourrit was to make Raoul in *Les Huguenots* his last creation at the Opéra.[9] It was this singer who suggested that the fourth act of *Les Huguenots* end with the *grand duo* for Raoul and Valentine.[10] After the momentous Blessing of the Daggers scene, in which some changes had also been made, Nourrit felt that anything other than the more intimate duet would be anticlimactic, yet that the work needed such a love duet between hero and heroine. Accordingly the project, no hurried task, was discussed thoroughly by Nourrit, Meyerbeer, and Deschamps before the actual text was written.[11] The rest, as they say, is history, for the duo is still the number in the opera to receive the largest number of laudatory comments.

Deschamps, however, apparently did not rewrite the entire fourth act but only made revisions and additions to what Scribe had already created. A note in Deschamps' hand on the first page of a copy of the *Huguenots* libretto preserved among his papers reads:

> Added by Emile Deschamps:
>
> 1° The entire role of Marcel throughout the five acts.
>
> 2° The Page's air at the end of the first act.

2 *bis* Valentine's romance, fourth act.
3° The grand love duet which ends the fourth act.
4° Raoul's air during the ball in the fifth act.
5° The grand trio of the fifth act.[12]

Other changes in Act IV involved the elimination of Queen Catherine de' Medici from the conspiracy scene. Chorley reports:

> It was orginally intended that the Saint Bartholomew massacre should be organized by *Queen Marguerite* [read "Catherine"; italics original], and not by the father of the heroine; but it was pointed out, that the interest attaching to the presence of *Valentine*, as an involuntary and horror-stricken witness, would be impaired by the predominance on the stage of another female character—and the change for the better was made.[13]

This change evidently was made before the music for the scene had been written, for Johannès Weber reports that there was never a part written for Catherine in Act IV.[14] His statement is confirmed by Théodore Lajarte in his catalogue of the Paris Opéra library, where he lists the following musical numbers as pieces composed but eliminated from the *Huguenots* score before the premiere.

> Very important fragments of *Les Huguenots*: entrance of Marcel and air for Valentine (unpublished); *orgie*, recitatives and beginning of Raoul's romance (Act I); grand air for Saint-Bris (unpublished) (Act II); monologue, chorale, and air for Valentine (unpublished) (Act III); recitatives for Valentine and Saint-Bris (unpublished) (Act IV); *pas de six* (unpublished).[15]

Among these numbers there is no mention of a part for Catherine written for any point in the opera.

The difference between the text in Meyerbeer's score and that in Scribe's *Oeuvres complètes* are too numerous to discuss in detail, and a few examples will have to suffice. In Act II the dialogue between Marguerite and Valentine after the latter returns from seeing Nevers is considerably longer in the libretto than in the score. It is difficult to agree with Newman that Meyerbeer's version does not make clear to the spectator that Marguerite plans the marriage between Raoul and Valentine primarily as a political move,[16] for the composer does include these essential details while at the same time eliminating a page of tedious recitative that would otherwise disturb the diversionary emphasis of the first part of this act. Since Marguerite's identity is known to the audience, they expect Raoul's arrival at any minute (because of the letter,

Act I) and expect that it will be he whom Marguerite intends for Valentine. Perhaps the inclusion of more of Scribe's narrative would make this more explicit but the action is surely not unclear as it stands. In fact, part of Scribe's dialogue complicates the plot unduly with news of Marguerite's own engagement to Henry of Navarre. Preparation for this event can wait for later in the opera.

According to Newman, Act II of the score also contains a quartet (not in Scribe), placed after Catholics and Protestants swear peace and friendship,"in which the four principals pray for brotherhood and peace. This quartet seems to have been omitted in Paris at an early stage in the opera's career."[17] It does appear in the scores consulted. Another number apparently omitted from Paris performances of *Les Huguenots* is Valentine's *romance* (Act IV).[18] This piece also appears in scores of the work, but its text is not that printed in the libretto. Whereas Scribe's text begins, "De mon amour faut-il, triste victime," Meyerbeer's *romance* begins, "Parmi les pleurs mon rêve se ranime." Since Deschamps claims to have written this text, perhaps the printed verses are those of Scribe's original. This seems strange, however, in view of the fact that Deschamps' other additions appear in the printed libretto more or less intact.

Like *Robert le Diable*, *Les Huguenots* is to some extent a derivative work in which both composer and librettist provide the spectator some basis in the familiar against which he can perceive—or think he perceives—the novelty of the new opera. For Scribe this familiarity stems from his basing the work not only on an important event in French history, the St. Bartholomew's Day masacre of 1572, but also on Prosper Merimée's novel, *Chronique du temps de Charles IX*. Specific relationships between libretto and novel will be discussed below.

Although the average spectator would probably not have been aware of it, Meyerbeer carried over specific ideas from his own earlier works and from those of others when he composed *Les Huguenots*. Saint-Bris' "Pour cette cause sainte" (Act IV) was taken from a trio in Act II of Meyerbeer's Italian opera *Margherita d'Anjou* (1820), performed in Paris in 1826.[19] Berlioz remarked of the triple chorus scene in Act III of *Les Huguenots* that no one had ever created this sort of "magnificent musical fabric" before,[20] but he was wrong. Meyerbeer himself had done so in Act I of *Il Crociato in Egitto*, the first of his operas to be performed in Paris, when he presented first a chorus of Egyptian priests, then a chorus of Crusaders, then a superimposition of the two.

*Il Crociato* influences *Les Huguenots* in still other ways. The Conspirators' Chorus and breaking of the swords has already been mentioned. There is at least one more situation which has a parallel in

*Les Huguenots.* In Act II of *Il Crociato* Palmira, an Egyptian, decides to embrace Christianity, whereupon Adriano permits her marriage to his nephew Armando and prays over the couple. This action is similar to that in the first part of the Marcel-Raoul-Valentine trio in Act V, a number added by Deschamps.

There are also dramatic and musical parallels between *Les Huguenots* and Rossini's *Guillaume Tell.* The latter also features a conspirators' scene set in responsorial style and a love affair between Arnold and Matilde, members of opposing political factions. Like Valentine, Matilde too eventually joins the revolutionaries because of the man she loves.

Earlier in *Les Huguenots*, Raoul's search for and subsequent rejection of Valentine is reminiscent of a similar situation in Scribe's opéra comique libretto *Fiorella* (Auber, 1826). Also from Scribe's repertoire of devices comes the journey of the blindfolded hero to an unknown destination *(Le Maçon)*, the flirtation scene between Marguerite and Raoul (Jenny and Georges in *Le Dame blanche*), the Sunday tableau (Palm Sunday in *Fra Diavolo*), and the struggle of two opposing forces, Valentine and Marcel, for the soul of the hero *(Robert le Diable).* From yet another source, Urbain is clearly the dramatic descendant of Rossinian vocalism.

Musically, Meyerbeer's "learned" style again calls up associations with the compositional greats of past and present. Castil-Blaze, cataloging Meyerbeer's musical allusions, found reminiscences of Mozart, Cimarosa, Handel, Rossini, Boieldieu, Beethoven, Gluck, Hérold, Spohr, and Spontini[21]; and Dauriac remarked that Marcel's song "Pif paf pouf" in Act I reminded him of the scherzo in Beethoven's Fifth Symphony.[22] Not the least of the musical effects was the use of the chorale to call up a host of religious associations, pro or con, among the spectators.[23] Throughout the opera Marcel is likely to sound forth a few phrases of "Ein feste Burg" at the drop of a downbeat, apparently neither knowing nor caring that the Huguenots are Calvinists, not Lutherans.[24]

No less important in giving the opera popular roots were its extra-musical associations. Although Heine comments that *Les Huguenots* does not refer directly to social questions of the day even though strongly rooted in them,[25] purely historical accounts of the mid-1830s refute this. After the death of Perier in 1832,

> France grew restive. The attacks in the press renewed their vigor, and revolutionary societies became more audacious. In 1834 and early in 1835 there was a whole series of riots. One of them, in Paris, developed into a republican insurrection which required three days to suppress. The whole situation came to a head in July, 1835,

> when on the anniversary of the revolution that had made Louis-Philippe king, there was a desperate attempt on his life.[26]

What indeed could be more relevant to current social questions than an opera about a brutal massacre of common people? George Sand found in it a reinforcement for a "new liberal theory of history acccording to which, far from being the exclusive property of revolutionists, terrorism was attributed primarily to the aristocratic nobles, kings, princes and gentlemen."[27] More abstractly, Théophile Gautier wrote:

> *Les Huguenots* is the spirit of analysis, rational fanaticism; the struggle of idea against faith, of duty against passion, of negation against affirmation; it is history which is substituted for legend, philosophy for religion.[28]

With such a context of universal emotions and conflicts, members of the audience could hardly help but feel that in *Les Huguenots* they were treading familiar ground, yet being offered new and lofty insights into their own particular condition of life.

### Novel and Libretto

As *Les Huguenots* begins, a group of young noblemen are gathered at Nevers' chateau for an afternoon of revelry and gambling. The Count has invited a young Huguenot, Raoul, to join them as his contribution to the king's avowed intention of reconciling Catholic and Protestant factions. The nobles begin to speak of their amorous adventures and Raoul admits that he has fallen in love with someone whose life he saved some days earlier but whose name he does not know. Marcel, a devout Huguenot and servant of Raoul, enters and is shocked to find his master in company with the Catholic nobles. One of the latter recognizes Marcel as the man who wounded him at an earlier battle and the gentlemen demand that he sing them a Huguenot battle song.

A messenger announces the arrival of an unidentified young woman to see Nevers, and the latter goes off to meet her. The nobles, curious, look through a window to try to see who she is and Raoul, recognizing the woman with whom he has fallen in love, declares now that he hates her. Nevers returns, confiding to a few friends that the woman, a lady-in-waiting to Queen Marguerite, was to have married him but that he has agreed to break the engagement at her request. Urbain, the queen's page, arrives with a message for Raoul saying that a carriage will come for him and that he will be taken, blindfolded, to an unknown location. The nobles recognize Marguerite's handwriting and become considerably more friendly toward Raoul. Marcel sees this favoritism as some sort of victory for the Huguenot cause.

Act II takes place at Marguerite's country estate, where the queen and her ladies are seated on the riverbank enjoying the fine summer weather, while the page Urbain plays Cherubino to Marguerite's Countess. Valentine reports that Nevers has agreed to break their engagement, whereupon Marguerite reveals that she has another match in mind for Valentine, one to which the latter's father has already agreed. Some of the ladies swim in the river, after which Raoul, blindfolded, is led in. The queen enjoys a brief flirtation with the young man, then tells him she wishes to cement the reconciliation between Protestants and Catholics by marrying him to the daughter of a Catholic noble, Saint-Bris. Raoul consents.

Saint-Bris, Nevers, Marcel, and a number of nobles arrive to pay their respects to Marguerite before leaving for Paris to discuss an as yet unspecified project with King Charles IX. Marguerite announces the planned marriage of Raoul and the latter swears eternal friendship with Saint-Bris and Nevers. The spell is broken when Raoul discovers that his intended is Valentine, whom he saw earlier at Nevers' chateau. Raoul refuses to marry her and only Marguerite's intervention prevents the Catholic nobles from avenging themselves at once for this insult. Marcel again rejoices at a victory for the Huguenots.

Act III takes place at the Pré-aux-Clercs, near which a number of soldiers, students, and other Parisians are enjoying a leisurely Sunday afternoon. Some friction develops between the Huguenot soldiers and a group of Catholics, but it is dispelled by the arrival of gypsy fortune-tellers who entertain the crowd. Saint-Bris and Nevers emerge from a chapel where Nevers and Valentine have just been married and where Valentine has remained to pray. Saint-Bris, still angry at Raoul's insult, receives a challenge to duel with the latter from Marcel and makes plans to ambush the young man when he arrives. The curfew is announced and the people leave the stage.

Valentine emerges from the chapel. She has overheard Saint-Bris' plans and seeks a way to warn Raoul without endangering her father's life. Seeing Marcel, she tells him that Raoul should not come to the duelling place alone. Marcel, however, does not know where his master is, but he is impressed with Valentine's devotion and prays for some way to save Raoul. Saint-Bris, his friends, and Raoul arrive simultaneously and the duel begins. Just as the other nobles are about to join the fray, Marcel draws his sword to defend his master. Both sides call for assistance and the melée of Catholics and Protestants is halted only by the arrival of Marguerite and her train. Accusations are hurled back and forth, and Raoul finally learns the reasons for Valentine's visit to Nevers' chateau. Nevers arrives to take his bride home and the act ends in mixed reactions from all sides.

Act IV takes place at Nevers' chateau, where Raoul has come to see Valentine once more before he dies. Hearing someone approach, he hides behind a tapestry where he overhears Saint-Bris tell the other nobles of their king's plan to surprise and massacre the Huguenots. All the Catholics swear to carry out the plan except Nevers, who breaks his sword rather than dishonor it by attacking defenseless people. After monks bless the Catholics' weapons, all leave to carry out the massacre.

Raoul emerges from his hiding place, determined to warn the Huguenots, but Valentine distracts him from his purpose by admitting she still loves him. Raoul is roused from his happy state only when sounds from outside the house indicate the battle has begun. He rushes off to join his friends.

The first scene of Act V takes place at a ball where Catholic and Protestant nobles and leaders are celebrating the marriage of Marguerite to Henry of Navarre. Raoul runs in to inform the gathering of the massacre. Shocked, the Huguenots follow Raoul to battle.

The scene changes to the exterior of a church where the wounded, nearly beaten Huguenots have taken refuge. Marcel sees no way the Protestants can win and hopes only that they will die honorably. Valentine arrives with news that Raoul's life will be spared if only he escapes with her and converts to Catholicism. Nevers has died trying to save Marcel, leaving Valentine free to marry again. When Raoul decides to stay with his friends, Valentine determines to remain as well and to embrace Raoul's religion. Marcel blesses the couple while, in the background, sounds from the church indicate that the soldiers are murdering those who have taken refuge there. Marcel sees a vision of heaven opening to receive the souls of the martyrs. The soldiers, led by Saint-Bris, move onstage to kill the three survivors. As Valentine calls out, Saint-Bris recognizes his daughter, but it is too late.

Rarely are the plots of Scribe's operas based on anything more than a suggestion taken from historical or fictional sources. *Les Huguenots* is an exception to this. According to Lang,[29] the opera is "vaguely inspired" by Prosper Merimée's *Chronique du temps de Charles IX*.[30] If one takes only an overview of the plot, Lang is unquestionably correct, for the story line and characters in libretto and novel are quite different. Nevertheless, in *Les Huguenots* there is little of any importance that is not based somehow on material from the Merimée tale. Indeed, it was never Scribe's practice to take over a play, a novel, or even a theme intact from another source for use in a libretto, as is well illustrated in the books for numerous of his opéras comiques. It was also not Merimée's practice to dwell on actual history but to work out from anecdotes about a particular period or event the atmosphere surrounding it. Thus in a sense his attitude was the same as Scribe's, to whom a suggestion sufficed for the creation of a tale and the recreation of a past and forgotten world.

The novel centers around the characters of two brothers, Bernard and George de Mergy, the former a Protestant newly arrived in Paris, the later a Catholic convert, captain in the Royal Guard, and long-time resident of Paris. The tale opens as Bernard, on his way to Paris to join the troops of Admiral Coligny, a powerful Huguenot leader, falls in with a troop of German mercenaries hired by the Huguenots and led by Captain Dietrich Hornstein. While asleep, Bernard is robbed by a gypsy girl traveling with the troops and awakens to find himself with little money and no horse. He does, however, make his way to Paris, where he meets his brother George and the latter's noble friends. They tell Bernard of some of the major social figures and customs of the city, after which George finds Bernard some suitable lodgings, clothing, and a good horse.

Bernard then pays a visit to Admiral Coligny. While he is there a mysterious messenger delivers a letter to the admiral which his aides believe may be poisoned. Bernard opens the envelope and finds that this is not the case, but his bravery is later rewarded with a cornet's commission.

The next day George takes Bernard to a royal hunt, where the latter sees again and falls in love with a beautiful and much admired lady of the court, Countess Diane de Turgis. The countess, however, is considered the probable mistress of the Count of Comminges. When Comminges jostles Bernard, the latter is persuaded to challenge him to a duel. Although Comminges is an accomplished swordsman, Bernard kills him and thus acquires some good fame in courtly society. Through the countess' influence he also receives a royal pardon for murdering his adversary.

Some time later the affair between Bernard and the countess begins in earnest when she sends for him by messenger and appears to him disguised as a Spanish lady. The disguise, however, does not deceive Bernard, and soon all the court is aware that the young Huguenot has won the Catholic countess as his mistress.

Meanwhile the king, although outwardly friendly to the Huguenots and their leader Coligny, is secretly more and more incensed that the admiral should be able to exert such power. At first he calls upon George to attempt to assassinate Coligny, but George refuses as a point of honor. The task is eventually accomplished by one Maurevel two days before the massacre, and is one of the events which stirs up the populace of Paris to a point where such a massacre becomes possible. When George, with his company, is ordered to take part in the mass murders, he resigns his captaincy and goes to warn Bernard of the king's plans.

George finds Bernard at the home of Countess de Turgis. The latter, knowing of the massacre plans but sworn to secrecy, tries in vain to convert Bernard to Catholicism. By the time George arrives and Bernard realizes what is happening, it is too late to escape. The countess hides both brothers, but George is discovered and imprisoned for disobeying orders. Bernard escapes a few days later, disguised as a monk, and meets Captain Hornstein in a similar disguise. The two make their way to La Rochelle, where they join other Huguenot forces in resisting the king. When Bernard's company ambushes a detachment of the Royal Guard, Bernard wounds its leader not knowing that the man is his brother. Hospitalization comes too late and George dies less than two hours afterward. The subsequent royal siege of La Rochelle and the return of peace are mentioned in passing at the end of the novel.

> But did Mergy console himself? And did Diane take another lover? I leave these questions to the decision of the reader, who can thus in every case suit the conclusion of the story to his own taste.[31]

In the matter of time limitations Scribe had a slightly easier time with the *Chronique* than with the novels of Scott or Dumas. The Scott novels are lengthy narratives highlighting numerous key incidents in tales which are drawn out over a number of years, whereas Merimée's *Chronique* covers only a few months. Nevertheless, a great deal of telescoping is necessary to bring the action into the space of two-and-one-half days. This task is made easier by Scribe's typical technique of a delayed-action plot for the drama as a whole and for each separate act. By the time the opera begins Raoul (Bernard) has already arrived in Paris, has been awarded the cornet's grade, and has met and fallen in love with a mysterious woman. Between Acts I and II Marguerite has made arrangements for Valentine's marriage to Raoul and has had the latter brought to her chateau. Between Acts II and III Valentine has married Nevers and plans are afoot for a duel between Saint-Bris and Raoul. Previously mentioned plans for the massacre are finalized between Acts III and IV, and between the fourth and the final acts the major part of the massacre has taken place.

There are few exact equivalents of the novel's main characters in the opera. Rather, most of Scribe's personae combine traits of several of Merimée's people. The only more-or-less direct transfers are the characters of Bernard de Mergy and Diane de Turgis, who become Scribe's Raoul and Valetine. However, whereas Raoul and Bernard are quite similar, Valentine is quite different from Diane. No mere daughter of a nobleman and lady-in-waiting, Diane is pictured as a strong-willed, self-sufficient, and very worldly member of the court in her own right. Yet she is, like Valentine, the hero's love interest—even though Valentine marries someone else—and her physical appearance has something in common with that of Valentine. In addition to being stunningly beautiful, Diane is described as one who "had skin of a dazzling whiteness and eyes of dark blue."[32] Again: "Her complexion, of dazzling whiteness, but tinged by no colour anywhere, set off her jet black hair; and her arched eyebrows, just meeting in the midst, gave to her expression an air of hardness, or rather of pride, without destroying her features as a whole."[33] In *Les Huguenots* Raoul's famed Act I *romance* begins:

> Whiter than the white ermine,
> Purer than a day in springtime,
> An angel, a divine virgin,
> The sight of her dazzles my senses.

The similarity of such prominent descriptions is surely no coincidence.

Although the person of Bernard's brother George is not included in *Les Huguenots*, his traits and actions appear in those of other Scribe characters. George's relationship to Bernard in matters of religion—opposing the latter's Protestantism with his own Catholicism—and his subsequent death at the hands of his brother find parallels in the actions of Scribe's Valentine. The latter is also a Catholic, the hero's nearest opposite number in matters of religious, who is killed in the massacre, albeit by her father rather than by the hero. Although the parallels are not strict, there is a definite and perceptible connection between these items in the novel and those in the opera.

Others of George's traits are taken over into the characters of Marcel and Nevers. Marcel's willingness to protect Raoul and to fight beside him in the Act III duel are actions performed by George in the *Chronique*. The character of Nevers is much more strongly related to that of George. Like George, Nevers is responsible for presenting the young Huguenot (Raoul-Bernard) to court society; and like George, Nevers refuses to participate in the massacre. In Act IV, iii, the following piece of dialogue occurs.

Nevers.

Let us strike the enemies, but not [when they are] defenseless;
It is not the dagger that should pierce their breasts.

Saint-Bris

When the king commands it!

Nevers.

He commands me in vain
To eliminate honor and bravery from my blood.
(Pointing to the portraits hung about the room)
And among these ancestors whose glory surrounds me
I count soldiers, and not one assassin!

Saint-Bris

What! By you our cause is betrayed and foiled!

Nevers.

No! But I am saving my sword from dishonor.
(He breaks it.)
Take it! Here it is! May God be our judge!

A direct parallel to this is found in Merimée.

"And am I expected to lend my hand to cut the throats of sleeping men?"

"Are you a Catholic, and do you acknowledge Charles IX as your King? . . ."

. . . . . . . . . . . . . . . . . . . . . . . . . . . . . . . . .

"My troopers will never do the work of assassins!" said George, . . .

"There is no question of assassination," said the priest coolly. "The matter concerns heretics; and what is to be done is to execute justice on them."

. . . . . . . . . . . . . . . . . . . . . . . . . . . . . . . . .

"Silence in the ranks!" thundered the captain. "No one but I has the right to give orders to these troopers. Comrades, this wretch's words cannot be true, and had the King himself ordered it, my troopers would never slay defenceless [*sic*] men."

The soldiers were silent, but Maurevel and his companion shouted together, "Long live the King!" "Death to the Huguenots!" And the troopers an instant later echoed "Long live the King!" "Death to the Huguenots!"

"Well, captain, will you obey?" said Maurevel.

"I am no longer captain!" cried George, tearing off his collar and scarf, the insignia of his rank.[34]

As Nevers is killed trying to save Marcel, so George is killed when he tries to come to the aid of Béville, an old friend.

If George's characteristics form the more admirable side of Scribe's Nevers, those of Comminges also contribute to the nobleman's traits. As Bernard wins Comminges' desired mistress, Diane, so Raoul wins the heart if not the hand of Nevers' fiancée, Valentine. The "young man about town" quality of Comminges is also preserved in Nevers.

Like Nevers, Scribe's Marcel (or, rather, Deschamps' Marcel) is also a composite figure. No mere substitute for Merimée's Admiral Coligny, he is rather a combination of George, the Admiral, Captain Hornstein, and perhaps even Bernard's father. His only real similarity to the Admiral lies in his function as a partiarchal figure among the Huguenots. In his Act I song ("Pif paf pouf") Marcel reveals some attitudes expressed by Captain Hornstein in the *Chronique.* Compare, for example, the two passages below.

Down with the cursed convents!
Let monks be struck to the ground!
Down with their rich habits!
Into the fire with their breviary!
Into the fire their splendid edifices,
Impure retreats!
The papists! Let us overwhelm them,
Let us strike them,
May they sob!
May they die!
But mercy . . . never!

. . . Mergy began again:

"Why did they hang you, captain?"

"For a mere trifle; a miserable convent in Saintonge that was sacked, and then burnt by accident."

"But the monks had not all got out of it," interrupted the cornet, roaring with laughter at his own wit.

"Well, what does it matter whether such rascals burn a little sooner or a little later?"

. . . . . . . . . . . . . . . . . . . . . . . . . . . . . . . . . . . . . . .

"Ah, what a sack was at the said town of Longnac! My mouth waters at the mere thought of it."

. . . . . . . . . . . . . . . . . . . . . . . . . . . . . . . . . . . . . . .

"What a time we had with the nuns of the great convent!" said the cornet . . .

> "'Twas there too," cried the captain, "that 'twas pretty to see our *argoulets* watering their horses with priests' chasubles on their backs, our horses eating their oats off the altar, and ourselves drinking the priests' good wine in their silver chalices."[35]

Although the father of Bernard and George does not appear in Merimée's novel, he is described in such a way that he appears the model of sternness and doctrinal severity in his Calvinist beliefs. These traits are also prominently displayed in the figure of Marcel, particularly as he appears in the first act.

Scribe's Marguerite takes much of her character from Merimée's Diane. Whereas Valentine is Diane's equivalent only in that she is in love with the hero, Marguerite takes on the personality of the countess. It is she, not Valentine, who is the worldly, self-assured court lady, and her elaborate arrangements to bring Raoul to her chateau are an echo of the mysterious circumstances surrounding Bernard's arrival for his first evening meeting with Diane.

Although there is no single parallel to Saint-Bris in the *Chronique*, Maurevel, popularly known as the King's Butcher, comes close, for it is he who assassinates Admiral Coligny and brings George the orders relating to the massacre. Like Merimée's Duke of Guise, Saint-Bris also functions as leader of the Catholics.

Other, minor characters in the opera are also drawn from the novel. Captain Bois-Rosé combines the zest for a merry life exhibited by Merimée's Captain Hornstein with the name of Merimée's Sergeant Belle-Rose, a member of the Catholic army. Even the gypsy fortune-tellers, brought in at the beginning of Act III as a *divertissement*, have their origin in the novel in the character of Mila, a gypsy who tells Bernard's fortune in Chapter I of the *Chronique*.

There are several other events in *Les Huguenots* that are rooted in Merimée's *Chronique*. The opening party scene at Nevers' chateau is similar to the scene which opens the novel, that of Bernard, Captain Hornstein, and the soldiers dining and carousing at an inn. In the course of the party, Scribe's noblemen discuss their various amorous exploits. Similarly, when George introduces Bernard to his friends in Paris, they immediately inform Bernard of the major figures in Paris society and of their reputations, particularly in matters of love. In Act I, vii, of *Les Huguenots* a letter comes to Raoul and the noblemen, recognizing the handwriting as that of Marguerite, immediately become more friendly. In the *Chronique*, two incidents could have served as models for Scribe's scene. Bernard shows some friends a letter he has received from his mysterious lady, the handwriting of which is identified as belonging to one Maria Rodriguez, an elderly lady in the service of Marguerite de

Valois. Earlier in the novel, after Bernard has killed Comminges, he suddenly finds the court circles more kindly disposed to him, several nobles seeking out his favor or friendship.

Although it ends quite differently, the duel between Saint-Bris and Raoul at the Pré-aux-Clercs is Scribe's equivalent of the Bernard-Comminges battle. Before the opera's duel, Valentine warns Marcel of Raoul's danger. So, in the novel, does Diane warn Bernard of Comminges' swordsmanship. There is also something in Valentine's warning of that of Béville to Bernard on the night of the massacre. Valentine tells Marcel, "May he [Raoul] only come to the combat suitably accompanied," and will say no more. Similarly Béville, meeting Bernard in the street, warns: "Cross the Seine, brave friend; that is my last word. If you come to harm by neglecting my advice, I wash my hands of it."[36] Although the situations and some of the characters involved are quite different, there is something of the same quality in the warnings and the conditions under which they are given.

The famous fourth act of *Les Huguenots* is also, quite amazingly, modeled on situations in the novel: amazingly, because parts of the act were not Scribe's idea. Yet the act as a whole telescopes and rearranges two scenes from the novel as closely as one might expect in any such adaptation. In the *Chronique* Merimée relates the following events. George (not Bernard-Raoul) is told by Maurevel and a priest (Saint-Bris and the monks) of the massacre and is assigned a particular area. After leaving his company, George goes to warn Bernard and finds him, like Scribe's Raoul, with his mistress. Meanwhile Diane, who also knows of the massacre, tries to save Raoul by converting him to Catholicism. By the time George arrives the massacre has already begun and escape is impossible. In *Les Huguenots* Valentine tries to convert Raoul to Catholicism to save his life (Act V) and Raoul leaves Valentine (Act IV) after the fighting has begun. It is the combination of several characters, actions, and incidents into one continuous dramatic line that characterizes Scribe's adaptation technique in general and this fourth act in particular.

From the preceding discussion it can readily be seen that Scribe's use of Merimée's novel for *Les Huguenots* cannot be written off. Although externally the two tales may differ considerably, closer analysis reveals that the majority of the characters and incidents in the opera have roots in Merimée's tale.

Artz has written that Merimée's *Chronique*

> . . . is really nothing but a series of pictures which [Merimée] attempts to hold together by carrying a love intrigue through the events of the Massacre of St. Bartholomew. On finishing the novel one finds it hard to decide what is the subject of the book. . . . If

> the book has a leading idea, it is that, beneath the superficial differences of Catholics and Protestants, love and ambition are the real motives of men.[37]

This description could be applied to *Les Huguenots* as well.

In bringing history to the stage of the Opéra Scribe has, of course, treated it imaginatively. More specifically, he has eliminated certain key figures in the actual massacre (Catherine de' Medici, Admiral Coligny), replacing them with others (Saint-Bris, Marcel) who serve similar functions in the plot but who are wholly fictitious. Moreover, he has made the historical event not the subject for the opera but a background of activity against which the tale of Raoul and Valentine is played. In doing so he was soundly criticized for having demeaned the historical event.[38] However, such critics fail to take into account that *Les Huguenots* is opera, not history. Written history can be expansive, can describe events, analyze their causes, and deal with the motivation of leaders. One way that so short and simple a dramatic form as an opera libretto could present history was to focus on two characters, one from each of the opposing sides, who could not only personalize the historical conflict but who could sing soprano and tenor arias as well. Without Raoul, Valentine, Marcel, Nevers, and Saint-Bris we would be left with nothing but large crowds of people, with a few leaders engaged in political rhetoric and diplomatic dealings. The dramatic result would hardly be interesting, and the musical result would verge on oratorio. Perhaps Rameau would have been willing to set a newspaper—or in this case a historical chronicle—to music, but even in his time few would have paid the price of admission to hear it nor have been so struck by the events thus presented.

## Words, Music, and Spectacle

By the time Scribe and his multitude of collaborators and sidewalk superintendents had finished with the libretto of *Les Huguenots*, they had produced a work that was both a continuation of the developments seen in *Robert le Diable* and *Gustave III* and a solidification of the generic traits of the grand opera libretto. In *Les Huguenots* grand opera had a composer capable of creating mammoth musical scenes filled with stunning effects, a librettist capable of drawing up those scenes, and a work which in no way relied on the crutch of opéra comique for its structure The subject was grand and based on historical events; the scenic effects were marvelous; the choruses were massive yet moved as groups of real people, not as human scenery; and each principal role was vocally and dramatically demanding.

The key word in this final crystallization of the genre is *tableau.* In *Robert le Diable* the influence of the visual tableau made itself felt especially in those portions of the opera not directly derived from the original opéra comique plan. For these scenes Meyerbeer created large-scale but relatively static musical numbers in which the spectator's sense of sight was called upon just as much as was his sense of hearing in order to appreciate fully the opera's dramatic power. In *Les Huguenots* this process is complete: the scenic tableau and the musical tableau replace the simple set-number as the dramatic unit into which the opera is subdivided. Because *Robert* is such a mixture of new ideas with previously developed Scribean traits, no real definition of a new genre emerges. With *Les Huguenots* both musical and dramatic traits of grand opera have reached that point of consistency at which a distinct pattern appears and particular traits of a new musico-dramatic form can be defined more fully.

The chart below outlines the musical numbers in *Les Huguenots* and a brief description of the action in each. Again, broken lines across the page indicate final cadences, and the sometimes superficial divisions produced point up the fact that Meyerbeer is indeed working in large scenic units.[39] Each unit has a theatrical point of focus, one which often forms a striking contrast to that of the scenes preceding and following it. The simplest and clearest example is Act IV, in which the three musical numbers focus successively on Valentine's personal dilemma, the madly grandiose preparation for the massacre, and the conflict between love and duty in the mind of Raoul.

Key to abbreviations:

R - Raoul
M - Marcel
S - Saint-Bris
N - Nevers
Nob - Catholic nobles
B - Bois-Rosé
V - Valentine
Marg - Marguerite
U - Urbain
Cho - Chorus

| Number | Form or technique | Action involved |
|---|---|---|
| | | ACT I |
| 1 a. | *Ouverture* | Orchestral. |
| b. | Introduction (N, Nob) | Soli and cho in praise of youth, pleasure. |
| c. | *Morceau d'ensemble et entrée de Raoul* (N, R, Nob) | N announces R, a Huguenot, is expected and should be well received because of king's plan to reconcile religious factions. R feels honored to be included. |
| d. | *Choeur d'orgie* (N, R, Nob) | Drinking chorus. |
| | Recit (N, R, Nob) | Nob talk of love adventures. R admits he loves someone whose name he does not know. |
| 2 | *Scène et romance* (R) | R tells of saving woman's life, describes her beauty. |
| 3 | Recit and chorale (N, R, M, Nob) | M shocked to see R with Nob, sings "Ein feste Burg" to get his attention and warn him of danger. |
| - - - | - - - | - - - |
| 4 | *Scène et Chanson Huguenot* (N, R, M, Nob) | A Nob recognizes M as one who wounded him. M responds to requests and sings Huguenot battle song. |
| - - - | - - - | - - - |
| | [Recit] | Valet announces woman to see N. |
| 5 | *Morceau d'ensemble* (R, M, Nob) | Men speculate on woman's identity. R recognizes her. Nob show mock pity; R is angry. |
| | [Recit] | N tells a few friends of broken engagement. |
| 6 | Finale | |
| a. | *Choeur* (Nob) | In praise of N's gallantry. U brings letter from a lady. N thinks letter is for him, but U gives it to R. R reads aloud. Nob, recognizing Marg's writing, become friendly to R. R is astonished. M sees victory for Huguenot cause. |
| b. | *Cavatine du Page* (U) | |
| c. | *Suite du Finale* (U, R, N, M, Nob) | |
| - - - | - - - | - - - |

## ACT II

| | | |
|---|---|---|
| 7 | *Entr' acte et Air* (Marg) [Recit] [Trio (Marg, U, a lady-in-waiting)] and continuation of air with U and 2 ladies. | General text in praise of countryside, fine weather. Marg is tired of religious squabbles. Love should reign in all hearts. |
| | [Recit] | V reports N's agreement to break engagement. M tells of planned marriage of V and R. |
| 8 | *Choeur des Baigneuses* | Ladies swim in river, sing of pleasures in such amusements. |
| | [Recit] | U announces arrival of R. |
| 9 | *Scène du Bandeau* (R, Marg, U, cho) | Cho comments on R and his mission as R is led in blindfolded. Marg sends all others away. |
| | [Recit] | R removes blindfold, wonders where he is. |
| 10 | Duo (Marg, R) | Flirtation scene. |
| 11 | Recit and *Entrée de la cour* (Marg, U, R, S, N, Nob, cho) | U announces arrival of court and R discovers Marg's identity. R agrees to marry S's daughter. Cho of honor to Marg. Marg asks all to swear peace and friendship. |
| 12 | Finale | |
| a. | *Serment* (R, S, N, M, Nob) | All swear eternal friendship. |
| b. | *Scène* (same, V) | Marg presents V as R's bride. R refuses to marry her. |
| c. | *Stretta* (same) | Reactons of all. Marg stops Nob from revenge. |

## ACT III

| | | |
|---|---|---|
| 13 | *Entr'acte et Choeur* | *Choeur des promeneurs* enjoying leisurely Sunday afternoon. |

| | | | |
|---|---|---|---|
| 14 | a. | *Couplets militaires des soldats huguenots* (B, cho) | Soldiers confident of victory. |
| | b. | *Litanies* (women's cho) | Cho of Catholic women praying to Virgin Mary and accompanying V to chapel. |
| | c. | *Morceau d'ensemble* (B, M, S, triple cho) | Combined cho of Huguenot soldiers (14a), Catholic women (14b), people. |
| 15 | | *Ronde bohémienne* (two Gypsies) | Gypsies arrive to tell fortunes, entertain people. |
| 16 | | *Danse bohémienne* (ballet) | Orchestral. |
| | | [Recit] | N has just married V, has left her in chapel to pray. M delivers R's challenge to S, who accepts it. |
| 17 | | *Le Couvre-feu* (a crier, cho) | Curfew announced. All people leave stage. |
| | | [Recit] | S and a Nob agree to bring friends and meet later to attack R. |
| 18 | | *Scène et Duo* (V, M) | V warns M of R's danger. M blesses her. |
| | | [Recit] | M tries to warn R, but he ignores it. |
| 19 | | *Septuor du duel* (M, R, S, Nob) | Duel begins. S's friends arrive to attack R. |
| | | [Recit] | M defends R, calls for help. |
| 20 | | *Choeur de la dispute* (same, cho) | People, soldiers, students return, take sides. |
| | | *Scène* (same, Marg and train) | Marg stops fight. R learns of V's warning to M. |
| 21 | | Finale (same) | R learns truth about V and that she is now married to N. |
| | | *Le Cortège de noces* (N, cho, dancers) | N arrives to escort V. Gypsies, others dance, celebrate marriage. Mixed reactions from all sides. |

ACT IV

| | | |
|---|---|---|
| 22 | *Entr'acte,* recit and *romance* (V) | V is troubled, still loves R. |
| | Recit (V, R) | R wants to see V again. Someone comes. R hides. |
| | Recit (S, N, V, Nob) | S announces plans for massacre. |
| 23 | *Conjuration et bénédiction des poignards* (same, monks, cho) | Nob swear to carry out plans. V is shocked. N refuses to join, breaks sword. S and Nob continue to make plans. V tries to think of a way to save R. Monks bless weapons. Monks, nuns, Nob look forward to victory, will meet again at midnight. |
| 24 | *Grand duo* (R, V) | R wants to warn friends, but V fears for lives of S and N, admits she still loves R. Massacre begins. R leaves to join Huguenots. |

ACT V

| | | |
|---|---|---|
| 25 | *Entr'acte et ballet* | Orchestral. Celebration of Marg's wedding. |
| 26 | Recit and Air (R, cho) | R tells Huguenot leaders about massacre. They leave join fight. |
| 27 | *Scène et grand trio* (M, V, R, cho) | M wounded, sees no hope of victory. V offers R plan to save his life; he rejects it. V decides to stay with R and convert to Protestantism. |
| a. | *Trio* | M blesses R and V. |
| b. | *Choeur des meurtriers* (same, double cho) | Catholics murder Huguenots in church offstage while R, V, M comment. |
| c. | *Vision* (M, R, V) | M sees heavens opening to receive martyrs. M, R, V prepare to die. Soldiers come for them. |
| 28 | *Scène final* (same, S, Cho, Nob) | Catholics kill M, R, V. S discovers V as she is dying. |

To say that the structure of *Les Huguenots* and other grand operas is based on a mosaic-like succession of strong emotional or theatrical contrasts is only to deal in surface impressions. Basically, the musical numbers in this opera fall into one of three categories: dramatic tableau, scenic tableau, and set-number. A few sections of recitative fall outside these categories. The classifications are not rigid ones, for some scenic tableaux may contain a small amount of action and some dramatic tableaux may be static enough at times, particularly at their endings, to border on the scenic.

In a dramatic tableau the primary accent is on action, but it is action of a different sort from that in spoken drama or even in opéra comique. Events move very slowly, for the musical divisions are large and center on one or two focal points. Normally the action in a dramatic tableau can be summarized in one or two sentences, yet the scene may last for dozens of pages in the score. At least a portion of the dramatic tableau's effectiveness is attributable to the exploitation of visual movement—as opposed to visual spectacle—and its combination with the clearest, most straightforward text and the most immediately attractive and striking musical setting.

Such a tableau is that in Act II, iv (Nos. 19-20), the duel scene. The action is slight: during a supposedly legitimate duel, Raoul is set upon by Saint-Bris' confederates and defended by Marcel; both sides call for aid, and groups of people arrive to join the fray. Yet Meyerbeer takes most of No. 19, some twenty pages in the piano-vocal score, to bring the combatants to the point at which they are actually ready to begin the duel. First, all the men declare their confidence in the rightness of their cause; then Marcel complains that he is too old to be of assistance to Raoul, the four witnesses pace off the dueling field, draw up the ground rules for the fray, and inspect the weapons. Finally all are ready to duel, but then Marcel hears others of Saint-Bris' friends arriving and calls out.

It would be an understatement to say that little has happened in these twenty pages. However, precisely at this point visual aids are called in to give the illusion of action. The audience sees the men mark off the dueling area, observes the weapons drawn and inspected, witnesses all the formalities connected with the ritual of dueling. Surely something momentous is afoot; surely it will break at any moment. Meanwhile, the spectator is like a slow motion camera following the players through an exciting tenth inning, bases loaded, score tied.

Here is no neat alternation of action and repose as in the typical opéra comique ensemble scene. Rather, librettist and composer work out a gradual intensification of the dramatic pace from relatively modest beginnings to a mammoth scene of confused near-riot. In this build-up the static qualities of Meyerbeer's music are an asset. Meyereer moves from one idea to the next, but does not develop any single motive or set of motives. Thus the listener always knows where he is: if the music changes, the action is moving forward; if it remains the same, nothing is happening and he can sit back and listen. So in this scene Raoul and the Catholic nobles begin with an ensemble based on a swaggering melody (Example 56a) which is repeated whole and in fragments by the six men for thirty-seven measures with little variation or relief. While the men pace off the dueling area Marcel sings in his usual Sarastro-like manner (Example 56b), after which the four witnesses lay the ground rules for the duel in an antiphonal section rhythmically similar to the opening of the number but devoid of melodic interest (Example 56c). Meyerbeer combines Marcel's plaints with a continuation of the business by the four witnesses, then returns to his opening material and adds a coda as the duel is about to begin. The call for help and the arrival of the Huguenot soldiers bring back Marcel's chorale and the previously heard "Rataplan" chorus. Meyerbeer has set each new event in a way that is immediately striking and effective, that at once tells the spectator where he is, yet carries him nowhere.

**Example 56a**

**Example 56b**

Example 56c

In a scenic tableau not even the illusion of action is necessary, although it may be present. Purely scenic tableaux do nothing more than preset a finely framed picture in which the subjects move. Frequently such tableaux involve spectacle and dance, as in the *Choeur des Baigneuses* of Act II or the opening numbers of Act III. In both cases large numbers of people are on the stage, colorfully costumed, moving against pleasant, unusual, or even spectacular scenery, but they do nothing to further the main plot of the opera. Often a tableau that is essentially dramatic may end as this kind of framed picture. Such, for example, is the Blessing of the Daggers scene in Act IV. Once the monks have blessed the weapons the participants do nothing but sing *fortissimo* for several pages, then depart to regroup at midnight. Such little action as exists in this scene is thus musically and dramatically frozen for the contemplation of the spectator.

The few set-numbers that occur outside the major tableaux of *Les Huguenots* are not unusual formally. For example, Raoul's *scène et romance* (No. 2) is nothing more than an accompanied recitative followed by a strophic song. Internally the song has some unusual features—e.g., the accompaniment by a solo viola d'amore, resulting in a texture and total sound not unworthy of Berlioz,[40] and the virtuosic cadenza passages—but in form and over-all presentation it is quite a conventional component of French opera.

If the musical numbers of *Les Huguenots* are placed in an appropriate category, recognizing a certain amount of flexibility, the following pattern emerges.

| Dramatic tableau | Scenic tableau |
|---|---|
| | Act I, i-iia (No. 1) |
| Act I, iib (No. 2; set-number) | |
| | Act I, iiia (No. 3) |
| Act I, iiib (No. 4; set-number) | |
| Act I, iv-vi (Recit, No. 5) | |
| Act I, vii-end (Recit, No. 6) | |
| | Act II, ia (No. 7) |
| Act II, ib-ii (Recit; not a tableau) | |
| | Act II, iiia (No. 8) |
| Act II, iiib-iva (Recit, No. 9) | |
| | Act II, ivb-v (Recit, No. 10) |
| Act II, vi-viii (Nos. 11-12) | |
| | Act III, ia (Nos. 13-14; 15-16) |
| Act III, ib (Recit; not a tableau) | |
| | Act III, ii (No. 17) |
| Act III, iii-iva (Recit, No. 18) | |
| Act III, ivb (Recit, Nos. 19-20) | |
| | Act III, ivc (No. 21) |
| Act IV, i-ii (No. 22, set-number; recit) | |
| Act IV, iiia (Recit; not a tableau) | |
| Act IV, iiib-v (No. 23) | |
| | Act IV, vi (No. 24) |
| | Act V, i (No. 25) |
| Act V, ii-v (Nos. 26-28) | |

The significance of this sort of division in defining the dramatic structure of the grand opera libretto becomes clear if one traces the course of action only through the dramatic tableaux and the non-tableau recitatives, with some assistance from recitatives preceding the set-numbers. The skeleton that emerges looks something like this.

Act I. Raoul tells of a woman he has met and with whom he has fallen in love. A valet announces that a woman wishes to see Nevers. Raoul discovers she is he woman of whom he spoke and thinks her faithless. Nevers tells of his broken engagement. Raoul receives a letter from Marguerite, which causes the nobles to look on him with more favor. In the letter Raoul learns he is to be taken somewhere blindfolded.

Act II. Valentine tells Marguerite that Nevers has agreed to break their engagement. Marguerite informs her of another marriage planned to cement Catholic and Protestant factions. Raoul arrives and agrees to Marguerite's plan. Catholics and Huguenots swear eternal friendship before the former leave for Paris on an unknown project. Raoul refuses to marry Valentine, thereby insulting the Catholics and arousing the personal animosity of Saint-Bris.

Act III. Nevers emerges from the chapel where he has just married Valentine and has left her to pray. Marcel delivers Raoul's challenge to Saint-Bris, who makes plans to insure Raoul's death. Valentine overhears and warns Marcel. During the duel Saint-Bris' friends arrive and Marcel calls for help. Marguerite stops the battle and Raoul learns the truth about Valentine.

Act IV. Valentine still loves Raoul. The latter, coming to see her, overhears plans for a massacre. He is prevented from leaving by her declaration of love.

Act V. Raoul's report on the massacre to guests at Marguerite's wedding celebration (a remnant of the earlier messenger scenes of classical drama and *tragédie-lyrique*) stirs up the crowd. Nevers dies trying to save Marcel, and Valentine joins Raoul and other Huguenots in martyrdom.

These bare bones of the plot, properly joined by Scribe, constitute nothing more than a less elaborate but no less strong frame for a well-made libretto. Most of the characteristics of this form are preserved intact. The play's point of attack occurs at the climax of a story in which Raoul and Valentine have already fallen in love, Marguerite has already arranged for their marriage, and the Catholic rulers, behind a facade of peace-making, have begun to plan the massacre. The hero's fortunes rise and fall in various points throughout the opera. Each act represents the well-made libretto structure in miniature and ends in a final yet suspense-giving theatrical *coup*. Throughout the work the smooth flow and tight integration of the action is supported by contrived entrances (e.g., Valentine's visit to Nevers, Raoul's visit to Valentine), overhead conversations (Valentine, Act III; Raoul, Act IV), and the careful and logical preparation for each successive event. The central misunderstanding or *quiproquo* is provided by Raoul's misunderstanding of Valentine's actions in Act I. The *scène à faire* occurs when Valentine's real motivation is revealed, and the recognition scene—really two scenes—includes Valentine's decision to remain with the Huguenots and her father's discovery of this fact.

Many critics have felt that Act V of *Les Huguenots* is anti-climatic, that the opera should end with the *grand duo* of Act IV.[41] Perhaps in terms of more recent trends in opera, particularly Italian *verismo*, this belief has some validity. However, in terms of Scribe's technique and the structure he created for this opera, to omit the fifth act would be to destroy a skillfully worked-out libretto and to subvert the writer's intentions. All actions in Act V have been prepared well in advance, and Scribe was not one to leave events up in the air. Today, post-curtain speculation is considered artistically desirable—the playwright should "leave you thinking"—but this was not the case in Scribe's work. Scribe wanted his audiences to think, but he also told them what to think and when to think it. It is precisely this function that is fulfilled by Act V of *Les Huguenots*, bringing this well-made libretto to what was for Scribe a satisfactory conclusion.

If the dramatic tableaux provide *Les Huguenots* with the outline of the well-made libretto, the scenic tableaux give it more substance. They embellish the story with flashes of color, blazes of sound, masses of participants, all keyed to provide the greatest enjoyment for the greatest number. As a group they present far more variety than do the dramatic tableaux. The conventional carousing nobles, the fresh country scenes, the colorful parade of Sunday *promeneurs*, the fanatical solemnity of the Blessing of the Daggers, Marguerite's ball provide the opera with a kind of dual structure. On the one level there is the basis provided by the well-made libretto, while on a second level there emerge the bright-hued contrasts of one theatrical *coup* with the next. Observers have often been so overwhelmed by this second level structure that they have failed to recognize the first. Yet both are equally valid, for without either one the genre of grand opera would have lost its particular traits.

There are many parallels between *Les Huguenots* and later works by Scribe and other librettists. Most interesting is that between Meyerbeer's opera and Auber's opéra comique, *La Barcarolle*, for many of the situations of the latter are like those in *Les Huguenots*. In *La*

*Barcarolle* there is the love affair between the Count and the daughter of a member of an opposing political faction; the situation of Fabio (Raoul) saving the life of an unknown woman (Gina-Valentine) in a carriage, falling in love with her, then believing her faithless; the scene in which Fabio (Raoul), hidden, overhears the details of a political conspiracy by the enemy (the Marquis-Saint-Bris) in time to act upon this information; and the invitation of an unknown young man (Fabio-Raoul) to court circles. It should be noted that none of the situations mentioned is derived from the *comédie-vaudeville* on which the plot of *La Barcarolle* is based.

Scribe's libretti for Donizetti's *Les Martyrs* and *La Favorite*, Gounod's *La Nonne sanglante*, and Verdi's *Les Vêpres siciliennes* also contain situations similar to those in *Les Huguenots*. *Les Martyrs* has a similar plot. Pauline, wife of Polyeucte, is still in love with Sévère, to whom she was once engaged. She is converted to Christianity by her husband and with him becomes a martyr for her faith. Punishment of the Christians is carried out by Félix, Pauline's father, and Sévère. Act I of *La Favorite*, beginning with Scene iii, is similar to the opening of Act II of *Les Huguenots*. The setting is the bank of a river, where Leonore's attendants are enjoying the fine country weather. Fernand (Raoul), who has been blindfolded and brought to this estate, has fallen in love with Léonore (Valentine), though he is unaware of her true identity. When he finally learns she has been the king's mistress he rejects her, but in the meantime she, like Marguerite in *Les Huguenots*, becomes his protectress.

In both *La Nonne sanglante* and *Les Vêpres sicilienes* a marriage is planned to help cement previously warring factions. The cast of *La Nonne sanglante* also includes a page named Urbain. *Les Vêpres siciliennes* is even closer to *Les Huguenots*. Like Valentine and Saint-Bris, Henri and Montfort, his father, are on opposing sides in political matters. The latter, hoping to win his son's love and at the same time insure peace, tries to arrange a marriage between Henri and Hélène, one of the leaders of the opposition to Montfort's government. Hélène, however, refuses to marry Henri even though she loves him, because he is Montfort's son and because she later learns that their wedding will be the signal for the start of the revolution in which both Henri and Montfort are likely to be killed. Like *Les Huguenots*, the *Vêpres* ends in a massacre of unarmed people.

Two other Verdi works end similarly to *Les Huguenots*. In *Rigoletto* the title character discovers that his own daughter has become the victim of his plot to kill the Duke, and in *Il Trovatore* Azucena reveals to the Count di Luna that Manrico, whom he has murdered, is not her son but his own brother. Scribe's *La Juive* concludes similarly.

*Les Huguenots* not just another in a succession of grand operas but rather illustrates the emergence of grand opera as a genre unto itself. Externally Scribe has created a varicolored theatrical mosaic of dramatic and scenic contrasts supported by the simplified but recognizable skeletal substructure of the well-made libretto. Internally, the set number has been replaced largely by the musico-dramatic or scenic tableau in which individual set-numbers may or may not have a part. Subjects are historical, casts huge, spectacle exploited to the fullest. Music is massive, demanding, virtuosic, eclectic, effective theatre. Grand opera thus emerges as the product of first-rate talents in all areas: composition, performance, writing, directing, scene designing, management, even applause-gathering. In the hands of any less than the best it could not endure.

# HISTORICAL OPERA: MEYERBEER'S *LE PROPHETE*

> *Le Prophète*! This great work of art, so long awaited, of which the very existence had finally been in doubt, and which so many times had amused the spare time of the press, *Le Prophète* has finally been revealed! For anyone other than the author of *Robert le Diable* and *Les Huguenots* these long delays in bringing out a work [—so long] that it almost passed into the state of myth [—] would have tired the public's attention. . . . But the public has no rancor for Meyerbeer; it treats him like a lover whose return causes his infidelities to be forgotten.[1]

So wrote critic François Fétis, without exaggeration, of the long-awaited premiere of Meyerbeer's penultimate grand opera on April 16, 1849. As early as 1837 plans for the opera had been announced[2] and by 1838 Meyerbeer had the complete libretto,[3] save for the inevitable changes and additions to be made before the opening night curtain rose. The first version of the score was finished by 1840 but not performed because Léon Pillet, then director of the Opéra, did not have a company suitable to the demands of the work. Only when Roqueplan and Duponchel assumed directorship in 1847 were Pauline Viardot and Roger engaged for the roles of Fidès and Jean, respectively,[4] and not until November 1848 did Berlioz report: ". . . Meyerbeer has begun rehearsing his *Prophète*: he is a courageous man to risk launching a work of such dimensions at a time when riots or a change of government can cut him short, however great his eloquence."[5]

Meanwhile Scribe himself was having his difficulties with Pillet. As early as 1838 Scribe had signed a contract for *Le Duc d'Albe*, an opera for Halévy which the latter did not set. Donizetti eventually took over this libretto, but performance of his opera was postponed repeatedly.[6] To replace *Le Duc d'Albe* Scribe and Donizetti agreed to produce *Jeanne la folle* in 1843, but Pillet had not liked the scenario.[7] By this time Scribe had become so angered at Pillet that he not only sued him to recover fees for the contracted work but determined not to write for the Opéra until Pillet had been replaced.[8]

Once a new administration was installed at the Opéra, once a suitable cast had been assembled, once the tremors of 1848 had subsided, and once librettist and composer had made changes in the original work to suit the new performers, *Le Prophète* was performed with the expected success. Within a year the work had been heard on forty stages, and within somewhat over two years it had enjoyed one hundred performances at the Opéra, where it was given until 1912.[9] So popular was the opera that transcriptions of the music were soon made for piano, two and four hands; two violins; one violin; two flutes; one flute; and even flageolet; and Berlioz was moved to exclaim: "When one dreams that there exist in the world beings in human form desirous of possessing the score of *Le Prophète transcribed* (the word is marvelous) for a flageolet!!!"[10]

## The Libretto as History

The first act of *Le Prophète* is set in the vicinity of Dordrecht in Holland, where peasants are gathering for their morning meal and enjoying the fine weather. Berthe enters, happy and excited that today Fidès, her future mother-in-law, is coming to take her away and that tomorrow she is to be married to Jean. Fides arrives, but Berthe cannot leave until she has permission from the ruling noble, Count Oberthal. As she is about to leave to find the Count, three Anabaptists—Jonas, Mathisen, and Zacharie—arrive and preach against the injustices the peasants must suffer at the hands of their rulers. The peasants, believing the Anabaptists correct, arm themselves with clubs and farm implements and begin to move toward the chateau. Just then Oberthal and some nobles emerge. Their appearance frightens the peasants, who hide their weapons and greet the Count with respect. The Count recognizes in Jonas an employee he discharged earlier for dishonesty, and he threatens to have all three Anabaptists hung if they come into the area again. Berthe comes forward to ask permission to marry Jean. Oberthal is impressed enough with Berthe's sweetness and beauty to want to keep her for himself, and Fidès tries in vain to persuade the peasants to demand justice for the girl. In the background the song of the Anabaptists is heard.

Act II takes place in Leyden, at an inn owned by Jean and his mother. Jean serves refreshments to the dancing villagers and is beginning to worry that Fidès and Berthe have not arrived. The crowd at the inn includes the three Anabaptists, who see in Jean a remarkable likeness to the image of Kind David at Münster. From the peasants the Anabaptists learn that Jean is brave and devout and that he knows the Bible by memory, and they conclude that he is the man they need to carry out their plans. When the villagers leave, Jean tells the three men of a dream he has had twice, in which he is in a vast cathedral wearing a crown and standing before a worshiping crowd who call him the Messiah, the Son of God; the scene then perishes in flames and he hears himself cursed by all but one. The Anabaptists try to convince him that his dream can become reality, but he replies that he only wishes to marry Berthe and lead a quiet, happy life. He breathes a sigh of relief when the three men leave but his peace is short-lived, for Berthe rushes in begging protection from Oberthal and the soldiers who are following her. She hides just as they enter. When Jean will not reveal her hiding place, Oberthal threatens to kill Fidès, whom he has captured, and Jean reluctantly delivers Berthe into his hands.

Jean now realizes how defenseless people of his station are against the arbitrary will of the nobility and vows to avenge this wrong. When the Anabaptists return he agrees to impersonate the expected Messiah before the Anabaptists in Germany, convinced that God has called him.

In a forest in Westphalia, where Act III takes place, the Anabaptist soldiers have won a battle and have taken prisoner several nobles and Catholic religious from whom they hope to obtain large ransoms. Over the frozen pond people from the area arrive on ice-skates bearing provisions for the war-weary soldiers. Night falls, and the scene changes to the interior of Zacharie's tent, where Mathisen reports that they must take Münster quickly, before the newly dispatched troops of the emperor can arrive to defeat them. Zacharie orders Mathisen to take some soldiers and march on Münster in the name of the Prophet Jean, who by this time has become a popular idol.

Jonas arrives with Oberthal, who pretends to have come to join the army in order to get to Münster, where his father is governor. Jonas and Zacharie recognize him once a lamp is lit, and Zacharie orders him executed on the spot.

Jean enters to tell Zacharie of his decision to return to Leyden. Seeing Oberthal being led to execution without his permission, Jean stops the soldiers and recognizes his former adversary. Oberthal reveals that Berthe, rather than sacrifice her virtue, tried to drown herself but that he has heard she is alive in Münster and was going there to beg her forgiveness. Jean orders Oberthal imprisoned, then concludes that God has chosen this means to tell him that he should go on to Münster. Mathisen reports that a detachment of Anabaptist soldiers has been defeated at Münster and urges Jean to lead them to victory once more.

The scene changes to the Anabaptist camp, where some rebellious soldiers are talking against Jean, saying that he lied when he promised them they would be able to take Münster. Jean appears, angry that the army attacked the city without his permission, and reprimands them for their lack of faith. He prays that God will forgive them. Stirred up once more, the soldiers sing a triumphal hymn and Jean sees a celestial vision predicting their victory.

Act IV begins in a public square of Münster. The bourgeoisie of that city, although they publicly acclaim the Prophet and his army, are privately angry that they are being forced to support these new tyrants or be killed. Rumor has it that the Prophet is to be crowned King of the Anabaptists in Münster Cathedral later in the day. Fidès arrives dressed as a beggar, asking alms to have a Mass said for a son whom she believes dead. Another pilgrim enters and Fidès is surprised to find that it is Berthe. The latter has come to Münster to find her only living relative, an elderly uncle who is employed as a palace guard. She despairs when Fidès tells her Jean has been killed by the Prophet. Berthe determines to kill the supposed murderer and at the same time deliver Germany of a tyrant.

The scene changes to Münster Cathedral, were Jean is being crowned king. In the crowd Fidès prays that Berthe will carry out her plan, but when Jean appears she recognizes that the Prophet is her son. Mathisen threatens to kill Fidès if Jean admits the truth, since Jean is supposed to have descended from God and to have had no human parents. Jean denies before the crowd that he is the woman's son. When the Anabaptists want to kill her as a blasphemer, however, Jean prevents them, saying that Fidès must simply be mad and should be left in peace. Finally Jean forces her to say that he is not her son by asking that the Anabaptists kill him as an impostor should she again swear her statement is true. As Jean proceeds out of the cathedral Fidès wonders how she will be able to find Berthe in time to stop her from killing the Prophet, while the people hail the "miracle" of Fidès' restored sanity.

In a vaulted room beneath the palace of Münster, where the fifth act begins, Jonas, Zacharie, and Mathisen are discussing the danger of the emperor's approaching armies. Jonas reveals that the troops will not harm them if only they turn over Jean. The other two agree that this is a wise course and depart.

Fidès is escorted into the room by some soldiers. Not knowing where she is, she fears that this imprisonment will prevent her from finding Berthe, but she soon learns that it is Jean who has sent for her. Jean has come to beg forgiveness, but Fidès can only remind him that he is an impostor and has shed innocent blood in religious warfare. She demands that he renounce his past deeds, saying that God will forgive him if he repents. Jean promises to do this.

Berthe enters. She has been admitted by her uncle and plans to set fire to some explosives in the palace to kill the Prophet and his associates. An officer runs in with news that some traitors have let enemy troops into the castle and calls upon Jean, the Prophet, to do something about them. Discovering that Jean is the Prophet, Berthe curses him for the evil he has done and stabs herself. Jean determines to stay in the palace and punish the guilty, but urges Fidès to leave at once and save herself.

In the great hall of the palace Jean and the other Anabaptists are carousing to celebrate their victory. The three traitors determine to distract Jean by drink so that he will not suspect that they have admitted the enemy troops. Amid the revelry Jean gives orders to some faithful soldiers to carry out his plans. The emperor's soldiers arrive to claim Jean, but before they can seize him an explosion fells the walls and flames shoot up from all sides, trapping traitors and tyrants alike. At that moment Fidès arrives to pardon her son and die with him.

*Le Prophète*, unlike *Les Huguenots*, is a historical opera based only on suggestions taken from descriptions of the events themselves, not on a novelist's conception of these events.[11] The historical John of Leyden (1509-1536) was a disciple of the Anabaptist preacher Jan Matthys, who believed "that the advent of the New Jerusalem could no longer be patiently awaited, but must be achieved at once, and, if necessary, by force."[12] John was an uneducated tailor with a creative mind who even engaged in writing poetry and dramas before he was won over by Anabaptism at the age of twenty-four. The same year (1533), believing himself to be divinely inspired, he went to preach at Münster, the capital of Westphalia, where people from the lower classes had become discouraged with the small role accorded them in the government of even so relatively democratic a city. In 1534, fearing revolution, the ruling party called in troops led by Bishop Franz von Waldeck, but the Anabaptist leaders and the people drove them out and won control of the city. A rule of fear began.

> Münster found itself at once in a state of war, besieged by the Bishop and his reinforced army, and fearful that soon all the powers of order and custom in Germany would unite against it . . . The new council decreed that all non-Anabaptists must accept rebaptism or leave the city. It was a cruel measure, for it meant that [people] . . . had to ride or trudge from the town at the height of a German winter. During the siege both sides executed without mercy any persons found working for the enemy. . . . [After April 5, 1534] John of Leyden ruled the city as its king.[13]

John's government became a kind of religion-inspired communism to which all with any wealth were required to contribute, but it soon seemed to the people that their king and other leaders were taking more than their share of the goods. Among the new laws passed was one allowing polygamy. Opposition to this led to a revolt in which John was taken prisoner, but the revolutionary soldiers, "soon besotted with wine, were slaughtered by the resurgent Anabaptist soldiery."[14]

Although according to some reports John was cruel and tyrannical ruler, he had many loyal followers among the people.

> When he asked for 'apostles' to venture forth and seek aid from other Anabaptist groups, twelve men tried to get through the enemy's lines, were all caught, and all killed. One fervent woman, inspired by the story of Judith, sallied out to assassinate the Bishop; she was intercepted and put to death.[15]

Germans, both Protestant and Catholic, took action to put down this and other "peasant" revolts, and John allowed anyone who wished to escape to leave Münster. However, most did not get far before they were felled by the enemy. "One of the *émigrés*," reports Durant, "saved his life by offering to show the besiegers an undefended part of the walls."[16] Led by him, large numbers of enemy troops entered the town, massacred most of the remaining inhabitants, and tortured John and two of his aides to death.

If the case of *Les Vêpres siciliennes* can stand as an example,[17] Scribe undoubtedly studied the historical reports of John of Leyden quite thoroughly. It was therefore not a lack of knowledge of the facts that led him to change John from a tailor to an innkeeper, to condense the action of three years into the space of a few months at most, and to create the supporting characters in *Le Prophète.* Rather, it was an eye to the exigencies of the operatic stage and the box office. Nevertheless, the historical account does provide many suggestions which Scribe embroidered to make them fit for musical setting.

To dispose of minor matters first, the condensation of time and events is an obvious operatic necessity, as demonstrated by Scribe's treatment of Scott's expansive novels in his opéras comiques. It is dictated by nothing more than the limitations of dramatic time and scenic space. The transformation of John from tailor to innkeeper is another, less obvious bow to operatic requirements or at least to traditions. A "Valse villageois" in a tavern was a popular, conventional type of scene in French opera. It is difficult to imagine what sort of equivalent Scribe could have dreamed up to take place inside a tailor's loft.

The historical account as summarized above does not reflect the over-all action of the opera very well. For example, the Anabaptists of history take Münster from inside the city, not from outside. Yet this account provides suggestions of events and even of characters in *Le Prophète.* The account of the Anabaptist rule in Münster quoted above describes events and attitudes similar to those in Act III of the opera, when some of the Anabaptists wish to execute prisoners willy nilly, or when Oberthal is ordered killed. Reaction to the communistic state set up by the Anabaptists at Münster is effectively reflected in the opening of the opera's fourth act, when the bourgeoisie of the city complain of being forced to support the new rulers with their goods and money or be killed. During the seige of Münster many Anabaptist supporters from outside the city tried to send supplies to its inhabitants, according to historical accounts. This conceivably could have provided one suggestion for the arrival of the skaters with provisions for the tired, hungry soldiers (Act III). The putting down of the conservative revolt may have suggested in part the scene of revelry forming the final tableau of the opera.

Particularly interesting associations exist between the events related in the second long quotation given above and those in the opera. The defeat of the first, unauthorized assault on Münster (Act III) may have been suggested by the fate of the twelve "apostles" mentioned here. More to the point, however, is the reference to the potential assassin of the bishop, for her case directly parallels that of Berthe in *Le Prophète.* At one point Fidès even refers to Berthe as "Judith novelle" (Act IV, iv, the scene in Münster Cathedral). Like the woman in the historical account, Berthe plans to assassinate an undesirable leader, in this case the Prophet. When she learns the latter's true identity she too dies, although by suicide. However, her original plan would also have been suicidal, for she had determined to set fire to the explosives and to die with the Anabaptists. Later, Jean uses the same plan to destroy his enemies.

The last scene of *Le Prophète* is also paralleled in the historical account. Like the real John, Jean tries to insure that his mother and his loyal followers will have left for safety once he knows the end is near. Like the *émigré* mentioned, the three Anabaptist leaders are responsible for allowing enemy troops into the city and hence for the destruction that follows.

Most of the less important fictional characters in the opera have some basis in the historical account. Oberthal personifies the many governmental leaders, including those of Münster, who oppressed the common people. In giving the audience just one such example and showing his actions in only one case (his dealings with Berthe), Scribe makes his message more direct and personal than if he had tried to picture nobles as a group or to portray a large number of oppressive and unjust actions by Oberthal himself. The three Anabaptists who convert Jean resemble many such preachers of the time, and their attitudes are not unlike that of Jan Matthys. As mentioned earlier, some of Berthe's actions may be based directly on history, and the general course of Jean's life, from his humble birth to his reign as king in Münster, is in accordance with actual events.

Such subtleties of characterization as exist, however, are the products of Scribe's imagination. Of the three main characters, two—Berthe and Fidès—are fictional, and Jean is largely so. The conception of Jean and his relationship to his mother has been ascribed by Legouvé to a source quite unrelated to any already mentioned.

> One of Scribe's least favorably disposed critics has ranked 'Le Prophète' among Shakespearian conceptions. Whence sprang that conception? From the simple perusal of an illustrated edition of the Bible. [Scribe] was reading the description of the marriage in Cana when he came upon the words, 'Woman, what have I to do with thee?' He read no further, for his imagination had been struck and had already began [*sic*] to transform the image of Christ.[18]

Knowing how Scribe's mind worked, there is no reason to doubt the truth of this anecdote.

Again Meyerbeer made a number of changes in the libretto which do not appear in the text as printed in the complete edition of Scribe's works. Some of these changes occur simply for the sake of shortening unnecessarily long dialogues or to make the text more easily set to music. Certain key changes, however, effect the characterization of the hero and show a subtle but clear difference between the conception of Jean as seen by Scribe and by his musical collaborator.

*Le Prophète* embodies many of Scribe's views of revolution, and one sees with clarity that both the rulers, as represented by Oberthal, and the three Anabaptist leaders are men of low ideals and high hopes of personal gain. Jean, however, is a different sort of man. Both Scribe and Meyerbeer viewed him as a basically honest, idealistic young man who becomes gradually but thoroughly convinced that he is everything people claim he is: chosen of God, a new Messiah, a great religious leader. Only the appearance of his mother at his coronation can make him realize that he is a fraud in whose name much evil has been done. Scribe, however, is still the realist. Fanatic though he be, Jean is still given personal, human reasons for each specific action in the opera. He has a dream of his coronation, yet he joins the Anabaptists because of Oberthal's cruelty. He wishes to return to Leyden, yet resolves to go to Münster because Berthe is there. It is precisely these realistic human traits that Meyerbeer omits or minimizes when he sets the libretto. Scribe's Jean is an angry young man with a cause; Meyerbeer's is a mad fanatic.

A few examples will illustrate this point. In Act II, vi, after Fidès' "Ah, mon fils," Meyerbeer eliminates a page of dialogue between mother and son in which Jean indirectly provides practical reasons for his eventual joining with the Anabaptists by speaking out at some length against the nobles and the oppression of the people. Then, in Scene vii, Scribe has provided the following.

**Jean** (alone).

O furies!
Who tear at my heart, come, guide my arms!
Heaven does not thunder over these ungodly heads!
It is to me then to punish, to me then their deaths!
Who must be killed?... who struck down?... All!!! I swear
To cleanse my shame and my injury in their blood!
Yes... their blood! but how?

(The song of the three Anabaptists is heard in the background.)
................................
Ah! it is God who hears me!... God who sends them to me
To serve my vengeance and deliver to me my prey.

Meyerbeer's score includes only the following lines.

**Jean** (alone).

O furies!
Heaven does not thunder over these ungodly heads!

(The song of the three Anabaptists is heard in the background.)
................................
Ah! it is God who hears me!... God who sends them to me.

Gone is all the logical motivation for Jean's act. In its place we find only the seeds of a sense of divine mission which will become stronger as the opera progresses.

Later, at the end of Jean's *prière* (no. 19), Scribe writes:

**Jean.**

Listen! listen! the trumpets make heard
Their proud challenge on the walls of Münster!
God inspires me... Let us march!... on your glorious heads
Victory will descend!

**All.**

Yes, it is the chosen one! it is the son of God!

**Jean** (aside, with love).

Berthe will be saved!
(Aloud, with exaltation.)
Yes, I shall be conqueror!
(With religious fervor and as if inspired.)
And you who appeared to me, great God! avenging God! . . .

Meyerbeer changed this and added some lines so that the speeches are:

**Jean.**

Listen! listen! these sounds are made heard,
The trumpets of Münster awaken our trumpets!
God inspires me . . . Come, and tomorrow, on your glorious heads
Holy victory will descend
And the grace of the Lord will be upon you!

**Mathisen.**

Great prophet, your people are awakened and you reign!
Yes, all the peasants, shaking their irons,
Rush to line up under your holy banners.

**First Anabaptist.**

A single cry goes up: assault on Münster!

**Jean** (seeing a vision).

What do I see!
The heavens are opening!
Over their harps the voices of angels
Sing in chorus: to Münster!

**All.**

To Münster!

By eliminating any reference to Berthe, by emphasizing the holy war aspect of the proposed siege, and by including a vision for Jean, Meyerbeer has deepened the psychological characterization of the hero. He is no longer doing what any strong man in the Paris audience might do under similar circumstances; he is a true, mad, wide-eyed religious fanatic, a man no longer part of Scribe's middle class world.

Many nineteenth-century critics noticed that *Le Prophète* contained little similar to the traditional love stories with which operas since *Orfeo* had been filled.[19] Indeed, the heroine of the opera is not Berthe, the young coloratura soprano, but Fidès, the mezzo soprano and mother of the hero. This is undoubtedly due in part to the fact that the famed singer Pauline Viardot created Fidès' role. Yet the structure of the opera and its message are sufficiently different from others of Scribe's grand operas to make the central position of Fidès only one indication of many pointing toward a type of oprea which was to be exploited later by Barbier and Carrè in their *Reine de Saba* and by Richard Wagner. *Le Prophète* may be viewed as the first in a long line of operas of the latter half of the nineteenth centry in which a philosophical idea is not just a by-product of the work—as in *La Muette*, *Robert*, or *Les Huguenots*—but is central to the work and is the primary theme around which the work revolves. In Scribe's own output the sort of philosophy-based opera is later represented, less successfully, by *Le Juif errant.*

*Les Huguenots* certainly presents Scribe's view of revolution, and it is certainly in tune with its own time, but it is still first of all a love story and secondly a tale of a historical event. It shows, it tells, but it does not advocate. The same cannot be said of *Le Prophète.* Here, long treatises-in-verse by the three Anabaptists spell out in more detail than ever before the crimes of rulers against the common man;[20] here a young man sees visions and dreams dreams; here an old woman sobs for page after page over the destruction wrought by one man, who happens to be her son, in the name of God. Everywhere the composer reinforces the sentiments of the text by some of his most skillful, restrained, and effective music.

Théophile Gautier caught some of this meaning when he wrote:

> These three operas [*Robert, Les Huguenots, Le Prophète*] compose an immense symbolic trilogy, filled with profound and mysterious meaning; the three principal phases of the human soul are found represented there: law, examination, illumination. Faith corresponds to the past, examination to the present, illumination to the future. In order to be made visible each one of these ideas has taken its necessary form: *Robert le Diable*, the fairy tale; *Les Huguenots*, the chronicle; *Le Prophète*, the *pamphlet.*[21]

## The Music

Fétis, in his review of the opera, caught some of the same idea as did Gautier when he observed that Meyerbeer had more difficulty composing *Le Prophète* because its basic idea of religious fanaticism was less close to human experience than was the good-evil conflict in *Robert* or the struggle between love and honor in *Les Huguenots.* He also observed that in *Le Prophète* one has less interest in the characters as people (except for Fidès in Acts IV-V) because of the strong emphasis on the historical-ideological background of the work.[22] And Gautier again: "*Le Prophète* is hypothesis, Utopia, the still confused form of things that are not, drawn in an extravagant outline."[23]

The structure of the libretto reinforces these claims. The following charts outline first the musical numbers in *Le Prophète* and a sketch of the action involved in each; then a profile of the musical numbers as they can be divided into dramatic scenes or tableaux, scenic tableaux, and set-numbers.

Key to abbreviations:

| | | | | | |
|---|---|---|---|---|---|
| Je | - | Jean | O | - | Oberthal |
| Z | - | Zacharie | F | - | Fidès |
| Jo | - | Jonas | B | - | Berthe |
| M | - | Mathisen | Cho | - | chorus |

| Number | Form or technique | Action involved |
|---|---|---|
| | | ACT I |
| 1 | *Prélude et Choeur Pastoral* | Peasants enjoying fine weather. |
| 1 *bis* | *Cavatine* (B) | B looks forward to F's arrival and her marriage tomorrow. |
| 2 | *Scène* (B, F) | F and B happy over marriage. B must get O's permission to leave. Anabaptists arrive. |
| 3 | *Le Prêche Anabaptiste* (*morceau d'ensemble*) (Jo, M, Z, cho) | Anabaptists try to stir up people against nobles. Peasants agree with their preaching, take up arms and move toward chateau. |
| | Recit (B, O) | O comes to investigate noise, condemns Anabaptists. B approaches O timidly. |
| 4 | *Romance à deux voix* (B, F) | B tells how she met Jean, asks permission to marry him. |

| | | |
|---|---|---|
| 5 | Recit and Finale (B, F, O, Jo, M, Z, cho) | O refuses to let B leave. People unhappy, hear Anabaptists singing and threatening O with revenge. |
| | | **ACT II** |
| 6 | *Valse villageois* (*morceau d'ensemble*) (Je, Jo, M, Z, cho) | Villagers dancing at Je's inn. Je worries that F and B have not arrived. Villagers leave. |
| 7 | *Le Songe* (Je, Jo, M, Z) | Je tells Anabaptists about dream (see plot summary). |
| 8 | *Romance* (Je) | Je wants to live quietly with B, although Anabaptists urge him to join them. |
| 9 | *Scène et morceau d'ensemble* (Je, B, O, F, soldiers) | Je, glad Anabaptists have gone, looks forward to marriage. B runs in and hides. O enters and demands information from Je, threatening to kill F if he does not give up B. Je delivers B to O. |
| 10 | *Arioso* (F) | F blesses her son for saving her life. |
| 11 | *Scène et Quatuor* (Je, Jo, M, Z) | Je, furious, hears Anabaptists returning. They gradually persuade him to join them even though he must leave without telling his mother. |
| | | **ACT III** |
| 12 | *Entr'acte et choeur des Anabaptistes* Recit (M, another Anabaptist) | Anabaptists victorious in battle, want to strike down all enemies. M stops execution of prisoners in hopes that some might pay ransom. |
| 13 | *Couplets* (Z, cho) | Boasting of Anabaptist victories. |
| | *Scène* (M, Z) | M says soldiers are tired and hungry. Z points to skaters coming across lake with provisions. |
| 14 | *L'Arrivée des Patineurs* (cho) | Skaters arrive with food. |

| | | |
|---|---|---|
| 15 | Ballet | Four "Airs de ballet," orchestral. |
| | *Scène* (Jo, M, Z, O) | Soldiers retire for night. Z and M discuss proposed assault on Münster, and M leaves to attack the city. Jo arrives with O. |
| 16 | *Trio bouffe* (Jo, Z, O) | O wishes to join Anabaptists and swears to abide by their aims and beliefs. Jo lights a lamp and recognizes O. Soldiers take O away. |
| | *Scène* (Jo, Je, O, M, Z,) | Z orders O killed without consulting Je. Je tells Z he wishes to return home. O enters with guards and tells Je that B is at Münster. Je determines to take the city. M announces return of defeated Anabaptist soldiers, in revolt aginst Prophet. Je goes to speak to them. |
| 17 | *Choeur des soldats révoltés* | Soldiers accuse Je of having deceived them, of being a false prophet. |
| 18 | *Scène* (Je, Jo, M, Z, cho) | Men reveal that Z sent them to battle without consulting Je. Je is angry, promises army victory if they follow him. |
| 19 | *Prière* (Je cho) | Je prays God will forgive them and promises them victory. |
| | Recit (M, Je, an Anabaptist, cho) | M and an Anabaptist report peasants flocking to join Je's army. Je sees vision of heaven opening, feels inspired to go to Münster. People agree. |
| 20 | *Hymne triomphal* (Je, cho) | Je praises God, predicts victory. People echo his words. |
| | | ACT IV |
| 21 | *Entr'acte et Choeur des Bourgeois* | Bourgeoisie publicly praise the Prophet but privately resent his oppression. One reports that Je is to be crowned in Münster Cathedral. |
| 22 | *Complainte* (F) | Begs for money to have Mass said for her dead son. |
| | *Scène* (F, people) | People give her money, warn of danger. |

| | | |
|---|---|---|
| 23 | *Scène et duo* (F, B) | F and B recognize each other. B explains how she came to Münster. B learns Je is dead and vows to kill Prophet. |
| 24 | *Marche du sacre* | Instrumental, using orchestras onstage and in pit. |
| 25 | Finale (all principals except B, cho) | |
| | a. *Prière et Imprecation* | Offstage *a cappella* chorus prays for Je, while F prays that B will succeed in killing Prophet. |
| | b. *Choeur d'enfants et choeur general* | During procession choirs sing praise of Prophet, saying he was not born of woman but is Son of God. Je believes he really is blessed. F recognizes Je. |
| | c. *Couplets et morceau d'ensemble* | F claimes to be Je's mother, chides him for not acknowledging her. Crowd becomes upset. |
| | Recit | Je claims F must be mad and he will restore her sanity. |
| | d. *L'Exorcisme* | Under Je's urging F claims she was mistaken. People think her senses have returned by a miracle. F wonders how to prevent B from killing Je. |
| | | **ACT V** |
| 26 | *Entr'acte et scène* (Jo, M, Z) | Jo, M, Z agree to turn Je over to emperor's troops in return for protection for themselves. |
| 27 | *Scène, Cavatine et Air* (F) | F, brought to palace, learns she is to see Je and hopes she will be able to return him to true God. |
| 28 | *Scène et Grand Duo* (F, Je) | Je begs F's pardon. F moves him to repentance. |
| 29 | *Scène et trio* (F, Je, B) | B, happy to see Je, then condemns him when she finds he is Prophet. B kills herself. Officer tells Je enemies are in |

| | | |
|---|---|---|
| | | palace. After F leaves Je determines to punish all guilty persons. |
| 30 | Finale (all principals except B, cho) | |
| | a. *Bacchanale* (*choeur dansé*) | Anabaptists reveling. Jo, M, Z decide to make Je drunk to keep him under control. Je makes arrangements to trap traitors. |
| | b. *Couplets bachiques* | Je drinks, promises all his friends will share his rewards. Emperior's troops enter to take Je. Explosions, flames, falling walls. F enters to die with Je. |

**Tableaux in *Le Prophète***

| Primarily Dramatic | | Primarily Scenic |
|---|---|---|
| | | Act I, i (No. 1) |
| | Act I, ii (No 1 *bis*; set-number) | |
| Act I, iii-iva (*Scène*, not a tableau) | | |
| Act I, ivb-va (No. 3, recit) | | |
| | Act I, vb (No. 4; set-number) | |
| Act I, vc (No. 5) | | |
| | | Act II, i (No. 6) |
| Act II, iia (No. 7) | | |
| | Act II, iib (No. 8; set-number) | |
| Act II, iii-v (No. 9) | | |
| | Act II, vi (No. 10; set-number) | |
| Act II, vii-viii (No. 11) | | |
| | | Act III, i-ii (No. 12; recit; No. 13) |
| | | Act III, iii (*Scène*, Nos. 14-15) |

Act III, iv-v (*Scène*, not a tableau)

Act III, via (No. 16; set-number)

Act III, vib-xi (*Scène*, not a tableau)

Act III, xiia (No. 17)

Act III, xiib (Nos. 18-19; recit; No. 20)

Act IV, i-ii (Nos. 21-22)

Act IV, iii (*Scène*, No. 23)

Act IV, iva (Nos. 24-25a-b)

Act IV, ivb (No. 25c-d)

Act V, i (No. 26)

Act V, ii-iii (No. 27; set-number)

Act V, iv (No. 28; partly scenic)

Act V, v-vi (No. 29)

Act V, vii (No. 30)

End of finale

The libretto of *Le Prophète* preserves those traits of grand opera illustrated by *Les Huguenots* in several respects. The primary musico-dramatic unit is the tableau, which *Le Prophète* possesses in abundance. The difference here is that in *Le Prophète* most of the numbers that can be considered tableaux are primarily scenic, whereas those numbers classified as dramatic and through which the well-made plot is carried out are often not tableaux at all. Rather they bear the designation *scène* and are recitative or arioso dialogues with no musical form. A similar type of number is the *morceau d'ensemble*, also frequently found in the "dramatic" column. It differs from the *scène* in length and in that it ordinarily has a musical form in effect at least for the last part of the number. Although this musical form can create a relatively short dramatic tableau the number as a whole is generally too filled with action to give it tableau status.

The substructure of *Le Prophète* is again a simplified version of the well-made libretto and is carried out through the dramatic scenes. The delayed-action plot begins after Jean and Berthe have become engaged and after the Anabaptists have begun to stir up the peasants and to dream of taking Münster. Each act starts after an important event has taken place and each ends with the logical conclusion of actions begun in the opening scenes, thus becoming structural miniatures of the well-made libretto. Contrived entrances and exits abound. Some good examples are the return of the Anabaptists immediately after Oberthal has taken Berthe away (Act II, vii); the entrance of Berthe after the Fidès-Jean duo of Act IV; and the officer's call to Jean, as the Prophet, to put down the conspiracy against him—which precipitates Berthe's condemnation of Jean and her suicide.

The *quiproquo* of *Le Prophète* is not some logical misunderstanding later straightened out by human means, but rather the whole mystical aura surrounding the character of Jean. Here, to a large degree because of Meyerbeer, the nature of the *quiproquo* changes from something the audience knows but certain characters do not to something that begins to involve the audience as well as the characters. In the beginning the spectator knows that Jean is not divine, that he is merely the son of a humble woman, an innkeeper. Then confusion sets in. As Jean himself seems more and more convinved of his divinity, might not the spectator too begin to wonder whether the Prophet would indeed turn out to be the chosen instrument of God? Only in Act V, when Fidès convinces Jean to repent and to tell the truth, is this confusion resolved.

The careful preparation of events through the opera is another trait of the well-made libretto preserved in *Le Prophète*. The first part of Act I is primarily expository: we meet Berthe, Fidès, the Anabaptists, and Oberthal, and learn enough about them and their purposes to anticipate subsequent events. The action proper begins only in the final scene, as Berthe requests and is refused permission to go to Leyden to be married. In Act II the Anabaptists' conversation and Jean's dream have their expected result when Jean agrees to go to Münster. Although specific events in this act involving Berthe and Fidès are not prepared, Oberthal's attitude and Fidès' response in Act I make something of the sort inevitable. Jean's hesitancy at leaving his home forecasts his desire in Act III to return to Leyden, and his eventual victory at Münster is prepared for by his dream, his earlier victories, the conversations of the Anabaptists, information from Oberthal, and Jean's vision.

Fidès' appearance at Münster is explained after the fact when she tells Berthe of her belief that the Prophet has killed Jean, and

Berthe's presence in the city is prepared for by Oberthal's information in Act III. The choir's song praising the Prophet as a man not born of woman and threats from the three Anabaptists are enough to prepare for the dramatic confrontation of Jean and Fidès in the cathedral.

Every event in Act V has also been well prepared. The treachery of the Anabaptists is made clear as early as Act I, when Oberthal reminds one of them that he was dismissed for dishonesty, and is further amplified in their decision (Act II) to use Jean as their tool. The love Jean has already expressed for his mother and the devout character Fidès has portrayed make the confrontation and its outcome inevitable, and Berthe's curse and suicide are no surprise once we hear her feelings about the Prophet (Act IV, iii; Act V, v) and learn that she had planned a suicide mission to destroy him. Hearing Berthe's plan and later hearing Jean give orders to his faithful officers, one is not surprised at the opera's outcome.

The large blocks of musical and dramatic time given over to scenic tableaux and set-numbers is symptomatic of the change that sets *Le Prophète* apart from others of Scribe's grand operas. It is quite a static work, with great amounts of stage spectacle particularly noticeable. In such scenes as the Skaters' Ballet and the Coronation Scene the various collaborators seem to have created nothing more than a spectacular background against which large masses of people could sing or move. Here the work becomes oratorio with scenery, but superb scenery. Gautier commented with regard to Act II that the decorator's art had never been carried so far: "this is no longer painting, it is reality itself."[24]

The musical equivalent of such scenic spectacle is the vocal spectacle found in the set-numbers. Berthe's *cavatine* in Act I, the half humorous - half hypocritical antics in the *trio bouffe* (No. 16), and Fidès grand scene in Act V (No. 27) are good examples. If, in the scenic tableaux, the choruses and dancers move within a picture frame, the soloists do the same in the set-numbers. They exult, sob, or express simple sentiments in a touching and effective manner, but they do nothing.

Despite the massive scenic tableaux, the music of *Le Prophète* is often remarkably restrained and even subtle. Alongside the usual ensembles with chorus, or even double and triple chorus, represented by parts of the Anabaptist-peasant scene (No. 3), the "Valse villageois" (No. 6), the arrival of the skaters (No. 11), the soldiers' chorus (No. 17), the triumphal hymn (No. 20), the chorus of the bourgeois (No. 21), and the scene in Münster Cathedral (No. 25), there are some striking pieces which depend more on texture and style, less on pure mass for their effect. The opening peasants' chorus, for example, evokes a pastoral mood by placing a delicate soprano melody over a chordal, dronelike accompaniment in the lower voices and the orchestra (Example 57a). The melody and the effect are similar to those in the trio of the Scherzo of Dvorak's New World Symphony (Example 57b). In the chorus of Anabaptists that begins Act II Meyerbeer includes some Handelian counterpoint rather unexpected in a number that begins with the words, "Du sang!" (Example 58). Later in the same number he interrupts the conventional choral cries of warfare with a five-bar statement of "Te Deum laudamus" set *a cappella* in a sustained, chordal style, an excellent musical reflection of the Anabaptists' hypocrisy.

During the refrain of Zacharie's *couplets* (No. 13), which resemble in spirit if not in actual notes Marcel's "Pif paf pouf" in *Les Huguenots*, Meyerbeer creates an interesting and unusual texture between chorus and soloist (Example 59). Rather than have the chorus repeat a previously sung solo refrain Meyerbeer orchestrates with voices, retaining the solo voice as a kind of obbligato and using the various choral parts in short comments on the solo text. A similar effect of vocal orchestration is created in the semichorus and full chorus combination during the entrance of the skaters (No. 14).

In view of the growing interest in church music reform and the renewed interest in Renaissance polyphony the opening of the scene in Münster Cathedral (No. 25) is particularly impressive and timely. Meyerbeer had written *a cappella* pieces for chorus and for ensembles as early as *Robert le Diable*; thus the device itself was nothing new. As in *Robert*, Meyerbeer even makes use of an organ in this scene. However, the *a cappella* portion of No. 25, introduced by a timpani roll and performed offstage, resembles the much admired antiphony of such works as Allegri's *Miserere* and Palestrina's settings of the *Reproaches* and the *Stabat Mater*, all popular with active reformers of church music, and may well have called up associations with this type of music among the listeners (see Example 60).

Much of the writing for solo voices, particularly for the female characters, is conventional, and the role of Berthe features many musical and dramatic clichés of operatic writing of the day. In many numbers, however, Meyerbeer makes use of a style of declamatory arioso that is particularly effective in the context of *Le Prophète*, with its explicit sermonizing. Good examples of this are to be found in Jean's dream and Fidès' well known arioso, "Ah, mon fils," both of which concentrate more interest on the dramatic situation than on considerations of absolute musical worth. In Jean's *prière* (No. 19) Meyerbeer creates an arresting musical texture by accompanying this sort of declamatory vocal

## Example 57a

## Example 57b

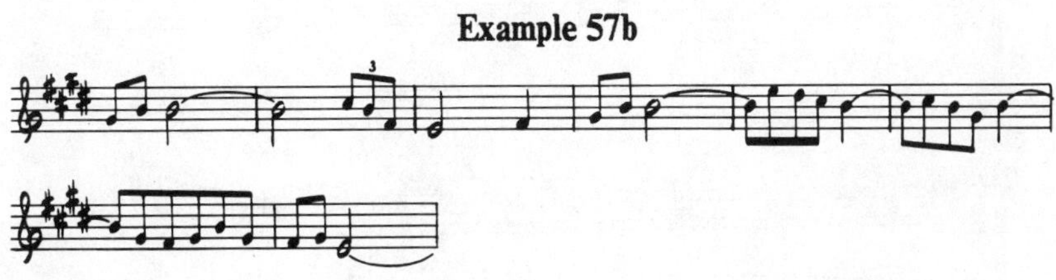

## Example 58

## Example 59

**Example 60**

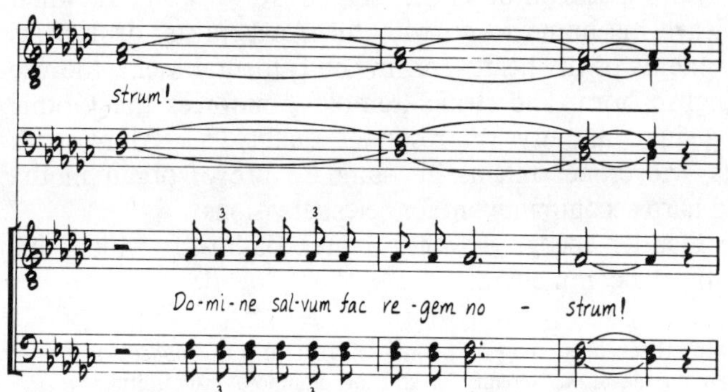


writing with a continuo-like bass line (Example 61), later adding soft choral statements of "miserere nobis" in a responsorial manner.

Even some of the more conventional writing, however, can be charming and appropriate: for example, Jean's *pastorale* (No. 8; example 62), which Bizet's subconscious mind may have called upon as the basis for the *Entr'acte* before Act II of *Carmen.*

In *Le Prophète* Meyerbeer makes considerable use of reminiscence motives and musical labels. The most obvious is the Anabaptist chorale (Example 63), a freely composed tune which returns at strategic points in the score (e.g., after Oberthal has forbidden Berthe to leave and after Jean has been forced to turn Berthe over to the Count). During his dream Jean tells of his coronation to the accompaniment of the song sung by the choirboys in the cathedral scene. Later, as he looks in on his sleeping mother and hears her praying for him, the orchestra plays a portion of Fidès' *arioso* (No. 10) and Jean hesitates to leave with the Anabaptists. When Jean announces in Act II that he wishes to return to Leyden, the accompaniment includes the melody of his *pastorale* (Example 62), the text of which expressed his desire to marry and lead a quiet, happy life. In his use of such reminiscences Meyerbeeer resembles Wagner far less than he resembles Scribe. Just as the librettist uses verbal preparations and pointers to make the spectator aware of dramatic connections between events, so Meyerbeer uses musical suggestions.

The greater extent of Meyerbeer's care and subtlety in creating the score of *Le Prophète* is also demonstrated in the orchestration, which Cooper considers, along with that of *L'Africaine*, to be Meyerbeer's most adventurous. Cooper particularly cites the use of four bassoons and two horns along with the three unison solo voices for the Anabaptist chorale as "giving a masterful impression of sinister hypocrisy." In Act II, when Jean hesitates to leave his home to go with the Anabaptists, drumbeats represent the movements of his heart; and in the cathedral scene the use of three flutes, English horn, and string tremolos reinforces the Gothic cathedral setting giving "an airy yet resonant quality."[25] Along with these novel effects, Meyerbeer retains his standard use of organ in the cathedral scene and harp accompaniment for celestial visions.

Théophile Gautier recognized the greater skill with which this score was written when he commented:

> Never has Meyerbeer been more of a master than in *Le Prophète.* He has taken on elevation, serenity, a sort of grandiose tranquility that one does not find in his other work . . . for Meyerbeer is, since Gluck, the most essentially dramatic composer to be heard at the Opéra: he has theatrical skill in the highest degree and this . . . is the distinctive quality of his genius . . . none has surpassed him in dramatic effect. . . .[26]

Some of the influences of *Le Prophète* on later music have already been mentioned, and it would be out of place here to try to trace every feature of the piece to find echoes in the works of later composers, for they are legion. One example of a work quite filled with such echoes is Gounod's *Faust*, with its catherdal scene and harp-accompanied celestial vision. Like *Le Prophète*, *Faust* also includes a peasant dance, the well-known *Faust* waltzes, in which a chorus pronounces homophonic, relatively uninteresting phrases over a singing orchestral melody.

## Example 61

## Example 62

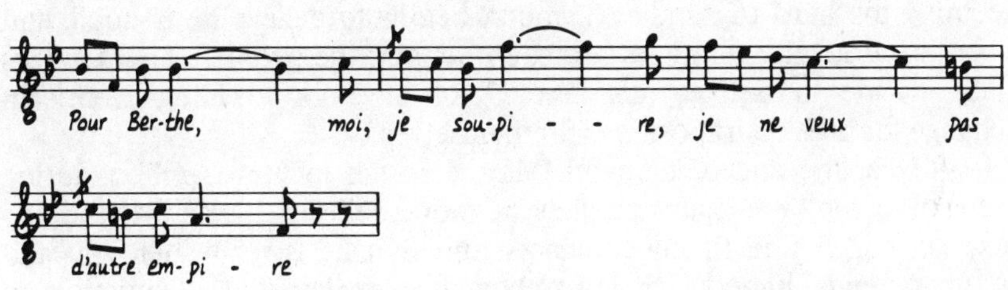


## Example 63

In the works of Scribe the libretto of *Le Prophète* has a distinct sucessor in the opéra comique *Lambert Simnel*, written in collaboration with Mélesville (September 14, 1843). In this work the hero, Lambert Simnel, is employed at a hotel. He lives with his elderly mother Marthe and is in love with a girl of his own social class. The partisans of the House of York, visiting the inn where Lambert is employed, notice a resemblance between the young man and the Count of Warwick, who opposes Henry VII as King of England. When Warwick dies unexpectedly, the York party decides to substitute Lambert as its candidate for king. To do this they must convince him that he is of royal blood, that Marthe is only his nurse, and that he has a patriotic duty to lead his followers in battle and to leave behind his home and the girl he loves. Problems arise when the conspirators find their puppet becoming too hard to handle. Lambert begins to believe he is noble and to command loyalty on his own account among the people. The Yorkists finally decide to deliver this false Duke of York to King Henry in exchange for high court positions for themselves.

Near the end of the work Marthe comes to find Lambert during a crucial battle, not knowing that he now believes himself to be the Duke of York. She finally convinces him that he is really her son, and the opera ends happily once Lambert has explained the situation to Edward, King Henry's son. The parallels between *Lambert Simnel* and *Le Prophète* are obvious.[27]

In many respects *Le Prophète* continued the line of grand opera begun in the years around 1830 and sustained, with a temporary sidetrack around this monumental work, for two decades more. One cannot ignore the fact, however, that the libretto in its final form breaks new ground in the use of opera as propaganda and in the raising of symbolism to a place of importance within the context of musical drama of the first half of the nineteenth century.

# FRENCH OPERA AFTER SCRIBE: BARBIER AND CARRE

Although produced in 1849, *Le Prophète* was in style and in fact a product of the pre-1848 world. The same could be said of most of the rest of Scribe's operas produced after the revolution. At least three of them—*La Nonne sanglante*, *Les Vêpres siciliennes*, and *L'Africaine*—are known to have been written or conceived before 1848. Of the six remaining libretti two (*La Tempète* and *Florinde*) were intended for London and were unsuccessful; one was an *opéra-ballet* adapted from Auber's earlier opéra comique, *Le Chéval de bronze*; and one (*Zerline*) was a three-act comic opera of the same type as *Le Serment* or *Le Philtre.* Only two—Auber's *L'Enfant prodigue* (1850) and Halévy's *Le Juif errant* (1852)—are grand operas, and both of these try to some extent to continue the trend begun by *Le Prophète*, although far less successfully. In both, mysticism or morality form a central element in the plot and the stories are less tightly constructed and less interesting dramatically than the works in which Scribe carries on the older traditions for which he had been in large part responsible.

*L'Enfant prodigue* and *Le Juif errant* contain in them symptoms of the decline that set into grand opera after 1850. In attempting to get away from the world of human concerns to an area of less clearly defined motivation and purpose, Scribe was the prophet of things to come. Unfortunately the times were taking a different turn, and the emphasis on even greater materialism and on things worldly had in it no place for a mystical never-never land nor any desire to return to subjects that might have interested earlier generations were the ballets sufficiently entertaining.

> The deliberate frivolity of the Second Empire, the shameless place-seeking and corruption of Napoleon and the Third's regime, had had a double effect on the artistic world. The serious artist . . . turned his back on public life in a gesture natural to those who inhabit and cultivate exclusive, 'private' universes. The less serious, but more extrovert, artist . . . frankly enjoyed, even if he did not make direct use of the comic indignities of the Second Empire.[1]

In this world Scribe started but could not sustain a new trend, not because he was weak but because the trend itself was not valid. Into this operatic void stepped one of the most skilled libretto-writing teams of all time, Jules Barbier and Michel Carré. Even they found themselves unable or unwilling to continue older traditions or to establish new ones at the Opéra, and they met their greatest successes at the Opéra-Comique and the Théâtre-Lyrique.

The Opéra after 1850 was becoming a musical museum. Whereas fresh, new works were being produced on other musical stages of Paris at a rate of about three or four per year between 1850 and 1900, the Opéra staged only thirty-two works sufficiently important to be included in Loewenberg's listings, half of them before the Franco-Prussian War in 1870. Of these works only nine can be considered great successes and another eight, moderate successes. Among the most popular operas few met the acclaim of a *Robert le Diable* or a *Les Huguenots*, and the most successful of all, *L'Africaine* (1865), was also the product of the Scribe-Meyerbeer team.[2] To flesh out these weak, often retrospective offerings the Opéra relied on the works that had made its reputation during the 1830s and '40s (*La Muette de Portici*, *Guillaume Tell*, Meyerbeer's works, *La Juive*), a few works by foreign composers, (e.g., Donizetti's *Lucia di Lammermoor*), and works revised from *opéra-lyrique* (e.g., Gounod's *Faust*). The picture was indeed grim and would not improve. "By the time the Second Empire reached its height," writes Mina Curtiss, "the opera was a kind of club of the upper classes, desiring no new members and requiring no fresh forms of entertainment."[3]

Jules Barbier (1825-1901), a native of Paris, had his first drama performed at the age of thirteen. After finishing his formal schooling he turned at once to the theatre, where each year he had produced on the Paris stages one or more of his works. Like Scribe, he wrote all types of comedies and dramas, including one (*La Loterie du mariage*, 1868) in which Sarah Bernhardt made her debut.

Michel-Florentin Carré (1822-1872) came to Paris in 1840 from his native Besançon to study painting, but soon turned to literature, publishing a collection of poems in 1842. In 1843 his first drama appeared and was followed by a large number of *comédies-vaudevilles* performed on various stages in Paris. In 1852 he and Barbier first collaborated on a libretto, *Galathée*, set by Massé for the Opéra-Comique. Thereafter the two provided libretti for some of the most significant works of their day, including Massé's *Les Noces de Jeannette*; Gounod's *Le Médecin malgré lui*, *Faust*, and *Roméo et Juliette*; Thomas' *Psyché* and *Mignon*; Offenbach's *Contes d'Hoffman*; and Meyerbeer's *Le Pardon de Ploërmel*.[4]

The joint career of Barbier and Carré reflects in miniature the operatic situation in Paris in the latter half of the nineteeth century. Their large output includes only four operas; Gounod's *La Reine de Saba* (1862) and *Polyeucte* (1878); and Thomas' *Hamlet* (1868) and

*Françoise de Rimini* (1882); Of these, two (Gounod's works) were not successful; one (*Françoise*) enjoyed moderate success; and one (*Hamlet*) became quite popular, although it caused nowhere near the furor of Meyerbeer's works. The most successful works of Barbier and Carré, those destined to be longest lived, were those listed in the preceding paragraph. All were produced at the Opéra-Comique or the Théâtre-Lyrique. One, Gounod's *Faust*, the most popular and successful work of its time, eventually outfitted with recitatives and ballet, helped revitalize the Opéra's repertoire later in the century. In their opéras comiques Barbier and Carré turned from Scribe's emphasis on situations and intrigues toward the depiction of characters and their emotions, producing works in which the heroine was usually the most important character. Although the opera libretti show the same emphasis on the individual characters, in three of the four the hero is the central figure.

It is difficult to determine the subjects of now obscure or forgotten operas by their titles. Recognizing the limited degree to which such conclusions are valid, perusal of any listing of the new operas produced between 1850 and 1900 demonstrates that one would have difficulty establishing any consistency in subject matter among these thirty-two operas. Most of the works that could be considered at all successful continued the tradition of subjects from modern history: for example, Verdi's *Les Vêpres siciliennes* and *Don Carlos*, Meyerbeer's *L'Africaine*, Poniatowsky's *Pierre de Medicis*, Massenet's *Le Cid*, Thomas' *Hamlet* and *Françoise de Rimini*. Another group of operas, most of them less successful than the history-based works, returned to subjects from antique legend or Roman history. Among these are two by Barbier and Carré—*La Reine de Saba* and *Polyeucte*—as well as Gounod's *Sapho*. A few operas on Gothic or exotic subjects were also performed, the remnants of tastes and traditions long since dead.

The table in Appendix D outlines the major musical features of the four Barbier and Carré operas. Comparison with the similar chart of Scribe's libretti in Apprendix C reveals that there are few features involving the nature and placement of the musical numbers that are not also found in Scribe's works.[5] The tendency in Scribe's later works to deemphasize strophic numbers and to create specific categories of form for specific occasions is continued by Barbier and Carré. The types of numbers normally used to open and close each act are similar to those in Scribe's libretti, with the possible exception of those in *Françoise de Rimini*, the most unconventional work of the four. Neither librettists nor composers were inclined to go beyond the bounds of form established by Scribe and his musical collaborators, especially Meyerbeer. All still work within the bounds of set-numbers and tableaux, showing little desire to move in the formal directions taken by Wagner.

Because Barbier and Carré place more emphasis on the individual characters than on situations their writing often tends to be more poetic and richer in imagery than Scribe's, although not so rich as to become lost in the musical setting. The greater poetic value could well be the result of the sources from which they drew their material, for all their works are based on literary models, three of them poetic, the other (*La Reine de Saba*) a mystical tale written by Gérard de Nerval and based on oriental sources. Scribe, on the contrary, relied very little on literary models for his operas, preferring to recast historical events or suggestions of events in the mold of the well-made libretto as adapted to suit the musical and scenic exigencies of the Opéra's stage.

Although they share the same traits of character emphasis, literary style, and musical forms employed, the four libretti are quite different from one another in various other respects. *La Reine de Saba* has a very obsure plot which cannot really be understood without some familiarity with the legendary tale of Adoniram and Balkis. Basically the story is quite simple: King Solomon, jealous of the master architect Adoniram, a descendant of Tubalcain, for winning from him the love of Balkis, the Queen of Sheba, cooperates with three former employees of Adoniram who have been dismissed for incompetence and excessive pride to have the architect murdered. However, this conventional love triangle is so overlaid with mysticism and presented in so inexplicit a manner that it gets lost. Amid talk of the spiritual legacy of Egypt passed down from Tubalcain to Adoniram and Balkis, a legacy that does not include either King Solomon or other members of the Jewish religion, the librettists have tried to suggest the drama and a higher meaning by concentrating on the character of Adoniram, his thoughts and inner conflicts. His love for Balkis is not the simple human love portrayed in most operas but is intermixed with symbolism, oriental mysticism, and a sense of divine destiny not unlike that in *Tristan und Isolde.* Wagner, however, was wise enough not to attempt to combine his love story with a complex intrigue involving several characters and a subplot. With Barbier and Carré, the queen disappears in the operatic incense and the plot's foggy outlines are difficult even for a reader, much less a spectator, to follow.

*Hamlet,* on the contrary, is quite a straightforward operatic drama. Indeed, one author considered this work to be "the only significant new French opera given between 1850 and 1870 at the Opéra."[6] The ghost of Hamlet's father as he appears in this opera has much in common with the operatic ghosts in earlier *tragédie-lyrique*—e.g., that in Catel's *Sémiramis*—and the allegorical ballet also has overtones of much earlier traditions. Some of the speeches—for example, Hamlet's soliloquy—are paraphrased from Shakespeare and the ending is softened in quite a conventional operatic manner: Hamlet kills Claudius, explains his actions to the assembled crowd, and becomes King of Denmark. Many of the conflicts in the original play are simplified, and the characters of Polonius, Horatio, and Laertes are eliminated or pushed into the background. However, the plot itself remains basically that of Shakespeare's drama. As in *La Reine de Saba*, various omissions in the opera indicate that the librettists were depending on the audience's knowledge of the source of the plot to fill in details. This is something Scribe's technique would never have admitted.

*Françoise de Rimini*, Thomas' last opera, seems to represent a middle ground between the style of *La Reine de Saba* and that of *Hamlet*. Like the former, it begins and ends in the clouds and mists, this time of the unfamiliar land of Dante's *Inferno*. The beginning of the story comes into focus only gradually, as out of that unknown land of spiritual symbolism. Once the action proper begins, however, the plot—not unlike that of *Romeo and Juliet*—is carried out in a straightforward manner. Like *Hamlet*, *Françoise* shows an emphasis on individual characters and a comparative lack of the Scribean stress on situations, their careful contrivance and preparation. Characters appear unexpectedly and their relationships to one another are explained slowly or grow before the eyes of the audience. One is unaware, for example, that Paolo and Malatesta are to be rivals for the hand of Francesca or even that Malatesta loved Francesca before the opera's action began. Had Scribe written on the same subject these ideas would surely have been related in the exposition before the real action of the opera began.

It is fortunate for purposes of this discussion that one of Scribe's libretti, *Les Martyrs*, is based on the same subject as that of Barbier's and Carré's *Polyeucte*. Although the plots and order of incidents in the two operas are similar, there is no sign that the later work was in any way an adaptation from Scribe. Comparison of the two works will show in concise form the similarities and differences between the techniques of libretto writing used by Scribe and by Barbier and Carré.

Scribe's libretto for Donizetti's *Les Martyrs* is unusual in several respects. First, it is based on a subject and on a period that had largely gone out of fashion at the Opéra, for it deals with an episode from Roman history in the early years of the Christian era and includes ceremonies to pagan gods similar to those found in traditional *tragédie-lyrique*. Second, unlike most of Scribe's grand operas, it is based on a literary model, Corneille's *Polyeucte*. This model is also from an era largely out of fashion by the 1840s. Third, Scribe was adapting not only Corneille but Cammarano as well, for the latter had written the original libretto, *Poliuto*, to which Donizetti had composed music. This opera, however, had been rejected by the censors in Naples and was not performed in Italy until 1848, a few months after Donizetti's death, when it was given in its original Italian form.[7] Meanwhile, Scribe had reworked the piece as a four-act work, trying to follow Corneille as closely as possible while at the same time taking into account the changes necessary for an operatic adaptation of any literary model and keeping in mind Donizetti's already-composed music.[8] The result was, by Donizetti's admission, a recomposed work, not just a translation. The composer not only had to rewrite all the recitatives but needed to add several numbers, delete some, and rearrange others. Scribe's libretto was closer to the original Corneille drama than was Cammarano's, though neither was overly faithful to its model.[9]

*Les Martyrs* was not very successful in Paris, enjoying only twenty performances, but it was later performed in other countries with moderate success.

*Les Martyrs* begins during a secret worship service of the Christians being held in the catacombs of Melitene, capital of Armenia. Néarque has brought his friend Polyeucte to the gathering to be baptized. Polyeucte is the son-in-law of Félix, governor of Armenia and a vigorous persecutor of Christians, and Néarque points out that his friend could be risking death or at least dishonor to himself and his wife by becoming a Chrisitian. Polyeucte recalls, however, that only when he turned to the Christian religion did his wife Pauline recover from a serious illness. Convinced of Polyeucte's sincerity, Néarque and other Christians retire to another part of the catacombs to baptise the convert.

Pauline enters with some attendants to place flowers at her mother's tomb and to make an offering to the goddess Proserpine. She prays that her mother's spirit will help her to forget a man she once loved and turn all her affections to Polyeucte instead. In the distance she hears the prayers of returning Christians but she cannot escape in time. Surprised to find Polyeucte among them, Pauline urges him to return to the pagan religion and threatens to denounce the Christians to Félix. Polyeucte reveals that he has already become a Christian and has just been baptized. A messenger reports that a Roman proconsul has arrived in Melitene with others from the emperor to renew persecution of the Christians. The Christians, however, are not afraid, and Polyeucte says he will not hide his faith.

Act II begins in Félix's study, where the governor issues new orders banishing all Christians, convinced that in this way he is serving the gods well. He shows Pauline a copy of the orders, which specify the death penalty for anyone who has been baptized, and declares that he will carry it out no matter who is affected. Félix asks why Pauline seems troubled. She replies that although she has come to respect and love Polyeucte, the husband her father chose for her, she still thinks of the man, now dead, to whom she was previously engaged.

Callisthènes, the high priest, enters to announce the arrival of the Roman proconsul. The latter is a military hero, once left for dead on the battlefield, then ransomed by the emperor after having been imprisoned for two years. Pauline's distress increases when she learns that the man is Sévère, her former lover, and wonders how she will escape this dilemma.

The scene changes to a public square, where choruses and dancing honor Sévère. The proconsul looks forward especially to seeing Pauline, not knowing that she is married. When she arrives and presents Polyeucte as her husband, Sévère hides his anger. Callisthènes reports that the Christians have recently baptized another convert and Sévère orders more vigorous persecution of the sect. The act ends amid mixed reactions, Néarque and Pauline urging Polyeucte to keep silent, Sévère overcome with jealousy of Polyeucte.

Act III begins in Pauline's room, where she is praying that memories of Sévère will leave her in peace. Sévère enters hopefully, since he has learned that Pauline's marriage was her father's wish, not her own. Pauline, however, reveals that she has come to love her husband. Sévère does not want to believe this and Pauline fears he may tempt her to want to return his love again. Finally both agree that they must part forever.

Polyeucte enters, troubled that he will be expected to attend a special sacrifice being prepared in the temple of Jupiter in honor of Sévère. Although he says he loves God even more than he loves Pauline, he finally yields to her pleas and agrees to attend the ceremony for her sake. Félix arrives with news that Néarque's affiliation with Christianity has been discovered and that he is being tortured to force revelation of the name of the person who was baptized in the catacombs. Since Félix knows that Néarque was Polyeucte's friend he excuses Polyeucte from attending the temple ceremony at which Néarque will be sacrificed. Now, however, Polyeucte wants to be there. In a monologue he reveals his intention to break the stone statues of the gods and to share Néarque's martyrdom.

The scene changes to the temple of Jupiter, where Callisthènes and Sévère demand that Néarque reveal the name of the Christians' most recent convert. Polyeucte stops them, admits he is the man, and overturns statues and sacred vessels of the temple. Sévère, Félix, and Callisthènes demand that Polyeucte be punished. Despite Pauline's pleading Polyeucte is led off to be executed.

In Félix's apartment, where Act IV begins, Pauline pleads in vain that her father spare Polyeucte's life. Even after she convinces Sévère that Polyeucte should not die, Félix refuses to free him unless he renounces Christianity.

The scene changes to a cell near the arena. Polyeucte has had a dream that he and Pauline went to heaven after she too embraced Christianity, and he prays that this dream will become reality. Pauline arrives to plead with him to renounce his faith and finds instead that she is miraculously converted. She and Polyeucte resolve to die together.

The scene changes to the arena, where the crowd calls for the execution of the Christians. Félix gives orders to begin the ceremony and is shocked to find his own daughter among the people led in by the guards. Although Sévère offers her the chance to renounce her new faith, she refuses to do so. Néarque and the other Christians are led in and all fall on their knees as Callisthènes and the priests turn the lions loose.

The libretto of *Les Martyrs* displays most of the same characteristics of French grand opera found in *Les Huguenots*, except that the historical period dealt with is earlier than that ordinarily found in grand opera. There is a loose but recognizable division of the musical numbers into dramatic tableaux, scenic tableaux, and set-numbers. The opening scene among the Christians, for example, is primarily dramatic, whereas the entrance of Pauline and her attendants begins a scenic tableau followed by a set-number (Pauline's air), then a dramatic finale. Dramatic scenes fill the first half of Act II, but the second part of the act is filled with processions and ballets and is, except for the finale, primarily scenic in nature. The last half of Act III is also scenic, but the first part of the third act is taken up with set-numbers. Most of Act IV is dramatic in nature, with the final scene comparable to that of *Les Huguenots* and including both scenic and dramatic elements.

As in *Les Huguenots*, the dramatic tableaux and some sections of the set-numbers of *Les Martyrs* outline the typical framework of the well-made libretto. The delayed-action plot begins after Polyeucte's conversion and during his baptism; after Sévère's supposed death and Pauline's marriage to Polyeucte; after Pauline has come to love her husband; after Sévère has been dispatched by the emperor to assist Félix in his ongoing persecution of the Christians. Actions are tightly woven together and carefully prepared. For example, Pauline's prayer for help to forget a man she once loved precedes the arrival of that man; her belief in pagan gods and her avowed love for Polyeucte prepare for the central conflict in the plot; and Félix's determination to kill all Christians even if they be members of his own family assures that there will be no *deus ex machina* to come save Polyeucte. This careful preparation is supported by the usual contrived entrances and exits, such as Pauline's arrival in the catacombs just as Polyeucte is being baptized or her entrance into her father's study just as he is signing the edict condemning all Christians. The action proper begins only in the finale of Act I. Thereafter each act presents the well-made libretto formula in miniature.

Characters in *Les Martyrs* are real in the usual Scribean sense. They are flat figures, the products of the librettist's instant characterization procedures, and their motivation derives from the logical workings of human minds and emotions. Even in his decision to die for his faith Polyeucte is just a strong, admirable human being, not a religious fanatic. He neither raves nor preaches; his prayers, declarations of faith, and attempts to convert Pauline are relatively direct and to the point, not overlaid with breast-beating emotionalism.

*Les Martyrs* contains several other features typical of Scribe's libretti. There is a *quiproquo* in that most members of the cast do not know until the end of the third act that Polyeucte is a Christian. In the course of the opera the hero's fortunes rise and fall until the *scène à faire*, when he makes known his religious faith, brings them to their lowest point. Thereafter his outlook gradually becomes brighter when, despite the threat of death, he is able to convert Pauline. In the recognition scene Félix, like Saint-Bris before him, finds too late that his daughter is among the martyrs.

Gounod's *Polyeucte* appeared nearly forty years after *Les Martyrs*. Like Donizetti's opera, Gounod's work was not very successful, for it was performed only twenty-nine times at the Opéra and saw performances in only two cities outside of Paris: Antwerp (1879) and Geneva (1882).[10] A five-act work, *Polyeucte* is viewed by Cooper as "a conscious attempt (on Gounod's part) to unite opera and oratorio,"[11] and was written during a time when Gounod was turning away from opera in favor of oratorio composition.[12] Thus, as one might expect, it is quite different in concept from *Les Martyrs* even though based on the same story.

Act I begins in Pauline's room at nightfall. Pauline tells Stratonice, her nurse, of a dream she has had which she believes to be prophetic. In it Polyeucte, her husband, worships before a Christian altar and is baptized. Suddenly Jupiter sends down thunder, which dissolves the altar into dust, and Polyeucte is killed. Stratonice tries unsuccessfully to reassure Pauline. Hearing Polyeucte approach, Pauline sends her attendants away.

Polyeucte is disturbed that Albin, the high priest, insists on sacrificing Christians to appease the gods, and thinks that Albin is using the gods as an excuse to conduct his personal crusade. He urges Pauline not to worry about her dream, especially since he is of royal blood and her father is governor, but rather to be concerned about the unfortunate victims of Albin's vengeance. He reveals that Sévère, a Roman envoy, has been sent from the emperor to help carry out the persecution of the Christians. Pauline confesses that she once loved Sévère and would have married him but that, believing him dead, she had yielded to her father's wishes and married Polyeucte instead. The latter, however, is not jealous, for he knows that Pauline now loves him. Néarque, a known Christian, arrives and Polyeucte departs with him. Again Pauline voices her fears that Polyeucte will die as in her dream.

The scene changes to a public square, where the people of Melitene honor Sévère. The hero is speechless when he learns that Pauline, whom he still loves, is married to someone else. A continuation of the chorus in honor of Sévère closes the act.

Beyond the garden where Act II begins an offstage chorus wishes Sévère a happy life and hopes he will enjoy the celebration prepared for him. Sévère, however, flees the crowd in despair, for his one hope was to be able to lay his honors and glory at the feet of Pauline and to marry her. He hides among the trees as Pauline enters. During her prayer to Vesta she mentions that marrying Polyeucte was her father's wish. Sévère comes forward hopefully, but Pauline declares that she now loves her husband. She finally persuades Sévère that the past cannot be recaptured and that the best thing he could do for her and for himself would be to find in his heart enough nobility and generosity to save Polyeucte from the fate she is certain awaits him. Sévère promises not to trouble Pauline again, and she enters the temple of Vesta to pray.

Polyeucte appears with Néarque. He sees Pauline in the temple and expresses his sadness that he must keep secrets from her. Néarque, however, observes that if Pauline knew, her tears might keep him from the true God. Agreeing that this is so, Polyeucte goes off with Néarque.

The scene changes to a site outside the city. A group of young patricians in a boat appears and one of them, Sextus, sings a *barcarolle* filled with references to pagan deities. After they leave Siméon appears, condemns their paganism, and greets the group of Christians that arrives for worship. After a prayer and an admonition that the people be willing to die for their faith if necessary, Siméon welcomes Néarque and

Polyeucte and baptizes the latter. Sévère, hidden among the rocks, observes the scene in amazement.

Act III begins in a room in the palace, where Albin reveals to Félix, Sévère, and Polyeucte that he has received news of a recent baptism at a meeting of the Christians. Furious, he demands that the pagan gods be avenged. Félix agrees, but Sévère refuses to take part in such mindless cruelty done in the name of the gods. He points out that the Christians are being accused of crimes they have not committed in order to justify their execution and that nobles, not just people of the lower classes, are also members of the sect. Félix, hostile, will not listen and swears he will punish anyone found to be a Christian, even members of his own family, because the gods will it.

Alone with Polyeucte, Sévère urges him to keep his faith secret or give it up for Pauline's sake, but Polyeucte declares himself willing to die if necessary. When Néarque arrives, Polyeucte persuades him to go along to the temple, overthrow the stone statues of the gods, and be martyred.

The scene changes to a public square before the temple of Jupiter. The people sing praises to their gods and begin the sacrifice ceremony with a ballet in which various pagan deities appear and are honored. Albin calls for the sacrifice of Christians, but Polyeucte stops the ceremony, admits he is a Christian, and denounces the false gods. He and Néarque break the statues of the gods and in the ensuing fray Néarque is killed. Only the intervention of Sévère and his soldiers prevents the mob from murdering Polyeucte as well.

Act IV takes place in a prison where Polyeucte is awaiting execution. In a monologue he declares that he has given up the world and that God has replaced Pauline as the central object of his love. Pauline arrives and tries to persuade him to renounce his religion and be released from prison, but he refuses. He takes out a scroll Néarque gave him and reads to her the biblical accounts of Epiphany and the crucifixion. Pauline, however, can think only of Polyeucte's fate and continues to urge him to return to the pagan religion. Sévère enters and tries to help Polyeucte escape, but the latter refuses to leave the prison. Félix and the guards arrive and take Polyeucte to the arena.

Act V opens in a public square near the entrance to the arena. The people call for the Christians' deaths. Before the assembly of people and priests Polyeucte sings a shortened textual parody of the *Credo*. As the infuriated crowd demands he be punished Pauline enters, saying she has been converted and wishes to die with Polyeucte. The two repeat Polyeucte's *Credo* in unison over the cries of the people.

The scene changes to the interior of the arena, with Polyeucte and Pauline kneeling in the center, illuminated by a light from heaven. As the people call for their execution they feel God calling them to the skies. An officer steps forward to release the lions.

Gounod's *Polyeucte* is musically and dramatically a static, slow-moving work. Like *Les Martyrs*, it has a delayed-action plot, but unlike Donizetti's work it does not present essential information in an exposition before the real action of the opera begins. Rather, bits and pieces of expository or background material are scattered about throughout Act I, often just suggested rather than stated clearly, and action proceeds slowly in the loosely knit fabric of the plot. A good example of these points is to be found in the events and actions relating to Polyeucte's conversion and baptism. In *Les Martyrs* the conflict between the pagan religion and Christianity is established immediately and elements of a subsidiary conflict—that of Pauline's love for her husband and her memory of a former lover—are introduced. In *Polyeucte* Pauline's dream prepares the spectator, albeit in a rather speculative way, for the outcome of the opera, but not until the last half of Act II is there any more than an indefinite suggestion that Polyeucte is indeed a Christian, not merely a sensitive man indignant over injustices being committed by a proud ruling class against a group of innocent and defenseless people.

Three elements of the Barbier and Carré libretto cause the action to seem much less vital and to move more slowly than in Scribe's grand operas. The first is the greater emphasis placed on the characters as individuals; the second is the larger amount of time and space devoted to scenic tableaux; and the third is the use of several prominent but unnecessary characters.

Because characters do develop psychologically, Barbier and Carré must necessarily devote a greater proportion of their libretto to set-numbers, especially monologues and duos, in which the various personae have room to express themselves and expand upon their own thoughts and emotions. Naturally, one cannot be expressing thoughts and catching Christians at the same time, and physical motion—i.e., situation—gives way before the static moment and portrait of the individual.

Frequently in *Polyeucte* a situation is barely allowed to develop before it is interrupted by a long scenic tableau. In Act I, for example, the possibility of Polyeucte's conversion is discussed for a time during the first half of the act, itself partly devoted to a scenic tableau, then interrupted for choruses and processions in honor of Sévère, whose speech before the crowd is less than concise. At the beginnings of Acts II and V Barbier and Carré make no pretense of plunging directly into a new situation but dwell on nondramatic tableaux. Indeed, Act II is even more thoroughly scenic than the second act of *Les Huguenots*. It begins with an empty stage and an offstage chorus, followed by two soliloquies and an overly long duo in which Sévère and Pauline express their thoughts and feelings on their former love. In half an act the only thing that has occurred is Sévère's decision to be honorable and to trouble Pauline no longer. In the last half of this act the finale alone presents an event: Polyeucte's baptism. Before this we are treated to a pleasant but hardly essential *barcarolle*, a procession of the arriving Christians, a textual parody of the Lord's Prayer, and a sermon extolling the virtues of martyrdom. In Act III only Scene i and the Finale contain any action, and Act IV is nothing more than a sermon-like attempt to convert Pauline. The fifth act is similar to the second and third in that it is primarily scenic, the only action taking place when Pauline arrives to join the Christians.

Three characters in *Polyeucte* are nonessential: Stratonice, Sextus, and Siméon. Stratonice exists only to provide Pauline with a confidante to whom she can tell her dream; after the first scene the nurse disappears. Sextus and Siméon, both included in Act II, have larger roles and could confuse or distract the spectator. Sextus has a long solo *barcarolle* to perform, yet we are never told his name and never know whether he will eventually play some important role or, indeed, why he is in the opera at all. Siméon is obviously the leader of the Christians and one expects more of him than a long but static appearance in one scene of one act of the opera. He is definitely a descendant of Scribe's Marcel, but not nearly so active: he preaches but does not practice.

Mention of Marcel and of the sermonizing not only by Siméon but by most of the other principals as well brings up the question of the relationship between the libretto of Barbier and Carré and the Scribe legacy. Clearly, the framework of the well-made libretto and the dependence on situation and action so prominent in Scribe's libretti have given way to a loosely woven plot filled with suggestions rather than clear statements, with expansive monologues and emotion-filled moments. Yet Scribe's influence remains. If the plot and at least one character are similar to those of *Les Huguenots*, the plan of the opera and the majority of its principal figures are descended from *Le Prophète*. Like *Le Prophète*, *Polyeucte* relies to an unusual degree on scenic tableaux. Like Scribe's characters, the figures created by Barbier and Carré advocate specific doctrines and beliefs and sermonize at length, thus taking the emphasis from the story and placing it on themselves and their beliefs. Gounod's Polyeucte is not like Donizetti's. Rather, he is a religious fanatic, a man with a mission, an Armenian John of Leyden. After his baptism no human means can sway him from his determination to be a martyr. He quotes scripture at his adversary, a temptress Eve, and one can imagine him going toward the lions glassy eyed, slightly mad, convinced he is but a step away from his heavenly reward. In their creation of this superhuman hero and in the spiritual, mystical overtones suggested in their libretto, Barbier and Carré show the probable joint influence of not one but two prophets: Scribe's John of Leyden and Germany's Richard Wagner.

## STRETTO

In the history of French opera of the nineteenth century the libretti of Eugene Scribe represent an area of stability and continuity which spanned two-and-one-half decades. In his craft Scribe crossed generic lines by bringing together a number of consistent structural principles and applying them with necessary modifications and great technical skill to a variety of theatrical genres including those of the musical theatre. Scribe's operas and opéras comiques not only had a strong basis in the popular theatre, but this popular theatre itself was in good part the result of Scribe's own contributions in his *comédies-vaudevilles.* A foundation in the popular theatre was one factor that contributed to Scribe's continued success in libretto writing, for his was a strongly social art rooted in the conditions not only of the Paris stages but of Paris itself.

Times changed, and so did Paris. Neither opera nor opéra comique could remain the same in the face of the Second Empire, and new trends arose to take the place of the old. Yet certain consistencies remained. The leading librettists after 1850—Meilhac, Halévy, Barbier, Carré—were, like Scribe, men of the theatre active in a variety of dramatic genres. Their plays were popular art in the best sense of the term. Inasmuch as their libretti retained something of the spirit, life and character of the popular theatre they were successful. When they tried to move out into more remote, unconventional, esoteric spheres, as did Barbier and Carré in their operas, they found themselves part of a tradition either dying or not valid for their modern world.

The legacy of Scribe was passed down to these later librettists not only in such general ways as similarities in their social backgrounds and the orientation of their pens. Changing times meant changing styles, but the basic strength and validity of Scribe's writing techniques is demonstrated by the fact that his influence can be traced in the works of later writers. Because Scribe provided libretti for the most popular operas and opéras comiques of his day, works that were performed with repeated success long after his death, his example was ever present in the world of French opera. Moreover, this influence extended not only beyond his own time, but beyond the boundaries of his own country. Creator of a tradition, Scribe sustained this tradition for years and in it provided a foundation for modern libretto techniques.

# NOTES

## LIFE OF EUGÈNE SCRIBE

[1]René Doumic, *De Scribe à Ibsen* (Paris: Perrin et Cie., 1901), pp. viii-ix.

[2]For a survey of criticisms of Scribe, cf. Stephen S. Stanton, *English Drama and the French Well-Made Play, 1815-1915* (Ann Arbor: University Microfilms, 1955).

[3]*Op. cit.*, p. 2.

[4]Stanton, *op. cit.*, p. 299.

[5]Henri Blaze de Bury, "Portraits d'hier et d'aujourd'hui I, Auber et Scribe," *Revue des Deux Mondes*, Ser. 3, Vol. XXXV (September-October 1879), pp. 54-55.

[6]*Ibid.*

[7]Théophile Gautier, *Histoire de l'art dramatique en France depuis vingt-cinq ans* (Leipzig: Edition Hetzel, 1858-1859), Vol. III, p. 15.

[8]Ernest Legouvé, *Sixty Years of Recollections*, trans. A. Vandam (London & Sydney: Eden, Remington, & Co. 1893), Vol. II, p. 105.

[9]Arthur Scherle, "Eugène Scribe und die Oper des 19. Jahrhunderts," *Maske und Kothurn*, Vol. III (1957), p. 141.

[10]For a study of Scribe's influence on the English theatre, see Stanton, *op. cit.*

[11]Legouvé, *op. cit.*, Vol. II, p. 126.

[12]J. Brander Matthews, *French Dramatists of the Nineteenth Century* (New York: Charles Scribner's Sons, 1901), p. 101.

[13]J. Brander Matthews, "Eugène Scribe," *Atlantic Monthly*, Vol. XLVII (1881), pp. 648-649.

[14]A. de Forges, "Scribe, son répertoire, ses collaborateurs," *Le Ménestrel*, Vol. XLII (1876), p. 67.

[15]Matthews, *French Dramatists*, pp. 100-102; and "Eugéne Scribe," p. 689.

[16]Scherle, *op. cit.*, pp. 156-158.

[17]The following have served as sources for biographical information on Scribe: Neil Cole Arvin, *Eugène Scribe and the French Theatre, 1815-1860* (Cambridge: Harvard University Press, 1924); Paul Bonnefon, "Scribe sous l'Empire et sous la Restauration d'après des documents inédits," *Revue d'Histoire littéraire de la France*, Vol. XXVII (1920), pp. 321-370; Paul Bonnefon, "Scribe sous la Monarchie de Juillet d'après des documents inédits," *Revue d'Histoire littéraire de la France*, Vol. XXVIII (1921), pp.

60-99, 241-260; and Lila Maurice-Amour, "Scribe, Auguste-Eugène," *Die Musik in Geschichte und Gegenwart* (Kassel & Basel: Bärenreiter, 1965), Vol. XII, cols. 437-440. Specific quotations will be noted separately as they occur.

[18]Bonnefon, "Scribe sous l'Empire," pp. 327-328.

[19]*Ibid.*, p. 330.

[20]Arvin, *op. cit.*, p. 10.

[21]Bonnefon, "Scribe sous l'Empire," p. 367.

[22]Arvin, *op. cit.*, p. 9.

[23]*Ibid.*, p. 13.

[24]Bonnefon, "Scribe sous l'Empire," p. 368.

[25]Bonnefon, "Scribe sous la Monarchie," p. 65. All italics are original.

[26]Arvin, *op. cit.*, p. 24.

[27]Matthews, *French Dramatists*, p. 82.

[28]Louis Véron, *Memoires d'un bourgeois de Paris* (Paris: G. de Gonet [1853-1855], Vol. III, p. 121.

[29]Bonnefon, "Scribe sous l'Empire," p. 356.

[30]J. G. Prod'homme, "Wagner, Berlioz, and Monsieur Scribe. Two Collaborations That Miscarried," *Musical Quarterly*, Vol. XII (1926), p. 361; and Véron, *op. cit.*, Vol. III, p. 126.

[31]Matthews, *French Dramatists*, p. 89.

[32]Véron, *op. cit.*, Vol. III, p. 122.

[33]Paul Smith (D. G. E. Monnais), "Eugene Scribe," *Revue et Gazette Musicale de Paris*, Vol. XXVIII, No. 8 (February 24, 1861), p. 57.

[34]Matthews, "Eugène Scribe," p. 686.

[35]*Ibid.*, p. 680.

[36]Paul Henry Lang, "The Literary Aspects of the History of Opera in France" (unpublished Ph.D. dissertation, Department of Music, Cornell University, 1934), pp. 7-8.

## SCRIBE AND HIS COLLABORATORS

[1]A. de Forges, *op. cit.*, p. 68.

[2]Véron, *op. cit.*, Vol. III, p. 126.

[3]Vapereau, *Dictionnaire des contemporains*, translated in Prod'homme, *op. cit.*, p. 360.

[4]Gautier, *op. cit.*, Vol. I, pp. 82-83.

[5]Bonnefon, "Scribe sous l'Empire," p. 344.

[6]Legouvé, *op. cit.*, Vol. II, pp. 119-120.

[7]*Ibid.*, pp. 52-53.

[8]Rey M. Longyear, *D. F. E. Auber: A Chapter in the History of the Opéra-Comique, 1800-1878* (Ann Arbor: University Microfilms, 1957), p. 245. All italics are original.

[9]Legouvé, *op. cit.*, pp. 120-121.

[10]David Owen Evans, *Le Théâtre pendant la période romantique (1827-1848)* (Paris: Les Presses Universitaires de France, 1925), p. 84.

[11]Matthews, *French Dramatists*, pp. 87-88.

[12]Longyear, *op. cit.*, p. 245.

[13]This term is used by Matthews, "Eugène Scribe," p. 649.

[14]Longyear, *op. cit.*, p. 254. All italics are original.

## THE THEATRES OF SCRIBE'S PARIS

[1]Lang, *op. cit.*, p. 3.

[2]D. O. Evans, *op. cit.*, 3.

[3]Gautier, *op. cit.*, Vol. III, p. 67.

[4]John B. Wolf, *France, 1815 to the Present* (New York: Prentice-Hall, Inc., 1940), p. 16.

[5]Frederick B. Artz, *France under the Bourbon Restoration, 1814-1830* (Cambridge, Mass.: Harvard University Press, 1931), p. 264.

[6]*Ibid.*, p. 258.

[7]Wolf, *op. cit.*, p. 17.

[8]Artz, *op. cit.*, p. 235.

[9] *Ibid.*, pp. 265-266.

[10] Gautier, *op. cit.*, Vol. III, p. 68.

[11] *Ibid.*, Vol. IV, p. 265.

[12] Victor Hallays-Dabot, *Histoire de la censure théâtrale en France (Paris: E. Dentu, 1862), p. 261.*

[13] *Ibid.*, p. 270.

[14] *Ibid.*, p. 250.

[15] *Ibid.*, pp. 248-249.

[16] *Ibid.*, p. 276.

[17] Artz, *op. cit.*, pp. 83-85.

[18] Hallays-Dabot, *op. cit.*, p. 281.

[19] Karl Mantzius, *A History of Theatrical Art*, trans. C. Archer (New York: Peter Smith, 1937), Vol. VI, p. 201.

[20] Hallays-Dabot, *op. cit.*, pp. 289-290.

[21] *Ibid.*, pp. 308, 314.

[22] *Ibid.*, p. 330.

[23] George Hogarth, *Memoirs of the Musical Drama* (London: Richard Bentley, 1838), Vol. II, p. 351.

[24] Artz, *op. cit.*, p. 247.

[25] Maurice Albert, *Les Théâtres des boulevards (1789-1848)* (Paris: *Société française d'imprimerie et de librairie,* 1907), p. 253.

[26] Bonnefon, "Scribe sous l'Empire," p. 364.

[27] Artz, *op. cit.*, p. 237.

[28] D. O. Evans, *op. cit.*, pp. 4-5.

[29] Cf. J. Brander Matthews, *The Theatres of Paris* (New York: Charles Scribner's Sons, 1880), Chapters 5-7.

[30]Information for the above from D. O. Evans, *op. cit.*, p. 9 ff; Mantzius, *op. cit.*, Vol. VI, pp. 190-204; Phyllis Hartnoll, ed., *Oxford Companion to the Theatre* (London: Oxford University Press, 1951), pp. 141-142, 289. Quotation from Mantzius, p. 201.

[31]Arvin, *op. cit.*, p. 81.

[32]Mantzius, *op. cit.*, Vol. VI, pp. 205-207.

[33]Hartnoll, *op. cit.*, p. 347; Matthews, *The Theatres*, p. 164; Bonnefon, "Scribe sous l'Empire," p. 347.

[34]Albert, *op. cit.*, p. 265.

[35]Bonnefon, "Scribe sous l'Empire," p. 339.

[36]Hartnoll, *op. cit.*, p. 824.

[37]*Ibid.*, p. 824; Matthews, *The Theatres*, p. 161.

[38]D. O. Evans, *op. cit.*, p. 83.

[39]Hartnoll, *op. cit.*, p. 288.

[40]Lang, *op. cit.*, p. 241.

[41]Arvin, *op. cit.*, p. 17.

[42]Hartnoll, *op. cit.*, p. 289.

[43]*Ibid.*, p. 626.

[44]Matthews, *The Theatres*, pp. 170-171.

[45]Hartnoll, *op. cit.*, p. 24.

[46]*Ibid.*, p. 297.

[47]*Ibid.*

[48]James Frederick Mason, *The Melodrama in France from the Revolution to the Beginnings of Romantic Drama, 1791-1830* (Baltimore: J. H. Furst Co., 1912), pp. 20-21.

[49]*Ibid.*, p. xii.

[50]Paul Ginisty, *Le Mélodrame* (Paris: Louis-Michaud [1910]), p. 15.

[51]For further information, see Jan van der Veen, *Le Melodrame musical de Rousseau au romantisme* (La Haye: M.. Nijhoff, 1955).

[52]Artz, *op. cit.*, p. 339.

[53]Ginisty, *op. cit.*, p. 213.

[54]*Ibid.*, p. 216.

[55]Matthews, *The Theatres*, pp. 18-19, 31, 51; Guy Ferchault, "Paris, D. 19. Jahrhundert," *Die Musik in Geschichte und Gegenwart* (Kassel & Basel: Bärenreiter, 1962), Vol. X, cols. 773-774; John Hullah, "Académie de Musique," *Grove's Dictionary of Music and Musicians* (Fifth edition; London: Macmillan & Co., 1954), Vol. I, *p. 21;* A. Peytel, "Les Théâtres musicaux subventionnés," *Encyclopédie de la musique et dictionnaire du Conservatoire*, edited by A. Lavignac (Paris: Librairie Delagrave, 1913-1931), Part II, Vol. VI, p. 3819.

[56]This theatre was twice restored or rebuilt during the latter half of the nineteenth century. See Ferchault, *op. cit.*, col. 775; "Paris," *Grove's Dictionary*, Vol. VI, pp. 547-548; Albert Soubies and Charles Malherbe, *Histoire de l'Opéra-Comique: La seconde Salle Favart, 1840-1860* (Paris: Librairie Marpon et Flammarion, 1892), pp. 11-13.

[57]Matthews, *The Theatres*, p. 60.

[58]Matthews, *The Theatres*, p. 160; Hartnoll, *op. cit.*, pp. 288, 579. The Odéon was also the scene of several performances of musical-theatrical works lying outside the realms of the Opéra and the Opéra-Comique: for example, *Robin des Bois*, Castil-Blaze's version of Weber's *Der Freischütz*, which enjoyed some success at this theatre. Cf. John Hullah, *op. cit.*, p. 21.

[59]"Paris," *Grove's Dictionary*, p. 548; Ferchault, *op. cit.*, col. 776.

[60]Matthews, *The Theatres*, pp. 65-66; Ferchault, *op. cit.*, col. 777; Soubies and Malherbe, *op. cit.*, pp. 170-171.

[61]Hartnoll, *op. cit.*, p. 663.

[62]Donald Jay Grout, *A Short History of Opera* (second edition; New York: Columbia University Press, 1965), p. 315.

[63]H. Sutherland Edwards, *History of Opera from Its Origins in Italy to the Present Time* (London: William H. Allen & Co., 1862), Vol. II, p. 189.

[64]Oliver Strunk, "Musical Life in Paris (1817-1848), a Chapter from the Memoirs of Sophie Augustine Leo," *Musical Quarterly*, Vol. XVII (1931), p. 261.

[65]*Ibid.*, p.. 267.

[66]Camille Bellaigue, "Les Epoques de la musique: *le grand opéra-français*," *Revue des Deux Mondes*, Ser. 5, Vol. XXXV (September-October 1906), p. 613; Strunk, *op. cit.*, pp. 262-263.

[67]Cf. Hector Berlioz, "Quelques mots sur les anciens compositeurs, et sur Grétry en particulier," *Revue et Gazette Musicale de Paris*, Vol. IV, No. 6 (February 5, 1837), 45-46; Jaques Barzun, *Berlioz and the Romantic Century* (Boston: Little, Brown & Co., 1950), Vol. I, chapter 3.

[68]Strunk, *op. cit.*, p. 262.

[69]Joseph d'Ortigue, *De la Guerre des dilettanti, ou de la révolution opérée par M. Rossini dans l'opéra françois [sic]* (Paris: Librairie de Ladvocat, 1829), p. 6.

[70]Strunk, *op. cit.*, p. 394.

[71]d'Ortigue, *op. cit.*, pp. 6-7.

[72]Jean-François Gail, *Reflexions sur le goût musical en France* (Paris: Paulin, 1832), p. 41.

[73]J.-G. Prod'homme, "Rossini and His Works in France," *Musical Quarterly*, Vol. XVII (1931), p. 111.

[74]Strunk, *op. cit.*, pp. 268-269.

[75]d'Ortigue, *op. cit.*, pp. 22-30.

[76]Lang, *op. cit.*, p. 231.

[77]*Ibid.*, p. 227.

[78]Gautier, *op. cit.*, Vol. I, p. 17.

[79]Gail, *op. cit.*, p. 4.

[80]*Ibid.*, p. 50.

[81]Bellaigue, *op. cit.*, p. 620.

[82]Subtitle of William L. Crosten's *French Grand Opera* (New York: King's Crown Press, 1948); italics my own.

[83]Véron, *op. cit.*, Vol. III, p. 171.

[84]*Ibid.*, Vol. III, p. 161.

[85]*Ibid.*, Vol. III, pp. 173-178.

[86]Lang, *op. cit.*, p. 279.

[87]Auguste Thurner, *Les Transformations de l'Opéra-Comique* (Paris: Castel, 1865), pp. 224-225.

[88]Gautier, *op. cit.*, Vol. II, pp. 142-143.

[89]Rey M. Longyear, "'*Le livret bien fait*': The Opéra Comique Librettos of Eugène Scribe," *Southern Quarterly*, Vol. I (1963), p. 171.

[90]Lang, *op. cit.*, pp. 294-295.

[91]Longyear, *D. F. E. Auber*, pp. 218-219.

[92]*Ibid.*, p. 111.

[93]*Ibid.*, p. 219.

[94]Grout, *op. cit.*, p. 331.

[95]Gail, *op. cit.*, p. 60.

[96]Thurner, *op. cit.*, p. 246.

[97]Longyear, *D. F. E. Auber*, p. 1.

[98]Maurice Cauchie, "The High Lights of French Opera Comique," *Musical Quarterly*, Vol. XXV (1939), p. 309.

[99]Longyear, *D. F. E. Auber*, p. 65.

[100]Gautier, *op. cit.*, Vol. II, pp. 142-143.

[101]Longyear, *D. F. E. Auber*, pp. 5-7.

[102]Marie-Antoinette Allévy [Akakia-Viala], *La Mise en scène en France dans la première moitié du XIX^e^ siècle* (Paris: E. Droz, 1938), pp. 69-71.

SCRIBE AND THE LIBRETTO: PERSPECTIVE

[1]*La Presse*, November 24, 1841, quoted in Raymond Leslie Evans, *Les Romantiques français et la musique* (Paris: Honoré Champion, 1934), p. 141.

[2]Gautier, *op. cit.*, Vol. V, pp. 288-289.

[3]*Ibid.*, Vol. V, p. 288.

[4]*Ibid.*, Vol. I, pp. 17-18.

[5]*Ibid.*, p. 143.

[6]Douglas Moore, "Something about Librettos," *Opera News*, Vol. XVI, No. 1 (September 30, 1961), p. 9.

[7]F. Castil-Blaze [François-Henri-Joseph Blaze], *De l'Opéra en France* (Paris: Janet et Cotelle, 1820), p. 72.

[8]*Ibid.*, pp. 70-72.

[9]F. Castil-Blaze [François-Henri-Joseph Blaze], *Sur l'Opéra français, verités dures mais utiles* (Paris: Castil-Blaze, 1856), p. 10.

[10]Lamartine, *XXX$^e$ Entretien*, Ch. xx; quoted in R. L. Evans, *op. cit.*, pp. 141-142.

[11]Pierre Lassere, *The Spirit of French Music*, trans. D. Turner (London: Kegan Paul, Trench, Trubner & Co., Ltd., 1921), pp. 127-128.

[12]Lang, *op. cit.*, pp. 45-46.

[13]S. A. Rhodes, *Gérard de Nerval* (New York: Philosophical Library, 1951), p. 83. This tale later served as the basis for Gounod's opera of the same title, with libretto by Barbier and Carré.

[14]Letter to his sister Adèle (April 17, 1835) in Hector Berlioz, *Les Années romantiques, 1819-1842*, ed. J. Tiersot (Paris: Calmann-Levy [1904]), p. 281.

[15]Loewenberg, *op. cit.*, Vol. I, cols. 783-785.

[16]Gautier, *op. cit.*, Vol. III, p. 15.

[17]L. de M., "Du Style et de la poésie des opéras français," *Revue et Gazette Musicale de Paris*, Vol. II, No. 50 (December 13, 1835), was sufficiently aware of such repetitions in libretti of the time to suggest that at least three of them—"La force m'abandonne," "A peine je respire," and "Je tremble d'effroi," no strangers to Scribe's pen—be used less frequently.

[18]Robert Freeman, "Apostolo Zeno's Reform of the Libretto," *Journal of the American Musicological Society*, Vol. XXI (1968), p. 334.

[19]Letter from Metastasio to Francesco Giovanni de Chastellux, 1766, translated in Ulrich Weisstein, *The Essence of Opera* (New York: Free Press of Glencoe, 1964), p. 99.

[20]A. A. Abert, "Libretto," *Die Musik in Geschichte und Gegenwart* (Kassel & Basel: Bärenreiter, 1960), Vol. VIII, col. 712.

[21]Aubrey S. Garlington, "The Concept of the Marvelous in French and German Opera, 1770-1840" (unpublished Ph.D. dissertation, School of Music, University of Illinois, 1965), p. 3.

[22]Gautier, *op. cit.*, Vol. V, p. 288.

[23]"L. de M.," *op. cit.*, pp. 405-406.

[24]Crosten, *op. cit.*, p. 87.

[25]Letter to M. Letellier, August 3, 1824, quoted in Arthur Pougin, *Boieldieu* (Paris: Charpentier et Cie., 1875), pp. 214-215, and summarized in Paul-Louis Robert, "Correspondance de Boieldieu," *Rivista Musicale Italiana*, Vol. XIX (1912), p. 99.

[26]Henri Blanchard, "De la poésie lyrique et musicale," *Revue et Gazette Musicale de Paris*, Vol. XII, No. 41 (October 12, 1845), p. 334.

[27]Antoine Reicha, *Art du compositeur dramatique* (Paris: Simon Richault, 1833), p. 14.

[28]Lang, *op. cit.*, p. 107.

[29]Véron, *op. cit.*, Vol. III, p. 248.

[30]Reicha, *op. cit.*, p. 11.

[31]Louis Spohr, *Autobiography*, translatled from the German (London: Reeves & Turner, 1878), Vol. II, p. 115.

[32]F. Castil-Blaze [François-Henri-Joseph Blaze], *Théâtres lyriques de Paris de 1645 à 1855*, (Paris: Castil-Blaze, 1855), pp. 211-212.

[33]Gautier, *op. cit.*, Vol. III, p. 16.

[34]Véron, *op. cit.*, Vol. III, pp. 252-253.

[35]Lang, *op. cit.*, p. 279.

[36]Reicha, *op. cit.*, p. 12.

## THE OPÉRA COMIQUE LIBRETTO BEFORE SCRIBE

[1]Georges Favre, *Boieldieu: sa vie, son oeuvre* (Paris: Librarie E. Droz, 1944-45), Vol. II, p. 44

[2]Loewenberg, *op. cit.*, Vol. I, cols. 320-321.

[3]*Ibid.*, Vol. I, col. 413.

[4]*Ibid.*, Vol. I, cols. 413-414.

[5]*Ibid*, Vol. I, col. 507.

[6]For further information on this question, see the discussion of the source of *Fra Diavolo* p. 98, and Chapter 6, n.19.

[7]F. Lamy, *Jean-François Le Sueur* (Paris: Librairie Fischbacher, 1912), p. 46.

[8]Loewenberg, *op. cit.*, Vol. I, col. 555. Boieldieu himself did the revision in the summer of 1824, and mentions in his letters that he worked as much on it as on a new work. Cf. P.-L. Robert, *op. cit.*, p. 99.

[9]This distribution of roles is similar to but not exactly the same as in Méhul's *Joseph.*

A SURVEY OF SCRIBE'S OPERAS COMIQUES

[1]Stanton, *op. cit.*, pp. 41-42.

[2]*Ibid.*

[3]*Ibid.*, p. 242.

[4]Reicha, *op. cit.*, p. 13.

[5]Longyear, "'*Le livret bien fait*,'" p. 175.

[6]Reicha, *op. cit.*, p. 70.

[7]*Ibid.*, p. 76.

[8]*Ibid.*, p. 13.

[9]Michael Kaufmann, *Zur Technik der Komödien von Eugène Scribe* (Hamburg: Lütcke & Wulff, 1911).

[10]Martin Cooper, *Opéra-Comique* (London: Max Parrish & Co., Ltd., 1949), p. 59.

[11]Wolf, *op. cit.*, 89.

[12]*Ibid.* pp. 168-169.

[13]Translated by Humphrey Searle, *Hector Berlioz, a Selection from His Letters* (New York: Harcourt, Brace, & World, Inc., 1966), pp. 108-109.

[14]Longyear, *D. F. E. Auber*, p. 192.

[15]Dates given are according to Loewenberg, *op. cit.*, Vol. I, *passim.*

[16]H. J. Holz, "Die Tradition des Opernbuches," *Musikblätter des Anbruch*, Vol. IV, No. 15-16 (September-October 1922) pp. 231-232.

[17]It was given 525 times at the Opéra-Comique between its premiere in 1825 and 1896. Cf. Loewenberg, *op. cit.*, Vol. I, col. 695.

[18]Benoît-Jean-Baptiste Jouvin, *D. F. E. Auber, sa vie et ses oeuvres* (Paris: Heugel et Cie., 1864), p. 30. According to Scherle, *op. cit.*, pp. 147-148, the opera is based on a short story with an unhappy ending. Since he names neither the tale nor its source, it is impossible to say whether he and Jouvin are referring to the same source.

[19]Arvin, *op. cit.*, p. 184. Several sources cite a connection between *Fra Diavolo* and Lesueur's *La Caverne.* Both Eduard Hanslick (*Die moderne Oper* [Zweite unveränderte Auflage; Berlin: A. Hofmann & Co., 1875], p. 133, n.) and Scherle (*op.*

*cit.*, p. 148) trace the connection via a version of *La Caverne* entitled *Fra Diavolo, Chef des Brigands dans les Alpes*, presented in Paris in 1808 by Cuvellier and Franconi as a spectacle piece and given in Germany as *Die Räuber in den Abruzzen* with great success in 1822. George Upton (*The Standard Operas* [new edition; Chicago: A. C. McClurg & Co., 1917], p. 7) simply states that Scribe's *Fra Diavolo* is based on *La Caverne.* However, in view of the great differences in plot between the two operas of Lesueur and Auber, this connection cannot be substantiated. Also, according to Arvin (*op. cit.*, pp.183-184), the person on whose life *Fra Diavolo* is supposed to have been based was active in Italy *ca.* 1810. If so, any connection between Auber's opera and *La Caverne* would have to be coincidental.

[20]Georg Knepler, *Musikgeschichte des 19. Jahrhunderts* (Berlin: Henschelverlag, 1961), Vol I, p. 262, states that the date is 1788, but there is no substantiation of this either in the libretto or in the score. In fact, certain statements made by various characters about the nature of freedom in France at the time the action is supposed to be taking place would suggest a date of *ca.* 1815-1820.

[21]Hermann Abert, *Gesammelte Schriften und Vorträge*, edited by Friedrich Blume (Halle an der Saale: Max Niemeyer Verlag, 1929), p. 410.

[22]Longyear, *D. F. E. Auber*, p. 47; general information on pp. 46-47 and in Knepler, *op. cit.*, Vol. I, pp. 262-265.

[23]Grout, *op. cit.*, pp. 304-305.

[24]Knepler, *op. cit.*, Vol. I, pp. 263-264.

[25]*Ibid.*, p. 259.

[26]Longyear, *D. F. E. Auber*, p. 47.

[27]Stanton, *op. cit.*, p.7.

[28]Longyear, *D. F. E. Auber*, p. 238.

[29]Félix Clément and Pierre Larousse, *Dictionnaire des Operas* (Paris: Librairie Larousse, 1897), p. 671.

[30]Longyear, *D. F. E. Auber*, p. 390; Loewenberg, *op. cit.*, Vol. I, col. 723; Alexander Ringer, "Fra Diavolo," *Musical Quarterly*, Vol. XXXVIII (1952), p. 642 ff.

[31]Stanton, *op. cit.*, p. 42.

[32]Ringer, *op. cit.*, p. 643.

[33]Grout, *op. cit.*, p. 305.

[34]Ringer, *op. cit.*, p. 643.

[35]Gerald Abraham, *A Hundred Years of Music* (second edition; London: Duckworth, 1955), p. 79.

[36]The vaudeville is printed in Eugène Scribe, *Oeuvres Complètes* (Paris: E. Dentu, 1877), Series 2, Vol. X, pp. 137-178.

[37]*Ibid.*, pp. 150-151.

[38]*Ibid.*, p. 141.

[39]*Ibid.*, p. 160.

[40]Longyear, *D. F. E. Auber*, p. 90.

[41]*Ibid.*, p. 91.

[42]Paul H. Beik, *Louis Philippe and the July Monarchy* (Princeton: D. Van Nostrand Co., Inc., 1965), p. 58.

[43]William Ashbrook, *Donizetti* (London: Cassell & Co. Ltd., 1965), p. 398, n. 2.

[44]Henri Blanchard, "Théâtre royal de l'Opéra-Comique. La Barcarolle ou l'Amour et la musique. . . ," *Revue et Gazette Musicale de Paris*, Vol. XII, No. 17 (April 27, 1845), p. 130.

[45]Loewenberg, *op. cit.*, Vol. I, cols. 413-414.

[46]Gautier, *op. cit.*, Vol. IV, p. 79.

[47]Clément and Larousse, *op. cit.*, p. 121.

[48]*Ibid.*, p. 217.

[49]Arthur Pougin, *Adolphe Adam* (Paris: G. Charpentier, 1877), pp. 90-91.

[50]Loewenberg, *op. cit.*, Vol. I, col. 562; Ashbrook, *op. cit.*, p. 487, n. 1.

[51]Lang, *op. cit.*, p. 246.

[52]Note the similarities here to the proposed duel between the Marquis and Lorenzo over Zerline in *Fra Diavolo.*

[53]In part this is due to the conventions of the time, for music was far less important or dramatically essential in eighteenth century singspiel or opéra comique than it became in the nineteenth century in both forms.

[54]Pougin, *op. cit.*, p. 90.

[55]*Ibid.*, pp. 93-94. Scribe apparently revised Adam's offending lines later, for they do not appear in the printed libretto or in the piano score in the form given by Adam.

[56]Clément and Larousse, *op. cit.*, p. 217.

[57]The general outlines of this number parallel those in the last act of *La Dame blanche*, when Georges Brown hears an old Scottish folk song and continues it when the chorus leaves off.

[58]It must be noted that although they do not follow the *Le Maçon-Le Chalet* pattern, the opening scenes of both *Fra Diavolo* and *Haydée* involve choruses, soli, and the beginnings of expository material, whereas *Le Timide* has no chorus and *La Barcarolle* begins with spoken dialogue.

[59]Longyear, *D. F. E. Auber*, p. 408.

[60]*Ibid.*, p. 91.

[61]The Domenico-Haydée affair resembles a situation used some years earlier by Scribe in his libretto for Clapisson's *Le Code noir* (June 9, 1842). In this work Palème, a freed slave, is always trying to tell Zoé, a slave girl, about an "idea" he has, that of marrying her. His approach is identical to Domenico's and he meets with the same degree of success.

[62]This song, in which Haydée, with pretended innocence, seems to turn Malipieri's leading questions toward good rather than evil ends, occurs in "a situation rather similar to that in which, in [Berton's recently revived] *Aline, reine de Golconde*, Zelie makes fun of the curiosity of the leader of the eunuchs." Cf. Henri Blanchard, "Theatre royal de l'Opéra-Comique. Haydée ou le Secret . . . ," *Revue et Gazette Musicale de Paris*, Vol. XV, No. 1 (January 2, 1848), p. 2.

[63]Soubies and Malherbe, *op. cit.*, p. 16.

[64]Longyear, *D. F. E. Auber*, p. 490. Longyear's summary of the story is inaccurate.

[65]Prosper Merimée, *Oeuvres Complètes*, edited by Pierre Trahard and Edouard Champion (Paris: Librairie Ancienne Honoré Champion, 1931), Vol. IX, pp. xiv-xxiii.

[66]Haidee is the heroine of Cantos II-IV of Byron's *Don Juan*. The reference is made in a comparison of Haidee with the heroine of Pushkin's *Le Prisonnier du Caucase*. Cf. Merimée, *op. cit.*, Vol. IX, pp. 13-14, 179.

[67]*Ibid.*, p. 436.

[68]Prosper Merimée, "The Game of Backgammon" in *Mosaic*, Vol. II of *The Works of Prosper Merimée*, trans. George Saintsbury (New York: Brown & Co., Inc., 1905), p. 116.

[69]Alfred Loewenberg, "Carafa (di Colobrano), Michele Enrico," *Grove's Dictionary of Music and Musicians* (fifth edition; London: Macmillan & Co., 1954), Vol. II, p. 57, says Ruggi and Fenaroli.

[70]Loewenberg (*ibid.*) adds Kalkbrenner.

[71]Eugène Borrel, "Carafa de Colobrano, Michel-Henry-François-Louis-Vincent-Paul," *Die Musik in Geschichte und Gegenwart* (Kassel & Basel: Bärenreiter, 1952), Vol. II, col. 831.

[72]Loewenberg, "Carafa," p. 57.

[73]Félix Clément, *Les Musiciens celèbres depuis le seizième siècle jusqu'à nos jours* (Paris: Librairie de L. Hachette et Cie., 1868), p. 399.

[74]Borrel, *op. cit.*, cols. 830-831.

[75]Information for the biography is taken from Borrel, *op. cit.*; Clément, *op. cit.*; and Loewenberg, "Carafa."

[76]Again, for convenience, references to the librettist will name only Scribe, while recognizing that the effort was a collaboration.

[77]Sir Walter Scott, *The Heart of Midlothian*, Vol. VII of *Waverly Novels Centenary Edition* (New York: The Baker & Taylor Co.; Edinburgh: A. & C. Black, 1871), p. 283. Incidentally, Scribe has written into his libretto at least one anachronism by causing the Duke of Argyle to come to Scotland after a civil war which took place in 1745, two years after the Duke's death.

[78]*Ibid.*, pp. 315-316.

[79]*Ibid.*, pp. 322-323.

[80]*Ibid.*, p. 145.

[81]*La Prison d'Edimbourg*, Act III, ii.

[82]Scott, *op. cit.*, pp. 164-165.

[83]*Ibid.*, p. 215.

[84]*Ibid.*, p. 218.

[85]There are also some similarities to *Léocadie* (Auber, 1824), which includes among its characters a poor girl (Léocadie) who has been given the education of a noblewoman, her illegitimate son, and a brother who must break his engagement to a village girl when the child's identity is discovered (the Jeanie-Reuben Butler situation in reverse). It is noteworthy that *Léocadie* is the first opéra comique libretto by Scribe in which all the musical and dramatic traits and conventions of his mature style appear fully formed.

[86]*La Prison d'Edimbourg*, Act III, iii.

[87]*Ibid.*, Act III, iv.

[88]Clément and Larousse, *op. cit.*, p. 906.

[89]Scribe has given everything the poet
Could best invent for the interpretive lyre;
And the inspired master lavished in turn
The charm which words have never known how to express,
The tone that brings dreaming, the tone that bring smiles,
The mirth of spirit, the ecstasy of love.

Quoted in Arvin, *op. cit.*, p. 183.

[90]Longyear, *D. F. E. Auber*, p. 183.

[91]Pougin, *Boieldieu*, p. 252.

[92]Longyear, *D. F. E. Auber*, p. 141.

[93]Loewenberg, *Annals*, Vol. I, cols. 698-699.

[94]The opera was referred to under this title by Boieldieu himself as late as March 7, 1825, in a letter to Pixérécourt. Cf. Robert, *op. cit.*, p. 104.

[95]Loewenberg, *Annals*, Vol. I col. 698; Cooper, *op. cit.*, p. 56.

[96]Arvin, *op. cit.*, p. 181; Favre, *op. cit.*, Vol. II, p. 116.

[97]Favre, *op. cit.*

[98]Elizabeth Forbes, "Sir Walter Scott and Opera," *Opera*, Vol. XIX, No. 11 (November 1968), p. 872.

[99]Victor Debays and Paul Locard, "L'Ecole romantique français de 1815 à 1837," *Encyclopédie de la Musique et Dictionnaire du Conservatoire*, ed. A. Lavignac (Paris: Librairie Delagrave, 1913-1931), Part I, Vol. III, p. 1682; François Fétis, *Biographie universelle des musiciens* (second edition; Paris: 1870-1875; reprint, Brussels: Culture et Civilisation, 1963), Vol. II, pp. 168-169.

[100]Longyear, *D. F. E. Auber*, p. 139.

[101]Robert, *op. cit.*, p. 88. Robert refers to the work as an *opéra* but it is unclear whether he really means opera or opéra comique. The piece was performed only in Russia and apparently never was revived when Boieldieu returned to Paris.

[102]Favre, *op. cit.*, Vol. II, pp. 122-124. Robert, *op. cit.*, p. 522, reprints a letter from Boieldieu to Castil-Blaze, critic of the *Journal des Débats*, in which the composer faults the *Journal* for having reported that the *ballade* of the White Lady was drawn from a Scottish tune and very badly arranged. The *ballade*, says Boieldieu, is his own, and adds: "How ridiculous it is to praise an air that does not exist at the expense of one that does!" As for the Scottish tune in Act III, Boieldieu states that he used it only "because it would have been a *gaucherie* for me not to have done so, since the situation demanded it."

[103]The situation is found in Scott's *Guy Mannering* (Boston: Dana Estes & Co., 1892), Book II, pp. 139-141.

[104]Adolphe Adam, *Dernièrs souvenirs d'un musicien* (Paris: Michel Lévy Frères, 1859), pp. 286-288. Scribe used a similar device again in his three-act opera *Zerline* (1851, muic by Auber), when Gemma, the illegitimate daughter of the Prince of Roccanera whom the latter has raised as his niece, recognizes a tune sung by Zerline, an orange-seller, as one she learned in her childhood from an unknown source. Gemma is able to sing the song back to the orange-seller. Since Zerline, who has returned to Palermo after fifteen years of slavery in Africa to look for the daughter she was forced to leave behind, wrote the song herself, Gemma's knowledge of it can only mean that she is Zerline's daughter. The orange-seller uses the knowledge of her daughter's identity gained by Gemma's recollection of the song to force the Prince to allow Gemma to marry the man she loves, but Gemma never learns the truth about her parentage.

[105]Scott, *Guy Mannering*, pp. 246, 249, 250.

[106]*La Dame blanche*, Act I, iv.

[107]Interestingly enough, this White Lady is modeled on La Motte-Fouqué's Undine. (Cf. Scott, *The Monastery*, Vol. X of *The Waverley Novels* [Philadelphia: John D. Morris & Co., n.d.], p. 12.) The operatic treatment of Undine by E. T. A. Hoffmann was one of the first German romantic operas. Such German operas in turn influenced the content of some French works, including *La Dame blanche*.

[108]Paul Bonnefon, "Les Métamorphoses d'un opéra. Lettres inédites de Eugène Scribe," *Revue des Deux Mondes*, Series 6, Vol. XLI (1917), p. 891.

[109]Arvin, *op. cit.*, pp. 215-216.

[110]Favre, *op. cit.*, Vol. II, pp. 119-120.

[111]Cooper, *op. cit.*, p. 56.

[112]Arvin, *op. cit.*, p. 182.

[113]Longyear, *D. F. E. Auber*, p. 139.

[114]Arvin, *op. cit.*, p. 182; Favre, *op. cit.*, Vol. II, pp. 119-120.

[115]Knepler, *op. cit.*, p. 261.

[116]Favre, *op. cit.*, Vol. II, p. 119, n. 3.

[117]Longyear, *D. F. E. Auber*, p. 130.

[118]Robert, *op. cit.*, p. 520.

[119]Never one to let a good thing die, Scribe used the auction idea for a similar scene in Clapisson's *Le Code noir* (1842). Here the scene is a slave auction in the West Indies, where the evil governnor of the island and Zamba, a free mulatto woman formerly a slave, bid against each other for Donatien, Zamba's son. Just as the governor's agent thinks he has won the bidding, Zamba steps in and offers a higher sum, finally gaining custody of her son.

[120]Longyear, *D. F. E. Auber*, p. 47. Longyear (*ibid.*, p. 7) is incorrect in stating that no full score of this work was published, for one was printed by I. Pleyel et Fils Ainé of Paris, probably in 1826.

[121]Julien Tiersot, "Auber," *Revue Musicale*, Vol. XIV, No. 140 (November 1933), p. 267.

**POST-SCRIBE: MEILHAC AND HALEVY**

[1]Rey M. Longyear, *Nineteenth Century Romanticism in Music* (Englewood Cliffs, N. J.: Prentice-Hall, Inc. 1969), p. 87.

[2]Grout, *op. cit.*, p. 426.

[3]Gabriel Grovlez, "Jacques Offenbach, A Centennial Sketch," *Musical Quarterly*, Vol V (1919), p. 330, credits Florimond Hervé with the creation of the "operetta as distinct from the *cafe-concert*," and Hugo Riemann, *Musik Lexikon*, revised and edited by Willibald Gurlitt (Twelfth edition; Mainz: B. Schott's Söhne, 1959), Vol I, p. 97, writes: "With *Galathée*, set by Massé in 1852, Barbier and Carré introduced the so-called Greek genre to comic opera."

[4]Grout, *op. cit.*, p. 337.

[5]Grovlez, *op. cit.*, p. 331.

[6]R. R. Palmer, *A History of the Modern World* (New York: Alfred A. Knopf, 1953), p. 514.

[7]*Ibid.*, p. 515.

[8]*Ibid.*, p. 518.

[9]Prosper Merimée, *Lettres à Madame de Montijo* (Paris, 1936), translated in Mina Curtiss, *Bizet and His World* (New York: Alfred A. Knopf, 1958), pp. 198-199.

[10]Biographical information on Meilhac and Halévy from Matthews, *French Dramatists*, p. 243 ff.; "Halévy, Ludovic," *Grand Larousse encyclopédique* (Paris: Librairie Larousse, 1960-1964), Vol. V, p. 759; "Meilhac, Henri," *ibid.*, Vol. VII, p. 228.

[11]Matthews, *French Dramatists*, pp. 245-246.

[12]Curtiss, *op. cit.*, p. 378.

[13]*Ibid.*, p. 397.

[14]Grout, *op cit.*, p. 426.

[15]Loewenberg, *Annals*, Vol. I, col. 989-990.

[16]Grovlez, *op. cit.*, p. 334.

[17]Curtiss, *op. cit.*, p. 199.

[18]*Ibid.*, pp. 198-199.

[19]Marcel Frémiot and Alphonse Silbermann, "Offenbach, Jacques," *Die Musik in Geschichte und Gegenwart* (Kassel & Basel: Bärenreiter, 1961), Vol. IX, col. 1899.

[20]L. Halévy, *Carnets* I, 156, translated in Curtiss, *op. cit.*, p. 199.

[21]Curtiss, *op. cit.*, p. 375.

[22]*Ibid.*, p. 377.

[23]Cf., for example, Winton Dean, *Bizet* (London: J. M. Dent and Sons Ltd., 1948); and Ernest Newman, *Great Operas* (New York: Vintage Books, 1958), Vol. 1.

[24]Ludovic Halévy, "Le millième représentation de Carmen," *Le Théâtre*, (January 1905), translated in Weisstein, *op. cit.*, pp. 223-224.

[25]Camille Saint-Saëns, *Outspoken Essays on Music*, trans. F. Rothwell (London: Kegan Paul, Trench, Trubner & Co., Ltd.; New York: E. P. Dutton, 1922), p. 59.

**THE FRENCH OPERA LIBRETTO BEFORE SCRIBE**

[1]Loewenberg, *Annals*, Vol. 1, col. 405.

[2]Loewenberg (*ibid.*) identifies the latter as King Louis XVI, remarking that he "is said to have had a share in the libretto." However, the preface to the piano-vocal score (Paris: E. Girod (*ca.* 1855-63) (vii), contains the information that the author was the king's brother, later Louis XVIII.

[3]Cf. Loewenberg, *Annals*, Vol, I, cols. 300, 304, 310, 320, 333, 344, 405, 461, 480.

[4]Act I, i; Oracle's speech.

[5]P. Desriaux, *Sémiramis* (Paris: Ballard, An 10 [1802]), unnumbered page in the preface.

[6]*Ibid.*

[7]Only in the 1804 version of the opera does Assur actually admit having killed Ninus or make clear his conspiratorial plans.

[8]Grout, *op. cit.*, p. 306.

[9]Translated in Gerald Abraham, *Slavonic and Romantic Music* (New York: St. Martin's Press, 1968), p. 227.

[10]The source is a collection of narrative poems on historical and religious subjects. Cf. author's prefce to *Les Bayadères* libretto (Paris: Roullet, 1810).

[11]Loewenberg, *Annals*, Vol. I, col. 616.

## THE BIRTH OF GRAND OPERA

[1]For a thorough survey of the development of grand opera and a discussion of the people involved in its rise, see Crosten, *op. cit.*

[2]Longyear, *D. F. E. Auber*, p. 55.

[3]For an excellent survey of the development of romantic ballet see Ivor Guest, *The Romantic Ballet in Paris* (Middletown, Conn.: Wesleyan University Press, 1966).

[4]*Ibid.*, p. 4.

[5]*Ibid.*, pp. 8-9.

[6]Crosten, *op. cit.*, p. 82.

[7]*Ibid.*

## SCRIBE'S OPERAS: AN OVERVIEW

[1]Grout (*op. cit.*, p. 315) does not list *Gustave III* among the earliest grand operas, even though some works he mentions were produced later, and even states flatly that its composer, Auber, wrote only one work "in the serious style of grand opera," *La Muette* (*ibid.*, p. 317).

[2]Einstein, *op. cit.*, p. 122.

[3]Martin Cooper, *Ideas and Music* (Philadelphia and New York: Chilton Books, 1967), pp. 78-79.

[4]Henry Sutherland Edwards, *The Life of Rossini* (Boston: Oliver Ditson Co., n.d.), p. 206.

[5]Cf. Crosten, *op. cit.*, p. 39.

[6]Scherle, *op. cit.*, p. 143.

## AUBER'S *LA MUETTE DE PORTICI* AND OPERA COMIQUE

[1]Loewenberg, *Annals*, Vol. I, col. 711; Théodore de Lajarte, *Bibliothèque musicale du Théâtre de l'Opéra* (Paris: Librairie des Bibliophiles, 1878), Vol. II, p. 129.

[2]Langer, *op. cit.*, p. 398

[3]Rey M. Longyear, "La Muette de Portici," *Music Review*, Vol. XIX (1958), p. 37, with corrections by the present writer. The libretto to Keiser's opera has recently been published by Johanna Rudolph and Horst Richter *(Masaniello oder Die neapolitanische Fischer-Empörung* [Leipzig: VEB Deutscher Verlag für Musik, 1968]).

[4]Bonnefon, "Les Métamorphoses," pp. 890-891.

[5]Crosten, *op. cit.*, pp. 93-94.

[6]Stanton, *op. cit.*, p. 34.

[7]Longyear, "La Muette," p. 41.

[8]Arvin, *op. cit.*, pp. 194-195.

[9]Of course, the degree of novelty is to an extent relative. Many of the seemingly commonplace elements of *La Muette* were in fact commonplace in opéra comique but new to opera.

[10]Longyear, "La Muette," p. 43; Helmut Wirth, "Auber, Daniel François Esprit," *Die Musik in Geschichte und Gegenwart* (Kassel & Basel: Bärenreiter, 1949-1951), Vol. I, col. 775.

[11]Hanslick, *op. cit.*, P. 129.

[12]Richard Wagner, "Reminiscences of Auber," *Richard Wagner's Prose Works*, trans, William Ashton Ellis (London: Kegan Paul, Trench, Trubner and Co., Ltd., 1896), Vol. V, p. 46.

[13]Longyear, *D. F. E. Auber*, p. 56.

[14]Crosten, *op. cit.*, pp. 2-3.

[15]Ginisty, *op. cit.*, pp. 60, 66.

[16]Longyear, *D. F. E. Auber*, p. 56, gives the date of this opera as 1798, but Loewenberg, *Annals*, lists it under 1806.

[17]René Dumesnil, *Histoire illustrée du théâtre lyrique* (Paris: Librairie Plon, 1953), p. 116.

[18]For more information, see Guest, *op. cit.*, Chapter 1.

[19]Hanslick, *op. cit.*, p. 130; Joseph Gregor, *Kulturgeschichte der Oper* (Vienna: Gallus-Verlag, 1941), p. 315; Jouvin, *Auber*, pp. 39-40; Henri Blaze de Bury, "Portraits d'hier et d'aujourd'hui I. Auber et Scribe," *Revue des Deux Mondes*, Series 3, Vol. XXXV (1879), p. 60.

[20]Camille Bellaigue, "Les Epoques de la musique: le grand opéra français," *Revue des Deux Mondes*, Series 5, Vol. XXXV (1906), p. 620.

[21]Allévy, *op. cit.*, p. 59.

[22]Cooper, *Ideas*, p. 73; Allévy, *op. cit.*, p. 59.

[23]For pictures see Hellmuth Christian Wolff, *Oper. Szene und Darstellung von 1600 bis 1900* (Leipzig: VEB Deutscher Verlag für Musik [1967]), pp. 166-167. The scenic libretto, published by Solomé, was entitled *Indications Génerales et Observations pour la Mise en Scène de la Muette de Portici* . . . (Paris, 1828).

[24]Heinrich Heine, *Sämtliche Werke*, ed. Jonas Fränkel, Ludwig Krähe, Albert Leitzmann, Julius Petersen, Oskar Walzel (Leipzig: Insel Verlag, 1911-1920), Vol. VIII, p. 117.

[25]Crosten, *op. cit.*, p. 69.

## *LA MUETTE* AND *GUILLAUME TELL*

[1]Loewenberg, *Annals*, Vol. I, *passim.*

[2]Longyear, *D. F. E. Auber*, p. 57.

[3]Joseph Bennett, *Giacomo Meyerbeer* (London and New York: Novello, Ewer and Co. [188-], p. 15.

[4]Adolphe Adam, "Académie Royale de Musique. Le Siège de Corinthe, de Rossini," *Revue et Gazette Musicale de Paris*, Vol, II, No. 47 (November 22, 1835), p. 383.

[5]A comparable scene of people swearing vengeance against a ruler also ends Act II of Meyerbeer's *L'Etoile du Nord* (1854), an opéra comique with libretto by Scribe.

[6]Like *La Muette de Portici* and *Guillaume Tell*, *Le Siège de Corinthe* was relevant to the contemporary political scene, for many Frenchmen were sympathetic to the current war being fought by the Greeks and Rossini himself conducted a concert in 1826 the proceeds from which went to aid the Greeks. Cf. Guiseppe Radiciotti, *Gioacchino Rossini* (Tivoli: Arti Grafiche majella di Aldo Chicca, 1927), Vol II, p. 63.

[7]*Ibid.*, Vol. I, p. 403.

## THE TRANSFORMATION OF A GENRE: MEYERBEER'S *ROBERT LE DIABLE*

[1]Quoted in Johannès Weber, *Meyerbeer, Notes et Souvenirs d'un de ses secrétaires* (Paris: Librairie Fischbacher, 1898), p. 6.

[2]Martin Cooper, "Giacomo Meyerbeer," *Fanfare for Ernest Newman*, edited by H. van Thal (London: Arthur Barker, 1955), p. 43.

[3]Bonnefon, "Scribe sous la Monarchie," p. 63.

[4]Loewenberg, *Annals*, Vol. I, cols. 736-737.

[5]Helmut Kirchmeyer, "Psychologie des Meyerbeer-Erfolges," *Neue Zeitschrift für Musik*, Vol. CXXV (1964), p. 471.

[6]Comparative statistics compiled by Kirchmeyer (*ibid.*) show that Weber's *Der Freischütz* took nearly twice as long to reach 213 performances on its home stage in Berlin as did *Robert* to reach 280 performances in Paris. In Dresden, Wagner's home base, *Rienzi* had seen sixty performances, *Tannhäuser* forty-eight performances, and *Der fliegende Holländer* four performances by 1861, whereas *Robert* enjoyed 103 performances and *Les Huguenots* 130 performances in the same years on the same stage. By 1885 Wagner's operas had surpassed those of Meyerbeer in popularity on German stages, but by then there were ten Wagnerian operas in production, as opposed to Meyerbeer's five.

[7]Honoré de Balzac, *Gambara*, edited by Maurice Regard (Paris: Librairie José Corti, 1964); the author puts these criticisms in the mouth of Andrea.

[8]Arvin, *op. cit.*, p. 202.

[9]Heine, *op. cit.*, Vol. VIII, p. 104.

[10]*Ibid.*, p. 108.

[11]Heine, fifth letter on "Conditions in France," March 25, 1832, translated by F. H. Martens in O. G. Sonneck [and F. H. Martens], "Heinrich Heine's Musical Feuilletons," *Musical Quarterly*, Vol. VIII (1922), pp. 147-148.

[12]Gautier, *op. cit.*, Vol. VI, pp. 82-83.

[13]Balzac, *op. cit.*, p. 96.

[14]*Ibid.*

[15]Dorothy Veinus Hagan, "French Musical Criticism Between the Revolutions (1830-1848)" (unpublished Ph.D. dissertation, School of Music, University of Illinois, 1965), p. 220.

[16]Cf. Johann Peter Eckermann, *Conversations of Goethe*, trans. John Oxenford (new edition; London: George Bell and Sons, 1879), conversations of January 29, 1827, and February 12, 1829; Heinz Becker, *Der Fall Heine-Meyerbeer* (Berlin: Walter de Gruyter & Co., 1958), pp. 69-70.

[17]Cooper, "Giacomo Meyerbeer," p. 47. see also Julius Kapp, *Meyerbeer* (Berlin: Schuster and Loeffler [1920]), p. 63.

[18]Herbert Weinstock, *Rossini: A Biography* (New York: Alfred A. Knopf, 1968), p. 159.

[19]Max Milner, *Le Diable dans la littérature française de Cazotte à Baudelaire* (Paris: J. Corti, 1960), p. 613, n. 105.

[20]Edouard Fournier, *Le Mystère de Robert le Diable. . . .* (Paris: E. Dentu [1878]), pp. xviii-xxvii.

[21]Milner, *op. cit.*, p. 612.

[22]Cf. Hermann Tardel, *Die Sage von Robert dem Teufel in neueren deutschen Dichtungen und in Meyerbeers Oper* (Berlin: Alexander Duncker, 1900), p. 11 ff., for details.

[23]Milner, *op. cit.*, p. 613.

[24]Cf. Fournier, *op. cit.*

[25]Georg Richard Kruse, "Meyerbeers Jugendopern," *Zeitschrift für Musikwissenschaft*, Vol. I (1918-1919), p. 404, quoting a statement made by Meyerbeer to Schucht regarding his Italian period.

[26]Hagan, *op. cit.*, p. 219.

[27]René Dumesnil, *La Musique romantique française* ([Paris:] Aubier [1944]), p. 100.

[28]Lionel Dauriac, *Meyerbeer* (Paris: Librairie Félix Alcan, 1930), p. 83-85.

[29]H. Abert, *op. cit.*, p. 418.

[30]J. Weber, *op. cit.*, p. 74.

[31]M. Cooper, "Giacomo Meyerbeer," p. 85.

[32]J. Weber, *op. cit.*, pp. 28-29.

[33]The device was a timely one when the opera was being planned, for in 1825 a law was passed making sacrilege a crime punishable by death. "Though it remained a dead letter and was never enforced," writes Artz (*op. cit.*, p. 162), "it gave a tremendous impetus to the growth of Liberal bitterness toward the government of Charles X." By the time the opera was finally produced, the authors could safely enlarge on the sensational effect of a reference to a burdensome law which was by then only a memory but which still had associations in the minds of the spectators to remind them how far they had come.

[34]Hagan, *op. cit.*, p. 231.

[35]Cooper, "Giacomo Meyerbeer," p. 44; Kapp, *op. cit.*, p. 63; Arthur Pougin, "Giacomo Meyerbeer," *Famous Composers and Their Works*, edited by J. K. Paine, T. Thomas and K. Klauser (Boston: J. B. Millet Co., 1891), Vol. I, p. 480.

[36]Véron, *op. cit.*, Vol. I, p. 259; Hanslick, *op. cit.*, p. 143; Adolphe Jullien, "Robert le Diable. Le Mystère. L'Opéra-comique avant l'opéra," *Revue et Gazette Musicale de Paris*, Vol. XLVI, No. 50 (December 14, 1879), p. 403.

[37]Véron, *op. cit.*, Vol. I, p. 261.

[38]Hector Berlioz, letter to his sister Adèle, August 2, 1835, *Les Années romantiques, 1819-1842*, edited by J. Tiersot (Paris: Calmann-Lévy [1904]), p. 293.

[39]Véron, *op. cit.*, Vol. III, p. 218.

[40]*Ibid.*, pp. 220-221.

[41]*Ibid.*, pp. 219-220.

[42]Cooper, "Giacomo Meyerbeer," p. 44.

[43]Letter from Meyerbeer to Count Redern, February 4, 1832, printed in Wilhelm Altmann, "Meyerbeer-Forschungen," *Sammelbände der Internationalen Musikgesellschaft*, Vol. IV (1902-1903), pp. 524-525.

[44]Jullien, *op. cit.*, and Vol. XLVI, No. 48 (November 30, 1879), pp. 386-388; No. 49 (December 7, 1879), pp. 395-396.

[45]Jullien, *op. cit.*, p. 403.

[46]*Ibid.*

[47]*Ibid.*

[48]Note here the similarity to *La Muette de Portici*, in which violent action takes place offstage and is reported by characters on the stage.

[49]Jullien, *op. cit.*

[50]*Ibid.*

[51]*Ibid.*

[52]*Ibid.*

[53]*Ibid.*

[54]*Ibid.*, p. 396.

[55]Lasserre, *op. cit.*, pp. 130-131.

[56]H. C. Wolff, *op. cit.*, p. 170; Allevy, *op. cit.*, pp. 102, 104; Crosten, *op. cit.*, p. 62.

[57]Artz, *op. cit.*, pp. 110-111.

[58]Altmann, *op. cit.*, p. 524.

[59]Felix Mendelssohn-Bartholdy, *Letters*, edited by G. Selden-Goth (New York: Pantheon Books, 1945), p. 186.

[60]Cooper, *Ideas*, p. 80, notes that Wagner "plagiarized" Raimbaut's *ballade* for Senta's *ballade* in *Der fliegende Holländer.* To be sure, there is a similarity between the two numbers, but not really to the degree of plagiarization. Dorothy Hagan, *op. cit.*, p. 221, has also pointed out the similarity of the *ballade* to the theme of the finale of Beethoven's sixth symphony.

[62]Henri Blaze de Bury, quoted in Bellaigue, *op. cit.*, p. 628.

[63]Hagan, *op. cit.*, pp. 274-275. Berlioz' words can be found in his *Les Musiciens et la musique* (Paris: Calmann-Lévy [1904]), pp. 88-89.

[64]Cooper, "Giacomo Meyerbeer," pp. 45-46.

[65]One possible exception to this statement is *Le Juif errant*, but here the supernatural character is supposed to be alive, not risen from the dead and not endowed with magical powers.

[66]H. Abert, *op. cit.*, p. 405.

[67]Cf. Ivor Guest, *op. cit.*, pp. 111-120 and *passim*.

COMIC OPERA AND OPERA COMIQUE: AUBER'S *LE PHILTRE*

[1]Cf. Tiersot, *op. cit.*, p. 273; Clément, *op. cit.*, p. 366; Clément and Larousse, *op. cit.*, p. 874; Longyear, *D. F. E. Auber*, p. 69.

[2]Loewenberg, *Annals*, Vol. I, col. 734; Lajarte, *op. cit.*, Vol. II, p. 138.

[3]For a comparison of the two operas, see Ebenezer Prout, "Auber's *Le Philtre* and Donizetti's *L'Elisire [sic] d'Amore:* A Comparison" *Monthly Musical Record*, Vol. XXX (1900), pp. 25-27, 41-46, 73-76.

[4]Weinstock, *Donizetti*, p. 82, no. 10.

THE TECHNIQUE OF GRAND OPERA AND THE TRANSFORMATION OF LITERARY MODELS: MEYERBEER'S *LES HUGUENOTS*

[1]J. G. Prod'homme, "Die Huguenotten-Premiere," *Die Musik*, Jg. III, Band IX (1903-1904), p. 187.

[2]R***, "Les Huguenots à Vienne," *Revue et Gazette Musicale de Paris*, Vol. VII, No. 16 (February 23, 1840), p. 130.

[3]"Les Huguenots à Munich," *Revue et Gazette Musicale de Paris*, Vol. V, No. 23 (June 10, 1838), p. 239. In this version the daggers are blessed by a group of sheriffs, "doubtless very astonished at having to bless anything" (*ibid.*, p. 240).

[4]Becker, *op. cit.*, p. 42.

[5]Henri Girard, *Emile Deschamps dilettante* (Paris: Librairie Ancienne Honoré Champion, 1921), p. 56.

[6]*Ibid.*, pp. 63-64.

[7]Léon Halévy, *F. Halévy, sa vie et ses oeuvres* (second edition, revised and enlarged; Paris: Heugel et Cie., 1863), pp. 24-25.

[8]Henri Blaze de Bury, *Musiciens contemporains* (Paris: Michel Lévy Frères, 1856), p. 228.

[9]Francis Rogers, "Adolphe Nourrit," *Musical Quarterly*, Vol. XXV (1939), pp. 12-15.

[10]Véron, *op. cit.*, Vol. III, p. 251; Girard, *op. cit.*, p. 61.

[11]Girard, *op. cit.*, pp. 62-63.

[12]*Ibid.*, p. 63.

[13]Henry Fothergill Chorley, *30* [*sic*] *Years' Musical Recollections* (London: Hurst & Blackett, 1862), Vol. II, p. 40-41.

[14]J. Weber, *op. cit.*, p. 65.

[15]Lajarte, *op. cit.*, Vol. II, p. 267.

[16]Ernest Newman, *More Stories of Famous Operas* (New York: Alfred A. Knopf, 1943), p. 198.

[17]*Ibid.*, p. 202.

[18]*Ibid.*, p. 210.

[19]*Ibid.*, p. 211; Kapp, *op. cit.*, p. 168; Loewenberg, *Annals*, Vol. I, col. 669.

[20]Berlioz, *Les Musiciens*, pp. 92-93. Berlioz copied the idea in a more complex form in a scene of his *Damnation of Faust.*

[21]Hagan, *op. cit.*, pp. 223-224.

[22]Lionel Dauriac, "Herbert Spencer et Meyerbeer," *Zeitschrift der Internationalen Musikgesellschaft*, Vol. V (1903-04), p. 107.

[23]In a letter to Gottfried Weber of October 20, 1837 (printed in Wilhelm Altmann, "Briefe Meyerbeers an Gottfried Weber," *Die Musik*, Jg.. VII, No. 21 [August 1908], p. 160), Meyerbeer himself mentions a precedent for his introduction of religious warfare and a chorale onto the operatic stage.

> . . . it is already this long [twenty-five years] ago that in Lutheran Berlin *Die Weihe der Kraft* by Werner was given, in which Luther himself was the hero and his religious conflicts with the Pope and

> the Emperor formed the subject of the drama and in which several of his chorales were also sung. . . . All this aroused no scandal at the time. . . .

[24]Not one to play favorites, Meyerbeer has Marcel sing "*Te Deum laudamus*" in the Act I finale. This text is not in the printed libretto.

[25]Heine, *op. cit.*, Vol. VIII, p. 110.

[26]Wolf, *op. cit.*, p. 88.

[27]Hagan, *op. cit.*, p. 243.

[28]Gautier, *op. cit.*, Vol. VI, p. 82.

[29]Lang, *op. cit.*, p. 276; see also Gautier, *op. cit.*, Vol. VI, p. 81; Crosten, *op. cit.*, pp. 89-90.

[30]Arvin, *op. cit.*, p. 207, refers to treatments of the same subject earlier by Arnaud Baculard, the Chevlier de Chantelouve, and Chénier. This last is not the part of an unfinished poem, *L'Amerique*, by André Chénier dealing with Charles IX, but the drama *Charles IX* by Marie-Joseph Chénier, brother of André. The drama was produced in 1790. Arvin also mentions a melodrama on the subject, but does not cite title or author.

[31]Prosper Merimée, *A Chronicle of the Reign of Charles IX*, Vol. 6 of *The Novels, Tales, and Letters of Prosper Merimée*, trans. George Saintsbury (New York and Philadelphia: Frank S. Holby, 1906), pp. 327-328.

[32]*Ibid.*, p. 48.

[33]*Ibid.*, p. 105.

[34]*Ibid.*, pp. 234-236.

[35]*Ibid.*, pp. 13-14, 16-17.

[36]*Ibid.*, p. 243.

[37]Artz, *op. cit.*, pp. 348-349.

[38]Cf. René Dumesnil, *La Musique*, pp. 91-92; Heinrich Bulthaupt, *Dramaturgie der Oper* (Leipzig: Breitkopf und Härtel, 1887), p. 21; Ernst Bücken, *Die Musik des neunzehnten Jahrhunderts bis zur Moderne* (Wildpart-Potsdam: Akademische Verlagsgesellschaft Athenaion, 1929), p. 168.

[39]Some of the cadences indicated on the chart are indeed final cadences but are written in the score as if the next number should follow at once without a break.

[40]Even this device was not strictly original, for Schneitzhoeffer included a viola d'amore solo in the score for his ballet on *Zémire et Azor* at the Opéra in 1824. Cf. Guest, *op. cit.*, p. 61.

[41]Cf., for example, Edgar Istel, "Act IV of Les Huguenots," *Musical Quarterly*, Vol. XXII (1936), p. 95.

## HISTORICAL OPERA: MEYERBEER'S *LE PROPHETE*

[1]François Fétis, "Le Prophète, . . . Opéra en 5 actes, paroles de M. Scribe, musique de Meyerbeer," *Revue et Gazette Musicale de Paris*, Vol. XVI, No. 16 (April 22, 1849), p. 121.

[2]Cf. Heine's comment of May 1837 that he was already anticipating the new opera "with great eagerness" (Heine, *op. cit.*, Vol. VIII, p. 106).

[3]Gustave Kobbé, *Kobbé's Complete Opera Book*, edited and revised by the Earl of Harewood (New York: G. P. Putnam's Sons, 1965), p. 709.

[4]Heinz Becker, "Meyerbeer, Giacomo," *Die Musik in Geschichte und Gegenwart* (Kassel & Basel: Bärenreiter, 1961), Vol. IX, col. 251.

[5]Letter to Count Wielhorsky, November 18, 1848, translated in Searle, *op. cit.*, pp. 109-110.

[6]An Italian version of the opera was given March 22, 1882, in Rome. Meanwhile Scribe had reused ideas from the French libretto as the basis of *Les Vêpres siciliennes.* Cf. Bonnefon, "Les Métamorphoses"; Loewenberg, *Annals*, Vol. I, col. 1096.

[7]This libretto was eventually set by Clapisson (1848).

[8]Bonnefon, "Les Métamorphoses," pp. 879, 885-886.

[9]Becker, "Meyerbeer," pp. 251-252; Loewenberg, *Annals*, Vol. I, col. 873.

[10]Berlioz, *Les Musiciens*, p. 119.

[11]Henry Sutherland Edwards (*The Lyrical Drama* [London:; W. H. Allen & Co., 1881], Vol. I, p. 257) says that *Le Prophète* is based not only on the story of John of Leyden, but on that of "the false Demetrius, who, when he had raised himself to the throne of Russia, was confronted with his humbly-born mother. . . ." This is surely not impossible, for Scribe could have read of Demetrius in histories of Russia or may even have reinforced his knowledge of history by reading Pushkin's *Boris Godunov*, although this drama does not contain the incident Edwards mentions. First published in 1831, the Pushkin work exposes a view of peasant revolts, fanaticism, and a leader being used as a tool by a revolutionary group which is not unlike that found in *Le Prophète.* Merimée's quite different version of the Demetrius story did not appear until 1852 (*Revue des Deux Mondes*, Vol. XVI, pp. 1001-1047), however, and could not have been used by Scribe.

[12]Will Durant, *The Reformation*, Part VI of *The Story of Civilization* (New York: Simon and Schuster, 1957), p. 398.

[13]*Ibid.*, p. 399.

[14]*Ibid.*, p. 400.

[15]*Ibid.*

[16]*Ibid.*, p. 401

[17]See Bonnefon, "Les Métamorphoses."

[18]Legouvé, *op. cit.*, Vol II, p. 127.

[19]Cf. Berlioz, *Les Musiciens*, p. 106; Fétis, "Le Prophète," p. 122; Clément and Larousse, *op. cit.*, p. 551.

[20]Gautier (*op. cit.*, Vol. VI, p. 82) observes: "The Anabaptists and the peasants have dialogue that one could believe [to be] drawn from the prose of communistic journals."

[21]Gautier, *op. cit.*, Vol. VI, p. 82; italics added.

[22]Fétis, "Le Prophète," pp. 121-122.

[23]Gautier, *op. cit.*, Vol. VI, p. 82.

[24]*Ibid.*

[25]Cooper, "Giacomo Meyerbeer," p. 53.

[26]Gautier, *op. cit.*, Vol. VI, p. 81.

[27]Because of the many delays in bringing out *Le Prophète* and because of Scribe's own problems with Pillet at the Opéra, it is not impossible that the librettist may have used ideas from the libretto for Meyerbeer in another work precisely because he saw so little hope that the grand opera would ever be performed.

**FRENCH OPERA AFTER SCRIBE: BARBIER AND CARRE**

[1]Martin Cooper, *French Music from the Death of Berlioz to the Death of Fauré* (London: Oxford University Press, 1951), p. 8.

[2]These conclusions are based on facts and figures in Loewenberg, *Annals*, Vol. I, cols. 873-1231, which are not complete but which nevertheless provide sufficient indication of the state of opera in Paris during this period.

[3]Curtiss, *op. cit.*, p. 125.

[4]Biographical information on Barbier and Carré from J. Balteau *et al.*, *Dictionnaire de Biographie Française* (Paris: Librairie Letouzey et Ané, 1733-1968), Vol. V, pp. 331-332; Vol. VII, p. 1230.

[5]As in the previous chart, italicized numbers indicate pieces placed in the appropriate column by the present writer, not by the librettists or the composers.

[6]John W. Klein, "Thomas, Charles-Louis-Ambroise," *Die Musik in Geschichte und Gegenwart* (Kassel and Basel: Bärenreiter, 1966), Vol. XIII, col. 354.

[7]Loewenberg, *Annals*, Vol. I, cols. 807-808.

[8]Scribe, *op. cit.*, Ser. 3, Vol. IV, p. 104, n.

[9]Ashbrook, *op. cit.*, pp. 227-228, 425-427. For specific details on the differences between Cammarano's *Poliuto* and Scribe's *Les Martyrs*, see *ibid.*, pp. 425-427.

[10]Loewenberg, *Annals*, Vol. I, col. 1073.

[11]Martin Cooper, "Gounod and His Influence on French Music," *Music and Letters*, Vol. XXI (1940), p. 55.

[12]Cooper, *French Music*, p. 13.

# APPENDIX A

## THE LIBRETTI OF EUGENE SCRIBE: THE OPERAS COMIQUES

Explanatory notes:

1. The order given is chronological.

2. Introductions and some large ensembles and Finales sometimes contain *couplet*, airs, etc. These have been counted as separate numbers.

3. Unless otherwise stated, "Intro" and "Finale" refer to pieces using chorus and one or more soloists.

Key to Abbreviations:

| | | |
|---|---|---|
| C | - | Cavatine |
| cho | - | chorus |
| ens | - | ensemble |
| Lg | - | ensemble scene involving chorus and soli or more than five soloists |
| Qt | - | quartet |
| Qtt | - | quintet |
| R | - | rondeau |
| w/ | - | with |

| Title, composer, date | No. of Acts | No. of characters | Act beginning | Act ending | Strophic forms | Airs | Duos | Trios | Qt | Qtt | Cho | Lg |
|---|---|---|---|---|---|---|---|---|---|---|---|---|
| *La Chambre à coucher* | 1 | 4 | Dialogue | Vaudeville | 2 | 2 | 1 | | | | | |
| Guénée; Apr. 20, 1813 | | | | | R-2 | | | | | | | |
| *La Meunière* | 1 | 6, cho | Dialogue | Ens w/ cho; | 3 | 1 | 1 | | | 1 | 1 | 2 |
| Garcia; May 16, 1821 | | | | dialogue; cho | | | | | | | | |
| *Le Paradis de Mahomet* | 3 | 11, cho | Intro | Finale | 1 | 1 | | 1 | 1 | | | 2 |
| Kreutzer & Kreubé; | | | Chorus | Finale | 1 | | | 1 | | | 1 | 3 |
| Mar. 23, 1822 | | | Monologue | Ens w/ cho; short monologue; cho | 1 | | 2 | | | | 1 | 1 |
| ***La Petite lampe merveilleuse*** | 3 | 7, cho | Intro | Air | 1 | 2 | | | 1 | | | 1 |
| Piccini; July 29, 1822 | | | Dialogue | Finale | | 1 | 1 | | | | 1 | 1 |
| | | | Monologue | Finale | 1 | | | 1 | | | 1 | 1 |
| *Leicester* | 3 | 10, cho | Monologue | Finale | 2 | C-1 | 2 | | | | | 1 |
| Auber; Jan. 25, 1823 | | | Cho & solo | Finale; 4 soli | | 1 | 2 | | 1 | | 1 | 2 |
| | | | Monologue | Chorus | 1 | 2 | 1 | 1 | | | 1 | |
| *Le Valet de chambre* | 1 | 7 | Dialogue | *Choeur final* | 2 | 1 | 1 | 1 | 1 | | (1) | |
| Carafa; Sept. 16, 1823 | | | | for all soli | R-1 | | | | | | | |
| *La Neige* | 4 | 9, cho | Dialogue | Duo | 1 | 2 | 1 | | | | | 1 |
| Auber; Oct. 8, 1823 | | | Cho & solo | Finale | 1 | | | 1 | | | | 2 |
| | | | Dialogue | Trio | 1 | | 1 | 2 | | | | |
| | | | Air | Chorus | | 1 | | 2 | | | 1 | |
| *Le Concert à la cour* | 1 | 5, cho | Monologue & air | Chorus | 2 | 2 | 1 | 1 | | | 1 | 1 |
| Auber; June 3, 1824 | | | | | | | | | | | | |

| Title, composer, date | No. of Acts | No. of characters | Act beginning | Act ending | Strophic forms | Airs | Duos | Trios | Qt | Qtt | Cho | Lg |
|---|---|---|---|---|---|---|---|---|---|---|---|---|
| *Léocadie* | 3 | 6, cho | Intro | Finale | 2 | C-1 | | | | | | 2 |
| Auber; Nov. 4, 1824 | | | Dialogue | Finale | | | 2 | | 1 | | | 1 |
| | | | Monologue & couplets | Finale | 1 | 1 | | | | | | 1 |
| *Le Maçon* | 3 | 10, cho | Intro | Finale | 2 | | 1 | | 1 | | | 2 |
| Auber; May 3, 1825 | | | Cho & solo | Finale | 2 | 1 | 2 | | | | | 2 |
| | | | Monologue & air | Finale | | 2 | 1 | | | | | 1 |
| *La Dame blanche* | 3 | 8, cho | Intro | Trio | 2 | 1 | 1 | 1 | | | | 2 |
| Boieldieu; Dec. 10, 1825 | | | Couplets | Finale | 1 | C-1 | 1 | 1 | | | | 1 |
| | | | Air | Finale | | 1 | 1 | | | | | 2 |
| *La Vieille* | 1 | 4, cho | Intro | Finale | | 1 | 1 | | | | | 2 |
| Fêtis; Mar. 14, 1826 | | | | | | | | | | | | |
| *Le Timide* | 1 | 6 | Trio | "Chorus" for all soli | 1<br>R-1 | | 2 | 1 | | 2 | | 1 |
| Auber; May 30, 1826 | | | | | | | | | | | | |
| *Fiorella* | 3 | 6, cho | Intro | Finale | 2 | | 2 | 1 | | | | 2 |
| Auber; Nov. 28, 1826 | | | Cho & solo | Finale | 2 | | 1 | | | | | 2 |
| | | | Dialogue | Finale | | | 2 | | | | | 1 |
| *Le Loup-Garou* | 1 | 5, cho | Intro | Finale | 2 | | 1 | | | 2 | | 2 |
| L. Bertin; Mar. 10, 1827 | | | | | | | | | | | | |
| *La Fiancée* | 3 | 6, cho | Intro | Finale | 3 | 3 | 1 | | | | | 2 |
| Auber; Jan. 10, 1829 | | | Cho & soli | Finale | 2 | | | 2 | | | | 2 |
| | | | Dialogue | Finale | | 1 | 3 | | | | | 2 |

| Title, composer, date | No. of Acts | No. of characters | Act beginning | Act ending | Strophic forms | Airs | Duos | Trios | Qt | Qtt | Cho | Lg |
|---|---|---|---|---|---|---|---|---|---|---|---|---|
| *Le Deux nuits* Boieldieu; May 20, 1829 | 3 | 16, cho | Intro | Finale | 1 | 1 | | | | | | 2 |
| | | | Dialogue | Finale | 1 | | 2 | | 1 | | 1 | 1 |
| | | | | | 1[a] | | | | | | | |
| | | | Air | Finale | | 1 | | 1 | 1 | | | 2 |
| *Fra Diavolo* Auber; Jan. 28, 1830 | 3 | 8, cho | Intro | Finale | 2 | | 1 | 1 | | 1 | | 2 |
| | | | Air | Finale | 1 | 1 | | 1 | | | | 1½ |
| | | | | | | 1[b] | | | | | | |
| | | | Air | Finale | 1 | 1 | | | | | 1 | 2 |
| *La Marquise de Brinvilliers* Auber, Batton, Berton, Blangini, Boieldieu, Carafa, Cherubini, Hérold, Paer; Oct. 31, 1831 | 3 | 10, cho | Intro | Finale | 2 | 1 | | 1 | | | | 2 |
| | | | Cho & Air | Finale | | 1 | 1 | | | | 1 | 1 |
| | | | Monologue | Finale | 1 | | 1 | | | | | 1 |
| *Le Médecine sans médecin* Hérold; Oct. 17, 1832 | 1 | 5 | Duo | Finale: all soli | 2 | 1 | 2 | 1 | 1 | 1 | | |
| *La Prison d'Edimbourg* Carafa; July 20, 1833 | 3 | 9, cho | Intro | Finale | 2 | | 2 | | | | | 2 |
| | | | Cho & air | Finale | 1 | 1 | 1 | 1 | | | | 2 |
| | | | Cho & soli | Finale | 2 | | | | | | | 2 |
| | | | | | R-1 | | | | | | | |

[a] Fabliau w/ ens

[b] w/ ens

| Title, composer, date | No. of Acts | No. of characters | Act beginning | Act ending | Strophic forms | Airs | Duos | Trios | Qt | Qtt | Cho | Lg |
|---|---|---|---|---|---|---|---|---|---|---|---|---|
| *Lestocq* Auber; May 24, 1834 | 4 | 9, cho | Intro | Finale | 2 | | 2 | 1 | | | 1 | 2 |
| | | | Air & couplets | Finale; soli only | 3 | 1 | 1 | 2 | | 1 | | 1 |
| | | | Dialogue | Finale | 1 | C-1 | 1 | 1 | | | | 1 |
| | | | Air | Finale | | 1 | | 1 | | | | 2 |
| *Le Fils du prince* A. de Feltre; Aug. 28, 1834 | 2 | 7, cho | Intro | Finale | 1 | 1 | 1 | | | | | 3 |
| | | | Monologue & air | Finale | 1 | 1 | | 1 | | | 1 | 1 |
| *Le Chalet* Adam; Sept. 25, 1834 | 1 | 3, cho | Intro | Finale | 3 | 2 | 2 | 1 | | | | 3 |
| *Le Cheval de bronze* Auber; Mar. 23, 1835 | 3 | 8, cho | Intro | Finale | 2 | 2 | | 1 | 1 | 1 | 1 | 2 |
| | | | Air | Finale | 1 | 2 | 1 | 1 | | | | 1 |
| | | | Chorus | Finale | 1 | 1 | 2 | | | | 1 | 1 |
| *Le Portefaix* Gomis; June 16, 1835 | 3 | 7, cho | Intro | Finale | 2 | 1 | | 1 | 1 | | | 2 |
| | | | Cho & soli | Duo | 2 | 1 | 2 | | | | | 1 |
| | | | Cho & soli | Finale | 1 | | | | 1 | | | 2 |
| *Actéon* Auber; Jan. 23, 1836 | 1 | 5, cho | Intro | Finale | | 2 C-1 1[a] | 2 | | 1 | | | 2 |

[a]Canzonetta

| Title, composer, date | No. of Acts | No. of characters | Act beginning | Act ending | Strophic forms | Airs | Duos | Trios | Qt | Qtt | Cho | Lg |
|---|---|---|---|---|---|---|---|---|---|---|---|---|
| *Les Chaperons blancs* Auber; Apr. 9, 1836 | 3 | 10, cho | Intro: soli only | Finale | | | 1 | 1 | | 1 | | 2 |
| | | | Air | Finale: soli only | | 3 | 1 | | 1 | | | 1 |
| | | | Couplets | Finale | 1 | | | 1 | | | | 1 |
| *Le Mauvais-Oeil* Loisa Puget; Oct. 1, 1836 | 1 | 7, cho | Intro | Finale | 3 | 2 C-1 | 2 | | | | | 3 |
| *L'Ambassadrice* Auber; Dec. 21, 1836 | 3 | 7 | Air | Dialogue | 3 | 3 | 1 | | | 1 | | |
| | | | Dialogue | Trio | | | 1 | 2 | | 1 | | |
| | | | Monologue & couplets | Finale: soli only | 1 | | 1 | 1 | | | | 1 |
| *Le Domino noir* Auber; Dec. 2, 1837 | 3 | 14, cho | Dialogue | End of duo (1 soloist) | 2 | | 1 | 1 | | | | |
| | | | Monologue & couplets | Finale | 3 | | | | | | | 2 |
| | | | Monologue & couplets | Finale | 2 | 1 | | | | | | 2 |
| *Le Fidèle berger* Adam; Jan. 11, 1838 | 3 | 8, cho | Intro | Finale: soli only | 2 | 1 | | 1 | | | | 2 |
| | | | Duo | Finale | 2 | 1 | 2 | | | | | 1 |
| | | | Air | Finale | | 1 | 1 | 1 | | | | 1 |
| *Marguerite* A. Boieldieu; June 18, 1838 | 3 | 7, cho | Intro | Finale | | 1 | 1 | 1 | | | | 2 |
| | | | Air | Finale | 1 R-1 | 1 | 1 | | | | | 2 |
| | | | Dialogue | Finale | 1 | | 1 | | | | | 2 |

| Title, composer, date | No. of Acts | No. of characters | Act beginning | Act ending | Strophic forms | Airs | Duos | Trios | Qt | Qtt | Cho | Lg |
|---|---|---|---|---|---|---|---|---|---|---|---|---|
| *La Figurante* | 5 | 9, cho | Intro | Finale | 2 | 1 | | | | | | 2 |
| Dupin; Aug. 24, 1838 | | | Dialogue | Duo | 1 | 1 | 3 | | | | | |
| | | | Dialogue | Finale | | | 1 | | | | | 1 |
| | | | Air | Finale: soli only | | 1 | 1 | | 1 | 1 | | |
| | | | Dialogue | Finale: soli only | | | 2 | | | 1 | | |
| *Régine* | 2 | 5, cho | Duo | Finale | 2 | 1 | 1 | | | | | 1 |
| Adam; Jan. 17, 1839 | | | | | | C-1 | | | | | | |
| | | | Monologue | Finale: soli only | 2 | 1 | 1 | | 1 | 1 | | |
| *Les Treize* | 3 | 6, cho | Intro | Finale | 1 | 1 | | | | | | 2 |
| Halévy; Apr. 15, 1839 | | | Monologue | Finale: soli only | 1 | | 1 | | 1 | | | |
| | | | Monologue | Finale | 1 | | 2 | | | | | 1 |
| | | | & rondeau | | R-1 | | | | | | | |
| *Polichinelle* | 1 | 4, cho | Duo | Finale | 2 | 2 | 2 | 1 | | | | 1 |
| Montfort; June 14, 1839 | | | | | | | | | | | | |
| *Le Shérif* | 3 | 8, cho | Intro | Finale | | 2 | | 1 | 1 | | | 2 |
| Halévy; Sept. 2, 1839 | | | | | | C-1 | | | | | | |
| | | | Duo | Finale | | | 2 | 1 | | | | 1 |
| | | | Air | Finale | 1 | 1 | | 1 | | | | 1 |

| Title, composer, date | No. of Acts | No. of characters | Act beginning | Act ending | Strophic forms | Airs | Duos | Trios | Qt | Qtt | Cho | Lg |
|---|---|---|---|---|---|---|---|---|---|---|---|---|
| *La Reine d'un jour* Adam; Sept. 19, 1839 | 3 | 7, cho | Dialogue | Finale | 1 | 1 C-1 | 1 | | | | | 2 |
| | | | Intro | Finale | 2 R-1 | | 1 | | | 1 | | 2 |
| | | | Air | Finale | | 1 | 1 | | | | | 2 |
| *Zanetta* Auber; May 18, 1840 | 3 | 8, cho | Chorus | Finale | 1 | 1 | 1 | 1 | | | 1 | 1 |
| | | | Dialogue | Duo | 2 | 1 | 2 | | | | | |
| | | | Air | Finale | 2 | 1 | 1 | | | 1 | | 1 |
| *L'Opéra à la cour* Grisar & A. Boieldieu; July 14, 1840 | 4 *parties* | 8 | Intro: soli only | Finale | 2 | 1 | | | | | | 2 |
| | | | Dialogue | Dialogue | | | | | | | | |
| | | | Couplets | Finale | 2 | 1 C-1 | 4 | | 1 | | | 3 |
| | | | Dialogue | Recap. of part of above finale | | | | | | | | 1 |
| *Le Guitarrero* Halévy; Jan. 21, 1841 | 3 | 8, cho | Dialogue | Finale | | 2 | 1 | | | | | 2 |
| | | | Dialogue | Finale | | 1 | 1 | | 1 | | | 1 |
| | | | Dialogue | Finale | 2 | | 1 | | | | | 2 |
| *Les Diamants de la couronne* Auber; Mar. 6, 1841 | 3 | 8, cho | Monologue & couplets + scène | Finale | 2 | | 2 | | | | | 3 |
| | | | Dialogue | Finale | | | 2 | | | | | 2 |
| | | | Dialogue | Finale | | 1 | | 1 | | 1 | | 1 |
| *Le Main de fer* Adam; Oct. 26, 1841 | 3 | 7, cho | Intro | Air | 1 | 2 | 1 | | | | | 2 |
| | | | Air | Finale | 3 | 1 | | | | 1 | | 1 |
| | | | Duo | Finale | 1 | | 1 | | | | | 1 |

| Title, composer, date | No. of Acts | No. of characters | Act beginning | Act ending | Strophic forms | Airs | Duos | Trios | Qt | Qtt | Cho | Lg |
|---|---|---|---|---|---|---|---|---|---|---|---|---|
| *Le Diable à l'école* Boulanger; Jan. 17, 1842 | 1 | 3 | Romance | Trio | 3 | 1 | 3 | 1 | | | | |
| *Le Duc d'Olonne* Auber; Feb. 4, 1842 | 3 | 10, cho | Dialogue | Finale | 2 | 1 | 1 | 2 | | | | 1 |
| | | | Cho & soli | Finale | 1 | 1 | 2 | | | | 1 | 4 |
| | | | Dialogue | Finale | | 1 | 1 | | | | | 2 |
| *Le Code noir* Clapisson; June 9, 1842 | 3 | 8, cho | Dialogue & duo | Duo | 1 | | 2 | 1 | 1 | 1 | | |
| | | | Recit. & couplets | Chorus | 2 | 1 | 1 | | | | 1 | 1 |
| | | | Dialogue | Finale | | 1 | | | | | | 2 |
| *Le Kiosque* Mazas; Nov. 2, 1842 | 1 | 7 | Quintet | Finale: soli only | 1 | C-1 1[a] | 1 | | | 2 | | 1 |
| *La Part du diable* Auber; Jan. 16, 1843 | 3 | 8, cho | Dialogue | Duo | 2 | 3 | 2 | 1 | | | | |
| | | | Cho & soli | Finale | 2 | | 1 | 1 | 1 | | | 3 |
| | | | Air | Finale | | 1 | 1 | | | | | |
| *Le Puits d'amour* Balfe; Apr. 20, 1843 | 3 | 7, cho | Intro | Duo, air | 1 | 2 1[b] | 2 | | | | | 1 |
| | | | Dialogue | Finale | 2 | | 1 | | | | | 3 |
| | | | Dialogue | Finale | | 1 | 1 | | | 1 | | 1 |

[a]Bolero
[b]Légende

| Title, composer, date | No. of Acts | No. of characters | Act beginning | Act ending | Strophic forms | Airs | Duos | Trios | Qt | Qtt | Cho | Lg |
|---|---|---|---|---|---|---|---|---|---|---|---|---|
| *Lambert Simnel*<br>Monpou; Sept. 14, 1843 | 3 | 9, cho | Intro | Finale | 1 | 1 | 1 | 1 | | | | 2 |
| | | | Air | Finale | 1 | 1 | | 1 | | | 1 | 2 |
| | | | Dialogue | Finale | 1 | | | 1 | | | | 2 |
| *Cagliostro*<br>Adam; Feb. 10, 1844 | 3 | 7, cho | Intro | Quartet | 2 | C-1 | 1 | | 1 | | | 2 |
| | | | 1 spoken line & couplets | Duo | 2 | 1 | 1 | | | 2 | | 1 |
| | | | Cho & soli | Finale | | 1[a] | | 1 | | | | 2 |
| *Oreste et Pylade*<br>Thys; Feb. 28, 1844 | 1 | 7 | Dialogue | Solo (1-stanza air) | 2<br>R-1 | 1 | 1 | 3 | | | | |
| *La Sirène*<br>Auber; Mar. 26, 1844 | 3 | 7, cho | Dialogue | Quartet | 1 | 1 | 1 | | 2 | | | |
| | | | Cho & soli | Finale | 2 | 1 | 1 | 1 | | | | 3 |
| | | | Cho & soli | Finale | | | 1 | | | | 1 | 2 |
| *La Barcarolle*<br>Auber; Apr. 22, 1845 | 3 | 6, cho | Monologue | Duo | 1 | 1<br>C-1 | 5 | | | | | |
| | | | Air | Finale | | 1<br>C-1 | 1 | | | 1 | | 1 |
| | | | Monologue | Finale | | | 1 | 1 | | | | 2 |
| *Le Ménétrier*<br>Labarre; Aug. 9, 1845 | 3 | 8, cho | Intro | Finale | 1 | 1 | 1 | | | | | 2 |
| | | | Chorus | Finale | 2 | 1 | 2 | | | | 1 | 2 |
| | | | Air | Finale | | 1 | 1 | 1 | | | 1[b] | 1 |

[a] 1-stanza romance
[b] Sung twice

| Title, composer, date | No. of Acts | No. of characters | Act beginning | Act ending | Strophic forms | Airs | Duos | Trios | Qt | Qtt | Cho | Lg |
|---|---|---|---|---|---|---|---|---|---|---|---|---|
| *La Charbonnière*<br>Montfort; Oct. 13, 1845 | 3 | 8, cho | Intro | Quintet | 2 | | | 1½ | | 1 | | 2 |
| | | | Couplets | Finale | 2 | | | 1 | 1 | | | 1 |
| | | | Romance | Finale | 1 | | 1 | | | | | 1 |
| *Ne touchez pas à la reine*<br>Boisselot; Jan. 16, 1847 | 3 | 6, cho | Dialogue | Finale | 1 | | 1 | 1 | | | | 1 |
| | | | Cho & soli | Finale | 1 | 2 | 1 | | | | | 2 |
| | | | Air | Finale | 1 | 1 | | | | 2 | | 1 |
| *Le Sultan Saladin*<br>Bordèse; Feb. 8, 1847 | 1 | 7, cho | Air → Qt | Finale, inter-rupted by dialogue | 2 | 1<br>1[a] | | 2 | 2 | | | 1 |
| *Haydée*<br>Auber; Dec. 28, 1847 | 3 | 6, cho | Couplets: solo & cho | Duo | 4<br>R-1 | 1 | 1 | | 1 | | 1 | |
| | | | Cho & solo | Finale | 1 | 2 | 1 | | | | | 2 |
| | | | Air | Finale, inter-rupted by dialogue | 2 | 1 | 1 | | 1[b] | | | 3 |
| *La Nuit de Nöel*<br>Reber; Feb. 9, 1848 | 3 | 6, cho | Romance | Quintet | 1<br>1[c] | 1<br>C-1 | 1 | | | 1 | | 2 |
| | | | Cho & soli | Duo | 1 | 2 | 2 | | | | | 1 |
| | | | Dialogue | Quintet | 1 | | 1 | 2 | | 1 | | |

[a]Chanson
[b]Recitative
[c]Légende

| Title, composer, date | No. of Acts | No. of characters | Act beginning | Act ending | Strophic forms | Airs | Duos | Trios | Qt | Qtt | Cho | Lg |
|---|---|---|---|---|---|---|---|---|---|---|---|---|
| *La Fée aux roses* Halévy; Oct. 1, 1849 | 3 | 7, cho | Air | Duo | 1 | 1 | 1 | 2 | | | | |
| | | | Monologue | Duo | 2 | 2 | 2 | | | | | 1 |
| | | | Dialogue | Finale | 2 | 2 | 2 | | | | 1 | 1 |
| *Giralda* Adam; July 20, 1850 | 3 | 9, cho | Intro | Finale | 1 | 2 | 2 | | | | | 4 |
| | | | Chorus | Finale | 1 | | 1 | 1 | | | 1 | 2 |
| | | | Air | Finale | 2 | 1 | 1 | 1 | | 1 | | 1 |
| *La Chanteuse voilée* Massé; Nov. 26, 1850 | 1 | 3, cho | Dialogue | Finale | 4 | 2 | 1 | 1 | | | 1 | 1 |
| *La Dame de pique* Halévy; Dec. 28, 1850 | 3 | 8, cho | Intro | Finale | 1[a] | 2 C-1 | 1 | | | | 1 | 3 |
| | | | Recit. & romance | Finale | 3 | | 2 | | | | 1 | 3 |
| | | | Monologue | Finale, interrupted by dialogue | 1 | | 1 | | | 1 | | 1 |
| *Mosquita la sorcière* Boisselot; Sept. 27, 1851 | 3 | 8, cho | Intro | Finale | | 1 | 1 | | | | | 4 |
| | | | Recit. & romance | Finale | 3 | | 1 | | | | | 2 |
| | | | Dialogue | Chorus | 1 | | 1 | 1 | | | 1 | 1 |
| *Les Mystères d'Udolphe* Clapisson; Nov. 4, 1852 | 3 | 6, cho | Monologue & couplets | Finale | 2 | | 1 | 1 | | | | 2 |
| | | | Chorus | Finale | 1 | 2 C-1 | | | | | 1 | 1 |
| | | | Romance | Finale | 1 | | 1 | 1 | | | | 1 1[b] |

[a] Légende
[b] Sextet

| Title, composer, date | No. of Acts | No. of characters | Act beginning | Act ending | Strophic forms | Airs | Duos | Trios | Qt | Qtt | Cho | Lg |
|---|---|---|---|---|---|---|---|---|---|---|---|---|
| *Marco Spada* Auber; Dec. 21, 1852 | 3 | 9, cho | Dialogue | Finale | 2 | 1<br>1[a] | 1 | | 1 | | | 2 |
| | | | Dialogue & air | Finale | 1 | 2 | | 1 | | | | 3 |
| | | | Cho & soli | Finale, interrupted by dialogue | 2 | 2 | | | | | | 4 |
| *La Lettre au bon Dieu* Duprez; Apr. 28, 1853 | 2 | 5, cho | Intro | Duo | 1[b] | 1 | 2 | | | | | 1 |
| | | | Monologue & romance | Finale | 1 | 1 | 1 | | | | | 2 |
| *Le Nabab* Halévy; Sept. 1, 1853 | 3 | 7, cho | Intro | Finale | | 3 | 1 | | | | | 2 |
| | | | 3 ll. dialogue; cho & soli | Finale | 2 | 1 | 3 | | | | | 2 |
| | | | Cho & soli | Finale, interrupted by brief dialogue | 1 | | | | | | | 3 |
| *L'Étoile du nord* Meyerbeer; Feb. 16, 1854 | 3 | 13, cho | Intro | Finale, interrupted by brief dialogue | 2 | 2<br>1[c]<br>1[d] | 2 | | | | | 3 |
| | | | Cho & soli | Finale | 3 | | | 1 | | 1 | 1 | 2 |
| | | | Recit. & romance | Finale | 2 | | 1 | 1 | | | | 1 |

[a] Recitative
[b] Légende
[c] Chanson
[d] Ronde bohémienne

| Title, composer, date | No. of Acts | No. of characters | Act beginning | Act ending | Strophic forms | Airs | Duos | Trios | Qt | Qtt | Cho | Lg |
|---|---|---|---|---|---|---|---|---|---|---|---|---|
| *La Fiancée du diable*<br>Massé; June 5, 1854 | 3 | 7, cho | Trio | Finale | 3 | 1 | 1 | 1 | | | | 2 |
| | | | Air | Finale | | 3<br>C-1 | | 1 | 1 | | | 1 |
| | | | Cho & soli | Finale | 1 | | 2 | 1 | | | | 2 |
| *Jenny Bell*<br>Auber; June 2, 1855 | 3 | 7, cho | Monologue & couplets | Finale | 4 | C-1 | 2 | 1 | | | | 1 |
| | | | Monologue | Finale | 1[a] | 2<br>1[b]<br>C-1 | 1 | 1 | | 1 | | 1 |
| | | | Dialogue | Finale | 2 | | 1 | | | | | 1 |
| *Manon Lescaut*<br>Auber; Feb. 23, 1856 | 3 | 12, cho | Dialogue | Finale | 2 | 2 | 1 | 1 | | | | 2 |
| | | | Monologue & couplets | Finale | 3 | 1 | 1 | | | | | 1 |
| | | | Cho & solo | Short finale | 1 | 1<br>1[c] | 1 | 1 | 1 | | | 3 |
| *La Chatte metamorphosée en femme*<br>Offenbach; Apr. 19, 1858 | 1 | 4 | Monologue & couplets | Quartet | 3 | 3 | 2 | 1 | | 1 | | |
| *Broskovano*<br>Deffès; Sept. 29, 1858 | 2 | 6, cho | 1 line spoken; intro | Finale | 2 | | 1 | 1 | 1 | | | 2 |
| | | | Cho & solo | Finale | | 1 | 1 | | 1 | | | 2 |

[a] Madrigal
[b] Recitative
[c] Chanson

| Title, composer, date | No. of Acts | No. of characters | Act beginning | Act ending | Strophic forms | Airs | Duos | Trios | Qt | Qtt | Cho | Lg |
|---|---|---|---|---|---|---|---|---|---|---|---|---|
| *Les Trois Nicolas* | 3 | 9, cho | Intro | Finale | 5 | 1 | | | | | | 4 |
| Clapisson; Dec. 16, 1858 | | | Dialogue | Finale | 2 | 2 | 2 | | | | | 1 |
| | | | Monologue | Finale | | 1 | | 1 | 1 | | | 2 |
| *Les Petits violons du roi* | 3 | 9, cho | Intro | Finale | 2 | 1[a] | 1 | | | | | 2 |
| Deffès; Sept. 30, 1859 | | | Dialogue | Finale | | 1 | 1 | 1 | | | | 2 |
| | | | | | | 1[b] | | | | | | |
| | | | Chorus | Finale | | 1 | | | | | 1 | 2 |
| | | | | | | 1[c] | | | | | | |
| *Yvonne* | 3 | 8, cho | Dialogue | Finale | 3 | 1 | 2 | | 1 | | | 1 |
| Limnander; Nov. 29, 1859 | | | Romance | Finale | 2 | 2 | 3 | 1 | | | | 2 |
| | | | Cho & solo | Short finale | | 1 | | | | | | 4 |
| | | | | | | C-1 | | | | | | |
| *Le Nouveau Pourceaugnac* | 1 | 6, cho | Intro | Finale, interrupted | 1 | 1 | 2 | | 1 | | | 3 |
| Hignard; Jan. 14, 1860 | | | | by dialogue | R-1 | | | | | | | |
| *Barkouf* | 3 | 8, cho | Intro | Cho & duo | 2 | 2 | 1 | | | | 1 | 3 |
| Offenbach; Dec. 24, 1860 | | | Dialogue | Finale | 2 | 1 | 1 | 1 | 1 | | | 1 |
| | | | Monologue & couplets | Finale | 4 | | | 1 | | | | 3 |

[a] Ronde
[b] Ariette
[c] Villanelle

| Title, composer, date | No. of Acts | No. of characters | Act beginning | Act ending | Strophic forms | Airs | Duos | Trios | Qt | Qtt | Cho | Lg |
|---|---|---|---|---|---|---|---|---|---|---|---|---|
| *La Circassienne* Auber; Feb. 2, 1861 | 3 | 13, cho | Intro | Finale | 1 | 2 | 1 | 1 | | | | 3 |
| | | | Cho & soli | Finale | | 2 | 1 | | | | | 4 |
| | | | | | | C-1 | | | | | | |
| | | | Cho & soli | Finale | 1 | 4 | 1 | | | | | 2 |
| *Madame Grégoire* Clapisson; Feb. 8, 1861 | 3 | 8, cho | Dialogue | Dialogue | 2 | | 1 | 1 | | | 1 | |
| | | | Cho & soli | Finale, interrupted by dialogue | 4 | | 2 | 1 | | | | 3 |
| | | | Air | Short air w/ cho | 1 | 2 | 1 | | | | | |
| *La Beauté du diable* Alary; May 28, 1861 | 1 | 4, cho | Intro | Quartet | 3 | 1 | 3 | 2 | 1 | | | 1 |
| *La Fiancée du roi de Garbe* Auber; Jan. 11, 1864 | 3 | 13, cho | Dialogue | Finale | 3 | 2 | 1 | | 1 | | | 1 |
| | | | Dialogue | Finale | 2 | | 3 | 1 | 1 | | | 1 |
| | | | | | | | | | | | | 1[a] |
| | | | Cho & soli | Finale | 2 | 2 | 1 | | | | | 3 |
| *L'Ours et le pacha* Bazin; Feb. 21, 1870 | 1 | 6, cho | Intro | Finale | 2 | 3 | 3 | | | | | 4 |
| | | | | | | C-2 | | | | | | |

[a]Septet

# APPENDIX B

## LIBRETTI OF MEILHAC AND HALÉVY

Key to abbreviations:

Ch – chanson
Cho – chorus
E-C – ensemble-chorus scene (two or more soloists with chorus)
Ff – fanfare
Intro – introduction

o b – *opéra-bouffe*
o c – *opéra-comique*
R – rondeau
Rec – recitative
Rom – romance

| Title, composer, date | Genre | No. of Acts | No. of characters | Act beginning | Act ending | Strophic forms | Air | Duo | Trio | Quartet | More than 4 | Intro | Finale | Chorus | "Melodrame" | Reprises (vocal) | Other |
|---|---|---|---|---|---|---|---|---|---|---|---|---|---|---|---|---|---|
| *La Belle Hélène* (Offenbach; Dec. 17, 1864) | o b | 3 | 14,cho | Chorus | Finale | 3, cho | R | | | | | | 1 | 1 | 4 | 2 | Ff-3 |
| | | | | Intro | Finale | 1<br>1, cho | | 1 | | | E-C | 1 | 1 | 2 | | 1 | |
| | | | | Chorus | Finale | 1<br>1, cho | | | 1 | | E-C | | 1 | | 1 | | |

| Title, composer, date | Genre | No. of Acts | No. of characters | Act beginning | Act ending | Strophic forms | Air | Duo | Trio | Quartet | More than 4 | Intro | Finale | Chorus | "Melodrame" | Reprises (vocal) | Other |
|---|---|---|---|---|---|---|---|---|---|---|---|---|---|---|---|---|---|
| *Barbe-bleue* (Offenbach; Feb. 5, 1866) | o b | 3 | 20, cho | Recitative | Finale | 2<br>2, cho | R | 1 | | | E-C-3 | | 1 | 1 | | | Rec |
| | | | | Intro | Finale | 2<br>4, cho | Rom | 1 | 1 | 2 | | 1 | 1 | | 1 | 2 | |
| | | | | Intro | Finale | 2, cho | 1 | | | | | 1 | 1 | | 1 | 2 | |
| *La Grande-Duchesse de Gérolstein* (Offenbach; Apr. 12, 1867) | o b | 4 | 12, cho | Intro | Finale | 1<br>3, cho | R | 1<br>1, cho | | | | 1 | 1 | 1 | | 2 | |
| | | | | Chorus | Reprise à 4 of trio | 1<br>1, cho | R-2 | 1 | 1 | | E-C | | | 1 | 2 | 3 | |
| | | | | Dialogue | Finale | 2 | | | | | E-C | | 1 | 1 | 2 | | |
| | | | | Intro | Finale | 2, cho | | | | | | 1 | 1 | | | | |
| *Carmen* (Bizet; Mar. 3, 1875) | o c | 4 | 10, cho | Intro | Finale | 1, cho | 1 | 2 | | | 2<br>E-C | 1 | 1 | 1 | 1<br>1,Ch | | |
| | | | | Chanson | Finale | 2, cho<br>1 | Ch | | | | E-C<br>1 (5) | | 1 | | | | |
| | | | | Intro | Finale | | 1 | 1 | 1 | | E-C | 1 | 1 | | | | |
| | | | | Chorus | Duo | | | 1 | | | E-C | | | 1 | | | |

# APPENDIX C

## THE LIBRETTI OF EUGÈNE SCRIBE: THE OPERAS

Key to abbreviations:

- C – cavatine
- Can – canzonetta
- Cho – chorus
- Ens-Cho – large scene involving one or more soloists and chorus
- Instr – instrumental
- Intro – introduction
- Lg – ensemble involving more than five soloists
- P – prière
- Qt – quartet
- Qtt – quintet
- Rec – recitative
- Rm – nonstrophic romance
- Rn – rondeau

| Title, composer, date | No. of Acts | No. of characters | Act beginning | Act ending | Rec | Strophic forms | Air | Duo | Trio | Qt | Qtt | Lg | Cho | Ens-Cho | Ballet | Miscellaneous |
|---|---|---|---|---|---|---|---|---|---|---|---|---|---|---|---|---|
| *La Muette de Portici* | 5 | 13, cho | Intro | Finale | *2* | | 2 | | | | | | | 2,*2* | | |
| (Auber; Feb. 29, | | (7 | Ens-Cho | Finale | *1* | 1 | | 1 | | | | | | 1,*1* | | |
| 1828) | | principals) | Duo | Finale | | | P-1 | 1 | | | | | 1 | 1 | 1 | |
| | | | Ens-Cho | Marche et choeur | *2* | | 2<br>C-1 | | | | | | | 1,*3* | | Pantomine |
| | | | Barcarolle | Finale | | 1 | | | | | | | | 1 | | Pantomime |

| Title, composer, date | No. of Acts | No. of characters | Act beginning | Act ending | Rec | Strophic forms | Air | Duo | Trio | Qt | Qtt | Lg | Cho | Ens-Cho | Ballet | Miscellaneous |
|---|---|---|---|---|---|---|---|---|---|---|---|---|---|---|---|---|
| *Le Comte Ory* | 2 | 12, cho | Intro | Finale | *2* | | 2 | 1 | | | | | | 2,*2* | | |
| **(Rossini; Aug. 20,** | | (7 | | | | | C-1 | | | | | | | | | |
| **1828)** | | principals) | Intro | Finale | *2* | | 1 | 1 | 1 | | | | | 2,*2* | | |
| *Alcibiade* | 2 | 6, cho | Cho | *Ens-Cho* | *1* | 1 | 3 | 1 | | | | | 2 | *3* | | |
| (Hanssens; Brussels, | | | Solo-Cho | *Ens-Cho* | 4 | 1 | 4 | | 1 | | | | | *2* | 1 | |
| Oct. 30, 1829) | | | | | | | | | | | | | | | | |
| *Le Dieu et la bayadère* | 2 | 9, cho | Intro | Finale | *1* | | 2 | | | | | | | 3,*3* | 1 | Short |
| (Auber; Oct. 13, 1830) | | | Rec & | Finale | *2* | 1 | 2 | 1 | | | | | | 1 | | pantomines |
| | | | pantomime | | | | | | | | | | | | | throughout |
| *Le Philtre* | 2 | 6, cho | Intro | Finale | *1* | | 2 | | | | | | | 3,*3* | 1 | |
| (Auber; June 20, 1831) | | | *Ens-Cho* | *Ens-Cho* | *2* | 1 | 2 | 1 | | | | | | 1 | | |
| *Robert-le-Diable* | 5 | 27, cho | Intro | Finale | *2* | 1 | | 1 | | | | | | 2 | | |
| (Meyerbeer; Nov. 21, | | (9 | Air | *Ens-Cho* | *2* | | 1 | 1 | | | | | 1 | *2* | 1 | |
| 1831) | | principals) | Duo | Finale | *2* | 1 | | 3 | 1 | | | | | 1,*1* | 1 | Valse in- |
| | | | | | | | | | | | | | | | | fernale-cho |
| | | | | | | | | | | | | | | | | Invocation- |
| | | | | | | | | | | | | | | | | solo |
| | | | Cho | Finale | | | C-1 | | | | | | 1 | 1 | | |
| | | | Cho | Cho | | | 1 | | 1 | | | | 2 | *1* | | |
| *Le Serment* | 3 | 7, cho | Intro | Trio | *1* | 2 | 2 | 1 | 2 | | | | | 1 | | |
| (Auber; Oct. 1, 1832) | | | *Rec* | *Ens-Cho* | *1* | | 2 | 2 | | | | | | *1* | | |
| | | | *Ens-Cho* | Finale | *1* | | | 1 | | | | | 1 | 1,*3* | | |

| Title, composer, date | No. of Acts | No. of characters | Act beginning | Act ending | Rec | Strophic forms | Air | Duo | Trio | Qt | Qtt | Lg | Cho | Ens-Cho | Ballet | Miscellaneous |
|---|---|---|---|---|---|---|---|---|---|---|---|---|---|---|---|---|
| *Gustave III* | 5 | 15, cho | Intro | Finale | *2* | 1 | 1 | 1 | | | | | | 2 | 1 | |
| (Auber; Feb. 27, | | (11 | *Ens-Cho* | Finale | | 2 | | | 1 | | | | | 1,*2* | | |
| 1833) | | principals | Air | Finale | *1* | | 1 | 1,*1* | 1 | | | | | 1 | | |
| | | | Duo | Qtt | | | 1-C | 1 | 1 | *1* | 1 | | | | | |
| | | | Air | Finale | *2* | 1 | 1 | 1 | | | | | 1 | 1,*1* | 1 | |
| *Ali Baba* | Pro- | 10, cho | Rec & Rm | *Ens-Cho* | *1* | 1-Rm | | | | | | | | *1* | | |
| (Cherubini; July 22, | log | | Intro | Qt | *3* | 1 | 1 | 1 | | 1 | | | | 1,*1* | | |
| 1833) | 4 | | Cho | Finale | *2* | | | 1 | | | | | 1 | 1 | 1 | |
| | | | Trio | Finale | | | 2 | | 2 | | | | | 1,*1* | | |
| | | | Rec | *Ens-Cho* | *2* | | | 1 | | | | 1(6) | | *2* | 1 | |
| *La Juive* | 5 | 16, cho | Intro | Finale | *2* | 1 | 1-C | | | | | | 1 | 2 | 1 | |
| (Halévy; Feb. 23, | | (7 | *Ens-Cho* | Trio | *2* | 1 | 1-C | 1 | 2,*1* | | | | | *1* | | Prière-cho |
| 1835) | | principals) | Cho | Sextet | | | | | | | | 1(6) | 1 | *1* | 1 | Malédiction-Brogni solo |
| | | | Rec | Air | *1* | | 1 | 3 | | | | | | | | |
| | | | Cho | Finale | *1* | | | | | | | | 1 | 1 | | |

| Title, composer, date | No. of Acts | No. of characters | Act beginning | Act ending | Rec | Strophic forms | Air | Duo | Trio | Qt | Qtt | Lg | Cho | Ens-Cho | Ballet | Miscellaneous |
|---|---|---|---|---|---|---|---|---|---|---|---|---|---|---|---|---|
| *Les Huguenots* (Meyerbeer; Feb. 29, 1836) | 5 | 19, cho (9 principals) | Intro | Finale | *2* | 2 | 1-C | | | | | | 1 | 2 | | Chorale-solo Morceau d'ensemble |
| | | | Air | Finale | *3* | | 1 | 1 | | | | | 1 | 1,*3* | | Serment-soli, cho |
| | | | Cho | Finale | *3* | 1 | 1-Rn | 1 | | | | 1(7) | 2 | 1,*1* | 1 | Litanies-cho Le Couvre-Feu-solo, cho |
| | | | Rm | Duo | *1* | | 1-Rm | 1 | | | | | | | | Conjuration et Bénédiction des Poignards-ens, cho |
| | | | Ballet | Finale | *1* | | 1 | | 1 | | | | | 1,*2* | 1 | Vision-solo |
| *Guido et Ginevra* (Halévy; Mar. 5, 1838) | 5 | 10, cho | Intro | Finale | *2* | 1 | 1 | | 1 | | | | | 2,*1* | 1 | |
| | | | Rec | Finale | *1* | | 1 | 1 | | 1 | | | 1 | 1,*1* | 1 | |
| | | | Cho | Finale | *1* | | 1-P<br>2 | | | | | | 1 | 1 | | |
| | | | *Ens-Cho* | Duo | | | 1 | 2 | | | | | | *2* | | 2 *Scenas*-solo |
| | | | Prière | Cho | | | 1-C | | 1 | | | | 1 | | | Prière-cho *Procession*-instr |

| Title, composer, date | No. of Acts | No. of characters | Act beginning | Act ending | Rec | Strophic forms | Air | Duo | Trio | Qt | Qtt | Lg | Cho | Ens-Cho | Ballet | Miscellaneous |
|---|---|---|---|---|---|---|---|---|---|---|---|---|---|---|---|---|
| *Le Lac des fées* (Auber; Apr. 1, 1839) | 5 | 11, cho | Intro | Air | | | 2 | | | | | | | 2,*1* | | |
| | | | *Ens-Cho* | Finale | *5* | 1 | 2 | 1 | | | | | | 1,*1* | | |
| | | | Duo | Finale | *1* | 1 | | 1 | | | | | | 1,*3* | 1 | *Procession*-instr |
| | | | *Rec* | Finale | *1* | | 1 | *1* | | 1 | | | | 1,*1* | | |
| | | | *Ens-Cho* | *Ens-Cho* | | | | 1 | | | | | | *2* | | |
| *La Xacarilla* (Marliani; Oct. 28, 1839) | 1 | 4, cho | Intro | Finale | *2* | 1 | 2 | 2 | 1 | 1 | | | | 2,*2* | | |
| *Le Drapier* (Halévy; Jan. 6, 1840) | 3 | 8, cho | Intro *[Trio]* | Finale | *2* | 1 | | 1 | 1 | | | | | 1 | | |
| | | | *Rec* | Finale | *1* | | 1 | *1* | | | | | | 1,*1* | | |
| | | | *Rec* | *Ens-Cho* | *1* | | | 2 | | | | | | *3* | | *Scena*-solo |
| *Les Martyrs* (Donizetti; Apr. 10, 1840) | 4 | 8, cho | Cho | Finale | *1* | | 1 | 1 | | | | | 2 | 1 | | |
| | | | Air | Finale | *4* | | 2 C-2 | | | | | | 1 | 1 | 1 | |
| | | | *Rec* & Duo | Finale | *4* | | Rm-1 | | | | | | 2 | 1 | | |
| | | | *Rec* & Trio | Finale | *2* | | 1 | 1 | 1 | | | | | 1,*1* | | *Scena*-solo |
| *La Favorite* (Donizetti; Dec. 2, 1840) | 4 | 7, cho | Intro [Cho] | Air | *3* | | 2 C-1 | 2 | | | | | 2 | | | |
| | | | *Rec* | Finale | *2* | | 1 | 1 | | | | | | 1 | 1 | |
| | | | *Rec* | Finale | *3* | | 1 | | 1 | | | | 1 | 1 | | |
| | | | *Cho* | Duo et Finale | *2* | | C-1 | 1 | | | | | 1 | 1,*1* | | |

| Title, composer, date | No. of Acts | No. of characters | Act beginning | Act ending | Rec | Strophic forms | Air | Duo | Trio | Qt | Qtt | Lg | Cho | Ens-Cho | Ballet | Miscellaneous |
|---|---|---|---|---|---|---|---|---|---|---|---|---|---|---|---|---|
| *Carmagnola* (Thomas; Apr. 19, 1841) | 2 | 7, cho | Intro | Finale | *1* | 1 | | 1 | | | | | | 2,*1* | | |
| | | | Air | Finale | *1* | | 1<br>C-1 | 1 | 1 | | | | | 1 | | |
| *Dom Sébastien* (Donizetti; Nov. 13, 1843) | 5 | 9, cho | Intro | Finale | *2* | | C-1<br>Rm-1 | | | | | | | 2,*1* | | Prophétie-solo |
| | | | Cho | Cavatine | *1* | | 2<br>C-1 | 1 | | | | | 1 | *3* | 1 | |
| | | | *Rec & procession* | Choeur et Marche funèbres | *2* | 1 | | 2 | | | | | | 1,*1* | | *Procession*-instr |
| | | | Cho | Finale | | | | | | | | | 1 | 1,*1* | | |
| | | | *Rec* | *Ens-Cho* | *1* | 1 | 1 | 1 | 1 | | | | | *1* | | |
| *Jeanne la folle* (Clapisson; Nov. 6, 1848) | 5 | 8, cho | *Cho* | *Ens-Cho* | *2* | 1 | *1* | | 1 | | | | 1 | *1* | | |
| | | | Air | *Ens-Cho* | *1* | 1 | 1 | 1 | | | | | | *2* | 1 | |
| | | | Air | *Ens-Cho* | *1* | 1 | 1<br>C-1 | 2 | | | | | | *2* | | |
| | | | Romance | *Trio* | *1* | 1 | | | *1* | | | | | *1* | | |
| | | | Cho | *Ens-Cho* | *1* | | | | | | | 1(6) | 1 | *1* | | *Scena*-solo |

| Title, composer, date | No. of Acts | No. of characters | Act beginning | Act ending | Rec | Strophic forms | Air | Duo | Trio | Qt | Qtt | Lg | Cho | Ens-Cho | Ballet | Miscellaneous |
|---|---|---|---|---|---|---|---|---|---|---|---|---|---|---|---|---|
| *Le Prophète* (Meyerbeer; Apr. 16, 1849) | 5 | 16, cho (7 principals) | Cho | *Ens-Cho* | *1* | 1 | C-1 | | | | | | 1 | *1* | | Prèche Anabaptiste-soli and cho |
| | | | Valse Villageois | *Qt* | *1* | 1 | | | | *2* | | | | *2* | | Valse Villageois-cho<br>Songe-solo<br>Arioso-solo |
| | | | Cho | *Ens-Cho* | *5* | 1 | P-1 | | 1 | | | | 3 | *2* | 1 | *Scena*-solo<br>Hymne triomphal-solo |
| | | | Cho | Finale | | 1 | | 1 | | | | | 1 | 1 | | Complainte-solo<br>*Procession*-instr<br>Prière et Imprécations-cho<br>Exorcisme-solo |
| | | | *Rec* | Finale | *1* | 1 | 1 | 1 | 1 | | | | | 1 | | Choeur dansé |

| Title, composer, date | No. of Acts | No. of characters | Act beginning | Act ending | Rec | Strophic forms | Air | Duo | Trio | Qt | Qtt | Lg | Cho | Ens-Cho | Ballet | Miscellaneous |
|---|---|---|---|---|---|---|---|---|---|---|---|---|---|---|---|---|
| *La Tempête* (Halévy; London, June 8, 1850) | Pro-log, 3 | 11, cho | *Ens-Cho* | Prière | | | | | | | | | | *1* | | Prière-cho |
| | | | Cho | Duo | | 1 | C-2 | 1 | 1 | | | | 1 | | | |
| | | | Air | Finale | | 1 | 1 | 1 | | | | | 1 | 1 | | Bacchanale-soli and cho |
| | | | *Rec* | Duo et Finale | *1* | | 1 | 1 | | | | | | 1 | | Short pantomimes for Ariel in all acts |
| *L'Enfant prodigue* (Auber; Dec. 6, 1850) | 5 | 13, cho | Intro | Finale | *1* | 1 | 2 | 1 | | | | | | 2 | | Short pantomimes in all acts for Lia |
| | | | Cho | Cho | *1* | 1 | 1<br>Rm-1 | | | | | | 3 | *2* | *1* | |
| | | | Cho | Finale | | | | 1 | | | 1 | | 1 | 1,*1* | | |
| | | | Cho | Romance | *1* | 1 | 1<br>Rm-1 | | | | | | 2 | *1* | | |
| | | | Cho | Finale | *2* | | C-1<br>Rm-1<br>1 | 1 | | | | | 1 | 1 | | |
| *Zerline* (Auber; May 16, 1851) | 3 | 6, cho | Cho | Finale | *2* | | 2<br>Can-1 | 1 | | | | | 1 | 1,*2* | | |
| | | | Air | Duo | *1* | 1 | 1 | 2 | 1 | | | | | | | *Scena*-solo |
| | | | Cho | Air | *2* | 1 | 1 | | | | | | 2 | *1* | 1 | |

| Title, composer, date | No. of Acts | No. of characters | Act beginning | Act ending | Rec | Strophic forms | Air | Duo | Trio | Qt | Qtt | Lg | Cho | Ens-Cho | Ballet | Miscellaneous |
|---|---|---|---|---|---|---|---|---|---|---|---|---|---|---|---|---|
| *Florinde* (Thalberg; London, July 3, 1851) | 4 | 7, cho | Intro | Finale | | 1 | C-2 | | | | 1 | | | 2 | | Marche-cho |
| | | | Cho | Finale | | | 2 | 1 | | | | | 1 | 1 | | |
| | | | *Rec* | Finale | *1* | | | 1 | 1 | | | | 1 | 1 | 1 | Chanson militaire-solo and cho |
| | | | Romance | Finale | | 1 | | 2 | | 1 | | | | 1 | | |
| *Le Juif errant* (Halévy; Apr. 23, 1852) | 5 | 16, cho (7 principals) | Intro | Duo | | | Rm-1 | 1 | | | | | | 1,*1* | | Légende-solo Couvre-feu-solo and cho Pantomime |
| | | | Trio | Finale | *2* | | | 2 | 1 | | | | 1 | 1,*1* | 1 | |
| | | | *Ens-Cho* | Finale | *1* | | 1 Rm-1 | | | | | | | 1,*1* | 1 | *Procession*-instr |
| | | | Air | Finale | *1* | | 2 | 1 | | | | | 1 | 1 | | |
| | | | Quartet | *Air* | | | *1* | | | | 1 | | | | | *Scena*-solo 3 Tableaux-cho, scenery |
| *La Nonne sanglante* (Gounod; Oct. 18, 1854) | 5 | 10, cho | *Ens-Cho* | Finale | | | 1 | 2 | | | | | | 1,*1* | | Légende-solo |
| | | | *Ens-Cho* | *Ens-Cho* | *1* | 1 | 1 | | | | | | 1 | *3* | | |
| | | | *Ens-Cho* | Duo | *1* | 1 | 1 | 2 | | | | | | *1* | | |
| | | | Couplets | Finale | | 1 | | *1* | | | | | | 1,*1* | 1 | |
| | | | Air | Finale | | | 1 | 1 | | | | | | 1,*1* | | |

| Title, composer, date | No. of Acts | No. of characters | Act beginning | Act ending | Rec | Strophic forms | Air | Duo | Trio | Qt | Qtt | Lg | Cho | Ens-Cho | Ballet | Miscellaneous |
|---|---|---|---|---|---|---|---|---|---|---|---|---|---|---|---|---|
| *Les Vêpres siciliennes* | 5 | 11, cho | Intro | Duo | *1* | | 1 | 1 | 1 | | | | | 1 | | |
| (Verdi; June 13, 1855) | | | Air | Finale | *2* | | 1 | 1 | | | | | | 1 | 1 | |
| | | | *Rec* | Finale | *2* | | 1 | 1 | 1 | | | | 1 | 1 | 1 | |
| | | | *Rec* & Air | Finale | *2* | 1 | 1 | 1 | | 1 | | | | 1 | | |
| | | | *Cho* | Finale | *1* | 2 | | | 1 | | | | 1 | 1 | | |
| *Le Cheval de bronze* | 4 | 10, cho | Intro | Finale | *6* | 2 | 2 | | 2 | | 1 | | | 2,*1* | | |
| (Auber; Sept. 21, | | | Air | Finale | *3* | 1 | 2 | 1 | 1 | | | | | 1 | | |
| 1857) | | | Cho | Duo | *2* | | 1 | 3 | | | | | 1 | | | |
| | | | *Ens-Cho* | Finale | | | | | | | | | | 1,*1* | 1 | |
| *L'Africaine* | 5 | 11, cho | *Rec* | *Ens-Cho* | *1* | | Rm-1 | | 1 | | | | | *1* | | |
| (Meyerbeer; Apr. 28, | | | *Rec* | Finale | *2* | | 2 | 1 | | | | | | 1 | | |
| 1865) | | | *Ens-Cho* | *Ens-Cho* | *1* | 1 | | 1 | | | | | | *3* | | Prière-double cho |
| | | | *Ens-Cho* | Finale | | | 1 C-1 | 1 | | | | | | 1,*2* | 1 | Marche et cortège-cho |
| | | | Duo | *Ens-Cho* | *1* | | 1 | 1 | | | | | | 1 | | |

# APPENDIX D

## LIBRETTI OF BARBIER AND CARRE

Key to abbreviations:

- Ar – arioso
- B – barcarolle
- C – cavatine
- cho – chorus
- Ens-Cho – large scene with one or more soloists and chorus
- Instr – instrumental
- Intro – introduction
- Lg – Ensemble of more than 4 soloists
- P – prière
- Qt – quartet
- Rec – recitative
- Sc – scène

| Title, composer, date | No. of Acts | No. of characters | Act beginning | Act ending | Rec | Strophic forms | Air | Duo | Trio | Qt | Lg | Cho | Ens-Cho | Ballet | Miscellaneous |
|---|---|---|---|---|---|---|---|---|---|---|---|---|---|---|---|
| *La Reine de Saba* (Gounod; Feb. 28, 1862) | 4 | 9, cho | Rec | Finale | 2 | 1 | | | 1 | 1 | | | 1 | | Cortège-instr |
| | | | Rec & air | Ens-Cho | 1 | | 1 | | | | | | 1 | | |
| | | | Chorus | Scène* | 2 Sc-1 | | C-1 | 1 | | | 1-7* | 3 | | | |
| | | | Chorus | Finale | 3 Sc-2 | | C-1 | | | 2 | | 1 | 2 | 1 | |

*Originally ended with a septet, which Gounod cut after the first performance.

| Title, composer, date | No. of Acts | No. of characters | Act beginning | Act ending | Rec | Strophic forms | Air | Duo | Trio | Qt | Qtt | Lg | Cho | Ens-Cho | Ballet | Miscellaneous |
|---|---|---|---|---|---|---|---|---|---|---|---|---|---|---|---|---|
| *Hamlet* (Thomas; Mar. 9, 1868) | 5 | 11, cho | Intro | Scène | 2 Sc-1 | | C-1 | 1 | | | | | | 2 | | Prelude to 2d tableau-instr |
| | | | Air | Finale | 3 Sc-1 | | 1 Ar-1 | 1 | | | | | | 3 | | Marche-instr Pantomime |
| | | | Monologue | Duo | 2 | | 1 | 1 | 1 | | | | | | | Monologue |
| | | | Ballet | Finale | | | | | | | | | 1 | 2 | 2 | |
| | | | Duo | Finale | 2 | | Ar-1 | 1 | | | | | | 2 | | |
| *Polyeucte* (Gounod; Oct. 7, 1878) | 5 | 10, cho | Intro | Chorus | *2* | | | 1 | | | | | 1 | 2 | | Marche & cortège-instr |
| | | | Chorus | Finale | *1* Sc-3 | | B-1 C-1 | 1 | | | | | 1 | 2 | | Invocation-solo |
| | | | Scène | Finale | 1 Sc-1 | | | 1 | | | | | | 2 | 1 | Cantilène-solo |
| | | | Stances | Scène | Sc-1 | | | 1 | 1 | | | | | | | Stances-solo |
| | | | Chorus | Finale | *1* Sc-1 | | | | | | | | 1 | 1 | | Credo-ens-cho |
| *Françoise de Rimini* (Thomas; Apr. 14, 1882) | Prolog, 4, epilog | 8, cho | Ens-Cho | *Rec* | 2,*1* | | 1 | 1 | | | | | 1 | 1 | | |
| | | | Duo | Finale | 2 Sc-1 | 1-cho | | 1 | 1 | | | | 1 | 3 | | Melopée-solo |
| | | | Rec | Air | 4 Sc-1 | | 2 P-1 C-1 | | 1 | | | | | 3 | | Cantabile-solo Entrée dans la chapelle-organ |
| | | | Rec | Ens-Cho | 2 Sc-1 | | Ar-1 | | | | | | | 2 | | Message-solo |
| | | | Rec | Duo | 2 Sc-1 | | 2 | 1 | | | | | | | | Chanson-solo |
| | | | Apotheosis | | | | | | | | | | | 1 | | |

# BIBLIOGRAPHY

## Books and Articles


Abert, A. A. "Libretto," *Die Musik in Geschichte und Gegenwart* (Kassel and Basel: Bärenreiter, 1960), Vol. VIII, cols. 709-732.

Abert, Herman. *Gesammelte Schriften und Vorträge.* Edited by Friedrich Blume. Halle an der Saale: Max Niemeyer Verlag, 1929.

Abraham, Gerald. *A Hundred Years of Music.* Second edition, reprinted. London: Duckworth, 1955.

________. *Slavonic and Romantic Music.* New York: St. Martin's Press, 1968.

Adam, Adolphe, "Académie royale de musique. Le Siège de Corinthe, de Rossini," *Revue et Gazette Musicale de Paris,* Vol. II, no. 47 (November 22, 1835), pp. 383-384.

________. *Derniers souvenirs d'un musicien.* Paris: Michel Lévy Frères, 1859.

________. *Souvenirs d'un musicien . . . précédés de notes biographiques écrites par lui-même.* Paris: Michel Levy Frères, 1857.

Albert, Maurice. *Les Théâtres des boulevards (1789-1848).* Paris: Société française d'imprimerie et de librairie, 1907.

Allévy, Marie Antoinette [Akakia-Viala]. *La Mise en scène en France dans la première moitié du XIX^e^ siècle.* Paris: E. Droz, 1938.

Altmann, Wilhelm. "Briefe Meyerbeers an Gottfried Weber," *Die Musik,* Jg. VII, no. 20 (July 1908), pp. 72-86; no. 21 (August 1908), pp. 155-161.

________. "Meyerbeer-Forschungen," *Sammelbände der Internationalen Musikgesellschaft,* Vol. IV (1902-1903), pp. 519-534.

Artz, Frederick B. *France under the Bourbon Restoration, 1814-1830.* Cambridge, Mass.: Harvard University Press, 1931.

Arvin, Neil Cole. *Eugene Scribe and the French Theatre, 1815-1860.* Cambridge, Mass.: Harvard University Press, 1924.

Ashbrook, William. *Donizetti.* London: Cassell & Co., Ltd., 1965.

Balteau, J., Baroux, M. Prevot, M. [and d'Amat, Roman]. *Dictionnaire de biographie française.* 11 volumes and 2 fascicles to date. Paris: Librairie Letouzey et Ané, 1933-1968.

Balzac, Honoré de. *Gambara.* Edited by Maurice Regard. Paris: Librairie José Corti, 1964.

Barzun, Jacques. *Berlioz and the Romantic Century.* 2 volumes. Boston: Little, Brown & Co., 1950.

Beik, Paul H. *Louis Philippe and the July Monarchy.* Princeton: D. Van Nostrand Co., Inc., 1965.

Becker, Heinz. *Der Fall Heine-Meyerbeer.* Berlin: Walter de Gruyter & Co., 1958.

________. "Meyerbeer, Giacomo," *Die Musik in Geschichte und Gegenwart* (Kassel and Basel: Bärenreiter, 1961), Vol. IX, cols. 249-261.

________. "Meyerbeers Beziehungen zu Louis Spohr," *Die Musikforschung,* Vol. X (1957), pp. 479-486.

Becker, Heinz. *Giacomo Meyerbeer: Briefwechsel und Tagebücher.* 3 volulmes. Berlin: Walter de Gruyter & Co., 1960-1975.

Bekker, Paul. *The Changing Opera.* Translated by A. Mendel. New York: W. W. Norton, 1935.

Bellaigue, Camille. "Les Epoques de la musique: Le grand opéra français," *Revue des Deux Mondes,* Ser. 5, Vol. XXXV (September-October 1906), pp. 612-649.

Bennett, Joseph. *Giacomo Meyerbeer.* London and New York: Novello, Ewer and Co., n. d.

Benoist, Antoine. "Les Opéras et les opéras-comiques de Scribe," *Revue des Cours et Conférences,* Vol. III (1895), pp. 80-96.

Berlioz, Hector. *A travers chants.* Paris: Calmann-Lévy, 1898.

________. *Les Années romantiques, 1819-1842.* Correspondence, edited by J. Tiersot. Paris: Calmann-Lévy [1904].

________. *Memoirs of Hector Berlioz from 1803 to 1865.* Translated by Rachel [Scott Russell] Holmes and Eleanor Holmes, annotated, and the translation revised by Ernest Newman. New York: Tudor Publishing Co., 1935.

________. *Les Musiciens et la musique.* Paris: Calmann-Lévy [1903].

________. "Quelques mots sur les anciens compositeurs, et sur Grétry en particulier," *Revue et Gazette Musicale de Paris,* Vol. IV, no. 6 (February 5, 1837), pp. 45-46.

________. "Théâtre de l'Opéra. Debut de Duprez dans les Huguenots," *Revue et Gazette Musicale de Paris,* Vol. IV, no. 21 (May 21, 1837), pp. 175-176.

Blanchard, Henri. "De la poesie lyrique et musicale," *Revue et Gazette Musicale de Paris,* Vol. XII, no. 41 (October 12, 1845), pp. 333-334; no. 42 (October 19, 1845), pp. 341-342; no. 43 (October 26, 1845), pp. 352-354.

________. "Théâtre Royale de l'Opéra-Comique: La Barcarolle ou l'Amour et la Musique. . . ," *Revue et Gazette Musicale de Paris,* Vol. XII, no. 17 (April 27, 1845), pp. 129-131.

________. "Théâtre Royale de l'Opéra-Comique: Haydée ou le Secret. . . ," *Revue et Gazette Musicale de Paris,* Vol. XV, no. 1 (January 2, 1848), pp. 1-3.

Blaze de Bury, Henri. *Meyerbeer et son temps.* Paris: Michel Lévy Frères, 1865.

________. *Musiciens contemporains.* Paris: Michel Lévy Frères, 1586.

________. "Portraits d'hier et d'aujourd'hui I. Auber et Scribe," *Revue des Deux Mondes,* Ser. 3, Vol. XXXV (September-October 1879), pp. 43-75.

Blum, Klaus. "Bemerkungen Anton Reichas zu Aufführungspraxis der Oper," *Die Musikforschung,* Vol. VII (1954), pp. 429-440.

Bombet, L. A. C. "Letters on the Genius of Metastasio [1812]," *The Lives of Haydn and Mozart, with Observations on the Present State of Music in France and Italy.* Translated by the author of the sacred melodies. Second edition. London: John Murray, 1818.

Bonnefon, Paul. "A travers les autographes," *Revue d'Histoire Littéraire de la France,* Vol. XXVI (1919), pp. 96-118.

________. "Les Métamorphoses d'un opéra. Lettres inédites de Eugène Scribe," *Revue des Deux Mondes,* Ser. 6, Vol. XLI (1917), pp. 877-899.

________. "Scribe sous l'Empire et sous la Restauration d'après des documens inédits," *Revue d'Histoire Littéraire de la France,* Vol. XVII (1920), pp. 321-370.

________. "Scribe sous la Monarchie de Juillet d'après des documents, inédits," *Revue d'Histoire Littéraire de la France,* Vol. XXVIII (1921), pp. 60-99, 241-260.

Borrel, Eugene. "Carafa de Colobrano, Michel-Henry-François-Louis-Vincent-Paul," *Die Musik in Geschichte und Gegenwart* (Kassel and Basel: Bärenreiter, 1952), Vol. II, cols. 830-832.

Bovet, Marie Anne de. *Charles Gounod, His Life and Works.* London: Sampson Low, Marston, Searle & Rivington, 1891.

Brent Smith, Alexander. "The Tragedy of Meyerbeer," *Music and Letters,* Vol. VI, (1925), pp. 248-255.

Breur, R. "Meyerbeer Revealed," *Opera News*, Vol. XVI (January 29, 1977), pp. 38-43.

Bücken, Ernst. *Die Musik des neunzehnten Jahrhunderts bis zur Moderne.* Wildpart-Potsdam: Akademische Verlags-gesellschaft Athenaion, 1929.

Bulthaupt, Heinrich Alfred. *Dramaturgie der Oper.* 2 volumes. Leipzig: Breitkopf und Härtel, 1887.

Castil-Blaze, François [François-Henri-Joseph Blaze]. *De l'opéra en France.* Paris: Janet et Cotelle, 1820.

________. *Sur l'opéra français, verités dures mais utiles.* Paris: Castil-Blaze, 1856.

________. *Théâtres Lyriques de Paris de 1645 à 1855.* 2 volumes. Paris: Castil-Blaze, 1855.

Cauchie, Maurice. "The High Lights of French Opera Comique," *Musical Quarterly*, Vol. XXV (1939), pp. 306-312.

Chantavoine, Jean, and Denombynes, Jean Gaudefroy. *L'Ere romantique: le romantisme dans la musique européenne.* Paris: A. Michel, 1955.

Chénier, André. *Oeuvres completes.* Edited by Gerard Walter. (*Bibliothèque de la Pl'éiade*, Vol. 57.) Paris: Librairie Gallimard, 1958.

Chorley, Henry Fothergill. *Music and Manners in France and Germany.* 3 volumes. London: Longmans, 1841.

________. *30 Years' Musical Recollections.* 2 volumes. London: Hurst & Blackett, 1862.

________. *National Music of the World.* Edited by H. G. Hewlett. London: Sampson Low, Marston, Searle, & Rivington, 1880.

Chouquet, Gustave. *Histoire de la musique dramatique en France depuis ses origines jusqu'à nos jours.* Paris: Firmin Didot, 1873.

Clément, Felix. *Les Musiciens célèbres depuis le seizième siècle jusqu'à nos jours.* Paris: Librairie de L. Hachette et Cie., 1868.

Clément, Félix, and Larousse, Pierre. *Dictionnaire de Opéras.* Paris: Librairie Larousse, 1897.

Coeuroy, André. *Musique et littérature; études de musique et littérature comparées.* Paris: Blond et Gay, 1923.

Cooper, Martin. *French Music from the Death of Berlioz to the Death of Fauré.* London: Oxford University Press, 1951.

Cooper, Martin, "Giacomo Meyerbeer," *Fanfare for Ernest Newman.* Edited by Herbert van Thal. London: Arthur Barker, 1955.

________. "Gounod and His Influence on French Music," *Music and Letters,* Vol. XXI (1940), pp. 50-59.

________. *Ideas and Music.* Philadelphia and New York: Chilton Books, 1967.

________. *Opéra-Comique.* London: Max Parrish & Co. Ltd., 1949.

Crosten, William L. *French Grand Opera: An Art and a Business.* New York: King's Crown Press, 1948.

Curtiss, Mina. *Bizet and His World.* New York: Alfred A. Knopf, 1958.

Curzon, Henri de. "Les Opéras-comiques de Boieldieu," *Revue Musicale,* Vol. XIV, no. 140 (November 1933), pp. 249-263.

Dauriac, Lionel. "Herbert Spencer et Meyerbeer," *Zeitschrift der Internationalen Musikgesellschaft,* Vol. V (1903-1904), pp. 103-109.

________. *Meyerbeer.* Paris: Librairie Félix Alcan, 1930.

________. *La Psychologie dans l'opéra français (Auber-Rossini-Meyerbeer).* Paris: F. Alcan, 1897.

Dean, Winton. *Bizet.* London: J. M. Dent & Sons, 1948.

Debays, Victor and Locard, Paul. "L'Ecole romantique française de 1815 à 1837," *Encyclopédie de la musique et Dictionnaire du Conservatoire,* edited by Albert Lavignac (Paris: Librairie Delagrave, 1913-1931), Part I, vol. II, pp. 1661-1697.

Dent, Edward J. *Opera.* Baltimore: Penguin Books, 1949.

________. *The Rise of Romantic Opera.* Edited by Winton Dean. Cambridge: Cambridge University Press, 1976.

________. "The Romantic Spirit in Music," *Proceedings of the Royal Music Association,* Vol. LIX (1932-1933), pp. 85-102.

Desriaux, P. *Sémiramis, tragédie lyrique . . . arrangée d'après la tragedie de Voltaire . . .* [music by Catel]. Paris: Ballard, An 10 [1802].

Doehring, S. "Les oeuvres tardives de Meyerbeer," *Schweizerische Musikzeitung,* Vol. CXV (1975), pp. 57-65.

d'Ortigue, Joseph. *De la guerre des dilettanti, ou de la révolution opérée par M. Rossini dans l'opera françois [sic].* Paris: Librairie de Ladvocat, 1829.

Doumic, René. *De Scribe à Ibsen.* Paris: Perrin et Cie., 1901.

Dumas, Alexandre. *The Count of Monte Cristo.* 2 volumes. Translated by Adolphe Cohn. New York: Charles Scribner's Sons, 1926.

Dumesnil, René. *Histoire illustrée du théâtre lyrique.* Paris: Librairie Plon, 1953.

________. *La Musique romantique française.* [Paris:] Aubier [1944].

________. *L'Opéra et l'opéra-comique.* Paris: Presses Universitaires de France, 1947.

Durant, Will. *The Reformation.* (*The Story of Civilization,* Part VI.) New York: Simon and Schuster, 1957.

Eckermann, Johann Peter. *Conversations of Goethe.* Translated from the German by John Oxenford. New edition. London: George Bell & Sons, 1879.

Edwards, Henry Sutherland. *Famous First Representations.* London: Chapman & Hall, Ltd., 1886.

________. *History of Opera from Its Origins in Italy to the Present Time.* 2 volumes. London: William H. Allen & Co., 1862.

________ *The Life of Rossini.* Boston: Oliver Ditson & Co., n.d.

________. *The Lyrical Drama.* 2 volumes in 1. London: W. H. Allen & Co., 1881.

Einstein, Alfred. "Die Huguenotten," *Musikblätter des Anbruch,* Vol. XIV (1932), pp. 52-53.

________. *Music in the Romantic Era.* New York: W. W. Norton & Co., 1947.

Evans, David Owen. *Le Théâtre pendant la période romantique (1827-1848).* Paris: Les Presses Universitaires de France, 1925.

Evans, Raymond Leslie. *Les Romantiques français et la musique.* Paris: Honoré Champion, 1934.

Favre, Georges. *Boieldieu: sa vie, son oeuvre.* 2 volumes. Paris: Librairie E. Droz, 1944-1945.

Ferchault, Guy. "Paris, D. 19. Jahrhundert," *Die Musik in Geschichte und Gegenwart* (Kassel and Basel: Bärenreiter, 1962), Vol. X, cols. 773-783.

Fétis, François. *Biographie universelle des musiciens et bibliographie géneral de la musique.* Second edition, revised and enlarged. 9 volumes. Brussels: Culture et Civilisation, 1963. (First published in 1870-1875.)

Fétis, François. "De la crise du goût en musique," *Revue et Gazette Musicale de Paris,* Vol. XIII, no. 1 (January 4, 1846), pp. 1-4; no 3 (January 28, 1846), pp. 17-19.

________. "Le Prophète, . . . Opéra en 5 actes, paroles de M. Scribe, musique de Meyerbeer," *Revue et Gazette Musicale de Paris,* Vol. XVI, no. 16 (April 22, 1849), pp. 121-126; no. 28 (May 6, 1849), pp. 137-140.

Forbes, Elizabeth. "Sir Walter Scott and Opera," *Opera,* Vol. XIX, no. 11 (November 1968), pp. 872-878.

Forges, A. de. "Scribe, son répertoire, ses collaborateurs," *Le Ménestrel,* Vol. XLII (1876), pp. 67-68.

Fournier, Edouard (ed.). *Le Mystère de Robert le Diable, mis en 2 parties avec transcription en vers modernes, en regard du texte du XIV$^{e}$ siecle.* Paris: E. Dentu [1879].

Freeman, Robert. "Apostolo Zeno's Reform of the Libretto," *Journal of the American Musicological Society,* Vol. XXI (1968), pp. 321-341.

Frémiot, Marcel, and Silbermann, Alphons. "Offenbach, Jacques," *Die Musik in Geschichte und Gegenwart* (Kassel and Basel: Bärenreiter, 1961), Vol. IX, cols. 1892-1901.

Frese, C. *Dramaturgie der grossen Opern Giacomo Meyerbeers.* Berlin: Robert Lienau, 1970.

Gail, Jean François. *Reflexions sur le goût musical en France.* Paris: Paulin, 1832.

Garlington, Aubrey S., Jr. "The Concept of the Marvelous in French and German Opera, 1770-1840: A Chapter in the History of Opera Esthetics." Unpublished Ph.D. Dissertation, School of Music, University of Illinois, 1965.

Gautier, Théophile. *Histoire de l'art dramatique en France depuis vingt-cinq ans.* 6 volumes. Leipzig: Edition Hetzel, 1858-1859.

Gibson, B. "Boieldieu (1775-1834)," *Music and Musicians,* Vol. XXIV (December 1975), pp. 26-30.

Gibson, R. Wayne. "The Ensemble Technique in the Grand Operas of Giacomo Meyerbeer (1891-1864)." Unpublished Ph.D. dissertation, Northwestern University, 1975.

Ginisty, Paul. *Le Mélodrame.* Paris: Louis-Michaud [1910].

Girard, Henri. *Emile Deschamps dilettante.* Paris: Librairie Ancienne Honoré Champion, 1921.

Goethe, Johann Wolfgang von. *Sämmtliche Werke.* 13 volumes. Stuttgart & Tübingen: J. G. Cotta'scher Verlag, 1851.

Gounod, Charles François. *Memoirs of an Artist.* Translated by Annette E. Crocker. Chicago and New York: Rand, McNally & Co., 1895.

*Grand Larousse encyclopédique.* 10 volumes. Paris: Librairie Larousse, 1960-1964.

Gregor, Joseph. *Kulturgeschichte der Opera.* Vienna: Gallus-Verlag, 1941.

Grout, Donald Jay. *A Short History of Opera.* Second edition. New York: Columbia University Press, 1965.

Grovlez, Gabriel. "Jacques Offenbach, a Centennial Sketch," *Musical Quarterly,* Vol. V (1919), pp. 329-337.

Guest, Ivor. *The Romantic Ballet in Paris.* Middletown, Conn.: Wesleyan University Press, 1966.

Guichard, Léon. *La Musique et les letters au temps du romantisme.* (Université de Grenoble Publications de la Faculté des Lettres No. 12.) Paris: Presses Universitaires de France, 1955.

Hagan, Dorothy Veinus. "French Musical Criticism between the Revolutions (1830-1848)." Unpublished Ph.D. dissertation, School of Music, University of Illinois, 1965.

Halévy, Jacques François Fromental Elie. *Souvenirs et portraits; études sur les beaux-arts.* Paris: Michel Lévy Frères, 1861.

Halévy, Léon. *F. Halévy, sa vie et ses oeuvres.* Second edition, revised and enlarged. Paris: Heugel et Cie., 1863.

[Halévy, Ludovic, and Meilhac, Henri.] *Théâtre de Meilhac et Halévy de l'Académie Française.* 8 volumes. Paris: Calmann-Lévy [1901-1902].

Hallays-Dabot, Victor. *Histoire de la censure théâtrale en France.* Paris: E. Dentu, 1862.

Hanslick, Eduard. *Die moderne Oper.* Zweite unveränderte Auflage. Berlin: A Hofmann & Co., 1875.

Haraszti, Emile. "Gounod, Charles François," *Die Musik in Geschichte und Gegenwart* (Kassel and Basel: Bärenreiter, 1956), Vol. V, cols. 594-605.

Hartnoll, Phyllis (ed.). *The Oxford Companion to the Theatre.* London: Oxford University Press, 1951.

Heine, Heinrich. *Sämtliche Werke.* Edited by Jonas Fränkel, Ludwig Krähe, Albert Leitzmann, Julius Petersen, Oskar Walzel. 10 volumes. Leipzig: Insel Verlag, 1911-1920.

Heinsheimer, Hans. "Libretti am laufenden Band: Eugene Scribe," *Neue Zeitschrift für Musik,* Vol. CXXXV (1974), pp. 237-240.

________. "The Scribe Factory," *Opera News,* Vol. XLI (January 29, 1977), pp. 16-19.

Hervey, Arthur. *French Music of the XIXth Century.* London: Grant Richards; New York: E. P. Dutton & Co., 1903.

________. *Masters of French Music.* New York: Charles Scribner's Sons, 1896.

Hogarth, George.. *Memoirs of the Musical Drama.* 2 volumes. London: Richard Bentley, 1838.

Holz, Herbert J. "Die Tradition des Opernbuches," *Musikblätter des Anbruch,* Vol. IV, no. 15-16 (September-October 1922), pp. 231-234.

"Les Huguenots à Munich," *Revue et Gazette Musicale de Paris,* Vol. V, no. 23 (June 10, 1838), pp. 239-240.

Hullah, John. "Académie de Musique," *Grove's Dictionary of Music and Musicians* (fifth edition; London: Macmillan & Co., 1954), Vol. I, pp. 19-22.

Istel, Edgar. "Act IV of Les Huguenots," *Musical Quarterly,* Vol. XXII (1936), pp. 87-97.

________. "Carmen: Novel and Libretto—a Dramaturgical Analysis," *Musical Quarterly,* Vol. VII (1921), pp. 493-510.

________. *Das Libretto.* Berlin: Deutsche Verlagsanstalt, 1914.

________. "Meyerbeer's Way to Mastership," *Musical Quarterly,* Vol. XII (1926), pp. 72-109.

Jean-Aubry, G. "A Romantic Dilettante: Emile Deschamps (1791-1871)," *Music and Letters,* Vol. XX (1939), pp. 250-265.

JNS. "Académie Royale de Musique. Les Huguenots. (Cent-septième représentation.)," *Revue et Gazette Musicale de Paris,* Vol. VII, no. 15 (February 20, 1840), pp. 121-122.

Jobe, Robert D. "The Operas of André-Ernest-Modeste Grétry." Unpublished Ph.D. dissertation, University of Michigan, 1965.

Jouvin, Benoît Jean Baptiste. *D. F. E. Auber, sa vie et ses oeuvres.* Paris: Heugel et Cie., 1864.

Jouy, V. J. Etienne de. *Les Bayadères* [music by Catel]. Paris: Roullet, 1810.

Jullien, Adolphe. "Ambroise Thomas," *Rivista Musicale Italiana,* Vol. III (1896), pp. 358-366.

________. "Robert le Diable: le Mystère. L'Opéra-comique avant l'opéra," *Revue et Gazette Musicale de Paris,* Vol. XLVI, no. 48 (November 30, 1879), pp. 386-388; no. 49 (December 7, 1879), pp. 395-396; no. 50 (December 14, 1879), pp. 403-404.

Kapp, Julius. *Meyerbeer.* Berlin: Schuster & Loeffler [1920].

Kaufmann, Michael. *Zur Technik der Komödien von Eugène Scribe.* Hamburg: Lutcke & Wulff, 1911.

Keiser, Reinhard, and Feind, Barthold. *Masaniello oder Die neapolitanische Fischer-Empörung.* Edited by Johanna Rudolph and Horst Richter. Leipzig: VEB Deutscher Verlag für Musik, 1968.

Kirchmeyer, Helmut. "Die deutsche Librettokritik bei Eugene Scribe und Giacomo Meyerbeer," *Neue Zeitschrift für Musik,* Vol. CXXV (1964), pp. 372-376.

________. "Psychologie des Meyerbeer-Erfolges," *Neue Zeitschrift für Musik,* Vol. CXXV (1964), pp. 471-476.

Klein, John W. "Daniel-François Auber," *Opera,* Vol. XXII (1971), pp. 684-690.

________. "Thomas, Charles-Louis-Ambroise," *Die Musik in Geschichte und Gegenwart* (Kassel and Basel: Bärenreiter, 1966), Vol. XIII, cols. 351-355.

Knepler, Georg. *Musikgeschichte des 19. Jahrhunderts.* 2 volumes. Berlin: Henschelverlag, 1961.

Kobbé, Gustave. *Kobbé's Complete Opera Book.* Edited and revised by the Earl of Harewood. New York: E. P. Putnam's Sons, 1965.

Kracauer, S. *Orpheus in Paris.* Translated by Gwenda David and Eric Mosbacher. New York: Alfred A. Knopf, 1938.

Kruse, Georg Richard. "Meyerbeers Jugendopern," *Zeitschrift für Musikwissenschaft,* Vol. I (1918-1919), pp. 399-413.

L. de M. "Du Style et de la poésie des opéras français," *Revue et Gazette Musicale de Paris,* Vol. II, no. 50 (December 13, 1835), pp. 405-408.

Lajarte, Théodore de. *Bibliothèque musicale du théâtre de l'Opéra.* 2 volumes in 1. Paris: Librairie des Bibliophiles, 1878.

Lamb, A. "Meilhac, Halévy and the Viennese Operetta," *Opera*, Vol. XXIII (1972), pp. 1060-1066.

Lamy, F. *Jean-François Le Sueur.* Paris: Librairie Fischbacher, 1912.

Lang, Paul Henry. "The Literary Aspects of the History of Opera in France." Unpublished Ph.D. dissertation, Cornell University, 1934.

________. *Music in Western Civilization.* New York: W. W. Norton, 1941.

Langer, William L. (compiler and editor). *An Encyclopedia of World History.* Third revised edition. Boston: Houghton Mifflin Co., 1952.

Lasserre, Pierre. *Le Romantisme français.* Third edition. Paris: Société de Mercure de France, 1908.

________. *The Spirit of French Music.* Translated by D. Turner. London: Kegan Paul, Trench, Trubner & Co., Ld., 1921.

Laurencie, Lionel de la. *Le Goût musical en France.* Paris: A. Joanin et Cie., 1905.

Legouvé, Ernest. "Eugène Scribe," *Le Menestrel*, Vol. XL (1874), pp. 108-109.

________. *Sixty Years of Recollections.* Translated by Albert Vandam. London & Sydney: Eden, Remington & Co., 1893.

Lippmann, Friedrich. "Rossini," *Die Musik in Geschichte und Gegenwart* (Kassel and Basel: Bärenreiter, 1963), Vol. XI, cols. 948-973.

Locke, Arthur Ware. *Music and the Romantic Movement in France.* London: Kegan Paul, 1920.

Loewenberg, Alfred. *Annals of Opera.* 2 volumes. Second edition. Geneva: Societas Bibliographica, 1955.

________. "Carafa (di Colobrano), Michele Enrico," *Grove's Dictionary of Music and Musicians* (fifth edition; London: Macmillan & Co., 1954), Vol. II, p. 57.

Longyear, Rey Morgan. *D. F. E. Auber: A Chapter in the History of the Opéra Comique, 1800-1878.* Ann Arbor: University Microfilms, 1957.

________. 'Le livret bien fait': the Opéra Comique Librettos of Eugène Scribe," *Southern Quarterly,* Vol. I (1963), pp. 169-192.

________. "La Muette de Portici," *Music Review*, Vol. XIX (1958), pp. 37-46.

________. *Nineteenth Century Romanticism in Music.* Englewood Cliffs, N. J.: Prentice-Hall, Inc., 1969.

Malherbe, Charles. *Auber.* Paris: Henri Laurens [1911].

Mantzius, Karl. *A History of Theatrical Art.* Vol. VI: *Classicism and Romanticism.* Authorised translation by C. Archer. New York: Peter Smith, 1937.

Marek, George. "Barnum of the Opera," *Opera News*, Vol. XLI (January 29, 1977), pp. 10-15.

________. *Opera as Theater.* New York; Harper & Row, 1962.

Martin, Ruth and Thomas. "The Good Libretto," *Opera News*, Vol. XXIX, no. 15 (February 20, 1965), pp. 12-15.

Marx, Adolf Bernhard. *Music of the Nineteenth Century and Its Culture.* Translated by August Heinrich Wehrhan. London: Robert Cocks and Co., 1854.

Mason, James Frederick. *The Melodrama in France from the Revolution to the Beginnings of Romantic Drama, 1791-1830.* Baltimore: J. H. Furst Co., 1912.

Matthews, J. Brander. "The Conventions of the Music Drama," *Musical Quarterly*, Vol. V (1919), pp. 255-263.

________. "Eugene Scribe," *Atlantic Monthly*, Vol. XLVII (1881), pp. 678-690.

________. *French Dramatists of the Nineteenth Century.* New York: Charles Scribner's Sons, 1901.

________. *The Theatres of Paris.* New York: Charles Scribner's Sons, 1880.

Maurice-Amour, Lila. "Scribe, Eugène," *Die Musik in Geschichte und Gegenwart* (Kassel and Basel: Bärenreiter, 1965), Vol. XII, cols. 437-440.

Mendelssohn-Bartholdy, Felix. *Letters.* Edited by G. Selden-Goth. New York: Pantheon Books, 1945.

Merimée, Prosper. *A Chronicle of the Reign of Charles IX.* (The Novels, Tales and Letters of Prosper Merimée, Vol. VI.) Translated by George Saintsbury. New York and Philadelphia: Frank S. Holby, 1906.

________. "Le faux Demetrius," *Revue des Deux Mondes*, Vol. XVI (December 15, 1852), pp. 1001-1047.

________. "The Game of Backgammon," *The Mosaic.* (Works of Prosper Merimée, Vol. II.) Translated by George Saintsbury. New York: Bigelow, Brown & Co., Inc., 1905.

________. *Oeuvres complètes.* Edited by Pierre Trahard and Edouard Champion. 10 volumes. Paris: Librairie Ancienne Honoré Champion, 1931.

Merrau, Charles. "Robert-le-Diable," *Revue et Gazette Musicale de Paris,* Vol. VI, No. 34 (October 27, 1839), pp. 431-432.

Milner, Max. *Le Diable dans la littérature française de Cazotte à Baudelaire.* Paris: J. Corti, 1960.

Mitchell, M. K. "Meyerbeer's *Les Huguenots:* A Dramatic Revision," *Opera Journal,* Vol. VI (1973), pp. 2-9.

Moore, Douglas. "Something about Librettos," *Opera News,* Vol. XXVI, no. 1 (September 30, 1961), pp. 8-13.

Newman, Ernest. *Great Operas.* Vol. I. New York: Vintage Books, 1958.

________. *More Essays from the World of Music.* Essays from the London 'Sunday Times' Selected by Felix Aprahamian. New York: Coward-McCann, Inc., 1958,

________. *More Stories of Famous Operas.* New York: Alfred A. Knopf, 1953.

Palmer, R. R. *A History of the Modern World.* New York: Alfred A. Knopf, 1953.

"Paris," *Grove's Dictionary of Music and Musicians* (fifth edition; London: Macmillan & Co., 1954), Vol. VI, pp. 547-55.

Pazmor, R. "The Librettists: Eugène Scribe," *Bulletin of the National Association of Teachers of Singing,* Vol. XXX (1974), pp. 22-26.

Pendle, Karin. "Eugène Scribe and French Opera of the Nineteenth Century," *Musical Quarterly,* Vol. LVII (1971), pp. 535-561.

________. "The Opéras-comiques of Grétry and Marmontel," *Musical Quarterly,* Vol. LXII (1976), pp. 409-434.

________. "Scribe, Auber and *The Count of Monte Cristo," The Music Review,* Vol. XXXIV (1973), pp. 210-220.

________. "The Transformation of a Libretto: Goethe's *Jery und Bätely," Music and Letters,* Vol. LV (1974), pp. 77-88.

Perris, Arnold. "French Music in the Time of Louis-Philippe: Art as a Substitute for the Heroic Experience," Unpublished Ph.D. dissertation, Northwestern University, 1967.

Peytel, A. "Les Théâtres musicaux subventionnés," *Encyclopedie de la Musique et Dictionnaire du Conservatoire*, edited by Albert Lavignac (Paris: Librairie Delagrave, 1913-1931), Part II, Vol. 6, pp. 3748-3833.

Pougin, Arthur. *Adolphe Adam.* Paris: G. Charpentier, 1877.

________. *Boieldieu.* Paris: Charpentier et Cie., 1875.

________. "Giacomo Meyerbeer," *Famous Composers and Their Works.* Edited by John Knowles Paine, Theodore Thomas and Karl Klauser. Boston: J. B. Millet Co., 1891.

Prod'homme, J. G. "Die Huguenotten-Premiere," *Die Musik*, Jg. III, Band 9 (1903-1904), pp. 187-200.

________. "Rossini and His Works in France," *Musical Quarterly*, Vol. XVII (1931), pp. 110-137.

________. "Wagner, Berlioz and Monsieur Scribe. Two Collaborations that Miscarried," *Musical Quarterly,* Vol. XII (1926), pp. 359-375.

Prout, Ebenezer, "Auber's *Le Philtre* and Donizetti's *L'Elisire* [sic] *d'Amore:* a Comparison," *Monthly Musical Record,* Vol. XXX (1900), pp. 25-27, 41-46, 73-76.

Pushkin, Alexander. *The Works of Alexander Pushkin.* Selected and edited, with an introduction by Avrahm Yarmolinsky. New York: Random House, 1936.

Reicha, Antoine. *Art du compositeur dramatique.* 2 volumes. Paris: Simon Richault, 1833.

Rhodes, S. A. *Gérard de Nerval.* New York: Philosophical Library, 1951.

Riehl, Wilhelm Heinrich. *Musikalische Charakterköpfe.* 3 volumes. Fifth edition. Stuttgart: J. G. Cotta'schen Buchhandlung, 1876-1878.

________. *Zur Geschichte der romantischen Oper.* Berlin: Weltgeist-Bücher Verlags-Gesellschaft [1928].

Riemann, Hugo. *Musik Lexikon.* 3 volumes. Twelfth completely revised edition, edited by Willibald Gurlitt. Mainz: B. Schotts Söhne, 1959.

Ringer, Alexander. "Fra Diavolo," *Musical Quarterly*, Vol. XXXVIII (1952), pp. 642-644.

Robert, Paul-Louis. "Correspondance de Boieldieu," *Rivista Musicale Italiana,* Vol. XIX (1912), pp. 75-107; Vol. XXII (1915), pp. 520-559.

Rogers, Francis. "Adolphe Nourrit," *Musical Quarterly*, Vol. XXV (1939), pp. 11-25.

Rolandi, Ulderico. *Il libretto per musica attraverso i tempi.* Rome: Ateneo, 1951.

Rosenthal, Harold. "American-Italian Rossini," *Opera,* Vol. XX, no. 6 (June 1969), pp. 482-486.

S. "Académie Royale de Musique. Début de M. Mario (de Candia) dans Robert-le-Diable," *Revue et Gazette Musicale de Paris,* Vol. V, no. 48 (December 2, 1838), p. 491.

Saint-Saens, Camille. *Outspoken Essays on Music.* Authorized Translation by Fred Rothwell. London: Kegan Paul, Trench, Trubner & Co., Ltd.: New York: E. P. Dutton, 1922.

Sauvigny, Guillaume Bertier de. *The Bourbon Restoration.* Translated by Lynn M. Case. Philadelphia: University of Pennsylvania Press, 1966.

Scherle, Arthur. "Eugène Scribe und die Oper des 19. Jahrhunderts," *Maske und Kothurn,* Vol. III (1957), pp. 141-158.

Scott, Sir Walter. *The Abbot.* Boston: Dana Estes & Co., 1893.

________. *The Complete Poetical Works.* Edited by Horace E. Scudder. Boston & New York: Houghton Mifflin Co., 1900.

________. *Guy Mannering.* Boston: Dana Estes & Co., 1892.

________. *The Heart of Midlothian.* (Waverly Novels Centenary Edition, Vol. 7.) New York: The Baker & Taylor Co., Edinburgh: A. & C. Black, 1871.

________. *The Monastery.* (The Waverley Novels, Vol. X.) Philadelphia: John D. Morris & Co., n.d.

Scribe, Eugène. *Oeuvres complètes.* 76 volumes. Paris: E. Dentu, 1874-1885.

Searle, Humphrey (editor and translator). *Hector Berlioz, a Selection from His Letters.* New York: Harcourt, Brace & World, Inc., 1966.

Séchan, Charles P. *Souvenirs d'un homme de théâtre, 1831 bis 1855.* Edited by Adolphe Badin. Paris: Calmann Lévy, 1883.

Smith, Patrick. *The Tenth Muse.* New York: Knopf; London: Gollancz, 1970.

Smith, Paul [D.G.E. Monnais]. "Eugène Scribe," *Revue et Gazette Musicale de Paris,* Vol. XXVIII, no. 8 (February 24, 1861), pp. 57-58.

Sonneck, O. G. [and Martens, F. H.]. "Heinrich Heine's Musical Feuilletons," *Musical Quarterly,* Vol. VIII (1922), pp. 119-159; 273-295; 435-468.

Soubies, Albert, and Malherbe, Charles. *Histoire de l'Opéra-Comique: la Seconde Salle Favart, 1840-1860.* Paris: Librairie Marpon et Flammarion, 1892.

Souriau, Maurice. *Histoire du romantisme en France.* Paris: Editions Spes, 1927.

Spohr, Louis. *Autobiography.* Translated from the German. London: Reeves & Turner, 1878.

Stanton, Stephen Sadler. *English Drama and the French Well-Made Play, 1815-1915.* Ann Arbor: University Microfilms, 1955.

Stedman, J. W. "Wizard of the North," *Opera News,* Vol. XXIX, no. 4 (December 5, 1964), pp. 22-27.

Strunk, Oliver. "Musical Life in Paris (1817-1848), a Chapter from the Memoirs of Sophie Augustine Leo," *Musical Quarterly,* Vol. XVII (1931), pp. 259-271, 389-403.

Suskin, Sylvan. "The Music of Charles-Simon Catel for the Paris Opéra." Unpublished Ph.D. Dissertation, Yale University, 1970.

Tardel, Herman. *Die Sage von Robert dem Teufel in neueren deutschen Dichtungen und in Meyerbeers Oper.* (Forschungen zur neueren Litteraturgeschichte, XIV.) Berlin: Alexander Duncker, 1900.

Ternant, Andrew de. "French Opera Libretti," *Music and Letters,* Vol. XI (1930), pp. 172-176.

"Théâtre Royal de l'Opéra-Comique: Le Chalet, Paroles de M. Scribe; musique de M. Ad. Adam," *Gazette Musicale de Paris,* Vol. I, no. 39 (September 28, 1834), pp. 314-315.

Thomson, Joan. "Meyerbeer and His Contemporaries." Unpublished Ph.D. Dissertation, Columbia University, 1972.

________. "Pathbreaker: Analyzing *Le Prophète,"* *Opera News,* Vol. XLI (January 29, 1977), pp. 34-35.

Thurner, Auguste. *Les Transformations de l'Opéra-Comique.* Paris: Castel, 1865.

Tiersot, Julien. "Auber," *Revue Musicale,* Vol. XIV (November 1933), pp. 265-278.

Toye, Francis. *Rossini, a Study in Tragi-Comedy.* New York: Alfred A. Knopf, 1934.

Trahard, Pierre, and Josserand, Pierre. *Bibliographie des Oeuvres de Prosper Merimée.* Paris: Librairie Ancienne Honoré Champion, 1929.

Upton, George Putnam. *The Standard Operas.* New edition. Chicago: A. C. McClurg & Co., 1917.

Veen, Jan van der. *Le Mélodrame musical de Rousseau au romantisme.* La Haye: M. Nijhoff, 1955.

Valentin, Erich. "Dichtung und Oper," *Archiv für Musikforschung,* Vol. III (1938), pp. 138-179.

Véron, Louis Désiré. *Mémoires d'un bourgeois de Paris.* 6 volumes. Paris: G. de Gonet, [1853-]1855.

Wagner, Richard. "Reminiscences of Auber," *Richard Wagner's Prose Works,* Vol. V, pp. 35-56. Translated by William Ashton Ellis. London: Kegan Paul, Trench, Trubner & Co., Ltd., 1896.

Weber, Heinrich. *Daniel François Esprit Auber.* (Neujahrsstück der Allgemeinen Musikgesellschaft in Zurich, 69.) Zurich: Orell Füssli & Co., 1881.

Weber, Johannès. *Meyerbeer, notes et souvenirs d'un de ses secrêtaires.* Paris: Librairie Fischbacher, 1898.

Weinstock, Herbert. *Donizetti and the World of Opera in Italy, Paris and Vienna in the First Half of the Nineteenth Century.* New York: Pantheon Books [1963].

________. *Rossini, a Biography.* New York: Alfred A. Knopf, 1968.

Weiss, Jean Jacques. *Le Théâtre et les moeurs.* Fifth edition. Paris: Calmann Lévy, 1889.

Weisstein, Ulrich. *The Essence of Opera; The Creative Process of Opera Revealed by Librettists and Composers in Original Writings from 1600 to the Present.* New York: Free Press of Glencoe, 1964.

White, Henry Adelbert. *Sir Walter Scott's Novels on the Stage.* (Yale Studies in English, LXXVI.) New Haven: Yale University Press, 1927.

Wirth, Helmut. "Adam, Adolphe Charles," *Die Musik in Geschichte und Gegenwart* (Kassel and Basel: Bärenretier, 1949-1951), Vol. I, cols. 76-77.

________. "Auber, Daniel François Esprit," *Die Musik in Geschichte und Gegenwart* (Kassel and Basel: Bärenreiter, 1949-1951), Vol. I, cols. 772-776.

Wolf, John B. *France, 1815 to the Present.* New York: Prentice-Hall, Inc., 1940.

Wolff, Hellmuth Christian. *Oper. Szene und Darstellung von 1600 bis 1900.* (Musikgeschichte in Bildern, Vol. IV: Musik der Neuzeit. Lieferung 1.) Leipzig: VEB Deutscher Verlag für Musik [1967].

## SCORES

Adam, Adolphe. *Le Chalet.* Piano-vocal score. Paris: Schonenberger, n.d.

________. *Le Chalet.* Piano-vocal score. Brussels: Henry Lemoine & Cie., n.d.

Auber, Daniel François Esprit. *La Barcarolle.* Full score. Paris: E. Troupenas & Cie. [1845].

________. *Fra Diavolo.* Piano-vocal score. Paris: G. Brandus, Dufour et Cie., n.d.

________. *Fra Diavolo.* Piano-vocal score. Edited and translated by N. Macfarren. London: Novello, Ewer & Co. [1934].

________. *Haydée.* Piano-vocal score. Paris: G. Brandus & S. Dufour, n.d.

________. *Le Maçon.* Piano-vocal score. Paris: Schonenberger, n.d.

________. *La Muette de Portici.* Piano-vocal score. Edited and translated into English by Natalia Macfarren. London: Novello, Ewer & Co., n.d.

________. *Le Philtre.* Piano-vocal score. Paris: G. Brandus et S. Dufour [185-].

________. *Le Philtre.* Full score. Paris: E. Troupenas, 1831.

________. *Le Timide.* Full score. Paris: I. Pleyel & Fils ainé [1826].

Bizet, Georges. *Carmen.* Full score. 2 volumes. Edited by Fritz Oeser. Kassel: Alkor-Edition, 1964.

Boieldieu, François Adrien. *Béniowsky* [*sic*]. Full score. Paris: Chez Mlles. Erard [1800].

________. *La Dame blanche.* Piano-vocal score. Braunschweig: G. M. Meyer, Jr., n.d.

Carafa, Michel. *La Prison d'Edimbourg.* Full score. Paris: Ph. Petit, 1833.

Catel, Charles-Simon. *Les Bayadères.* Full score. Paris: Janet et Cotelle, 1810.

________. *Sémiramis.* Full score. Paris: Madame Le Roy, An 12 [1804].

Cherubini, Luigi. *Démofoon.* Piano-vocal score. Leipzig and Berlin: C. F. Peters, n.d.

________. *Les Deux journées.* Piano-vocal score. Edited by J. Pittman. London and New York: Boosey & Co., n.d.

Gounod, Charles. *Faust.* Piano-vocal score. New York: G. Schirmer [1902].

________. *La Nonne sanglante.* Piano-vocal score. Paris: Choudens [1854].

________. *Polyeucte.* Piano-vocal score. Paris: Henry Lemoine, n.d.

________. *La Reine de Saba.* Piano-vocal score. Fourth edition. Edition conformé au manuscrit de l'auteur revue par Henri Büsser. Paris: Choudens fils, Editeurs, n.d.

Grétry, André Ernest Modeste. *La Caravane du caire.* Piano-vocal score. Paris: E. Girod [between 1855 and 1863].

________. *Richard Coeur-de-Lion.* Piano-vocal score. Paris: Brandus, n.d.

________. *Zémire et Azor.* Piano-vocal score. Paris: Launer, n.d.

Lesueur, François. *La Caverne.* Full score. Paris: Naderman, n.d.

Meyerbeer, Giacomo. *Il Crociato in Egitto.* Piano-vocal score. Paris: Maurice Schlesinger [1836].

________. *Les Huguenots.* Piano-vocal score. Paris: G. Brandus, Dufour & Cie., n.d.

________. *Les Huguenots.* Piano-vocal score. Paris: Brandus et Cie., n.d.

________. *Le Prophète.* Piano-vocal score. Paris: Brandus et Cie., n.d.

________. *Robert le Diable.* Piano-vocal score. Paris: G. Brandus, Dufour & Cie., n.d.

Offenbach, Jacques. *Barbe-Bleue.* Piano-vocal score. Paris: Heugel et Cie., 1866.

________. *La Belle Hélène.* Piano-vocal score. Paris: Heugel et Cie., 1864.

________. *La Grande-Duchesse de Gérolstein.* Piano-vocal score. Edited by J. Pittman. London: Boosey & Co., n.d.

Rossini, Gioacchino. *L'Assedio di Corinto.* Piano-vocal score. Milan: Gio. Ricordi [1826?].

________. *L'Assedio di Corinto.* Piano-vocal score. Milan: G. Ricordi, 1949.

________. *Guillaume Tell.* Piano-vocal score. Edited by B. Tour, translated by N. Macfarren. London: Novello, Ewer & Co., n.d.

________. *Maometto Secondo.* Piano-vocal score. Paris: Pacini, n.d.

________. *Stabat Mater.* Piano-vocal score. New York: G. Schirmer, n.d.

Spontini, Gaspard. *La Vestale.* Full score. Paris: Chez Mlles. Erard, n.d.

Thomas, Ambroise. *Françoise de Rimini.* Piano-vocal score. Paris: Heugel et Fils, n.d.

________. *Hamlet.* Piano-vocal score. Paris: Heugel et Cie., n.d.

# INDEX

Cover illustrations: watermark examples selected from the *French Harpsichord Music of the 17th Century* by Bruce Gustafson, published by UMI Research Press.